PUBLIC EDUCATION
IN THE UNITED STATES

*A Study and Interpretation of American
Educational History*

BY

ELLWOOD P. CUBBERLEY

DEAN EMERITUS, SCHOOL OF EDUCATION
LELAND STANFORD JUNIOR UNIVERSITY

Revised and Enlarged Edition

HOUGHTON MIFFLIN COMPANY

The Riverside Press Cambridge

The Riverside Press
CAMBRIDGE · MASSACHUSETTS
PRINTED IN THE U.S.A.

AUTHOR'S PREFACE

IT IS now fifteen years since the first edition of this textbook appeared, and the wide and generous reception which the work has received has been a source of much gratification to both the publishers and the author. It is not too much to say that at the time of its publication it represented a method of treatment of the history of education that was new. Instead of offering the usual cyclopædic treatment of our educational development, the text furnished, for beginning students, a connected story of our educational evolution which was closely tied up with the social, political, and industrial forces that shaped the nineteenth century. An effort was made to set forth the outstanding events of our educational history in graphic manner, to point out their close relation to the social, political, and national movements then taking place, and to help the teacher to see the educational problems of the twentieth century in the light of their historical development. Throughout, an effort was made to explain the connection between the history of education and the institutional efforts of the State in the matter of the training of the young; to set forth our educational history as an evolving series of events from which the recent advances in educational practice and procedure have had their origin; and to make clear the relation between our educational development and the great social and industrial changes which have given the recent marked expansion of state educational effort its meaning. In particular, the author tried to catch the spirit of our educational development and to use the facts as a background upon which to paint the picture which our national evolution presents. Believing that the history of education, and particularly the history of our American educational development, is too important a subject in the proper orienting of teachers to lose, an effort was made to create a textbook that would restore the subject to its old-time popularity.

In preparing this revised and enlarged edition the lines and method of the earlier edition have been retained throughout, but a somewhat more detailed treatment has been provided and gaps have been filled in. The book remains, however, as before a history of administrative progress and curriculum change and expansion, rather than a history of theories about education. An additional chapter has been given to the Colonial period, and a fuller treatment of this interesting stage in our development has been provided, particularly more complete as regards the private school, apprenticeship training, and the work of the colleges of the time. Two additional chapters, dealing with education in the South, aim to set forth the effects of the Civil War on education there and the important developments which have since taken place in that section of our country. Another new chapter deals with professional organization, both of the subject of education itself and of teachers' organizations. Throughout all the chapters much new factual material has been included in the text and in a series of footnotes which were not in the previous edition. Throughout, changes and additions have been so numerous that scarcely a single page remains as it was in the earlier volume, yet the main lines and method of treatment of the previous work have been retained. In this new form it is felt that the volume is destined for a new lease of life and, it is hoped, a new manifestation of popular favor as a textbook for classroom use.

The lines upon which the text has been built up may be stated, as follows:

Education, with us in America, was a fruit of the movements which resulted from the Protestant Revolt of the sixteenth century and the general awakening of Europe which was at that time taking place. Back beyond this historic event the beginning student scarcely need go. One short chapter will give the beginner the necessary historic background, and the study can then begin with the transfer of European civilization and educational zeal to our shores. Much time, too, need not be spent on our development before the first quarter of the nineteenth century, when the forces — national, state, philanthropic, social, political, and economic — which were potent in our educational development first began to find expression. The battle for taxation for education; the battle to eliminate the pauper-school idea; the battle to do away with the rate bill and the fuel tax, and make the schools entirely free; the battle to establish supervision; the battle to eliminate sectarianism; the battle to extend and complete the system by adding the high school and the state university; the struggle to establish normal schools, and begin the training of teachers; the gradual evolution of the graded system of instruction; and the opening of instruction of all grades to women — these are the great milestones in our early national educational history which are of real importance for the beginning student of education to know. Of the educational reformers, the beginning can be made with Rousseau, as the inspirer of Pestalozzi's labors. Then Pestalozzi, Fellenberg, Froebel, and Herbart are the Europeans whose main ideas the student needs to grasp, and it was not until near the middle of the nineteenth century that the work of the first two of these began to be made known to us by returning travelers and to influence the current of our national educational progress. The other educational reformers with whom the beginning student should become familiar are the practical constructive American thinkers who fought through our early state educational battles and shaped the traditions of our American state school systems.

Up to the time of our Civil War we were engaged in laying foundations and establishing principles of action. The great period of our educational development and expansion has been since 1860, since which time we have twice reorganized our elementary instruction, first in the light of the "faculty" psychology which came in with Pestalozzian ideas, and again in the light of the vast and far-reaching social and industrial changes of the past fifty years. We are now at the beginnings of a third reorganization, this time to include the high school and the college as well. The kindergarten, manual training, domestic arts, and Herbartian ideas have also come from abroad since 1860, and been incorporated into our educational theory and practice. The great stream of immigration which has come to our shores, the vast industrial revolution which has taken place, the destruction of the old-type home, the virtual disappearance of the apprenticeship system of training, the institution of compulsory education, new conceptions as to the education of delinquents and defectives, new child-welfare legislation, and the rise of a rural-life problem of great dimensions — these are the more important changes and forces of the past three decades which have necessitated extensive modifications in almost every aspect of our educational service. To enable our schools to meet these new problems of our changing democratic life we have been forced to change their direction and to adapt the instruction given to the new needs and conditions of society. A new educational theory has been evolved, adjustments and differentiations in school work have had to be worked out, the education of defectives and delinquents has required new classes and new state institutions, child-welfare work has been given an importance before unknown, the high school has had to be made over, vocational education and the improvement of agriculture and rural-life conditions have recently been made great national undertakings, the education of adults for literacy and intelligent citizenship has awakened a wide national interest, and the original one-course colleges have been transformed into great universities, training leaders for and ministering unto the needs of the State. The new problems in education have developed so rapidly, and have become matters of such national importance, that questions of educational reorganization and educational readjustment — the curriculum, the organization of the school, city education, rural and village education, county organization, state organization, national aid and oversight, and the study of education as a science — these and others have now everywhere been pushed to the front, and are matters of everyday discussion with which teachers and students of education should be familiar. Within the past quarter of a century we have come to see, with a clearness of vision not approached before, that education is our Nation's greatest constructive tool, and that the many problems of national welfare which education alone can solve are far greater than the schoolmaster of two or three decades ago dreamed.

To be familiar with recent development, to be able to view present-day educational problems in the light of their historical evolution and their political and social bearings, and to see educational service in its proper setting as a great national institution evolved by democracy to help it solve its many perplexing problems, the writer holds to be of fundamental importance to the beginning student of education and the teacher in our schools. Such a study offers for education what a beginning course in history or economics or science does, in that it gives the student the cardinal points of the compass for the journey in the study of the subject, gives the larger developments of the field their proper historical setting, states the problems of the present and near future in terms which give them significance, displays the ignorance and prejudice against which those who labored to make possible the educational organization which we inherit worked, shows the relations existing between the different institutions of society engaged in the educational service, reveals the forces which circumscribe and condition and direct and limit all our educational endeavors, and sets forth the fundamental principles in the light of which we labor.

It is from such a point of view that this book has been written. The first chapter gives the needed European background; the next three describe the establishment of education on our shores, and trace its development through the Colonial and early national periods; the next five treat the half-century of struggle to establish education as a function of the State, describe the schools established, and cover the period up to about 1850; the next two chapters give the background, in the work of Rousseau and Pestalozzi, needed to understand the great reorganization of elementary education traced in Chapter XIII, and cover the period from 1860 up to about 1890; the far-reaching consequences of the vast social and industrial changes of the latter half of the nineteenth century are traced in Chapter XIV, and the nine remaining chapters deal with the twentieth-century problems which have arisen as a result of the social and industrial and political changes of the nineteenth century, and the attempts which have been made and are being made to find a solution for them. Chapters XII and XX trace the effect of the Civil War on education, and sketch the educational revival which has since taken place in the South. All but the first three chapters deal with educational development since the beginning of our national period; half of the book deals with the period since 1860; and one third of the book with the problems which have arisen since about 1890, the attempts we have made to find solutions for them, and a look ahead.

To add concreteness to this new edition, a parallel book of *Readings* (Volume II) has been built up, and this is being issued as a companion volume of illustrative source material, designed to back up the historical record of educational development and progress as presented in the *Text* (Volume I). These source selections have been listed herein, and fully cross-referenced (**R. 64; R. 147;** etc.) in the pages of this Text. The chapter arrangement of the two volumes is the same, so that the *Readings* may be used as a reference book of sources to which the student of the *Text* may turn for the documents from which the history of American educational development has been written. It is believed that this companion volume contains sufficient supplementary reading to meet the needs of most classes studying the subject, without recourse to other reading material.

To make the *Text* of greater teaching value there has been appended to the different chapters a series of questions for discussion, and to most of the chapters a short list of topics for investigation and report.

The *Readings* in the parallel chapter of the accompanying volume have also been listed at the ends of the different chapters, and a series of questions bearing on these *Readings* added. To make the references given of greatest value they have been carefully selected, those not likely to be found in an average college library omitted unless of great importance, an asterisk prefixed to the most important, and some brief indication as to the size and value of each reference has been added. In this form it is hoped that the *Text* and the *Readings* together will add materially to the ability of instructors to make this interesting subject live in their classrooms and in the minds and lives of their students.

ELLWOOD P. CUBBERLEY

STANFORD UNIVERSITY

CONTENTS

CHAPTER I. OUR EUROPEAN BACKGROUND I

CHAPTER II. THE BEGINNINGS OF AMERICAN EDUCATION . . 12
    I. Origin of Our Type Attitudes Toward Education . . . 12
        1. The compulsory-maintenance attitude 14
        2. The parochial-school attitude 20
        3. The pauper-school non-state-interference attitude . 22
    II. Types of Schools Transplanted and Developed . . . 26

CHAPTER III. GENERAL CHARACTER OF THE COLONIAL SCHOOLS 41
    I. Early Instruction, and Teachers 41
    II. Change in Character after about 1750 58
    III. Rise of the Civil or State School 68

CHAPTER IV. EARLY NATIONAL AND STATE ATTITUDES . . 82
    I. The National Government and Education . . . 82
    II. What the States were doing 94
    III. The North-West-Territory Development 105
    IV. The Real Interest in Advanced Education 112

CHAPTER V. EARLY INFLUENCES TENDING TO AWAKEN AN EDU-
        CATIONAL CONSCIOUSNESS 120
    I. Philanthropic Influences 120
        1. The Sunday-School movement 121
        2. The City School Societies. 123
        3. The Lancastrian Monitorial System 128
        4. The Infant-School Societies 137
    II. Social, Political, and Economic Influences . . . 142
        1. The growth of the cities 142
        2. The rise of manufacturing 144
        3. The extension of the suffrage 150
        4. New public demands for schools 154

CHAPTER VI. THE BATTLE FOR FREE STATE SCHOOLS . . . 163
    I. Alignment of Interests, and Propaganda 163
    II. Phases of the Battle for State-Supported Schools . . 176
        1. The battle for tax support 177
        2. The battle to eliminate the pauper-school idea . 189
        3. The battle to make the schools entirely free . . 198

CHAPTER VII. THE BATTLE TO CONTROL THE SYSTEM . . . 212
        4. The battle to establish school supervision . . . 212
        5. The battle to eliminate sectarianism . . . 230

CHAPTER VIII. THE BATTLE TO EXTEND THE SYSTEM . . . 245
    6. The battle to establish the American high school . . 245
    7. The state university crowns the system 264
  III. The Rise of Professional and Technical Education . . . 275

CHAPTER IX. CHARACTER OF THE SCHOOLS ESTABLISHED . . 288
  I. New Textbooks Change the Old Instruction 289
  II. Evolution of the Graded Elementary School 300
  III. The Great Day of the District System 315
  IV. The Teachers, Their Methods, and Equipment . . . 323

CHAPTER X. NEW IDEAS FROM ABROAD 340
  I. English Origins and Early Independence 340
  II. Work and Influence of Pestalozzi 344
  III. Early American Travelers and Official Reports . . . 354

CHAPTER XI. THE BEGINNINGS OF TEACHER-TRAINING . . 371
  I. The Rise of the Normal School 371
  II. Introduction of Pestalozzian Methods 384

CHAPTER XII. THE CIVIL WAR CHECKS DEVELOPMENT . . 408
  I. Ante-Bellum Development in the South 408
  II. General Character of Ante-Bellum Southern Schools . 421
  III. General Effect of the Civil War on Education . . . 427
  IV. The Post-War Reconstruction Period 431

CHAPTER XIII. MORE NEW IDEAS FROM ABROAD . . . 449
  I. New Ideas from Herbartian Sources 449
  II. The Kindergarten and Play 455
  III. Instruction in the Manual Activities 461
  IV. The Addition of Art and Science Study 467
  V. The Elementary School now Reorganized and Complete . 471

CHAPTER XIV. NEW MODIFYING FORCES 480
  I. Changes in the Character of our People 480
  II. The Industrial Revolution 489
  III. Effect of These Changes on the Home 496
  IV. Effect of These Changes on the School 501

CHAPTER XV. NEW EDUCATIONAL CONCEPTIONS AND ADJUSTMENTS 513
  I. New Conceptions of the Educational Process . . . 513
  II. Necessary Adjustments and Differentiations . . . 519
  III. More Fundamental Reorganizations 528

CHAPTER XVI. CURRICULUM AND SCHOOL REORGANIZATION . 539
  I. Curriculum Reorganization 539
  II. Reorganization of Form and Scope 549

CONTENTS

CHAPTER XVII. PUBLIC SCHOOL EXTENSIONS 563
  I. Compulsory Attendance and Child Labor 563
  II. Education of Handicapped Children 577
  III. Adult Education and Citizenship 587

CHAPTER XVIII. CHILD HEALTH AND WELFARE 604

CHAPTER XIX. NEW DIRECTIONS OF EDUCATIONAL EFFORT . 627
  I. The Expansion of the High School 627
  II. The Development of Vocational Education . . . 638
  III. University Expansion and Extension 651

CHAPTER XX. THE EDUCATIONAL REVIVAL IN THE SOUTH . . 663

CHAPTER XXI. PROFESSIONAL ORGANIZATION 688
  I. The Scientific Study of the Problem 688
  II. Organization of the Teaching Profession 704

CHAPTER XXII. ADMINISTRATIVE REORGANIZATION OF AMERI-
         CAN EDUCATION 717
  I. Reorganization and Redirection of Rural and Village Educa-
     tion 718
  II. State Educational Reorganization 727
  III. Taxation Reform a Necessity 734
  IV. The National Government and Education . . . 739

CHAPTER XXIII. FUNDAMENTAL PRINCIPLES AND PROBLEMS . 750

INDEX 767

PORTRAITS

	FACING
DeWitt Clinton	124
Joseph Lancaster	128
Samuel Galloway	182
The Reverend Samuel Lewis	182
Caleb Mills	186
The Reverend Calvin E. Stowe	186
Gideon Hawley	214
John Swett	214
Horace Mann	222
Henry Barnard	228
Mary Lyon	274
James G. Carter	274
Jean Jacques Rousseau	342
Thomas Jefferson	342
Pestalozzi Monument at Yverdon	346
The Reverend Samuel R. Hall	372
Cyrus Peirce	372
Dr. Edward A. Sheldon	386
Professor Hermann Krüsi	386
G. Stanley Hall	402
Johann Friedrich Herbart	454
Friedrich Wilhelm Froebel	454
Dr. William T. Harris	472
Colonel Francis W. Parker	472
John Dewey	506
Charles William Eliot	550
Edward Lee Thorndike	690
Charles Hubbard Judd	690

FIGURES IN THE TEXT

1. Results of the Protestant Revolts 7
2. Religious Faiths of the Early Colonists in America 13
3. John Harvard 16
4. Town School at Dedham, 1648 17
5. A Dame School 28
6. Location of 39 Grammar Schools Founded before 1700 . . . 30
7. The Boston Latin School 31
8. "Old Nassau," at Princeton 32
9. Apprenticing an Orphan Boy, 1694 35
10. A Horn-Book 43
11. A Page from the Westminster Catechism 44
12. Two Specimen Pages from the New England Primer . . . 45
13. Thomas Dilworth, and His Book 47
14. Title-Page of Hodder's Arithmetic 48
15. Part of a Page from a Colonial MS. Arithmetic 49
16. Title-Page of Cheever's *Accidence* 50
17. A Colonial Teacher's Tuition Bill 53
18. Advertisement for a Teacher to Let 54
19. Indentured Servants for Sale 55
20. A Schoolmaster of the Old Type 56
21. A School Whipping-Post 57
22. How the Early New England Towns were Located 60
23. Advertisement for a Colonial Schoolmaster 62
24. Two Early College Presidents 66
25. The College of William and Mary, 1776 67
26. The First Meeting-House of Center Church, New Haven . . 69
27. Showing the Evolution of the District System in Massachusetts . 70
28. Map of the Town of New Haven, in 1724 71
29. Showing the Evolution of the Modern State School *Between* 74 and 75
30. The United States in 1783 83
31. A Congressional Township 92
32. Showing Land Grants for Common Schools 93
33. Showing Western Expansion of New England, by 1810 . . . 100
34. Early Attitude Assumed Toward Public Education 104
35. One of the New Yales in the Wilderness 106
36. Showing the Western Expansion of New England by 1840 . . 107
37. A Pennsylvania Academy 113
38. Columbia College, 1784–1850 115
39. Where Indiana University Began Instruction, 1824 116
40. The First Schoolhouse Built by the Free School Society, New York City 125

41. The First Free School in Baltimore 128
42. A Lancastrian School in Operation 130
43. Monitors Teaching Reading 131
44. Monitor Inspecting Written Work 133
45. "Model" School Building of the Public School Society . . 139
46. Evolution of the Essential Features of the American Public School System 140
47. The First Commercial Cotton Mill in the United States . . 144
48. Threshing Wheat with Flail and Roller 146
49. Distribution of Industrial Plants in the United States in 1833 . 147
50. Dates of the Granting of Full Manhood Suffrage . . . 151
51. Organizing Work of the Western Literary Institute . . . 170
52. The Indiana Referendum of 1848 186
53. The Pennsylvania School Elections of 1834 193
54. Thaddeus Stevens 195
55. The New York Referendum of 1850 201
56. Noah Porter 204
57. Early District Organization 213
58. Status of School Supervision in the United States by 1861 . 217
59. The Alphabet, from *The Columbian Primer* 232
60. A Typical New England Academy 247
61. The First High School in the United States 253
62. The Development of Secondary Schools in the United States . 255
63. The First High School in New York City, 1825 . . . 256
64. The First High School at Providence, Rhode Island . . 258
65. The Chicago High School of 1856 261
66. High Schools in the United States by 1860 262
67. Colleges and Universities Established by 1860 268
68. The American Educational Ladder 273
69. Emma Willard 275
70. Two Pioneers in the Establishment of Technical Education . 278
71. A Summer School 289
72. Frontispiece to Noah Webster's American Spelling Book . 290
73. Making the Preliminary Bow to the Audience . . . 292
74. Noah Webster 293
75. William H. McGuffey 293
76. Warren Colburn 294
77. An Early English Grammar 295
78. Two Early Textbook Writers, Morse and Murray . . . 296
79. An Early American School Geography, 1795 297
80. A "Sampler" of 1813 299
81. How and What a Providence Teacher Taught, in 1820 . . 302
82. The Boston School System in 1823 306
83. Exterior and Interior of a Providence Grammar School . . 308
84. An "Usher" and his Class 310
85. Floor Plans of the Quincy Grammar School, Boston, 1848 . 312
86. The First Free Public School in Detroit, 1838 . . . 317

87. Chicago in 1832 318
88. The First Schoolhouse in Cleveland 319
89. How the District System Organized a County 320
90. The Old-Time District School 322
91. Teacher Training in the United States by 1860 324
92. A Reward of Merit 327
93. Early School Architecture and Contracting 328
94. One of the "Weather-Boarded Boxes" 329
95. School Desks Before 1860 330
96. One of the Arithmetical Puzzles 331
97. The Springfield Tests, Then and Now 333
98. The Scene of Pestalozzi's Labors 347
99. German State School Systems before 1914 352
100. Two Early American Travelers 355
101. Victor Cousin 356
102. Alexander Dallas Bache 360
103. David P. Page 377
104. The Reverend Charles Brooks 379
105. Where the First Normal School in America Opened . . . 380
106. The First State Normal School Building in America . . . 382
107. Growth of Public and Private Normal Schools in the United
    States 384
108. Distribution of Oswego Graduates, 1861–86 389
109. Arnold Henry Guyot 394
110. A Pestalozzian Number Chart 395
111. Early Spencerian Writing Exercises 398
112. The Decreasing Percentage of Men Teachers 401
113. Calvin H. Wiley 412
114. A "Field School" Interior 424
115. The University of Georgia as it was Before the Civil War . . 426
116. Per Pupil Costs, 1876–1926 430
117. George Peabody 439
118. The Two Agents of the Peabody Fund, Sears and Curry . . 440
119. John F. Slater 441
120. The First Manual-Training High School 464
121. Redirected Manual Training 465
122. Herbert Spencer 470
123. The Evolution of the Elementary School Curriculum . . . 473
124. Nationality of the White Population in 1790 481
125. Foreign-Born in the United States as Shown by the Census of 1930 485
126. Urban and Rural Population Distribution in 1930 493
127. Farm Tenantry in 1930 495
128. Distribution by Nationalities in Two Elementary Schools in
    Cleveland 504
129. Promotional Results under Average Course of Study . . . 520
130. The Batavia Plan 522
131. The New Cambridge Plan 524

132. The Differentiated-Course Plan 525
133. The Gary School Building Plan 531
134. A Twelve-Section Platoon School 533
135. Two of the Puzzles we no Longer Teach 541
136. Problems of the Coming Industrial Age 548–549
137. Public Junior Colleges by 1930 556
138. The Reorganization of American Education 559
139. Gallaudet Teaching the Deaf and Dumb 578
140. The Sign Manual of Speech 579
141. The American Braille Alphabet 581
142. Special Educational Institutions Maintained by the State . 585
143. Evolution of the Extension of American Public Education . 589
144. Distribution of the Male Voting Population of the United States . 591
145. Who Constitute our Illiterates 595
146. Space Distribution of an Elementary School of Today . . 605
147. Five Years' Work in Reducing Physical Defects . . . 609
148. Percentage of Drafted Men Passing Physical Examination, by States 616
149. Reduction of Death-Rate in a Century 619
150. Number per Thousand of Public School Pupils in High Schools . 628
151. Number of Junior High Schools 631
152. Redirection of the Secondary School 634
153. Destruction of the Trades in Modern Industry . . . 638
154. A Year's Work in Industry and in School 646
155. Increasing Production by Correct Training Methods . . 647
156. Recent Expansion of the High School and the College . . 649
157. What Vocational Training and Guidance Can Do . . . 650
158. University Extension Work in Wisconsin 656
159. The Founders of Industrial Training for the Colored Race . 667
160. Edwin A. Alderman 670
161. Grade Norms for Handwriting 694
162. Army Intelligence Test Results 699
163. The Distribution of Intelligence among Children . . 701
164. Growth of the N.E.A. Since the World War . . . 710
165. One of the Landmarks 719
166. A Consolidated Community-Center School 723
167. Rural School Reorganization 724
168. Progress in Eliminating the Elected County Superintendent . 725
169. Methods used for Securing the Chief State School Officer . 729
170. Sources of Revenue for School Support, 1890–1930 . . . 738

CHAPTER I

OUR EUROPEAN BACKGROUND

Sources of our civilization. The problems which we are facing today in American education have not come about by accident, but are the result of a long historical evolution, and are best understood if considered in the light of their historical development. The history of education is essentially a phase of the history of civilization, and is easier to comprehend if it is studied from this point of view. School organization and educational theory represent but a small part of the historical evolution, and must be considered after all as but an expression of the type of civilization which a people has gradually evolved. The road that man has traveled since the days when might made right and children had no rights which even parents were bound to respect, to a time when the child is regarded as of first importance and adults represented in the State declare by law that the child shall be cared for and educated for the welfare of the State, is a long road and at times a very crooked one. Its ups and downs have been those of the progress of civilization itself, and in consequence any history of education must be in part a history of the progress of the civilization of the people whose educational history is being traced.

The civilization which we today enjoy is a very complex thing, made up of many contributions, some large and some small, and from people in many different lands and ages. To trace the different educational contributions back to their sources might be interesting, but it would take too long, and for our purposes would not be important. All we need to sketch in is sufficient background to give perspective and color to the story of the development of our American educational history and problems which it is here proposed to give. Even this takes us back to European lands, and especially to the stirring events which took place in Europe after about 1500.

The three foundation elements. The civilization which we have inherited has come down to us from three main sources, and in a fairly continuous stream. The Greeks, the Romans, and the Christians laid the foundations, and in the order named. On these three foundation stones, superimposed upon one another, our modern European and American civilization rests. We have made many additions in modern times, building an entirely new superstructure on these old foundations, but the foundations for the structure of our civilization nevertheless were laid by Greece and Rome and Christianity.

The work of Greece underlies all else. This wonderful people introduced a new force into the world by placing a premium on personal and political freedom and initiative, by daring to trust themselves to follow the truth as they saw it, and by developing a literature, an art, and a philosophy which was to be a heritage to all succeeding civilizations. In the lines of culture and philosophic thought the world will always remain debtor to this small but active, imaginative, artistic, and creative people.

To the Romans we are indebted for an entirely different type of inheritance. They were weak where Greece was strong, and strong where Greece was weak. Their strength lay in law and government and the practical arts. Rome absorbed and amalgamated the whole ancient world into one Empire, to which she gave a common language, dress, manners, religion, literature, and government. By imposing law and order and government on an unruly world, and unifying the ancient civilizations into one organized whole, Rome laid the necessary basis for the success of Christianity, and thus saved civilization from an even greater disaster when the Germanic hordes poured over her Empire (**R. 1**).

Into this Roman world, united by Roman arms and government, came the first of the modern forces of our present-day civilization — that of Christianity. Building on Greek philosophic ideas and Roman governmental forms, and with its new message for an old world, Christianity forms the connecting link and the preserving force between the old and the new civilizations. A new ethical force of first importance was by it added to the effective energies of mankind, and a basis for the education of all, not to be realized for many centuries, to be sure, was laid for the first time in the history of the world.

Christianity, too, came at just the right time to enable it to organize and establish itself to meet and in time overcome and civilize the barbarian deluge from the North which, in the fifth and sixth centuries, poured over the boundaries of the Empire and almost obliterated the ancient civilizations. The fall of the Roman Empire, and the long struggle of the Christian Church to preserve civilization from complete destruction at the hands of the Germanic barbarians, is a story with which almost every one is familiar. Progress ceased in the ancient world. The creative force of antiquity seemed exhausted. The digestive and assimilative powers of the old world were gone. Greek was forgotten. Latin was corrupted. The knowledge of the arts and sciences was lost. Schools disappeared. Only the Christian Church remained to save civilization from the wreck, and it too almost went under. It took ten centuries to partially civilize, educate, and reduce to national order this heterogeneous horde of new peoples, and to preserve enough of the ancient civilization that the modern world has been able to reconstruct its main outlines from the fragments which remained. During this long period the Church had to rely on oral and scenic teaching, and prohibition and punishment (**R. 2**). The day of literary learning was still far off.

The period of the awakening. Finally, however, first in Italy, and later in the new nations formed from the tribes which raided the ancient Empire, there came a period of awakening and discovery which led to a wonderful revival of ancient learning, a great expansion of men's thoughts, a general questioning of all ancient authority, a great religious awakening, a wonderful period of world exploration and discovery, the founding of new nations in new lands, the reawakening of the old Greek spirit of scientific inquiry, and the evolution of our modern civilization. It was out of these new impulses and forces that America was discovered; out of the contests incident to the great revolt against religious authority, known among Protestants as the Reformation, that America was in large part colonized; and out of the rediscovery of the ancient literature and learning in the days of the Renaissance, and the Protestant belief in general education as a means to salvation, that the early traditions of American education were derived. The three main forces to which we owe our settlement and educational beginnings were the Renaissance, the Protestant Revolts, and the beginnings of scientific inquiry and world exploration and trade. Let us examine each of these, briefly, in order.

The thirteenth century has often been called the wonderful century of the medieval world. It was wonderful largely in that the forces struggling against the oppressive medievalism which had grown up as a result of the long effort of the Church to Christianize the barbarian and reduce him to some form of civilized order, in this century first find clear expression. It was a century of rapid and unmistakable progress in every line. It saw the evolution of the first of the universities, the beginnings of modern scholarship, the great era of guild-hall and cathedral building, a rapid expansion of reviving commerce, the rise of a burgher and lawyer class, distinct from the clergy and the nobility on the one hand and the craftsmen and apprentices on the other, and the evolution of modern States and modern languages as expressive of the new feeling of nationality which was beginning to pervade Europe. The fourteenth century was a period of even more rapid change. New objects of interest were brought to the front, and new standards of judgment were applied. The medieval man, with his feelings of personal insignificance and lack of confidence, began to give way to men possessed of the modern spirit — men conscious of a past behind and a future before them, and capable of independence, action, initiative, and enjoyment. With this transformation in the character of life and change in the nature of human interests, Europe was ready for a revival of learning (**R. 3**).

The revival of learning. The revival began in Italy, Petrarch (1304–74) being regarded as the first modern scholar and man of letters in the Western World. In time the old monastic treasures were brought to light, the study of Greek was revived in the West, the first modern libraries and scientific academies were founded, and the history, literature, religion, and political and social life of the ancient world were reconstructed. It was the curious and enthusiastic Italians, and the wealthy merchant princes and reigning dukes who supported them (**R. 4**), more than the Greeks who taught them the language, who opened up the literature and the history of Athens to the comprehension of the modern world. In 1396 the first professorship of Greek in a university was created at Florence, then the center of art and literature and learning in the Western World.

So slowly did new ideas travel at that time that it was nearly a century before this revival began to be heard of north of the Alps. A professorship of Greek was created at Paris, in 1458; one at Seville in Spain, in 1473; and one at Vienna, in 1523. The German

university of Erfurt established a professorship of Poetry and Elo-
quence, in 1493. Greek came to Oxford about 1490. Very fortunately for the spread of the new learning, an important process
and a great invention now came at a most opportune time. The
new process was the manufacture of paper, obtained from Moham-
medan sources, the first paper-mill being set up in Italy, in 1276.
By 1450 paper was in common use throughout Europe, and the way
was open for one of the world's greatest inventions. This was made
in German lands, the first engraved page dating from 1423, the first
movable types from 1438, and the first printed book from 1456. By
1475 the printing-press had been set up in the leading cities of
Europe. From then on the way was open for a rapid extension of
schools and learning, and the press was destined in time to surpass in
importance the pulpit and the sermon, and to become one of the
world's greatest instruments for human progress and individual
liberty.

The new classical secondary school. The important and outstanding educational result of the revival of ancient learning by
Italian scholars was that it laid the basis for a new type of school below that of the recently created universities, and one destined in
time to be much more widely opened to promising youths than the
cathedral and monastic schools of the Middle Ages had been. This
new school, basing its curriculum on the intellectual inheritance re-
covered from the ancient world by Italian scholars, dominated the
secondary-school training of the middle and higher classes of society
for the next four hundred years. This type of school was well under
way by 1450, and it clearly controlled education until after 1850.
Out of the efforts of Italian scholars to resurrect, reconstruct, understand, and utilize in education the fruits of our inheritance from the
Greek and Roman worlds, modern secondary education arose.
Classical schools, known as Court Schools in Italy, Collèges and
Lycées in France, Gymnasia in German lands, and Latin Grammar
Schools in England, were founded. The reformed Latin Grammar
School, founded by Dean Colet, at Saint Paul's in London, in 1510,
thoroughly established the type, and was copied throughout England
during the succeeding century. Many of the old cathedral and
monastic schools of England were made over, after his model, into
reformed Latin Grammar Schools to teach pure Latin and Greek and
some elementary mathematics. In particular these schools were to

teach Latin as a restored and living tongue. This type of secondary school had become common all through England by 1600, and it was the type our early New England settlers knew and brought to and set up in the American colonies.

The revolt against authority. Another outgrowth of the Italian Renaissance, and for the history of education in America a much more important development, was the change in attitude toward the dogmatic and repressive rule of the Church which came as a somewhat natural result of the work of the Renaissance scholars, the new life in Christendom consequent upon the Crusades, the revival of commerce, the rise of city governments, the formation of lawyer and merchant classes, the founding of new States, the evolution of the university organizations, and the discovery and spread of the art of printing. All these forces united to stimulate thinking, to awaken a new attitude toward the old religious problems, and to prepare Western Europe for a rapid evolution out of the medieval conditions which had for so long dominated all action and thinking. In fact, about 1500 was the most stimulating period intellectually that Europe had known since the days of ancient Greece and Rome (**R. 4**), and the world seemed ready for rapid advances in many directions, but the promise was not to be fulfilled.

Had the Church assumed a tolerant attitude toward the many progressive tendencies of the time, the whole history of modern life, and particularly the history of educational development in America, with which in this volume we are to be particularly concerned, might have been different. It did not, however, and whether we be Catholic or Protestant makes no difference with the facts of history. So far as the Protestant Revolts which now broke are concerned, we may believe that Luther and Zwingli and Calvin and Knox were merely ambitious and selfish disturbers who made trouble without cause, or we may go to the opposite extreme and believe that they were inspired men, leading the world back to a truer religion. The facts of history remain the same in either case, and our religious beliefs need in no way enter into the problem. The great outstanding fact remains that one Martin Luther, in 1517, disputed the practices of the Church, later defied its authority, and was excommunicated by it in 1520; that the German people, and especially the German princes, largely adopted Luther's point of view and revolted; and that the revolt spread to other countries in the North and West of

Europe, and as a result the Western or Roman Catholic Church, which had remained one for so many centuries and been the one great unifying force in Western Europe, was permanently divided. How much of Europe was lost to the Church is shown by the accompanying map.

FIG. I. RESULTS OF THE PROTESTANT REVOLTS

The resulting conflict. Of course the revolt against the authority of the Church, once inaugurated, could not easily be stopped. This is nearly always the case when revolution has to be resorted to to secure progress or reform. The same right of freedom in religious belief which Luther claimed for himself and his followers had of course to be extended to others. This the German, the English, and other Protestants were not much more willing to do than had been the Catholics before them. The world was not as yet ready for such rapid advances, and religious toleration, though established in principle by the revolt, was an idea to which the world required a long time to accustom itself. It took a century and a half of intermittent religious warfare, during which Catholic and Protestant waged war on one another, plundered and pillaged lands, and killed each other for the salvation of their respective souls, before the people of Western Europe were willing to stop fighting and recognize for others that for which they were fighting for themselves. For still another century the world was divided into hostile camps as a result of the hatreds engendered by this religious warfare. When religious toleration finally became established by law, civilization had made a tremendous advance.

The result of this long religious strife was to check the orderly progress of civilization, spread misery and suffering abroad, and drive from the countries persecuted those who would rather leave than conform. From the point of view of the student of the history of education in America, this last was a very important result, as it was from among these irreconcilable non-conformists that the early settlers of most of our American Colonies were drawn. The early educational history of America is hardly to be understood without some knowledge of the different religious forces and hatreds awakened as a result of the Protestant Revolts.

The dominant idea, and its educational consequences. What we are primarily concerned with, however, are the educational consequences of this break with authority. To understand this we need to know the dominant idea underlying Luther's action, and for that matter the action of Zwingli, Calvin, and Knox as well. The idea was that of substituting the authority of the Bible in religious matters for the authority of the Church, and this in turn was one of the results of the revival of the study of Greek and the recovery of the Gospels in the original. Such a change meant the substitution of individual responsibility for salvation for the collective responsibility of the Church, and this meant that those who were to be saved, in theory at least, must be able to read the word of God, participate intelligently in the Church service, and shape their lives in accordance with the commands of the Heavenly Father. Whether one accepts the Protestant position as sound or not depends largely on one's religious training and beliefs, and need not concern us here, as it makes no difference with the course which history actually has taken. We can believe either way, and the course of history remains the same.

The educational consequences of this position, though, were very important, and are our chief concern. Under the older religious theory of collective judgment and collective responsibility for salvation — that is, the judgment of the Church rather than that of individuals — it was not important that more than a few be educated. Under the new theory of individual responsibility promulgated by the Protestants the education of all became a vital necessity. To provide this education meant the creation of an entirely new type of school — the elementary, for the masses, and in the native tongue — to supplement the secondary Latin schools of the Renaissance and the still older cathedral and monastic Latin schools for the education of those who were to become the leaders in Church and State. Never before had such schools seemed necessary. These schools were in time created, and the result of the evolution in the centuries since has been the development, all through Europe, of a double school system, the two parts of which — an elementary school system for the masses, and a secondary school system for the classes — have had but little in common. We in America started this way also, but before such a development had made much headway it was turned aside by the rise of a distinctively American and democratic spirit, as will be explained in subsequent chapters, which in time demanded one common school system for all.

The modern elementary vernacular school, then, may be said to be essentially a product of the Protestant Revolts. This is true in a special sense among those peoples which embraced some form of the Lutheran or Calvinistic faiths. These were the Germans, Moravians, Swedes, Norwegians, Danes, Dutch, Walloons, Swiss, Scotch, Scotch-Irish, French Huguenots, and the English Puritans. As the Renaissance gave a new emphasis to the development of secondary schools by supplying them with a large amount of new subject-matter and a new motive, so the Reformation movement gave a new motive for the education in religion and the elements of learning of children not intended for the service of the State or the Church, and the development of elementary vernacular schools was the result. Only in England, of all the revolting countries, did this Protestant conception as to the necessity of education for salvation fail to take firm root, with the result that elementary education in England awaited the new political and industrial impulses of the latter half of the nineteenth century for its development. These educational attitudes were all faithfully reflected in the settlement of the American Colonies, as we shall see in the next chapter.

The discovery and settlement of America. The discovery of America was another development of the desire for travel and discovery awakened by the Crusades, the revival of commerce which now sought a sea-route to the riches of the Indies, and the new intellectual life in Christendom which stimulated thinkers to question the old theories as to the shape and position of our earth. These impulses led to the perfecting of the compass in the fourteenth century, the revival of geographical discovery, the rounding of the Cape of Good Hope (1487), the discovery of the new world (1492), and the circumnavigation of the globe by Magellan (1519–21).

After the first century of exploration of the new continent had passed, and after the claims as to ownership had been largely settled, colonization began. The first colonization, that of Virginia, was actuated wholly by gain, and rested on a commercial basis, and this also was largely true of the other Southern Colonies. To the northward, however, the settlements were mostly due to the desire to secure religious freedom, and resulted from the warfare and persecution following the Protestant Revolts in Europe. Those who came to establish new homes along the bleak North Atlantic coast did so that here, in a new land, they might establish their churches, order their civil life, and bring up their children to worship God after the dictates of their own conscience (**R. 5**).

It took a high degree of courage and deep religious conviction to cause men, at that time, to take such a step, as it meant the giving up of all the associations of a lifetime and the bringing of their families to a new and unbroken land to start life over again. (**R. 6**). The result was that the American Colonies settled from religious motives were from the first peopled by a sturdy and self-reliant stock, and the character of this stock has repeatedly shown itself in the history of the different Colonies, and later in the history of our Nation. Just what our different colonists came for, what they tried to do by means of education, what types of schools and educational attitudes they established here, and how their belief in education for salvation or lack of such has colored our whole colonial and national history, it will be the purpose of the chapters which follow to set forth.

QUESTIONS FOR DISCUSSION

1. Would any type of general education be possible among a people where might made right?
2. Give a number of illustrations to show the presence of Greek and Roman elements in the foundations of our civilization.
3. Compare the barbarian invasions of the fifth and sixth centuries with the Bolshevik destructions of the twentieth.
4. Why did it take so long for the revival of the study of Greek to extend over Western Europe?
5. Show how the evolution of Latin higher schools for the education of boys from the middle and higher classes of society was a perfectly natural evolution.
6. Show how the elementary vernacular school for the masses was a natural outgrowth of the Protestant Revolts and the invention of printing.
7. Show that a class, instead of a common or mass system of education, has been a perfectly natural development for European States.
8. Show that a mass system of education has been a perfectly natural development with us.

SELECTED READINGS

In the accompanying volume of *Readings* the following selections, related to the subject-matter of this chapter, are reproduced:

1. Cubberley: Greece and Rome Contrasted.
2. Draper: Educational Influences of the Church Services.
3. Cubberley: The Thirteenth and Fourteenth Centuries.
*4. Cubberley: About A.D. 1500, a Stimulating Time.
*5. Bradford: The Puritans Leave England.
*6. Tudor: Character and Motives of the Early New England Colonists.

QUESTIONS ON THE READINGS

1. Show the large importance of such sharply contrasted peoples as the Greeks and Romans (1) in laying the foundations for a great civilization.
2. Can you explain the greater simplicity of the church services in modern Protestant churches than in the Roman (2) or Greek Catholic churches?
3. Show how the printing press soon became a formidable rival of the pulpit (2) as a means for education and human progress.
4. How do you explain the lack of self-confidence and historical perspective (3) of the medieval man?
5. Characterize the educational significance of the Renaissance (3).
6. How do you account for such checks to human progress as took place shortly after A.D. 1500 (4), to cite one instance?
7. Characterize the feelings and the emotions of the Puritans, as expressed in the extract (5) from Governor Bradford's narrative.
8. Show the future values, in the founding of a State, of such characteristics and motives as the early New England colonists exhibited (6).

---

* If only a portion of the Readings can be used, the more important ones are indicated by an asterisk, and this plan will be followed in subsequent chapters.

CHAPTER II

THE BEGINNINGS OF AMERICAN EDUCATION

I. ORIGIN OF OUR TYPE ATTITUDES TOWARD EDUCATION

Religious origin of our schools. Schools, with us, as with the older European countries from which our early settlers came, arose largely as children of the Church. From instruments of religion they have been changed gradually into important instruments of the State. The first schools in America were clearly the fruits of the Protestant Revolts in Europe. The reformers everywhere had insisted upon the necessity of a knowledge of the Gospels as a means to personal salvation. This meant, carried to its logical conclusion, that each child, girls as well as boys, should be taught to read so that they might become acquainted with the commandments of God and learn what was demanded of them. Not being able to realize their ideals of life and worship in the old home lands, large numbers of religious congregations left Europe and came as bodies (**R. 5**) to America. Here they settled in the wilderness, set up a civil government (**R. 7**) and began life anew. Among other things they brought with them their European ideas as to religion and the training of children, and hence a European background lies behind all the beginnings of American education.

The religious basis for type attitudes. Practically all of the early settlers of America came from among those people and from those lands which had embraced some form of the Protestant faith, and most of them came to America to enjoy a religious freedom impossible in the countries from which they came. This was especially true of the French Huguenots, who settled along the coast of the Carolinas; the Calvinistic Dutch and Walloons, who settled in and about New Amsterdam; the Scotch and Scotch-Irish Presbyterians, who settled in New Jersey, and later extended along the Allegheny Mountain ridges into all the Southern Colonies; the English Quakers about Philadelphia, and a few English Baptists and Methodists in eastern Pennsylvania; the Swedish Lutherans along the Delaware; the German Lutherans, Moravians, Mennonites, Dunkers and Reformed-Church Germans who settled in large numbers in the mountain valleys of Pennsylvania; and the Calvinistic dissenters from the English National Church, known as Puritans, who settled the New England Colonies.[1] and who, more than any others, gave

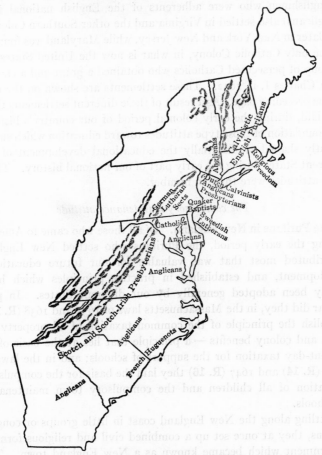

FIG. 2. SHOWING THE RELIGIOUS FAITHS OF THE EARLY COLONISTS IN AMERICA

direction to the future development of education in our American States. With practically all these early religious groups the edu-

[1] Educationally, the concern is with four Colonies, two in Massachusetts, which united in 1692, and two in Connecticut, which united in 1665. The founders of Rhode Island wanted nothing in common with the people who banished them — not even their education.

cation of the young for membership in the Church, and the perpetuation of a learned ministry for the congregations, immediately elicited serious attention.

Englishmen who were adherents of the English national faith (Anglicans) also settled in Virginia and the other Southern Colonies, and later in New York and New Jersey, while Maryland was founded as the only Catholic Colony, in what is now the United States, by a group of persecuted Catholics who obtained a grant and a charter from Charles I, in 1632. These settlements are shown on the map on the preceding page. As a result of these different settlements there was laid, during the early colonial period of our country's history, the foundation of those type attitudes toward education which subsequently shaped so materially the educational development of the different States during the early part of our national history. These type attitudes were three in number.

1. *The compulsory-maintenance attitude*

The Puritans in New England. Of all those who came to America during the early period, the Puritans who settled New England contributed most that was valuable for our future educational development, and established in practice principles which have finally been adopted generally by our different States. In particular did they, in the Massachusetts laws of 1634 and 1638 (**R. 13**), establish the principle of the common taxation of all property for town and colony benefits — a principle that lies at the basis of all present-day taxation for the support of schools; and in the laws of 1642 (**R. 14**) and 1647 (**R. 16**) they laid the basis for the compulsory education of all children and the compulsory town maintenance of schools.

Settling along the New England coast in little groups or congregations, they at once set up a combined civil and religious form of government which became known as a New England town. The "Meeting House" was the center of their civil and religious life, and in it they met both as a religious congregation and as a civil government. The two were one in membership and spirit. Being deeply imbued with Calvinistic ideas as to religion and government, the Puritans founded here a series of little town governments, but loosely bound together in colony federations, the corner stones of which were religion and education (**Rs. 7, 8**). The attitude of the early Puritans toward religion and learning is well expressed in the following extract[1] from an early New England pamphlet, *New England's First Fruits*, printed in London in 1643:

After God had carried vs safe to New England
And wee had builded our houses
Provided necessaries for our liveli hood
Reard convenient places for Gods worship
And setled the civill government
One of the next things we longed for
And looked after was to advance learning
And perpetuate it to posterity
Dreading to leave an illiterate ministry
To the churches when our present ministers
Shall lie in the Dust.

Educational beginnings. At first home instruction and the old established type of apprenticeship training were depended upon to furnish the necessary ability to read and to participate in the home and church religious services, the great religious purpose which had brought the colonists to America being the motive which was to insure such instruction. Very early (1636) an English type college was founded in the Massachusetts Colony, partly by colony action,[2] but more by the gift of John Harvard[3] (**R. 10**), that "the tongues

[1] The extract given above, together with the order of the General Court granting £400 "towards a schoale or colledge" in the Colony, are carved in stone tablets placed on either side of the west gateway to the Harvard College yard.

[2] The Records of the General Court, for October 28, 1636, contains the following vote:
"The Court agree to give Four Hundred Pounds toward a School or College, whereof Two Hundred Pounds shall be paid the next year and Two Hundred Pounds when the work is finished, and the next Court to appoint where and what building."
The next General Court appointed twelve of the most eminent men of the Colony "to take order for a college at Newtown," and the Court then changed the name Newtown to Cambridge, "in grateful tribute" to the old-world university in whose colleges so many of the early settlers had been educated.

[3] "But that which laid the most significant stone in the foundation, was the last will of Mr. John Harvard, a reverend, and excellent minister of the gospel, who dying at Charlstown, of a consumption, quickly after his arrival here, bequeathed the sum of seven hundred, seventy nine pounds, seventeen shillings and two pence (half his property, together with his entire library) towards the pious work of building a Colledge, which was now set a foot. A committee then being chosen, to prosecute an affair, so happily commenced, it soon found encouragement from several other benefactors: the other colonies sent some small help to the undertaking, and several particular gentlemen did more, than whole colonies to support and forward it: but because the memorable Mr. John Harvard, led the way by a generosity exceeding the most of them, that followed his name was justly æternized, by its having the name of Harvard Colledge imposed upon it...." (Cotton Mather, in his *Magnalia Christi Americana*, 1698.)
The catalogue of his library of 260 volumes is still treasured among the archives of Harvard College.

and arts" might be taught and learning and piety maintained. In 1701 the Connecticut Assembly provided for a college (Yale) in that Colony (**R. 19**) also. In addition, the town religious governments early began the voluntary establishment [1] of town Latin

Schools (**Rs. 11, 12**) to prepare boys for the colleges (Harvard, Yale) which the colonial legislatures had established.[2] Clergymen also, in many instances, undertook, in addition to their regular duties, the instruction of a few boys in classical learnings, acting either as a tutor for them or receiving them into their families as boarding pupils. The next step was the organization of town free schools, though where the first free school was established is not certain (**R. 9**).

FIG. 3. JOHN HARVARD
(1607–38)

From French's Statue in Cambridge

In this establishment in the wilderness of New England of a typical English educational system of the time — that is, private instruction in reading and religion in the homes and by the master of apprentices, Latin grammar schools in the larger towns to prepare boys for the colony college, and an English-type college to prepare ministers for the churches — we see

[1] A few examples will illustrate:

Boston, in town meeting in 1635, laid the foundations of the Boston Latin School by the adoption of the following order:

"Likewise, it was then generally agreed upon that our brother Philemon Pormont shall be entreated to become schole-master for the teaching and nourtering of children with us."

A year later Charlestown voted to arrange with William Witherell "to keep a school for a twelvemonth," and fixed his salary at £40 a year.

Cambridge, in 1638, established its first school by voting certain lands for "the vse of mr Nath Eaten as long as he shall be Imployed" in the work of teaching the school.

Newbury, the year following, granted to Anthony Somerby "foure akers of upland" and "sixe akers of salt marsh" as an "encouragement to keepe schoole for one year."

Salem opened a grammar school in 1637, Dorchester in 1639, Ipswich in 1641, and Roxburie in 1645.

[2] "And by the side of the Colledge a faire Grammar Schoole, for the training up of young schollars, and fitting of them for Academical learning, that still as they are judged ripe they may be received into the Colledge of this Schoole." (Note on the founding of the grammar school at Cambridge, in *New England's First Fruits.*— **R. 10.**)

"The Erection of ye said Schoole being principally for ye Institucion of hopeful youth in ye Latin tongue, and other learned Languages soe far as to prepare such youths for ye colledge and publique service of ye Country in Church, & Commonwealth. (Statement of purpose of founding the Hopkins Grammar School at New Haven, in 1684. — **R. 12.**)

manifested the deep Puritan-Calvinistic zeal for education as a bulwark of Church and State. As in England, the system was voluntary, and clearly subordinate to the Church. The Church, though, in early New England, was the State and more, and from the first (Law of 1638 — **R. 13**) it had required equalized contributions from all for the support of the undertakings of "both church and commonwealth."

FIG. 4. TOWN SCHOOL AT DEDHAM, MASSACHUSETTS, BUILT IN 1648

The Massachusetts Law of 1642. It early became evident, however, that these voluntary efforts on the part of the people and the towns would not be sufficient to insure that general education which was required by the Puritan religious theory. Under the hard pioneer conditions and the suffering which ensued, many parents and masters of apprentices apparently proved neglectful of their educational duties. Accordingly the leaders in the Puritan Church appealed to what was then their servant, the State as represented in the colonial legislature, to assist them in compelling parents and masters to observe their obligations. The result was the famous Massachusetts Law of 1642 (**R. 14**), which directed the officials of each town to ascertain, from time to time, if parents and masters were attending to their educational duties; if all children were being trained "in learning and labor and other employments profitable to the Commonwealth"; and if the children were being taught "to read and understand the principles of religion and the capital laws of the country." The officers were empowered to impose fines on those who failed to give proper instruction, or to report to the officer when required, and the courts were insistent that the towns be compelled to obey the law (**R. 15**). This Law of 1642 is remarkable in that, for the first time in the English-speaking world, a legislative body representing the State ordered that all children should be taught to read. This was a distinctively Calvinistic contribution to our new-world life, and a contribution of large future importance.

The Massachusetts Law of 1647. The Law, however, did not establish schools, nor did it direct the employment of schoolmasters.

After true English fashion, the provision of education was still left with the homes. The results still continuing unsatisfactory, five years later the colonial legislature enacted the famous Law of 1647 (**R. 16**), by means of which it has been asserted that "the Puritan government of Massachusetts rendered probably its greatest service to the future." After recounting in a preamble that it had in the past been "one chief point of that old deluder, Satan, to keep men from a knowledge of the Scriptures... by keeping them in an unknown tongue," so now "by persuading from the use of tongues,"... learning was in danger of "being buried in the grave of our fathers in church and commonwealth," the Law then ordered:

1. That every town having 50 householders should at once appoint a teacher of reading and writing, and provide for his wages in such manner as the town might determine; and

2. That every town having 100 householders must provide a (Latin) grammar school to fit youths for the university, under a penalty of £5 for failure to do so.

This Law represents a distinct advance over the Law of 1642. The State here, acting again as the servant of the Church, enacted a law for which there were no English precedents. Not only was a school system ordered established — elementary for all towns and children, and secondary [1] for the youths in the larger towns — but, for the first time among English-speaking people, there was the assertion of the right of the State to require communities to establish and maintain schools, under penalty of a fine if they refused to do so. That the law was not always popular, and that the courts had to be appealed to, here and there, to enforce the law, does not alter the importance of this early legislation.

Importance of these two laws. It can safely be asserted that these two Massachusetts laws of 1642 and 1647 represent not only new educational ideas in the English-speaking world, but that they, together with the laws of 1634 and 1638 (**R. 13**) providing for the equalized and compulsory taxation of all for all town charges, also represent the very foundation stones upon which our American public school systems have later been constructed.

Mr. Martin, the historian of the Massachusetts public school

[1] The grammar schools of Massachusetts did much, during the seventeenth century, to contribute to the fame of the Colony as an educational center. Many of the schools, and their teachers, were locally famous, and numerous grants of land were made for their maintenance.

system, states the fundamental principles which underlie this legislation as follows:

1. The universal education of youth is essential to the well-being of the State.

2. The obligation to furnish this education rests primarily upon the parent.

3. The State has a right to enforce this obligation.

4. The State may fix a standard which shall determine the kind of education, and the minimum amount.

5. Public money, raised by a general tax, may be used to provide such education as the State requires. This tax may be general, though the school attendance is not.

6. Education higher than the rudiments may be supplied by the State. Opportunity must be provided, at public expense, for youths who wish to be fitted for the university.

Mr. Martin then adds the following significant comment:

It is important to note here that the idea underlying all this legislation was neither paternalistic nor socialistic. The child is to be educated, not to advance his personal interests, *but because the State will suffer if he is not educated*. The State does not provide schools to relieve the parent, nor because it can educate better than the parent can, but because it can thereby better enforce the obligation which it imposes.

These laws became the basis for legislation in all the other New England Colonies, except Rhode Island, which had been founded on the basis of religious freedom. Connecticut, in 1650, adopted the Massachusetts Law of 1647, word for word, with an amplifying preamble making the demand for the teaching of children still more definite (**R. 17**), and in 1657 gave further orders[1] for "the setting up of schools"; while Plymouth Colony, which was not joined to Massachusetts until 1692, enacted a series of laws which first (1658) recommended that every town provide a schoolmaster (**R. 18b**), then virtually adopted (1671) the Massachusetts Law of 1642 (**R. 18c**), set aside money (1673–74) from the proceeds of the Cape Cod fisheries as aid for schools (**R. 18e**), ordered the establishment of Latin grammar schools (1677) with aid for such (**R. 18f**), and appealed to the towns (1672) for aid for "that Nursery of Learning att harveard Colledge in Cambridge" (**R. 18d**). Still later, Massachusetts, in 1654, commended to the Selectmen of the towns that they exercise

---

[1] In 1657 the Connecticut Court ordered "that in every plantation, where a schoole is not already set up and maintayned, forthwith indeavors shall be used that a schoolemaster be procuried that may attend the worke." One third of the teacher's salary was to be paid by the town, and two thirds by parents of the pupils.

some supervision over the character of the teachers employed by the towns, and again, in 1693, charged the Selectmen and the towns jointly to see that schools were maintained, with power to tax therefor.   In 1680, New Hampshire adopted the Massachusetts law almost unchanged.   The conceptions as to the compulsory establishment and maintenance of schools which these laws embodied deeply influenced the educational development of all the States to which New England people later migrated in any numbers.

In the early New England Colonies, then, was established the first of the three important type attitudes to which we earlier referred — that of the State compelling the towns to establish schools, and parents to send their children to school to learn to read and to receive instruction in religion.   The State here, acting as the servant of the Church, enacted legislation which formed a precedent and fixed a tradition as to school management and support, and one which was retained after State and Church had parted company.

2. *The parochial-school attitude*

Pennsylvania as a type.   In New England the Puritan-Calvinists had had a complete monopoly of both Church and State.   Into the Middle Colonies, best represented by New Jersey and Pennsylvania, there had come a mixture of peoples representing different Protestant faiths, and no such monopoly was possible there.   The English and Dutch had mixed in New York; the English, Dutch, Swedes, Scotch-Irish, and Germans had settled in New Jersey; while in Pennsylvania, which Penn had founded on the basis of religious freedom, a large number of English and German Protestant sects had settled. All were Protestant in faith, though representing different creeds and nationalities; all believed in the importance of being able to read the Bible as a means to personal salvation; and all made efforts looking toward the establishment of schools as a part of their church organizations.   Unlike New England, though, no sect was in a majority.   Church control by each denomination was, as a result, considered to be most satisfactory, and hence no appeal to the State was made by the churches for assistance in carrying out their religious purposes.[1]   The clergymen usually were the teachers in the paro-

---

[1] The conflict between the English and the German settlers was unfavorable to the development of any public form of education, and the long struggle between the different races and sects proved to be a serious drawback to educational development.

chial schools established (**R. 45**) until a regular schoolmaster could be had, while private pay schools were opened in a few of the larger towns. These, as were the church services, were conducted in the language of the different immigrants. Girls were educated as well as boys, the emphasis being placed on reading, writing, counting, and religion, rather than upon any form of higher training.

The result was the development in Pennsylvania, and to some extent in the other Middle Colonies as well, of a policy of depending upon Church and private effort for educational advantages. As a consequence, the provision of education, aside from certain rudimentary and religious instruction thought necessary for religious purposes, and aside from the apprenticing of orphans and the children of the very poor (**R. 33**), was left largely for those who could afford to pay for the privilege.[1] Of the different denominations, the Quakers, in particular, rendered notable service in the founding of schools in both New Jersey (**R. 20**) and Pennsylvania (**R. 21**). The Lutherans in Pennsylvania also did important work.

Under the freedom thus allowed many communities made but indifferent provisions, or allowed their schools to lapse entirely. In the primitive conditions of the time the interest, even in religious education, frequently declined almost to the vanishing point. Two attempts were made, later on, to enforce the maintenance of schools in the Colony; but one, the Law of 1683, was vetoed by William and Mary as foreign to English practices, and the other (1693) proved unenforceable (**R. 22**). In consequence, except in a few of its cities (**R. 23**) Pennsylvania settled down to a policy of leaving education to private and parochial effort, and in time this attitude became so firmly established that the do-as-you-please idea persisted up to 1834, and was only overcome then after bitter opposition. In New Jersey and New York this same policy prevailed during the whole of the colonial period. Each parochial group did as it wished, and private and church effort, in pay and charity schools, with apprenticeship training for the children of the poor and for orphans (**Rs. 25, 33**), provided practically all the educational facilities available until well into our national period.

In secondary education little more was accomplished. Though secondary schools were opened at a number of places in Pennsylvania.

---

[1] "The educational policy for 150 years after the coming of Penn was to make those who were able to do so pay for the education of their children, and to educate the children of others free." (Wickersham, Jas. P., *History of Education in Pennsylvania*, p. 180.)

the efforts often were short-lived. Economic conditions and the pressure of wars were not favorable. Brave efforts were made by some of the German sects to maintain schools of a high grade, and the Quakers exerted themselves to the same end, often uniting with other denominations to secure results. Here and there the Episcopalian churches, in co-operation with the Society for the Promotion of the Gospel, maintained a school, as did the Log College Presbyterians. Yet it was an up-hill road that they all traveled.[1]

3. *The pauper-school non-state-interference attitude*

Virginia as the type. In the settlement of Virginia and the Southern Colonies, almost all the attending conditions were in contrast with those of the New England Colonies. The early settlers were from the same class of English people, but with the important difference that, whereas the New England settlers were dissenters from the English National Church and had come to America to obtain freedom in religious worship, the settlers in Virginia were adherents of that Church and had come to America for gain. The marked differences in climate and possible crops led to the large-plantation type of settlement, instead of the compact little New England town; the introduction of numbers of "indentured white servants,"[2] and later negro slaves, led to the development of classes in society instead of to the New England type of democracy, making common schools impossible; and the lack of any strong religious motive for education naturally led to the adoption of English practices instead of the development of distinctively colonial schools. The tutor in the home, education in small private and select pay-schools, or edu-

---

[1] Of these various efforts Wickersham writes:

"By 1775 not only was the number of scholarly men in the Province small, but comparatively few grown persons could do more than read, write, and calculate according to the elementary rules of Arithmetic, and many remained wholly illiterate. There was little demand for higher institutions of learning, and few existed. The College and the Friends' Public School in Philadelphia, the Academy at Germantown, and scarcely half a dozen private classical schools in the older settled counties, with in all an attendance of three to four hundred students, absolutely exhaust the advantages enjoyed at home by our Revolutionary fathers." (*History of Education in Pennsylvania*, p. 255.)

[2] This unfortunate and dispossessed class was composed of political offenders, convicted criminals, paupers from the workhouses, vagabonds from city streets, and some fairly well-educated persons who were so poor that they would bind themselves to a period of service for a chance in a new land. The ship captain brought them to the planter, who paid their transportation in return for the right to their labor for the period of indenture — usually five years, but ranging from two to seven. Some of these indentured servants later became renters or tenants, and a few eventually became planters. On the other hand, many others, unable to gain a foothold, came in time to form the "poor white" class of the South.

cation in the mother country for the sons of the well-to-do planters were the prevailing methods adopted among the wealthier people,[1] while the poorer classes were left with only such advantages as apprenticeship training and the few pauper schools of the time (R. 25) might provide.   The education of the leading class may have been "wider and more generous" than in the New England Colonies, but it was the education of a small class rather than that of the great bulk of a people.

Practically all the Virginia colonial legislation relating to education refers either to William and Mary College, founded in 1693, "that the church of Virginia may be furnished with a seminary of the ministers of the gospel, and that the youth may be piously educated,[2] in good letters and manners, and that the Christian faith may be propagated among the Western Indians" (R. 24), or to the education of orphans and the children of the poor "in Christian religion and in the rudiments of learning and to provide for their necessaries according to the competents of their estate" (R. 25).   Both these interests were typically English.   The seventeenth-century legislation included the compulsory apprenticeship of the children of the poor (R. 33), training in a trade, the requirement that the public authorities must provide opportunities for this type of education, and the use of both local and colony funds for the purpose — all, as the Statutes state, "according to the aforesaid laudable custom in the Kingdom of England."   It was not until 1705 that Virginia reached the point, reached by Massachusetts in 1642, of requiring that "the master of the (apprenticed) orphan shall be obliged to teach him to read and write," while New York did not enact such legislation until 1788 (R. 34).

During the entire colonial period the indifference of the mother country to general education was steadily reflected in Virginia and the other Colonies which followed the English example.   As in the mother country, education was not considered as any business of the State, nor did the Church give any great attention to it.   Vir-

---

[1] When the royal governor of Virginia, William Berkeley, reported to the authorities in England on conditions in the Colony, in 1671, he wrote, concerning educational practices: "The same course that is taken in England out of towns; every man according to his ability instructing his children."

[2] When the English attorney general learned of the grant of the Charter and £2000, he flew into a rage and for a time refused the order for the money.   Upon being told by the Virginia emissary that "the people of Virginia had souls to be saved," the irate custodian of the Crown's purse exclaimed: "Souls!   Dam your souls!   Make *tobacco!*"

ginia thus stands as the clearest example of the third type of colonial attitude toward education — viz., tutors and private schools for those who could afford them, with church charity schools for some of the children of the poorer members, but no state interest in the problem of education except to see that orphans and children of the very poor were properly apprenticed and trained in some useful trade, which in Virginia usually was agriculture.

This type in other Colonies. In the other American Colonies which followed the example of Virginia — New York, New Jersey, Delaware, Maryland, the Carolinas, and Georgia — the English charity-school idea largely dominated such education as was provided, with the apprenticing of orphans always a prominent feature, and a "free school," supported by assessments, found here and there with a master "capable of teaching the learned languages and the useful parts of Mathematics." The "Society for the Propagation of the Gospel in Foreign Parts," an English society, chartered in 1701, to act as an auxiliary of the Church of England "to train children in the tenets and worship of the Church, through the direct agency of schools," provided for these Anglican Colonies probably the best charity schools in America during the later colonial period. The work of this Society in New York was specially noteworthy (**R. 27**), though valuable work was done in other Colonies. Its schoolmasters were well selected and sound in the faith,[1] and the children were taught reading, writing, a little arithmetic, the catechism, and the religious observances of the English National Church.[2] The church charity schools of this Society furnished the nearest ap-

---

[1] The Society's regulations as to schoolmasters required:

"1. That no person be admitted as Schoolmaster till he bring certificate of the following particulars: (1) his age, (2) his condition of life, whether single or mary'd, (3) his temper, (4) his prudence, (5) his learning, (6) his sober and pious conversation, (7) his zeal for the Xtian Religion and diligence in his calling, (8) his affection to the present government, and (9) his conformity to the doctrines and discipline of the Ch. of England.

"2. That no person shall be sent as a Schoolmaster by Soc. till he has been tryed and approved by 3 members appointed by the Soc. or Com^ee. who shall testify by word or writing his ability to teach reading, writing and the Catechism of the Ch. of England and such exposition thereof as the Soc. shall order." (Adopted, Feb. 15, 1711-12.)

[2] The original plan for the organization of this Society, drawn up in 1697, provided, among other purposes, the following:

"That they proceed also to set up Cathechetical Schools for the Education of Poor Children in Reading, Writing, and more especially in the Principles of the Christian Religion."

A certificate of the Mayor of New York, dated 1713, states that one "Wm. Huddlestone, Schoolmaster of said City, received into his school forty poor Boyes... which he hath dilligently and faithfully instructed in reading the English tongue, the Church Catechism, the English Liturgy and singing of Psalms, with writing and arithmetic, of which several are already put out to trades."

proach to a free school system found in the Anglican Colonies before the Revolution. They were, though, intended for a class, the free places usually being open only to the children of the poorer communicants in the Anglican Church.

Type attitudes represented by 1750. The seventeenth century thus witnessed the transplanting of European ideas as to government and religion and education to the new American Colonies, and by the eighteenth century we find three clearly marked types of educational practice or conceptions as to educational responsibility established on American soil.

The first was the strong Calvinistic conception of a religious State, supporting a system of common schools, higher Latin schools, and a college, both for religious and civic ends. This type dominated New England, and is best represented by Massachusetts and Connecticut. From New England it spread westward, and deeply influenced the later educational development of all States to which New England people migrated. It was the educational contribution of Calvinism to America. Out of it, by the later separation of Church and State, our modern state school systems have been evolved.

The second was the parochial school conception of the Dutch, Moravians, Mennonites, German and Swedish Lutherans, German-Reformed Church, Quakers, Presbyterians, Baptists, and Catholics. This type is best represented by Protestant Pennsylvania and Catholic Maryland. It stood for church control of all educational effort, resented state interference, was dominated only by church purposes, and in time came to be a serious obstacle in the way of state organization and control.

The third type, into which the second type tended to fuse, was the attitude of the Church of England, which conceived of public education, aside from collegiate education, as intended chiefly for orphans and the children of the poor, and as a charity which the State was under little or no obligation to assist in supporting. All children of the upper and middle classes in society attended private or church schools, or were taught by tutors in their homes, and for such instruction paid a proper tuition fee. Paupers and orphans, in limited numbers and for a limited time, were provided with some form of useful education at the expense of either the Church or the State.

These three types or attitudes toward public education became fixed American types, and deeply influenced subsequent American educational development, as we shall see in the chapters which follow.

TYPES OF SCHOOLS TRANSPLANTED AND DEVELOPED

Transplanting the old home institutions. At the time the early colonists came to America the parish elementary school for religious training had become an established institution in Scandinavian, Dutch, and German lands, while in England certain main types of schools had been developed. All of these types were transplanted to America, and established here in much the same form that they had developed in the home lands. The Dutch in New Amsterdam, the Swedes along the Delaware, and the different German sects in Pennsylvania and the other Colonies where they settled, reproduced in America the Lutheran parish school of Europe, with its instruction in reading, singing, religion, and sometimes writing, and taught not uncommonly by the pastor, but sometimes by the sexton or other type of teacher. The Quakers, in the Central Colonies, similarly established a type of parish school in their communities (**Rs. 20, 21**), as did the Dutch in and about New York (**R. 44**). This type of school continued largely unchanged throughout the whole of the colonial period.

The English, who formed the great bulk of the early immigrants to the American Colonies, reproduced in the different Colonies the main types of schools at that time existing in the mother country. These were, for those who could afford to pay for education, excepting in Massachusetts and Connecticut, where schools were maintained in part by the towns and in part by fees: (1) the petty or dame school, (2) the writing school, (3) the Latin grammar school, and (4) the English-type college, for preparation for the ministry and the service of the State; and (5) the charity or pauper elementary school for a limited number of indigents, and (6) apprenticeship training for orphans and the children of pauper parents. The first three became the characteristic schools of New England, the English-type college was found from Massachusetts to Virginia, the fifth type largely characterized English educational work in the Central and Southern Colonies, while apprenticeship training was utilized in all the Colonies. It was these English-type schools, rather than the continental European type of parochial school of the Central Colonies, which ultimately exerted the greatest influence on our early American educational development.

The petty or dame school. The primary teaching at first was done at home, but the dame school soon developed to supply the place of home instruction in the rudiments of learning. The dame school was a very elementary school, kept in a kitchen or living room by some woman who, in her youth, had obtained the rudiments of an education, and who now desired to earn a pittance for herself by imparting to the children of her neighborhood her small store of learning. For a few pennies a week [1] the dame took the children of neighbors into her home and explained to them the mysteries connected with learning the beginnings of reading and spelling,[2] with the Catechism usually added. Occasionally a little writing and counting also were taught, but not often, and not infrequently a little sewing and knitting.[3] Sometimes, however, a younger woman who had received some advantages kept such a school. In time, the daughters of schoolmasters were fitted purposely to keep a dame school, as preparatory, for boys, for the town grammar school.

Originating in England after the Reformation, and introduced into New England by the early colonists, the dame school flourished greatly in America during the eighteenth century, while in England it continued popular until well into the nineteenth. While men teachers were employed at first in the town schools, the dame school soon became the primary school of colonial New England, and the instruction in the A B C's and the elements of reading and writing given in it soon became a prerequisite for admission to the town grammar school. Outside of Boston it was possible, in all the towns, for children to begin their schooling at a very early age. If

[1] "The selectmen agreed with Goodwife Mirick, to encourage her in the good work of training up of children and teaching children to read, that she should have 3d a week for every child that she takes to perform this good work for." (Selectmen's orders, Springfield, Massachusetts, 1682.)

[2] The school dame usually did not find the labor of teaching very heavy. An interesting instance to show this is found in the annals of Northfield, Massachusetts. The first teacher in the town was a dame, with four children of her own, who was hired to care for a class of little ones for "twenty-two weeks in the warm season." The semi-leisure of the school room allowed her to work making shirts for the Indians at 8 pence each, and breeches at 1s 6d a pair, besides caring for her own household.

[3] "Mary goes to Mrs. Thair's to learn to Read and Knit," is an entry in a Boston diary of 1696. (*Judge Sewell's Diary*, vol. I, p. 436.)

FIG. 5. A DAME SCHOOL

they could "stand up and keep their places" and could read they usually were permitted to come to school.[1]

Origin of the school of the 3-Rs. The second type of school brought over by the early colonists was the writing school, a school in which writing, reckoning, and the simplest elements of merchants' accounts were taught. The masters in this type of school also gave instruction in writing to the boys in the third type (**R. 12**) brought over — the Latin grammar school. Sometimes the instruction was given in a separate school, taught by a "scrivener" and arithmetic teacher, and sometimes the writing and reckoning were taught by a peripatetic scrivener, who moved about as business seemed to warrant. The writing school never became common in New England, as the exigencies of a new and a sparsely settled country tended to force a combination of the dame and the writing school into one, thus forming the school of the so-called 3-Rs — "Readin, Ritin, and Rithmetic" — from which our elementary schools later were evolved. Among the Dutch, Quakers, and Germans of the middle Colonies as well this combination was commonly found in their parochial schools, and from it their elementary schools also evolved.

The charity or pauper elementary school, which came to exist quite commonly in the Central and Southern Colonies, in which a limited number of the children of indigents were given a limited amount of schooling and which was supported largely by voluntary contributions and by church societies, also was of the dame, primary, or 3-R-school type.

The Latin grammar school. The third type of school brought over, and for New England the important school of the early period, was the Latin grammar school. In this the great teachers of the early time were found (**R. 40**). By this was meant a school for beginners in Latin, still the sacred language of religion and learning, and upon the study of which the main energy of the schools was spent. The location of the thirty-nine such schools established prior to 1700 is shown in Figure 6. The school took the boy from the dame school at the age of seven or eight, and prepared him for en-

---

[1] One contract is illustrative. In 1668 Master John Prudden made an agreement with the authorities for the Roxburie Grammar School in which he:

"promised and engaged to use his best endeavor, both by precept and example, to instruct in all scholasticall, morall, and theological discipline, the children soe far as they are or shall be capable, of the signers, all A B C darians excepted."

trance to college at fifteen,[1] or thereabout, the boy in the meantime having learned to read, write, and make his own quill pens, and hav-

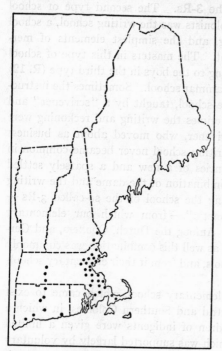

ing mastered sufficient Latin to enter the college of the Colony (**R. 28**). He was usually ignorant of numbers, and was usually unable to write English with any degree of fluency or accuracy. He was, however, well schooled in the Latin tongue and usually, in the last years of the course, in the elements of Greek as well. The purpose of the Latin school is well stated by the admission requirements of Harvard College,[2] in 1642, which read (**R. 28a**):

When any Schollar is able to understand Tully, or such like classicall Latine Author *extempore*, and make and speake true Latine in Verse

FIG. 6. LOCATION OF THE 39 NEW ENGLAND GRAMMAR SCHOOLS FOUNDED PRIOR TO 1700

After Table in Grizzell, pp. 7–8. Vermont was not settled until 1762, and Maine remained a part of Massachusetts until 1820. So little is known as to the beginnings of education in Rhode Island that it is uncertain whether the school at Newport was a Latin grammar school.

[1] One contract here also is illustrative. In 1658 Ichabod Wiswell agreed with the selectmen of Dorchester:

"to instruct and teach in a free school all children as by the inhabitants shall be committed unto his care in English, Latin, and Greek, as from time to time the children shall be capable, and also instruct them in writing as he shall be able; which is to be understood such children as are so far entered all ready to know their letters and to spell somewhat."

[2] Yale College, for some years after its foundation, was governed by the Harvard laws. In 1745 a body of laws was drawn up for its own government, with the following admission requirements stated:

"That none may expect to be admitted into this College unless, upon Examination of the President and Tutors, They shall be found able Extempore to Read, Construe and Parce Tully, Vergil, and the Greek Testament; and to write True Latin in Prose and to understand the Rules of Prosodia, and Common Arithmetic, and Shall bring Sufficient Testimony of his Blameless and inoffensive Life."

and Prose, *suo ut aiunt Marte;* and decline perfectly the Paradigms of *Nounes* and *Verbes* in the *Greek* tongue: Let him then, and not before, be capable of admission into the Colledge.

The Latin grammar school attained its greatest development in New England, where such schools had been required by the law of 1647 (**R. 16**), and where the attitude toward classical study was distinctly more friendly than in the Colonies to the southward.[1] Latin grammar schools were, however, found here and there in the few large towns of the Middle and Southern Colonies, though in these the commercial demands early made themselves felt and the tendency in the higher schools was toward the introduction of more practical studies, such as merchants' accounts, navigation, surveying,[2] and the higher mathematics (**Rs. 55, 56, 57**). This in time led to the evolution of a distinctively American type of higher school, with a more practical curriculum — the English grammar school (**R. 56**), and the Academy — and this latter in time displaced the Latin grammar school, even in New England.

FIG. 7. THE BOSTON LATIN GRAMMAR SCHOOL

Showing the school as it was in Cheever's day, with King's Chapel on the left, the school facing on School Street.

The English-type college. In the founding of Harvard (**R. 10**) College in Massachusetts Bay Colony, in 1636; William and Mary College in Virginia, in 1693 (**R. 24**); Yale College in Connecticut Colony, in 1701 (**R. 19**); and Princeton in New Jersey [3] in 1746

---

[1] Small, in his *Early New England Schools*, page 30, lists twenty-seven grammar schools that were founded in Massachusetts and Connecticut before 1700, and seven others that probably were. The list of Harvard graduates before 1700 shows that the main feeders to the college were the grammar schools at Boston, Braintree, Cambridge, Charlestown, Dorchester, Roxbury, and Salem.

[2] Due to the rapid settlement of the then West, and the rapid rise of ocean commerce after the close of the War for Independence, both Surveying and Navigation, together with Bookkeeping, were much in demand as practical studies.

[3] Originally chartered as the College of New Jersey, in 1746, and opened for instruction at Elizabethtown (now Elizabeth) in 1747, but moved to Newark, five miles distant, later that same year. Both were temporary locations, while determining a permanent location for the college. The offer of the residents of Princeton of 200 acres of woodland, 10 acres of cleared land, and £1000 in money was accepted, the first building, "Old Nassau," was erected, and instruction began at Princeton in 1756.

(opened for instruction in 1747),we find the transplanting of the English-type college and English collegiate traditions to the shores of the new world. The Harvard statutes of 1642, as laid down by President Henry Dunster (**R. 28 a-d**), were a clear copy of the Arts course of the English college, and particularly of Magdalene College, at Cambridge, from which Dunster[1] had been graduated twelve

FIG. 8. "OLD NASSAU," AT PRINCETON

The original building in which the "College of New Jersey" began instruction, in 1756. Though wrecked internally by revolutionary armies, and twice partially destroyed by fire (1802, 1854), the original walls of Nassau Hall are still intact.

years before and in which many of the early Massachusetts colonists had studied. The purpose was to train up a class of learned men for the Christian ministry. Latin, Greek, Hebrew, the Bible, ethics, logic, rhetoric, composition, a little mathematics, and a chronological type of history constituted the curriculum (**Rs. 28c, 29**), and

[1] Dunster (1640–1654) was the first real president, though nominally he succeeded Nathaniel Eaton, who had been master of the new college for two years (1638–1640). Dunster was an indefatigable worker, and during the fourteen years of his presidency he organized the institution and "carried it from what were scarcely pre-natal squirmings to at least a healthy infancy." He was both president and faculty with a student body of less than twenty. He held the first commencement in the new world in 1642. His salary was never over £60 per year, and frequently in arrears. In 1654, because he had advanced doubts as to the validity of the doctrine of infant baptism, he was required to resign the presidency of the college. He died five years later, at the age of 50.

with training in disputation the core of the whole (**Rs. 28d, 30**). Dunster brought to Harvard the enthusiasm for disputation that he had acquired at Cambridge in the days of John Milton and Jeremy Taylor. As Merriwether states it:

> Discussion became a passion, dialectics a creed, disputation was almost an act of worship, textual study was almost a superstition, and the polemical faculties were sharpened.

Yale followed the Harvard plan in its curriculum and organization, placed the collegiate program on the basis of discipline and intellectual culture, and profoundly affected the trend of collegiate instruction for the next century and a half.[1] The traditions and practices which Yale received from Harvard she in turn passed on to Princeton, founded in 1746. William and Mary College, though more a copy of Oxford, was not essentially different from Harvard, Yale, and Princeton in its instruction.[2] Drill and mental discipline, obtained through an intimate knowledge of the classics and the Bible, training in logical thinking and speaking (**Rs. 30, 31**), and preparation of a class of learned men for the Christian ministry, became the ruling ideas in collegiate training in the new, as well as in the old, home lands. The effect of this type of collegiate training in preparing ministers for the churches and leaders for the stormy days that were ahead (**R. 31**), was large indeed.[3]

As President Barnard once aptly said:[4]

> Our earliest American Colleges were founded on the model of those of British universities: and here, as there, their avowed design, at the time of their foundation, was not merely to raise up a class of learned men,

[1] The Report of the Yale faculty in 1727–28, on the course of study, profoundly influenced the trend of educational thinking for nearly 150 years. This report introduced a fixed course, based on discipline and intellectual culture. Drill and mental discipline, based on a study of the classics, became the ruling ideas in college training. By 1840 nearly all the northern colleges, following the Yale ideas, had a fixed and similar curriculum.

[2] The only colonial college not to follow the Dunster-Yale plan and ideas was the new College of Pennsylvania. There the first Provost, William Smith, set forth (1756) a new notion that a college should aim to supply a nation with leadership, and should train for the future as well as give training in the studies of the past. Smith's plan greatly influenced Madison in his reform of William and Mary College in 1776, and was influential elsewhere in the South.

[3] "When these disputations turned toward pointed inquiry into matters of government, commerce, and political liberty, as they did in the Colonies during the last half of the eighteenth century, they became the raw winds of a coming storm. The flames of the Revolution fired all this arsenal. Out of it flashed the Declaration of Independence, the Federalist Papers, the Constitution, and the Monroe Doctrine." (A. F. Blanks, unpublished thesis.)

[4] F. A. P. Barnard, in *Annual Report of the President of Columbia College*, 1872, p. 31.

but specifically to raise up a class of learned men for the Christian Ministry. Here, as there, accordingly, the teachings consisted largely in the classics, with logic, geometry, and physics (such modest and not wholly accurate physics as existed in that day); to which was added Hebrew, Syriac, Chaldaic, and dogmatic theology. This was the system which time had honored at Oxford and Cambridge, and which time continued to honor on this continent, with very slight modifications, down nearly to the close of the eighteenth century.

Apprenticeship training. The binding out of both boys and girls as apprentices, to learn a trade or some useful calling, was an old custom that had existed in Europe for centuries. There were two kinds of apprenticing — the voluntary, and the forced or compulsory. A boy of average means — or his parent or guardian for him — chose his future calling and apprenticed himself to some master willing to take him and give him the necessary instruction (**R. 32**). Orphans and children of the poor, on the other hand, were bound out by town officials to masters willing to take apprentices under the provisions of the poor law (**R. 33**). When a master took an apprentice, a formal Indenture of Apprenticeship (**Rs. 32, 33**) was drawn up, signed, witnessed, and recorded. Compulsory apprenticeship needed, in addition, the approval of a court. Both forms were so commonly more favorable to the master than to the apprentice [1] that, in time, it became common, in the Northern Colonies, to enact rather stringent regulations (**R. 34a, b**) protecting apprentices from neglect in the matter of their education.

In England the practice of apprenticeship had been general long before the time the colonists came to America. Until 1562 it had been a locally regulated custom, but in that year the *Statute of Artificers* changed the practice into a nationally regulated system. The English *Poor Law of 1601*, which consolidated and strengthened all previous legislation on the subject, required the church wardens and the overseers of the poor to bind out orphans and the children of indigents under apprenticeship agreements.

---

[1] The apprenticeship training of colonial days was that of the Old World, and exhibited alike its advantages and its disadvantages. Its advantages were in the direct association of the apprentice and a master workman. When the master was conscientious and efficient, the apprentice doubtless learned much that was useful. If the master neglected him, or employed him mostly for chores and errands, as was common, he learned but little. The common term, seven years, was far too long for the needs of the trade. Pioneer youth, too, were restless and objected to the conditions. It is not hard to see why, in a new country where opportunity for independent activity was so easy to find, such training was confined chiefly to orphans and public charges.

The colonists brought this English practice with them to America, and we find many recorded evidences of its use in the different American Colonies.   Plymouth Colony, in 1641 (**R. 18a**), accepted the principle of the English law of 1601 as a colony responsibility, re-enacted the law in 1658, and in 1671 enacted a still more carefully worded statute covering the education of all types of children (**R. 18c**); the Massachusetts law of 1642 directed the apprenticing of "the children of such (parents) as they shall find not to be able and

FIG. 9. APPRENTICING AN ORPHAN BOY, 1694

William Pead, indigent orphan, bound to the Honorable Thomas Harvey, 1694, "Said Harvey to teach him to read." From M. C. S. Noble: *A History of Schools in North Carolina.* Reproduced by permission.

fitt to imploy and bring them up" (**R. 14**); the Virginia law of 1643 ordered the overseers and guardians of "orphants...to educate and instruct them according to their best endeavors in Christian religion and the rudiments of learning" (**R. 25a**); the New York law of 1665, drawn up shortly after the English occupation, paraphrased the Massachusetts law of 1642 (**R. 14**); and similar legislation was enacted by nearly all the Colonies.   The practice of apprenticing early became general, as the number of recorded Indentures reveals, but with the difference that in the New England, and to a large degree in the Middle Colonies as well, the practice was supplemental to other educational means, while in Virginia and the Southern Colonies apprentice training tended rather to be the only type of public training provided. In the Northern Colonies, too, the right of the apprentice to instruction in the rudiments of an education was in time carefully safeguarded by laws (**R. 34**).

QUESTIONS FOR DISCUSSION

1. State the change in the importance of education which resulted from the Protestant Reformation in Europe.
2. Explain what is meant by "the Puritan Church appealed to what was then its servant, the State," etc.
3. State the important contributions of Calvinism to our new-world life.
4. Explain the significance of the prelude to the Massachusetts Law of 1647, which begins by stating that it had been "one chief point of that old deluder, Satan," etc.
5. Do the fundamental principles stated by Mr. Martin as underlying the Massachusetts Laws of 1642 and 1647 still hold true?
6. What does the wide copying of the Massachusetts legislation by the other New England Colonies, Rhode Island excepted, indicate as to a common attitude toward religion and learning?
7. Explain why a parochial-school system in colonial times was certain to be less effective than the Massachusetts state system.
8. Explain how climate and crop differences between Massachusetts and Virginia in themselves would have tended to develop different governmental and educational attitudes, even had there been no difference in religion.
9. What explanation can you give for the great indifference to education of the English Church during the entire colonial period?
10. Why did the charity school, designed to encourage the founding of schools, eventually serve to retard the development of state school systems?
11. Explain the origin of the American school of the 3-Rs.
12. Characterize the Dame School, and estimate its usefulness.
13. Explain the establishment, in the New England wilderness, of the Latin grammar school as the important school of the early colonial period. The English-type college.
14. Explain what you understand by disputation in the early colleges.
15. Explain the general use of apprenticeship training in all the Colonies.

SELECTED READINGS

In the accompanying volume of *Readings* the following selections, related to the subject-matter of this chapter, are reproduced:

*7. Bradford: The Mayflower Compact.
*8. Fiske: The Puritan Theory of Life.
9. Monitor: The First Free School in America.

*10. First Fruits: The Founding of Harvard College.
*11. Town Records: Founding of the Free School of Dedham.
  12. Dillaway: Founding of the Free School of Roxburie.
  13. Colony Records: Massachusetts Laws of 1634 and 1638.
*14. Colony Records: Massachusetts Law of 1642.
  15. Court Records: Presentment of Town of Topsfield.
*16. Colony Records: Massachusetts Law of 1647.
  17. Colony Records: Connecticut Law of 1650.
*18. Colony Records: The Plymouth Colony Legislation.
  19. Colony Records: Act Incorporating Yale College.
*20. Woody: Early Quaker Education in New Jersey.
  21. Woody: Early Quaker Education in Pennsylvania.
*22. Colony Records: The Pennsylvania Law of 1683.
  23. Wickersham: The First School in Philadelphia.
*24. Colony Records: The Charter of William and Mary College.
  25. William and Mary Quarterly: Endowed Parish Schools in Virginia.
*26. Colony Records: Apprenticeship Laws in the Southern Colonies.
*27. Kemp: Schools of the S.P.G. in New York.
*28. First Fruits: First Rules for Harvard College.
  29. Colony Records: Harvard College Course in 1690 and 1725.
  30. A Letter: The Harvard College Commencement of 1642.
*31. Merriwether: The Food that Made Giants.
*32. Stiles: A Voluntary Indenture of Apprenticeship.
*33. New England Register: A Compulsory Indenture of Apprenticeship.
*34. Colony Laws: Protecting Apprentices from Neglect.
   * If only a portion of the Readings can be used, the more important ones are indicated by an asterisk, and this plan will be followed in subsequent chapters.

QUESTIONS ON THE READINGS

   1. What form of government was set up by The Mayflower Compact (7)?
   2. Show how the Reformation spirit was expressed in the Puritan theory of life (8).
   3. Characterize the spirit behind the founding of Harvard College, as expressed in the extract (10) from New England's First Fruits.
   4. What type of school was the "Free School" at Dedham (11)?
   5. What does the extract from Dillaway (12) reveal as to the nature of the Roxburie foundation, and the type of school?
   6. Show how the Massachusetts Laws of 1634 and 1638 laid the foundations (13) for the present type of state and school support.
   7. State the essential requirements (14) of the Massachusetts Law of 1642.
   8. What does the court citation of Topsfield (15) reveal?
   9. What new principle is added by the Law of 1647, and what does this new law (16) indicate as to the need for classical learning in the Colony?
  10. Show how the Connecticut Law of 1650 (17) was based on the Massachusetts Law (14) of 1642.
  11. Compare the Plymouth Colony legislation as to schools (18c, 18d) with that of Massachusetts Colony (14, 16).

12. What does the Plymouth Colony appeal for Harvard College (**18d**) indicate as to community of ideas in New England?
13. Compare the purpose in the founding of Yale (**19**) and Harvard (**10**).
14. Characterize the early Quaker zeal for education, as described by Woody (**20, 21**), and describe the kind of schools provided.
15. Compare the proposed Pennsylvania Law of 1683 (**22**) and the Massachusetts Law of 1642 (**14**).
16. Just what kind of school was the first one (**23**) established in Philadelphia?
17. Compare the forces behind the founding of William and Mary College (**24**) and those behind the founding of Harvard College (**10**).
18. Just what type of schools were the endowed parish schools of Virginia (**25**)?
19. What conception as to education is revealed by the Virginia apprenticeship laws (**26, I, 1-3**) and the North Carolina court records (**26, II, 1-3**)?
20. Characterize the type of school provided by the S.P.G. in New York (**27**), and the purposes of the Society in establishing them.
21. What was the nature and purpose of the early Harvard instruction, as revealed by the selection **28 a-d**?
22. Reconstruct the time-schedule of instruction (**28c**), and evaluate it.
23. Compare the Harvard course of 1690 (**29**) with that offered in 1642 (**28c**).
24. Just what was done at the Harvard Commencement of 1642 (**30**)? What type of curriculum is indicated?
25. Describe and evaluate the early collegiate training in disputation (**31**). What takes its place today?
26. List what a boy agreed to when apprenticed (**32, 33**).
27. Why were the Northern Colonies more solicitous as to the education of apprentices (**34**) than were the southern?

TOPICS FOR INVESTIGATION AND REPORT

Intended for brief reading and quite brief written or class report.

1. Indebtedness to England for our early educational traditions and practices. (Brown, E. E.; Eggleston.)
2. The early New England Latin grammar schools, and their work. (Brown, E. E.; Barnard; Small.)
3. The work of Ezekiel Cheever and Elijah Corlett as types of grammar-school masters. (Barnard; Brown, E. E.)
4. The founding of Harvard College. (Barnard.)
5. Early parochial schools in the Central Colonies. (Murray; Wickersham — See Bibl. to Chap. IV.)
6. Dutch schools in colonial New Amsterdam. (Fitzpatrick.)
7. The work of the Quakers in establishing schools. (Jones; Klain; Woody.)
8. The schools of the "Society for the Propagation of the Gospel."
9. The dame school of colonial times. (Updegraff; Small.)
10. Life and instruction in the colonial colleges. (Merriwether.)
11. Franklin and the founding of the University of Pennsylvania.

12. The support of schools in colonial New England.   (Brown; Jackson; Small; Updegraff.)
13. The apprenticeship system in the Colonies.   (Heatwole; Knight; Seybolt.)

SELECTED REFERENCES

The most useful and most easily accessible references for the general reader are indicated by a *.

Barnard, Henry.   "Ezekiel Cheever"; in Barnard's *American Journal of Education*, vol. 1, pp. 297–314.

An interesting sketch of the life and work of this famous New England schoolmaster, with notes on the early free grammar school of New England.

Boone, R. G.   *Education in the United States.*   402 pp.   New York, 1889.

Chapters I and II form good supplemental reading for this chapter.

*Brown, Elmer E.   *The Making of our Middle Schools.*   547 pp.   New York, 1903.

A standard history of the rise of the Latin grammar school and the later high schools. The first seven chapters bear particularly on the subject-matter of this chapter.

*Dexter, E. G.   *A History of Education in the United States.*   656 pp.   New York, 1904.

A collection of facts rather than an interpretation. The first five chapters deal with the period covered by this chapter.

*Heatwole, C. J.   *A History of Education in Virginia.*   382 pp.   New York, 1916.

The first four chapters give a good general account of educational efforts in Virginia, and the English attitude expressed there.

Jackson, G. L.   *The Development of School Support in Colonial Massachusetts.*   95 pp.   Teachers College Contributions to Education, No. 25, New York, 1909.

A study of the different methods employed in supporting schools, and the evolution of the town-supported school.

Kemp, W. W.   *The Support of Schools in Colonial New York by the Society for the Propagation of the Gospel in Foreign Parts.*   279 pp.   Teachers College Contributions to Education, No. 56, New York, 1913.

A very full and detailed study of the work of this Society in the different parts of the colony.

Kilpatrick, Wm. H.   *The Dutch Schools of New Netherlands and Colonial New York.*   239 pp.   United States Bureau of Education, Bulletin No. 12, Washington, D.C., 1912.

An excellent detailed study of Dutch education, with good descriptions of the schools and school work.

Klain, Zora.   *Educational Activities of New England Quakers.*   228 pp.   Philadelphia, 1928.

A very useful source book for studying the work of the Quakers.

Klain, Zora.   *Quaker Contributions to Education in North Carolina.*   351 pp.   University of Pennsylvania, Philadelphia, 1925.

A detailed history, with records, by "Quarters."

*Knight, Edgar W.   *Public School Education in North Carolina.*   384 pp. Boston, 1916.

> Chapter II contains a very good brief account of the apprentice system in the State during the colonial period.

*Martin, Geo. H.   *The Evolution of the Massachusetts Public School System.*   284 pp.   New York, 1894.

> A standard interpretative history of the rise of the Massachusetts schools. Chapters I and II deal with the early period represented by this chapter, and Chapter III with the decline in school spirit and the rise of the district system and the Academy.

Maurer, Chas. L.   *Early Lutheran Education in Pennsylvania.*   294 pp. Philadelphia, 1932.

> A careful study of Lutheran colonial education.

*Merriwether, Colyer.   *Our Colonial Curriculum.*   Washington, 1907.

> A very good analysis of the college curriculum of colonial times.

*Monroe, Paul, Editor.   *Cyclopedia of Education.*   New York, 1911–13. 5 volumes.

> The following articles are specially important.
> > 1. "Colonial Period in American Education," vol. II, pp. 115–22.
> >   Very good on the period covered by this chapter.
> > 2. "Society for the Propagation of the Gospel in Foreign Parts," vol. V, pp. 254–56.
> >   Good on the charity-school work of the Church of England in the Colonies.
> > 3. The historical portion of the different articles on the school systems of the American States, as Connecticut, Massachusetts, New York, Pennsylvania, Virginia, etc.

Murray, David.   *History of Education in New Jersey.*   344 pp. United States Bureau of Education, Circular of Information No. 1, Washington, 1899.

> Chapter VIII very good on colonial schools in New Jersey.

Seybolt, R. F.   *Apprenticeship and Apprenticeship Education in Colonial New York and New England.*   121 pp.   Teachers College Contributions to Education, No. 85, New York, 1917.

> An interesting study of old records relating to apprenticeship education.

Small, W. H.   "The New England Grammar School," 1635–1700; in *School Review*, vol. X, pp. 513–31.   (Sept., 1902.)

> A description of the founding of the early grammar schools, with interesting extracts from the records.

*Small, W. H.   *Early New England Schools.*   401 pp.   Boston, 1914.

> A very interesting collection of source extracts, copied from the early records, and classified into chapters describing all phases of early school life.

Updegraff, H.   *The Origin of the Moving School in Massachusetts.*   186 pp. Teachers College Contributions to Education, No. 17.   New York, 1908.

> Contains good pictures of schools and school conditions in Massachusetts.

Woody, Thos.   *Early Quaker Education in Pennsylvania.*   391 pp. Teachers College Contributions to Education, No. 105, New York, 1920.

Woody, Thos.   *Quaker Education in the Colony and State of New Jersey.*   400 pp.   University of Pennsylvania Press, Philadelphia, 1923.

> Two valuable histories and source books.

CHAPTER III

GENERAL CHARACTER OF THE COLONIAL SCHOOLS

I. EARLY INSTRUCTION, AND TEACHERS

Dominance of the religious purpose. The most prominent characteristic of all the early colonial schooling was the predominance of the religious purpose in instruction (**Rs. 8, 20, 21, 27, 44**). One learned to read chiefly to be able to read the Catechism and the Bible, and to know the will of the Heavenly Father. There was scarcely any other purpose in the maintenance of elementary schools. In Connecticut Colony the law required that the pupils were to be made "in some competent measure to understand the main grounds and principles of Christian Religion necessary to salvation," and "to learn some orthodox catechism" (**Rs. 17, 42**). In the Latin grammar schools and the colleges, which existed mainly to insure a supply of learned ministers for service in the Church and the State, the students were instructed to consider well the main end of life and studies (**Rs. 28, 42**). Such studies as history, geography, science, music, drawing, secular literature, and physical training were unknown during the early colonial period.

Children were constantly surrounded, week days and Sundays, by the somber Calvinistic religious atmosphere in New England,[1] and by the careful religious oversight of the pastors and elders in the Colonies where the parochial school system was the ruling plan for education. As one writer (Clifton Johnson) puts it:

> The children were perpetually enveloped, week days and Sundays, in an atmosphere saturated with religious forms, services, ideas, and language. Powers of darkness and of light were struggling for the possession of every youthful soul, and it was the duty of parents, ministers, and teachers to lose no opportunity to pluck the children as brands from the burning.

Schoolmasters were required "to catechise their scholars in the principles of the Christian religion," and it was made "a chief part of

[1] In 1651, in New Haven Colony, there is a record of a little girl being brought into court charged with "prophane swearing." She was charged with using such expressions as "by my soul," and "as I am a Christian."

the schoolmaster's religious care to commend his scholars and his labors amongst them unto God by prayer morning and evening [1] (R. 42, §5), taking care that his scholars do reverently attend during the same." Religious matter constituted the only reading matter, outside the instruction in Latin in the grammar schools. The Catechism was taught,[2] and the Bible was read and expounded. Church attendance was required, and grammar school pupils were obliged to report each week on the Sunday sermon. This insistence on the religious element was more prominent in Calvinistic New England than in the Colonies to the south, but everywhere, during the early colonial period, the religious purpose was dominant. The church parochial and charity schools were essentially schools for instilling the church practices and the beliefs of the churches maintaining them (Rs. 20, 21). This state of affairs continued until well toward the beginning of our national period.

This dominance of the religious purpose in the early colonial instruction was well shown in the textbooks used. Down to the time of the American Revolution, these were English in their origin and largely religious in their purpose. The *Hornbook*, the religious *Primer*, the *Psalter*, the *Testament*, and the *Bible* were the books used, supplemented during the last fifty years of the colonial period by newer English textbooks, the most notable of which were those by Hodder and Dilworth. It was not until about the time of the Revolution that the first American secular textbook appeared. In the grammar schools the atmosphere was deeply religious, and the teaching of the classics was permeated by the religious attitude. [3]

The textbooks used. Instruction at first everywhere began with the *Hornbook*, from which children learned their letters and began to read. This was a thin board on which a printed leaf was pasted

[1] For example, in 1789 the Boston School Committee

"Voted, That it be the indispensable duty of the several schoolmasters, daily to commence the duties of their office by prayer, and reading a portion of the sacred Scriptures, at the hour assigned for opening the school in the morning; and close the same in the evening with prayer."

[2] Also a little later in 1789 Boston ordered:

"That the several schoolmasters instruct the children under their care, or cause them to be instructed, in the Assemblie's Catechism, every Saturday, unless the parents request that they be taught any particular catechism of the religious society to which they belong; and the masters are directed to teach such children accordingly."

[3] Cotton Mather, in his lines written at the time of the death of the celebrated colonial schoolmaster, Ezekiel Cheever (R. 40), described such instruction when he wrote:

"He taught us *Lilly*, and he *Gospels* taught;
And us poor Children to our Savior brought."

(**R. 35**), and this was covered with a thin sheet of transparent horn to protect it from dirty fingers. Figure 10 shows a common form of this early type of primer, the mastery of which usually required some time. Cowper thus describes this little book:

> Neatly secured from being soiled or torn
> Beneath a pane of thin translucent horn,
> A book (to please us at a tender age
> 'Tis called a book, though but a single page)
> Presents the prayer the Savior designed to teach,
> Which children use, and parsons — when they preach.

After the *Hornbook*, in later Colonial times, came the *Battledoor*, a sort of enlarged and advanced Hornbook, or Primer. This was a sheet of cardboard, folded to form four to six pages, and with an illustrated alphabet on the inner pages, with a verse beneath each illustrated letter. A copy in the library of Teachers College, New York, contains the following good advice:

> He that ne'er learns his A B C,
> Forever will a blockhead be;
> But he that learns his letters fair,
> Shall have a coach and take the air.

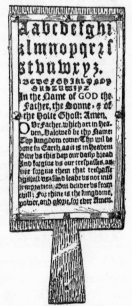

The Battledoor was used much less in America than in England, but it was known in all the Northern Colonies during the closing years of the colonial era; and it was used especially by Church of England schools. Having learned to read, the child next passed to the *Catechism*, the Psalter, and the *Bible;* these constituted the entire range of reading in the early schools.

FIG. 10. A HORN-
BOOK

The Catechism. The use of a Catechism was common in all Protestant lands. The *Shorter Catechism* prepared by Luther was used by the Germans, while in England and the American Colonies the *Westminster Catechism* was commonly used. In the New England Colonies much use also was made of one prepared by the Rev. John Cotton, entitled *Spiritual Milk for American Babes,*

Drawn out of the Breasts of Both Testaments, for their Soul's Nourishment. The Catechism formed the backbone of the religious instruction given in the home, the school, and the church (**Rs. 36, 38**).

THE
SHORTER CATECHISM,
Agreed upon by the Reverend ASSEMBLY of DIVINES at *Westminster.*

Q. *WHAT is the chief End of Man?*
A. Man's chief End is to glorify God and enjoy him forever.

Q. *What Rule hath God given to direct us how we may glorify and enjoy him?*
A. The Word of God which is contained in the Scriptures of the Old and New Testament, is the only rule to direct us how we may glorify and enjoy Him.

Q. *What do the Scriptures principally teach?*
A. The Scriptures principally teach what Man is to believe concerning God, and what Duty God requires of Man.

Q. *What is God?*
A. God is a Spirit, Infinite, Eternal and Unchangeable, in his Being, Wisdom, Power, Holiness, Justice, Goodness and Truth.

Q. *Are there more Gods than One?*

FIG. 11. THE WESTMINSTER CATE-CHISM

A page from the *New England Primer*, natural size

Teachers drilled their pupils on it, writing masters set as copies sentences from the book, children were required to memorize the answers, and the religious doctrines it contained were emphasized by teacher and preacher so that the children were saturated with the religious ideas it set forth.

The New England Primer. In 1690 there appeared a wonderful little volume, known as *The New England Primer*, which at once leaped into popularity and soon superseded the *Hornbook* as the beginning reading text, not only in New England but in the schools of all the Colonies except those under the control of the Church of England. It also contained both the *Westminster Catechism* and the *Spiritual Milk*, and at once made the use of both of these common in colonial schools. For the next century and a quarter it was the chief school and reading book in use among the Dissenters and Lutherans in America. Such spelling as was taught was taught from it also. A digest of its contents, with a few pages reproduced, is given in **R. 36**.

Being religious in the nature of its contents it was used both in the school and the church, the schoolmasters drilled the children in the reading matter and the catechism in the schools, and the

In Adam's Fall
We finned all.

Thy Life to mend,
This Book attend.

The Cat doth play,
And after flay.

A Dog will bite
A Thief at Night.

An Eagle' flight
Is out of fight.

The idle Fool
Is whipt at School.

A page of the Illustrated Alphabet

Praife to GOD for learning to Read.

THE Praifes of my Tongue
I offer to the LORD,
That I was taught and learnt fo young
To read his holy Word.

2 That I was brought to know
The Danger I was in,
By Nature and by Practice too
A wretched flave to Sin:

3 That I was led to fee
I can do nothing well ;
And whether fhall a Sinner flee
To fave himfelf from Hell.

A page of the Reading Matter

FIG. 12. TWO SPECIMEN PAGES FROM THE NEW ENGLAND PRIMER

people recited the catechism yearly in the churches. Every home possessed copies of it, and it was for sale at all bookstores, even in the smaller places, for a century and a half. It was reprinted throughout the Colonies under different names, but the public preferred the title *New England Primer* to any other. Its total sales have been estimated to have been at least three million copies. It was used in the Boston dame schools as late as 1806, and in the country districts still later, but was gradually discarded for newer types of secular readers. Compared with the primers and first readers of today it seems poor and crude, but probably no modern textbook will ever exercise the influence over children and adults which was exercised by this little religious reader, 3¼ by 4½ inches in size, and but 88 pages thick. It has been said of it that "it taught millions to read, and not one to sin." This important little book Ford has well characterized, in the following words:

> As one glances over what may truly be called "The Little Bible of New England," and reads its stern lessons, the Puritan mood is caught with absolute faithfulness. Here was no easy road to knowledge and salvation; but with prose as bare of beauty as the whitewash of their churches, with poetry as rough and stern as their storm-torn coast, with pictures as crude and unfinished as their own glacial-smoothed boulders, between stiff oak covers which symbolized the contents, the children were tutored, until, from being unregenerate, and as Johnathan Edwards said, "young vipers, and infinitely more hateful than vipers" to God, they attained that happy state when, as expressed by Judge Sewell's child, they were afraid that they "should goe to hell," and were "stirred up dreadfully to seek God." God was made sterner and more cruel than any living judge, that all might be brought to realize how slight a chance even the least erring had of escaping eternal damnation.

The *Psalter*, the *Testament*, and the *Bible* were its natural continuation, and constituted the main advanced reading books [1] in the Colonies before about 1750 (**R. 38**).

Dilworth's *Guide*. In 1740, there appeared in England a notable book that soon became popular in both old and New England. It was by a noted English schoolmaster by the name of Thomas Dilworth, and was entitled *A New Guide to the English Tongue.* This book (**R. 37**) contained, as the title page declared, selected lists of words with rules for their pronunciation, a short treatise

---

[1] As late as 1812, in Dorchester, the school had three classes, the lowest being known as the Psalter class, the intermediate as the Testament class, and the highest as the Bible class. Such a classification was very common half a century earlier.

on grammar, a collection of fables with illustrations for reading, some moral selections, and forms of prayer for children. This volume ran through many editions, was reprinted in New England, and was used extensively in the more advanced colonial schools. The title page of the book states the nature and content of the volume well.

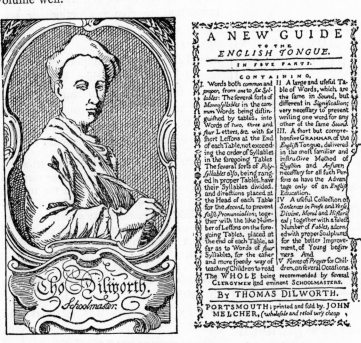

FIG. 13. THOMAS DILWORTH (?–1780) AND HIS BOOK
Frontispiece and Title-Page of the *New Guide*

Arithmetic. A textbook seldom was used in teaching arithmetic by the colonial schoolmasters (**R. 50c**), though a few texts had been published. One much used by the English was that of Hodder, a reprint of which appeared in Boston as early as 1719. Another early text was Isaac Greenwood's *Arithmetick, Vulgar and Decimal*, an American work, which also was issued at Boston, in 1729. The most popular text, however, was the English Dilworth's *Schoolmaster's Assistant* (**R. 37**), published in 1743. This book retained its popularity in both England and America until after the beginning of the nineteenth century. The study itself was common after the first quarter of the eighteenth century, but not universal.[1] It was not until near the beginning of our national period that arithmetic was anywhere made a required subject of instruction. The subject was for some time regarded as one of much difficulty, and one in which few teachers were competent to give instruction, or few pupils competent to understand.[2] To possess a reputation as an "arithmeticker" was an important recommendation for a teacher, while for a pupil to be able to do sums in arithmetic was a matter of much pride to parents. Teacher's contracts frequently required that the teacher should

— do his faithful, honest and true endeavor to teach the children or servants of those who have subscribed the reading and writing of English, and also arithmetick, if they desire it; as much as they are capable to learn and he capable to teach them within the compas of this year.

The teacher might or might not possess an arithmetic of his own, but the instruction to pupils was dictated and copied instruction. Each pupil made his own written book of rules and solved problems (**R. 39**), and most pupils never saw a printed arithmetic. It was not until near the middle of the eighteenth century that printed arithmetics came into use, and then only in the larger towns, while it was not until the nineteenth century that the use of arithmetics as textbooks became common.

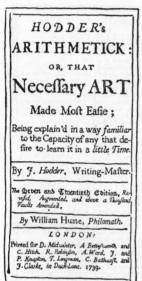

HODDER's
ARITHMETICK:
OR, THAT
Neceſſary ART
Made Moſt Eaſie ;
Being explain'd in a way *familiar* to the Capacity of any that deſire to learn it in a *little Time*.

By *J. Hodder*, Writing-Maſter.

The Seven and Twentieth Edition, Reviſed, Augmented, and above a Thouſand Faults Amended.

By William Hume, *Philomath*.

LONDON:

Printed for D. Midwinter, A Bettſſworth, and C. Hitch, R. Robinſon, A. Ward, J. and P. Knapton, T. Longman, C. Bathurſt, and J. Clarke, in Duck-Lane. 1739.

FIG. 14.   TITLE-PAGE OF HODDER'S ARITHMETIC

An early reprint of this famous book appeared in Boston, in 1719

---

[1] The early eighteenth century records mention "cyphering," and "numeration and addition," and the "art of arithmetic," and teachers' contracts require him "to set sums," and to "learn youth to read and cypher."

[2] Few pupils in the colonial schools ever got beyond "vulgar fractions" and the "Rule of three" (simple proportion). In fact, the introduction of arithmetic into the school was frequently opposed by the people. The first general requirement of the subject was made by the Massachusetts law of 1789.

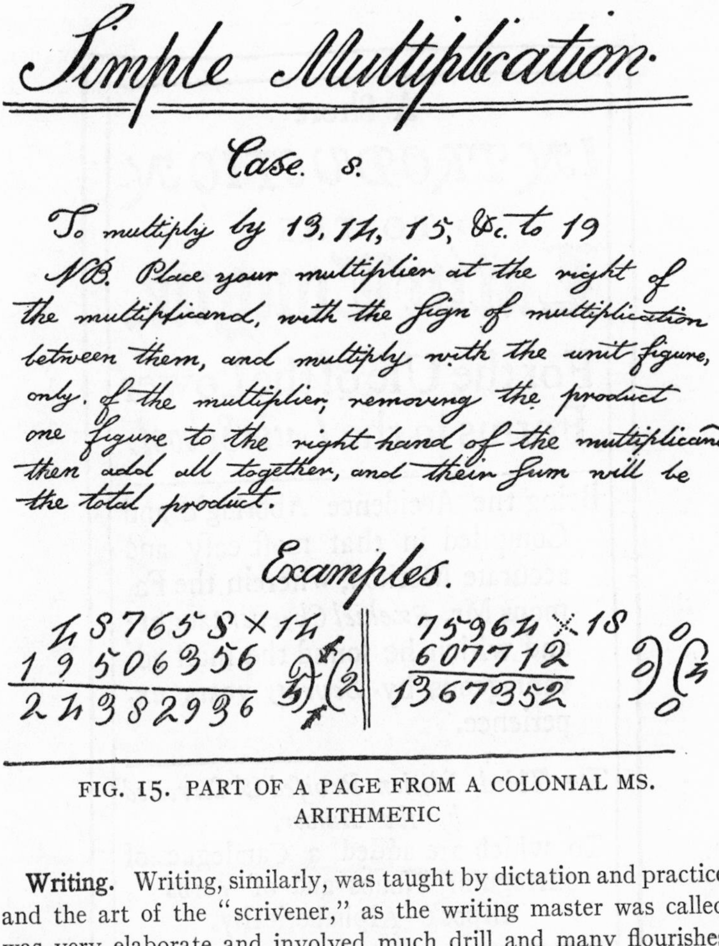

Simple Multiplication.

Case 8.

To multiply by 13, 14, 15, &c. to 19

NB. Place your multiplier at the right of the multiplicand, with the sign of multiplication between them, and multiply with the unit figure, only, of the multiplier; removing the product one figure to the right hand of the multiplicand then add all together, and their sum will be the total product.

Examples.

$$\begin{array}{r} 487658 \times 14 \\ 19506356 \\ \hline 24382936 \end{array} \qquad \begin{array}{r} 75964 \times 18 \\ 607712 \\ \hline 1367352 \end{array}$$

FIG. 15. PART OF A PAGE FROM A COLONIAL MS.
ARITHMETIC

Writing. Writing, similarly, was taught by dictation and practice, and the art of the "scrivener," as the writing master was called, was very elaborate and involved much drill and many flourishes. The difficulty of mastering the art, its lack of practical value to most children, the high cost of paper, and the necessity usually for special lessons, all alike tended to make writing a much less commonly known art than reading.

Cheever's Accidence. For the Latin grammar schools the great American textbook was *Cheever's Accidence* (**R. 40**), prepared by perhaps the most famous of all early American schoolmasters, Ezekiel Cheever. This volume was an outgrowth of Cheever's seventy years of teaching in the grammar schools of New England,

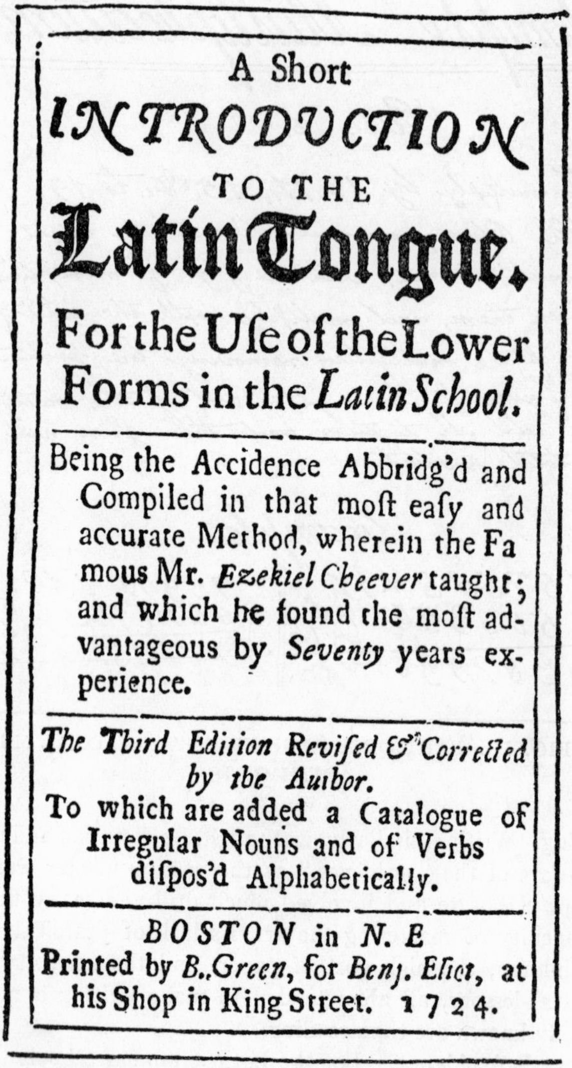

A Short

INTRODUCTION

TO THE

Latin Tongue.

For the Ufe of the Lower Forms in the *Latin School.*

Being the Accidence Abbridg'd and Compiled in that moft eafy and accurate Method, wherein the Famous Mr. *Ezekiel Cheever* taught; and which he found the moft advantageous by *Seventy* years experience.

The Third Edition Revifed & Corrected by the Author.
To which are added a Catalogue of Irregular Nouns and of Verbs difpos'd Alphabetically.

BOSTON in *N. E*
Printed by B. Green, for *Benj. Eliot*, at his Shop in King Street. **1724.**

FIG. 16. TITLE-PAGE OF CHEEVER'S ACCIDENCE

Third Edition, Boston, 1724. Photogravure from p. 253 of George E. Littlefield's *Early Schools and Schoolbooks in New England*, Boston, 1904.

but it was not published until the year following his death. A little volume of 79 pages, it was the best introductory textbook for Latin instruction that had appeared, and for more than a hundred years it was the textbook of the Latin grammar schools of all New England. It also was extensively used as a text wherever Latin was taught in the other American Colonies. The last edition [1] was printed in Boston in 1838.

The college studies. In **R. 29** is given the type of college curriculum in force at Harvard in 1690 and 1725, itself but little changed from that laid down by Master Dunster in 1642 (**R. 28**). Its chief purpose was "to raise up a class of learned men for the Christian ministry." Yale, and in turn Princeton, had followed the same plan, and the celebrated *Report* of the Yale faculty on the college curriculum, in 1727–1728, largely shaped the college course of study and profoundly affected the trend of educational thought for the next century. This *Report* placed the college program on a basis of discipline and intellectual culture and uniformity, in turn based on a knowledge of the classics and disputation. Only at Philadelphia, as we shall see a little further on, was a different idea as to the college curriculum set forth.

The teachers. The best teachers during the earlier colonial period were the teachers in the Latin grammar schools of New England. They were usually well-educated men, strict in the faith, and capable as teachers. A few attained a fame which has made them remembered to the present time. Among these Ezekiel Cheever [2] (1614–1708), mentioned above, a graduate of Cambridge, in England, who came to America at the age of twenty-three, and who served for seventy-one years as a teacher in New England and for thirty-eight years as head of the Boston Latin School; and

---

[1] The following news item appeared in the *American Annals of Education* for December, 1838:

"If it were possible for mere antiquity to give claims to excellence in a school book, that before us should certainly be regarded as among the first in our own country. It is an elementary work, compiled by Ezekiel Cheever, who for seventy years was a teacher of Latin, and was used in this country almost two centuries. The copy before us has just been carefully revised, corrected, and stereotyped from the eighteenth edition. It is designed for beginners. We cannot now enter deeply into an examination of the work, but it is at least a great curiosity. It comes to us highly recommended by those who ought to be judges of its merits."

[2] Cheever began his teaching in New Haven, where he remained twelve years, or until he was thirty-five years old. Then he taught eleven years at Ipswich, "making his school famous in all the country." Next he taught nine years in Charlestown, and at fifty-six was called to Boston, where he taught for thirty-eight years, dying in harness at the age of ninety-four, with seventy-one years of teaching to his credit.

Elijah Corlett [1] (1611–1687), for forty-three years head of the Cambridge Latin School, were the most famous. Of these, Cotton Mather wrote (**R. 40**) at the time of the death of Cheever:

> Tis CORLETS pains, & CHEEVER'S, we must own.
> That thou, *New England*, art not *Scythia* grown.

In the grammar schools of the smaller towns the teachers taught not only Latin and Greek, but quite often the common branches as well to the younger children. It would seem, too, that their work was never done, for, in addition, they had numerous town and church duties to perform, ranging from town clerk to ministerial duties.

Many of the early teachers in the reading schools were men of some learning, capable of serving as assistants to the ministers,[2] but the meager pay, and often the difficulty in collecting the pay that was due (**R. 41**), in time turned the instruction in these schools over to college students and local or itinerant schoolmasters in winter,[3] and to women in summer, and eventually the dame school supplanted the town elementary school. Girls usually were admitted to the summer, but not to the winter school, and hence were taught only reading, writing, and religion, with sometimes a little cyphering added. Only toward the close of the colonial period, and then only for girls "of the best families," was anything additional provided, aside from the domestic training of the home.[4]

---

[1] Corlett and the early history of the grammar school at Cambridge were one. He was master of the school at least as early as 1643, and continued in this position until his death in 1686–1687. "He had few students, some of them Indians, and he was very poor."

[2] A few votes of New England towns will illustrate. Newbury, in 1693, voted, "that Mr. John Clarke be called to assist in the work of the ministry at the west end of the town,... and also to keep a grammar school."

In 1718 Lynn instructed the selectmen to employ a schoolmaster and to make an agreement with him that should "have relation to some help for Mr. Shepard in preaching."

Rowley, in 1726, voted the schoolmaster "one pound for preaching on the Sabbath day."

Bradford, in 1729, voted "to hire as schoolteacher one who could also be helpful in the ministry as occasion required."

[3] The local farmer who taught school in the winter for a small sum, and the transient teacher who "kept school" for a small sum and board, later became common in New England. In Providence, the first schoolmaster kept a public house, in Milton a shoemaker also taught, at Woburn the town clerk also taught, etc.

[4] "In the eighteenth century the daughters of men holding important offices in town and church were obliged to make their mark instead of writing their signatures." (W. B. Weeden, *Economic and Social Conditions in New England,* I, p. 419.)

"Of all the women whose names appear in the recorded deeds of the early part of the eighteenth century, either as grantors of property or as relinquishing dower, something less than forty per cent sign their names; all the others make their marks." (G. H. Martin, *The Evolution of the Massachusetts School System,* p. 75.)

The teachers in the middle-colonies parochial schools were usually good, carefully selected by their churches, sound in the faith,[1] and rendered service which for the time was reasonably satisfactory. Often they rendered many types of service — teacher, chorister,

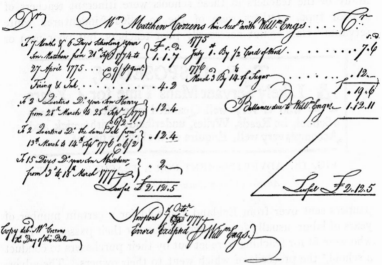

FIG. 17. A COLONIAL TEACHER'S TUITION BILL

William Engs, teacher, presents the above tuition bill to Mr. Matthew Cozzens for a balance due of 1£, 12s, 11d, over and above the wood and sugar previously paid, for teaching his two sons between September 21, 1774, and March 18, 1777.

bell-ringer, sexton, and janitor at times being combined in one person (**R. 45**) — and for a small amount of pay.[2] Often, too, this pay was difficult to collect. Probably the best of the teachers in the schools supported by the churches were found in the schools of the Anglican Church "Society for the Propagation of the Gospel

[1] The following is from the orders given by the English Society for the Propagation of the Gospel to the successive governors of New York:

"38 And wee doe further direct that noe schoolmaster bee henceforth permitted to come from England & to keep school within our province of New York, without the license of the said Archbiship of Canterbury; And that noe other person now there or that shall come from other parts, bee admitted to keep school without your license first had."

[2] The following agreement, made in Lancaster, Pa., in 1747, is illustrative:

"I, the undersigned John Hoffman, parochial teacher of the church at Lancaster, have promised, in the presence of the congregation, to serve as chorister, and as long as we have no pastor, to read sermons on Sunday. In summer I promise to hold cathecetical instruction with the young, as becomes a faithful teacher, and also to lead them in singing, and to attend to the clock."

in Foreign Parts" (**R. 27**), which operated in many towns and cities in the English Colonies between 1702 and 1782. Probably the poorest teachers were to be found in the private adventure schools of the Central and Southern Colonies, and in the charity schools. Many of the teachers in these schools were itinerant teachers of a poor type. Others were of the so-called "indentured white servants" class — not necessarily poor teachers, but poor men or

To Be DISPOSED of,

A Likely Servant Mans Time for 4 Years who is very well Qualified for a Clerk or to teach a School, he Reads, Writes, underſtands Arithmetick and Accompts very well, Enquire of the Printer hereof.

FIG. 18. ADVERTISEMENT FOR A TEACHER TO LET

American Weekly Mercury, Philadelphia, 1735

paupers sent over from England and sold for a certain number of years of labor, usually four or five, to pay for their passage. Those who were fit for teaching were let out by their purchasers to conduct a school,[1] the proceeds of which went to their owners. The advertisement given above shows such a teacher for sale. Many somewhat similar advertisements for teachers to let, and for runaway teachers, are to be found in the newspapers of the time (**R. 47**) of the Central Colonies. Other servants of this type were sold directly to those wanting them by the ship captains, who brought them over.[2] One such cargo is listed as for sale at Baltimore,[3] as late as

---

[1] "Once in a while a planter would start a little school for the benefit of his own children and the other white children who chanced to live near or on his plantation. The teachers of such plantation schools were apt to be redemptioners and exported convicts. In Europe at this time the lot of the poor was extremely hard, and many persons came across the Atlantic solely to escape the misery at home. The captain of the ship that brought over a penniless man of this class was allowed to sell him for four years to pay his passage. It was also customary to transport men who had been convicted of small crimes and sell them for periods of greater or less length. When one of these unfortunates could read and write, he sometimes was purchased for a schoolmaster, and teachers of this kind were common in both Southern and Middle Colonies." (Clifton Johnson, *Old Time Schools and Schoolbooks*, p. 32.)

[2] "When a ship arrives in the River," wrote an English missionary preacher at Newcastle, Delaware, in 1727, "it is a common expression with those who stand in need of an Instructor for their children — Let us go and buy a School-Master."

[3] Maryland seems to have depended heavily on servant schoolmasters for the instruction of its youth. McCormac, in his *White Servitude in Maryland* (p. 76), estimates that at least two thirds of the teachers of Maryland were of this class.

1786, in the advertisement given below. A few indentures of youths to be apprenticed to learn the trade of schoolmaster (**R. 48**) also are to be found, showing that the apprenticeship route also was occasionally employed, in the early period, in securing teachers for the schools.

Men and Women Servants
JUST ARRIVED

In the Ship *Paca*, Robert Caulfield, Master, in five Weeks from Belfast and Cork, a number of healthy Men and Women SERVANTS.

Among them are several valuable tradesmen, viz.

Carpenters, Shoemakers, Coopers, Blacksmiths, Staymakers, Bookbinders, Clothiers, Diers, Butchers, Schoolmasters, Millwrights, and Labourers.

Their indentures are to be disposed of by the Subscribers,

Brown, and Maris,'
William Wilson.

FIG. 19. INDENTURED SERVANTS FOR SALE

Maryland Gazette or Baltimore Advertiser, May 30, 1786

Licensing of teachers. The licensing of teachers was carefully looked after [1] in so far as religious faith was concerned, though private teachers usually were unlicensed. Where this was done locally, as in New England, the minister usually examined the candidate thoroughly to see that he was "sound in the faith and knew his Latin." Little else mattered. In the parochial schools to the southward, where there was a connection with a home church in continental Europe, the license to teach not infrequently came, in theory at least, from a church synod or bishop in the home land.

A modicum of learning was of course assumed on the part of the applicant, but this was not especially inquired into. The great consideration was that the teacher should adhere closely to the tenets of the particular church, and should abstain from attendance upon the services of any other church. For example, the Bishop of London issued the license to teach in schools under the direction of the English Church in the Colonies. To hold such a license the

[1] In the records of Portland, Maine, for 1761, for example, we find "John Montague Richard, of Falmouth, yeoman" under bonds of £10 "to appear at the General Session to be held at Falmouth to answer his being presented for getting up and keeping a school in said Falmouth without the approbation of the selectmen."

applicant must conform to the Church liturgy, must have received the Sacrament in some Anglican church within a year, and for attending any other form of worship was usually subject to imprisonment and disbarment from teaching. Such conditions illustrate the intense religious bitterness of the times, and the dominance of the religious motive in all instruction. Had there not been churches to recruit for, and a feeling of the deep importance of church membership, there would have been little need for schools. It was the one compelling motive of the time for maintaining them.

Character of the early school instruction. Viewed from any modern standpoint the early colonial schools attained to but a low degree of efficiency. The dominance of such an intense religious motive[1] in itself precluded any liberal attitude in the instruction.

FIG. 20. A SCHOOLMASTER OF THE OLD TYPE

In addition, the school hours were long (**Rs. 42, §3; 45, §1**) and most of the time was wasted as the result of an almost complete lack of any teaching equipment, books, and supplies, and of poor methods of teaching. The schoolhouses commonly were of logs with a rough puncheon floor, and with seats and a rough board desk running around the walls (**R. 49**). Paper, greased with lard, often took the place of glass in the windows. There were no black-boards or maps. Slates were not used until about 1820, and pencils and steel pens did not come into use until much later. The first printed writing "Copy Books" were those of Caleb Bingham, printed in Boston in 1795, but it was half a century and more

---

[1] Among many school regulations of the time, the following is illustrative. Ipswich, as ate as 1792, voted:

"that in both schools of the town parishes the Catechism of the Assembly of Devines, with Dr. Watt's explanatory notes, and the Catechism by the same author, be constantly used as much as three or four times a week, according to the different grades of the scholars, until the same are committed to memory."

before they came into common use.   Paper was expensive and
not particularly good in quality, and hence used but sparingly.
Sometimes birch bark was used for ciphering, and
often the figures were traced in sand.   The pens
were goose quills, and one of the prerequisites for
a schoolmaster was the ability to make and repair
quill pens.   The ink was home-made, and often
poor.

The discipline in all classes of schools was
severe.   Even boys in college were still whipped,[1]
much time in the grammar schools was devoted
to imposing discipline, while in the lower schools
little else than hard punishments were the rule.[2]
Whipping-posts were sometimes set up in the
schoolroom, or in the yard or street outside.
Pictures of schools of the time, especially European schools, usually show the schoolmaster
with a bundle of switches near at hand.   The
ability to impose some sort of order on a poorly
taught and, in consequence, an unruly school, was
another of the prerequisites for a schoolmaster.

FIG. 21.   A
SCHOOL WHIP-
PING-POST

Drawn from a pic-
ture of a five-foot
whipping-post which
once stood in the
floor of a schoolhouse
in Sunderland, Mas-
sachusetts. Now in
the Deerfield mu-
seum.

The greatest waste of time came from the poor
methods used in teaching and the individual
methods of instruction universally followed.   Reading and spelling were taught everywhere by first
learning the letters, then syllables, and finally words.   Children
came forward to the teacher's desk and recited individually to the
master or dame, and so wasteful was the process that children
might attend school for years and get only a mere start in reading
and writing (**Rs. 51, 52**).   Hearing lessons, assigning new tasks,

[1] The Harvard College rules of 1660, in force for a long time thereafter, contained the
following:

"It is hereby ordered that the president and fellows of Harvard College have the power
to punish all misdeeds of the young men in their college.   They are to use their best judgment, and punish by fines or whipping in the hall publicly, as the nature of the offense shall
call for."

Illustrative of the way the rule was enforced, Thomas Sargent, a Harvard student, convicted in 1674 of speaking blasphemous words, was publicly whipped in the library before
all the scholars.   The punishment was inflicted under the supervision of the president,
who preceded the chastisement with prayer.

[2] "Both at home and in school the rod — the rawhide — was freely used; nor did either
sex or age afford any immunity from corporal punishment which would now excite indigna-
tion if inflicted on dogs."   (Adams: *Three Episodes in New England History*.)

setting copies, making quill pens, dictating sums, and keeping order completely absorbed the teacher's time (**R. 53**). Only in the Latin grammar schools, which enrolled a small but select body of pupils and which were taught by college graduates, and the English grammar schools of the few cities, whose teachers employed the best methods of the time, do we find a better condition. Teachers, even in these, had their difficulties in preparing for college the rough material that came to their hands. After this "material" reached the college it seems to have had its troubles also.[1]

II. CHANGE IN CHARACTER AFTER ABOUT 1750

The period of establishment. The seventeenth century was essentially a period of transplanting, during which little or no attempt at adaptation or change was made. The customs of the mother countries in manners, morals, dress, religious observances, education, and classes in society were all carefully transplanted. In most of the Colonies the early settlements were near the coast. This was particularly the case in New England, where the danger from Indian massacres had been greater than farther south. King Philip's War (1675–78) had cost the New England colonists half a million dollars — a large sum for that time — and had almost exhausted the people. Twelve out of the ninety existing towns had been destroyed, and forty others had witnessed fire and massacre. A number of towns were so poor they could not pay their colony taxes, and the maintenance of schools, either by tuition or tax, became exceedingly difficult.[2]

The general result, though, of the war was such a punishment of the Indians that the colonists felt free thereafter to form settlements inland, and a marked expansion of New England took place. The same was true of the Central Colonies, new settlements now being founded farther and farther inland. These new towns in

[1] The following extract from the diary of a Harvard student, under date of 1758, is illustrative:

> "Came to college, began Logick,
> Fit with the sophomores,
> Mowed President's grass,
> Did not go to prayers,
> President sick, wherefore much deviltry carried on in college."

[2] Life and liberty in the new land had proved costly. The colonists were wearied by the struggle to establish a new civilization in the wilderness, the conquering of the Indians had been difficult, and taxation had been found to be a heavy burden. The firmness of purpose remained, but the early zeal for education had largely given way.

the wilderness, owing their foundation to an entirely different cause than the original towns, and being founded by younger people who had never known European religious zeal or oppression, at once gave evidence of less interest in religion and learning than had been the case with the towns nearer the coast. Even in these earlier coast towns, the second and third generation then in control began to turn from religion and agriculture to shipping and commerce, and with the rise of trade new interests began slowly to displace the dominant religious concern of the early colonists.

Waning of the old religious interest. As early as 1647 Rhode Island had enacted the first law providing for freedom of religious worship ever enacted by an English-speaking people, and two years later Maryland enacted a similar law. Though the Maryland law was later overthrown, and a rigid Church-of-England rule established there, these laws were indicative of the new spirit arising in the New World. The witchcraft persecutions at Salem (1691–1692) and elsewhere in New England did much to weaken the hold of the ministry on the people there. By the beginning of the eighteenth century a change in attitude toward the old problem of personal salvation and church attendance became evident. New settlements amid frontier conditions, where hard work rather than long sermons and religious disputations were the need; the gradual rise of a civil as opposed to a religious form of town government; the increase of new interests in trade and shipping, and inter-colony commerce; the beginnings of the breakdown of the old aristocratic traditions and customs, originally transplanted from Europe; the rising individualism in both Europe and America — these all helped to weaken the hold on the people of the old religious doctrines. The importation of many "indentured white servants," who for a time were virtually slaves, and the deportation from England of many paupers and criminals from the English jails, most of whom went to the Central and Southern Colonies, likewise tended not only to reduce the literacy and religious zeal of the Colonies, but also to develop a class of "poor whites" who later deeply influenced educational progress in the States in which they settled.

By 1750 the change in religious thinking had become quite marked. Especially was the change evidenced in the dying out of the old religious fervor and intolerance, and the breaking up of the old religious solidarity. While most of the Colonies continued

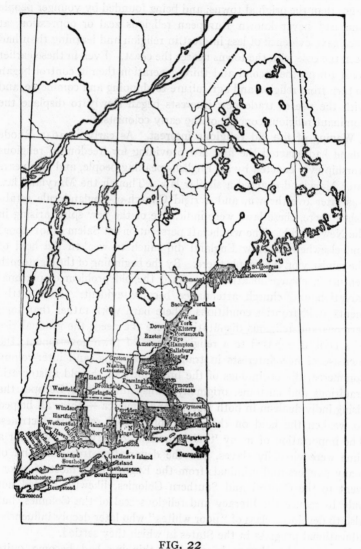

FIG. 22

HOW THE EARLY NEW ENGLAND TOWNS WERE LOCATED

From L. K. Mathews's *The Expansion of New England*, p. 35.   Houghton
Mifflin Co., Boston, 1909.   By permission.

to maintain an "established church," other sects had to be admitted to the Colony and given freedom of worship, and, once admitted, they were found not to be so bad after all. The Puritan monopoly of New England was broken, as was also that of the Anglican Church in the Central Colonies. Expressive of the new attitude was the founding at Philadelphia, in 1753–1755, on a non-denominational basis of what later evolved into the University of Pennsylvania; the opening of King's College in New York City, in 1754, with a published announcement:

> That as to Religion, there is no Intention to impose upon the Scholars the peculiar Tenets of any particular Sect of Christians... as to any peculiar Tenets everyone is left to judge freely for himself and to be required to attend only such Places of Worship on the Lord's Day as their Parents or Guardians shall think fit to order or permit;

and the founding of Brown at Providence, in 1764, as a Baptist college but with the following clause in its charter:

> Furthermore it is hereby enacted and declared: That into the liberal and Catholic institution shall never be admitted any religious tests. But on the contrary all members hereof shall forever enjoy full free, absolute, and uninterrupted liberty of conscience.

The day of the monopoly of any sect in a Colony was over. New secular interests began to take the place of religion as the chief topic of thought and conversation. Secular books began to dispute the earlier monopoly of the Bible, and a few colonial newspapers (seven by 1750) were founded and began to circulate. All these changes materially affected both the support and the character of the education provided in the schools of the time.

Changing character of the schools. These changes manifested themselves in many ways in the matter of education. The maintenance of the Latin grammar schools, required by the Law of 1647, had been found to be increasingly difficult of enforcement, not only in Massachusetts, but in the other New England Colonies which had followed the Massachusetts example.[1] As far back as Cheever's day we find even Boston having difficulty in paying him

---

[1] Throughout much of the seventeenth century the records of the New England towns abound with protests, citations, payment of fines, and various attempts to comply with the law on some partial basis. The inland towns in particular found its support a heavy burden. There was a constant struggle between the law on the one side, and ability and desire to support on the other, with the result that often as much ingenuity was displayed in escaping the fine as zeal in maintaining the school.

his salary (**R. 41**).   The expenses incurred in King Philip's War (1675–1678) had borne heavily on the New England Colonies, and with the changing attitude of the people, which had become clearly manifest by 1750, the demand for relief from the maintenance of this school in favor of a more practical and less aristocratic type of higher school, if higher school at all were needed, became marked. By the close of the period the more American Academy, with its more practical studies, had begun to supersede the old Latin Grammar School, even in New England, while in the cities of the middle Colonies the English grammar school (**Rs. 55, 56**), with its much more modern curriculum, had become the prevailing type of secondary school.

This is to give NOTICE,

THat the Subscribers hereof, living in the Township of Ewr. him. Burlington County, and Province of West New Jersey, do want a Schoolmaster, and chance to have a single Man such Person applying, qualified for the said Service, may expect good Wages, and good Treatment, by us.

⊙   ABRAHAM HAINES, and THOMAS SMITH, Senior.

FIG. 23. ADVERTISEMENT FOR A COLONIAL SCHOOLMASTER

Pennsylvania Gazette, November 22, 1759

The elementary schools experienced something of the same difficulties.   Many of the parochial schools died out, and others declined in character and importance.   Teachers for the schools became hard to obtain.   In Church of England Colonies all elementary education now was left to private initiative and philanthropic or religious effort.   In the Southern Colonies the classes in society made common tax-supported schools impossible, though in a number of the parishes some form of endowed school frequently was maintained [1] (**R. 53b**).   In New England the eighteenth century

[1] Two Virginia records are illustrative: The minister of Elizabeth City Parish reported, in 1724:

"There are two schools endowed, though very meanly, whereof John Mason and Abram Paris are teachers.   There is also a very good private school where, besides reading, arithmetic and writing, Latin and Greek are very well taught."   (Perry, W. S. *Historical Collections*, I, 294.)

The minister of Accomack Parish reported, the same year:

"a school, endowed by one Mr Sandford, late of London,... for the benefit, better learning, and education of poor children, whose parents are esteemed unable to give them learning, living in the upper part of Accomack county."

was a continual struggle on the one hand to prevent the town school from dying out, and on the other to establish in its place a series of scattered and inferior district schools, while tuition fees and taxation for support became harder and harder to obtain.   Among other changes of importance the reading school and the writing school now became definitely united in all smaller places and in the rural districts to form the American elementary school of the 3-Rs, while the dame school was definitely adopted as the beginners' school (**R. 53a**).   Both these changes were measures of economy, as well as distinctively American adaptations.   Only in a few New England cities did the Reading and the Writing Schools retain their earlier character (**R. 54**).

New textbooks, containing less of the gloomily religious than the *New England Primer* (**R. 36**), and secular rather than religious matter, appeared and began to be used in the schools.   Dilworth's *A New Guide to the English Tongue* (**R. 37**), first published in England in 1740, began to be used in the American Colonies by 1750. This contained words for spelling and a number of fables, and was the first of a line of some half-dozen so-called spelling books which finally culminated in the first distinctively American textbook — Noah Webster's blue-backed *Spelling Book* (**R. 174**), first published at Hartford, in 1783.

The English Grammar School.   The Latin Grammar School had its home in New England, and there it retained its character throughout the colonial period.   In New York and the cities of the middle Colonies, however, the instruction in the secondary school was materially modified to adapt it better to the needs of a new country rapidly becoming interested in trade and commerce.   Beginning probably with the Grammar School of the City of New York, established in 1732 to offer instruction in writing, Latin, and "all Branches of Mathematicks, Geometry, Algebra, Geography, Navigation Merchants Bookkeeping after the most Perfect Manner"; and carried further by the founding of Franklin's Academy at Philadelphia, in 1749 (opened in 1751), we soon find developed in the Middle Colonies a secondary school of a new type which became known as the English School, or the English Grammar School (**R. 56**), by way of distinguishing it from its New England prototype.

In the days before the War for Independence the English Grammar School played an important part in the few cities of the Middle Colonies in the education of youth destined for the more practical pursuits of the time. The New England Academy, a few of which had been established before the beginning of the national period, was in large part an adaptation of the English Grammar School which had been developed in the Middle Colonies. These institutions offered a comprehensive program of studies (**R. 56**), and possessed a clear aim as to the purposes of their work. In the founding of Franklin's Academy at Philadelphia, in 1749 (**R. 144**), an institution that later developed into the University of Pennsylvania, we see these new ideas as to studies and purposes in full swing.

The private and evening schools. During the colonial period schools supported by the towns were commonly known as "town schools," and seldom as "public schools." Supported as they were, in New England, by the public, they naturally were open to all. In the later colonial period we find the rise in the cities, and particularly the cities of the Middle Colonies (**R. 58**), of a number of private schools, of various types which often took the name of "public schools" because they were open to anyone prepared to undertake the studies and pay the tuition fees. Sometimes they also were called "academies," but were of the proprietorship type. The masters of some of the publicly-supported schools also came in time to supplement their public income by announcing "private" pay hours (**R. 57f**), at their homes. Other teachers, not employed by the public, opened private (pay) schools, often termed public schools (**R. 57**), in which they engaged to offer the type of practical and vocational instruction desired by the public. Some of the classes were for "Young Ladies" only (**R. 57h**).

As these schools were private-venture undertakings, the masters were free to develop them along such lines as seemed desirable, and they were forced to keep the instruction in them good to make them prosperous. Freed from a prescribed program of studies, as was the Latin Grammar School (**R. 54**), and aiming at the adaption of their instruction to the needs of their pupils, the private secondary school of the later colonial period made a distinct contribution to the development of a liberal and modern-type of secondary school curriculum in America (**R. 58**), and one adapted to the needs of a people becoming conscious that the period of transplanting and of colonial dependence was rapidly drawing to a close.

Beginnings of change in the college. In 1754 an advertisement announcing the opening of King's College (later Columbia) appeared in a New York paper (**R. 59**). While the entrance requirements as stated (§ II) were much the same as for other colleges of the time, it proposed larger religious freedom for the students (see p. 61), and a much wider curriculum (§ V), including many of the mathematical and scientific and commercial studies then being offered in the English grammar schools of the city. Theological discussion is not mentioned, though disputation is retained in the 1762 program. The first professor appointed, significantly, was a professor of "Mathematics and Natural History."

While the college was still in embryo a pamphlet was published and circulated in New York under the title of *General Idea of the College of Mirania,*[1] which embodied so many reforms that have since been accepted in college administration that its importance as a document in the history of the college curriculum is large.[2] It is our first comprehensive plan of a college course intended to form "a succession of sober, virtuous, industrious citizens." The author, William Smith, was to be the first Provost of what later evolved into the University of Pennsylvania,[3] and there he embodied his ideas into a "Scheme of Liberal Education," which was approved by the Board of Trustees in 1756, and which remained

[1] The author of the pamphlet was a young man but recently returned from his ordination as a minister at the hands of the Bishops of Lincoln and Carlisle. In England he had been studying the educational problem, "trying to devise plans for the educating a class of persons who had not been reached by the ordinary methods then in use.

"The object which the Miranians always kept in sight was the easiest, simplest, and most natural method of forming youth to the knowledge and exercise of private and public virtue."

The proposals bear a striking resemblance to the revised course of study introduced in 1753, by Alexander Girard, at the University of Aberdeen, and it is presumed that the author, William Smith, drew his inspiration from that source.

[2] Provost Stille (1868-80), writing of the work of Provost Smith, says of the plan he inaugurated:

"Its best eulogy is that it formed the basis of our American college system.... It may be safely affirmed that in 1756 no such comprehensive scheme of education existed in any college in the American colonies." (C. J. Stille, *Memoir of Rev. William Smith*, p. 12, Philadelphia, 1869.)

[3] In 1749 Benjamin Franklin had issued a pamphlet, *Proposals Relating to the Education of Youth in Pennsylvania*, which awakened much interest. A charity school had been maintained in Philadelphia since 1740, but no effort had been made for more advanced instruction. What Franklin proposed was an Academy, and he soon found himself at the head of a board of directors to organize the school. It began instruction in 1751, and was chartered in 1755 as "The College, Academy, and Charitable School of Philadelphia," with the power to grant degrees. The first commencement was in 1757. In 1777 the legislature changed the name to "University of the State of Pennsylvania."

practically unchanged as the college course through the whole period of its existence as a colonial college. Up to the Revolution, when the work of the college was suspended, Pennsylvania offered the most liberal course of instruction found in any college in the Colonies; in fact, it was, with the partial exception of Columbia, the only

FIG. 24. TWO EARLY COLLEGE PRESIDENTS

PROVOST WILLIAM SMITH
University of Pennsylvania
(b. 1727; d. 1803)
Provost, 1755-1791.

PRESIDENT JAMES MADISON
College of William and Mary
(b. 1749; d. 1812)
President, 1777-1812.

American college not to follow the plan laid down at Harvard in 1642 by Dunster, and further amplified by the Yale faculty in 1727-28. Dexter [1] gives the following brief digest of the Pennsylvania curriculum:

> The course covered three years, and comprised readings in Juvenal, Livy, Cicero, Horace, Quintilian, and the Tuscular Questions; the Iliad, Thucydides, Epictetus, and Plato's *De Legibus* formed the work in Greek. Mathematics occupied a prominent place in the course of study, and during the last two years considerable work was done in natural philosophy, chemistry, hydrostatics, prismatics, optics, and astronomy. Ethics and politics, natural and civil law, formed a group of subjects to which more than usual attention was given. In 1765 it established a medical department, the first in the country.

In 1756, no such comprehensive scheme for collegiate education existed in any other American college, yet it marked the way that the post-revolutionary college would in time follow.

[1] E. G. Dexter. *History of Education in the United States*, p. 251.

Much the same ideas were carried into effect by President Madison in the reform of the William and Mary curriculum in 1779, partly with the assistance of Thomas Jefferson, and later by Thomas Jefferson in the University of Virginia at its opening in 1825. The reforms at William and Mary in 1779 were especially thorough-

FIG. 25. THE COLLEGE OF WILLIAM AND MARY, AS IT WAS
WHEN THE PARENT CHAPTER OF PHI BETA KAPPA
WAS ORGANIZED THERE, IN 1776

going,[1] and a radical departure from the restricted Oxford curriculum which had been in force from the founding of the institution. When carried through, the institution had a broader and a more liberal curriculum than any other colonial college, while in the complete freedom in electives it anticipated the Harvard reforms of a century later. Summing up its colonial history,[2] President Tyler said:

> It was the first college in the United States to have a full faculty of professors (1729); the first to adopt the lecture system (1758); the first to establish the elective and the honor systems (1779); the first to widen its scope into that of a university (1779); the first to establish courses in municipal and constitutional law (1779), modern languages (1779), politi-

[1] "In 1779 I was... elected one of the Visitors of William and Mary College, a self-electing body. I effected, during my residence in Williamsburg that year, a change in the organization of that institution, abolishing the Grammar School, and the two Professorships of Divinity and Oriental Languages, and substituting a Professorship of Law and Police, one of Anatomy, Medicine, and Chemistry, and one of Modern Languages: and, the charter confining us to six professorships, we added the Law of Nature and of Nations and Fine Arts to the duties of the Moral Professor, and Natural History to the Professor of Mathematics and Natural Philosophy." (Thomas Jefferson. *Memoir*, vol. I, p. 43.)

[2] William and Mary, like Harvard, trained an illustrious body of sons who rendered a good account of themselves in the days of the Revolution and the organization of the Government. Peyton Randolph, first president of the Continental Congress; Thomas Jefferson, author of the Declaration of Independence; John Tyler, Sr., and Edmund Randolph, noted revolutionary leaders; John Marshall, who interpreted the constitution; three early presidents of the United States; and 16 of the 27 Senators from Virginia between 1789 and 1861 looked to her as mother.

cal economy (1779), and history (1803); and the first to organize a Greek letter intercollegiate fraternity, the Phi Beta Kappa (1776).

Despite a largely unchanged curriculum in the older colleges, there was nevertheless a change in direction and spirit. In particular did the long training in disputation begin to bear fruit when it turned toward inquiry into matters of government, commerce, and political liberty, as it clearly did after about 1750. Many of the brightest minds of the time received their forensic training in the debating societies which now arose,[1] and disputation now changed into a debate as to human rights and liberties — a vast explosive store which the flames of the Revolution fired, and out of it flashed the Declaration of Independence, the Federalist Papers, and the Constitution.

III. RISE OF THE CIVIL OR STATE SCHOOL

Disintegration of the New England town. One of the most fundamental changes which now took place among New England people, and one which vitally modified future educational administration in almost all our American States, was the breakdown of the unity of the old New England town and the rise of the school district as the unit for school maintenance in its stead. It came about in this way.

Originally each New England settlement was a unit, and the irregular area included — twenty to forty square miles, a little smaller than a western township — was called a town. At the

---

[1] A few colonial examples will illustrate:

Samuel Adams entered Harvard in 1736, at the age of 14. He attracted attention to himself by his debate on "Liberty."

John Witherspoon entered Edinburgh in 1734, at 14, and later (1768) became president of Princeton. An active debater in college, he encouraged two famous debating societies at Princeton, both of large influence. The only clergyman to sign the Declaration of Independence.

James Otis entered Harvard in 1739, at 14. He was a noted debater, and delivered a syllogistic disputation on taking his A.B. degree.

John Hancock entered Harvard in 1750, at 13; was a noted student of Ramus' *Disputations*, and a noted debater.

John Adams entered Harvard in 1751, at 16. He became a noted public speaker while a student.

James Madison entered Princeton in 1769, at 18, founded the American Whig Society, a noted debating society.

Alexander Hamilton entered King's in 1774, at 17, and was noted as an able logician and debater.

Benjamin Franklin, at 22, organized the "Junto," a literary and debating society which flourished for forty years, and finally evolved into the American Philosophical Society, of Philadelphia.

center, and usually facing on the town common, were the Meeting-House, and later the town school, and the town hall. Often at first the school and the town office were in a part of the Meeting House building. All citizens were required by law to live within one half-mile of the Meet-ing-House, to attend the town meetings, and to send their children to the town school. In the town meet-ing, at first held in the churches, all matters relat-ing to the interests of the town were discussed, taxes were levied, and town by-laws were enacted. In time these towns, originally founded as little religious republics, became centers for the discussion of all forms of public questions, and schools for training the people in the principles of government and parlia-mentary procedure. In

FIG. 26. THE FIRST MEETING-HOUSE OF CENTER CHURCH, NEW HAVEN

Church organized in 1639; building erected in 1640. Built of logs, with a watch-tower at the top for protection against surprise attacks of Indians.

them the people learned how to safeguard their own interests.

By the close of the seventeenth century, as has been stated, many of the forces which at first required a compact form of settlement had begun to lose their hold. With the decline in dominance of the old religious motive, new interests arose. One of these was to scatter out and live on the farming land. New settlements accord-ingly arose within the towns, miles away from the meeting- and schoolhouses. To attend church or town meeting in winter was not always easy, and for children to attend the town school was impossible.[1] The old laws as to place of residence accordingly had

[1] In a petition of the town of Wilton, New Hampshire, asking relief from a fine for not having maintained a grammar school, as required by law, it is recited that:

"From the view of its local situation — mountainous land, long winters, deep snows, inhabitants scattered, town divided by a rapid stream rendering passage to its center at some seasons of the year inconvenient and impracticable... and the inability of the people to provide schooling in the extreme parts, while obliged to support a grammar school in the center..."

to be repealed or ignored, and as a result church enthusiasm, town as opposed to individual interests, and zeal for education alike declined. New towns also arose farther inland, which soon broke up into divisions or districts. By 1725 the population of most of the towns had been scattered over much of the town's area, and small settlements, cut off from that of the central town by hills, streams, forest, or mere distance, had been formed. Due to the difficulties of communication, these little settlements tended to become isolated and independent.

The rise of the district system. As the tendency to subdivide the town became marked, these subdivisions demanded and obtained local rights. The first demand was for a minister of their own, or at least for separate services. As a result parishes were created within the town, and each parish, with its parish officers, became a new center for the rise of democracy and the assertion of parish rights (**R. 60**). The town was next divided into road districts for the repair and maintenance of roads, and then into districts for recruiting the militia, and for assessing and collecting taxes. All these decentralizing tendencies contributed toward

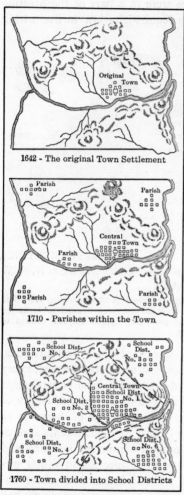

1642 - The original Town Settlement

1710 - Parishes within the Town

1760 - Town divided into School Districts

FIG. 27. SHOWING THE EVOLUTION OF THE DISTRICT SYSTEM IN MASSACHUSETTS

the growth of a district consciousness and the breakdown of town government. The establishment of dame schools in the district

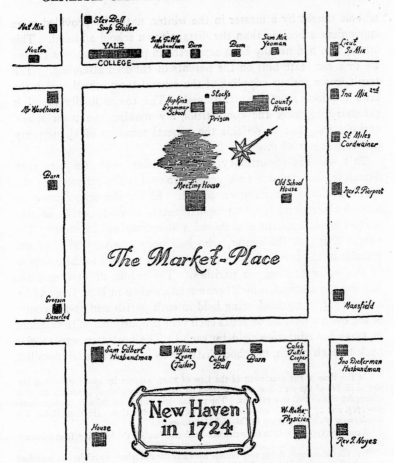

FIG. 28. MAP OF THE TOWN OF NEW HAVEN, IN 1724

Based on Brown's "Map of New Haven in 1724." Reproduced, by permission, from Edwin Oviatt's *The Beginnings of Yale, 1701–1726.* Yale University Press, 1916.

parishes [1] in the summer, which had become an established institution in New England by 1700, and the presence of private tuition-

---

[1] For example, the Worcester records for 1731 contain the following vote:

"Whereas many small children cannot attend ye school in ye center of ye town by reason of ye remoteness of their dwellings, and to ye intent that all children may have ye benefit of education, &c., voted, that a suitable number of school dames, not exceeding five, be provided by ye selectmen, at ye charge of ye town, for the teaching of small children to read, and to be placed in ye several parts of ye town as ye selectmen may think most convenient, and such gentlewomen to be paid by the poll as ye selectmen and they may agree."

schools taught by a master in the winter, naturally provided more convenient schooling than the distant town school afforded. This latter, too, had usually been supported in part at least by a tuition fee or a tax (rate bill) on the parents of children attending.[1] The result was a serious crippling of the central town school, which the laws required must be maintained. The towns finally found it necessary to meet the competition by making the town school entirely free, but to do this the general taxation of all property had to be resorted to.

This was the opportunity of the parishes, and the price they demanded for consent to a general town tax for schools was the division of the central town school. Either the school must be moved about, and taught proportionately in each parish, or separate schools must be established and maintained in each.[2] The people living at the center, who had been receiving most of the benefits of the town school, were compelled to yield to the demands of the outer sections, or parishes. The result, at first, was the moving town school, which became established in New England by about 1725, the school being held in each parish and at the center of the town a number of weeks each year proportional to the amount of taxes for education paid by each.[3] The next step was to give back to each parish, or school district [4] as it now came to be called,

---

[1] At the time of the enactment of the Law of 1647, support by contribution was employed in five of the six towns whose records on the point are clear. Gradually the plan of support was shifted to a rate tax. The median date of rate adoption in Massachusetts was 1715, and by 1764 only one town studied still collected tuition. (Jackson, G. L. *The Development of School Support in Colonial Massachusetts.*)

[2] A common type of petition for such a subdivision of funds is the following, from Swanzey, in 1775:

"We, the subscribers, living very remote from any district where we might be convenient to a school for our children, do humbly petition that the town do vote us off as a district, and grant that "the money which we pay towards maintaining a school in this town be laid out for schooling in the said district, as near the center as may be convenient."

[3] For example, the selectmen of the town of Harwich, in 1719, were directed "to divide the town into societies, each to have the benefit of the school its part of the time," and in 1725 a committee was appointed "to settle the school and proportion the six removes, both as to the number of families and children belonging to each remove, till the school hath gone once around the town." Six removes were provided for, with three and a half years to complete the circuit.

Another example is Amesbury, which voted, in 1711, "that the school shall be kept the first four months at the meetinghouse, the next four months at Pond's Hill fort, and the last four months at Left. Foote's fort or thereabouts."

[4] "Society," "precinct," "division," "parish," "quarter," and "squadron" were all used to define school limits, but the most common term was "district," which finally became the accepted word, was incorporated into the law, and "district" it has ever since remained.

the money it had paid and let it maintain its own school.[1] (**R. 61**). This step was taken during the latter part of the eighteenth century and the right to elect school trustees, levy district school taxes, and select a teacher alone were needed to complete the establish‑ ment of the full district system.   These were legally granted in Connecticut [2] in 1766 and in Massachusetts [3] in 1789, and from New England the district system, thus created, in time spread over nearly all of the United States.   The practical effect of these laws was that the school system, instead of embracing schools of different types and grades, was gradually narrowed down to a one-room district school for children of all ages and in every variety of study.

Rise of the civil or state school.   As has been stated earlier, the school everywhere in America arose as a child of the Church.   In the Colonies where the parochial-school conception of education became the prevailing type, the school remained under church con‑ trol until after the founding of our national government.   In New England, however, and the New England evolution in time be‑ came the prevailing American practice, the school passed through a very interesting development during colonial times from a church into a state school.

As we have seen, each little New England town was originally established as a religious republic, with the Church in complete control.   The governing authorities for church and civil affairs were much the same.   When acting as church officers they were known

[1] For example, the town of Waltham, in 1745, required each squadron "to furnish a place for the school and convenient board for the teacher."

Middletown, in 1754, voted that each " squadron shall have the sole power of managing their own schoolhouse and lands, by leasing out the same, and employing schoolmasters as it shall be most agreeable to them."

Hingham, in 1763, voted to "the inhabitants of each parish their just proportion of money raised the year ensuing, for the use of schools."

Winchendon, in 1768, allowed "the extreme parts of the town to have a school by them‑ selves, they providing a place and a keeper."

Braintree, in 1790, voted that "the money be divided in each precinct according to what they pay for polls and estates, and each precinct to lay out their own money (for schools) as the committee shall direct."

[2] The Connecticut law of 1766 enacted:

"That each town and society shall have full power and authority to divide themselves into proper and necessary districts for keeping their schools, and to alter and regulate the same from time to time, as they shall have occasion; which districts so made shall draw their equal proportion of said monies as well as all other public monies, for the support of schools belonging to such respective towns or societies, according to the lists of each respective district therein."

[3] This law Horace Mann declared to have been " the most unfortunate law on the sub‑ ject of education ever enacted by the State of Massachusetts."

as Elders and Deacons; when acting as civil or town officers they were known as Selectmen. The State, as represented in the colony legislature or the town meeting, was clearly the servant of the Church, and existed in large part for religious ends. It was the State acting as the servant of the Church which enacted the laws of 1642 and 1647, requiring the towns to maintain schools for religious purposes. Now, so close was the connection between the religious town which controlled church affairs, and the civil town which looked after roads, fences, taxes, and defense — the constituency of both being one and the same, and the meetings of both being held at first in the Meeting-House — that when the schools were established the colony legislature placed them under the civil, as involving taxes and being a public service, rather than under the religious town. The interests of one were the interests of both, and, being the same in constituency and territorial boundaries, there seemed no occasion for friction or fear. From this religious beginning the civil school, and the civil school town and township, with all our elaborate school administrative machinery, were later evolved (R. 62).

The erection of a town hall, separate from the Meeting-house, was the first step in the process. School affairs were now discussed at the town hall, instead of in the church. Town taxes, instead of church taxes, were voted for buildings and maintenance. The minister continued to certificate the grammar-school master [1] until the close of the colonial period, but the power to certificate the elementary-school teachers passed to the town authorities early in the eighteenth century. By the close of this century all that the minister, as the surviving representative of church control, had left to him was the right to accompany the town authorities in the visitation of the schools.[2] Thus gradually but certainly did the

[1] A sample certification, dated at Sudbury, Massachusetts, in 1701, and given by the ministers of the town, reads:

"We,... being desired by the town of Sudbury to write what we could testify concerning the justification of Mr. Joseph Noyes of Sudbury for a legal grammar schoolmaster, having examined the said Mr. Joseph Noyes, we find that he hath been considerably versed in the Latin and Greek tongues, and do think that upon his dilligent revisal and recollection of what he hath formerly learned, he may be qualified to initiate and instruct the youth in the Latin tongue."

[2] The annual appointment of a Visiting Committee "to go the rounds to examine the teaching of children and youth" was an old New England institution, dating back at least to 1660, and continued throughout all the eighteenth century. For example, in the *Massachusetts Historical Collections* for 1794 we read, for Boston:

"In the month of July annually the selectmen, and gentlemen of science chosen by the

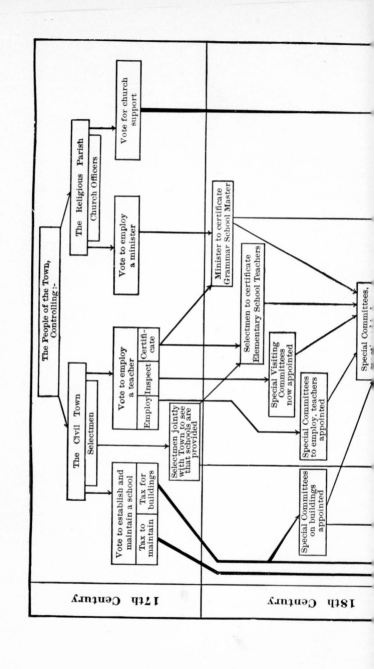

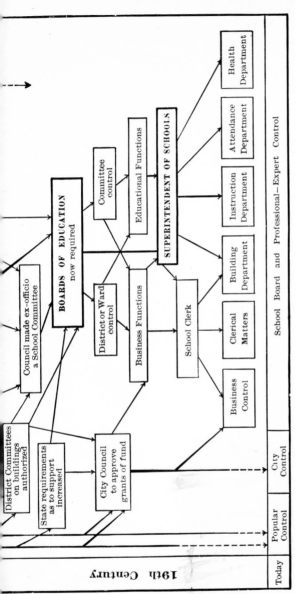

FIG. 29. CHART SHOWING THE EVOLUTION OF THE MODERN STATE SCHOOL, WITH ITS COMPLICATED ADMINISTRATION, OUT OF THE LITTLE RELIGIOUS SCHOOL OF THE EARLY NEW ENGLAND TOWN

earlier religious school pass out from under the control of the Church and become a state school. When our national government and the different state governments were established, the States were ready to accept, in principle at least, the theory gradually worked out in New England that schools are state institutions and should be under the control of the State.

European traditions no longer satisfy. The changes in the character and in the administration of the schools alike reflect the spirit of the times, which was one of rising individualism in both Europe and America. By 1750 it is clearly evident that European traditions and ways and manners and social customs and types of schools were no longer completely satisfactory. There is clearly manifest a desire to modify all these various forces so as to adapt them better to purely American needs. There is also a tendency, strongly marked in the South, to discard schools for all but a few as being unnecessary under new-world conditions, and to develop a new and more practical type of school for the training of these few. The growing exasperation with the mother country for her foolish colonial policy tended to emphasize this feeling of independence, while Braddock's defeat, after his insulting boastfulness, had a great effect in giving the people of all the Colonies a new confidence in their ability to care for themselves.

The evolution of the public or state school in New England from the original religious school; the formation generally of the American common school; the rise of the district system; the introduction of new types of textbooks; the decline of the Latin Grammar Schools; the rise of the English Grammar School and a little later of the essentially American Academy; the establishment of two new colleges (Pennsylvania, 1749; Kings, 1754), which from the first placed themselves in sympathy with the more practical studies; and the abandonment by Yale in 1767 and Harvard [1] in 1772 of the practice of listing the students in the Catalogue [2] according to

town as a school committee, with other reputable characters invited by them, visit these schools to examine into the regulations and proficiency of the scholars, at which times specimens of their writings are shown and there are exhibitions of their reading and speaking. The visitors then dine together at Fanuel Hall at the expense of the town."

[1] For example, when John Adams, later second President of the United States, entered Harvard College in 1751, he was ranked 14th in a class of 24 in social position, yet in scholarship he later stood among the first three in what was a notable class.

[2] Distinctions of rank, based on family lineage, wealth, social standing, or position, were common for long in the American Colonies. The privileged were separated from the underprivileged, and property rights were closely identified with natural rights. Congregations

the rank and social standing of their parents; — all these were clear indications that the end of the colonial period marked the abandonment of the transplanting of English educational ideas and schools and types of instruction. Instead, the beginnings of the evolution of distinctively American types of schools, better adapted to American needs, are clearly evident. This evolution was checked by the war which closed the period of colonial dependence, and something like half a century of our national life passed before we note again the rise of a distinctively American educational consciousness and the development of distinctively American schools once more begins.

QUESTIONS FOR DISCUSSION

1. Judged by conditions in England at the same time, was the dominance of the religious purpose in education in America anything exceptional?
2. Did the books used in reading form a good graded system?
3. What does the excerpt from the teacher's contract, given on page 48, indicate as to the character of both teachers and schools?
4. How do you explain the elimination of girls from all early instruction in the grammar schools?
5. Were the conditions demanded for a teacher's license perfectly legitimate for the time?   Compare these conditions with conditions demanded of teachers for licensing today.
6. What explanation can you give for the general prevalence of the individual instead of the class method of instruction during colonial times?
7. What explanation can you give for the heavy corporal punishments in the schools in a day of such deep religious feeling?
8. Explain how the seventeenth century was essentially a period of transplanting, or, as Eggleston states it, a period of the "transit of civilization."
9. Why did the rising individualism of later colonial times tend to weaken the religious zeal of earlier times?
10. Why was it natural that the English grammar school and the more practical higher studies should first find a place in the Middle Colonies, rather than in New England?
11. Explain why New York City and Philadelphia should have been centers for the new secondary schools.
12. What do the rise of private and evening schools in the cities of the Middle Colonies indicate?

in New England seated their members according to rank, family descent, wealth, age, and social standing. In the South, those of lower social position waited outside the church until their betters had seated themselves in their pews. One's place at table and in processions was similarly regulated. The dominating influence of English aristocratic traditions was marked in the life of the early colonial period, and the casting off of these, after about 1750, was clear evidence of the change in colonial attitude.

13. Why should the private, rather than the town school, have been the pioneers in developing the newer studies?

14. Explain the stages of development of the Massachusetts district-school system.

15. Explain the steps in the evolution of the modern state school, as shown on the chart, Figure 29.

16. Explain the development of the civil state school out of the religious town school.

17. Show how the moving school was merely a first step in the creation of district schools.

18. Why should the South have tended to discard schools altogether, except for the few?

SELECTED READINGS

In the accompanying volume of *Readings* the following selections, related to the subject matter of this chapter, are reproduced:

*35. Horn Book: Description and Picture of.
*36. New England Primer: Description and Digest of.
*37. Cubberley: The School Texts, by Dilworth.
 38. Gay: Catechism and Bible in the Connecticut Schools.
*39. Allen: Pages from a Colonial M S Arithmetic.
*40. Cheever's *Accidence*: Description of and Title Page.
*41. Jenks: Cheever asks for his Place and his Pay.
*42. Baird: Rules for the government of the New Haven Grammar School.
*43. Town Records: Schoolmaster Contracts in Massachusetts Towns.
*44. New Amsterdam: Rules regulating a Schoolmaster.
*45. Flatbush: Contract with a Dutch Schoolmaster.
*46. Newburg: Contract with a Minister to teach.
*47. Colony Newspapers: Advertisements for Run-away Schoolmasters.
*48. New Yorke: Learning the Trade of a Schoolmaster.
 49. Scharfe: A Late 18th Century Schoolhouse.
*50. Fitzpatrick: Content, Method, and Spirit of Late 18th Century Schools
*51. Middlesex County: How the School Day was Spent.
*52. Burton: The District School as it Was.
 53. Home and School Training in the Colonial Period.
     (*a*) Brainerd: In New England.
     (*b*) Wertenbaker: In Virginia.
*54. Boston: The New Curriculum of 1790.
*55. Newspaper Advs.: Late Colonial English Grammar Schools.
 56. N. Y. Gazetteer: An English Grammar School Program.
 57. Newspaper Advs.: Colonial Evening Schools.
*58. Seybolt: Significance of the Private School in Colonial America.
 59. Newspaper Adv.: The Opening of Kings College.
*60. Farmington: Division of a Town into Parishes and School Districts.
*61. Town Records: The Moving School ordered.
*62. Cubberley: Evolution of the School Committee.

QUESTIONS ON THE READINGS

1. Summarize your impressions of the New England Primer (**36**).
2. Show the importance of Dilworth's texts (**37**) from the teaching point of view.
3. What do the Farmingham rules of 1815 indicate (**38**) as to the survival values of the earlier instruction?
4. What is your impression of Cheever as a schoolmaster (**40**)?
5. Just what type of school was the one at New Haven (**42**)?
6. Characterize the early Dutch school at New Amsterdam (**44**).   Characterize the Dutch school at Flatbush (**45**).
7. What, if any, essential difference was there in the school at Newburg (**46**)?
8. What types of people constituted the run-away teacher group (**47**)?
9. What do you think of the apprenticeship method, time and conditions considered, for learning to be a schoolteacher (**48**)?
10. Regarding the description of the schoolhouse (**49**) as typical for the time, was it adapted to the needs of the curriculum of the period?
11. What percentage, would you estimate, went on for the "good English education" (**50**) described by Fitzpatrick?
12. Explain the new spirit in education (**50c**) which Fitzpatrick describes.
13. From the two descriptions given (**51, 52**), characterize the late colonial district school.
14. Contrast the home and school training of the colonial period in Massachusetts (**53a**) and Virginia (**53b**).
15. Does the Boston curriculum of 1790 (**54**) represent an advanced position, or otherwise?
16. From the newspaper advertisements given (**55a-d**), outline the curriculum of the new English Grammar School.
17. From the program of studies given (**56**), state the nature and the purpose of the instruction in this type of school.
18. From the newspaper advertisements given (**57a-h**), outline the types of evening schools.
19. What was the contribution of the private school (**58**) to early American education?
20. From the Farmington description (**60**), show the steps in the process of dividing the town into school districts.
21. Show how the moving school (**61**) was a natural evolution in early New England society.
22. Trace, briefly, the steps in the evolution of the school committee (**62**), and indicate the forces that produced each forward step.

TOPICS FOR INVESTIGATION AND REPORT

1. The New England Primer.   (Ford; Johnson.)
2. Cheever's Accidence, and Cheever.   (Barnard; Brown.)
3. Indentured servants as teachers.
4. The schoolroom of colonial times.   (Johnson.)

5. The religious aim in early New England education (Brown, E. E., and S. W.; Ford.; Johnson.)
6. The teaching of arithmetic in colonial times (Monroe, W. S.)
7. Teaching method in colonial times.
8. The change in character of New England after c. 1725.
9. The English Grammar School of the Central Colonies.
10. Franklin's plan, and the Academy.
11. Teachers and teaching in colonial times.
12. The moving school in Massachusetts. (Small; Updegraff.)
13. Rise of the district system in Massachusetts. (Martin; Updegraff.)
14. Parish educational activity in Colonial Virginia. (Wells.)
15. The Dutch schools of Colonial New York. (Kilpatrick.)
16. Early history of Harvard College.
17. Early history of Yale College.
18. Early history of William and Mary College.

SELECTED REFERENCES

*Barnard, Henry. "Ezekiel Cheever"; in *Barnard's American Journal of Education*, vol. I, pp. 297–314; vol. XII, pp. 531–60.

> An interesting sketch of the life and work of this famous New England schoolmaster, with notes on the early free grammar school of New England. Vol. XII, article also good on the history of the Boston Latin School.

*Brown, E. E. *The Making of our Middle Schools.* 547 pp. Longmans, New York, 1903.

> A standard history of the rise of the Latin grammar school, the academy, and the later high schools. The first seven chapters bear particularly on the subject matter of this chapter.

Brown, S. W. *The Secularization of American Education.* 160 pp. Teachers College Contributions to Education, No. 49, New York, 1912.

> Chapters I and II contain many extracts from old records relating to the religious aim of education, and to the instruction of orphans and dependents.

Dexter, E. G. *A History of Education in the United States.* 656 pp. The Macmillan Co., New York, 1904.

> A collection of facts rather than an interpretation. The first five chapters deal with the period covered by this chapter.

Dexter, E. G. "On Some Social Distinctions at Harvard and Yale before the Revolution"; in *Proceedings of the American Antiquarian Society*, New Series, vol. IX.

*Eggleston, Edw. *The Transit of Civilization.* 344 pp. New York, 1901.

> A very interesting description of the transfer of English civilization to America in the seventeenth century. Chapter V, on the transfer of educational traditions, is specially important.

*Fitzpatrick, E. A. *The Educational Views and Influence of De Witt Clinton.* 156 pp. Teachers College Contributions to Education, No. 44. New York, 1911.

> Part I is a very interesting study of educational conditions in New York State during the later colonial period.

*Ford, Paul L.   *The New England Primer.*   New York, 1899.

A reprint, with an historical introduction, of the earliest known edition of this famous book.

Hansen, A. O.   *Liberalism and American Education in the Eighteenth Century.*   317 pp.   New York, 1927.

Dominant ideas of the eighteenth century, and plans for a national system of schools.

*Johnson, Clifton.   *Old-Time Schools and School Books.*   381 pp.   234 Ills. New York, 1904.

A very interesting collection of pictures and bits of historical information, woven together into fourteen chapters descriptive of old schools and school books.

Junegan, W. N.   "Compulsory Attendance in the American Colonies"; in *The School Review*, vol. 26, pp. 731–49.

Kilpatrick, Wm. H.   *The Dutch Schools of New Netherlands and Colonial New York.*   239 pp.   United States Bureau of Education, Bulletin No. 12, 1912.

An excellent and detailed study of Dutch education, with good descriptions of the schools and school work.

Klain, Zora.   *Quaker Contributions to Education in North Carolina.*   351 pp. Philadelphia, 1925.

Klain, Zora.   *Educational Activities of the New England Quakers.*   228 pp. Philadelphia, 1928.

Two important studies of their educational work, with sources.

*Martin, Geo. H.   *The Evolution of the Massachusetts Public School System.* 284 pp.   Appleton, New York, 1894.

A standard interpretive history of the Massachusetts schools.   Chapter III deals with the decline in school spirit, and the rise of the district system and the Academy.

*Maurer, Chas. L.   *Early Lutheran Education in Pennsylvania.*   294 pp. Philadelphia, 1932.

Detailed information as to the educational work of the Lutheran churches in the later colonial period.   Good bibliography.

Merriwether, Colyer.   *Our Colonial Curriculum.*

An interesting and important volume on the college curriculum in colonial times.

*Monroe, Paul, Editor.   *Cyclopedia of Education.*   Macmillan Co., New York, 1911–13.   5 volumes.

Vol. II, pp. 115–22, contains a very good article on the "Colonial Period in American Education."

*Monroe, W. S.   *Development of Arithmetic as a School Subject.*   170 pp. United States Bureau of Education, Bulletin No. 10, Washington, 1917.

Contains an interesting introduction on the teaching of arithmetic in colonial times.

Seybolt, R. F.   *The Evening School in Colonial America.*   68 pp.   University of Illinois Bulletin, vol. XXII, No. 31.   Urbana, 1925.

Contains many records relating to the evening school in colonial America, its methods, personnel, and work.   Lists 100 typical evening schools, with curricula, between 1723 and 1770.

*Seybolt, R. F.   *Source Studies in American Colonial Education; The Private School.*   96 pp.   University of Illinois Bulletin, vol. XXIII, No. 4. Urbana, 1925.

>Contains many records, and much information as to types of private schools, and the importance of their work.   Lists fifty schools in Boston, New York, and Philadelphia, between 1709 and 1758.

Seybolt, R. F.   *Apprenticeship and Apprentice Education in Colonial New England and New York.*   121 pp.   Teachers College Contributions to Education, No. 85.   New York, 1916.

>A careful study of documents, with a good description of practice.

Suzzallo, Henry.   *The Rise of Local School Supervision in Massachusetts, 1635–1827.*   154 pp.   Teachers College Contributions to Education, No. 3, New York, 1906.

>A study of the evolution of the School Committee and its powers out of the town meeting.

*Updegraff, H.   *The Origin of the Moving School in Massachusetts.*   186 pp. Teachers College Contributions to Education, No. 17, New York, 1908.

>A very readable account of colonial education in Massachusetts, and of how the district school evolved out of the town school.

Vose, Caroline E.   "Placing Students in Colonial Days"; in *North American Review*, vol. 219, pp. 115–22 (January, 1924).

>How done in the colleges, based on social position.

Weber, S. E.   *Charity School Movement.*   74 pp.   Philadelphia, 1905.

>Deals with the charity school movement in the Middle Colonies.

*Wells, Guy F.   *Parish Education in Colonial Virginia.*   95 pp.   Teachers College Contributions to Education, No. 138, New York, 1923.

>A careful study of the records relating to parish educational activity as to schools, workhouses, and apprenticeship training.

Woody, Thos.   *Quaker Education in the Colony and State of New Jersey.* 391 pp.   Teachers College Contributions to Education, No. 105, New York, 1923.

Woody, Thos.   *Early Quaker Education in Pennsylvania.*

>Two important volumes, containing many sources.

CHAPTER IV

EARLY NATIONAL AND STATE ATTITUDES
(1775–1820)

I. THE NATIONAL GOVERNMENT AND EDUCATION

Effect of the war on education. The effect of the War for Independence, on all types of schools, was disastrous. The growing troubles with the mother country had, for more than a decade previous to the opening of hostilities, tended to concentrate attention on other matters than schooling. Political discussion and agitation had largely monopolized the thinking of the time.

With the outbreak of the war education everywhere suffered seriously. Most of the rural and parochial schools closed, or continued a more or less intermittent existence. In some of the cities and towns the private and charity schools continued to operate, but in others they were closed entirely. Usually the charity schools closed first, the private pay schools being able to keep open longest. In New York City, then the second largest city in the country, practically all schools closed with British occupancy and remained closed until after the end of the war. The Latin grammar schools and academies often closed from lack of pupils, while the colleges were almost deserted. Harvard, Kings, Princeton, and Pennsylvania, in particular, suffered grievously, and practically all the colleges sacrificed much for the cause of liberty.[1] The war engrossed the energies and the resources of the peoples of the different Colonies, and schools, never very securely placed in the affections of the people, outside of New England, were allowed to fall into decay or entirely disappear. The war, too, closed effectually what had been the avenue to new educational ideas, and the question of mere subsistence became too vital to the colleges to permit of

[1] The buildings of Harvard, Kings, and Princeton were used for troops, and were badly damaged. Harvard moved its library and classes to Concord for the duration of the war, while Kings was closed from 1776 to 1782 and its buildings used for hospital purposes. At Princeton, Nassau Hall was used alternately by both armies, its library was destroyed, and the college closed. At Pennsylvania instruction was suspended, property depreciated, and funds were reduced. Yale scattered its work, the students being taught in different towns. William and Mary, relatively well off before the war, lost its income property in the struggle.

much thought of anything else.   The period of the Revolution and the period of reorganization which followed, up to the beginning of our national government (1775–1789), were together a time of

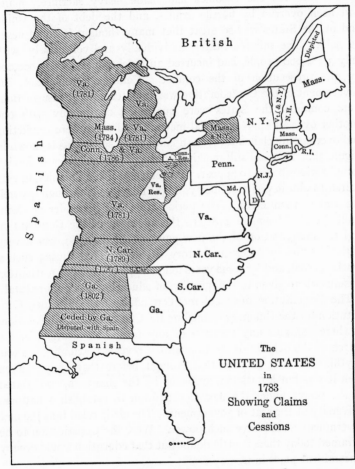

FIG. 30. THE UNITED STATES IN 1783
Showing conflicting claims to Western lands

rapid decline in educational advantages and increasing illiteracy among the people. Meager as had been the opportunities for schooling before 1775, the opportunities by 1790, except in a few cities

(**Rs. 63, 64**) and in some of the New England districts, had shrunk almost to the vanishing point (**R. 65**).

The close of the war found the country both impoverished and exhausted. All the Colonies had made heavy sacrifices, many had been overrun by hostile armies, and the debt of the Union and of the States was so great that many thought it could never be paid. The thirteen States, individually and collectively, with only 3,380,000 people, had incurred an indebtedness of $75,000,000 for the prosecution of the conflict. Commerce was dead, the government of the Confederation was impotent, petty insurrections were common, the States were quarreling continually with one another over all kinds of trivial matters, and there were conflicting and overlapping claims to western lands to be settled, as is shown in Figure 30. England still remained more or less hostile, and foreign complications began to appear. It seemed as if the Colonies, having united to obtain political liberty, might now lose it through quarreling among themselves. The period from the surrender of Cornwallis at Yorktown, in 1781, to the adoption of the Constitution and the inauguration of the new government, in 1789, was a very critical period in American history (**R. 66**). That during such a crucial period, and for some years following, but little or no attention was anywhere given to the question of education was only natural.[1]

The Constitution does not mention education. The new Constitution for the Union, as framed by the Constitutional Convention, nowhere contains any mention of any form of education, and a search of the debates of the Convention reveals that only once was anything relating to education brought before that body. Even then it was but a question, answered by the chairman, and related to the power under the new Constitution to establish a national university at the seat of government. The chair ruled that the new government would have such power. Were the Constitution to be reframed today there is little doubt but that education would occupy a prominent place in it.

It is not surprising, however, when we consider the time, the men, and the existing conditions, that the founders of our Republic

[1] "Neglect of education is among the evils consequent on war — perhaps there is scarce anything more worthy your attention than the revival and encouragement of seminaries of learning; and nothing by which we can satisfactorily express our gratitude to the Supreme Being for his past favors, since piety and virtue are generally the offspring of an enlightened understanding." — (Message of Governor George Clinton to the New York Legislature, January 21, 1784.)

did not deem the subject of public education important enough to warrant consideration in the Convention or inclusion in the document. Education almost everywhere was still a private matter, and quite generally under the control of the Church. The New England Colonies had formed a notable exception to the common practice, both in this country and abroad.

Everywhere in Catholic countries education as an affair of the State had not been thought of. In France elementary education had been left to the Brothers of the Christian Schools, and secondary education to the Jesuits. In 1792 the Brothers of the Christian Schools, after over a century of effort, had but 121 teaching communities in all France, about 1000 teaching brothers, and approximately 36,000 pupils enrolled, out of an estimated total population of 26,000,000, or about 1 child in each 150 of the population. In England education had, since the days of Elizabeth, been considered as "no business of the State," and the great nineteenth-century agitation for state schools had not as yet been started.[1] Even in Scotland, where schools were opened generally in the church parishes following the Reformation there, and had continued to be well maintained, they were church and not state schools. Only in the larger German Protestant States had education been declared a state function and subject to state supervision, but even in these States the schools were still partially under church control, through the pastors of the churches being appointed school inspectors and superintendents for the State.

Even the theory of education, aside from that relating to instruction in Latin secondary schools and colleges, had not been thought out and formulated at the time the Constitution was framed. Pestalozzi had not as yet done his great work in Switzerland, or written out his ideas as to the nature of elementary education. Herbart was a small child at the time, and Froebel a mere infant in arms. Herbert Spencer was not born for more than a quarter of a century afterward.

Again, it must be remembered that the Constitutional Convention embraced in its membership the foremost men of colonial times. Practically every one of them was a product of the old aristocratic

[1] England was still in the charity school conception of education for the children of the poor, and the Sunday-School movement just beginning at the time the Constitutional Convention met. The monitorial schools had not yet been thought out, or the parliamentary agitation for education begun.

and private type of tuition training, and probably few had any particular sympathy with the attempts at general education made by the charity-school type of instruction provided by the churches or with the indifferent type of teachers found in most of the pay schools before 1775. The Convention, too, it must be remembered, had weighty problems of State to find a solution for, serious differences between the States to reconcile, and important compromises to work out and make effective. Its great task was to establish a stable government for the new States, and in doing this all minor problems were left to the future for solution. One of these was education in all its forms, and accordingly no mention of education occurs in the document.

By the tenth amendment to the Constitution, ratified in 1791, which provided that "powers not delegated to the United States by the Constitution, nor prohibited by it to the States, are reserved to the States respectively, or to the people," the control of schools and education passed, as one of the unmentioned powers thus reserved, to the people of the different States to handle in any manner which they saw fit. The state governments, in turn, were too weak and too deeply engaged in trying to solve their own political and economic problems to give any real attention to, at that time, so relatively unimportant a subject as public education. In consequence educational interest, as New England had known it, awaited the educational revival of the second quarter of the nineteenth century.

How the Constitution helped solve the religious question. A reference to Figure 2 (page 13) will show that this Nation was settled by a large number of different religious sects, and this number was further increased with time. While the Colonies were predominantly Protestant, these Protestant sects differed greatly among themselves, and between them there was often as bitter rivalry as between Protestants and Catholics. This was almost as true of their schools as of their churches. At the beginning of the War of Independence the Anglican (Episcopal) faith had been declared "the established religion" of the seven English Colonies, and the Congregational was the established religion in three of the New England Colonies, while but three Colonies (Rhode Island, Pennsylvania, and Maryland) had declared for religious freedom and refused to give a state preference to any religion. Catholics in particular were under the ban, they not being allowed to vote or hold religious services except in Pennsylvania and Maryland.

This religious problem had to be met by the Constitutional Convention, and it handled it in the only way it could have been intelligently handled in a nation composed of so many different religious sects as was ours. The solution worked out was both revolutionary and wholesome. It simply incorporated into the Constitution provisions which guaranteed the free exercise of their religious faith to all, and forbade the establishment by Congress of any state religion, or the requirement of any religious test or oath as a prerequisite for holding any office under the control of the Federal Government. We thus took a stand for religious freedom at a time when the hatreds of the Reformation still burned fiercely, and when tolerance in religious matters was as yet but little known.[1]

Importance of the solution arrived at. The far-reaching importance for our future national life of these sane provisions, and especially their importance for the future of public education, can hardly be overestimated. This action led to the early abandonment of state religions, religious tests, and public taxation for religion in the old States, and to the prohibition of these in the new.[2] It also laid the foundations upon which our systems of free, common, public, tax-supported, non-sectarian schools have since been built up. How we ever could have erected a common public school system on a religious basis, with the many religious sects among us, it is impossible to conceive. Instead, we should have had a series of feeble, jealous, antagonistic, and utterly inefficient church school systems, confined chiefly to elementary education, and each largely intent on teaching its peculiar church doctrines and struggling for an increasing share of public funds. The high school, except for a few sects, would have been impossible.

How much we as a people owe the Fathers of our Republic for

[1] An early indication of the tendency to throw off church control is found in a letter, dated 1780, from the president of William and Mary College to the president of Yale College, describing the course of instruction there. In this letter he tells him that:

"The Professorship of Divinity is also abolished. It was formerly instituted for ye purpose of ye Church of England, wh. was established, but it is now thought that Establishments in Favr. of any particular Sect are incompatible with ye Freedom of a Republic, and therefore, ye Professorship is entirely dropped."

[2] The new Western States would not tolerate a state religion, and from the first forbade any favors or distinctions. Among the older States church support continued for a time, the last States to give it up being New Hampshire in 1817, Connecticut in 1818, and Massachusetts in 1833.

this most intelligent provision few who have not thought carefully on the matter can appreciate. To it we must trace not only the almost inestimable blessing of religious liberty, which we have for so long enjoyed, but also the final establishment of our common, free, public school systems. It still required a half century of struggle with the churches to break their strangle hold on the schools and to create really public schools, but the beginning of the emancipation of education from church domination goes back to this wise provision inserted in our National Constitution.

The new motive for education. Up to near the time of the outbreak of the War for Independence there had been but one real motive for maintaining schools — the religious. To be sure, this had clearly begun to wane by 1750, but it still continued to be the dominant motive. The Declaration of Independence had asserted that "all men are created equal," that "they are endowed by their Creator with certain inalienable rights," and that "to secure these rights Governments are instituted among men, deriving their just powers from the consent of the governed." The long struggle for independence, with its sacrifice and hardships, had tended to clinch firmly this belief among the colonists, and the new Constitution, with its extension of the right to vote for national officers to a largely increased number of male citizens, had carried the theory expressed in the Declaration of Independence over into practice. By 1830 most States had abolished property qualifications for voting, and general manhood suffrage was a concrete reality (see Fig. 50). These new political beliefs tended to create a new political motive for education, which was destined to grow in importance and in time entirely supersede the old religious motive.

At first those responsible for the government in the States and the Nation were too busy with problems of organization, finance, and order to think much of other things, but soon after a partial measure of these had been established we find the leading statesmen of the time beginning to express themselves as to the need for general education in a government such as ours. As early as 1784 we find Governor George Clinton of New York saying, in his message to the legislature:

Neglect of the Education of Youth is among the Evils consequent on War. Perhaps there is scarce any Thing more worthy of your Attention, than the Revival and Encouragement of Seminaries of Learning; and nothing by which we can more satisfactorily express our Gratitude to the supreme Being, for his past Favours; since Piety and Virtue are generally the Offspring of an enlightened Understanding.

Jefferson, as early as 1779, had proposed a comprehensive plan to the legislature of Virginia for education in that State (**R. 67**), but had failed to secure approval for his bill.[1] Writing to James Madison from Paris, in 1787, he had said:

Above all things, I hope the education of the common people will be attended to; convinced that on this good sense we may rely with the most security for the preservation of a due degree of liberty.

Writing from Monticello to Colonel Yancey, after his retirement from the presidency, in 1816, Jefferson again said:

If a nation expects to be ignorant and free in a state of civilization it expects what never was and never will be.... There is no safe deposit [for the functions of government], but with the people themselves; nor . can they be safe with them without information.

Washington, in his first message to Congress, in 1790, declared:

There is nothing which can better deserve your patronage than the promotion of science and literature. Knowledge is in every country the surest basis of public happiness. In one in which the measure of government receives their impressions so immediately from the sense of the community as in ours, it is proportionally essential.

In his Farewell Address to the American people, written in 1796, Washington said:

Promote then, as an object of primary importance, institutions for the general diffusion of knowledge. In proportion as the structure of a government gives force to public opinion, it is essential that public opinion should be enlightened.

General Francis Marion, in a statement on the need of popular education in South Carolina, wrote:

God preserve our legislature from penny wit and pound foolishness. What! Keep a nation in ignorance rather than vote a little of their own money for education! What signifies this government, divine as it is, if it be not known and prized as it deserves? This is best done by free schools. Men will always fight for their government according to

[1] The chief reason for the failure of this proposal was that there was no precedent upon which Jefferson could depend except parish and county participation in apprenticeship under the poor law, and certain endowed parish schools of the pauper type. There was no historic background of sentiment for education to which Jefferson could appeal.

their sense of its value.   To value it aright they must understand it.
This they cannot do without education.

John Jay, first Chief Justice of the United States, in a letter to
his friend, Dr. Benjamin Rush, wrote:

I consider knowledge to be the soul of a Republic, and as the weak
and the wicked are generally in alliance, as much care should be taken
to diminish the number of the former as of the latter.   Education is
the way to do this, and nothing should be left undone to afford all ranks
of people the means of obtaining a proper degree of it at a cheap and
easy rate.

James Madison, fourth President of the United States, wrote:

A satisfactory plan for primary education is certainly a vital desidera-
tum in our republics.

A popular government without popular information or the means of
acquiring it is but a prologue to a farce or a tragedy, or, perhaps, both.
Knowledge will forever govern ignorance; and a people who mean to be
their own governors must arm themselves with the power which knowledge gives.

John Hancock, in his message to the legislature as Governor of
Massachusetts, in 1793, said:

Amongst the means by which our government has been raised to its
present height of prosperity, that of education has been the most efficient; you will therefore encourage and support our Colleges and Academies; but more watchfully the Grammar and other town schools.   These
offer equal advantages to poor and rich; should the support of such institutions be neglected, the kind of education which a free government
requires to maintain its force, would be very soon forgotten.

John Adams, with true New England thoroughness, expressed
the new motive for education still more forcibly when he wrote:

The instruction of the people in every kind of knowledge that can
be of use to them in the practice of their moral duties as men, citizens,
and Christians, and of their political and civil duties as members of
society and freemen, ought to be the care of the public, and of all who
have any share in the conduct of its affairs, in a manner that never yet
has been practiced in any age or nation.   The education here intended
is not merely that of the children of the rich and noble, but of every
rank and class of people, down to the lowest and the poorest.   It is
not too much to say that schools for the education of all should be placed
at convenient distances and maintained at the public expense.   The
revenues of the State would be applied infinitely better, more charitably,
wisely, usefully, and therefore politically in this way than even in main-

taining the poor. This would be the best way of preventing the existence of the poor....

Laws for the liberal education of youth, especially of the lower classes of people, are so extremely wise and useful that, to a humane and generous mind, no expense for this purpose would be thought extravagant.

Having founded, as Lincoln so well said later at Gettysburg, "on this continent a new Nation, conceived in liberty, and dedicated to the proposition that all men are created equal," and having built a constitutional form of government based on that equality, it in time became evident to those who thought at all on the question that that liberty and political equality could not be preserved without the general education of all. A new motive for education was thus created and gradually formulated, and the nature of school instruction came in time to be colored through and through by this new political motive. The necessary schools, however, did not come at once. On the contrary, the struggle to establish that general education required the best efforts of those interested in the highest welfare of the Republic for more than a half-century to come.

Beginnings of national aid for education. By cessions made by the original States, the new National Government was given title to all the lands lying between the Alleghenies and the Mississippi. (Fig. 30). This it was agreed was to constitute a great National Domain, from which future States might be carved.[1] The Revolutionary War had hardly ceased before a stream of soldiers and other immigrants began to pour into this new territory. These people demanded to be permitted to purchase the land, but before it could be sold it must be surveyed. Accordingly Congress, in 1785, adopted a rectangular form of land survey, under which the new territory was laid out into "Congressional Townships," six miles square. Each township was in turn subdivided into sections one mile square, and into quarter sections, and a regular system of numbering for each was begun. In adopting the Ordinance for the government

[1] While the treaty of 1783 had recognized the boundary of the new Nation as extending westward to the Mississippi, there were many conflicting claims to the land west of the Alleghenies. By way of settling the matter, the Continental Congress, in 1780, proposed that the different States cede their claims to the National Government and thus create a national domain. New York, in 1781, was the first to do so, followed by Virginia (1784), Massachusetts (1785), Connecticut (1786), South Carolina (1787), North Carolina (1790), and Georgia (1802). The "common estate" thus created served as a real bond of union between the States during the critical period in the life of the new Nation.

of that part of the territory lying north of the Ohio, in 1787, Congress provided that

> Religion, morality, and knowledge being necessary to good government and the happiness of mankind, schools and the means of education shall be forever encouraged

in the States to be formed from this territory. This provision, and the ultimate settlement of the territory largely by people of New England stock, settled the future attitude as to public education of the States eventually erected therefrom.

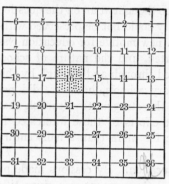

FIG. 31. A CONGRESSIONAL TOWNSHIP

Showing sections, quarter sections, plan of numbering, and location of Section 16

Ohio establishes a type and a policy. When the first State came to be admitted, Ohio, in 1802, the question arose as to the right of the new State to tax the public lands of the United States. By way of settling this question amicably Congress offered to the new State that if it would agree not to tax the lands of the United States, and the same when sold for five years after sale (the purchase price usually being paid in five annual installments), the United States would in turn give to the new State the sixteenth section of land in every township for the maintenance of schools within the township.[1] The offer was accepted, and was continued in the case of every new State admitted thereafter, except Texas, which owned its own land when admitted, and West Virginia and Maine, which were carved from original States. With the admission of California, in 1850, the grant was raised to two sections in each township, the sixteenth and the thirty-sixth, and all States since admitted have received two sections in each township for schools. In the ad-

[1] In 1787 and 1788 two large parcels of land on the Ohio had been sold to companies, and to effect the sale the Continental Congress had been forced to grant each a township of land for a future college, and to reserve section 16 in every township for schools and section 29 for religion. The actuating motive was more to raise much needed cash than to aid either education or religion, but these reservations and grants became the basis for a future national land policy.

mission of Utah, Arizona, and New Mexico, due to the low value of much of the land, four sections were granted to each of these States. To these section grants some other lands were later added — saline lands, swamp lands, and lands for internal improvements, and these constitute the National Land Grants for the endowment of public education, and form the basis of the permanent school funds in all the States west of the Alleghenies.   In all, the National Government has given to the States for common schools, in these sections and

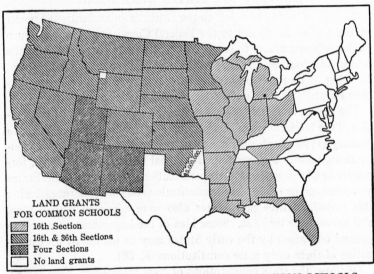

LAND GRANTS
FOR COMMON SCHOOLS

16th Section

16th & 36th Sections

Four Sections

No land grants

FIG. 32. SHOWING LAND GRANTS FOR COMMON SCHOOLS

other grants, a total of approximately 145,000,000 acres (226,562 square miles) of public lands.[1]   This, at the traditional government price of $1.25 an acre, would constitute a gift for the endowment of common school education in the different States of approximately $181,250,000.   As a matter of fact, due to the better care taken of their lands by the newer Western States, and the higher prices for more recent sales, these grants will produce at least half a billion dollars for educational endowment.

These gifts by Congress to the new States of national lands for

[1] This is an area nine tenths as large as the entire old North-West Territory, nearly four times the area of New England, five sixths of the size of the State of Texas, and a tenth larger than France.

the endowment of public education, though begun in large part as a land-selling proposition, helped greatly in the early days to create a sentiment for state schools, stimulated the older States to set aside lands and moneys to create state school funds of their own, and did much to enable the new States to found state school systems instead of relying on the district or charity type of schools of the older States to the east.

II. WHAT THE STATES WERE DOING

Education having been left to the States as an unmentioned power by the tenth amendment to the Federal Constitution, we next turn to the different States to see what action was taken by them in the matter of education during the early years of our national history. In doing so we need to examine both the state constitutions which they framed and their early educational legislation.

The early state constitutions. During the period from the adoption of the Declaration of Independence to the close of the eighteenth century (1776–1800), all the States, except Rhode Island and Connecticut, which considered their colonial charters satisfactory, formulated and adopted new state constitutions. A number of the States also amended or revised their constitutions one or more times during this period. Three new States also were admitted before 1800, and seven more by 1820. Some idea of the importance attached to general education by the early States may be gained by an examination of these early state constitutions (**R. 68**).

Of these, the state constitutions of New Hampshire, New Jersey, Delaware, Maryland, Virginia, and South Carolina, all framed in 1776; New York, framed in 1777; South Carolina, revised in 1778 and again in 1790; Kentucky, framed in 1792, and revised in 1799; Tennessee, framed in 1796; Louisiana, framed in 1812; and Illinois, framed in 1818 — all were equally silent on the matter of schools and education. New Hampshire and Delaware, in later revisions, included a brief section on the subject. Maryland amended its constitution four times before 1864, New York adopted a new constitution in 1872, and Illinois in 1848, all without including any mention of education. Of the twenty-three States forming the Union in 1820, ten had by that time made no mention of education in any of their constitutions.

The constitutions of the thirteen States which had made some

mention fall into three classes. The first, represented by Delaware and the first Georgia constitution (**R. 68**), merely briefly direct the establishment of schools, or, as in the Alabama and Mississippi constitutions, merely repeat the declaration as to "schools and the means of education" contained in the 1787 ordinance (p. 92) for the government of the North-West Territory; the second, represented by Massachusetts, New Hampshire, Vermont, Maine (**R. 68**), Ohio (**R. 69**), and Indiana (**R. 70**), have good sections directing the encouragement of learning and virtue and the protection and encouragement of school societies; while the third, represented by North Carolina and the first Pennsylvania and Vermont constitutions (**R. 68**), direct the establishment of schools wherein tuition shall be cheap. In its second constitution Pennsylvania went over completely to the maintenance of a pauper-school system.

Delaware made no mention of education in its first (1776) constitution, but in its second (1792) very briefly directed the Legislature, when it saw fit, to provide schools, as may be seen from the following section:

> Art. VIII, Sec. 12. The Legislature shall, as soon as conveniently may be, provide by law for... establishing schools, and promoting arts and sciences.

Georgia had given somewhat similar directions as to schools in 1777, but in 1798 withdrew these directions and substituted a section relating only to the promotion of arts and sciences in seminaries of learning, and directed the Legislature to protect the endowment funds of such.

Massachusetts and New Hampshire, in almost identical words, gave the most complete directions of any of the older States as to the encouragement of learning and private school societies and the establishment of schools, and Massachusetts included a long article making detailed provisions for the protection and maintenance of Harvard College (**R. 68**). Connecticut, in its first constitution, in 1818, confirmed the charter of Yale College, and Maine, in its first constitution of 1820, made careful provision for the protection of Bowdoin College. North Carolina, in its first constitution of 1776, made provision for the creation of a state university (**R. 68**). For the two dozen colleges in the Colonies at the close of the eighteenth century, and the beginnings of eight state universities made by 1820, no other constitutional mention is made except the general provision inserted in the Indiana constitution of 1816 making it the duty of the general assembly (R. 70):

> to provide by law for a general system of education, ascending in a regular gradation from township schools to a State university, wherein tuition shall be gratis, and equally open to all.

The Massachusetts and New Hampshire provision for the encouragement of learning are so excellent, and so much ahead of the general conception of the time, that they deserve careful reading (R. 68).

Vermont, in its first constitution (1777), directed the establishment of schools in each town "with such salaries to the masters, paid by the town," as would "enable them to instruct youth at low prices," and also directed the establishment of a grammar school in each county, and a university for the State. North Carolina, in its constitution of the preceding year, had inserted a similar provision for low-priced instruction. In a supplemental section Vermont also directed the encouragement of learning and private school societies, somewhat after the Massachusetts example. In the revision of 1787, all was omitted from the Vermont constitution except the supplemental section.

Pennsylvania, in its constitution of 1776, directed the establishment of a school in each county, "with such salaries to the masters, paid by the public, as may enable them to instruct youth at low prices"; directed the encouragement of learning in one or more universities; and then added a supplemental section, as had Vermont, directing the encouragement of learning and school societies. In the revision of 1790 all this was abandoned for a brief and indefinite direction for the establishment of a pauper-school system, and the encouragement of arts and sciences in one or more seminaries of learning.

These constitutional provisions represent the mandates relating to public education which seven States, of the sixteen States up to 1800, had thought desirable or necessary. Compared with a modern western state constitution, the mention of education made in them seems very hesitating and feeble. As in the earlier period of American education, it was Calvinistic New England which provided the best constitutional provisions for learning. On the other hand, it was the old Anglican Church Colonies and the new States of Kentucky and Tennessee which were silent on the subject.

With the admission of Ohio in 1802, and Indiana in 1816, we find

(**Rs. 69, 70**) a strong and emphatic stand for religious freedom, opposition to any discrimination against children of the poor in the new schools, and provision for broad and generous state educational systems. The new West here first expressed itself, and it is in the constitutions of the Western States that one finds today the most complete provisions for state systems of public instruction.

The early state school laws. Turning next to the early state laws regarding schools, we find in them a still better index as to state interest in and effort for general education. Examining the legislation relating to the establishment of public schools which was enacted by 1820, and omitting legislation relating to colleges and academies, we find that the twenty-three States in the Union before 1820 classify themselves into four main groups, as follows:

1. *The good-school-conditions group*

Maine	Connecticut
Vermont	New York
New Hampshire	Ohio
Massachusetts	

2. *The mixed-conditions group*

Indiana	Illinois

3. *The pauper-parochial-school group*

Pennsylvania	Virginia
New Jersey	Georgia
Delaware	South Carolina
Maryland	Louisiana

4. *The no-action group*

Rhode Island	North Carolina
Kentucky	Mississippi
Tennessee	Alabama

The good-school-conditions group. It is the five New England States, settled originally by Calvinistic Puritans, and the States of New York and Ohio, which by 1820 had become virtually a westward extension of New England by reason of the settlement of all central New York (see Fig. 33) and all northern Ohio (see Fig. 36) by New England people, which early made the best provisions for schools. Beside providing for the four colony colleges, Bowdoin, Dartmouth, Harvard, and Yale, and maintaining grammar schools and academies, the laws made, for the time, good provisions for elementary education. Summarized briefly by States the laws enacted provided as follows:

Maine. A part of Massachusetts up to 1820, when admitted as the twenty-third State. Town school records go back to 1701. The Massachusetts laws of 1642 and 1647 had applied. By 1800 there were 161 organized towns. District system established by law of 1789. Constitution of 1820 required the towns to provide suitable support for schools. Good school law adopted by the first legislature in 1821.

Vermont. First general state school law in 1782. District system authorized. Support of schools by district tax or rate bill on parents optional. State aid granted. 1797 — Districts failing to provide schools to receive no state assistance. Reading, writing, and arithmetic to be taught in all schools. 1810 — Town school tax obligatory, and gradually increased from 1 per cent to 3 per cent by 1826. 1825 — State school fund created. 1827 — New school law required towns to build school buildings; required certificates of teachers; made the beginnings of school supervision; and added spelling, grammar, history, geography, and good behavior to the list of required school subjects.

New Hampshire. First general state school law in 1789. Town tax required, and rate fixed; teachers' certificates required; English schools and Latin schools required in the larger towns. 1791 — Town taxes for schools increased. 1821 — State school fund created. 1827 — Poor children to be provided with schoolbooks free.

Massachusetts. First general state school law in 1789. This legalized the practices in education of the past hundred and fifty years, and changed them into state requirements. A six-months elementary school required in every town, and twelve-months if having 100 families. Also a six-months grammar school required of every town having 150 families, and twelve-months if 200 families. All teachers to be certificated, and all grammar school teachers to be college graduates or certificated by the minister as skilled in Latin. These laws also applied to Maine, which was a part of Massachusetts until 1820.

Connecticut. Laws of 1700 and 1712 required all parishes or school societies operating schools to maintain an elementary school for from six to eleven months a year, varying with the size of the parish. Law of 1714 required inspection of schools and teachers. These laws continued in force by the new State. A permanent school fund had been created (**R. 107**) in 1750 by the sale of some Connecticut lands, and in 1795, on the sale of the Western Reserve in Ohio for $1,200,000, this sum was added to the permanent school fund. 1766, district system established by law, and in 1798 school visitors and overseers ordered appointed.

New York. Little of an educational nature had been done in this State before the Revolution, except in the matter of church charity schools. In 1795 a law, valid for five years, was enacted (**R. 71**) which distributed $100,000 a year to the counties for schools. By 1798 there were 1352 schools in 16 of the 23 counties, and 59,660 children were enrolled (**Rs. 72, 73**). On the expiration of the law, in 1800, it could not be re-enacted. By 1812, when the first permanent school law was enacted, New England immigration into the State had counterbalanced the private-parochial-charity-school attitude which up to that time had prevailed in New York City (**R. 74**). The Massachusetts district system was now instituted, local taxation required, state aid distributed on the basis of school census, and the first State Superintendent of Schools provided for. In 1814 teachers were ordered examined. By 1820 New York schools were probably the best of any State in the Union.

Ohio. Admitted as a State in 1802; constitution adopted in 1803 (**R. 69**). Schools in Cleveland date from 1800 (**R. 75**), and other early local developments. School township organization laws in 1806 and 1810. General incorporation act for libraries and academies in 1817. First public school law in 1821, superseded by a better law in 1825. State school fund established in 1827, and minimum school tax ordered levied. New school laws in 1829, 1831, 1834, and 1836, culminating in the great school law of 1838.

The mixed-conditions group. The conflict in the two States belonging to this group was due to the northern portion of each being settled by New England stock, and the southern portion of each by southern stock. This created a conflict of ideas which materially delayed the development of education in each State. Only as the northern element gained control was the educational situation cleared up.

Indiana. First missionary school at Vincennes in 1793. In 1806 Vincennes University established, on basis of congressional grant of seminary townships to the Territory, and began instruction in 1810. Constitution adopted on admission in 1816 (**R. 70**) made good provision for schools, and first school law adopted that year. No revenue provision made, however. Law of 1824 created a system composed of rural schools, county seminaries, and state university. In 1833 district system substituted for township system, and decentralizing forces operative until new constitution of 1851, and new township school law of 1852.

Illinois. First constitution of 1818 made no mention of education. First general school law, in 1825, provided for free district schools, supported by local taxation and income, from school lands and fund. In 1827 payment of taxes made optional with each taxpayer; not repealed until 1841. Better school support provided in 1845. New constitution of 1848 again made no mention of education. Beginnings of a real state school system dates from law of 1856.

The pauper-parochial-school group. The eight States of this group are the five Middle Colonies, where the parochial-school and the pauper-school attitudes, described under Chapter II, had been most prominent, and three Southern States. The idea had become

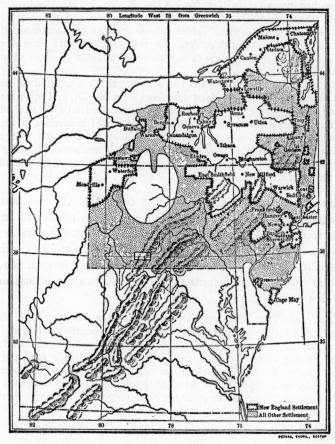

FIG. 33. SHOWING THE WESTERN EXPANSION OF NEW ENGLAND INTO NEW YORK, NEW JERSEY, AND PENNSYLVANIA, BY 1810

From L. K. Mathews's *The Expansion of New England;* Houghton Mifflin Co., Boston, 1909. By permission.

so fixed in these Middle Colonies that education belonged to the Church and to charitable organizations or to private effort that any interference by the State, beyond assisting in the maintenance of pauper schools, came in time to be bitterly resented.[1] Briefly summarized, by States, the legislation enacted provided as follows:

Pennsylvania. The constitution of 1776 had directed the establishment of a school in each county, where youths should be taught at low prices, but the constitution of 1790 had directed instead the establishment, at the convenience of the legislature, of a series of pauper schools. The first law was in 1802, and this provided only for the education of the pauper children in each county. In 1824 a better law was enacted, but its acceptance was optional, and in 1826 it was repealed and the pauper-school law of 1802 continued. The first free-school law dates from 1834. Even this was optional, and was at first accepted by but little more than half of the school districts in the State.

New Jersey. This State should be classed in the no-action group. Nothing was done until 1816, when a state school fund was begun. In 1820 permission to levy a local tax for schools was granted. In 1828 a report showed that one third of the children of the State were growing up without a chance for any education. Largely in consequence of this the first general school law was enacted, in 1829, but the next year this was repealed, as a result of bitter opposition from the private and church-school interests, and the State followed Pennsylvania's example and went over to the pauper-school idea of state action. In 1830 and 1831 laws limited state educational effort to aiding schools for the education of the children of the poor. In 1838 the beginnings of a state public school system were made, and in 1844 state aid was limited to public schools. First constitutional mention of education in 1844.

Delaware. In 1796 a state school fund was created from the proceeds of tavern and marriage licenses. This accumulated unused until 1817, when $1000 a year was appropriated from the income to each of the three counties for the instruction of the children of the poor in reading, writing, and arithmetic. In 1821 aid was extended to Sunday Schools. In 1821 a so-called free-school law was enacted, by which the State duplicated amounts raised by subscription or contribution, but by 1833 only 133 districts in the State were operating under the law. The schools of Wilmington date from 1821. In 1843 an educational convention adopted a resolution opposing taxation for free schools. First real school law in 1861.

Maryland. No constitutional mention until 1864. Many academies chartered, and lotteries much used for their aid between 1801 and 1817. 1812 — School fund begun by a tax on banks. 1816 — First property

---

[1] "Back of the practices in Virginia there was an idea that the public should be concerned with the education of the poor, but no general feeling of real public responsibility and no sense of an obligation to do anything which might involve the levying of taxes.... The association of the idea of public education with that of provision for the poor alone made it seem natural, in the early part of the federal period, to confine the efforts made to an improvement of arrangements for the poor... As a step toward the later development of common schools, it probably was an obstacle rather than a help." (G. F. Wells. *Parish Education in Colonial Virginia*, p. 92.)

tax to aid schools for the poor. 1826 — First general school law, but acceptance optional with the counties; too advanced and never in operation, except in Baltimore. No school system until after the Civil War.

Virginia. The efforts of Jefferson to establish a complete school system for the State (**R. 67**) failed. 1796 — Optional school law, but little done under it. 1810 — Permanent school fund started, to be used (1811) for the education of the poor only. 1818 — Law providing for a charity school system enacted, and a state university created. 1829 — District free-school optional law enacted; by 1835 partially adopted by six counties, but later discontinued by all but one, and law of 1818 continued to govern up to Civil War period. By 1843 estimated that half the indigent children in the State were receiving sixty days schooling. 1846 — Better school law enacted, but optional, and only nine counties ever used it. 1851 — First constitutional mention of education. 1870 — First real school law.

Georgia. In 1817 a fund of $250,000 was created for free schools. 1822 — Income of fund designated to pay the tuition of poor children. Schools for poor children were opened in Savannah in 1818, and Augusta in 1821. 1837 — Free school system established, but law repealed in 1840. 1858 — Word "poor" eliminated from law. Real state school system dates from after Civil War.

South Carolina. In 1811 the beginning of a state system of schools was made (**R. 76**). Though every white child of suitable age had a right to attend, the preference given orphans and children of the poor virtually limited the schools to charity schools. 1835 — Act passed providing penalties for neglect of Act of 1811, but largely ineffective. 1836 — Report made recommending a state system of charity schools; not adopted. 1847 — Legislative committee recommends a state system of education, but no action taken. 1854 — Charleston petitioned to be permitted to make its schools free; granted in 1856. State school system dates from after the Civil War.

Louisiana. In 1806 a free school law enacted, but repealed in 1808. Admitted as a State in 1812, but no mention of education in the constitution. A few primary schools established, and these placed under some supervision in 1819. In 1821 parish (county) tax for academies in return for instruction of indigent children, and aid to parish and parochial schools for indigents continued up to 1845, when new state constitution definitely provided for a system of public schools.

The no-action group. This group contains the religious-freedom State of Rhode Island, one of the States which for long was imbued with the Anglican "no-business-of-the-State" attitude, North Carolina, the two new States of Tennessee and Kentucky, settled largely by "poor whites" and adventurers from the Carolinas and Virginia, and Alabama and Mississippi. Examining the legislation, or rather lack of legislation in these States, we find the following:

Rhode Island. First constitutional mention in 1842. The first school law for the Colony was enacted in 1800, at the instance of a group of citizens of Providence. Schools were ordered established in every town in the State for instruction in reading, writing, and arithmetic, and some state aid was given. Providence and a few other towns established schools, but so great was the opposition to the law that it was repealed in 1803. In 1825 Newport was permitted to start schools for its poor children. It was not until 1828 that a permissive state school law was enacted, and by 1831 there were only 323 public schools and 375 public teachers in the State.

North Carolina. A School Society for the education of females was chartered in 1811. In 1816 legislature appointed a commission to report a school law. 1817 — Good plan reported, but legislature would not approve. 1824 — Another commission appointed. 1825 — Reported a bill for a pauper-school system, which also was not approved. 1825 — Permanent state school fund begun. 1839 — First bill creating an elementary school system, with county and local taxation.

Kentucky. Constitutions of 1792 and 1799 made no mention of education. Numerous land grants to academies between 1798 and 1808, with 47 in existence by 1820. Six colleges chartered between 1819 and 1829. Governor recommended public schools yearly from 1816 to 1819, but no action taken. Literary Fund created in 1821, but not used for schools. Louisville began schools in 1819. First provision for aid for common schools in 1830, but a dead letter, largely through lack of any interest in schools. New constitution in 1850 made first mention of education, and by 1853 a school in each county for first time.

Tennessee. No mention of education in the constitution of 1796; first mention in the new constitution of 1835. Act of 1823 made beginnings of schools for the poor. 1827, school fund begun. First school law in 1830, establishing the district system, and schools open to all. This law in force to time of Civil War.

Alabama. Constitution of 1819 contained rather good statement as to education, but it remained unredeemed until 1854. — A district system for education of children of the poor provided in 1823. — School system for Mobile dates from 1826. — First school law of any importance dates from 1854.

Mississippi. Admitted as twentieth State in 1817. Only a few private schools and academies then. First constitution merely embodied North-West Territory provision. Literary Fund established in 1821, and county commissioners to apply the income for education of poor children, and for building schoolhouses. Law virtually repealed in 1824, and in 1833 state system virtually abandoned. First real school law in 1846.

State attitudes summarized. Figure 34 sets forth graphically the state attitudes toward education which have just been summarized, as well as the attitude assumed toward Education by the

two remaining States carved from the old North-West Territory. From this map it will be seen, even better than from the descriptions of constitutional enactments and early legislation, what an important part religion played, with us, in the establishment of a public school attitude. It was the Calvinistic-Puritan States of New England which most deeply believed in education as a necessity for salvation, and they so established the school idea among their people that this

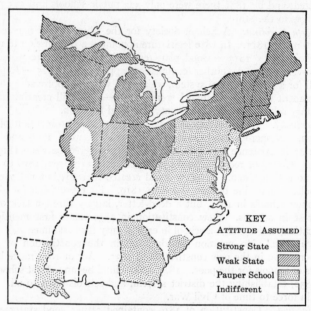

FIG. 34. EARLY ATTITUDE ASSUMED TOWARD PUBLIC EDUCA-
TION BY THE ORIGINAL STATES, AND THE STATES LATER
CARVED FROM THE CEDED NATIONAL DOMAIN

belief in schools persisted after the religious motive for education had died out. Spreading westward, they carried their belief in education into the new States in which they settled. In the Middle and Southern Colonies, where the parochial and pauper school ideas and the plan of apprenticing and educating orphans and paupers dominated, we see States where all elementary educational effort was turned over to private, church, and pauper schools, the State aiding only the last, or at most the last two. In the religious-freedom State of Rhode Island, and the old Anglican Colonies of New Jersey and North Carolina, we see the English "no-business-of-the-State" attitude for a time reflected in the indifference of the State to the education of the people. The five new States west of these southern Colonies — Kentucky, Tennessee, Mississippi, Alabama, and Louisiana — in large part reflected the attitude of the States to the eastward from which their early immigrants had largely come.

III. THE NORTH-WEST-TERRITORY DEVELOPMENT

The North-West-Territory States. The settlement of the States of the North-West Territory is an interesting exemplification of the influence on education of the early settlements we have so far studied, and much of the early educational history of these States is to be understood when viewed in the light of their settlement.

Immediately after the close of the Revolutionary War settlers from the different States of the new Union began to move to the new territory to the westward. To the north, a great movement of New England people began into central New York and northern Pennsylvania, and from then until 1810, when the tide of immigration turned farther westward, the history of these two regions is in large part the history of the westward expansion of New England.[1] By 1810 more than one half of New York, one fourth of Pennsylvania, portions of New Jersey (see map, Fig. 33), and the Western Reserve in Ohio (see map, Fig. 36) had been settled by New England people. In New York they counterbalanced the earlier predominance of the Anglicans, helped materially in securing the first permanent school law for the State, in 1812, and in carrying the State for free schools in the referenda of 1849 and 1850. They also helped to counteract the German Lutheran parochial element in the battle for free schools in Pennsylvania, in 1834 and 1835.

After 1810 the tide of migration of New England people set in to the new States to the west of New York, following the northern route. This migration of New-Englanders became strong after the completion of the Erie Canal in 1825, and by 1850 one half of the

[1] The then West was a land of great opportunity. Those who wanted more or better land, renters who wanted land of their own, servants who desired to be their own masters, artisans and tradesmen who wanted to establish themselves in the new towns, young people who found the old home place too small, and restless adventurers who wanted to try their luck in the new land — all these were found in the stream of Conestoga wagons that poured westward along the established trails, or on the flatboats that floated down the rivers. Among such classes there naturally was a democracy and economic equality unknown in the older States from which they came.

settled portions of the old North-West Territory had been populated by New England stock (see map, Fig. 36), while many settlements had been founded beyond the Mississippi River. The history of these migrations often repeated the old story of the Puritan migrations to New England. Congregations, with their ministers, frequently migrated to the West in a body. A new Granville, or Plymouth, or Norwalk, or Greenwich in the wilderness was a child of the old town of that name in New England. An almost ceaseless train of wagons poured westward, and the frontier was soon pushed

FIG. 35. ONE OF THE NEW YALES IN THE WILDERNESS

Illinois College in the early nineteenth century. Founded in 1829, by a "Yale Band" of seven men.

out to and beyond the Mississippi. Wherever the New-Englander went he invariably took his New England institutions with him. Congregational churches were established, new Yales [1] and Dartmouths were founded, common schools (**R. 75**) and the Massachusetts district system were introduced, and the town form of government and the town meeting were organized in the new Congressional townships — a ready-made unit which the New-Englander found easily adaptable to his ideas of town government.

Into these new States and Territories to the westward came also other settlers, along the southern route, with different political,

[1] Illinois College, at Jacksonville, an early picture of which is given above, is one illustration. A Yale Band of seven young men established the college, in 1829, and secured a charter for it in 1835. The college played an important part in the early history of the Middle West. The first president, from 1830 to 1844, was Edward Beecher, a brother of Henry Ward Beecher.

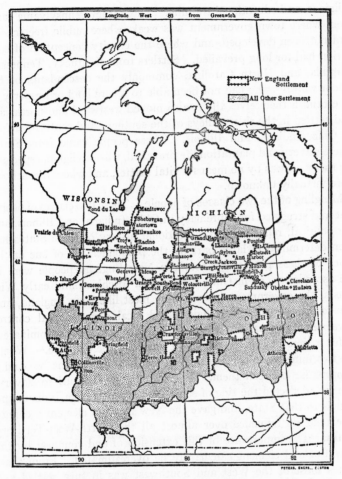

FIG. 36. SHOWING THE WESTERN EXPANSION OF NEW
ENGLAND INTO THE OLD NORTH-WEST TERRITORY
BY 1840

From L. K. Mathews's *The Expansion of New England;* Houghton Mifflin Co.,
Boston, 1909. By permission.

religious, and educational training. Those from Pennsylvania came from where town government was weak, where public free schools had not been developed, and where the charity conception of education had for long prevailed. Settlers from Kentucky, Tennessee, Virginia, and North Carolina, commonly the descendants of the "poor whites" who had not been able to secure land or property or to establish themselves there, also moved westward and northward and settled in the river valleys of the southern and central portions of Ohio, Indiana, and Illinois. These people came from States where slavery and plantation life prevailed, where religion, especially for the poor, was by no means a vital matter, and where free schools were virtually unknown.

Mingling of the two classes of people. These two classes of people met and struggled for supremacy in Ohio, Indiana, and Illinois, and the political, religious, and educational history of these States has been determined in large part by the preponderance of one or the other of these people. Where the New England people were in the ascendancy, as in Ohio, and also in Michigan and early Wisconsin, the governmental forms were most like New England, and the zeal for education, religion, and local governmental control have been most marked. Where the southern element predominated, as for a time in Illinois, the result has been the opposite.[1] Where the two mingled on somewhat even terms, as in Indiana, we find a compromise between them. The opening of Missouri to slavery, in 1820, deflected the tide of southern migration from Indiana and Illinois to that State, and gave the New England element a chance to extend its influence over almost all the North-West-Territory States. The importance of this extension of and conquest by the New England element can hardly be overestimated. From these States most of the West and Southwest was in turn settled and organized into state governments, and to these new regions New England educational ideas in time were spread.

Educational attitudes in the North-West States. The effect of the predominance or mingling of these two classes is clearly shown in the early state attitudes toward education, as written in their constitutions and laws.

[1] The Illinois legislature of 1833, according to Turner, contained 58 members from the Southern States (including Tennessee and Kentucky), 19 from the Middle States, and only 4 from New England. Missouri, at that time, was settled chiefly by Kentuckians and Tennesseans.

The Ohio constitutional provision of 1802 (**R. 69**) is noteworthy for its strong stand for the encouragement of learning and the interdiction of pauper schools in the State, and as reflecting the influence of the national land grants and the national attitude regarding religious freedom. In 1821 a permissive school law was enacted, and in 1825 a new school law laid the foundations of a state system, based on the Massachusetts district system, county taxation, and the certification of teachers.

The Indiana constitution of 1816 (**R. 70**) threw safeguards about the national land grants for schools, and was the first to issue a comprehensive mandate to the legislature ordering the establishment of a complete free state system of schools, "ascending in regular gradations from township schools to a State university." So evenly balanced were the northern and southern elements in Indiana, however, that this mandate of the constitution was difficult to carry out, and, despite legislation which will be described in Chapter V, the real beginning of a state school system in Indiana dates from the new constitution of 1851.

Illinois shows the southern element in control. Neither the constitution of 1818 nor the one of 1848 made any mention of education, and the constitution of 1862, containing a fair Article on education, was voted down by the people. It was not until 1870 that Illinois embodied a mandate as to education in its fundamental law. A good school law, said to have been the best outside of New England, was enacted in 1825, but this was nullified two years later by legislation which provided that no man could be taxed for schools without his written consent, and which permitted the maintenance of schools in part by tuition fees. It was not until 1841, and after the New England people had become a majority, that this nullifying legislation of 1827 could be repealed.

Michigan was not admitted as a State until 1835, but the territorial legislature, in 1827, adopted a good school law, modeled on the Massachusetts legislation. In 1829 the property of nonresidents was made subject to taxation for schools — at that time rather advanced legislation. The first state constitution, of 1835, adopted the Massachusetts district system, ordered a three-months' school maintained in each school district, and provided for the appointment of the first permanent State Superintendent of Public Instruction in any State.

Wisconsin was a part of Michigan until 1836, and the Michigan legislation applied to Wisconsin territory. In 1840 the first Wisconsin school law provided for the Massachusetts district school system, a school census, and district taxation for schools, and when the State was admitted, in 1848, the New England traditions as to education had become so firmly fixed, and the new forces working for popular education in the State had begun to have such an influence, that the school code of 1849 was quite modern in character.

No real educational consciousness before about 1820. Regardless of the national land grants for education made to the new States, the provisions of the different state constitutions, the beginnings made here and there in the few cities of the time, and the early state laws, we can hardly be said, as a people, to have developed an educational consciousness, outside of New England and New York, before about 1820, and in some of the States, especially in the South, a state educational consciousness was not awakened until very much later. Even in New England there was a steady decline in education, as the district system became more and more firmly fixed, during the first fifty years of our national history.

There were many reasons in our national life for this lack of interest in education among the masses of our people. The simple agricultural life of the time, the homogeneity of the people, the absence of cities,[1] the isolation and independence of the villages, the lack of full manhood suffrage in a number of the States, the continuance of old English laws,[2] the want of any economic demand for education, and the fact that no important political question calling for settlement at the polls had as yet arisen, made the need for schools and learning seem a relatively minor one. There were but six cities of 8000 inhabitants or over in the country as late as

[1] In 1790, twenty-nine out of every thirty inhabitants lived in villages or the country, and as late as 1820 nineteen out of every twenty inhabitants were classified as rural. In 1820, too, there were but thirteen cities having ten thousand inhabitants in all the twenty-three States. During the three decades from 1790 to 1820 the city population gained only 1.6 per cent over the rural, though the country as a whole increased approximately 140 per cent in population.

[2] Such as the laws of entail and primogeniture — laws designed to prevent the distribution of wealth. Jefferson waged war on these in Virginia, and secured their abolition. His work was copied elsewhere, and by 1820 these laws had been abolished generally. Everywhere to the westward girls were placed on an equal footing with boys in the inheritance of property.

1810, and even in these life was far simpler than in a small western village today.   There was little need for book learning among the masses of the people to enable them to transact the ordinary business of life.   A person who could read and write and cipher in that time was an educated man, while the absence of these arts was not by any means a matter of reproach.

The country, too, was still very poor.   The Revolutionary War debt still hung in part over the Nation, and the demand for money and labor for all kinds of internal improvements was very large. The country had few industries, and its foreign trade was badly hampered by European nations.   France gave us trouble for a decade, while England made it evident that, though we had gained our political independence, we should have to fight again if we were to win our commercial freedom.   Ways and means of strengthening the existing government and holding the Union together, rather than plans which could bear fruit only in the future, occupied the attention of the leaders of the time.   "The Constitution," as John Quincy Adams expressed it, "was extorted from the grinding necessities of a reluctant people" to escape anarchy and the ultimate entire loss of independence, and many had grave doubts as to the permanence of the Union.   It was not until after the close of the War of 1812 that belief in the stability of the Union and in the capacity of the people to govern themselves became the belief of the many rather than the very few, and plans for education and national development began to obtain a serious hearing.   When we had finally settled our political and commercial future by the War of 1812–14, and had built up a national consciousness on a democratic basis in the years immediately following, and the Nation at last possessed the energy, the money, and the interest for doing so, we then turned our energies toward the creation of a democratic system of public schools.

In the meantime, education, outside of New England, and in part even there, was left largely to private individuals, churches, incorporated school societies, and such state schools for the children of the poor as might have been provided by private or state funds, or the two combined.   Such pictures as we have of the schools of the time (**R. 64**) evidence a rather simple and primitive type of school.   Even in the cities of the period (**R. 63**) the schools had changed but little from late colonial times.

IV. THE REAL INTEREST IN ADVANCED EDUCATION

The rise of the academy. In so far as we may be said to have possessed a real interest in education, during the first half-century of our national existence, it was manifested in the establishment and endowment of academies and colleges rather than in the creation of schools for the people. The colonial Latin grammar school had been almost entirely an English institution, and never well suited to American needs. As democratic consciousness began to arise, the demand came for a more practical institution, less exclusive and less aristocratic in character, and better adapted in its instruction to the needs of a frontier society. Arising about the middle of the eighteenth century a number of so-called Academies and English Grammar Schools (**Rs. 55, 56, 57**) had been founded in the Middle Colonies, before the new National Government took shape.[1] While essentially private institutions, arising from a church foundation, or more commonly a local subscription or endowment, it in time became customary for towns, counties, and States to charter them (**R. 78**) and to assist in their maintenance, thus making them semi-public institutions. Their management, though, usually remained in private hands, or under boards or associations. After the beginning of our national life a number of the States founded and endowed a state system of academies.[2]

Besides what may be termed official Academies, managed by boards of trustees, there also arose a numerous class of small private academies whose master and proprietor was responsible to no one but himself. These schools often were quite small, but when the proprietor was well educated they probably offered a fair type of secondary training. Candidates for the ministry often taught for a short time in these schools Such teaching doubtless was good for their own scholarship, as it caused them to polish up their learning, but not so good for the pupils because they left about the time they came to be efficient teachers.

[1] The academy movement will be dealt with, much more in detail, further on, in Chapter VIII.

[2] Massachusetts, in 1797, granted land endowments to approved academies. Georgia, in 1783, created a system of county academies for the State. New York extended state aid to its academies, in 1813, having put them under state inspection as early as 1787. Maryland chartered many academies between 1801 and 1817, and authorized many lotteries to provide them with funds, as did also North Carolina. Ohio, Kentucky, and Indiana, among Western States, also provided for county systems of academies.

Character of the academy training. The study of Latin and a little Greek had constituted the curriculum of the old Latin grammar school, and its purpose had been almost exclusively to prepare boys for admission to the colony colleges. In true English style, Latin was made the language of the classroom, and even attempted for the playground as well. As a concession, reading, writing, and arithmetic usually also were taught.

The new academies which began early (**R. 77**), and the work of which we shall consider more at length further on (Chap. VIII), while retaining the study of Latin, and usually Greek, though now taught through the medium of English, added a number of new studies adapted to the needs of a new society (**Rs. 55, 56, 78**). English grammar was introduced and soon rose to a place of great importance, as did also oratory and declamation. Arithmetic, algebra, geometry, geography, and astronomy were in time added, and survey-ing, rhetoric (including some literature), natural and moral philosophy, and Roman antiq-uities frequently were taught,

FIG. 37. A PENNSYLVANIA ACADEMY

The York Academy, York, Pennsylvania, founded by the Protestant Episcopal Church, in 1787.

though in New England these newer subjects usually were offered in a separate course, or Department (**R. 148**). Girls were admitted rather freely to the new academies, whereas the grammar schools had been exclusively for boys. For better instruction a "female department" frequently was organized. The academies, beside offering a fair type of higher training before the days of high schools, also became training schools for teachers, and before the rise of the normal schools were the chief source of supply for the better grade of elementary teachers. These institutions rendered an important service during the first half of the nineteenth century, but were in time displaced by the publicly-supported and publicly-con-trolled American high school, the first of which dates from 1821. This evolution we shall describe more in detail in a later chapter.

The colleges of the time. Some interest also was taken in college education during this early national period. To the nine colonial foundations,[1] existing at the outbreak of the Revolution, fifteen additional colleges were founded by 1800, and fourteen more before 1820. College attendance, however, was small, as the country was still new and the people were poor. As late as 1815 Harvard graduated a class of but 66; Yale of 69; Princeton of 40; Williams of 40; Pennsylvania of 15; and the University of South Carolina of 37; while for the college year 1829–30 the entering class at Harvard had but 55 students, at Williams 22, and at Amherst 37. In 1832, Columbia was still a small college of 6 professors and 125 students, while Harvard, after almost two centuries of existence, had but 10 professors and 216 students.

After the organization of the Union the nine old colonial colleges were reorganized, and an attempt was made to bring them into closer harmony with the ideas and needs of the people and the governments of the States. Kings (now rechristened Columbia), and Pennsylvania were for a time changed into state institutions, and unsuccessful attempts were made to make a state university for New Hampshire out of Dartmouth, and for Virginia out of William and Mary. There was some change in the curriculum, too, the better to adapt it to changed conditions. At Harvard, Yale, and Princeton a decline in the importance of divinity and a neglect of Hebrew are clearly in evidence, with history and the modern languages rising to new importance. At Pennsylvania and Columbia new subjects of study had been begun. At William and Mary the chair of Divinity was abolished,[2] and a reformed curriculum introduced. Here and there, too, an individual professor broke away from the established order. The general tone of the intellectual life in the colleges, however, during the first three decades of our national history at least, was exceedingly low and devoid of intellectual stimulation. Yet in these early colleges lay, as it were in embryo,

---

[1] These were Harvard (1636), William and Mary (1693), Yale (1702), Princeton (1746), the Academy and College of Pennsylvania (1753–55), Kings (1754), Brown (1764), Rutgers (1766), and Dartmouth (1769).

[2] In a letter of President Madison of William and Mary, to President Stiles of Yale, under date of August 27, 1780, he says:

"The Professorship of Divinity is abolished. It was formerly instituted for ye purpose of ye Church of England, wh. was here established, but it is now thought that Establishments in Favr. of any particular Sect are incompatible with ye Freedom of a Republic, and therefore, ye Professorship is entirely dropped."

the "hope of the future" for the intellectual life of the United States (**R. 79**).

Beginnings of the state universities. Before 1825 eight States [1] had laid the foundations of future state universities. North Carolina provided for the establishment of a state university in its constitution of 1776, chartered it in 1789, it opened for instruction in 1795, and it graduated its first class in 1798. Georgia enacted a law providing for a state university in 1784, and it opened for instruc-

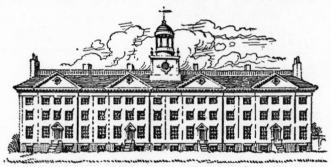

FIG. 38. COLUMBIA COLLEGE, 1784–1850

As it was on Church Street, New York City, during the first half of the nineteenth century, prior to the removal to Forty-Ninth Street.

tion in 1801. South Carolina passed an Act providing for a state college in 1801, and the institution opened for instruction in 1805. Of the two "seminaries of learning" provided for in the early Ohio land grants (p. 92), the one at Athens (Ohio University) was chartered in 1802 and began instruction in 1809, with one professor and three students, while the one at Oxford (Miami University) was chartered in 1809 and began instruction as an Academy, changing into a college in 1824. Tennessee made the beginnings of a state college in 1807, but it did not open for instruction until 1820. Virginia made the beginnings of a state university in a law enacted

[1] Some writers include two more States, but in the opinion of the author these two hardly qualify. They are Vermont, which passed an Act establishing a state university on admission of the State in 1791, and further confirmed its establishment in 1838. In 1865 the Vermont Agricultural College was combined with the University. The State, however, has given the institution but little aid, and it is not generally classed as a state university. The other State is Michigan, which made provision for a French administrative type of state university in 1817, but it never really got under way and the real establishment of the University of Michigan dates from the first constitution of 1835 and the legislative act of 1837. Instruction began in 1841.

in 1818, founded the institution in 1819, and it opened for instruction in 1825. Indiana made the beginnings of a territorial university at Vincennes in 1806, but later deserted this institution and founded the present university in 1820, opening it for instruction in 1824,

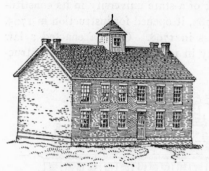

with one professor and ten students. Alabama appointed a committee in 1819 to select a site, and in 1820 incorporated the university, though it did not open for instruction until 1831. The National Government further stimulated the development of state higher educational institutions by granting to

FIG. 39. WHERE INDIANA UNI-VERSITY BEGAN INSTRUCTION, IN MAY, 1824

each new Western State, beginning with Ohio in 1802, two entire townships of land to help endow a "seminary of learning" in each — a stimulus which eventually led to the establishment of a state university in every new State.

QUESTIONS FOR DISCUSSION

1. Why does education not make much progress during periods of warfare or intense political agitation?
2. Contrast conditions as regards education in 1789 and today.
3. Explain how the religious-freedom attitude of the national constitution conferred an inestimable boom on the States in the matter of public schools.
4. Explain the change from the religious to the political motive for maintaining schools.
5. Does the quotation from Washington evidence as clear a conception of educational needs in a democracy as those from Jefferson?
6. What conception of education had John Jay in mind?
7. After the leaders of the time had come to see the need for the education of the masses, why did it take so long to obtain the establishment of state school systems?
8. Try to picture what might have been the educational conditions and development in this country: (a) Had the New England element had small families and remained in New England; (b) Had New England been settled by Anglicans, and no Calvinistic Puritans had ever come to North America; (c) Had the Puritans settled in Virginia, as they started out to do.

9. Explain why we were so slow in developing an educational consciousness.

10. Explain the early dependence on educational societies, churches, and private schools for elementary-school instruction, while providing academies and colleges for advanced instruction.

11. Explain why Oratory and Declamation naturally played such a prominent part in the work of the early academies and colleges.

12. Explain the great popularity of the academy, as compared with the older Latin grammar school.

13. Explain the large interest in the creation of institutions for advanced education, during the first quarter of a century of our national history.

14. How might the educational history of the North-West-Territory States have been different had the Nation never made the Louisiana purchase?

15. What and when were the beginnings of the state university in your State (if there is one)?

SELECTED READINGS

In the accompanying volume of *Readings* the following selections, related to the subject matter of this chapter, are reproduced:

*63. Everett: Character of the Boston Schools of 1803–07.
*64. A Teacher: A New England School of about 1810.
 65. Hartman: Schools in Wyoming Valley before the Awakening.
*66. Fiske: The Critical Period of American History.
*67. Jefferson: Plan for Education in Virginia.
*68. State Constitutions: Early Provisions as to Education in.
 69. Ohio: Educational Provisions of the First Constitution.
 70. Indiana: Educational Provisions of the First Constitution.
 71. New York: The Law of 1795 for Schools.
 72. Westchester: Organizing Schools under the 1795 Law.
*73. N. Y. Sun: Beginnings of Public Education in Albany.
*74. New York City: The Law of 1795 as applied in.
*75. Cleveland: How Schools began in.
*76. South Carolina: The Orphan and Indigent Law of 1811.
*77. News Item: Early Academies in North Carolina.
*78. Faught: Character of the Early Academies.
*79. Snow: The Early Colleges the "Hope of the Future."

QUESTIONS ON THE READINGS

1. Evaluate the Boston elementary and secondary schools (**63**) in terms of schools of today.

2. Do the same for the rural schools of the Wyoming Valley (**65**).

3. How good and how useful were these schools of about 1810? (**R. 64**).

4. Show why education, either public or private, could not be an important matter under such conditions as Fiske portrays (**66**).

5. Just what type of an educational system did Jefferson propose (67) to organize for Virginia?

6. Classify the constitutional provisions (68) according to the type of school system proposed.

7. In what respects were the educational provisions of the first Ohio constitution (69) remarkable?

8. In what respects were the educational provisions of the first Indiana constitution (70) remarkable?

9. Evaluate the New York law of 1795 (71) in terms of the type of school system proposed to be established, the time and period considered.

10. Compare the proceedings for organization under the law (72) with district organization of a later period.

11. Evaluate the Albany schools (73) in terms of present standards.

12. Do the same for the schools established (74) in New York City.

13. Show how the beginnings of schools at Cleveland (75) were typical of most other early western cities.

14. Who was provided for under the South Carolina law (76), and how was the benefit obtainable?

15. Evaluate these early North Carolina academies (77) in terms of the advanced instruction then offered.

16. Show that the early academies (78) were strong pioneer institutions.

17. Indicate how the early colleges (79) were the hope of the future.

TOPICS FOR INVESTIGATION AND REPORT

1. The National land grants for education, and their influence. (Cubberley, Cubberley & Elliott; Monroe.)

2. The rise and early influence of the Academy. (E. E. Brown; Miller; Seybolt.)

3. Early state constitutional provisions. (Cubberley.)

4. The early American colleges and the nature of their work. (Dexter; Monroe.)

5. The westward expansion of New England. (Mathews.)

6. Early education in Rhode Island. (Carroll.)

7. Early education in any of the Colonies.

8. The establishment of any one of the early state universities. (Brown; Monroe.)

9. Jefferson and the University of Virginia.

SELECTED REFERENCES

*Arrowood, C. F. *Thomas Jefferson and Education in a Republic.* 184 pp. New York, 1930.

> An appraisal of Jefferson's services, and selections from his writings on educational affairs.

*Brown, E. E. *Origin of the American State Universities.* 45 pp. Univ. California Pubs. on Educ., vol. III, no. 1. Berkeley, 1903.

> A very good sketch of the early colonial colleges, and the rise of a demand for state universities. Good bibliography.

Cubberley, E. P. *State School Administration.* 773 pp. Houghton Mifflin Co., Boston, 1927.

Chapter I deals with the beginnings of American education, and Chapter II describes the various land grants made to the States.

Cubberley, E. P., and Elliott, E. C. *State and County School Administration; Source Book.* 728 pp. New York, 1915.

Chapter II gives all the important sources relating to the national land grants to the States.

Davis, C. O. *Public Secondary Education.* 270 pp. Chicago, 1917.

Chapters III and IV good on early Michigan and the Northwest.

Dexter, E. G. *History of Education in the United States.* 656 pp. New York, 1904.

Contains a good brief summary of the work of the early colleges.

Fiske, John. *The Critical Period in American History.* Boston, 1888.

A very interesting picture of the problems and conflicts of the period 1783–89.

*Martin, G. H. *The Evolution of the Massachusetts Public School System.* 284 pp. New York, 1894.

*Mathews, Lois K. *The Expansion of New England.* 301 pp. Boston, 1909.

Chapters VI–VIII are excellent on the great migrations to the westward, and the planting of new commonwealths in the wilderness.

Merriwether, Colyer. *Our Colonial Curriculum.* Washington, 1907.

Good on the early college curriculum.

*Miller, G. F. *The Academy System of New York State.* 181 pp. Albany, New York, 1922.

A careful and very useful study of the academy in New York State.

Monroe, Paul. *Cyclopedia of Education.* New York, 1911–13.

The following article is especially important:
"Colonial Period in American Education"; vol. II, pp. 115–22.
"National Government and Education"; vol. II, pp. 372–82.

Seybolt, R. F. *Source Studies in American Colonial Education; The Private School.* 109 pp. University of Illinois Bulletin, vol. XXIII, no. 4. Urbana, 1925.

Contains many records as to private schools and their work.

*Snow, L. F. *The College Curriculum in the United States.* 186 pp. Teachers College Publications, New York, 1907.

Devoted chiefly to the older eastern colleges. Contains much good source material.

Ten Brook, Andrew. *American State Universities and the University of Michigan.* Cincinnati, 1875.

Chapter II presents an interesting picture of the state of culture in the West from about 1800 to about 1840.

CHAPTER V

INFLUENCES TENDING TO AWAKEN AN EDUCATIONAL CONSCIOUSNESS

I. PHILANTHROPIC INFLUENCES

A half-century of transition. The first half-century of our national life may be regarded as a period of transition from the church-control idea of education over to the idea of education under the control of and supported by the State. It required time to make this change in thinking. Up to the period of the beginnings of our national development education had almost everywhere been regarded as an affair of the Church, somewhat akin to baptism, marriage, the administration of the sacraments, and the burial of the dead. Even in New England, which formed an exception, the evolution of the civic school from the church school was not yet complete. A number of new forces — philanthropic, political, social, economic — now combined to produce conditions which made state rather than church control and support of education seem both desirable and feasible. The rise of a new national government based on the two new principles of political equality and religious freedom, together with the rise of new economic conditions which made some education for all seem necessary for economic as well as for political ends, changed this age-old situation.

The church charity school had become, as we have seen, a familiar institution before the Revolution. The English "Society for the Propagation of the Gospel in Foreign Parts," which maintained schools in connection with the Anglican churches in the Anglican Colonies (**R. 27**), and provided an excellent grade of charity-school master, withdrew at the close of the Revolutionary War from work in this country. The different churches after the war continued their efforts to maintain their church charity schools, though there was for a time a decrease in both their numbers and their effectiveness. In the meantime the demand for education grew rather rapidly, and the task soon became too big for the churches to handle. For long the churches made an effort to keep up, as they were loath to relinquish in any way their former hold on the training of the young. The churches, however, were not interested in the problem except in the old way, and this was not what the new democracy wanted. The result was that, with the coming of nationality and the slow but gradual growth of a national conscious-ness, national pride, national needs, and the gradual development of national resources in the shape of taxable property — all alike combined to make secular instead of religious schools seem both desirable and possible to a constantly increasing number of citizens. This change in attitude was facilitated by the work of a number of semi-private philanthropic agencies, the most important of which were: (1) the Sunday School Movement; (2) the growth of City School Societies; (3) the Lancastrian Movement; and (4) the coming of the Infant-School Societies. These will be described briefly, and their influence in awakening an educational consciousness pointed out.

1. *The Sunday School Movement*

Secular schools before the religious. One of the earliest of these philanthropic movements designed to afford a minimum of edu-cation for the children of the poor was the co-called Sunday School Movement. This originated in England shortly after the middle of the seventeenth century, but amounted to little until 1780, when a publisher by the name of Robert Raikes, of Gloucester, gathered together the children in the pin factories of that city and paid four women a shilling each to spend their Sundays in instructing these poor working children "in reading, and the Church cate-chism." In 1783 Raikes published a description of the plan and its results, and soon the idea spread to many parts of England. So successful did the plan prove that in 1785 there was organized "The Society for promoting Sunday Schools throughout the British Dominions." The historian Green has declared that "the Sunday Schools established by Mr. Raikes were the beginnings of popular education" in England.

Raikes's idea was soon brought to the United States. In 1786 a Sunday School after the Raikes plan was organized in Hanover County, Virginia, at the house of one Thomas Crenghaw. In 1787 a Sunday School for African children was organized at Charles-ton, South Carolina, and in 1790 a Methodist conference in session at Charleston ordered the establishment of Sunday Schools in or near each place of worship.[1] In 1791 "The First Day, or Sunday School Society," was organized at Philadelphia, for the establishment of Sunday Schools for the poor children in that city. In 1793 Katy Ferguson's "School for the Poor" was opened in New York, and this was followed by an organization of New York women for the extension of secular instruction among the poor. In 1797 Samuel Slater's Factory School was opened at Pawtucket, Rhode Island. Other cities opening Sunday Schools were Boston, Pittsburgh, Paterson, Jersey City (N.J.), and Portsmouth (N.H.). In the two decades following 1800 the secular Sunday School rendered its largest service.

The Sunday School Movement was particularly useful in the South, as it stirred the land-holding classes, much as the better-to-do in the towns and cities had been stirred, to do something for the education of the children of the poor.[2] These schools, too, being open to all as well as to the poor and lowly, had a small but an increasing influence in leveling class distinctions, and in making a common day school seem possible.[3] The movement for secular instruction on Sundays, though at first it met with some success and for a time awakened interest,[4] particularly in the cities, soon met in America with the opposition of the churches, and before

[1] An effort was to be made to secure teachers who would "teach gratis all who will attend and have capacity to learn, from six o'clock in the morning till ten, and from two o'clock in the afternoon till six, when it does not interfere with public worship."

[2] "Though the Sunday School may not be said to have substituted for the common school, it can be justly claimed to have played a peculiarly significant part in the development of the free school idea as modern society has evolved it…. It established a new relation between the Rich and the Poor; it was the only common school in which the sting of Pauperism was not felt by the Poor. On Sundays, the spirit of Jeffersonianism was realized; all the children of all the classes met together on perfect equality." (W. A. Maddox. *The Free School Idea in Virginia before the Civil War*, pp. 40–41.)

[3] "The Sunday school movement indirectly promoted the political ideal of common schools by bringing the children of all classes together in the name of religion on terms of perfect equality. Certainly it involved no political theory nor suggested change in government. It is not curious then that the Sunday school was a prime factor in drawing the attention of the rich to the educational needs of the poor with an impressiveness that political theory could never have for the conservative. At the same time it accustomed a neighborhood to schools." (W. A. Maddox. *The Free School Idea in Virginia*, p. 31.)

[4] The following note regarding Sunday Schools appeared in the *Annals of Education* for March, 1931:

"Governor Vroom of New Jersey, Hon. Theodore Frelinghuysen, a member of the United States Senate, and ten or twelve of the most distinguished lawyers of that State, are Sunday School teachers. Governor Tomlinson and General Whittlesey, of Connecticut, Mr. Starr, an eminent lawyer of Cincinnati, the Mayor of Philadelphia, and two or three Judges in Pennsylvania, are consecrating their gifted minds and their time, on the Sabbath to the instruction and benefit of the rising generation."

long they took over the idea, superseded private initiative and control, and changed the character of the instruction from a day of secular work to an hour or so of religious teaching. The American Sunday School Union, organized in 1824, and after 1832 operating from Cincinnati, waged so successful a campaign for the establishment of Sunday Schools (**R. 80**) in the then West that some 2800 Sunday Schools had been opened in that region by 1834. In a few cases the Union asked for state aid for the work it was doing.[1]

Though there had been some Sunday instruction earlier at a few places in New England, the introduction of the Sunday School from England, in 1786, marks the real beginning of the religious Sunday School in America. After the churches had once caught the idea of a common religious school on Sundays for the instruction of any-one, a number of societies were formed to carry on and extend the work. The most important of the earlier foundations were:

1808. The Evangelical Society of Philadelphia.
1816. The Female Union for the Promotion of Sabbath Schools (New York).
1816. The New York Sunday School Union.
1816. The Boston Society for the Moral and Religious Instruction of the Poor.
1817. The Philadelphia Sunday and Adult School Union.
1824. The American Sunday School Union.

2. *The City School Societies*

Before 1825 a number of subscription societies, many of which were able to effect financial connections with the city or the State, were formed in the few cities of the time to develop schools "for the education of such poor children as do not belong to, or are not provided for by any religious society." These societies were usually organized by philanthropic citizens, willing to contribute something yearly to provide some little education for a few of the many children in the city having no opportunities for any instruction.[2]

[1] Knight tells of a memorial to the North Carolina legislature, in 1825, from the Orange County Sunday School Union, asking for a grant of twenty-five cents a year per pupil for books, and stating that the Union had, at that time, twenty-two Sunday Schools, instructing "from 800 to 1000 children, many of whom, the children of the poor who would otherwise have been brought up in utter ignorance and vice, have been taught to read and trained in habits of moral reflection and conduct."

A legislative committee, to whom the petition was referred, recommended against the making of such a grant.

[2] There were many paupers and poor families in the cities of the Atlantic seaboard, unable to pay for the education of their children in even the rudiments of learning. Many

Early New York City societies.   One of the first of these societies was "The Manumission Society," organized in New York in 1785, for the purpose of "mitigating the evils of slavery, to defend the rights of the blacks, and especially to give them the elements of an education."   Alexander Hamilton and John Jay were among its organizers. A free school for colored pupils [1] was opened, in 1787.   This grew and prospered and was aided from time to time by the city, and in 1801 by the State, and finally, in 1834, all its schools were merged with those of the "Public School Society" of the city.   In 1801 the first free school for poor white children "whose parents belong to no religious society, and who, from some cause or other, cannot be admitted into any of the charity schools of the city," was opened. This was provided by the "Association of Women Friends for the Relief of the Poor," which engaged "a widow woman of good education and morals as instructor" at £30 per year.   This Association also prospered, and received some city or state aid up to 1824.   By 1823 it was providing free elementary education for 750 children.   Its schools also were later merged with those of the "Public School Society."

"The Public School Society."   Perhaps the most famous of all the early subscription societies for the maintenance of schools for the poor was the "New York Free School Society," which later (1826) changed its name to that of "The Public School Society of New York."   This was organized in 1805 under the leadership of De Witt Clinton, then mayor of the city, he heading the subscription list [2] with a promise of $200 a year for support, and an Address

of their children consequently were left to run the streets, subject to all kinds of temptations.   Public-spirited men and women saw the social menace involved, and undertook, as in England, to in part abate it by providing, at personal expense, some schooling for such children.

[1] The following note regarding this school appeared in the *Annals of Education* of February, 1831:

"The first African free school in New York was founded in 1787.   Only about forty pupils at first attended, but in 1791 a female teacher was employed to instruct the girls, and the school appeared to promise increased usefulness.   For nearly twenty years the number of scholars continued to vary from forty to sixty; but the introduction of the monitorial system, in 1809, improved the condition of the school, and added much to the number of pupils.   About 700 pupils are now attending this institution, about 500 being in the boys' department, in the brick building fronting on Mulberry Street."

[2] The original subscription book shows the name of De Witt Clinton for $200 annually, followed by one name for $50, quite a number for $25, gradually decreasing to thirty-six names for $8 each, and still smaller sums.   A total of $6501 was entered on the book, practically all of the subscriptions being for annual sums.   The first page of the original subscription book has been reproduced photographically in A. E. Palmer's *The New York Public School*, p. 22.

DE WITT CLINTON

(1769–1828)

First President of the Free School Society
Mayor of the City of New York
Governor of the State of New York

(**R. 81**) to the public, stating the purpose of the proposed Society, was issued that same year. For the next twenty-three years, until his death in 1828, he was its president and guiding genius (**R. 82**).

On May 14, 1806, the following advertisement appeared in the daily papers:

FREE SCHOOL

The Trustees of the Society for establishing a Free School in the city of New York, for the education of such poor children as do not belong to, or are not provided for by any religious Society, having engaged a Teacher, and procured a School House for the accommodation of a School, have now the pleasure of announcing that it is proposed to receive scholars of the descriptions alluded to without delay; applications may be made to, &c.

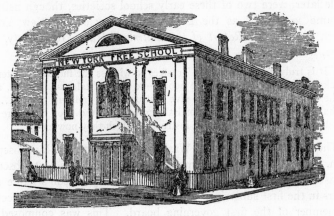

FIG. 40. THE FIRST SCHOOLHOUSE BUILT BY THE FREE SCHOOL SOCIETY IN NEW YORK CITY

Built in 1809, in Tryon Row. Cost, without site, $13,000.

This Society was chartered by the legislature "to provide school-ing for all children who are the proper objects of a gratuitous edu-cation." [1] It organized free public education in the city, secured funds, built schoolhouses, provided and trained teachers, and ably

[1] "Previous to the establishment of the Free School Society in 1806, there were but five charity schools in the City of New York (then a city of approximately 50,000 inhabit-ants), and these were small and for the exclusive benefit of the children of members of the several religious sects supporting them. The children of a large proportion of the poor population were constantly left a prey to all the evils of ignorance and idleness, and were growing up in habits calculated to fit them for the tenantry of pauper and prison estab-lishments." (*Report of the New York Free School Society*, 1823.)

supplemented the work of the private and church schools. By its energy and its persistence it secured for itself a large share of public confidence, aroused a constantly increasing interest in the cause of popular education (**R. 82**), and was granted financial aid in its work by both the city council and the legislature.[1] In 1853, after it had educated over 600,000 children and trained over 1200 teachers, this Society, its work done, surrendered its charter and turned over its buildings and equipment to the public school department of the city, which had been created by the legislature in 1842.

School Societies elsewhere. The "Benevolent Society of the City of Baltimore for the Education of the Female Poor," founded in 1799, and the "Male Free Society of Baltimore," organized a little later, were two of these early school societies, though neither became so famous as the Public School Society of New York. From the *Annual Report of the Baltimore Male Free Society*, for 1822, we read:

> It is truly gratifying to the Trustees to witness the increasing interest taken in the education of the poor, — to see the talents, the zeal, and the means now employed to give instruction to indigent youth.... To the liberality of the citizens of Baltimore, they (the poor boys) are indebted for the ample means of instruction which they now enjoy.

The schools of the city of Washington were started by subscription, in 1804, and for some time were in part supported by subscriptions from public-spirited citizens. Thomas Jefferson's name appears in the first subscription list as giving $200, and he was elected a member of the first governing board. This was composed of seven citizens appointed by the city council, and six elected from among the subscribers. The chief sources of support of the schools, which up to 1844 remained pauper schools, were subscriptions, lotteries,[2] a tax on slaves and dogs, certain license fees, and a small appropriation ($1500) each year from the city council "for the education of children whose parents reside in the city and are unable to defray the expense of their education." No child was ad-

[1] Beginning the first year with $6501 in subscriptions, a grant of $500 a year was made by the common council in 1807, the State adding $4000 for a building and $1000 annually for maintenance. From 1815 on the Society shared in the state Common School Fund, and from 1819 on half of a tax on lotteries. In 1829 the Society was granted a tax of one eighth of a mill, which in 1831 was raised to one half a mill.

[2] Between 1812 and 1838 Congress passed fourteen joint resolutions authorizing lotteries for the support of schools in the District of Columbia. Eventually a permanent fund of $40,000 was accumulated for their maintenance.

mitted if financially able to attend any other school.[1] This society did an important work in accustoming the people of the capital city to the provision of some form of free education.

In 1799 "The Philadelphia Society for the Free Instruction of Indigent Boys" was formed, which a little later changed to "The Philadelphia Society for the Establishment and Support of Charity Schools" (**R. 83**). This organization opened the first schools in Philadelphia for children regardless of religious affiliation, and for thirty-seven years rendered a useful service there. The first year twenty to thirty poor children were taught, at a total cost of $16.37. In 1804 the first school building of the Society was erected, in 1811 girls were taught for the first time, and by 1830 the Society had provided the rudiments of education to 5235 boys and 3596 girls at a per capita cost of around $4.00 a year. In 1814 "The Society for the Promotion of a Rational System of Education" was organized in Philadelphia, and four years later the public sentiment awakened by a combination of the work of this Society and the coming of the Lancastrian system of instruction enabled the city to secure a special law (1818) permitting Philadelphia to organize a system of city schools for the education of the children of its poor, and constituting the city the "first school district" of the State.

Other educational societies which rendered useful service include the "Mechanics and Manufacturers Association," of Providence,[2] Rhode Island, organized in 1789; "The Albany Lancastrian School Society," organized in 1826, for the education of the poor of the city in monitorial schools; and the school societies organized in Savannah, in 1818, and Augusta, in 1821, "to afford education to the children of indigent parents." Both these Georgia societies received some support from state funds.

Another type of free school, of which a number came to exist, resulted through establishments by will. Of these the bequest of Christopher Ludwick of about $13,000 to the Philadelphia charity-

---

[1] In 1831 the schools were made even more inaccessible, probably as a result of increasing financial burdens, by a requirement that only children whose parents earned less than $1.50 a day, or those coming from families having more than four children, could be admitted.

[2] One of the leading spirits in this Association was John Howland (1757–1854) of Providence. In 1799 he was one of a committee to memorialize the legislature to enact a school law, and wrote the memorial. The law was enacted in 1800, and Providence opened schools in October of that year. He was a member of the school committee for twenty years, and drew up the first rules and regulations for the schools.

school Society (**R. 83**) in 1801; the bequest of $600, annually in ground rents for the support of a free school in Baltimore, by John McKim, in 1817; the bequest of John Kidd, a wealthy baker of Cincinnati, who died in 1818 and bequeathed $1000 per year "for the education of poor children and youths of Cincinnati"; the bequest made to the same city and for the same purpose, in 1824, by Thomas Hughes; and still another bequest to the same city by a citizen named Woodward, in 1829, from which the Woodward High School [1] marks its origin, are examples.

FIG. 41.   THE FIRST FREE SCHOOL IN BALTIMORE

The McKim School, the oldest free school in Baltimore. It was founded by John McKim, who in 1817 bequeathed $600 annually in ground rents for the support of a free school under the direction of the Friends Society. The public school system of Baltimore was not established until 1829. The front of the building is copied faithfully from the old Greek temple of Theseus, at Athens, one of the finest remains of the age of Pericles. The McKim School ranks among the architectural treasures of Baltimore. A kindergarten is now maintained in the building.

The formation of these school societies, the subscriptions made by the leading men of the cities, the bequests here and there for education, and the grants of some city and state aid to these school societies, all of which in time became somewhat common, indicate a slowly rising interest in providing schools for the education of at least the children of the poor.   This rising interest in education was greatly stimulated by the introduction from England of a new and what for the time seemed a wonderful system for the organization of education, which we next describe.

3. *The Lancastrian monitorial system of instruction*

Origin of the idea.   In 1797 Dr. Andrew Bell, a clergyman in the Established Church, published in England an account of *An Experiment in Education* by means of monitors, which he had made

[1] This institution was founded in November, 1829, by a gift from Woodward, and was opened in October, 1831, with "three professors; one for Mathematics, one for Languages, and one for the Academic Department."   The number of students that winter was 95, and

JOSEPH LANCASTER
(1778–1838)

some years earlier in an orphan asylum in Madras, India. About the same time a young English Quaker schoolmaster, by the name of Joseph Lancaster, was led independently to a similar discovery of the advantages of using monitors by reason of his needing assistance in his school and being too poor to pay for additional teachers. The idea attracted attention from the first, and was spread rapidly over England, in part by reason of a bitter church quarrel between the followers of the two men as to which was entitled to credit for originating the system. The plans of the two men were much the same. Bell's system [1] was taken up and his claims supported by the Church-of-England educational organizations, while Lancaster's [2] was supported by the Dissenters. The plan was so cheap, and so effective in teaching reading and the fundamentals of religion, that it soon provided England with a sort of a substitute for a national system of schools. It was the Lancastrian plan which was brought to this country, Church-of-England ideas not being in much favor after the Revolution.

Once introduced into the United States, where the first school was opened in New York City, in 1806, the system quickly spread from Massachusetts to Georgia, and as far west as Cincinnati, Louisville, and Detroit. In New York and Philadelphia (**Rs. 84, 85**) in particular was the system adopted with enthusiasm, and the governors of both New York and Pennsylvania recommended the general adoption of the system by their legislatures. In 1826 Maryland instituted a state system of Lancastrian schools, with a Superintendent of Public Instruction, but in 1828 abandoned the idea and discontinued the office. Many private Lancastrian schools were opened, from New York to North Carolina, as rapidly as teachers could learn the method (**R. 87c**) and find pupils for them (**Rs. 87, 88**). In North Carolina the system made such headway that a state Lancastrian system was proposed in 1832, but failed of adoption by the legislature. In 1829 Mexico organized higher

approximately 150 were expected in the spring term. The avails of the property granted by the founder, at that time, paid for the gratuitous instruction of about 50 students, who also were provided with free books and stationery by the trustees. (Abstract of a news item of March, 1832.)

[1] Bell, Rev. Dr. Andrew. *An Experiment in Education made at the Male Asylum at Madras, Suggesting a System by which a School or a Family may teach itself under the Superintendence of a Master or Parent.* London, 1797.

[2] Lancaster, Joseph. *Improvements in Education as it Respects the Industrial Classes of the Community.* London, 1803; New York, 1807.

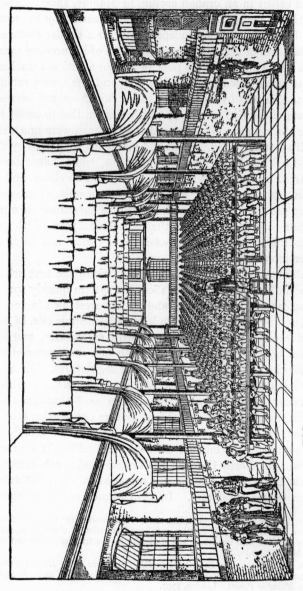

FIG. 42. A LANCASTRIAN SCHOOL IN OPERATION

This shows 365 pupils seated, monitors standing at the left, and "stations" around the walls.

Lancastrian schools for the Mexican State of Texas. In 1818 Lancaster himself came to America, and was received with much distinction. Official receptions were given for him in New York City, Albany, and Philadelphia, and the year following, when he visited Washington, he was, on motion of a member of the House from Virginia, accorded the privilege of the Speaker's chair while Congress was in session. He lectured extensively in the eastern cities explaining his plan of instruction, and most of the remaining twenty years of his life were spent in organizing and directing schools in various parts of the United States, and in expounding the merits of his system.

Essential features of the plan. The essential features of the Lancastrian plan were the collection of a large number of pupils in one room, from 200 to 1000 being possible. The picture on page 130

FIG. 43. MONITORS TEACHING READING

Three drafts of ten each, with their toes to the semicircles painted on the floor, are being taught by monitors from lessons suspended on the wall.

shows a monitorial school seating 365. The pupils were sorted and seated in rows, and to each row was assigned a clever boy who was known as a monitor, and who was the key to the entire system.[1] A common number for each monitor to instruct and look after was ten. The teacher first taught these monitors a lesson from a printed card, and then the monitors, "youthful corporals of the teacher's

[1] "The master," writes Lancaster, "should be a bystander and inspector. What the master says should be done. When the pupils, as well as the schoolmaster, understand how to act and learn on this system, the system, not the master's vague, discretionary, uncertain judgment, will be in practice.... In a common school the authority of the master is personal, and the rod is his sceptre. His absence is an immediate signal for confusion. But in a school conducted on my plan, when the master leaves the school, the business will go on as well in his absence as in his presence, because the authority is not personal." (Joseph Lancaster. *British System of Education*, p. 45.)

regiment," took their rows to "stations" about the wall and proceeded to teach the other boys what they had just learned.

At first used only for teaching reading and the catechism, the plan was soon extended to the teaching of writing, simple sums, and spelling, and later to instruction in the higher branches. A number of private monitorial schools (**R. 87**) and academies (**R. 88**) were organized in the different Eastern States, a number of monitorial high schools were organized in different cities, and it was even proposed that the plan should be adopted in the colleges. In many of the then rapidly rising cities the first free schools established were Lancastrian schools. It was the official system employed by the New York School Society from 1805 on. Lancastrian societies were incorporated in Albany in 1812, and Schenectady in 1816, and in five other New York cities before 1828. Between 1825 and 1836 the New York legislature passed 13 special acts for the incorporation of Monitorial high schools in the cities and counties of the State.[1] The first public free schools in Philadelphia (1818) were an outgrowth of Lancastrian influence, as was also the case in many other Pennsylvania cities — Lancaster, Columbia, Harrisburg, Pittsburgh, Milton, Erie, New Castle, and Greencastle being among the number. Baltimore began a Lancastrian school six years before the organization of public schools was permitted there by law. In Virginia the movement awakened interest, and the cities of Winchester, Petersburg, Norfolk, and Richmond, among others, gave their quotas from the Literary Fund to Lancastrian schools for the children of the poor.[2] In Kentucky, a free Lancastrian school was established at Louisville in 1829. Hartford, New Haven, Baltimore, and Washington were other cities which early established schools on the Lancastrian plan.

Such schools naturally were highly organized, the organization

[1] For a list of these, see Gifford, W. J. *Historical Development of the New York High School System*, p. 24.

[2] Efforts were begun in Richmond, in October, 1815, to establish a charity school by public subscription, and in June, 1816, the cornerstone of a Lancastrian school was laid, bearing the inscription:

"Dedicated to the Elementary Principles of Education, founded by the municipality and worthy, liberal-minded citizens. The children of the Wealthy are taught on the most moderate terms, and those of the Poor, gratis."

The following year the cornerstone of a Lancastrian school was laid in Norfolk, bearing the inscription:

"The Norfolk Lancastrian School, founded by the Common Council of Norfolk Borough, August 1, 1817."

being largely mechanical. The *Manuals of Instruction* gave complete directions for the organization and management of monitorial schools, the details of recitation work, use of the apparatus, order, and classification being minutely laid down.[1] These details teachers were forbidden to depart from, so that the final breakdown of the system in New York City, as elsewhere, was due to faults inherent in the system itself. By carefully studying and following these any person could soon learn to become a successful teacher in a monitorial school. The schools, mechanical as they now seem,

FIG. 44. MONITOR INSPECTING WRITTEN WORK AT SIGNAL, "SHOW SLATES"

rendered valuable service in introducing group instruction in place of the individual method upon which colonial schoolmasters had wasted so much of their own and their pupils' time. In place of their idleness, inattention, and disorder, Lancaster introduced activity, emulation, order, and a kind of military discipline which was of much value to the type of children attending these schools. Lancaster's biographer, Salmon, has written of the system that so thoroughly was the instruction worked out that the teacher had only to organize, oversee, reward, punish, and inspire:

> When a child was admitted a monitor assigned him his class; while he remained, a monitor taught him (with nine other pupils); when he was absent, one monitor ascertained the fact, and another found out

[1] The utter inadequacy of the Lancastrian plan has been well pointed out by Gordy, when he says:

"It is hardly necessary to point out that the hopes entertained of Lancastrian schools were based on two misconceptions: (1) that teaching consists merely in imparting knowledge; and (2) that all that is necessary to impart this knowledge is simply to know as much as is to be imparted. Dr. Bell said, 'Give me 24 pupils today and I will give you back 24 teachers tomorrow.'" (Gordy, J. P. *Rise and Growth of the Normal School Idea*, p. 23.)

the reason; a monitor examined him periodically, and, when he made progress, a monitor promoted him; a monitor ruled the writing paper; a monitor had charge of slates and books; and a monitor-general looked after all the other monitors. Every monitor wore a leather ticket, gilded and lettered, "Monitor of the First Class," "Reading Monitor of the Second Class," etc.

Value of the system in awakening interest. The Lancastrian system of instruction, coming at the time it did, exerted a very important influence in awakening a public interest in and a sentiment for free schools. For a time it seems to have awakened much enthusiasm (**R. 85**), and it undoubtedly did much toward making people see the advantages of a common school system, and become willing to contribute to the support of the same. Under the plans previously in use education had been a slow and an expensive process, because it had to be carried on by the individual method of instruction, and in quite small groups. Under this new plan it was now possible for one teacher to instruct 300, 400, 500, or more pupils in a single room, and to do it with much better results in both learning and discipline than the old type of schoolmaster had achieved. It is not strange that the new plan aroused widespread enthusiasm in many discerning men, and for almost a quarter of a century was advocated as the best system of education then known. As a step in the direction of class instruction, in place of individual instruction, it marked a long advance in the direction of free public education. Three quotations will illustrate what leading men of the time thought of it. De Witt Clinton, for twenty-three years president of the New York "Free School Society," and later governor of the State (from 1817–22, and 1824–28), wrote, in 1809:

When I perceive that many boys in our school have been taught to read and write in two months, who did not before know the alphabet, and that even one has accomplished it in three weeks — when I view all the bearings and tendencies of this system — when I contemplate the habits of order which it forms, the spirit of emulation which it excites, the rapid improvement which it produces, the purity of morals which it inculcates — when I behold the extraordinary union of celerity in instruction and economy of expense — and when I perceive one great assembly of a thousand children, under the eye of a single teacher, marching with unexampled rapidity and with perfect discipline to the goal of knowledge, I confess that I recognize in Lancaster the benefactor of the human race. I consider his system as creating a new era in education, as a blessing sent down from heaven to redeem the poor and distressed of this world from the power and dominion of ignorance.

Governor Heister of Pennsylvania, in 1821, in recommending the system to the consideration of the legislature of that State, said:

> For the establishment of schools in which the terms of tuition are greatly reduced, and in which those who are not able to meet the expenses are taught gratuitously, the citizens of Philadelphia stand pre-eminent. Their schools, established under different acts of Assembly, on the Lancastrian system of education, are, at this time, preparing for future usefulness five thousand, three hundred and sixty-nine scholars, many of whom would otherwise be permitted to grow up in ignorance, and become a prey to those vices of which it unfortunately is so fruitful a source.
>
> From the great success attending the introduction of the Lancastrian system of education in the First School District, embracing the city and county of Philadelphia, and the representations made to me of its being equally successful in some of our sister states, I think it worth the experiment of being attempted in other sections of the state as far as it can be adapted to the peculiarities of the respective situation and circumstances.

In a message to the legislature of Connecticut, a State then fairly well supplied with schools of the Massachusetts district type, Governor Wolcott said, in 1825:

> If funds can be obtained to defray the expenses of the necessary preparations, I have no doubt that schools on the Lancastrian model ought, as soon as possible, to be established in several parts of this state. Wherever from 200 to 1000 children can be convened within a suitable distance, this mode of instruction in every branch of reading, speaking, penmanship, arithmetic, and bookkeeping, will be found much more efficient, direct, and economical than the practices now generally pursued in our primary schools.

Value in preparing the way for taxation for education. One of the main difficulties up to this time had been the cost of education among people who were relatively poor, and unwilling to spend money for anything for which they did not clearly see the need. The private tutor as a means for education was out of the question for any except the well-to-do. The churches had their hands more than full in supporting schools, largely by tuition fees, for the children of those of their members able to contribute something toward their education, with a few free places for their deserving poor. So long as the time-honored individual method of instruction, with its accompanying waste of time and disorder, continued to be the prevailing method, only a small number of pupils could be placed under the control of a single teacher. The expense for this made general education almost prohibitive.

All at once, comparatively, a new system had been introduced which not only improved but tremendously cheapened education.[1] In 1822 it cost but $1.22 per pupil per year to give instruction in New York City, though by 1844 the per-capita cost, due largely to the decreasing size of the classes, had risen to $2.70, and by 1852 to $5.83. In Philadelphia, in 1817, the expense was $3, as against $12 in the private and church schools. One finds many notices in the newspapers of the time as to the value and low cost of the new system. The following note, from *The Recorder* of Boston, for August 21, 1816, is typical:

> A school on the Lancastrian plan has been recently established in Chillicothe, Ohio. The progress of the children is much more rapid than in the common schools; their exercises highly conducive to health; their lessons calculated to promote the purest morality; their books furnished; and the expenses no more than $2.50 by the quarter.

These sums are very low compared with present-day costs, or costs of even two decades ago.

At the beginning of the century it would not have been possible to have secured public support for any general state system of education. The Lancastrian schools accustomed the people to schools and to contribute something toward their support. Once accustomed to the practice they continued though education became more expensive, and they did this the more willingly as they slowly grasped the conception that a free public school was after all implied in a democratic theory of government.

The Lancastrian schools thus materially hastened the adoption of the free school system in all the Northern States by gradually accustoming people to bearing the necessary taxation which free schools entail. They also made the common school common and much talked of, and awakened thought and provoked discussion on the question of public education. They likewise dignified the work of

---

[1] "Having participated in the first establishment of the Lancastrian system in this country, having carefully observed its progress, and witnessed its benefits, I can confidently recommend it as an invaluable improvement which by a wonderful combination of *economy in expense* and *rapidity of instruction*, has created a new era in education; and I am desirous that all our common schools should be supplied with teachers of this description. As this system operates with the same efficiency in education that *labor-saving machinery* does in the useful arts, it will be readily perceived that it is peculiarly adapted to this country." (Message of Governor Clinton to the New York legislature, 1818.)

the teacher by showing the necessity for teacher training. The Lancastrian Model Schools, first established in 1818, were the precursors of our normal schools.

The system was very popular from about 1815 to about 1830, though by 1830, as the defects of the monitorial plan became evident (**Rs. 85, 89**), its popularity as a means for providing education was clearly on the wane. By 1840 it had almost generally been abandoned, outside of New York City, where it continued in partial use until 1853. "It was born in poverty, and poverty was ever its best excuse for being." While the development of education owes to Lancaster an improved organization for charity schools and a system of instruction based on rigid economy, we have to look to other workers for a system better adapted to the mental and cultural needs of the child.[1]

4. *The Infant-School Societies*

Origin of the Infant-School idea. A curious condition in this country was that in some of the cities where public schools had been established, by one agency or another, no provision had been made for beginners. They merely followed the older New England practice of expecting the pupils to be able to read when they came to the school. They were supposed to obtain the elements of reading at home, or in the dame schools. In Boston, for example, where public schools were maintained by the city, no children could be received into the schools who had not learned to read and write. This made the common age of admission somewhere near eight years. The same was in part true of Hartford, New York, Philadelphia, Baltimore, and other cities. When the monitorial schools were established they tended to restrict their membership in a similar manner, though not always able to do so.

In 1816 there came to this country, also from England, a valuable supplement to education, as then known, in the form of the so-called Infant-School idea. It had originated at New Lanark, in Scotland, in 1799, where a manufacturer by the name of Robert

---

[1] The adoption of the Lancastrian system by the Free School Society of New York City was due primarily to its cheapness, and to the impression made by the completeness of its organization. It appeared to be particularly adapted to charity schools such as were proposed by the Society. The editor of the *Academician* (1818, vol. 1, p. 270) viewed the Lancastrian system as better adapted to charitable institutions where there are many pupils, but the Pestalozzian as superior for private schools as it "addressed itself more to the understanding and elicited thought."

Owen had established a school for the children in his town and factories. The factory children were poor children of the town who had been bound out to him at five, six, and seven years of age, for a period of nine years. They worked as apprentices and helpers twelve to thirteen hours a day in the factories, and at early manhood were turned free to join the ignorant mass of the population. Owen sought to remedy this situation by opening a school which took the children at three years of age, and by amusements and instruction tried to give them moral, physical, and intellectual training. They were taught "whatever might be supposed useful and that they could understand," the instruction was combined with much singing and dancing to "render them active, cheerful, and happy." In good weather they were much out of doors. There was no punishment, and "the children were not to be annoyed with books." The idea, in the hands of his teachers, worked well; but in the hands of others elsewhere it was soon formalized, some of the new Pestalozzian procedures were introduced, and book learning was made a prominent feature of the Infant Schools.

Infant Schools in the Eastern cities. In this formalized state the idea reached Boston, in 1816, and for the next two years an agitation was carried on for the establishment of Infant or Primary Schools. In 1818 the city appropriated $5000 for the purpose of organizing such schools to supplement the public school system, and appointed a supplemental school committee of three citizens in each of the then twelve wards to organize and direct the so-called primary schools. These schools were to admit children at four years of age, were to be taught by women, were to be open all the year round, and were to prepare the children for admission to the city schools, which by that time had come to be known as English grammar schools.[1] The schools, though, were to be of quite a different type (**R. 90**) from the dame schools which had previously prepared the pupils for entrance. Separate schools were established, separate school

---

[1] Concerning these schools the *Boston Daily Advertiser*, in November, 1831, said:

"At a recent quarterly meeting of the Primary School Committee of this city, the Report of the semi-annual examination of the Standing Committee was read, from which it appears that there are now 62 of these schools in successful operation, containing 3913 pupils, 3228 of whom were present and 685 absent. The average number in each school is 63; 52 upon the average being present. Of the number, 467 are prepared for admission to the grammar schools, and 450 have been sent within the last six months. The children attending these schools are between the ages of four and seven. These schools are under the supervision of 70 gentlemen, 62 of whom visit them monthly and the other 8 semi-annually."

buildings were erected, and a new set of teachers was employed.[1]
An infant school was thus described by William Russell, in a
lecture before the American Institute of Instruction, in 1830:

A well-regulated Infant School furnishes a happy contrast to the
defects of the elementary school: it exhibits a spacious, airy, cheerful,
and comfortable apartment, prepared expressly for every good influence
on the infant being; a frequent
change of attitude and of employment; the presence of pictures and other objects as
calculated to inspire the mind
with activity and delight, or to
diffuse tranquillity and tender-
ness of feeling; mental employments interspersed with appropriate juvenile exercises, or
judicious intervals of entire rest;
lessons adopted to the capacities
and desires of infancy; mental
exertion rendered agreeable and
voluntary; discipline consisting
chiefly of rational and affec-
tionate measures addressed to
sympathy and moral feeling,
and, as far as practicable, to
reason, and turning upon the
incidents arising from the pupils'
intercourse with each other.

FIG. 45. "MODEL" SCHOOL
BUILDING OF THE PUBLIC
SCHOOL SOCIETY

Erected in 1843. Cost, with site, $17,000.
A typical New York school building, after
1830. The infant or primary school was on
the first floor, the second floor contained the
girls' school, and the third floor the boys'
school. Each floor had one large room seating
252 children; the primary schoolroom could be
divided into two rooms by folding doors, so
as to segregate the infant class. This building
was for long regarded as the perfection of the
builder's art, and its picture was printed for
years on the cover of the Society's *Annual
Reports*.

The management of the
primary schools remained separate from that of the grammar schools until 1854, when
the two were combined under
one city School Committee.
Providence, similarly, estab-
lished primary schools in 1828 for children between the ages
of four and eight, to supplement the work of the public schools,
there called writing schools. For New England, the establishment

[1]An infant school may be best described as something which resembled, not so much
a school as a large nursery, and the object of which was to provide for its little inmates
employment and amusement, not less than instruction. In England the ages in the infant
schools were from eighteen months to six years, while in Boston, where entrance was made
to the primary school at the age of four, children between two and four enjoyed the benefits
of the infant schools.

of primary schools virtually took over the dame-school instruction as a public function, and added the primary grades to the previously existing school (**R. 91**). We have here the origin of the division, often still retained at least in name in the Eastern States, of the "primary grades" and the "grammar grades" of our elementary school.

An "Infant-School Society" was organized in New York in 1827. The first Infant School was established under the direction of the Public School Society as the "Junior Department" of School No. 8,

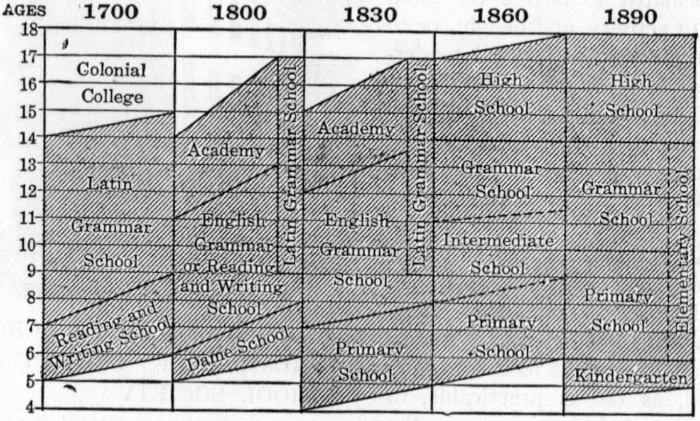

FIG. 46. EVOLUTION OF THE ESSENTIAL FEATURES OF THE AMERICAN PUBLIC SCHOOL SYSTEM

with a woman teacher in charge, and using monitorial methods.[1] A second school was established the next year. In 1830 the name was changed from Infant School to Primary Department,[2] and where possible these departments were combined with the existing schools. In 1832 it was decided to organize ten primary schools, under women

[1] "The first Infant School was established in New York, in May, 1827, and the experience of six years has placed beyond dispute the practicability of instructing infants, not only in the branches of primary education, but also in the principles of morals and religion.

"There are now (1833) in the city 16 schools, wherein 2370 infant children receive instruction — 1400 in the charity schools, and 970 in those attached to the Public Schools. There are also 11 private schools, conducted upon the infant plan, comprising about 490 children. There are still 6000 children, under four years of age, who are not embraced in any of the schools." (*American Annals*, June, 1833.)

[2] "The manifest superiority for young children of the schools established by the Infant School Society, in 1827, led to the withdrawal of the four lower classes of the monitorial school and the formation of primary schools and primary departments, and the substitution of women teachers for boy monitors." (J. F. Reigart. *The Lancastrian System of Instruction in the Schools of New York City*, p. 97.)

teachers, for children from four to ten years of age, and after the Boston plan of instruction. This abandoned the monitorial plan of instruction for the new Pestalozzian form, described in Chapter X, which was deemed better suited to the needs of the smaller children. By 1844 fifty-six Primary Departments had been organized in connection with the upper schools of the city.

In Philadelphia there were three Infant-School Societies founded in 1827–28, and such schools were at once established there. By 1830 the directors of the school system had been permitted by the legislature of the State to expend public money for such schools, and seven such, under women teachers, were in operation in the city [1] by 1832, and thirty by 1837.

Primary education organized. The Infant-School idea was soon somewhat generally adopted by the Eastern cities, and soon changed somewhat to make of it an American primary school. Where children had previously not been admitted to the schools without knowing how to read, as in Boston, they supplemented the work of the public schools by adding a new school beneath. Where the reverse had been the case, as in New York City, the organization of Infant Schools as Junior Departments enabled the existing schools to advance their work. Everywhere it resulted, eventually, in the organization of primary and grammar school departments, often with intermediate departments in between, and, with the somewhat contemporaneous evolution of the first high schools, the main outlines of the American free public school system were now complete.

Unlike the monitorial schools, the infant schools were based on the idea of small-group work, and were usually conducted in harmony with the new psychological conceptions of instruction which had by that time been worked out by Pestalozzi in Switzerland, and introduced into the Infant Schools of England. The Infant-School idea came at an opportune time, as the defects of the mechanical Lancastrian instruction were becoming evident and its popularity was waning. It gave a new and a somewhat deeper philosophical interpretation of the educational process, created a stronger demand

---

[1] In 1832, the *Fourth Annual Report* of the Managers announced seven schools — four of them charity, and three of them pay schools. In the four charity schools, 922 children had been instructed during the year, with a smaller number in the pay schools. In the five years since the Society began work, over 4000 children had been instructed, "many of whom are the children of parents who are poor and grossly ignorant, some of them unable to read, and not a few of them intemperate."

than had before been known for trained teachers, established a preference for women teachers for primary work, and tended to give a new dignity to teaching and school work by revealing something of a psychological basis for the instruction of little children.   It also contributed its share toward the awakening of a sentiment for intelligently directed public education.

These four important educational movements — the secular Sunday School, the semi-public city School Societies, the Lancastrian plan for instruction, and the Infant-School idea — all arising in philanthropy, came as successive educational ideas to America during the first half of the nineteenth century, supplemented one another, and together accustomed a new generation to the idea of a common school for all.

II. SOCIAL, POLITICAL, AND ECONOMIC INFLUENCES

It is hardly probable, however, that these philanthropic efforts alone, valuable as they were, could have resulted in the great battle for tax-supported schools, at as early a date as this took place, had they not been supplemented by a number of other movements of a social, political, and economic character which in themselves materially changed the nature and direction of our national life.   The more important of these will be described briefly.

1. *The growth of the cities*

Growth of city population.   At the time of the inauguration of our National Government nearly everyone lived on the farm or in some little village.   There were but five cities of 8000 or over in the new Nation, and Philadelphia, the largest of them all, had but 28,522 inhabitants.   The first forty years of our national life were essentially an agricultural and a pioneer period.   Even as late as 1820 there were but thirteen cities of 8000 inhabitants or over in the whole of the twenty-three States at that time comprising the Union, and these thirteen cities contained but 4.9 per cent of the total population of the Nation.   New York City, the largest of the thirteen, contained only 123,706 inhabitants, while Cincinnati, at that time the metropolis of the then "West," contained only 9642. Under such conditions education was largely a rural affair and, except in the more settled portions of the country, was almost certain to be generally neglected for the more important duties of cutting down the forests, draining the swamps, establishing farms and homes, and providing food and shelter for family and stock. Every child was then an asset, and was put to work at as early an age as possible. Few could be spared to go to school. It was a time of hard work, with few comforts and pleasures, and with but little need for the school of books.

GROWTH OF CITY POPULATION, 1790–1860

YEAR	NUMBER OF CITIES HAVING A POPULATION OF					PERCENTAGE OF TOTAL POPULATION IN CITIES
	8000 or over	8000 to 20,000	20,000 to 75,000	75,000 to 250,000	250,000 or over	
1780.....	5	4	1			2.7
1790.....	6	4	2			3.3
1800.....	6	1	5			4.0
1810.....	11	6	3	2		4.9
1820.....	13	7	4	2		4.9
1830.....	26	19	4	3		6.7
1840.....	44	28	11	4	1	8.5
1850.....	85	56	21	6	2	12.5
1860.....	141	96	35	7	3	16.1

After about 1825 these conditions began to change. By 1820 many little villages were springing up, and these frequently proved the nuclei for future cities. In New England many of these places were in the vicinity of some waterfall, where cheap power made manufacturing on a large scale possible. Lowell, Massachusetts, which in 1820 did not exist and in 1840 had a population of over twenty thousand people, collected there largely to work in the mills, is a good illustration. Other cities, such as Cincinnati, Chicago, and Detroit, grew because of their advantageous situation as exchange and wholesale centers. With the revival of trade and commerce after the second war with Great Britain the cities grew rapidly both in number and size, as may be seen from the table above.

The rise of the new cities and the rapid growth of the older ones materially changed the nature of the educational problem, by producing an entirely new set of social and educational conditions for the people of the Central and Northern States to solve. The South, with its plantation life, negro slavery, and absence of manufacturing was largely unaffected by these changed conditions until well after the close of the Civil War. In consequence the educational awakening there did not come for nearly half a century after it came in the North.

2. *The rise of manufacturing*

The beginnings in our country.   During the colonial period manufacturing was still in the home or village stage of development.   Almost all articles of use and wear were made by the family in the home. Wagons and furniture were made in the villages, and the traveling shoemaker came around from time to time to make up shoes for all the family (**R. 92**).   In 1787 the first American factory is said to have been started, at Beverly, Massachusetts.   In 1791 the first cotton spinning-mill was set up on the falls of the Pawtucket River,

"Old Slater Mill."

FIG. 47.   THE FIRST COMMERCIAL COTTON MILL IN THE
UNITED STATES

in Rhode Island, and the beginnings of New England's supremacy in the cotton-spinning industry were made.[1]   By 1804 there were four cotton-mills in operation, and by 1807, fifteen.   By 1815 approximately $50,000,000 had been invested in textile factories, and that year 90,000 bales of cotton were manufactured into cotton cloth.

Up to 1807, though, the development of our country was almost wholly agricultural.   This had meant a scattered and an isolated population, with few common ideas, common interests, or common needs.   Nearly all the manufactured articles not made in the homes

[1] The British had jealously guarded the machinery they had developed, and the export of models or machinery was prohibited.   Slater had worked in the Arkwright factory in England, and in 1790 came to America.   Not daring to bring any models of English machines with him, he drew plans, directed mechanics, and supervised the construction of a complete spinning mill, with carding, roving, and spinning machines, and operated by water power.   He then trained workmen to operate the machinery, and a new New England industry had its beginning.

or the villages were made in Great Britain. The Embargo of 1807, laid by Congress on American shipping, cut off articles of English manufacture and soon led to the rise of many "infant industries." Many of the legislative acts of the next five years had to do with the granting of charters and privileges to various kinds of manufactories. The War of 1812, the troubles with Napoleon, and the general westward movement of the population, all tended for a time to build up manufacturing faster than agriculture. At the end of the struggle with Napoleon (1815) this country, due to the lack of any adequate protective tariff, was for a time flooded with manufactured articles from Europe. As a result, the "infant industries" were paralyzed, and an era of hard times set in which continued to about 1820. This condition was in time corrected by the protective tariff, and following its enactment a great industrial development took place.[1]

The industrial transformation. The three decades from 1820 to 1850 were characterized by a rapid development of manufacturing and a rapid growth of cities, in which most of the new manufacturing plants were established. The introduction of the steamboat (1809) and the steam railroad (1826), together with the digging of many canals (the famous Erie Canal,[2] which cut the time from Albany to Buffalo from twenty to ten days, was opened in 1825), and the completion of the National Turnpike to Vandalia, Illinois, in 1838, at a cost of over $4,000,000, opened up the possibility of doing business on a scale before unthought of, and led to a great demand for manufactured articles and labor-saving machinery of every sort. The first steam railroad, three miles long, was built in 1826, by 1840 there were nearly 3000 miles of railways, and by 1850, 9021 miles had been constructed in the United States. One could now travel by rail from Maine to North Carolina, to Buffalo on Lake Erie, and from the western end of Lake Erie to Cincinnati or Chicago. By 1860 steam railways had been built westward into Iowa, Missouri, and Arkansas, and thirty thousand miles of rails were carrying agri-

[1] The tariff of 1828 served to swing capital in New England from shipping, where it had been invested for long, to the factory and industrial expansion. This led to the industrialization of the North and the expansion of the West, while the South remained largely unaffected. Industrialism completely changed, in time, the old agrarianism of the North, and created a new world in which the institution of slavery was an anachronism.

[2] This job was done by men who had had no technical training for such work. It was the first great pioneer work of American engineering. What they did not know how to do they studied and found out, and by the constant exercise of common sense, diligent study, and unwearied zeal they laid the foundations of a profession of civil engineering in the United States.

cultural products from the interior and manufactured products from the seaboard cities back to the interior. The invention of the telegraph (first line, 1844) also tremendously increased the possibilities of doing business on a large scale.

The inventive genius of our people was now called into play, and Yankee ingenuity manifested itself in every direction.[1] After 1825 the threshing machine began to supplant the flail and the roller; after 1826 edge tools began to be made in this country; and shortly

FIG. 48. THRESHING WHEAT WITH FLAIL AND ROLLER
From an old illustration.

after this time the Fairbanks platform scale, the mower, the reaper, and the lockstitch sewing machine were invented. Kerosene lamps were devised, improved cook-stoves were put on the market, and the friction match superseded the flint. The coal measures west of the Alleghenies were opened, and anthracite in the East was put to use. The great work of steam had begun, the chimneys of factories were rising over the land, and the steam engine was applied to both boat and train, to running the power loom and the printing-press, and to the steam hammer for working iron and steel. Between 1820 and 1850 the industrial methods in America were revolutionized.[2]

[1] "The twenty years from 1837 to 1857 have been called the Golden Age. In this brief period the total wealth of the country quadrupled, and the per capita wealth more than doubled... Industry flourished on every hand. This unprecedented prosperity and expansion of the mechanic arts made the need of more definite and accurate knowledge of the mechanic arts apparent." (C. R. Mann. *The American Spirit in Education*, p. 36.)

[2] "The period from 1825 to 1860 was marked by the rapid expansion of industry and invention, the reorganization of the social structure from an agricultural to a manufacturing

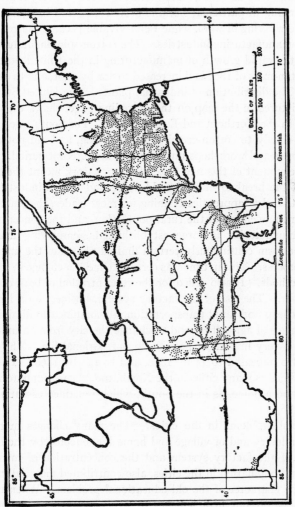

FIG. 49. DISTRIBUTION OF INDUSTRIAL PLANTS IN THE UNITED STATES IN 1833

From W. E. Dodd's *Expansion and Conflict*; Houghton Mifflin Co., 1915. Reproduced by permission.

How manufacturing changed the position of the city.   In the cities in the coast States north of Maryland, but particularly in those of New York and New England, manufacturing developed very rapidly. Cotton-spinning in particular became a New England industry, as did also the weaving of wool, while Pennsylvania became the center of the iron-manufacturing industries.   The cotton-spinning industry illustrates the rapid growth of manufacturing in the United States. The 15 cotton-mills of 1807 had increased to 801 by 1831, and to 1240 by 1840.   The distribution of industrial plants in the United States by 1833, pictured in the map on the preceding page, shows the development in the Northern and Eastern cities.   The South owed its prosperity chiefly to cotton-growing and shipping, and did not develop factories and workshops until a much more recent period.

The development of this new type of factory work meant the beginnings of the breakdown of the old home and village industries, the ultimate end of apprentice training for most trades, the start of the cityward movement of the rural population, and the concentration of manufacturing in large establishments, employing many hands to perform continuously certain limited phases of the manufacturing process.   This in time was certain to mean a change in educational methods.   It also called for the concentration of both capital and labor.   The rise of the factory system, business on a large scale, and cheap and rapid transportation, all combined to diminish the importance of agriculture and to change the city from an unimportant to a very important position in our national life.   The 13 cities of 1820 increased to 44 by 1840, and to 141 by 1860.   There were four times as many cities in the North, too, where manufacturing had found a home, as in the South, which remained essentially agricultural.

New social problems in the cities.   The many changes in the nature of industry and of village and home life, effected by the development of the factory system and the concentration of manufacturing and population in the cities, also contributed materially in changing the character of the old educational problem.   When the cities were as yet but little villages in size and character, homogeneous in their populations, and the many social and moral prob-

type, and an increase in the respect paid to manual work.   Several schools (to aid mechanical workers) were established by private benefactions.   It was thus a period of winning fortunes and opening up the resources of the country and of inauguration of the age of machinery."   (C. R. Mann, *ibid.*, p. 38.)

lems incident to the congestion of peoples of mixed character had not as yet arisen, the church and charity and private school solution of the educational problem was reasonably satisfactory. As the cities now increased rapidly in size, became more city-like in character, drew to them diverse elements previously largely unknown, and were required by state laws to extend the right of suffrage to all their citizens, the need for a new type of educational organization began slowly but clearly to manifest itself to an increasing number of citizens. The church, charity, and private school system completely broke down under the new strain. School Societies and Educational Associations, organized for propaganda, now arose in the cities; grants of city or state funds for the partial support of both church and society schools were demanded and obtained; and numbers of charity organizations began to be established in the different cities to enable them to handle better the new problems of pauperism, intemperance, and juvenile delinquency which arose.[1]

In 1833 it was estimated that one eighth of the total population of New York City was composed of public paupers or criminals, while the city had one saloon for every eighty men, women, and children in the total population. Other cities presented somewhat similar conditions. Child labor and woman labor, for long hours and for very low wages, became very common.[2] The powerful restraining influences of the old home, with its strict moral code and religious atmosphere, seriously weakened. Idle and uneducated children, with little or no home control, appeared in numbers on the streets, and the prevalence of juvenile crime and juvenile arrests began to turn attention to education as a possible remedy. The disintegrating effects of the new city and manufacturing life on the family, its

[1] "Thousands of men, women, and children were drained off from the farms and firesides, and to these were added other thousands from Europe. The problems of ignorance concentrated in congested communities, of pauperism, of delinquency and dependency, and of vagrancy and crime now appeared for the first time in American life. Neither science nor the law offered the workers protection from the destitution and disease, vermin and vice, that were certain results from long and unregulated hours of labor, unsanitary and unhygienic conditions in blocks of ugly tenements, the liability of imprisonment for debt, the lack of fit water supply or sewage system or garbage collection, and the scanty opportunities of schooling for their children — all united to crush down this new class of workers." (Knight, E. W. *Education in the United States*, p. 174.)

[2] "As factories developed the Puritanic conception that idleness and iniquity go together, combined with the argument that efficient male workers should be reserved for shipping, agriculture, and the skilled trades, suggested factory labor for children, even to some of the humanitarians. A journal in 1816 [*Niles Register*] made a serious calculation of the added wealth to the United States if all children went to mills and factories." (P. R. V. Curoe. *Educational Attitudes and Policies of Organized Labor*, p. 39.)

demoralizing effect upon the children, and the inability of families to send their children even to the charity schools of the time (**R. 94**) because of the long hours at which they and their children must labor, made a deep impression upon those possessed of humanitarian impulses, as it did also on many of the parents of the children concerned. We soon find these two very dissimilar groups of people — the humanitarians on the one hand and the new city laboring classes on the other — uniting in a propaganda for tax-supported schools.[1]

3. *The extension of the suffrage*

Breaking the rule of a class. As was stated in the preceding chapter, the Constitution of the United States, though framed by the ablest men of the time, was framed by men who represented the old aristocratic conception of education and government.[2] The same was true of the conventions which framed practically all the early state constitutions. The early leaders in our government — Washington, Madison, Hancock, Adams, Hamilton, Jay — had been of this older aristocratic class. The Federalist Party, a party which rendered very conspicuous service in welding the States into a strong and enduring Union, had nevertheless represented this older privileged group, and by 1817 had done its work and been broken up. The early period of our national life was thus characterized by the rule of a class — a very well educated and a very capable class, to be sure — but a class elected by a ballot based on property qualifications and belonging to the older type of political and social thinking.[3]

[1] "Without wishing to interfere with subjects not perfectly within the sphere of its office, this Board would suggest the propriety of adopting such legal restraints as should prevent the employment of children in manufactories until they shall have had an opportunity to obtain the rudiments of an education in the Public Schools, or require the proprietors of all establishments, of the kind alluded to, to furnish moral and scholastic instruction to the children engaged in these departments of industry." (*Annual Report, Controllers, Public Schools of Philadelphia, Fourth Report*, 1822.)

[2] "The Fathers who wrote the Constitution and presented it to the States for adoption strongly believed that landless men, non-taxpayers, and all persons who had no property to be affected by legislation were unfit to participate in the making of laws and their administration. It has been estimated that less than one-fifth of the entire white male population in the thirteen original States enjoyed the right to vote on the adoption of the Federal Constitution." (E. H. Reisner. *The Evolution of the Common School*, p. 273.)

[3] In Virginia, for example, only 45,000 who held property out of 140,000 free, white males, in 1829, were voters. In an argument over the question of broadening the suffrage, in the constitutional convention of that year, a typical remark, typical of other States as well as Virginia, was made by Governor Giles, when he said:

"Extend the right of suffrage to every man, dependent as well as independent, and you immediately open the flood gates of corruption, and undermine the public and private virtue of your people."

This class, too, viewed with alarm attempts to change existing conditions.[1]

Notwithstanding the statements of the Declaration of Independence, the change came but slowly. Up to 1815 but four States had granted the right to vote to all male citizens, regardless of property holdings or other somewhat similar restrictions. After 1815 a democratic movement, which sought to abolish all class rule and all political inequalities, arose and rapidly gained strength. In this the new States to the westward, with their absence of old estates or large fortunes, and where men were judged more on their merits than in an older society, were the leaders. As will be seen from the map, every new State admitted east of the Mississippi River, except Ohio (admitted in 1802), where the New England element predominated, and Louisiana (1812), with its French traditions, provided for full manhood suffrage at the time of their admission to statehood. Five additional Eastern

States shaded granted full suffrage at the time of admission to the Union

FIG. 50. DATES OF THE GRANTING OF FULL MANHOOD SUFFRAGE

Some of the older States granted almost full manhood suffrage at an earlier date, retaining a few minor restrictions until the date given on the map.

States had extended the same full voting privileges to their citizens by 1845, while the old requirements had been materially modified in most of the other Northern States. Writing on the influence of the West, Professor Turner says:

[1] Even such broad-minded men as Daniel Webster in Massachusetts and Chancellor Kent in New York feared the results of universal suffrage, and opposed the movement. Webster held that under universal suffrage the wealth of individuals would be subject to "the rapaciousness of a merciless gang," while Chancellor Kent likened manhood suffrage to a mighty engine which would "destroy property, laws, and liberties."

The frontier States that came into the Union in the first quarter of a century of its existence came in with democratic suffrage provisions, and had reactive effects of the highest importance upon the older States whose people were being attracted there. An extension of the suffrage became essential. It was western New York that forced an extension of the suffrage in the constitutional convention of that State in 1821; and it was western Virginia that compelled the tide-water region to put in a more liberal provision in the constitution of 1830, and to give the frontier region a more nearly proportional representation with the tide-water aristocracy.

Significance of the election of Jackson. The struggle for the overthrow of the old class government came to a head in 1828, when Andrew Jackson was elected President. From Washington down to John Quincy Adams each of the six Presidents had been drawn from the old aristocratic class, all had attended college except Washington, and the educated and propertied classes of Massachusetts, New York, and Virginia had largely furnished the leaders for the Nation. Jackson, on the other hand, represented the frontier, and was everywhere regarded as "a man of the people." His election was a reaction against trained leadership in governmental affairs and was a precursor of a change in the character of education itself (**R. 93**). The period when the people were to follow men of education and good breeding was now for a time largely past. The people had become impatient of the old claims as to the superiority of any class, and the demand for equal suffrage and for full participation in the functions of government now became too insistent to be disregarded longer.

This impatience and distrust expressed itself also with reference to governors and legislatures, and a popular demand for changes here now arose. In place of the former plan of electing a governor and allowing him to appoint most of the other officials, a long list of elected officials now appeared. In the sparsely settled West, in particular, the individualism of the settlers in the little, self-reliant communities had an opportunity for an almost unchecked growth (**R. 126**). All this stimulated ideas of equality and self assurance, and led to a firm belief in the localized administration of all civil affairs. The people consequently demanded and usually obtained the right to vote for every possible officer, and short terms in office became the rule. Legislatures, too, instead of being allowed to meet when and for as long as they pleased, were now closely limited as to length of session, and allowed to meet only at stated times. This democratic movement for the leveling of all distinctions between white men became very marked after 1820, and the final result was full manhood suffrage in all the States. This gave the farmer in the West and the new working classes in the cities a preponderating influence in the affairs of government. Jackson represented both these elements, and was elected by an electoral vote of 178 to 83 over John Quincy Adams, in 1828, and by a vote of 219 to 49 over Henry Clay, in 1832.

Educational significance of the extension of the suffrage. The educational significance of the extension of full manhood suffrage to all was enormous and far reaching. Up to the time of the separation of Church and State, education had not been conceived of as a function with which the State was specially concerned. Since the right to vote was closely limited by religious or property qualifications, or both, there was no particular reason why the State should assume the rôle of schoolmaster. Such citizens as were qualified by faith or property holdings to vote or hold office were amply able to pay for the education of their children privately. It was not necessary, either, for more than a small percentage of the people to be educated. The small educated class conducted the affairs of Church and State; the great majority formed "the hewers of wood and the drawers of water" for society.

With the extension of the suffrage to all classes of the population, poor as well as rich, laborer as well as employer, the whole situation was changed, and there came to thinking men, often for the first time, a realization that general education had become a fundamental necessity for the State, and that the general education of all in the elements of knowledge and civic virtue must now assume that importance in the minds of the leaders of the State that the education of a few for the service of the Church and of the many for simple church membership had once held in the minds of ecclesiastics. The agitation of the States' rights issue, which arose shortly after the close of the War of 1812 and grew in intensity each decade, increased as it was by the new States which came into the Union with frontier ideas as to rights and privileges, called for some real statesmanship to steer the country away from disaster. From about 1820 to about 1845 were years of marked intellectual and social agitation, and those who realized the danger most completely turned to the

general education of the people as a supplement to the political
nationalism which the fathers of the Republic had created.

This new conception is well expressed in the preamble to the first
(optional) school law enacted in Illinois (1825), which declared:

> To enjoy our rights and liberties, we must understand them; their
> security and protection ought to be the first object of a free people; and
> it is a well-established fact that no nation has ever continued long in
> the enjoyment of civil and political freedom, which was not both virtuous
> and enlightened; and believing that the advancement of literature al-
> ways has been, and ever will be the means of developing more fully the
> rights of man, that the mind of every citizen in a republic is the common
> property of society, and constitutes the basis of its strength and happi-
> ness; it is therefore considered the peculiar duty of a free government, like
> ours, to encourage and extend the improvement and cultivation of the
> intellectual energies of the whole.

4. New public demands for schools

Utterances of public men. Governors now began to call the attention of legislatures to the importance of public education, and to
recommend the establishment of tax-supported schools, and public
men began to take a stand for state action and state control.   A few
examples, selected from among many, will be illustrative.   In his
message to the Pennsylvania legislature, in 1813, Governor Simon
Snyder said:

> The preservation of morals and our free institutions, together with the
> true interests of humanity, would be much promoted and their perpetua-
> tion secured by the general diffusion of knowledge amongst all our citizens.
> A solemn injunction contemplating these important objects, by the es-
> tablishment of schools throughout the State, though contained in the
> instrument from which the departments constituting the government
> derive their powers, remains yet to be filled, on the broad plan and liberal
> principles which actuated those who enjoined the duty.   The laws in
> force have done much good; a careful revision of them would probably do
> much more, by extending the benefits of this important branch of re-
> publican polity.

In 1810, and again in 1811, Governor Tompkins of New York
urged action on the legislature, as there had been no state schools
in that State since the expiration of the five-year law in 1800.

> I cannot omit this occasion of inviting your attention to the means of
> instructing the rising generation.   To enable them to perceive and duly
> to estimate their rights, to inculcate correct habits of morality and religion,

and to render them useful citizens, a competent provision for their education is all-essential.

In 1811, the legislature authorized the Governor to appoint a committee to consider the matter and report a bill the following year. This was done, and in the introduction to the committee report they pointed out (**R. 95**) forcefully the fundamental importance of a state system of education in a republic such as ours, where the government is so immediately expressive of the intelligence and virtue of the citizenship.

DeWitt Clinton, for nine years (1817–22; 1824–28) governor of New York, and one of our important early educational leaders,[1] in a message to the legislature, in 1826, defending the schools which had been established as a result of the report of this committee, said:

> The first duty of government, and the surest evidence of good government, is the encouragement of education. A general diffusion of knowledge is a precursor and protector of republican institutions, and in it we must confide as the conservative power that will watch over our liberties and guard them against fraud, intrigue, corruption, and violence. I consider the system of our common schools as the palladium of our freedom, for no reasonable apprehension can be entertained of its subversion as long as the great body of the people are enlightened by education.

Again in his message of 1827, this "obstinate and intelligent friend of education" added:

> The great bulwark of republican government is the cultivation of education; for the right of suffrage cannot be exercised in a salutary manner without intelligence.

In an address delivered before the Pennsylvania legislature, in 1835, defending the Free School Law of 1834, which it was then proposed to repeal, Thaddeus Stevens declared:

> If an elective Republic is to endure for any length of time, every elector must have sufficient information not only to accumulate wealth and

[1] "As a practical reformer, Clinton deservedly ranks with Mann and Barnard in a trinity of educational leadership in American education during the early nineteenth century. He did for New York what Mann did for Massachusetts and Barnard did for Connecticut — and his work, like theirs, was not confined to his own state....

"A similar achievement by almost any other man would have been sufficient to elevate him into the ranks of our foremost educational formers and reformers. But in Clinton's case his achievement in the sphere of education has been overshadowed by his great — though not greater — service in many other spheres." (E. A. Fitzpatrick. *Educational Views and Influence of DeWitt Clinton*, p. 154.)

take care of his pecuniary concerns, but to direct wisely the legislature, the ambassadors, and the Executive of the Nation — for some part of all these things, some agency in approving or disapproving of them, falls to every freeman. If, then, the permanency of our Government depends upon such knowledge, it is the duty of Government to see that the means of information be diffused to every citizen. This is a sufficient answer to those who deem education a private and not a public duty.

In an address before the Western Literary Institute and College of Professional Teachers at Cincinnati, in 1837, a speaker, Mr. Ells, said: [1]

> We boast it as a distinguishing feature of our institutions, that all power lies with the people. This is well, while the people are capacitated to use it intelligently and wisely; otherwise it is but a knife in the hands of a maniac. A republic in which the great mass of the people who hold the sovereign power is given up to ignorance and degradation is the greatest treason against humanity.... Let us then no longer hug the delusion that in a popular government a free constitution and an impartial representation are all that is necessary for the preservation of liberty. I repeat — Virtue and Intelligence are the great pillars on which you must rest the fabric of republican institutions.

Daniel Webster, in an address delivered at Plymouth, Massachusetts, in 1822, and again in an address delivered at Madison, Indiana, in 1837, expressed his conception of the importance of education (**R. 96**) in a nation such as ours. In the Madison address, he said:

> Education, to accomplish the ends of good government, should be universally diffused. Open the doors of the schoolhouses to all the children in the land. Let no man have the excuse of poverty for not educating his offspring. Place the means of education within his reach, and if he remain in ignorance, be it his own reproach.... On the diffusion of education among the people rests the preservation and perpetuation of our free institutions.

In the *Sangamon (Illinois) Journal*, of March 15, 1832, there appeared an interesting communication from a future president of the United States, a part of which read:

> To the People of Sangamo(n) County:
> Fellow Citizens: Having become a candidate for the honorable office of one of your Representatives in the next General Assembly of this State, in accordance with an established custom and the principles of true republicanism, it becomes my duty to make known to you, the people

[1] *Transactions, College of Teachers*, 1837, p. 113.

whom I propose to represent — my sentiments with regard to local affairs....

Upon the subject of education, not presuming to dictate any plan or system respecting it, I can only say that I view it as the most important subject which we as a people can be engaged in. That every man may receive at least a moderate education, and thereby be enabled to read the histories of his own and other countries, by which he may duly appreciate the value of our free institutions, appears to be an object of vital importance, even on this account alone, to say nothing of the advantages and satisfaction to be derived from all being able to read the Scriptures and other works, both of a religious and moral nature, for themselves. For my part, I desire to see the time when education, and by its means, morality, sobriety, enterprise, and industry, shall become much more general than at present, and should be gratified to have it in my power to contribute something to the advancement of any measure which might have a tendency to accelerate the happy period.

A. LINCOLN

Workingmen join in demanding schools. The representatives of the newly organized labor movement [1] joined in the demands for schools and education, urging the free education of their children as a natural right. In 1829 the workingmen of Philadelphia asked each candidate for the legislature for a formal declaration of the attitude he would assume toward the provision of "an equal and a general system of education" for the State. In 1830 the Workingmen's Committee of Philadelphia submitted a detailed report, after five months spent in investigating educational conditions in Pennsylvania, vigorously condemning the lack of provision for education in the State, and the utterly inadequate provision where any was made.[2] Seth Luther, in an address on "The Education of Workingmen," delivered in 1832, declared that "a large body of human beings are ruined by a neglect of education, rendered miserable in the extreme, and incapable of self-government." Stephen Simpson, in

---

[1] Formed to combat the bad conditions under which men and women labored, the labor union developed rapidly in number and power during the years following 1825. By 1836 there were 53 unions in Philadelphia, nearly as many in New York, about 25 in Baltimore, and 16 in Boston, while labor journals, speakers, and agitators began to urge the rights of the "laborin' man an' laborin' woman."

[2] This same year a statement was published in a labor journal of the city describing the bad conditions under which children worked in the factories of Philadelphia. The hands, it stated, were boys and girls, "not one-sixth of whom could read or write." A report, made to a labor convention in Boston two years later, stated that two-fifths of all laborers in the factories there were children, and seldom was one taken from the mills to be put in school. As early as 1816 a congressional committee had estimated that of the 100,000 employed in the cloth industry, nearly one-fourth were boys and approximately 66,000 were women and girls, and that most of these were illiterate.

his *A Manual for Workingmen*, published in 1831, declared that "it is to education, therefore, that we must mainly look for redress of that perverted system of society, which dooms the producer to ignorance, to toil, and to penury, to moral degradation, physical want, and social barbarism."

With the invention of the steam printing-press the first modern newspapers at a cheap price appeared. These usually espoused progressive measures, and tremendously influenced public sentiment. Those not closely connected with church or private-school interests usually favored public tax-supported schools. The *Delaware Free Press*, for example, in 1835, declared a part of its mission to be:

> To awaken the attention of Working People to the importance of coöperation in order to attain the rank and station in society to which they are justly entitled by virtue of their industry, *but from which they are excluded by want of a system of Equal Republican Education.*

In 1837 the Providence (Rhode Island) Association of Mechanics and Manufacturers petitioned the city council (**R. 97**) for an improvement of the schools of the city, in particular asking for more schools, smaller classes, and better salaries for the teachers, and affirming that "no subject can be of more importance to the inhabitants of this city than the education of the rising generation."

At first various substitutes for state support and control were tried. School Societies, as we have seen, were chartered. Religious and benevolent schools were subsidized. Numerous lotteries for the support of schools were authorized by law. Grants of public land for their endowment were made. State support only of pauper schools was tried. Freedom of taxation to schools and educational societies was granted. Finally, all these makeshifts failing to meet the needs of the time,[1] they were gradually discarded as unsatisfactory and insufficient, and the battle for free, tax-supported, nonsectarian, and publicly controlled and directed schools, to serve the needs of society and the State, was begun.

---

[1] A census was taken, in 1829, of all the pupils under instruction in the city of New York, from Columbia College to the smallest Dame or Infant School, from which it appeared that the whole number of pupils being instructed was 24,952. From the results of this census the committee of the Common Council concluded that there were at least 20,000 more, between the ages of 5 and 15, who attended no school whatever — at least 10,000 of whom were growing up in entire ignorance.

The whole number of schools, of every description, was 463. Of this number, 432 were private schools, 3 were incorporated schools, 19 were charity schools, and 11 were public schools. Of the 432 private schools, there were two grades of masters' schools, two of female's schools, male and female minor schools, and some schools for colored children.

QUESTIONS FOR DISCUSSION

1. Explain why the development of a national consciousness was practically necessary before an educational consciousness could be awakened.
2. Show how the many philanthropic societies for the education of the children of the poor came in as a natural transition from church to state education.
3. Show the importance of the School Societies in accustoming people to the idea of free and general education.
4. Show how the Lancastrian system formed the necessary bridge between private philanthropy in education and tax-supported state schools.
5. Why were the highly mechanical features of the Lancastrian organization so advantageous in its day, whereas we of today would regard them as such a disadvantage?
6. Account for the Lancastrian system's great superiority over the methods of colonial schoolmasters.
7. Explain how the Lancastrian schools dignified the work of the teacher by revealing the need for teacher training.
8. What were two of the important contributions of the Infant-School idea to American education?
9. Why are schools and education much more needed in a country experiencing a city and manufacturing development than in a country experiencing an agricultural development?
10. Show how the development of cities caused the old forms of education to break down, and made evident the need for a new type of education.
11. Show how each extension of the suffrage necessitates an extension of educational opportunities and advantages.
12. Show how the utterances of public men on education, quoted in this chapter, evidence a much clearer conception of the need for public education than do those quoted in the preceding chapter, with the possible exception of the quotation from John Adams.

SELECTED READINGS

In the accompanying volume of *Readings* the following selections, related to the subject matter of this chapter, are reproduced:

80. Annals: Meeting in Favor of Sunday Schools.
81. Newspaper Adv.: The Beginnings of Public Education in New York City.
82. Fitzpatrick: Work of the New York Public School Society.
83. Annals: Philadelphia Society for Charity Schools.
84. Newspaper Adv.: Early Lancastrian Schools in Philadelphia.
85. Ellis: Report of a Lancastrian School Visiting Committee.
86. Boston: Report on the New York Lancastrian Schools.
87. Advertisement: A Private Lancastrian School in North Carolina.
88. Advertisement: The Lancastrian Plan in a North Carolina Academy.
89. Committee Report: Difficulties beset the Lancastrian Schools.
90. Russell: Work of the Infant Schools Described.

91. Boston Rept.: Real Purpose of the Infant Schools.
92. Routledge: Economic Status in Ohio in 1830.
93. Russell: The American Change in Social Philosophy.
94. Operatives: Children in the Philadelphia Factories in 1830.
95. New York Com.: The Importance of Education.
96. Webster: Addresses on Education.
97. Providence: A Memorial for Better Schools.

QUESTIONS ON THE READINGS

1. What would you say were the purposes and the outcomes of the Washington meeting (80)?
2. For whom were the schools (81) provided, and what kind of instruction was to be offered?
3. Summarize briefly the work and accomplishments of this Society (82).
4. Describe briefly the work and importance of this Philadelphia Society (83).
5. What are the expectations indicated by this advertisement (84)?
6. What kind of a school did this Visiting Committee (85) find?
7. What expectations does this advertisement (87) set forth?
8. What preparation did this teacher's certificate (88c) call for?
9. What type of a school does this academy (88) seem to have been?
10. Were the difficulties described (89) unusual? Why had these difficulties not been seen before?
11. Characterize the Infant Schools, as described (90), in terms of modern primary training.
12. Were the real purposes (91) different from those of preceding schools? In what respects?
13. Indicate the type of schooling adapted to such (92) economic conditions.
14. Enumerate other social ways in which this changing social philosophy expressed itself (93).
15. Why have we today so different an attitude toward child labor (94) from that of one hundred years ago?
16. Would you say that the statement (95) was accurate for the time, and why?
17. Restate, briefly, the arguments of Webster (96), and compare his reasoning with that of the public men quoted in the text.
18. Were the demands of the Providence Committee (97) reasonable, time considered?

TOPICS FOR INVESTIGATION AND REPORT

1. The Sunday School movement in the Colonies.
2. Work of the New York Public School Society. (Boese, Palmer, Reigart.)
3. Work of the Philadelphia Society for the support of Charity Schools. (Ellis.)
4. Educational services of De Witt Clinton. (Fitzpatrick.)
5. Organization and work of the Lancastrian schools. (Reigart, Manuals.)

6. The workingmen's movement of 1825–40. (Curoe; Carleton; Carmen; Simons.)
7. Messages of early Governors on Education. (Barnard; State Histories.)
8. The Infant Schools of Boston.

SELECTED REFERENCES

*Barnard, Henry, Editor. *The American Journal of Education*. 31 vols. Consult *Analytical Index* to; 128 pp. Published by United States Bureau of Education, Washington, 1892.

Binns, H. B. *A Century of Education, 1808–1908*. 330 pp. London, 1908.

A centenary history of the British and Foreign School Society, which promoted Lancastrian schools. Chapter I contains a sketch of Lancaster.

Boese, Thomas. *Public Education in the City of New York*. 288 pp. New York, 1869.

A history of the development, taken from the official records. An important work, though now out of print, but listed because still found in many libraries.

Bogart, E. L. *The Economic History of the United States*. 522 pp. New York, 1908.

Contains good chapters (X–XII) on the introduction and growth of the factory system.

*Carleton, F. T. *Education and Social Progress*. 320 pp. New York, 1908.

Chapters I and II deal with epochs in American educational progress, and point out the relation between educational advance and industrial progress.

Carmen, H. J. *Social and Economic History of the United States*. Boston, 1829–31.

Covers the period from colonial times to the Civil War.

*Curoe, P. R. V. *Educational Attitudes and Policies of Organized Labor in the United States*. New York, 1926. Teachers College Contributions to Education, No. 201.

*Dodd, W. E. *Expansion and Conflict*. 329 pp. 1915.

Chapter I is good on the significance of the election of Jackson, and Chapter XI gives a very good brief general sketch of American culture between about 1830 and 1860.

Ellis, Chas. C. *Lancastrian Schools in Philadelphia*. 88 pp. University of Pennsylvania Thesis, 1907.

A good study of Lancastrian schools in Philadelphia.

*Fitzpatrick, E. A. *The Educational Views and Influence of De Witt Clinton*. 156 pp. Teachers College Contributions to Education, No. 44. New York, 1911.

A study of educational conditions in New York at the time, Clinton's educational views, and his influence.

Knight, Edgar W. *Public School Education in North Carolina*. 384 pp. Boston, 1916.

An excellent example of a brief history of education in a State. Chapters 6, 7, and 8 are good on the establishment of the permanent school fund, the awakening of educational sentiment, and the beginnings of public education.

*Manuals of the Lancastrian System. ca. 90 pp. Various dates, 1805–50.

Various forms of these are found in libraries. Some are of the British and Foreign School Society, and others of the New York School Society, of various dates. Any one will usually outline the system of instruction employed in the Lancastrian schools.

*McManis, J. T. "The public school society of New York City"; in Educational Review, vol. 29, pp. 303–11. (March, 1905.)

A brief but sympathetic sketch of the work of this Society.

*Monroe, Paul. Cyclopedia of Education. New York, 1911–13.

The following articles are particularly important:
1. "Joseph Lancaster," III, pp. 621–22.
   A brief biography.
2. "Monitorial System," IV, pp. 296–99.
   A brief description of the rise and spread of the idea.
3. "New York City," IV, pp. 451–53.
   Sketches briefly the history of early education in.

*Palmer, A. E. The New York Public School. 440 pp. New York, 1905.

The first sixteen chapters describe the work of the Public School Society in some detail, and contain many important data.

Parker, S. C. "Free Schools and the Lancastrian System"; in Elementary School Teacher, vol. x, pp. 388–400. (April, 1910.)

A good brief statement on their work and influence.

*Reigart, J. F. The Lancastrian System of Instruction in the Schools of New York City. 105 pp. Teachers College Contributions to Education, No. 81, New York, 1916.

An excellent study of the introduction of the system, and the methods of instruction employed in the schools.

*Salmon, David. Joseph Lancaster. 76 pp. London, 1904.

The standard biography of Lancaster.

*Simons, A. M. Social Forces in American History. 325 pp. New York, 1911.

Very simple and well-written chapters on the birth of the factory system (XIII), changing interests of the people (XIV), condition of the workers (XVI), and the first labor movement (XVII).

CHAPTER VI

THE BATTLE FOR FREE STATE SCHOOLS

I. ALIGNMENT OF INTERESTS, AND PROPAGANDA

Stages in the development of a public school sentiment. Speaking broadly and of the Nation as a whole, and always excepting certain regions in New England where the free-school idea had become thoroughly established, a study of the history of educational development in the older States to the North and East reveals, as we have so far partially pointed out, approximately the following stages in the development of a public school sentiment and the establishment of a state school system:

1. An attempt to solve the problem through private benevolence or church charity, often aided by small grants of public funds.
2. Aid granted to private or semi-private schools or school societies, in the form of small money grants, license taxes, permission to organize lotteries, or land endowments, to enable such schools or societies to extend their instruction or to reduce their tuition rates, or both.
3. Permission granted generally, or to special districts requesting it, to form a tax district and organize schools — at first often only for pauper children, but later for others.
4. Laws requiring the education of the indigent poor.
5. Laws requiring a certain local effort for the maintenance of schools, in return for state aid received, with permission to supplement these sums with tuition fees.
6. Elimination of the tuition fees, thus establishing free schools.
7. Elimination of the pauper-school idea and aid to sectarian schools, thus establishing the American common school.

Something like half a century of agitation and conflict, again speaking broadly and of the Nation as a whole, was required to produce the succession of changes indicated above, but by 1850 it may be said that the question of providing a common-school education for all children at public expense had been settled, in principle at least, in every Northern State. In some of the Southern States, as well, quite a respectable beginning [1] looking toward the creation

---

[1] Notably North Carolina, which created a school fund in 1825, and an elementary school system, with local and county taxation, in 1839. In 1852 the office of State Superintendent of Common Schools was created.

of state school systems had been made before the coming of the Civil War for a time put an end to all educational development there.

The alignment of interests. The second quarter of the nineteenth century may be said to have witnessed the battle for tax-supported, publicly controlled and directed, and non-sectarian common schools. In 1825 such schools were the distant hope of statesmen and reformers; in 1850 they were becoming an actuality in almost every Northern State. The twenty-five years intervening marked a period of public agitation and educational propaganda; of many hard legislative fights; of a struggle to secure desired legislation, and then to hold what had been secured; of many bitter contests with church and private-school interests, which felt that their "vested rights" were being taken from them; and of occasional referenda in which the people were asked, at the next election, to advise the legislature as to what to do. Excepting the battle for the abolition of slavery, perhaps no question has ever been before the American people for settlement which caused so much feeling or aroused such bitter antagonisms. Old friends and business associates parted company over the question, lodges were forced to taboo the subject to avoid disruption, ministers and their congregations often quarreled over the question of free schools, and politicians avoided the issue. The friends of free schools were at first commonly regarded as fanatics, dangerous to the State, and the opponents of free schools were considered by them as old-time conservatives or as selfish members of society.

Naturally such a bitter discussion of a public question forced an alignment of the people for or against publicly supported and controlled schools, and this alignment of interests may be roughly stated to have been about as follows:

I. For public schools.
    Men considered as:
        1. "Citizens of the Republic."
        2. Philanthropists and humanitarians.
        3. Public men of large vision.
        4. City residents.
        5. The intelligent workingmen in the cities.
        6. Non-taxpayers.
        7. Calvinists.
        8. "New-England men."

II. Lukewarm, or against public schools.

Men considered as:

1. Belonging to the old aristocratic class.
2. The conservatives of society.
3. Politicians of small vision.
4. Residents of rural districts.
5. The ignorant, narrow-minded, and penurious.
6. Taxpayers.
7. Lutherans, Reformed-Church, Mennonites, and Quakers.
8. Southern men.
9. Proprietors of private schools.
10. The non-English-speaking classes.

It was, of course, not possible to so classify all persons, as a man might belong to two or more of the above classes. An example of such would be a Lutheran and a non-taxpaying workingman in a city, or a Calvinist and a heavy taxpayer. In all such cases there would be a conflict of interests with the stronger one prevailing, but, in a general way, the above classification of the alignment of interests is approximately correct.

Arguments for and against free schools. Both sides to the controversy advanced many arguments for and against state tax-supported schools, the more important on each side being the following:

I. Arguments for public tax-supported schools.

1. That education tends to prevent pauperism and crime.
2. That education tends to reduce poverty and distress.
3. That education increases production, and eliminates wrong ideas as to the distribution of wealth.
4. That a common state school, equally open to all, would prevent that class differentiation so dangerous in a Republic.
5. That the old church and private school education had proved utterly inadequate to meet the needs of a changed society.
6. That a system of religious schools is impossible in such a mixed nation as our own.
7. That the pauper-school idea is against the best interests of society, inimical to public welfare, and a constant offense to the poor, many of whom will not send their children because of the stigma attached to such schools.
8. That education as to one's civic duties is a necessity for the intelligent exercise of suffrage, and for the preservation of republican institutions.
9. That the increase of foreign immigration (which became quite noticeable after 1825, and attained large proportions after 1845) is a menace to our free institutions, and that these new elements

can be best assimilated in a system of publicly supported and publicly directed common schools.

10. That the free and general education of all children at public expense is the natural right of all children in a Republic.

11. That the social, moral, political, and industrial benefits to be derived from the general education of all compensate many times over for its cost.

12. That a general diffusion of education among the people would contribute to the increased permanency of our institutions, and to the superior protection of liberty, person, and property.

13. That a State which has the right to hang has the right to educate.

14. That the taking over of education by the State is not based on considerations of economy, but is the exercise of the State's inherent right to self-preservation and improvement.

15. That only a system of state-controlled schools can be free to teach whatever the welfare of the State may demand.

II. *Arguments against public tax-supported schools.*

1. Impractical, visionary, and "too advanced" legislation.

2. Will make education too common, and will educate people out of their proper position in society.

3. Would not benefit the masses, who are already as well cared for as they deserve.

4. Would tend to break down long-established and very desirable social barriers.

5. Would injure private and parochial schools, in which much money had been put and "vested rights" established.

6. Fear of the churches that state schools might injure their church progress and welfare.

7. Fear of the non-English speaking classes that state schools might supplant instruction in their languages.

8. The "conscientious objector" claimed that the State had no right to interfere between a parent and his child in the matter of education.

9. That those having no children to be educated should not be taxed for schools.

10. That taking a man's property to educate his neighbor's child is no more defensible than taking a man's plow to plow his neighbor's field.

11. That the State may be justified in taxing to defend the liberties of a people, but not to support their benevolences.

12. That the industrious would be taxed to educate the indolent.

13. That taxes would be so increased that no State could long meet such a lavish drain on its resources.

14. That there was priestcraft in the scheme, the purpose being first to establish a State School, and then a State Church.

15. That education is something for a leisure class, and that the poor have no leisure.

The work of propaganda. To meet the arguments of the objectors, to change the opinions of a thinking few into the common opinion of the many, to overcome prejudice, and to awaken the public conscience to the public need for free and common schools in such a democratic society as ours, was the work of a generation. With many of the older citizens no progress could be made; the effective work everywhere had to be done with the younger men of the time. It was the work of many years to convince the masses of the people that the scheme of state schools was not only practicable, but also the best and most economical means for giving their children the benefits of an education; to convince propertied citizens that taxation for education was in the interests of both public and private welfare; to convince legislators that it was safe to vote for free-school bills; and to overcome the opposition due to apathy, religious jealousies, and private interests. In time, though, the desirability of common, free, tax-supported, non-sectarian, state-controlled schools became evident to a majority of the citizens in the different American States, and as it did the American State School, free and equally open to all, was finally evolved and took its place as the most important institution in our national life working for the perpetuation of our free democracy and the advancement of the public welfare.

For this work of propaganda hundreds of School Societies, Lyceums, and Educational Associations were organized; many conventions were held, and resolutions favoring state schools were adopted; many "Letters" and "Addresses to the Public" were written and published; public-spirited citizens traveled over the country, making addresses to the people explaining the advantages of free state schools; many public-spirited men gave the best years of their lives to the state-school propaganda; and many governors sent communications on the subject to legislatures not yet convinced as to the desirability of state action. At each meeting of the legislatures for years a deluge of resolutions, memorials, and petitions for and against free schools met the members (**R. 98**).

Propaganda societies. The decades of the thirties and the forties witnessed the formation of a large number of these associations, organized to build up a sentiment for public education. They were founded not only in the older States of the East, but also in such widely scattered States as Georgia, Florida, and Tennessee.

One of the earliest of these propaganda societies for state schools was the "Pennsylvania Society for the Promotion of Public Economy," organized in 1817. Ten years later a branch of this Society became the "Pennsylvania Society for the Promotion of Public Schools" throughout the State of Pennsylvania. This Society organized branches throughout the State, corresponded with the leaders of opinion, utilized the newspapers of the time to inform the public, repeatedly memorialized the legislature, and for many years kept up a vigorous campaign for a state free-school law (**R. 99**).

Another early organization that rendered important work was the American Lyceum, originated by Josiah Holbrook,[1] in 1826, "to establish on a uniform plan, in every town and village, a society for mutual improvement and the improvement of schools." Local, county, and state lyceums developed rapidly in many States, and in 1831 a National Lyceum was organized and a constitution adopted (**R. 100**) which declared the purpose of the national organization to be "the advancement of education,[2] especially common schools, and the general diffusion of knowledge." Teachers as well as citizens were invited to join the Lyceums. Lecture courses for adults, the establishment of libraries, and the equipment of schools with scientific apparatus were means used supplemental to the general work of propaganda for taxation for education and trained teachers for the schools. Meetings were held annually in New York, Hartford, and Philadelphia until 1839, when the national movement seems to have come to an end, though many of the State Lyceums continued until 1845 or after. Gradually, however, their activities became more and more limited to the maintenance of a good yearly lecture course.[3]

---

[1] Holbrook (1788–1854) was a graduate of Yale (1810) who had organized one of the earliest industrial schools, at Derby, Connecticut, in 1819, after the model of Fellenberg's institution in Switzerland. For years he devoted his entire time to the Lyceum movement, which aimed to establish libraries, provide lecture courses, and aid schools in obtaining scientific appliances, in addition to its work of propaganda.

[2] The *American Journal of Education* (vol. 16, p. 312; 1842) gives a list of the titles of papers and addresses at the various meetings of the National Lyceum. These include such topics as the condition and improvement of schools, studies, books, apparatus, the schoolhouse, methods of instruction and discipline, and the whole field of educational legislation. An excellent history of the movement is to be found in Cecil B. Hayes's *The American Lyceum; Its History and Contribution to Education*. Bulletin 12, 1932, of the United States Office of Education.

[3] The more modern Chautauqua movement, first organized in 1874, and which by 1910 had spread over most of the United States, may be regarded as a more recent development of the adult education and the lecture course phases of the original Lyceum. The Chautauqua

Another early society of importance was the "Hartford Society for the Improvement of Common Schools," founded in 1827. Another was the Boston "Society for the Diffusion of Useful Knowledge," organized in 1829, with the promotion of public education as one of its objects.

The Western Academic Institute. In 1829 the "Western Academic Institute and Board of Education" was formed at Cincinnati by Albert Pickett, with such men as Samuel Lewis, Lyman Beecher, and Calvin E. Stowe being prominent in its organization. For more than a decade this association and its successor, the "Western Literary Institute and College of Professional Teachers" (1832) made Cincinnati the center of educational propaganda in the then West. By 1835 state auxiliary organizations had been formed in eight States, and by 1840 in nine additional States and two Territories (Iowa and Wisconsin). Its field of work was the central Mississippi Valley and the Southern States. Each of these auxiliaries was in turn to call educational conventions and form county associations in their respective States. It raised money, employed an agent to visit the schools of the State, published its proceedings in good form, diffused information as to education, tried to elevate the character of the teachers of the State, and repeatedly sent delegations to the legislature to ask for action. In addition it sent out lecturers to arouse the public, through its state auxiliaries it memorialized legislatures in behalf of schools (**R. 101**), and enlisted the support of the newspapers for its work. For two years (1837–38) Pickett edited the *Western Academician and Journal of Education and Science*, which was published at Cincinnati as part of the propaganda work. It sent Professor Stowe to Europe to investigate education there, and on his return induced the legislature (1837) to print 10,000 copies of his *Report on Elementary Education in Europe* for distribution. This *Report* was also reprinted afterward by the legislatures of Pennsylvania, Michigan, Massachusetts, North Carolina, and Virginia. In 1836 it called a state convention in Ohio of the "Friends of Education," in 1837 induced the legislature to create the office of Superintendent of Common Schools, and in 1838 the culmination of its efforts came in what has been frequently

movement has in turn been displaced, since the World War, by other forms of adult educational activity, chiefly the adult education movement in the public school and the university extension movement in the university.

called "the great school law of Ohio." Its annual conventions were attended by men of prominence from all the then West and South, who came to obtain light on their problems and the inspiration

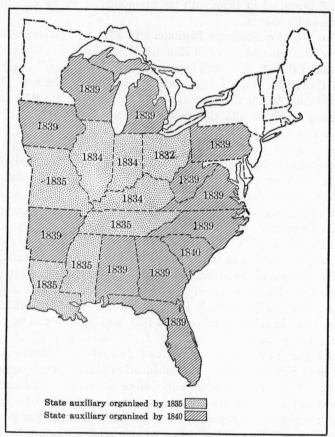

FIG. 51. ORGANIZING WORK OF THE WESTERN LITERARY INSTITUTE AND COLLEGE OF PROFESSIONAL TEACHERS

First organized at Cincinnati in 1829 as a local institute. Reorganized in 1832 for general propaganda, with auxiliary state branches, as shown on the map.

necessary to meet them. It has been said of this institution that it was "the commencement of a new era in education in the West." Its great work was done between 1832 and 1840.

In 1830 the "American Institute of Instruction" was organized at Boston,[1] and in 1838 this Association offered a prize of $500 for the best essay on "A System of Education best adapted to the Common Schools of our Country." A number of societies for propaganda were organized in New York State between 1830 and 1840. In New Jersey the "Society of Teachers and Friends of Education" held conventions, drew up memorials and petitions, and its members visited all parts of the State advocating general education at public expense, and especially the elimination of pauper-school education.

Much valuable work was done by associations of teachers in Pennsylvania, between 1838 and 1852. In 1831 the North Carolina Institute of Education was organized to promote the education of the people of that State, and the Florida Education Society was formed "to endeavor to procure the establishment of such a general system of instruction as is suited to the wants and conditions of the Territory."

Educational conventions. In 1838 a convention of the "Friends of Education" was held at Trenton, and a committee was appointed to prepare an "Address" to the people of the State. The result was a new school law which instituted a partial state school system, and secured an increase in the state appropriation for schools from $20,000 to $30,000 yearly. In 1839 a national convention was held in Philadelphia to discuss the needs of education in the United States. In 1841 an educational convention was held at Clarksburg (now in West Virginia), which was attended by over 100 delegates, and which urged state action for schools. Shortly afterward another convention was held at Lexington, Virginia. This latter prepared a report for the legislature on the defects and needs of Virginia's schools.[2] Still later in 1841 a state-wide assembly of elected delegates met in Richmond. The most distinguished and representative men of eastern Virginia were members of the convention. Their memorial to the legislature embraced all types of schools, with special emphasis on primary instruction. After

[1] Holbrook was one of the organizers of this Institute also. Annual meetings of this organization have been held since 1830. Its membership has been confined chiefly, but not wholly, to New England.

[2] This report, known as the Ruffner Plan for District Schools, and which bears a strong resemblance to what was finally created in 1870, recommended a district free school, supported by state and local funds, a state board of education, a state superintendent of schools, appointed county school superintendents, a normal school to train teachers, and school libraries. This plan was given wide publicity, and many organizations adopted resolutions approving it and urging legislative action.

stating why the charity system had failed to provide primary education,[1] the report recommended a general system of primary schools at public charge, county taxation for schools, competent teachers, and vigilant and constant school supervision. In 1845 another convention, meeting in Richmond, adopted a somewhat similiar memorial.

In 1847 an educational convention meeting at Knoxville, Tennessee, prepared a memorial to the legislature of that State on the need for schools.[2] This same year a called convention in Indiana, meeting in Indianapolis, similarly adopted a memorial to the legislative. In 1850 an important education convention was held in Harrisburg, the proceedings of which were printed and widely circulated. In 1858, sixty Georgia counties sent delegates to an educational convention held at Marietta, which adopted a memorial to the legislature much after the plan of those adopted in Virginia and Tennessee.

In 1834 over half the counties of Illinois sent delegates to an "Illinois Educational Convention" at Vandalia, which appointed a committee of seven to draft a memorial to the legislature and outline a plan for common schools and an "Address" to the people of the State.[3] In 1844 a convention of "Friends of Education," held at Peoria, demanded of the legislature the appointment of a State Superintendent of Schools and the levying of a state school tax. In 1845 the Democratic Convention of Wilkinson County, Kentucky, adopted elaborate resolutions in favor of the establishment of free public schools, and instructed its delegates to the state convention to press the matter. In 1841 three educational conventions were held in Virginia, and another in 1848, all of which urged the establishment of a state system of common schools. In 1847 a number of "State Common School Conventions" were held in

---

[1] "Education is represented as a gratuity, and men are not accustomed much to value what is cheap.... As only the poor and ignorant are interested in the schools that take the indigent children, they must be badly conducted... This imperfect system has failed also for want of systematic superintendence, and careful selection of teachers by competent persons." ("To the People of Virginia," in *Richmond Enquirer*, November 22, 1842.)

[2] The Tennessee report asked for state support, state supervision, the examination and certification of teachers, and the publication of a monthly school journal.

[3] The meeting was held December 5, 1834. Judges, members of the legislature, and others interested were invited to come, and 61 delegates from 31 counties took their seats. An *Address* to the people of Illinois, expressive of the sense of the Convention, was prepared by a committee appointed for the purpose, approved by the delegates, and 5000 copies of it ordered printed and distributed throughout the State.

Indiana to build up sentiment for taxation for schools. These are but examples of the work of the numerous propaganda societies formed, and conventions held, in increasing numbers between 1825 and 1850.

Support from associations of workingmen. Workingmen, too, through their newly formed organizations, also took for a time a prominent part in the propaganda for the establishment of public tax-supported schools. Their work, however, was confined to a few States, was most prominent between 1828 and 1832 during the period of workingmen's political parties,[1] and had practically ceased before 1840. Among the many resolutions adopted by these wage-earners, during the early period of their political activity, the following are typical:

At a General Meeting of Mechanics and Workingmen held in New York City, in 1829, it was:

> *Resolved*, that next to life and liberty, we consider education the greatest blessing bestowed upon mankind.
>
> *Resolved*, that the public funds should be appropriated (to a reasonable extent) to the purpose of education upon a regular system that shall insure the opportunity to every individual of obtaining a competent education before he shall have arrived at the age of maturity.

Again, in 1830, this same New York body adopted a resolution (**R. 102**) for "a general system of instruction, at the expense of the State."

At a meeting of workingmen held in Philadelphia, in 1829, it was declared that:

> No system of education, which a freeman can accept, has yet been established for the poor; whilst thousands of dollars of the public money has been appropriated for building colleges and academies for the rich.

Each candidate for the state legislature was formally asked to declare his attitude toward "an equal and general system of Education."

---

[1] "In the first period (1828–1840) they educated their own membership to the value of education, thus counteracting the inertia or avarice of laboring parents, and changing apathy towards education into active interest. They worked with other groups towards stirring up an interest in educational reform among the complacent members of legislatures and among the general public. They helped to 'sell' the idea that a voting citizen cannot discharge his obligations without a modicum of education and some leisure for self-improvement.

"In the two decades following the points of contact between our educational development and organized labor were neither many nor important." (P. R. V. Curoe. *Educational Attitudes and Policies of Organized Labor in the United States*, p. 190.)

In 1830 they adopted a long *Report* on the conditions of education in Pennsylvania, demanded schools, and declared that there could be "no real liberty in a republic without a wide diffusion of real intelligence." (**R. 103**).

In 1830 the Workingmen's Party of Philadelphia included, as the first plank in its platform:

> *Resolved*, that the time has arrived when it becomes the paramount duty of every friend to the happiness and freedom of man to promote a system of education that shall embrace equally all the children of the state, of every rank and condition.

In 1830 an Association of Workingmen was formed at New Castle, Delaware, and in their constitution they provided:

> Let us unite at the polls and give our votes to no candidate who is not pledged to support a rational system of education to be paid for out of the public funds.

At a Boston meeting of "Workingmen, Mechanics, and others friendly to their interests," in 1830, it was:

> *Resolved*, that the establishment of a liberal system of education, attainable by all, should be among the first efforts of every lawgiver who desires the continuance of our national independence.

In 1830 the "Farmers,' Mechanics,' and Workingmen's" Party of New York State, in convention at Salina, included as one of the planks in its platform the following:

> *Resolved*, that a scheme of education, more universal in its effects, is practicable, so that no child in the republick, however poor, should grow up without an opportunity to acquire at least a competent English education; and that the system should be adapted to the conditions of the poor both in the city and country.

In 1835 the workingmen of the city of Washington enumerated as as one of their demands the establishment of "a universal system of education," and in 1836 the "General Trades Union" of Cincinnati, in an "Appeal to the Workingmen of the West," urged that they try to elevate their condition by directing their efforts toward obtaining "a national system of education."

Recommendations of governors. A number of the early governors were public men of large vision, who saw the desirability of the State establishing a general system of education years before either the legislature or the people had clearly sensed the need (**R. 104**). In

Kentucky, for example, Governor Slaughter, in 1816, 1817, 1818, and 1819, called attention to the need for schools. In 1821 the legislature appointed a commission to study the need, but in 1822 refused to accept the recommendations made, as the people were judged not yet ready for taxation. In Delaware, almost every year from 1822 to 1829 succeeding governors urged the legislature to establish a genuine state system of education, as provided for in the state constitution. The people, however, were unwilling to tax themselves for schools, and only the city of Wilmington made any real headway in providing them. In Pennsylvania, in 1813 (page 154), and again in 1821 and 1825, the governor made a strong plea for a system of education, and in 1828, 1831, and 1833 (**R. 118**), the legislature was further urged to establish a public school system, but the first free school law dates from 1834. The messages of the New York governors from 1800 on, and especially those of DeWitt Clinton (governor, 1817–22, 1824–28), form famous documents in favor of free tax-supported schools. The messages of Governor Lewis in 1804, and Governor Tompkins in 1809 and 1811, especially urged that something be done for "the instruction of the rising generation." In 1829, 1831, 1835, and 1836, other New York governors urged the State's duty, and held that the establishment of a good system of public instruction was an evidence of good government. In Connecticut (1825, 1828), Massachusetts (1826, 1837), and Maine (1831) governors recommended an improvement in the schools, and a dependence upon a wide diffusion of education for the happiness and security of the State. In Ohio, Indiana, and Illinois governors repeatedly urged attention to the subject of public education. In South Carolina Governor Hamilton recommended action (1831) and Governor Patrick Noble (1838) asked the legislature to appoint a legislative commission to study the needs of the State in the matter of schools. In 1835 Governor McDuffie rebuked the legislature for its continued neglect of primary schools "in which a great part of the community obtain all the instruction they ever receive at schools," outlined a plan for the organization of school districts, and recommended action. The messages of Governor Campbell of Virginia, from 1837 to 1839, constantly urged better educational conditions and laws, and in 1843 Governor McDowell recommended the substitution of a better system for the indigent school system which had for so long been in use in the State.[1]   Still later in 1856 and 1857, Governor Wise was a militant advocate of tax-supported common schools.   In an open letter to his people he had said:

> Educate your children — every one of them — in common schools at state expense... Distrust all men who make false promises of freedom from taxation, but tax yourself and learn to believe in it as the *only* means of getting what you need... There is no royal road to paying debts or to education.   Industry, honesty, economy, and education alone can make you a free and happy people.   Educate your children — every one of them!   Don't wait for a tardy legislature, but organize yourself and make money by a voluntary system.

In 1853 Governor Andrew Johnson of Tennessee, in a message to the legislature, declared that the existing schools did not meet the demands of the constitution, and urged that the subject of education be dealt with in a strong and earnest manner.   In 1858 Governor Joseph Brown of Georgia urged the legislature to establish an adequate school system for the State.

After 1825, and especially through the decade of the thirties, governors generally began to give emphasis to education in their messages.   In the new Western States the messages often were clear and emphatic, and the arguments for education strong.   While usually at the time not influencing a legislature to action, these messages were influential in effecting a change in the attitude of the people toward the question of tax-supported schools.

II. PHASES OF THE BATTLE FOR STATE-SUPPORTED SCHOOLS

The problem which confronted those interested in establishing state-controlled schools was not exactly the same in any two States, though the battle in many States possessed common elements, and hence was somewhat similar in character.   Instead of tracing the struggle in detail in each of the different States, it will be much more profitable for our purposes to pick out the main strategic points in the contest, and then illustrate the conflict for these by describing conditions in one or two States where the controversy was most severe or most typical.   The seven strategic points in the

[1] "If sixty days' tuition to one half of the indigent children of the state," he says, "is the grand result which our present system is able to accomplish after so many years of persevering effort to enlarge and perfect its capacity, it is little more than a costly and delusive *nullity* which ought to be abolished and another and a better one established in its place."

struggle for free, tax-supported, non-sectarian, state-controlled schools were:

1. The battle for tax support.
2. The battle to eliminate the pauper-school idea.
3. The battle to make the schools entirely free.
4. The battle to establish state supervision.
5. The battle to eliminate sectarianism.
6. The battle to extend the system upward.
7. Addition of the state university to crown the system.

In this and the two following chapters we shall consider each of these, in order.

1. *The battle for tax support*

Early support and endowment funds. In New England, land endowments, local taxes, direct local appropriations, license taxes, and rate bills (that is, a per-capita tax levied on the parents of the children attending school) had long been common. Land endowments began early in the New England Colonies, while rate bills date back to the earliest times and long remained a favorite means of raising money for school support. These means were adopted in the different States after the beginning of our national period, and to them were added a variety of license taxes, while occupational taxes, lotteries, an insurance premium tax, and bank taxes also were employed to raise money for schools. A few examples of these may be cited:

Connecticut, in 1774, turned over all proceeds of liquor licenses to the towns where collected, to be used for schools. New Orleans, in 1826, licensed two theaters on condition that they each pay $3000 annually for the support of schools in the city. New York, in 1799, authorized four state lotteries to raise $100,000 for schools, a similar amount again in 1801, and numerous other lotteries before 1810. Kentucky, between 1805 and 1808, authorized its thirty academies to raise $1000, each, by lotteries. Delaware authorized a number of lotteries, between 1810 and 1835, to aid academies and Newark College,[1] as did North Carolina (**R. 105**) after 1814, and

---

[1] "The State of Delaware, with strange inconsistency, gave license to its citizens to gamble in a lottery, to a large amount, in order to secure a moderate endowment to Newark College; or, in other words, permitted a great number of its people to be led to wastefulness, in order to secure the benefits of education to a few. The Trustees hesitated concerning the acceptance of this ill-gotten gain, and in passing the vote, we are happy to see, that

Mississippi after 1817. Michigan authorized four lotteries for its new university in the Act of 1817, and Louisiana conducted two lotteries in 1820 for the support of schools. Maryland authorized five lotteries, to raise $50,000 a year for five years for schools, between 1816 and 1821. Individual cities often set up their own lotteries (**R. 106**) without any special authorization. Congress passed joint resolutions, between 1812 and 1836, authorizing fourteen lotteries to help provide schools and public buildings for the city of Washington.[1] For years the funds of the New York Public School Society were augmented by the license of dealers in lottery tickets. Bank taxes were a favorite source of income for schools, between about 1825 and 1860, banks being chartered on condition that they would pay over each year for schools a certain sum or percentage of their earnings. These all represent what is known as indirect taxation, and were valuable in accustoming the people to the idea of public schools without appearing to tax them for their support.

The National Land Grants, begun in the case of Ohio in 1802 (p. 92), soon stimulated a new interest in schools. Each State admitted after Ohio also received the sixteenth section for the support of common schools (see Fig. 32, page 93), and two townships of land for the endowment of a state university. The new Western States, following the lead of Ohio (p. 93), dedicated these section lands and funds to free common schools. The sixteen older States, however, did not share in these grants, so most of them now set about building up a permanent school fund of their own, though at first without any very clear idea as to how the income from the fund was to be used. Connecticut and New York[2] both had set aside lands, before 1800, to create such a fund, Connecticut's

several of the leading men protested and withdrew. If their opposition should prove fruitless, we have no doubt that an appeal to public benevolence, on behalf of an institution founded on endowments *honestly obtained*, would be promptly met." (*American Annals of Education*, August, 1835.)

[1] The early labor groups fought the lottery as "the most pernicious of all modes of taxation." Seth Luther, an early labor leader, said:

"The poor are generally the persons who support this legalized gambling; for the rich seldom buy lottery tickets. This fund, then, said to be raised by the rich, for the education of the poor, is actually drawn from the pockets of the *poor*, to be expended by the rich, on *their own children*." (*Address to Workingmen*, 1832, p. 22.)

[2] A New York act of 1782 had provided that: "always in every such township there shall be laid out one lott containing four hundred acres for the support of the gospel, and two other lotts containing each two hundred acres for the use of schools...."

fund dating back to 1750. Delaware, in 1796, devoted the income from marriage and tavern licenses to the same purpose, but made no use of the fund for twenty years. Connecticut, in 1795, sold its "Western Reserve" of 3,800,000 acres in northeastern Ohio for $1,200,000, and added this to its school fund (**R. 107**). New York, in 1805, similarly added the proceeds of the sale of half a million acres of state lands, though the fund then formally created accumulated unused until 1812. Tennessee began to build up a permanent state school fund in 1806; Virginia in 1810; South Carolina in 1811; Maryland in 1812; New Jersey in 1816; Georgia in 1817; Maine, New Hampshire, Kentucky, and Louisiana in 1821; Vermont and North Carolina in 1825; Rhode Island in 1828; Pennsylvania in 1831; and Massachusetts in 1834. These were established as permanent state funds, the annual income only to be used, in some way to be determined later, for the support of some form of schools.[1] Some of these funds, as has just been stated, accumulated for years before any use was made of the income (New York for twelve; Delaware for twenty; New Jersey for thirteen), while the income in other of the States was for a time used exclusively for the support of pauper schools. New Jersey, Pennsylvania, Delaware, Maryland, Virginia, and Georgia all for a time belonged to this latter class. These permanent funds also represented a form of indirect taxation, and formed important accumulations of capital, the income of which later went for school support and to that extent relieved taxation.

The beginnings of school taxation. The early idea, which seems for a time to have been generally entertained, that the income from land grants, license fees, and these permanent endowment funds would in time entirely support the necessary schools, was gradually abandoned as it was seen how little in yearly income these funds and lands really produced, and how rapidly the population of the States was increasing. There was also some expectation, for a time, that the surplus revenues of the States and the

[1] The development of the New Jersey fund is typical. In 1816 the first legislation for schools was enacted, in the form of a bill creating a state school fund, and appropriating $15,000 annually to it. The money was to be invested in United States six per cent bonds, and the interest was to be added to the principal until otherwise provided. In 1824 a change was made in that one tenth of the income from state taxes was substituted for the fixed appropriation, but in 1831 this was changed back to a yearly appropriation of $30,000. In 1829 the income from insurance and corporation taxes was added.

National Government [1] might be sufficient in time to maintain a system of free schools (**R. 108**), but after 1837 this idea too was abandoned. By 1825 it may be said to have been clearly recognized by thinking men that the only safe reliance of a system of state schools lay in the general and direct taxation of all property for their support. "The wealth of the State must educate the children of the State" became a watchword (**R. 109**), and the battle for direct, local, county, and state taxation for education was clearly on by 1825 to 1830 in all the Northern States. Now for the first time direct taxation for schools was likely to be felt by the taxpayer, and the fight for and against the imposition of such taxation was on in earnest.

The course of the struggle and the results were somewhat different in the different States, but, in a general way, the progress of the conflict was somewhat as follows:

1. Permission granted to communities so desiring to organize a school taxing district, and to tax for school support the property of those consenting and residing therein.
2. Taxation of all property in the taxing district permitted.
3. State aid to such districts, at first from the income from permanent endowment funds, and later from the proceeds of a small state appropriation or a state or county tax.
4. Compulsory local taxation to supplement the state or county grant.

Types of early permissive legislation. In the older States, always excepting the five Calvinistic New England States, the beginnings of this permissive legislation were usually obtained by the cities. With their pressing new social problems they could not afford to wait for the rural sections of their States. Accordingly they sought and obtained permissive city school-tax legislation, and proceeded to organize their schools independently, incorporating them later into the general state organization. Thus Providence began schools in 1800, and Newport in 1825, whereas the first Rhode

---

[1] Great expectations were for a time held as to the extinction of the national debt and such a surplus in the national treasury, from the income from the protective tariff, that there would be plenty of money to distribute among the States. In 1831 the legislature of Pennsylvania passed a resolution asking for such a distribution. In 1835 Clay's bill for a distribution passed Congress, but was vetoed by President Jackson. Finally, in 1836, a distribution, then termed a "Deposit," was ordered, and in all $28,171,453.86 was apportioned among the then twenty-six States. The panic of 1837 left the treasury empty, and put an end to further talk as to the distribution of surplus monies. Of the sum distributed, all but about one fourth of it was squandered or lost by the States, and over one half of what was saved is in the State of New York.

Island general law was not enacted until 1828; the "Free School Society" of New York City was chartered by the legislature in 1805, and the first permanent state school law dates from 1812; Philadelphia was permitted to organize schools by special legislation in 1812 and 1818, Harrisburg and Pittsburgh in 1821, and Lancaster in 1822, while the first general school law for Pennsylvania dates from 1834; Baltimore secured a special law in 1825, a year ahead of the first Maryland general but optional school legislation; Charleston was permitted to organize schools in 1811, and to make them free in 1856, whereas no general school system was established in South Carolina until after the Civil War; and Mobile was given special permission to organize schools in 1826, though the first general state school law in Alabama dates from 1854.

As other examples typical of early permissive state legislation may be mentioned the Maryland law of 1816, giving permission to the voters of Caroline County to decide whether they would support a school by subscription or taxation; the Maryland optional county law of 1826, practically a dead letter outside of Baltimore; the New Jersey law of 1820, which permitted any county in the State to levy a county tax for the education of the children of the poor; the Missouri law of 1824, which permitted a district tax for schools, on written demand of two thirds of the voters of the district, to maintain a school the length of time each year the majority of the parents should decide; the Illinois optional tax law of 1825, nullified in 1827 by providing that the voters might decide to raise only half the cost of the school by taxation, and that no man could be taxed for schools unless he filed his consent in writing; the Rhode Island law of 1828, giving the towns permission to levy a tax for schools, if they saw fit; the optional district tax laws of 1830 in Kentucky, 1834 in Pennsylvania, and 1840 in Iowa; the Mississippi optional tax law of 1846, which permitted a district tax only after a majority of the heads of families in the district had filed their consent in writing; and the Indiana optional county tax law of 1848. Many of these early laws proved to be dead letters, except in the few cities of the time and in a few very progressive communities, partly because it was made too difficult to initiate and too easy to prevent action, and partly because they were too far ahead of public sentiment to be carried into force.

The struggle to secure such legislation, weak and ineffective as it seems to us today, was often hard and long.[1] "Campaigns of education" had to be prepared for and carried through. Many thought that tax-supported schools would be dangerous for the State, harmful to individual good, and thoroughly undemocratic. There was danger, too, of making education too common. Schools of any kind were, or should be, for the few, and chiefly for those who could afford private instruction. It was argued that education demands a leisure class and that the poor do not have the necessary leisure (**R. 110**), that it was not possible for the government to provide a general educational system (**R. 111**), and that all such proposals represented the deliberate confiscation of the property of one class in society for the benefit of another class (**R. 108**). These and other arguments were well answered some years later by Horace Mann when he stated, at some length, the political and economic "Ground of the Free School System" (**R. 112**). Others were afraid that free schools were only a bait, the real purpose being to "religiously traditionalize the children," and then later unite Church and State. Many did not see the need for schools at all, and many more were in the frame of mind of the practical New England farmer who declared that "the Bible and figgers is all I want my boys to know." Strangely enough, the most vigorous opposition often came from the ignorant, improvident, hand-to-mouth laborers, who most needed schools, and free schools at that. Often those in favor of taxation were bitterly assailed, and even at times threatened with personal violence. Henry Barnard, who rendered such useful service in awakening Connecticut and Rhode Island, between 1837 and 1845, to the need for better schools, tells us that a member of the Rhode Island legislature told him that a bill providing a small state tax for schools, which he was then advocating, even if passed by the legislature could not be enforced in Rhode Island at the point of the bayonet. A Rhode Island farmer threatened to shoot him if he ever caught him on his property advocating "such heresy as the partial confiscation of one man's

[1] "The scheme of Universal Equal Education at the expense of the State is virtually 'Agrarianism.' It would be a compulsory application of the means of the richer for the direct use of the poorer classes, and so far an arbitrary division of property among them... Here, we contend, would be the action, if not the name, of the Agrarian system. Authority — that is, the State — is to force the more eligibly situated citizens to contribute a part of their means for the accommodation of the rest, and this is equivalent to an actual compulsory partition of their substance." (Editorial in *Philadelphia National Gazette*, August 19, 1830.)

SAMUEL GALLOWAY
(1811–1872)
Ex-officio State Superintendent of
Common Schools, 1844–1851

REV. SAMUEL LEWIS
(1799–1854)
First State Superintendent of
Common Schools, 1837–1840

TWO EARLY OHIO STATE SCHOOL SUPERINTENDENTS

property to educate another man's child." A member of the Indiana legislature, of 1837, declared that when he died he wanted engraved on his tombstone, "Here lies an enemy to free schools."

Growth of a public school sentiment illustrated by taxation in Ohio. The progress of the struggle to secure taxation for the maintenance of public schools differed somewhat in detail in the different States, but Ohio and Indiana offer us good illustrative examples — the first of a slow but peaceful settlement of the question, the other of a settlement only after vigorous fighting. The history in Ohio may be summarized as follows:

1802. State admitted to the Union.

1806, 1816. Organization of schools permitted. Only means of support rents of school section lands and rate-bills.

1821. All property of residents of district made taxable for schools; district taxation permitted.

1825. Building of schoolhouses permitted; site must be donated.

1825. A county school tax of one half mill required to be levied; raised to three quarters of a mill in 1828.

1827. State permanent school fund created.

1827. Building repairs limited to $300, and two thirds vote required to authorize this expenditure.

1829. Special organization and tax law enacted for Cincinnati. A three months school ordered.

1831. Non-resident property holders also made liable for district school taxes. Apportionment basis changed from householders to census children.

1834. Each parent sending a child to school must provide his quota of wood. County tax increased to one mill.

1836. County tax increased to one and one half mills, and to two mills in 1838.

1838. Purchase of a school site permitted. Majority vote for repairs reduced to one half. First state school tax of one half mill levied.

1839. County school tax reduced to one mill.

1853. Rate-bill abolished, and schools made free. County tax abolished; state tax of two mills substituted.

1854. State tax reduced to one and a half mills, and a township tax of two mills authorized to prolong the term.

Some of the older States and a number of the newer States have had a somewhat similar history of a slow but gradual education of the people to the acceptance of the burdens of school support.

The battle for taxation illustrated by Indiana. Ohio was predominantly New England in stock (see map, p. 107), but Indiana represented a more mixed type of population. The New England element dominated the northern part of the State, and was prominent along the eastern edge and down the Ohio, especially near Cincinnati. The Southern element was in the majority in the southern and central portion of the State. Between these two elements there was a conflict for a generation over the question of tax-supported schools. Even more was it a battle between the charity and pauper-school conception of education of the Southern element, and the strong-state conception of theNew England Yankee.

Though admitted in 1816, with a constitution making careful provision for a complete state system of schools (**R. 70**), the first general school law was not enacted until 1824. This merely introduced the district system into the townships, authorized schools where wanted, and permitted their support by a district tax or by the rate-bill. Nothing more was done until 1836. In this year two laws were enacted which provided a form of compulsory township taxation for schools. The first gave back to each township one fourth of its state poll taxes, and the second gave back five per cent of the general state taxes collected therein, with the provision that these moneys should be used to help maintain schools in the townships. This, however, was regarded by the Southern element as an entering wedge to state taxation for a system of public education, and was so bitterly opposed that it became the chief election issue in 1837. The opponents of tax-supported schools carried the day, and the legislature then elected met and promptly repealed the law. Nothing more was done until 1848.

In the meantime conditions in the new State grew steadily worse. By 1840, the illiteracy in Indiana had increased alarmingly, Indiana exceeding all Northern States, except Illinois, six to one, and almost equaling the most illiterate Southern States.[1] Of nearly 300,000 children of school age in the State, less than 50,000 were in any sort of school. In 1833, liability for school charges was limited to those sending children to school, and parents could make their own contracts with teachers for tuition, fuel, and board. Religious and private schools were considered as district schools and entitled to share in the public funds. In 1837 any householder could employ a teacher to teach his own children and so share, and in 1841 the

[1] A contemporary wrote: "The state of common education (in Indiana) is alarming. Only about one child in eight between five and fifteen years of age is able to read. The common schools and competent teachers are few... A large majority of the teachers ought to be seized by the public authorities and sent to school themselves."

requirement of a trustee's certificate for such a teacher was made optional (**R. 126**).

As the legislature of 1846 was about to meet, there appeared an Address to the Legislature of Indiana entitled "Education and the Schools of Indiana," and signed "One of the People." The author was Caleb Mills, a professor in Wabash College. It was the first of six Annual Addresses which he prepared and published (**R. 113**), and which, more than any other single influence, helped to shape public opinion and prepare the way for the new constitution of 1851 and the new school law and state tax of 1852. Early in 1847 a meeting of citizens in Indianapolis issued a call for a convention of the friends of education, to meet later in the year. Accordingly a "State Common School Convention" was held to consider the situation, an "Address" to the people was adopted, and a bill was prepared which provided for a personal poll tax of 25 cents, a state tax of .6 of a mill, and a similar township tax for schools. This was presented to the legislature of 1848, along with a copy of Mills' second "Address," and with a demand for action. The legislature, however, was cautious and undecided, and voted to obtain first a referendum on the subject at the election of 1848. This was done, with the result shown on the map on the following page. The New England element in the population came out strong for tax-supported schools, the Southern element opposing.[1] Though 66 per cent of the counties and 56 per cent of the population favored tax-supported schools, the majority favoring was not very large, and the legislature of 1849 was still afraid to act. Finally an optional law, providing for a 25-cent poll tax, a general county tax of 1 mill, and an insurance-premium tax was enacted, with permission to levy additional taxes locally. The law, however, was not to apply to any county until accepted by the voters thereof, and a new referendum on the law was ordered for 1849. The vote in 1849 was not essentially different from that of 1848. Two counties that had favored the tax in 1848 by very small margins now fell below,

---

[1] The attitude of those opposing was well stated in an article in the Richmond (Va.) *Enquirer*, of January 17, 1840, in the following words:

"Literary training does not appeal to men who have toiled many days and, by severe economy, have laid up a little money to enter new lands, to lose the time of their children from domestic labors... They do not see the necessity of educating their children for their own benefit or for the benefit of the state, and are, therefore, unwilling to yield any of their scant physical comforts for, to them, the ideal advantage in dangerous luxuries of learning."

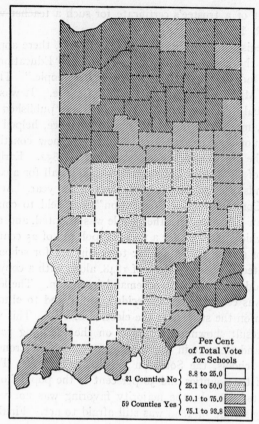

FIG. 52. THE INDIANA REFERENDUM OF 1848

Thirty-four per cent of the counties and forty-four per cent of the electors voted No.

while four counties reversed themselves the other way.   The map
for the referendum of 1848 is essentially true also for the referendum
of 1849.   The two referenda gave the following results:

	1848	1849
Total vote on the question	140,410	142,391
Vote for tax-supported schools	78,523	79,079
Vote against tax-supported schools	61,887	63,312
Majority for tax-supported schools	16,636	15,767
Voters favoring tax-supported schools	56%	55%
Voters opposing tax-supported schools	44%	45%
Counties favoring tax-supported schools	66%	68%
Counties opposing tax-supported schools	34%	32%

CALEB MILLS
(1806–1879)
President of Wabash College
Author of six *Messages* "by one of the people"

REV. CALVIN E. STOWE
(1802–1886)
Professor in Lane Theological Seminary, Cincinnati
Author of *Report on Elem. Educ. in Europe* (1837)

TWO LEADERS IN THE COMMON SCHOOL AWAKENING IN INDIANA AND OHIO

In 1850 a convention met to draft a new constitution for the State, and Mills' Fifth Address, dealing with the educational questions a new constitution should settle, met the delegates as they assembled.   A long summer campaign was waged, a suitable Article on education was incorporated in the new constitution, and the new fundamental law was approved by the people, despite much opposition to its provisions.   The new constitution of 1851 settled the matter by providing for a state tax-supported school system, and in 1852 the first general state school tax (of 1 mill) was levied on all property in the State.[1]   This ended the main battle in Indiana.

The struggle to prevent misappropriation as illustrated by Kentucky. At approximately the same time as the struggle in Indiana a conflict was also taking place in Kentucky which was illustrative of early political standards regarding education and educational funds.   The Kentucky Act of 1830 had provided for schools and local taxation, but so great was the indifference of the people to education and their unwillingness to bear taxation that the law remained practically a dead letter.   In 1837 the State received $1,433,754 as a virtual gift from the National Government in the distribution of the so-called Surplus Revenue, and $850,000 of this was put into a state school fund and invested in state internal improvement bonds.   At that time an investigation showed that one half of the children of school age in the State had never been to school, and that one third of the adult population could not read or write.

In 1840 the State refused to pay the interest on the bonds in the school fund, and in 1845 the legislature ordered the bonds destroyed and repudiated the State's debt to the school fund.   Now began a battle to change conditions, led by the Reverend Robert J. Breckinridge, a descendant of a Scotch Covenanter who had come to Kentucky from Pennsylvania, and who became State Superintendent of Common Schools in 1847.   He first obtained from the legislature of 1848 a new bond for the confiscated school funds for $1,225,768, thus adding all unpaid interest to the principal of the bond.   The

[1] As the legislature of 1851 met to enact legislation putting the provisions of the new constitution into effect, Mills' Sixth Address, recommending desirable school legislation, was placed on the desks of the members.   By now "One of the People" had won his right to be heard, and the legislature ordered 5000 copies of the Address printed for circulation throughout the State.

next year he secured legislation permitting the people to vote at the fall elections for a two-mill state school tax, stumped the State for the measure, and carried the proposal by a majority of 36,882. In the constitutional convention of 1850 he not only secured the first constitutional mention of education and made provision for a state system of schools, but also had the debt of the state school fund recognized at $1,326,770, and the fund declared inviolable. In the legislature of 1850, against the determined opposition of the governor, he secured further legislation making the interest on the school fund due to the schools a first charge on any moneys in the state treasury. This closed the fight of ten years to force the State to be honest with and support education in the State. Similar fights, involving school lands or funds, took place in some of the other States, though not always so successfully as in Kentucky.

State support fixed the state system. With the beginnings of state aid in any substantial sums, either from the income from permanent endowment funds, state appropriations, or direct state taxation, the State became, for the first time, in a position to enforce quite definite requirements in many matters. Communities which would not meet the State's requirements would receive no state funds.

One of the first requirements to be thus enforced was that communities or districts receiving state aid must also levy a local tax for schools. Commonly the requirement was a duplication of state aid. Generally speaking, and recognizing exceptions in a few States, this represents the beginnings of compulsory local taxation for education. As early as 1797 Vermont had required the towns to support their schools on penalty of forfeiting their share of state aid. Massachusetts, in 1827, made taxation for school support compulsory on all towns, thus definitely putting into effect, after 180 years, the principles laid down in the law of 1647. On the creation of the school fund in 1834, towns, to share, were required to levy a tax of $1 (soon raised to $3) per child of school age. New York in 1812, Delaware in 1829, and New Jersey in 1846 required a duplication of all state aid received. Wisconsin, in its first constitution of 1848, required a local tax for schools equal to one half the state aid received. The next step in state control was to add still other requirements, as a prerequisite to receiving state aid. One of the first of such was that a certain length of school term, commonly three months, must be provided in each school district. Another was schoolhouse repairs

at the expense of the district instead of by a labor quota, the provision of free heat in place of the cord-wood quota,[1] and later on
free school books and free school supplies.

When the duplication-of-state-aid-received stage had been reached,
compulsory local taxation for education had been established, and
the great central battle for the creation of a state school system
had been won. The right to tax for support, and to compel local
taxation, was the key to the whole state system of education. From
this point on the process of evolving an adequate system of school
support in any State has been merely the further education of
public opinion to see new educational needs. The process generally
has been characterized by a gradual increase in the amount of the
required school tax, the addition of new forms of or units for taxation, and a broadening of the scope and purpose of taxation for
education. The development has followed different lines in different
States, and probably no two States today stand at exactly the same
place in the evolution of a system of school support. So vital is
school finance, however, that the position of any state school system
today is in large part determined by how successful the State has
been in evolving an adequate system of public school support.

2. *The battle to eliminate the pauper-school idea*

The pauper-school idea. The home of the pauper-school idea
in America, as will be remembered from the map given on page 104,
was the old Central and Southern States. New Jersey, Pennsylvania, Delaware, Maryland, Virginia, and Georgia were the chief
representatives, though the idea had friends among certain classes
of the population in other of the older States. Connecticut, for
example, in the middle of the last century, had for a time a bad
attack of the pauper-school idea under the guise of the rate bill.
The new and democratic West, to the contrary, would not tolerate
it. The pauper-school conception was a direct inheritance from
English rule, belonged to a society based on classes, and was wholly
out of place in a Republic founded on the doctrine that "all men

[1] For example, in one of the school districts in the town of Hartford, Connecticut, where
the winters are long and cold, the district voted, in 1825, "That each scholar furnish ten
feet of seasoned hard wood, or green walnut, or white ash, to be inspected by the master,"
and in 1829 raised the amount to "eleven feet, or 40 cents a foot in money," and that
"each scholar deliver his wood or money when they commence the school." In other
places the children of parents who did not furnish their quota of wood were "denied the
privilege of warming themselves by the schoolhouse fire."

are created equal, and endowed by their Creator with certain inalienable rights." Still more, it was a very dangerous conception
of education for a democratic form of government to tolerate or to
foster. Its friends were found among the old aristocratic or conservative classes, the heavy taxpayers, the supporters of church
schools, and the proprietors of private schools. Citizens who had
caught the spirit of the new Republic, public men of large vision,
intelligent workingmen, and men of the New England type of thinking were opposed on principle to a plan which drew such invidious
distinctions between the future citizens of the States. To educate
part of our children in church or private pay schools, they said,
and to segregate those too poor to pay tuition and educate them
at public expense in pauper schools, often with the brand of pauper
made very evident to them, was certain to create classes in society
which in time would prove a serious danger to our democratic
institutions.

Large numbers of those for whom the pauper schools were intended
would not brand themselves as paupers by sending their children to
the schools,[1] and others who accepted the advantages offered, for
the sake of their children, despised the system. Concerning the
system "The Philadelphia Society for the Establishment and
Support of Charity Schools" in an "Address to the Public," in
1818, said:

> In the United States the benevolence of the inhabitants has led to
> the establishment of Charity Schools, which, though affording individual
> advantages, are not likely to be followed by the political benefits kindly
> contemplated by their founders. In the country a parent will raise
> children in ignorance rather than place them in charity schools. It is
> only in large cities that charity schools succeed to any extent. These
> dispositions may be improved to the best advantage, by the Legislature,
> in place of Charity Schools, establishing Public Schools for the education
> of all children, the offspring of the rich and the poor alike.

The battle for the elimination of the pauper-school idea was fought
out in the North in the States of Pennsylvania and New Jersey,
and the struggle in these two States we shall now briefly describe.

[1] "It is said, ample provision is made for the poor, as their bills may be abated. True,
if they are willing to stand in the attitude of town paupers. Ought the honest laborer to
be thus humiliated? His pride and self respect revolts at seeing his name recorded among
the town indigents. That it is regarded as degrading I have the fullest means of knowing....
Even the poor washerwoman scorns to send her children to the pauper school, proudly
saying, 'I havn't come to that yet — indeed I havn't.'" (Rev. B. C. Northrop, on *Pauper
Schools*.)

The Pennsylvania legislation. In Pennsylvania we find the pauper-school idea fully developed. The constitution of 1790 (**R. 68**) had provided for a state system of pauper schools, but nothing was done to carry even this constitutional direction into effect until 1802. A pauper-school law was then enacted (**R. 114**), directing the overseers of the poor to notify such parents as they deemed sufficiently indigent that, if they would declare themselves to be paupers, their children might be sent to some specified private or pay school and be given free education. The expense for this was assessed against the education poor-fund, which was levied and collected in the same manner as were road taxes or taxes for poor relief. No provision was made for the establishment of public schools, even for the children of the poor, nor was any standard set for the education to be provided in the schools to which they were sent. Still more, no provision was made for ascertaining the number of children entitled to the privileges of the law, or to require their attendance when the proper recipients were known. No other general provision for elementary education was made in the State until 1834.

With the growth of the cities, and the rise of their special problems, something more than this very inadequate provision for schooling became necessary. "The Philadelphia Society for the Establishment and Support of Charity Schools" had long been urging a better system, and in 1814 "The Society for the Promotion of a Rational System of Education" was organized in Philadelphia for the purpose of educational propaganda. Bills were prepared and pushed, and in 1818 Philadelphia was permitted, by special law, to organize as "the first school district" in the State of Pennsylvania, and to provide, with its own funds, a system of free Lancastrian schools for the education of the children of its poor.[1] The spirit in which these schools were organized, and the Christian citizenship purposes the organizers had in mind, are well set forth in one of the *Annual Reports* of the Philadelphia board (**R. 115**). In 1821 the counties of Dauphin (Harrisburg), Allegheny (Pittsburgh), Cumberland (Carlisle), and Lancaster (Lancaster) also were exempted from

---

[1] By 1833, the *Sixteenth Annual Report* of the district reported 6767 pupils in the schools, with 1098 provided for in nearer private schools, or a total of 7865 educated at public expense. About 60 per cent of these were boys. The total cost for the year for maintenance was $33,550, or a per-capita cost of $4.26. The population of Philadelphia, in 1833, was approximately 135,000.

the state pauper-school law, and allowed to organize schools for the education of the children of their poor. Outside of these cities but little had been done, the chief dependence throughout the State,[1] so far as there were elementary schools at all, being on a rather inferior grade of private school (**R. 116**).

That the Law of 1802 plan for the education of the children of the poor reached but few children in the State, not otherwise provided for, was shown by a *Report* made to the legislature, in 1829. At that time but 31 of the then 51 counties of the State reported children as being educated under the poor-law act, and these showed that the number of poor children being paid for had been only:

4940, in 1825;	9014, in 1827;
7943, in 1826;	4477, in 1828.

There were at that time estimated to be 400,000 children in the State between the ages of 5 and 15, not over 150,000 of whom were attending any kind of school. The existing situation was well set forth in a Memorial to the legislature of 1830, by the Pennsylvania Society for the Promotion of Public Schools (**R. 117**). In 1833, the last year of the pauper-school system, the number educated had increased to 17,467 for the State, and at an expense of $48,466.25 to the counties, or an average yearly expense per pupil of $2.77. No wonder the heavy taxpayers regarded favorably such an inexpensive plan for public education.

In 1824 an optional free-school law was enacted which permitted the organization of public schools, but provided that no child could attend school at public expense longer than three years. Even this law was repealed in 1826, and the old pauper-school law was reinstated.

The Law of 1834. In 1827 "The Pennsylvania Society for the Promotion of Public Schools" began an educational propaganda which did much to bring about the Free-School Act of 1834. In an "Address to the Public" (**R. 99**) it declared its objects to be the pro-

---

[1] "The educational policy enforced in Pennsylvania for fifty years after the close of the Revolutionary War embraced two objects; first, the establishment in all parts of the State of endowed academies, in which a small number of indigent pupils were to be taught gratuitously, mostly with reference to their becoming teachers; and second, the free instruction of poor children in existing church or neighborhood schools." (J. F. Wickersham. *A History of Education in Pennsylvania*, p. 273.)

motion of public education throughout the State of Pennsylvania, and the "Address" closed with these words:

This Society is at present composed of about 250 members, and a correspondence has been commenced with 125 members, who reside in every district in the State. It is intended to direct the continued attention of the public to the importance of the subject; to collect and diffuse all information which may be deemed valuable; and to persevere in their labors until they shall be crowned with success.

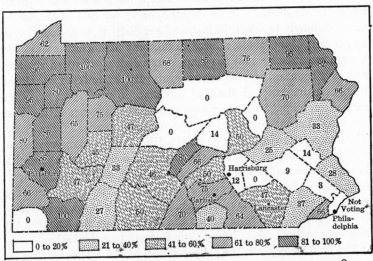

FIG. 53. THE PENNSYLVANIA SCHOOL ELECTIONS OF 1834

Showing the percentage of school districts in each county organizing under and accepting the School Law of 1834. Percentage of districts accepting indicated on the map for the counties.

Memorials were presented to the legislature year after year (**R. 117**), governors were interested and they in turn urged action (**R. 118**), "Addresses to the Public" were prepared (**R. 99**) and a vigorous propaganda was kept up until the Free-School Law of 1834 (**R. 119**) was the result.[1]

This law, though, was optional. It created every ward, township, and borough in the State a school district, a total of 987 being created for the State. Each school district was ordered to vote that autumn

[1] Petitions for and against a general school system were presented in both houses of the legislature during the session, those opposed protesting against the use of any portion of the public money for the support of common schools.

on the acceptance or rejection of the law. Those accepting the law were to organize under its provisions, while those rejecting the law were to continue under the educational provisions of the old Pauper-School Act.

The results of the school elections of 1834 are shown, by counties, on the above map. Of the total of 987 districts created, 502, in 46 of the then 52 counties (Philadelphia County not voting), or 52 per cent of the whole number, voted to accept the new law and organize under it; 264 districts, in 31 counties, or 27 per cent of the whole, voted definitely to reject the law; and 221 districts, in 46 counties, or 21 per cent of the whole, refused to take any action either way. In 3 counties, indicated on the map, every district accepted the law, and in 5 counties, also indicated, every district rejected or refused to act on the law.[1] A study of this map, in comparison with the map given on page 100, shows once more the influence of the New England element settled along the northern border of the State. The democratic West, with its Scotch-Irish Presbyterian population, also is in evidence. It was the predominantly German counties, located in the east-central portion of the State, which were strongest in their opposition to the new law. One reason for this was that the new law provided for English schools; another was the objection of the thrifty Germans to taxation; and another was the fear that the new state schools might injure their German parochial schools.

The final victory over the pauper-school forces. The real fight for free *versus* pauper schools was yet to come. Legislators who had voted for the law were bitterly assailed, and, though it was but an optional law, the question of its repeal and the reinstatement of the old Pauper-School Law became the burning issue of the campaign in the autumn of 1834. Many legislators who had favored the law were defeated for re-election. Others, seeing defeat, refused to run. Undismayed, however, by the rising storm of opposition, Governor Wolf took a strong stand, in his message to the new legislature, in

[1] "In many districts the contest between those in favor of accepting the new law, and those determined to reject it, became so bitter that party and even church ties were for a time broken up, the rich arrayed themselves against the poor, and the business and social relations of whole neighborhoods were greatly disturbed. Cases are known in which father and son took different sides, and in certain districts an outspoken free school man was scarcely allowed to live in peace and transact his ordinary business. The newspapers of the day were crowded with communications on the subject; and it was the leading topic for discussion for months." (J. F. Wickersham. *A History of Education in Pennsylvania*, p. 318.)

favor of a retention of the new law.[1]   Petitions for the repeal of the
law, and remonstrances against its repeal, flooded the legislature
as soon as it met in session.   Some 32,000 persons petitioned for a
repeal of the law, 66 of whom signed by
making their mark, and "not more than
five names in a hundred," reported a
legislative committee (**R. 120**) which investigated the matter, "were signed in
English script."   It was from among the
Germans that the strongest opposition to
the law came.   This same committee
further reported that so many of the
names were "so illegibly written as to
afford the strongest evidence of the
deplorable disregard so long paid by
the Legislature to the constitutional in-
junction to establish a general system of
education."

FIG. 54.   THADDEUS
STEVENS
(1792–1868)

The Senate at once repealed the law, but the House, largely under
the leadership of a Vermonter by the name of Thaddeus Stevens,
refused to reconsider, and finally forced the Senate to accept an
amended and a still stronger bill.   In support of the free-school act
he made a memorable address [2] (**R. 121**), and probably rendered
here the greatest public service of his entire public career,[3] though

[1] "That the system of education for which the Act in question provides is decidedly
preferable, in every conceivable point of view, to that now in operation, no man, who will
give himself the trouble to draw a faithful comparison between the two, can for a moment
hesitate about or doubt.   If the Act now under consideration goes into operation, the
odious distinction between rich and poor, wealth and indigence, which has heretofore precluded the children of many poor, but honest and respectable parents, from a participation
in the advantages of education under the present system, will be ended." (Extract from
Governor Wolf's message.)

[2] Two members of the House who heard the address, later wrote their recollections of it.
One wrote: "It was one of the most powerful addresses I ever heard.   The House was
electrified.   The wavering voted for the House sections, and the school system was saved
from ignominious defeat." Another wrote: "The address was so convincing that the friends
of education were brought in solid column to the support of the measure, and thus saved
the common school system."

[3] Writing, in 1864, to a lady who had written him appreciatively regarding his efforts,
thirty years before, for free schools, Stevens, then a member of Congress, wrote:
"When I review all the measures in which I have taken part, I see none in which I take
so much pleasure, perhaps I may be excused for saying pride, as the free school system of
Pennsylvania.   You probably give me too much credit, but I think I may, without arro-
gance, admit that my efforts contributed something.... As the mother of eight children
you thank me for it.   Such thanks, while I am living, and if I could hope for the blessings
of the poor when I am no more, are a much greater reward than silver and gold."

later he became a Republican leader in Congress.[1] This defeat finally settled, in principle at least, the pauper-school question in Pennsylvania, though it was not until 1873 that the last district in the State accepted the new system. The law provided for state aid, state supervision of schools, and county and local taxation, but districts refusing to accept the new system could receive no portion of the new funds. During the first year a three and one half months' free school was provided. By 1836 the new free-school law had been accepted by 75 per cent of the districts in the State, by 1838 by 84 per cent, and by 1847 by 88 per cent. In 1848 the legislature ordered free schools in all districts, but, not attaching a compulsory feature to the enactment beyond the forfeiting of any state aid, it was twenty-five years longer before the last district gave in and accepted the law. In 1849 a four months' free school was made necessary to receive any state aid.

Eliminating the pauper-school idea in New Jersey. No constitutional mention of education was made in New Jersey until 1844, and no educational legislation was enacted before 1816. In that year a permanent state school fund was begun, and in 1820 the first permission to levy taxes "for the education of such poor children as are paupers" was granted. In 1828 an extensive investigation showed that one third of the children of the State were without educational opportunities, and as a result of this investigation the first general school law for the State was enacted, in 1829. This law provided for district schools, school trustees and visitation, licensed teachers, local taxation, and made a state appropriation of $20,000 a year to help establish the system. The next year, however, this law was repealed and the old pauper-school plan re-established, largely due to the pressure of church and private-school interests. In 1830 and 1831 the state appropriation was made divisible among private and parochial schools, as well as the public pauper schools, and the use of all public money was limited "to the education of the children of the poor."

Between 1828 and 1838 a number of conventions of friends of free

---

[1] Charles Sumner, speaking in eulogy of Thaddeus Stevens in the United States Senate, at the time of his death, in 1868, said:

"Not a child in Pennsylvania, conning his spelling book beneath the humble rafters of a village school, who does not owe him gratitude; not a citizen rejoicing in that security which is found only in liberal institutions, founded on the equal rights of all, who is not his debtor."

public schools were held in the State, and much work in the nature
of propaganda was done.   At a convention in 1838, "the most notable convention of the friends of the common schools ever held in
the State," a committee was appointed to prepare an "Address to
the People of New Jersey" on the educational needs of the State.
This Address (**R. 122**), coupled with the speakers sent over the State
to talk to the people on the subject, so aroused the people that positive action soon followed.   That "every free State must provide for
the education of all its children," and that the education of the people
is indispensable to the preservation of free institutions, were held
to be axiomatic.   The pauper-school idea was vigorously condemned.
Concerning this the "Address" said:

> We utterly repudiate as unworthy, not of freemen only, but of men,
> the narrow notion that there is to be an education for the poor as such.
> Has God provided for the poor a coarser earth, a thinner air, a paler sky?
> Does not the glorious sun pour down his golden flood as cheerily on the
> poor man's hovel as upon the rich man's palace?   Have not the cotter's
> children as keen a sense of all the freshness, verdure, fragrance, melody,
> and beauty of luxuriant nature as the pale sons of kings?   Or is it on
> the mind that God has stamped the imprint of a baser birth, so that the
> poor man's child knows with an inborn certainty that his lot is to crawl,
> not climb?   It is not so.   God has not done it.   Man cannot do it.
> Mind is immortal.   Mind is imperial.   It bears no mark of high or low,
> of rich or poor.   It asks but freedom.   It requires but light.

The campaign against the pauper school had just been fought to a
conclusion in Pennsylvania, and the result of the appeal in New
Jersey was such a popular manifestation in favor of free schools that
the legislature of 1838 instituted a partial state school system.   The
pauper-school laws were repealed, and the best features of the short-
lived law of 1829 were re-enacted.   In 1844 a new state constitution
limited the income of the permanent state school fund exclusively
to the support of public schools.

With the pauper-school idea eliminated from Pennsylvania and
New Jersey, the North was through with it.   The wisdom of its
elimination soon became evident, and we hear little more of it among
Northern people.   The democratic West never tolerated it.   It
continued some time longer in Maryland, Virginia, and Georgia, and
at places for a time in other Southern States, but finally disappeared
in the South as well in the educational reorganizations which took
place following the close of the Civil War.

One of the most vigorous attacks on the pauper system made in the South took place in Virginia in 1856–57. Governor Wise had severely criticized the plan of using the proceeds of the public school fund largely for the maintenance of pauper schools, and had urged the organization of an effective state school system. At the same time a state educational convention meeting in Richmond severely condemned the pauper-school idea, and questioned the propriety of so using the income from the school fund. A few quotations from the report of this convention will reveal the spirit of the attack.

> Is it right to take the property of the many and bestow it exclusively on the few?... They are the privileged class, the aristocracy of poverty. Now is it right to exclude from all the benefits of the literary fund all the children of this glorious old commonwealth, except those who put in the plea of rags and dirt?... Can this injustice and partiality benefit the poor children? Is it a law of humanity, that to lift up, you must first degrade; that to elevate the soul and spirit of a child, you must first make him a public pauper?... Has the pauper system of education diminished the number of your intellectual paupers? Or is it, like every other system of legally supported pauperism, a fire that feeds itself?

The South was rapidly moving toward the abolition of the pauper-school system also when the outbreak of the Civil War put an end, for a time, to educational progress there.

3. *The battle to make the schools entirely free*

The schools not yet free. The rate-bill, as we have previously stated, was an old institution, also brought over from England, as the term "rate" signifies. It was, as we have said, a charge levied upon the parent to supplement the school revenues and prolong the school term, and was assessed in proportion to the number of children sent by each parent to the school. In some States, as for example Massachusetts and Connecticut, its use went back to colonial times; in other States it was introduced as a transition plan in changing from private pay schools to state-aided and rate-supported common schools; in still other States it was added as the cost for education increased, and it was seen that the income from permanent funds and authorized taxation was not sufficient to maintain the school the desired length of time. The deficiency in revenue was charged against the parents sending children to school, *pro rata*, and collected as ordinary tax-bills (**R. 123**). The charge was small, but it was sufficient to keep many poor children away from the schools. It thus tended to be a bounty on absence.[1] It also tended to build up the private schools,[2] as its abolition was accompanied generally by a decreased attendance at private schools, as well as an increase at the public schools.

The effect of the charge in keeping children away is well illustrated by the case of New York City, where The Public School Society, finding its funds inadequate to meet its growing responsibilities, attempted, in 1826, to raise additional funds by adding the rate-bill for those who could afford to pay. The rates were moderate, as may be seen from the following schedule of charges:

	Per quarter
For the Alphabet, Spelling, and Writing on Slates, as far as the 3d Class, inclusive	$0.25
Continuance of above, with Reading and Arithmetical Tables, or the 4th, 5th, and 6th Classes	0.50
Continuance of last, with Writing on Paper, Arithmetic, and Definitions, or the 7th, 8th, and 9th Classes	1.00
The preceding, with Grammar, Geography, with the use of Maps and Globes, Bookkeeping, History, Composition, Mensuration, Astronomy, etc.	2.00

No additional charge for Needlework, nor for Fuel, Books, or Stationery.

Two days before the system went into effect there were 3457 pupils in the schools of the Society; six months later there were but 2999, while the number taking the $2 per quarter studies dropped from 137 to 13. The amount received from fees in 1826 was $4426, but by 1831 this had fallen to $1366. What to do was obvious, and, securing additional funds, the schools were made absolutely free again in 1832.

The rising cities, with their new social problems, could not and would not tolerate the rate-bill system, and one by one they secured

[1] "Many scholars stay away from school to avoid paying balance of term bill. It is a wretched policy to tax parents in proportion to the attendance of their children. It is a premium on non-attendance. Societies (districts) should be obliged to see that every child is in school at least four months to be entitled to public money for that child." (*Connecticut Common School Journal*, 1834, p. 222.)

[2] "The present mode of supporting common schools, principally by public funds and by taxation on scholars, has operated to encourage men of property to abandon them and patronize private schools. Judging from official returns, there cannot be less than 10,000 children under 16 years of age in private schools, at an aggregate expense of not less than $200,000 for tuition alone... Nay, more, I have found an antagonist interest arrayed against every effort to improve the common schools." (Henry Barnard, in *Connecticut Common School Journal*, 1838, vol. I, p. 173.)

special laws from legislatures which enabled them to organize a city school system, separate from city council control, and under a local "board of education." One of the provisions of these special laws nearly always was the right to levy a city tax for schools sufficient to provide free education for the children of the city. In New York State, to illustrate, though the State of New York did not provide for free schools generally until 1867, we find special legislation, providing free schools for the city, enacted as follows:

1832. New York City	1848. Syracuse
1838. Buffalo	1849. Troy
1841. Hudson	1850. Auburn
1841. Rochester	1853. Oswego
1843. Brooklyn	1853. Utica
1843. Williamsburg	

In other States, it might be added, that the schools in Providence, Baltimore, Charleston, Mobile, New Orleans, Louisville, Cincinnati, Chicago, and Detroit were free for about a quarter-century before the coming of free state schools in their respective States.

The fight against the rate-bill may be well illustrated by describing the struggle in two States where the conflict was most prolonged and most hotly contended, on both sides — New York and Connecticut.

The fight against the rate-bill in New York. The attempt to abolish the rate-bill and make the schools wholly free was vigorously contested in New York State, and the contest there is most easily described. From 1828 to 1868, this tax on the parents produced an average annual sum of $410,685.66, or about one half of the sum paid all the teachers of the State for salary. While the wealthy districts were securing special legislation and taxing themselves to provide free schools for their children, the poorer and less populous districts were left to struggle to maintain their schools the four months each year necessary to secure state aid. Finally after much agitation, and a number of appeals to the legislature to assume the rate-bill charges in the form of general state taxation, and thus make the schools entirely free, the legislature, in 1849, referred the matter back to the people to be voted on at the elections that autumn. The legislature was to be thus advised by the people as to what action it should take. The result was a state-wide campaign [1] for free, public, tax-supported schools, as against partially free, rate-bill schools (R. 124).

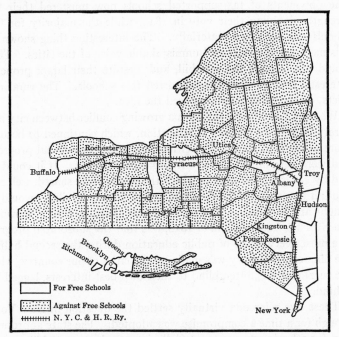

FIG. 55. THE NEW YORK REFERENDUM OF 1850

Total vote: For free schools, 17 counties and 209,346 voters; against free schools, 42 counties and 184,308 voters.

The result of the 1849 election was a vote of 249,872 in favor of making "the property of the State educate the children of the State," and 91,952 against it. This only seemed to stir the opponents of free schools to renewed action, and they induced the next

[1] Great public battles usually have slogans and songs. There were many of each for this New York fight. A stanza from one of the best of the songs read:

"Then free as air should knowledge be —
    And open wisdom's portal,
To every thirsty, earnest soul,
    Who longs to be immortal.
Here rich and poor stand side by side,
    To quaff life's purest chalice,
And never dream that deathless names
    Belong to cot or palace."

legislature to resubmit the question for another vote, in the autumn of 1850.

The result of the referendum of 1850 is shown on the last map. The opponents of tax-supported schools now mustered their full strength, doubling their vote in 1849, while the majority for free schools was cut down materially. The interesting thing shown on this map was the clear and unmistakable voice of the cities. They would not tolerate the rate-bill, and, despite their larger property interests, they favored tax-supported free schools. The rural districts, on the other hand, opposed the idea.

We have here clearly set forth a growing conflict between city and rural interests, in matters of education, which continued to become more acute with time. The cities demanded educational progress, and were determined to have it, regardless of cost. If it could be had by general legislation in which the whole State shared, well and good; if not, then special laws and special taxing privileges would be sought and obtained. The result of this attitude, clearly shown in the New York referendum of 1850, was that the substantial progress in almost every phase of public education during the second half of the nineteenth century was made by the cities of our country, while the rural districts, often blind to their own best interests, lagged far behind.

These two referenda virtually settled the question in New York, though for a time a compromise was adopted. The state appropriation for schools was very materially increased, the rate-bill was retained, and the organization of "union districts" to provide free schools by local taxation where people desired them was authorized. Many of these "union free districts" now arose in the more progressive communities of the State, and finally, in 1867, after rural and other forms of opposition had largely subsided, and after almost all the older States had abandoned the plan, the New York legislature finally abolished the rate-bill and made the schools of New York entirely free.

The struggle in Connecticut. Connecticut, it will be remembered (p. 91), had created a state school fund as early as 1750, and in 1795 had added the proceeds of the sale of the Western Reserve (**R. 107**) to this fund. By 1849 a permanent fund of $2,000,000 had been built up. The new school fund in time produced so large an income that, in 1821, the old law of 1700, requiring the levy of a two-mill town tax for schools, was repealed, and the income from the fund was now depended on for school support.[1] As school expenses increased, the rate-bill (**R. 123**) was used to provide the needed additional funds. A pernicious practice, thus begun, finally became in time so established by practice that to uproot it required a long and hard-fought educational campaign. This dependence on the school fund income eventually almost led to the ruin of the schools through the destruction of the willingness of the people to bear taxes, while the rate-bill tended both to keep children out of school and to turn children from the public school.[2]

By 1830 the low condition of the Connecticut schools had begun to attract general attention, and in 1831 Governor Peters recommended a required one cent tax for schools as a means for overcoming the "general apathy" as to their proper maintenance. In 1838, following the example of Massachusetts of the preceding year, Connecticut created a State Board of Education to institute some supervision of the rampant district system. Henry Barnard was elected its first Secretary, and he at once entered into a vigorous campaign against the rate-bill [3] as a means for school support. What promised to be the beginning of a new era in the State, however, was soon (1842) cut short by a new governor and legislature not in sympathy with such advanced ideas. This action drew a stinging and well deserved rebuke from Horace Mann (**R. 125**).

[1] "The prevailing method of managing our common schools renders them comparatively useless. Exclusive reliance is placed on the avails of the Fund, and, in a great majority of cases, no addition is made to the amount obtained from this source, by tax or otherwise. Consequently adequate means are not provided for employing competent instructors... The public money is used while it lasts, and when this is exhausted the school is discontinued. A cheap instructor is employed for a few months, and the remainder of the year the schoolhouse is closed." (*Connecticut Courant*, July 13, 1830.)

[2] "To place the schools on their old footing, I have advocated the abandonment of quarter-bills, or charge per scholar, and making property, whether it represented children or not, chargeable with their support. This is the cardinal idea of the free school system, and with the aid now furnished from the school fund, this charge cannot be considered burdensome. This too is the practice of every city which has an efficient system of schools. The practical abandonment of the rate in our cities, has led to the withdrawal of the children, and the active interest, of the wealthy, from the private schools. Many parents who now send to private schools would send to the common schools, if they were taxed annually for their support." (Henry Barnard. *Annual Report, Commissioners, Common Schools, Connecticut,* 1842, p. 25.)

[3] "It would be difficult to frame a law to operate more unfavorably, unequally, and, in many instances, more oppressively than this one. There is not only the ordinary pecuniary interest against it, but it is increased from the fact that all the abatements for poor children must come upon them who send to schools.... Many of them who are required to pay the bills of their poorer neighbors are just able to pay their own, and the addition of a single penny is oppressive so long as the burden is not shared by the whole community." (Henry Barnard, in *Connecticut Common School Journal,* 1838, vol. I, p. 162.)

Between 1840 and 1868, the date of the final abolition of the rate-bill in the State, a long series of laws relating to tuition bills was enacted, and after 1850 governors began to recommend a substitution of the general taxation of all for the rate-bill. In 1849 Barnard

FIG. 56. NOAH
PORTER
(1811–92)
Twelfth President of Yale

returned to Connecticut and took service as a campaigner, and in 1851 he once more became Secretary to the State Board of Education. Though Barnard left the State for other work in 1855, others succeeded him who carried on the needed education of the people. A vigorous campaign for taxation to replace the rate-bill was now waged.[1] The services of public men were enlisted. An essay on the proper basis of school support by Noah Porter, a professor at and later president of Yale, and urging that free schools be supported by general taxation, was reprinted and given wide circulation (**R. 109**). Cities and towns threw off the rate-bill voluntarily, and made their schools free.

In 1856 a one-mill state tax for schools was enacted, but the use of the rate-bill was still permitted. That year, 776 out of 1624 school districts in the State had levied a tax and established free schools. By 1860 there were 846 free districts; by 1864, 1025; and by 1867, 1225. The slow process of building up public sentiment and re-educating the people to tax themselves took time. Finally, in 1868, Governor English recommended the abolition of the rate-bill and the creation of a uniform free school system, a recommendation with which the legislature concurred.[2] It took

[1] "The greatest hindrance to the improvement of our schools is the Rate-Bill. It is wrong in principle and mischievous in practice. It is alike the duty and the interest of the State to furnish substantially equal common school privileges to the children of all classes. Self protection is the right and duty of the government. For this purpose it may maintain armies and navies. But cheaper, safer, every way better than forts and fleets, indispensable as they may be, better for its peace and security, its prosperity and protection, is universal education." (See Cyrus Northrop, in *Connecticut State School Report*, 1868, p. 38.)

[2] The effect was as had been predicted. Commenting on the school statistics for 1870, Secretary Northrop said:

"The increase in the whole number registered the first term of free schools, as reported last year, was 6208, and for the corresponding term now reported, 5744, or an increase in two years of 11,952. How beneficent that legislation which has led nearly 12,000 children to school and thus to a higher future. The proof now before the public, that over 10,000

forty years of argument and struggle to recall Connecticut to its ancient duty. When it finally did away with the rate-bill but two States using it still were left.

The dates for the abolition of the rate-bill in the other older Northern States were:

1834. Pennsylvania	1867. New York
1852. Indiana	1868. Connecticut
1853. Ohio	1868. Rhode Island
1855. Illinois	1869. Michigan
1864. Vermont	1871. New Jersey

The New York fight of 1849 and 1850 and the long struggle in Connecticut were the pivotal fights; in the other States it was abandoned by legislative act, and without a serious contest. In the Southern States free education came with the educational reorganizations following the close of the Civil War.

Other school charges. Another per-capita tax usually levied on parents, in the early days of public education, was the fuel or wood tax. Unless each parent had hauled, or paid someone to do so, his proper "quota of wood" to the schoolhouse during the summer,[1] it was assessed against him as was the rate-bill. This was vexatious, because small, and often hard to collect. Finally State after State abandoned the charge and assessed it, with other necessary expenses, against the property of the school district, thus making wood or coal a public charge.

The provision of textbooks has been another charge gradually assumed by cities and States. The earliest provision of free textbooks, as in the case of free schooling, was made by the cities. The earliest city to provide free textbooks probably was Philadelphia, in 1818. New Hampshire ordered free textbooks for indigent children as early as 1827. Jersey City began to provide free textbooks in 1830, and Newark in 1838. Charleston, South Carolina, began in 1856; and Elizabeth and Hoboken, New Jersey, some time before 1860. Massachusetts gave all its towns permission to furnish free textbooks in 1873, and made them obligatory in 1884. Maine fol-

children were barred from school by the rate bill, buries it beyond the possibility of resurrection." (*Connecticut State School Report*, 1871, p. 19.)

[1] For example, the following New Hampshire town vote of about 1810:

"Voted that three-eighths of a cord of hard wood be laid on the head of each scholar in the district, under eighteen and over five years of age, to be good sound wood and to be delivered at the schoolhouse, cut and corded, before the opening of the school."

lowed in 1889, and New Hampshire in 1890. Many other States have since ordered free textbooks provided for their schools.

Free school supplies — pens, ink, paper, pencils — have also been shifted gradually from an individual charge to general taxation, and, within recent years, as we shall see in later chapters, many new charges have been assumed by the public as in the interests of better school education.

QUESTIONS FOR DISCUSSION

1. Explain the theory of "vested rights" as applied to private and parochial schools.
2. How do you explain the intense bitterness developed over the transition from church to state education?
3. Take each of the leading arguments advanced for tax-supported state schools and show its validity, viewed from a modern standpoint.
4. Take each of the leading arguments advanced against tax-supported state schools and show its weakness, viewed from a modern standpoint.
5. Does every great advance in provisions for human welfare require a period of education and propaganda? Illustrate.
6. Explain why the legislatures were so unwilling to follow their governors in the matter of establishing schools.
7. What items have gone into the building up of the permanent state school fund in your State? What are its present total and per-capita-income values?
8. What is the size of the permanent state school fund in your State, how is its income apportioned, and what percentage of the total cost per pupil each year does it pay?
9. What has been the history of the development of school taxation in your State?
10. Explain just what is meant by "the wealth of the State must educate the children of the State."
11. Show how, with the beginnings of state support, general state requirements could be enforced for the first time.
12. Show how the retention of the pauper-school idea would have been dangerous to the life of the Republic.
13. Why were the cities more anxious to escape from the operation of the pauper-school law than were the towns and rural districts?
14. Why were the pauper-school and rate-bill so hard to eliminate?
15. Enumerate the items furnished free, in your State, in addition to tuition.

SELECTED READINGS

In the accompanying volume of *Readings* the following selections, related to the subject matter of this chapter, are reproduced:

*98. Philadelphia: Resolution favoring a Public School Law.
*99. Address: Pennsylvania Society for Promotion of Public Schools.

100. Annals: Organization of the American Lyceum.
*101. Western Academic Institute: Form of Petition for Schools.
*102. Mechanics Free Press: "Address" to Workingmen on Education.
*103. Philadelphia: Report of Working-Men's Committee.
 104. Annals: Messages of the Governors on Education, 1831.
 105. Advertisement: A North Carolina Lottery.
*106. Murray: A New Jersey School Lottery.
 107. Connecticut: Act Creating the Connecticut School Fund.
*108. National Gazette: Early Expectations as to School Support.
*109. Porter: The Sound Basis for School Support.
*110. National Gazette: Education Demands a Leisure Class.
*111. National Gazette: Government cannot Provide General Education.
*112. Mann: The Ground of the Free School.
*113. Mills: The Messages of "One of the People."
*114. Pennsylvania: Pauper School Laws of 1802–09.
*115. Philadelphia Report: Spirit of the Early Schools.
*116. Address: Educational Conditions in Pennsylvania, 1828.
*117. Memorial: Status of Education by 1830.
*118. Wolf: Message to the Pennsylvania Legislature, 1833.
*119. Pennsylvania: The Free School Law of 1834.
*120. Pennsylvania: Report of the House Committee, 1835.
*121. Stevens: Speech Opposing Repeal of the Law of 1834.
*122. Address: To the People of New Jersey.
*123. New York: A Rate Bill of 1825.
*124. N.Y. Tribune: The New York School Referendum of 1849.
 125. Mann: Repeal of the Connecticut School Law.

QUESTIONS ON THE READINGS

1. Hundreds of resolutions such as **98** were adopted, without much effect. What was the best part of this resolution?
2. Does this Address (**99**) seem important?   Evaluate the effectiveness of the organization as set up.
3. Estimate the importance of the Lyceum (**100**) in awakening interest in education, as judged by the constitution and topics for discussion proposed.
4. Estimate the effectiveness of such a petition (**101**), at the time, if presented from many organized bodies in many States.
5. Do you consider the argument in **102** sound, and why?
6. Just what kind of schools existed in the cities of Pennsylvania in 1830, judging from the Report (**103**) of this Committee?
7. Was the Report (**103**) correct as to a monopoly of talent?
8. Do the Messages of 1831 (**104**) appear to be very hopeful of results, or are they perfunctory in nature?
9. What would be the net proceeds of such a (**105**) lottery, and its value in aiding schools?
10. What kind of a school did the honorable gentlemen (**106**) propose?

11. In establishing the Connecticut school fund (**107**), was aid to education the main object?
12. Just what were the expectations of the "less-eligibly situated fellow-citizens" (**108**) as to how they were to obtain educational advantages?
13. Do you consider Porter's argument (**109**) particularly sound? Why?
14. At the time **110** was written it seemed plausible; what has changed the situation so greatly in a century?
15. At the time **111** was written it also seemed plausible; why?
16. Do Mann's three propositions (**112**) hold equally true today?
17. What do you see in the extract from one of Mills' "Messages" (**113**) to explain their great influence in effecting reform?
18. Explain the process of obtaining education for a child under the Pennsylvania pauper school law (**114**).
19. What purposes and educational conceptions do **115** reveal?
20. What educational conditions (**116**) did exist in 1828?
21. What educational conditions (**117**) did exist in 1830?
22. In view of existing conditions, do you consider Gov. Wolf's message (**118**) a strong one, or not?
23. Just what did the Law of 1834 (**119**) propose to do?
24. How do you explain such a petition (**120**) appearing?
25. Do you consider Stevens' arguments sound and reasoning good? Why?
26. Explain the strong appeal of the New Jersey address (**122**).
27. Point out the essential soundness of the New Jersey reasoning (**122**).
28. Explain the willingness of people, a hundred years ago, to do business on such a scale as the New York rate-bill (**123**) indicates.
29. Was Greeley's reasoning (**124**) sound?
30. What light do thele tter and the editorial (**124**) throw on educational conditions in 1849?
31. Assuming Mann's description of Connecticut progress (**125**) to be correct, how do you account for the legislature's following so readily the recommendations of the governor?

TOPICS FOR INVESTIGATION AND REPORT

1. Thaddeus Stevens and the Pennsylvania school law of 1834. (Monroe; Stevens; Wickersham.)
2. Caleb Mills and the Indiana awakening. (Barnard; Boone.)
3. A comparison of educational development in Ohio and Indiana before 1850. (Boone; Miller; Orth; Rawles.)
4. The fight for free schools in New Jersey. (Murray.)
5. Use of the lottery for school endowment and support.
6. History of the Connecticut state school fund. (Barnard; Griffin.)
7. History of the New York state school fund.
8. Work of the western Academic and Literary Institutes. (Hansen.)
9. Education in Virginia before 1860. (Maddox; Heatwole.)
10. Education in North Carolina before 1860. (Knight; Noble.)

SELECTED REFERENCES

Barnard, Henry, Editor. *The American Journal of Education*, 31 vols. Consult *Analytical Index* to; 128 pp. Published by United States Bureau of Education, Washington, 1892.

See especially vols. IV and V, for a history of the Connecticut school system; and vol. VI, for a history of the Connecticut school fund.

Barnard, Henry. "Thomas H. Burrowes, with a Sketch of the History of Common Schools in Pennsylvania"; in *Barnard's Journal*, vol. VI, 1859, pp. 107–24.

Organization of schools under the law of 1834.

Barnard, Henry. "The School Fund of Connecticut"; in *Barnard's Journal*, vol. VI, p. 859, pp. 365–425.

A detailed history of the Fund, with many extracts from documents.

Boone, R. G. *Education in the United States*. 402 pp. New York, 1889.

Chapter VI forms good supplemental reading on the formation of permanent school funds.

*Boone, R. G. *History of Education in Indiana*. 454 pp. New York, 1892.

Chapters VIII and IX give very good descriptions of the awakening, the enactment of the law of 1848, and the referendum of 1849.

*Curoe, P. R. V. *Educational Attitudes and Policies of Organized Labor in the United States*. 201 pp. Teachers College Contributions to Education, No. 201. New York, 1926.

A study of attitudes assumed from the beginning of the movement, and with special reference to education.

*Fairlie, John A. *Centralization of Administration in New York State*. Columbia University Studies in History, Economics, and Public Law, vol. XI, No. 3, New York, 1898.

Chapter II describes briefly the centralizing tendencies in educational administration in New York State.

*Fitzpatrick, E. A. *The Educational Views and Influence of De Witt Clinton*. 155 pp. Teachers College Contributions to Education, No. 44, New York, 1911.

His educational views, and work as an educational advocate.

*Hansen, A. O. *Early Educational Leadership in the Ohio Valley*. 120 pp. Journal Education Research Monographs, No. 5, Bloomington (Ill.), 1923.

Study of the work and influence of the Western Literary Institute and College of Professional Teachers, 1829–41.

Hayes, Cecil B. *The American Lyceum*. 72 pp. Bulletin 12, 1932, United States Bureau of Education.

An excellent history of the rise and constitution and work of this early educational and propaganda organization. Good bibliography. Constitution, resolutions, etc.

*Heatwole, C. J. *A History of Education in Virginia*. 381 pp. New York, 1916.

A good history of educational development in the State.

Knight, Edgar W. *Public School Education in North Carolina.* 384 pp. Boston, 1916.

Good on the development of public education in the State.

*Maddox, Wm. A. *The Free School Idea in Virginia before the Civil War.* 225 pp. Teachers College Contributions to Education, No. 93. New York, 1918.

Studied as a phase of the State's political and social evolution.

Mayo, Rev. A. D. "Original Establishment of State School Funds"; in *Report of the United States Commissioner of Education, 1874–95, vol. II, pp. 1505–11.

A brief descriptive article.

*Mead, A. R. *The Development of Free Schools in the United States.* 236 pp. Teachers College Contributions to Education, No. 91. New York, 1918.

A study of taxation and the rate-bill, as found in the historical development of the school system of Connecticut and Michigan.

*Miller, E. A. *History of Educational Legislation in Ohio, 1803–1850.* 286 pp. University of Chicago Press, 1918.

A good digest of educational legislation and progress.

Monroe, Paul. *Cyclopedia of Education.* New York, 1911–13. 5 vols.

The following articles form good supplemental references:
1. "District of Columbia"; vol. II, pp. 342–45.
2. "Philadelphia, City of"; vol. IV, pp. 666–67.
3. "School Funds"; vol. V, pp. 269–73.
4. The historical portions of the articles on state school systems, such as Indiana, New York, Ohio, Pennsylvania, etc.

Murray, David. *History of Education in New Jersey.* 344 pp. United States Bureau of Education, Circular of Information, No. 1, Washington, 1899.

Chapter III describes the struggle to establish free schools in New Jersey.

Noble, M. C. S. *A History of Public Schools in North Carolina.* 463 pp. Chapel Hill, 1930.

An excellent history of education in a State.

*Orth, S. P. *Centralization of Administration in Ohio;* Columbia University, Studies in History, Economics, and Public Law, vol. XVI, No. 3, New York, 1903.

Chapter II gives a good sketch of the centralization in educational affairs, and the development of taxation for education.

*Randall, S. S. *The Common School System of the State of New York.* 94 pp. Troy, New York, 1851.

An old classic, now out of print, but still found in many libraries. Pages 72–79 describe the battle to abolish the rate-bill in New York.

*Rawles, W. A. *Centralizing Tendencies in the Administration of Indiana.* Columbia University Studies in History, Economics, and Public Law, vol. XVII, No. 1, New York, 1903.

Pages 26 to 141 very good on the development of educational administration in Indiana.

Stevens, Thaddeus. "Speech in defense of the Pennsylvania Free School System"; in *Report of the United States Commissioner of Education*, 1898–99, vol. 1, pp. 516–24.

Historical note, and the speech made in the Pennsylvania House of Representatives, in 1835, in opposition to the attempt to repeal the Law of 1834.

*Wickersham, J. P.   *A History of Education in Pennsylvania.*   683 pp. Lancaster, Pa., 1886.

A very valuable volume, now somewhat rare. Chapters XIII, XV, and XVI very good on pauper education and the fight to establish free schools.

CHAPTER VII

THE BATTLE TO CONTROL THE SYSTEM

II. PHASES OF THE BATTLE FOR STATE—SUPPORTED
SCHOOLS — *continued*

4. *The battle to establish school supervision*

Local nature of all early schools. The history of our educational evolution so far described must have clearly revealed to the reader how completely local the evolution of schools has been with us. Everywhere development has been from the community outward and upward, and not from the State downward. At first the schools were those of individual teachers, churches, philanthropic societies, towns, or districts, organized and maintained without much if any thought of connection or state relationship. Even in Massachusetts and Connecticut the local nature of the education provided was one of its marked characteristics.

After the New England towns, in response to the demand for greater local rights and local control of affairs, had split their town governments up into fragments, known at first as parishes and later as school districts, as described in Chapter III, and after the Massachusetts district school system thus evolved had been confirmed in the new state laws (1789), it spread to other States and soon became the almost universal unit to the North and West for school organization and control. The reasons for its early popularity are not hard to find. As an administrative and taxing unit it was well suited to the primitive needs and conditions of our early national life. Among a sparse and hard-working rural population, between whom intercourse was limited and intercommunication difficult, and with whom the support of schools by taxation was as yet an unsettled question, local control answered a very real need. The simplicity and democracy of the system was one of its chief merits. Communities or neighborhoods which wanted schools and were willing to pay for them could easily meet and organize a school district, vote to levy a school tax on their own property, employ a teacher, and organize and maintain a school. Figure 57 shows how this process took place.

On the other hand, communities which did not desire schools or were unwilling to tax themselves for them could do without them, and let the free-school idea alone. The first state laws generally, as we have pointed out in Chapter VI, were permissive in nature and not mandatory, and under these permissive laws the progressive communities of each State gradually organized a series of local schools.

These have since been brought together into township, county, and state organizations to form the state systems which we know today.

The schools thus established would naturally retain their local character so long as their support was entirely local. Schools might even be ordered established, as in the case of the town schools of Massachusetts and Connecticut, or the pauper schools of Pennsylvania, and, so long as the State contributed nothing to their maintenance, their organization, management, and control would almost of

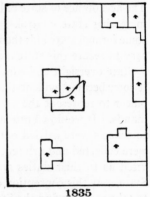

1835

FIG. 57. EARLY DISTRICT ORGANIZATION

necessity be left to local initiative. The more progressive communities would obey the law and provide schools supported largely or wholly by taxation; the unwilling communities would either ignore the law or provide schools dependent upon tuition fees and rate-bills.

Beginnings of state control. The great battle for state schools, which we have briefly described in the preceding chapter, was not only for taxation to stimulate their development where none existed, but was also indirectly a battle for some form of state control of the local systems which had already grown up. The establishment of permanent state school funds by the older States, to supplement any other aid which might be granted, also tended toward the establishment of some form of state supervision and control of the local school systems. Under the early permissive laws all state aid for schools might of course be rejected, and frequently was, and usually large option and power of initiative had at first to be left to the local units, but the State, once any aid from permanent state endowment funds or any form of state taxation was accepted by a community school system, was now in position to make and enforce demands in return for the state aid granted. In return for the state aid accepted the local school authorities must now make reports as to attendance, length of term, kind of teacher, and income and expenses, and must comply with the requirements of the state school laws as to district meetings, levying of local taxes to supplement the state aid, subjects to be taught, certificate for the teacher, and other similar matters. The acceptance of state aid inevitably meant a small but a gradually increasing state control. The first step was the establishment of some form of state aid; the next was the imposing of conditions necessary to secure this state aid.

State oversight and control, however, does not exercise itself, and it soon became evident that the States must elect or appoint some officer to represent the State and enforce the observance of its demands. It would be primarily his duty to see that the laws relating to schools were carried out, that statistics as to existing conditions were collected and printed, and that communities were properly advised as to their duties and the legislature as to the needs of the State. As this conception of the duty and power of the State began to take root, we find the States beginning to create a series of school officers to represent the State, the enactment of new laws extending control, and a struggle to integrate, subordinate, and reduce to some semblance of a state school system the hundreds of community school systems which had grown up. The communities usually were very willing to accept the state aid offered, but many of them resented bitterly any attempt to curb their power to do as they pleased, or to force them to make reports and meet general state requirements.[1]

The first state school officers. The first American State to create a state officer to exercise supervision over its schools was New York, in 1812. It will be remembered that this State had enacted an experimental school law (**R. 71**), and had made an annual state grant for schools from 1795 to 1800. Then, unable to re-enact the law, a school fund had been created (1800), and the system was allowed to lapse. It was not until the New England element gained control, in 1812, that a state school system was re-established. The Massachusetts district school system was now substituted for the previous town system, district taxation for schools was permitted, and the

[1] As each citizen claimed the right to give his children the kind and amount of education which he deemed sufficient, so the districts insisted on the same right, regardless of any larger interests or attempted control.

GIDEON HAWLEY
(1785–1870)

State Superintendent, New York, 1812–1821
From a painting in the State Department of Education,
at Albany

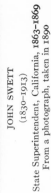

JOHN SWETT
(1830–1913)

State Superintendent, California, 1863–1869
From a photograph, taken in 1890

TWO EARLY FOUNDERS OF STATE SCHOOL SYSTEMS

income from the state school fund, created in 1800, was put to use. In enacting the new law [1] providing for state aid for schools the first State Superintendent of Common Schools in the United States was created. So far as is known this was a distinctively American creation, uninfluenced by the practice in any other land. It was to be the duty of this officer to look after the establishment and maintenance of the schools throughout the State. By his vigorous work in behalf of schools [2] the first appointee, Gideon Hawley, gave such offense to the politicians of the time that he was removed from office, in 1821, and the legislature then abolished the position and designated the Secretary of State to act, *ex officio*, as Superintendent.[3] This condition continued until 1854, when New York again created the separate office of Superintendent of Public Instruction. Maryland created the office in 1826, but two years later abolished it and did not re-create it until 1864. Illinois directed its Secretary of State to act, *ex officio*, as Superintendent of Schools in 1825, as did also Vermont from 1827 to 1833, Louisiana in 1833, Pennsylvania in 1834, and Tennessee in 1835. Illinois did not create a real State Superintendent of Schools, though, until 1854, Vermont until 1845, Louisiana until 1847, Pennsylvania until 1857, or Tennessee until 1867.

The first States to create separate school officials who have been continued to the present time were Michigan and Kentucky. In 1829, while a Territory, Michigan had created the office of Territorial Superintendent of Common Schools, and in 1836 this was

[1] The Act of 1812 followed a report of a legislative committee on a plan for the "organization and establishment of common schools." It accepted the principle of state responsibility and aid, with state oversight, while at the same time establishing the Massachusetts district system in place of the town system previously used.

[2] "The first superintendent did not limit himself to the duties specified in the statute. By his activity he demonstrated the possibilities of his position, and the successful establishment within eight years of 5500 schools, with an enrollment of over 300,000 pupils, has been ascribed in very large degree to his work. The uncalled for removal of Superintendent Hawley, in 1821, caused the legislature, as a means of censuring this action of the Council of Appointment, to transfer the duties of his office to the Secretary of State." (J. A. Fairlie. *The Centralization of Administration in New York State*, p. 23.)

[3] "To no individual in the state are the friends of common school education more deeply indebted for the impetus given to the cause of elementary education, in its infancy, than to Gideon Hawley. At a period when everything depended upon organization; upon supervision; upon practical acquaintance with the most minute details; and upon a patient, persevering, laborious process of exposition, Mr. Hawley united in himself all the requisites for the efficient discharge of the high functions devolved upon him by the legislature. From a state of anarchy and confusion, and complete disorganization, within a period of eight years arose a beautiful and stately structure, based on impregnable foundations." (S. S. Randall. *The Common School System of the State of New York*, p. 18.)

evolved into the position of State Superintendent of Public Instruction. Influenced by Cousin's *Report* (Chapter X) on the organization of schools in Prussia, the educational leaders in the Michigan constitutional convention of 1835 — Pierce and Crary — insisted on the title of Superintendent of Public Instruction, and on constitutional provisions which would insure, from an administrative point of view, a state school system [1] rather than a series of local systems of schools. Kentucky, on the other hand, in 1838 evolved, as had New York, a purely American-type official, known as Superintendent of Common Schools. The Michigan title in time came to be the one commonly used, though few States in adopting it have been aware of its Prussian origin. Other States followed these two, creating a state school officer under one of a number of titles, and in some States, such as Connecticut, Ohio, Iowa, and Missouri, the office was created, abolished, and re-created one or more times before it became permanently established. Often quite a legislative struggle took place to secure the establishment of the office, and later on to prevent its abolition. Today, however, all our American States have such an official.

By 1850 there were *ex-officio* state school officers in nine, and regular school officers [2] in seven, of the then thirty-one States, and by 1861 there were *ex-officio* officers in nine and regular officers in nineteen of the then thirty-four States, as well as one of each in two of the organized Territories. The map opposite shows the growth of supervisory oversight by 1861 — forty-nine years from the time the first American state school officer was created. The map also shows the ten of the thirty-four States which had, by 1861, also created the office of County Superintendent of Schools, as well as the twenty-six cities which had, by 1861, created the office of City Superintendent of Schools. Only three more cities — Albany, Washington, and

[1] "About this time, Cousin's report on the Prussian system came into my hands and was read with much interest. Sitting one pleasant afternoon upon a log, General Crary and myself discussed, for a long time, the fundamental principles which were deemed important for the [constitutional] convention to adopt, in laying the foundations of a new State. The subject of education was the theme of special interest. It was agreed, if possible, that it should be made a distinct branch of government, and that the constitution ought to provide for an officer who should have the whole matter in charge." (Statement by John D. Pierce, quoted by Putnam, p. 21.)

[2] Other early state school officers which have been continued down to the present time were created in Rhode Island in 1845, New Jersey in 1846, Iowa and Louisiana in 1847, and California in 1849. The title of Superintendent of Public Instruction was used in the last three.

Kansas City — were added before 1870, making a total of twenty-nine, but since that date the number of city superintendents has increased to something like three thousand today.

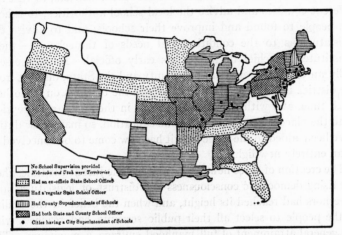

FIG. 58. STATUS OF SCHOOL SUPERVISION IN THE UNITED STATES BY 1861

For a list of the 26 city superintendencies established up to 1861 (29 up to 1870), see Cubberley's *Public School Administration*, p. 75. For a history of the state educational office in each State see Cubberley and Elliott, *State and County School Administration, Source Book*, pp. 283–87.

Early duties; selection by election. The office of State Superintendent of Common Schools, Superintendent of Free Schools, Superintendent of Education, Superintendent of Public Instruction, or Commissioner of Education — terms which are significant of the educational evolution through which we have passed — was thus evolved with us to represent the State in its dealings with the local school systems to which it now proposed to extend some financial aid. At the time the office arose there were few of our present-day problems to be solved, and the early functions attached to the office were almost exclusively clerical, statistical, and exhortatory. These early functions have become crystallized in the laws and have formed the traditions of the office.

Even more have they formed the traditions of the office of County Superintendent of Schools, which also was an evolution, arising out of the increasing state need for additional oversight and control.[1] To collect, tabulate, and edit the school statistics as to attendance, teachers, term, and finances demanded by the law; to advise as to the law; to apportion the state aid to the school districts; to visit the different counties and advise the local school authorities; to exhort the people to found and improve their schools; and to advise the legislature as to the condition and needs of the schools — these constituted the chief duties of this early official. He was essentially an officer to represent the county and the State, distinct from the district trustees on the one hand and the teachers on the other. With time, and with the gradual change in the popular conception as to the place and purpose of public education, so many new duties have been added to the office that it has now come to be conceived of in an entirely new light.

The creation of these new state officials came just at the time when the rising democratic consciousness and distrust of legislatures and governors had reached its height, and when the belief in the ability of the people to select all their public servants had reached, with the general attainment of full manhood suffrage, a maximum. The appointed city school superintendent had not as yet arisen to point the way to a better method of selection — there were but twelve such in the United States by 1850 — the analogy to a state auditor or a county clerk seemed clear, the expert functions which now ought to characterize the office had not developed, there was no business that an average member of the electorate could not handle satisfactorily, and nomination and election by the people seemed the perfectly natural method to follow.

In consequence of this situation, almost everywhere these new state and county school officials were placed in the elective column, instead of being appointed to office. Even in the cities the elective method was at first tried, though all cities have now discarded it as a means for selecting a city superintendent of schools. In the earlier period, when the duties of these new officials were far simpler than they now are, when they were largely those of a clerical and auditing

---

[1] This office arose about 1830, became common by 1860, and may be said to have become definitely established by about 1880. In a few States, as New York and Michigan, it was evolved out of the township superintendency which preceded it; in others, as Ohio and Indiana, it came through the subdivision of the work of some other county official; and in still others, as Georgia and Louisiana, by appointment as executive officer for the board of county commissioners in the oversight of the schools.

official, and when almost no professional functions had arisen, the elective method of choosing a person to fill these educational offices naturally gave much better results than it does today.   Only in New England and New York was a better method followed from the first.[1]

Curbing the district system.   One of the chief duties of these early state school officials, aside from the collection of statistics and exhorting the people to establish and maintain schools, was that of trying to institute some control over the local school communities, and the introduction of some uniformity into school practices.   By the time the States began to create state and county school officers, the Massachusetts district system, the origin of which we described in Chapter III, had overrun the country.   The first school law enacted by Massachusetts (1789) recognized and legalized the district system of school organization and control,[2] as it had evolved in the State during the preceding hundred years.   In 1800 the districts were given full local power to tax for schools; in 1817 full power was given them to contract and to sue and be sued; and in 1827 the full culmination of the district system was attained by laws which authorized the districts to select district school trustees, and gave to these trustees the power to choose the textbooks and employ and certificate their teachers.   Starting as a social convenience, the school district had now evolved into a political institution.

Maine, Vermont, New Hampshire, Rhode Island, and Connecticut also accepted the district system early.   It spread to New York in 1812, and was carried by New England people in their great migration toward the West and South.   Ohio definitely accepted the district system of organization in 1821, Illinois in 1825, Tennessee in 1830, Indiana in 1833 (**R. 126**), Michigan in 1837, Kentucky and Iowa in 1838, North Carolina in 1839, and Virginia in its optional law of 1846.   Once established amid pioneer people it became firmly rooted and has since been changed only after much effort, though almost all the conditions which gave rise to it have since passed away.

In most of the States the system soon ran rampant.   The district

[1] In the six New England States and New York the people have never been permitted to elect, at popular election, what is so manifestly an expert professional officer.

[2] The law of 1789 Horace Mann termed "the most unfortunate law on the subject of common schools ever enacted in this State," and Mr. Martin, the historian of the Massachusetts school system, declared that the law of 1827, by which the school district became a body politic, "marks the utmost limit to the subdivision of American sovereignty — the high-water mark of modern democracy, and the low-water mark of the Massachusetts school system."

meeting became a forensic center in which questions the most remote and personal animosities of long standing were fought out. Petty local interests and a "dog-in-the-manger spirit" too often prevailed, to the great detriment of the schools.[1] District jealousies prevented needed development. An exaggerated idea of district rights, district importance, and district perfection became common (R. 126). Possessed of no machinery for the consideration of policies or for the adoption of progressive plans, the school district meeting was moved by antipathies and ruled by sentiment. If a fight was on, a full attendance could be counted on. District independence often was carried to a great extreme. In Massachusetts, for example, Horace Mann found that in two thirds of the towns teachers were allowed to begin teaching without any examination or certification, and frequently were paid without either; that the trustees refused generally to require uniform textbooks, or to furnish them to poor children, as required by the law; and that one third of the children of school age in the State were absent from school in the winter and two fifths in the summer, without the trustees concerning themselves in any way about the situation. In Ohio the trustees "forbade the teaching of any branches except reading, writing, and arithmetic," and in 1840 the early laws requiring schools in the English language were repealed and the districts were permitted to authorize schools in the German language. In Indiana, the system went to such an extreme as almost to destroy the schools. In 1836 and 1837 laws were passed which permitted householders to make individual contracts with teachers to teach their children, and in 1841 the requirement of any form of a teacher's certificate was made optional with the district trustees. In Illinois, in 1827, the whole or half support of a school by taxation was made optional with the voters of each district, and no man could be taxed for schools without first obtaining his consent in writing. In many States school district trustees were allowed to determine what subjects should be taught and how, and the people in district meeting determined who should teach and how long a term of school should be maintained.

[1] "Questions involving the fate of nations have been decided with less expenditure of time, less stirring of passions, less vociferation of declamation and denunciation, than the location of a 15 x 20 schoolhouse. I have known such a question to call for ten district meetings, scattered over two years, bringing down from mountain farms three miles away men who had no children to be schooled, and who had not taken the trouble to vote in the presidential election of the period." (G. H. Martin. *Evolution of the Massachusetts Public School System*, p. 93.)

To enforce reports giving statistics as to the schools, to enforce local taxation to supplement the state aid, to enforce the requirement of some form of a teacher's certificate, to see that the school subjects required in the law were taught in the schools, and that the schools were maintained at least the length of time demanded by the State, were among the early functions of these state, county, and township school superintendents. All these were important as establishing some form of state control over the school districts, and marked the beginnings of their integration into a series of county and state school systems.

Creating supervision in Massachusetts. The struggle to subordinate and control the district system and establish state control is well illustrated by the history of Massachusetts. Once foremost in general education, a great decline had set in after the coming of statehood, and this decline continued steadily up to about 1826. The decline in the importance of its schools was closely paralleled by the growth in importance of the district system of school control. The growth of manufacturing, the social changes in the cities, and the philanthropic and humanitarian movements we have described in Chapter V, all tended in Massachusetts, as elsewhere, to awaken an educational consciousness and a demand for educational reform. As early as 1821 a young Harvard graduate and teacher, by the name of James G. Carter (1795–1845), had published a series of *Letters...on the Free Schools of New England.* In these letters Carter traced the history of legislation relating to free and public schools in Massachusetts, pointed out the condition of the schools, laid bare the glaring defects of the district system and the decline in importance of the schools, and dwelt on the depressing influence which the establishment of academies and private schools, and the neglect of grammar schools in the towns, had exerted on the common schools of the State (**R. 127**). Deeply impressed with conditions, he soon became a leader in educational propaganda and educational reform.

The first result of the agitation he started was the law of 1826, whereby each town (township) was required to appoint a Town School Committee (School Board) to exercise general supervision over all the district schools in the town, select the textbooks, and examine and certificate all the teachers employed. This law met with bitter opposition from many districts, it being regarded as an infringement of district "rights." In 1834 the state school fund [1] was created, and, profiting by the experience of Connecticut, to share in the income all towns were required to raise a town tax of one dollar per child of school age and to make statistical reports as required. In 1837 came the culmination of Mr. Carter's labors, when he, as chairman of the House Committee on Education, secured passage of a bill creating the first real State Board of Education in the United States. Instead of following the practice of the time, and creating an elected State Superintendent of Schools, Mr. Carter, much more wisely, provided for a small appointed State Board of Education which in turn was to select a Secretary, who was to act in the capacity of a state school officer and report to the Board, and through it to the legislature and the people. Neither the Board nor the Secretary were given any powers of compulsion, their work being to investigate conditions, report facts, expose defects, and make recommendations as to action to the legislature.[2] The permanence and influence of the Board thus depended very largely on the character of the Secretary it selected.

The new Secretary and his problems. A prominent Brown University graduate and lawyer in the State Senate, by the name of Horace Mann (1796–1859), who as president of the Senate had been of much assistance in securing passage of the bill creating the State Board of Education, was finally induced by the Governor and the Board to accept the position of Secretary. He entered on his duties in June, 1837. The choice proved to be a particularly fortunate one, as Mr. Mann possessed the characteristics needed for such an office — enthusiasm, courage, vision, lofty ideals, and practical legislative experience (**R. 128**). Few State Superintendents of Public Instruction since his time have risen to a higher conception of the importance of their office, and his career forms a worthy study for anyone interested in educational leadership. He gave up a promising

[1] This fund was to be made up from all money in the state treasury obtained from the sale of Maine lands, from the claims of the State on the United States for military services, and one half of all future income from Maine lands, the total not to exceed one million dollars.

[2] "The measure was very mild and inoffensive. It was evident that the State intended to lay no violent hands on the people's schools. The new board had some simple duties, but no power. It was to prepare an abstract of the school returns; it was to make an annual report to the legislature of the condition and efficiency of the common school system, and to suggest means of improving it — only this and nothing more could the board do. Its mission was to control by enlightening, not to control by authority." (G. H. Martin. *Evolution of the Massachusetts Public School System*, p. 156.)

HORACE MANN
(1796–1859)
(From a painting in the Westfield, Massachusetts, Normal School)

career in the law and in politics to accept the office at a beggarly salary [1] that often left him without money for his dinner, but, once he had made up his mind to do so, he entered upon the work with all the energy he possessed. To a friend he wrote:

> I no longer write myself attorney, counsellor, or lawyer. My law books are for sale. My office is "to let." The bar is no longer my forum. My jurisdiction is changed. I have abandoned jurisprudence and betaken myself to the larger sphere of mind and morals.

On the day he accepted the office he wrote in his diary:

> Henceforth so long as I hold this office I devote myself to the supremest welfare of mankind upon earth.... I have faith in the improvability of the race — in their accelerating improvability. This effort may do, apparently, but little. But mere beginning in a good cause is never little. If we can get this vast wheel into any perceptible motion, we shall have accomplished much.

When he learned that his friends and the public were surprised that he would give up his profession and the chances for political preferment for an office whose salary was meager and the title of which was without honor, he said:

> If the title is not sufficiently honorable now, then it is clearly left for me to elevate it. I had rather be creditor than debtor to the title.

The problems which Mr. Mann faced, growing out of bad legislation in the past and the resulting state of affairs, are thus stated by Hinsdale:

1. The whole State needed to be thoroughly aroused to the importance and value of public instruction.

2. The public schools needed to be democratized; that is, the time had more than come when they should be restored to the people of the State, high as well as low, in the good old sense of the name.

3. The public necessities demanded an expansion of public education in respect to kinds of schools and range of instruction.

4. The legal school organization and machinery, as existing, were not in harmony with the new social conditions. Moreover, current methods of administration were loose and unbusinesslike.

5. The available school funds were quite insufficient for maintaining good schools, and called loudly for augmentation.

6. The schools were, to a great extent, antiquated and outgrown in respect to the quantity and quality of the instruction that they furnished,

---

[1] The Act of 1837 made no provision for funds, beyond $1000 a year for the Secretary to be elected. This was increased by the legislature to $1500, but with no provision for any contingent expenses, office rent, or clerical assistance. This left about $500 a year for the Secretary. Mann's comment was: "Well, one thing is certain, I will be revenged on them; I will do them more than $1500 worth of good."

as well as in methods of teaching, management, discipline, and supervision.[1]

The time for beginning such a work was anything but propitious. The great panic of 1837 was just breaking, and this grew in intensity until 1841. Internal development was at a standstill, money was hard to get, and the times seemed anything but favorable for launching a campaign for education reform and increased taxation for education. Yet Mann, undaunted, went ahead.

The work of Horace Mann. Mr. Mann now began a most memorable work of educating public opinion, and soon became the acknowledged leader in school organization in the United States. State after State called upon him for advice and counsel, while his twelve *Annual Reports* to the State Board of Education will always remain memorable documents. During the first five years after the organization of the Board of Education, a common school convention was held in each county annually, and in some of the larger counties two or more were held. At these Mann gave addresses on education, and strove to awaken some interest and enthusiasm for the work he had undertaken.[2] Public men of all classes — lawyers, clergymen, college professors, literary men, teachers — were laid under tribute and sent forth over the State explaining to the people the need for a reawakening of educational interest in Massachusetts. His "campaigns" resembled somewhat the recent national campaign to explain to our people the meaning and moral significance of our participation in the World War in Europe. Though he at times met with much discouragement,[3] he nevertheless was so successful, and

[1] In two thirds of the towns teachers were allowed to commence school without being previously examined and certificated by the School Committee, as required by law, and teachers' wages were paid without evidence of certification. The selection of textbooks was neglected in one third of the towns. Schools were not visited, as required by law. On an average, one third of all the children four to sixteen years of age were absent from school in winter, and two fifths in summer.

[2] On his return to Boston from his first circuit, he wrote in his Journal:

"My great circuit is now completed. The point to which, three months ago, I looked forward with so much anxiety, is reached. The labor is done. With much weariness, with almost unbounded anxiety, with some thwartings, but, on the whole, with unexpected and extraordinary encouragement, the work is done. That, however, is but the beginning. I confess life begins to have a value which I have not felt for five years before."

[3] Some of Mann's comments on his efforts are interesting:

To make an impression in the Berkshires, he said, was like trying to batter down Gibraltar with one's fist. At Wellfleet, the convention was miserable, contemptible, deplorable. At Dedham, his former home, it was meager, spiritless, and discouraging. If the schoolmaster was abroad in the county, he would like to meet him. A little dent was made in Worcester. At Pittsfield, the meeting was small, but two or three individuals who attended were of themselves equal to a meeting. At Hanover, where ex-President Adams and Daniel Webster spoke, it was "a great day for common schools."

so ripe was the time for such a movement, that he not only started a great common school revival in Massachusetts which led to the regeneration of the schools there, but one which was felt and which influenced development in every Northern State.

His controversy with the Boston schoolmasters (**R. 129**), whose sensibilities he had wounded by his praise of European schools in his *Seventh Report*, attracted much attention, made a deep impression on the public mind, and did much to fix Mr. Mann's place in educational history. His controversy with the religious societies marked the beginning of the struggle in the United States for non-sectarian schools. Everywhere he preached the doctrine of liberal taxation for public education, with the result that during the twelve years of his secretaryship the appropriations for public education were more than doubled, salaries of teachers greatly increased, and a full month added to the length of the school term. He organized the first three state normal schools in America, and some of the earliest teachers' institutes. He labored continually at the improvement of teaching method, and especially worked for the introduction of Pestalozzian reforms and the substitution of the word-method in teaching reading for the slow, wasteful, and unintelligent alphabet method. He edited the *Massachusetts Common School Journal*,[1] wrote a careful report on schoolhouse hygiene, introduced school libraries throughout the State, and stimulated the development of the high school. In his hands the printed "school returns," first required by the law of 1826, became "powerful instruments in educating the public." His vigorous condemnation of the district system, to which he devoted his *Fourth Report*, contributed to its ultimate abandonment. The Massachusetts Law of 1789, which legalized it, he repeatedly stated to have been "the most unfortunate law on the subject of common schools ever enacted in the State," and he declared that "no substantial and general progress can be made so long as the district system exists." So entrenched was the system "behind statutory rights and immemorial usage" that it required forty-one years longer to free the State from its inimical influence.

---

[1] Of this Journal, Mr. Mann said, later: "It came to the public rather as their fate than as a consequence of their free will. It was born, not because it was wanted, but because it was needed." Its object was to be the improvement of common schools by making what was known to the few known to the many. It was a 16 pp. semi-monthly, octavo magazine, the annual volume containing 384 pp., and its price was $1.00 a year The ten annual volumes which Mr. Mann edited are a mine of information.

His twelve carefully written *Reports* (**R. 130**) on the condition of education in Massachusetts and elsewhere, with his intelligent discussion of the aims and purposes of public education, occupy a commanding place in the history of American education, while he will always be regarded as perhaps the greatest of the "founders" of our American system of free public schools.[1] No one did more than he to establish in the minds of the American people the conception that education should be universal, non-sectarian, and free, and that its aim should be social efficiency, civic virtue, and character, rather than mere learning or the advancement of sectarian ends. Under his practical leadership (**R. 131**) an unorganized and heterogeneous series of community school systems was reduced to organization and welded together into a state school system, and the people of Massachusetts were effectively recalled to their ancient belief in and duty toward the education of the people.

Henry Barnard in Connecticut and Rhode Island. Almost equally important, though of a somewhat different character, was the work of Henry Barnard in Connecticut and Rhode Island. A graduate of Yale, and also educated for the law, he turned aside to teach and became deeply interested in education. The years 1835–37 he spent in Europe studying schools, particularly the work of Pestalozzi's disciples. On his return to America he was elected a member of the Connecticut legislature, and at once formulated and secured passage of the Connecticut law (1839) providing for a State Board of Commissioners for Common Schools, with a Secretary, after the Massachusetts plan. Mr. Barnard was then elected as its first Secretary, and reluctantly gave up the law and accepted the position at the munificent salary of $3 a day and expenses. Until the legislature abolished both the Board and the position, in 1842, and again from 1851 to 1855, he rendered for Connecticut a service (**R. 133**) scarcely less important than the better-known reforms which Horace Mann at about the same time was carrying on in Massachusetts.

It will be remembered that Connecticut had established a state school fund as early as 1750 (page 179), and on the sale of the West-

[1] Mr. Mann's influence was neither slight nor transient. It survived both his resignation of the Secretaryship and his death; it has continued strong to the present time, and promises to be one of the spiritual powers of the country. The centennial of his birth was commemorated throughout the land, the memorial services that were held, and the essays and articles that were published, testifying in a most eloquent manner to the hold that he has on the intellect and conscience of the Nation." (B. A. Hinsdale. *Horace Mann*, p. 279.)

ern Reserve for $1,200,000, in 1795, had added this sum to the fund (**R. 107**). The fund experienced excellent management, and by the time of the creation of the State Board had reached nearly $2,000,000 in value, producing a yearly income large enough to pay a substantial portion of the then cost of maintaining the schools. This had made the people negligent as to taxation (**R. 132**), and this, combined with the growing strength of the district system, led to a decline in interest in education in Connecticut [1] similar to that which had taken place in Massachusetts. The schools were poor, private schools were increasing, the people objected to taxation, the teachers were without training or professional interest, the pauper-school idea began to be strongly advocated, and a general decline in educational affairs had set in. An investigation, made in 1838, showed that not one half of the children of the State were attending school. From probably the best schools of any State at the end of the colonial period, the Connecticut schools had fallen to a very inferior position.

It was the work of Barnard to recall Connecticut to her ancient duty. He visited and inspected the schools, and made many public addresses. In 1839 he organized the first teachers' institute in America which met for more than a few days (his was for six weeks, with daily instruction in classes), and he used this new instrument extensively to awaken the teachers of the State to proper conceptions of their work. He established (1838) the *Connecticut Common School Journal*, after the plan of Mann's *Journal* in Massachusetts, to disseminate his ideas. He also organized school libraries, and urged the establishment of evening schools. He strove to improve the physical condition of the schools by writing much on schoolhouse construction. He studied the "school returns," and used the statistical data, as Mann had done, to arouse interest. In 1842, through the animus of a governor who objected to the "useless expense," [2] and the "dangerous innovation" of union schools to pro-

---

[1] One of Connecticut's able statesmen, Hon. R. M. Sherman, writing on the results of the Fund, in 1830, said:

"It may be justly questioned whether the school fund, as used, has been of any use in Connecticut. It has furnished a supply, when there was no deficiency. Content with the ancient standard of school instruction, the people have permitted the expense of sustaining it to be taken off their hands, and have aimed at nothing higher. They expended about an equal sum before the school fund existed.... A higher value would consist in its being made *an instrument for exciting general exertion* for the attainment of some important end."

[2] "By way of experiment, the Legislature established a Board of Commissioners of Common Schools; and, under the belief that some essential improvements might be made, an officer has been employed, at considerable expense, to visit the various schools in the State

vide advanced education, the Board was abolished, the laws repealed, and Mr. Barnard was legislated out of office. For this action Mr. Mann delivered himself of some caustic comments (**R. 125**).

In 1843 Barnard was called to Rhode Island to examine and report upon the existing schools,[1] and from 1845 to 1849 acted as State Commissioner of Public Schools there, where he rendered a service similar to that previously rendered in Connecticut. Like Mann, he was a great campaigner and organizer, holding public meetings all over the State and awakening public interest.[2] In 1845 he organized the Rhode Island Institute of Instruction, one of the oldest teachers' associations in the United States. In addition he organized a series of town lecture courses and town libraries throughout the State. For his teachers' institutes he devised a traveling model school, to give demonstration lessons in the art of teaching.

From 1851 to 1855 he was again in Connecticut, as principal of the newly established state normal school and *ex-officio* Secretary of the Connecticut State Board of Education. He now rewrote the school laws, increased taxation for schools, checked the power of the districts, there known as "school societies," and laid the foundations of a state system of schools.

Barnard as the scholar of the "awakening." In 1855 he began the editing of his famous *American Journal of Education*, a vast encyclopædia of educational information which finally reached thirty-one volumes, of around 800 pages each. Dr. Harris has

with reference to their improvement... Without questioning the motives of those by whom these experiments were suggested and adopted, I think it obvious that the public expectations, in regard to their consequences, have not been realized; and that to continue them will only entail on the State a useless expense." (*Message to the Legislature* of Governor Cleveland, May, 1842.)

[1] What is often termed the first school survey report was his first printed *Report* as Commissioner of Public Schools for Rhode Island, which summarized his two years of observation of the State's schools, and was almost encyclopædic in character. He had visited every section of the State, examined the schoolhouses, questioned the teachers, consulted with the school officers, conducted and addressed public meetings, and drafted school legislation to remedy the defects which he found. See article by Wells, in the References at the close of this chapter.

[2] "During the five years of service of Mr. Barnard, more than 1100 meetings were held expressly to discuss topics connected with public schools, at which upwards of 1500 addresses were delivered. One hundred and fifty of these meetings continued through the day and evening, upwards of 100 through two evenings and a day, 50 through two days and three evenings, and 12 through the entire week. In addition, upwards of 200 meetings for teachers and parents were held for lectures and examination of schools. In addition, more than 16,000 educational pamphlets were distributed, and one year no almanac was sold in Rhode Island without at least sixteen pages of educational matter attached." (E. M. Stone. *History of the Rhode Island Institute of Instruction.*)

HENRY BARNARD
(1811–1900)
From a picture taken about 1890

termed the *Journal* "an educational course of reading of 24,000 pages and 12 million words." In this venture he sunk his entire private fortune, and in his old age was a poor man. The collection still remains a great storehouse of educational information and biography, covering almost every phase of the history of education from the earliest times down to 1870. It gave to American educators, who had so long been isolated and who had been slowly evolving a thoroughly native school system out of the English inheritance, a needed conception of historical development in other countries and a useful knowledge of recent development and practice in other lands and nations. From 1858 to 1860 he served as president of the University of Wisconsin, and from 1867 to 1870 as the first United States Commissioner of Education. He published much, was distinctively the scholar of the great public school awakening of the second quarter of the nineteenth century, and was closely associated with the most progressive movements in American education for approximately forty years. Mann and Barnard stand out as the two conspicuous leaders during the formative period of American education. Mann in particular pointed the way to many subsequent reforms in the administration of public education, while to Barnard we owe a special debt as our first great educational scholar.

The "awakening" elsewhere; the leaders. The work of Mann and Barnard had its influence throughout all the Northern States, and encouraged the friends of education everywhere. Almost contemporaneous with them were leaders in other States who helped fight through the battles of state establishment and state organization and control, among the more prominent of whom should be mentioned Calvin Stowe, Samuel Lewis, and Samuel Galloway in Ohio; Caleb Mills in Indiana; Ninian W. Edwards in Illinois; John D. Pierce and Isaac E. Crary in Michigan; Robert J. Breckinridge in Kentucky; Calvin H. Wiley in North Carolina; and John Swett in California.

It is not perhaps without its significance, as showing the enduring influence of the Calvinistic educational traditions, that of these Stowe was a graduate of Bowdoin College in Maine, and that the Stowe family goes back to 1634, in Roxbury, Massachusetts; that Lewis was born in Massachusetts, was descended from one of the first colonists in Plymouth, and floated down the Ohio with his parents to Cincinnati in the great westward migration of New England people; that Galloway was of Scotch-Irish ancestry, and was educated among New England people in Ohio; that Mills was born in New Hampshire, and had been graduated from Dartmouth; that Pierce was born in New Hampshire, educated in Massachusetts, and had been graduated from Brown; that Crary was of Puritan ancestry, born and educated in Connecticut, and a graduate of Trinity College; that Breckinridge was a descendant of a Scotch Covenanter who fled to America, at the time of the restoration of the Stuarts in England, and settled in Pennsylvania; that Wiley was of early Scotch-Irish Presbyterian stock; and that Swett was born and educated in New Hampshire, taught school in Massachusetts in the days of Horace Mann, and was descended from a family of that name which landed at Massachusetts Bay in 1642.

5. *The battle to eliminate sectarianism*

The secularization of American education. The Church, with us, it will be remembered, was from the earliest colonial times in possession of the education of the young. Not only were the earliest schools controlled by the Church and dominated by the religious motive, but the right of the Church to dictate the teaching in the schools was clearly recognized by the State. Still more, the State looked to the Church to provide the necessary education, and assisted it in doing so by donations of land and money. The minister, as a town official, naturally examined the teachers and the instruction in the schools. After the establishment of our National Government this relationship for a time continued. New York and the New England States specifically set aside lands to help both church and school. When Connecticut sold its Western Reserve, in 1795, and added the sum to the Connecticut school fund, it was stated to be for the aid of "schools and the gospel." In the sales of the first national lands in Ohio (1,500,000 acres to The Ohio Company, in 1787; and 1,000,000 acres in the Symmes Purchase, near Cincinnati, in 1788), section 16 in each township was reserved and given as an endowment for schools, and section 29 "for the purposes of religion." After about 1800 these land endowments for religion ceased, but grants of state aid for religious schools continued for nearly a half-century longer. Then it became common for a town or city to build a schoolhouse from city taxation, and let it out rent-free to any responsible person who would conduct a tuition school in it, with a few free places for selected poor children. Still later, with the rise of the state schools, it became quite common to take over church and private schools and aid them on the same basis as the new state schools.

In colonial times, too, and for some decades into our national period, the warmest advocates of the establishment of schools were those who had in view the needs of the Church. Then gradually the emphasis shifted, as we have shown in Chapter IV, to the needs of the State, and a new class of advocates of public education now arose. Still later the emphasis has been shifted to industrial and civic and national needs, and the religious aim has been almost completely eliminated. This change is known as the secularization of American education. It also required many a bitter struggle, and was accomplished in the different States but slowly. The two main factors which served to produce this change have been:

1. The conviction that the life of the Republic demands an educated and intelligent citizenship, and hence the general education of all in common schools controlled by the State; and
2. The great diversity of religious beliefs among our people, which has forced tolerance and religious freedom through a consideration of the rights of minorities.

The secularization of education with us must not be regarded either as a deliberate or a wanton violation of the rights of the Church, but rather as an unavoidable incident connected with the coming to self-consciousness and self-government of a great people.

So long as there was little intercommunication and migration, and the people of a community remained fairly homogeneous, it was perfectly natural that the common religious faith of the people should enter into the instruction of the school. When the schools were purely local and voluntary this was not a serious objection. With the rise of state support, and the widening of the units for maintenance and control from the lonely community or district to the town, the county, and the State, the situation changed. With the development of the West, after 1800, with its indifference as to distinctions still powerful in the older States to the East; the coming of foreign immigration, which began to be marked after about 1825; and the intermingling of peoples of different faiths in the rapidly evolving cities and towns, religious uniformity ceased to exist. Majority rule now for a time followed, but this was soon forced to give way to the still more important governmental principle of religious freedom.[1] As necessity gradually compelled the State to provide education for its children, sectarian differences made it increasingly evident that the education provided must be non-sectarian in character. As Brown (S. W.) has so well stated it:

> Differences of religious belief and a sound regard on the part of the State for individual freedom in religious matters, coupled with the necessity for centralization and uniformity, rather than hostility to religion as such, lie at the bottom of the movement toward the secular school.

Gradual nature of the change. The change to non-sectarian schools came very gradually, and it is hard to assign a date for its beginning. The chart between pages 74 and 75, showing the process of evolving the civic out of the earlier religious schools, discloses a gradual fading out of religious influence and control during the eighteenth century, and the gradual assumption of state control early in the nineteenth century. The change began early in our national history — in a way it was but a sequel to the waning religious interest which characterized the last fifty years of the colonial period — but it was not until the decade of the forties that the question became at all acute. At first it was largely a matter of change in the character of instruction, marked by a decreasing emphasis on the religious element and an increasing emphasis on secular material. The use of the English Dilworth's *A New Guide to the English Tongue* (**R. 37**), after about 1760; the publication of Noah Webster's *American Spelling Book* (**R. 173**), a combined speller and reader, in 1783; and the *Columbian Primer* and the *Franklin Primer*, in 1802; soon broke the almost exclusive hold of the *New England Primer*, with its

Cc *Stands for* Camel, who lives in the east;   Dd *Stands for* Drunkard, a worse looking beast.

FIG. 59. THE ALPHABET

From *The Columbian Primer*, 1802. A small, 84-page, modernized and secularized imitation of the *New England Primer*. Each letter was illustrated; the illustrations for C and D are here reproduced.

---

[1] A good illustration of this new western liberality in matters of religious faith is found in the Act chartering the University of Michigan, in 1821, which contained the following clause:

"*Be it enacted*, That persons of every religious denomination shall be capable of being elected trustees; nor shall any person, as president, professor, instructor, or pupil, be refused admittance for his conscientious persuasion in matters of religion, provided he demean himself in a proper manner and conform to such rules as may be established."

Shorter Catechism, on the schools. By 1806 the *Primer* had been discarded in the dame schools of Boston, as well as in the lower schools in most other cities, though it continued to be used in the rural districts until near the beginning of the second quarter of the nineteenth century. Other American textbooks, more literary and less religious in character, also helped along the process of change. Some of the more prominent of these were Caleb Bingham's *American Preceptor* (1794) and *Columbian Orator* (1806), Lindley Murray's *English Reader* (1779) and *Grammar* (1795), and the *Franklin Primer* (1802). Readings from these new books in time began to take the place of, or at least materially to supplement, readings from the Bible.

The Lancastrian schools had also given but little attention to religious instruction as such, though having religious exercises, and these, it will be remembered, became for a time exceedingly popular throughout the country. The most significant single fact, and one clearly expressive of the process which had for long been under way, was the Massachusetts Act of 1827 which declared that School Committees should "never direct to be used or purchased in any of the town schools any school books which were calculated to favor the tenets of any particular sect of Christians." This Act merely registered what the slow operation of public opinion had already decided.[1] In 1833 Massachusetts gave up taxing for church support, as had Connecticut in 1818.

The fight in Massachusetts. The educational awakening in Massachusetts, brought on by the work of Carter and Mann, was to many a rude awakening. Among other things, it revealed that the old school of the Puritans had gradually been replaced by a new and purely American type of school, with instruction adapted to democratic and national rather than religious ends. Mr. Mann stood strongly for such a conception of public education, and being a Unitarian, and the new State Board of Education being almost entirely liberal in religion, a series of attacks was launched against them, and for the first time in our history the cry was raised that

[1] "This law had enjoined the teaching of religion and morality, while forbidding sectarianism in the schoolbooks used. It was drawn up and defended by a committee, themselves Orthodox, as expressing the desire of the citizens of the Commonwealth, Orthodox and Unitarians alike, that the religious controversies then raging in the churches should not invade the common schools." (R. B. Culver. *Horace Mann and Religion in the Massachusetts Public Schools*, p. 28.)

"The public schools are Godless schools." Those who believed in the old system of religious instruction, those who bore the Board or its Secretary personal ill-will, and those who desired to break down the Board's authority and stop the development of the public schools, united their forces in this first big attack against secular education. Horace Mann was the first prominent educator in America to meet and answer the religious onslaught.

The first attack came in the winter of 1838–39 in the form of *Four Letters*, a pamphlet of 25 pages, published anonymously, and five Letters published in the *Boston Recorder* attacking Mr. Mann and signed "Clericus Hampdenensis." In these the Law of 1827, the policy of the Board, and the writing of Mr. Mason, as they related to moral but non-sectarian instruction, were vigorously attacked, and it was held that:

> The Bible — in the naked simplicity of its annunciations; the Bible — unwarped, undiluted by sectarian expositions; the Bible, insisting on the great facts of man's moral ruin, of his need of a Redeemer, of regeneration and sanctification to fit him for the highest measure of usefulness on earth, and for the holy employments of the redeemed in heaven — should be daily and thoroughly taught in the schools.

Though a number replied in the press, Mr. Mann thought it wise at this time not to do so.

In the legislatures of 1840 and 1841 the religious forces attempted to abolish the State Board of Education, but the attempts failed dismally. Most of the orthodox people of the State took Mr. Mann's side.

The next important assault came, in 1844, from an Episcopalian paper in Boston, and became known as the *Christian Witness* controversy. In this the Board and its Secretary were violently assailed for their attitude toward sectarian instruction. Mr. Mann prepared three carefully drawn statements in reply, and a number of other writers came to his aid (**R. 134**), a number of whom pointed out the danger of denominational control or instruction.

A third and a much more virulent attack was opened on Mr. Mann and the State Board, late in 1846, by a Rev. Mr. Smith, who asserted in a sermon, and later at a public meeting, that the increase in intemperance, crime, and juvenile depravity in the State was due to the "Godless schools" they were sponsoring (**R. 135**). It was claimed that the Board was trying to eliminate the Bible from the schools, to abolish correction, and to "make the schools a counter-poise to religious instruction at home and in Sabbath schools." The local right to demand religious instruction (**R. 135**) was insisted upon.[1] In two courteous and carefully prepared personal letters Mr. Mann called his attention to the facts, answered the criticisms, and pointed out the errors in the argument (**Rs. 136, 137**). The Bible, he said, was an invaluable book for forming the character of children, and should be read without comment in the schools, but it was not necessary to teach it there. He showed that most of the towns had given up the teaching of the Catechism before the estab-lishment of the Board of Education. He contended that any attempt to decide what creed or doctrine should be taught would mean the ruin of the schools. The Rev. Mr. Smith then shifted his ground, and later published the correspondence, with a detailed reply, with-out first sending the reply to Mr. Mann.[2] Mann now felt that a great public issue had been raised which should be answered care-fully and fully. This he did in a published document of 56 pages, in which he answered the various accusations, in "decided tones" and closed his reply with a scathing arraignment (**R. 137**) of the man as a professed minister of the Gospel.

This ended the controversy in Massachusetts so far as the public was concerned. In his inaugural address, in 1847, Governor Briggs, a strong Baptist, commended the work of Mr. Mann in the follow-ing terms:

> Justice to a faithful public officer leads me to say that the indefatigable and accomplished Secretary of the Board of Education has performed services in the cause of common schools which will earn him the lasting gratitude of the generation to which he belongs.

The attempt to divide the school funds. As was stated earlier, in the beginning it was common to aid church schools on the same

---

[1] Religious fires and feelings still burned fiercely. Even as conservative a journal as the *Princeton Review* declared:

"The people of each school district have the right to make the schools as religious as they please; and if they cannot agree they have the right severally of withdrawing their proper proportion of the public stock of funds."

[2] In the first letter Mr. Mann very politely called the Rev. Mr. Smith's attention to the facts in the case, and asked him for proofs of his charges. Mr. Smith made an evasive reply, accompanied by four specific charges against Mr. Mann and his work. Mr. Mann again replied, still courteously, and pointed out the utter impossibility of deciding as to what religious instruction should be given. To this Mr. Smith drew up a long and detailed reply, and published the entire correspondence under the title of *The Bible, the Rod, and Religion, in the Common Schools* (59 pp., 1847).

basis as the state schools, and sometimes, in the beginnings of state aid, the money was distributed among existing schools without at first establishing any public schools. In many Eastern cities church schools at first shared in the public funds. In Pennsylvania church and private schools were aided from poor-law funds up to 1834. In New Jersey the first general school law of 1829 had been repealed a year later through the united efforts of church and private school interests, who fought the development of state schools, and in 1830 and 1831 new laws had permitted all private and parochial schools to share in the small state appropriation for education.

After the beginning of the forties, when the Roman Catholic influence came in strongly with the increase in Irish immigration to the United States, a new factor was introduced and the problem, which had previously been a Protestant problem, took on a somewhat different aspect. Largely through the demands of the Catholics one of the most interesting fights in the whole process of secularizing American education was precipitated in the City of New York.

It will be remembered that the Public School Society, founded in 1805, had become the greatest single educational organization in the city, and had received state money, after 1807, to assist it in its work. In 1820 the Bethel Baptist Church, which had opened a school for poor children of all denominations, was admitted by special act to a share in the state appropriation.[1] To this the Public School Society objected, and the legislature in 1825 turned over the quota of New York City to the city council, to divide as it thought best. The council cut off the Baptist schools, three of which were by that time running, and refused to grant public money to any religious society. In 1828 the Public School Society was permitted to levy a local tax to supplement its resources, it being estimated that at that time there were 10,000 children in the city with no opportunities for education. The Society was regarded as a non-denominational organization, though chartered to teach "the sublime truths of religion and morality contained in the Holy Scriptures" in its schools.

In 1831 the Roman Catholic Benevolent Society applied to the

[1] The passage of this law, and the almost immediate application of other religious societies for additional shares, alarmed the Public School Society. All such grants not only cut down the amount available for the work of the Public School Society, but it opened the door wide for the perversion of the school fund for church ends. The Public School Society accordingly asked for a repeal of the law, which was done, despite the opposition of the church societies, and the whole matter was turned over to the New York city council for settlement.

city council for a grant of funds for their Orphan Asylum School, which was allowed. The Methodists at once applied for a similar grant, in behalf of the orphan and destitute children attending the school under their management, and were refused.[1] The religious question now became more and more prominent, though without any progress being made toward its settlement. By 1840 the Massachusetts conflict was on, and in that year Governor Seward, of New York, urged the establishment of schools in the cities of the State in which the teachers should be of the same language and religion as the foreign patrons. This dangerous proposal encouraged the Catholics, and they immediately applied to the New York City council for a division of the city school fund, and, on being refused, carried their demand to the legislature of the State. A Hebrew and a Scotch Presbyterian Church also applied for their share, and supported the Catholics in their demands. On the other hand, the Methodists, Episcopalians, Baptists, Dutch Reformed, and Reformed Presbyterians united with the Public School Society in opposing all such division of the funds (**R. 138**).

The legislature deferred action until 1842, and then did the unexpected thing. The heated discussion of the question in the city and in the legislature had made it evident that, while it might not be desirable to continue to give funds to a privately organized corporation, to divide them among the quarreling and envious religious sects would be much worse. The result was that the legislature created for the city a City Board of Education, to establish real public schools, and stopped the debate on the question of aid to religious schools by enacting that no portion of the school funds was in the future to be given to any school in which "any religious sectarian doctrine or tenet should be taught, inculcated, or practiced." Thus the real public school system of New York City was evolved out of this attempt to divide the public funds among the churches. The Public School Society continued for a time, but its work was now done, and in 1853 it surrendered its buildings and property to the City Board of Education and disbanded.

---

[1] The request was about to be granted by the council, when the Public School Society entered so vigorous a protest, with legal reasons, that the council at first hesitated and later refused. The Society reiterated its conviction, previously expressed in 1825, "that the school fund ought not to be diverted, in whole or in part, to the purposes of sectarian instruction, but should be kept sacred to the great object, emphatically called COMMON EDUCATION."

The contest in other States. As early as 1831, Lowell, Massachusetts, had granted aid to the Irish Catholic parochial schools in the city, and in 1835 had taken over two such schools and maintained them as public schools. In 1848 the question of establishing parochial schools in Massachusetts, as an alternative to the nonsectarian state schools, was agitated, chiefly by the Catholics and the Episcopalians. Even the General Assembly of the Presbyterian Church had passed a resolution declaring for primary schools by congregations, as Governor Seward had recommended for New York State. In 1853 the representatives of the Roman Catholic Church made a demand on the state legislature, not only of Massachusetts but of several other States as well, for a division of the school fund of the State. To settle the question once for all a constitutional convention then in session included a clause providing that all state and town moneys raised or appropriated for education must be expended only on regularly organized and conducted public schools, and that no religious sect should ever share in such funds.[1] This new constitution failed of adoption at the election of 1853 by a vote of 65,111 for and 65,512 against, but the same provision as to aid to religious schools was reproposed as an amendment to the existing constitution, and approved by the people in 1855. This settled the question in Massachusetts, as Mann had tried to settle it earlier (**R. 139**), and as New Hampshire had settled it in its constitution of 1792 and Connecticut in its constitution of 1818.

Other States now faced similar demands, as the Catholics had presented their petitions in a number of States. One interesting case was that of the petition for division in Michigan (**R. 140**), also in 1853, to which the Bishop of the Episcopal Diocese of Michigan offered a counter-petition (**R. 141**) which set forth the issue involved in division. No demand for a share in or a division of the public school funds, after 1840, however, was successful. The demand everywhere met with intense opposition, and with the coming of enormous numbers of Irish Catholics after 1846, and German

[1] "By the time Mann left the leadership of the educational system of Massachusetts, its non-sectarian character had become definitely fixed... The elimination of sectarian teaching had been accomplished with no sectarian change since the law of 1827. The Bible was still used in the schools for devotional exercises, but with no legal sanction. The coming of the Catholics, who refused to acquiesce in the arrangement, but who insisted on a division of the funds and their own schools, united the Protestants to make constitutionally and legally permanent the existing status of public religious education in Massachusetts." (S. M. Smith. *Religious Education in Massachusetts*, pp. 183, 188.)

Lutherans after 1848, the question of the preservation as unified state school systems of the schools just established now became a burning one. Petitions deluged the legislatures, and these were met by counter-petitions. Mass meetings on both sides of the question were held. Candidates for office were forced to declare themselves. Anti-Catholic riots occurred in a number of cities. The Native American Party was formed, in 1841, "to prevent the union of Church and State," and to "keep the Bible in the schools." In 1841 the Whig Party, in New York, inserted a plank in its platform against sectarian schools. In 1855 the national council of the Know-Nothing Party, meeting in Philadelphia, in its platform favored public schools and the use of the Bible therein, but opposed sectarian schools. This party carried the elections that year in Massachusetts, New Hampshire, Connecticut, Rhode Island, Maryland, and Kentucky.

To settle the question in a final manner legislatures now began to propose constitutional amendments to the people of their several States which forbade a division or a diversion of the funds, and these were almost uniformly adopted at the first election after being proposed. The States, with the date of adoption of such a constitutional prohibition, are:

States amending constitution		*Adopted when admitted*	
New Jersey	1844	Wisconsin	1848
Michigan	1850	Oregon	1857
Ohio	1851	Kansas	1859
Indiana	1851	Nevada	1864
Massachusetts	1855	Nebraska	1867
Iowa	1857	Colorado	1876
Mississippi	1868	North Dakota	1889
South Carolina	1868	South Dakota	1889
Arkansas	1868	Montana	1889
Illinois	1870	Washington	1889
Pennsylvania	1872	Idaho	1890
West Virginia	1872	Wyoming	1890
Alabama	1875	Utah	1896
Missouri	1875	Oklahoma	1907
North Carolina	1876	New Mexico	1912
Texas	1876	Arizona	1912
Minnesota	1877		
Georgia	1877		
California	1879		
Louisiana	1879		
Florida	1885		
Delaware	1897		

In 1875 President Grant, in his message to Congress, urged the submission of an amendment to the Federal Constitution making it the duty of the States to support free public schools, free from religious teaching, and forbidding the diversion of school funds to church or sectarian purposes. In a later message he renewed the recommendation, but Congress took no action because it considered such action unnecessary. That the people had thoroughly decided that the school funds must be kept intact and the system of free public schools preserved may be inferred from the fact that no State admitted to the Union after 1858, excepting West Virginia, failed to insert such a provision in its first state constitution. Hence the question may be regarded as a settled one in our American States. Our people mean to keep the public school system united as one state school system, well realizing that any attempt to divide the schools among the different religious denominations (*The World Almanac* for 1930 lists 79 different denominations and 160 different sects in the United States) could only lead to inefficiency and educational chaos.

QUESTIONS FOR DISCUSSION

1. Explain why with us schools naturally developed from the community outward.
2. Why did state organization and compulsion eventually become necessary?
3. Do state support and state control always go together?
4. State your explanation for the older States beginning to establish permanent school funds, often before they had established a state system of schools.
5. What was the reason the local school communities so resented state control, when anxious to accept state funds?
6. Compare the duties of the chief state school officer in your state today with those described for the early state officials.
7. Explain how the different titles for the chief state school officer, given on page 217, are "significant of the educational development through which we have passed."
8. Explain how the district system naturally became what it did.
9. Show the gradual transition from church control of education, through state aid of church schools, to secularized state schools.
10. Show why secularized state schools were the only possible solution for the United States.
11. Show that the quotation from Brown, on page 232, represents the statesman-like manner in which we have handled the question.

12. Show that secularization would naturally take place in the textbooks and the instruction before manifesting itself in the laws.

13. What would be the effect on education if everyone followed the declaration of the writer in the *Princeton Review* (p. 235)? Would the attempt of the Catholics to divide the school funds have resulted in the same thing?

14. What would have been the probable result had the New York legislature followed Governor Seward's recommendation?

15. Would a good system of high schools ever have been possible had we divided the school funds among the churches?

SELECTED READINGS

In the accompanying volume of *Readings* the following selections, related to the subject matter of this chapter, are reproduced:

*126. Rawles: Why the District System displaced the Township.
*127. Carter: Decline of the Massachusetts School System.
*128. Martin: Mr. Mann's Personal Qualifications.
*129. Mann: Reply to the Boston Schoolmasters.
 130. Digest: Horace Mann's Annual Reports.
*131. Barnard: The Work and Character of Horace Mann.
 132. Humphrey: Decline of Interest in Schools of Connecticut.
 133. Ellsworth: On the Work of Henry Barnard.
 134. Editorials: Mann and the Christian Witness Controversy.
*135. Smith: Rev. Mr. Smith and the Godless Schools.
*136. Mann: Letter to Rev. Mr. Smith, and Reply.
*137. Mann: On Religious Instruction in the Schools.
*138. Hall: Change in Attitude toward Sectarian Schools.
 139. Smith: Results of the Struggle in Massachusetts.
*140. Catholics: Petition for a Division of the School Fund.
*141. Episcopal Bishop: Counter Petition against Division.

QUESTIONS ON THE READINGS

1. What was the basis of the "deep-seated conviction of the sacredness of local government" in the Indiana townships and school districts (**126**) of the early period?

2. Was Carter probably right as to the depressing effect of the academies (**127**) on the old grammar schools? Could this effect have been prevented?

3. Summarize Mr. Martin's statement as to Mann's strength for the position (**128**).

4. Explain the extreme sensitiveness of the Boston schoolmasters (**129**), and state what you think of Mann's reply.

5. Our state superintendents no longer issue such *Reports* as did Horace Mann (**130**). Why?

6. What estimate would you put on the educational contribution of Mann in his twelve Reports (**130**)?

7. Compare the article by Barnard (**131**) with that of Martin (**128**), as revealing Mr. Mann's ability for the work to be done.

8. Why should the Connecticut school fund have produced such disastrous results (**132**)?

9. Would Governor Ellsworth's statement (**133**) indicate that the people of Connecticut were very much in earnest as to the advancement of education? Why?

10. What do the two articles quoted from the Massachusetts press (**134**) indicate as to public opinion in the religious controversy matter?

11. Characterize the attack of the Rev. Mr. Smith (**135, 136**).

12. Characterize Mr. Mann's replies (**135, 136**), from the point of view of a public servant.

13. Evaluate Mr. Mann's statement as to religious instruction in the schools (**137**), for validity.

14. Is the change in attitude in New York, as described by Hall, (**138**) one typical of the American people generally? Illustrate.

15. Estimate Mr. Mann's place in history in the religious controversy (**139**).

16. What is the weakness, from a public education point of view, of the Catholic petition (**140**) to the legislature of Michigan?

17. What were the strong points, from a legislative point of view, of the counter petition (**141**)?

TOPICS FOR INVESTIGATION AND REPORT

1. The work of Horace Mann.
2. The work of Henry Barnard.
3. The work of James G. Carter. (Barnard.)
4. The messages of Caleb Mills. (Boone; Tuttle.)
5. Barnard's Rhode Island school survey report. (Wells.)
6. The work of Lewis and Stowe in Ohio. (Barnard.)
7. The work of Pierce and Crary in Michigan. (Hoyt-Ford.)
8. The work of Breckinridge in Kentucky. (Barnard.)
9. The work of Calvin Wiley in North Carolina. (Barnard; Knight.)
10. The work of John Swett in California.
11. The secularization fight in Massachusetts. (Culver, Confrey, Smith.)
12. The secularization fight in New York. (Hall, Boese.)
13. Mann's conflict with the Boston schoolmasters.

SELECTED REFERENCES

Barnard, Henry, Editor. *The American Journal of Education.* 31 vols. Consult *Analytical Index* to; 128 pp. Published by United States Bureau of Education, Washington, 1892.

Barnard, Henry. *American Teachers and Educators.* 526 pp. Syracuse, New York.

A reprint of articles found in different volumes of the *American Journal of Education.* Contains biographies with portraits of Carter, Lewis, Mann, Peirce, Stowe, and others.

*Barnard, Henry. Memorial Addresses on; in *Proceedings of the National Education Association*, 1901, pp. 390–439.

    1. Influence in establishing normal schools — Lyte.
    2. Influence on schools in West — Dougherty.
    3. Home Life and Work in Connecticut and Rhode Island — Keyes.
    4. As an educational critic — Parker.
    5. His relation to the establishment of the office of United States Commissioner of Education, with historical reviews — Harris.

"Henry Barnard: His Labors in Connecticut and Rhode Island"; in Barnard's *American Journal of Education*, vol. I, pp. 659–738.

    A detailed statement of his work, reproducing many documents.

Boese, Thos. *Public Education in the City of New York.* 288 pp. New York, 1869.

    An important work, compiled from the documents. Still found in many libraries.

Boone, R. G. *Education in the United States.* 402 pp. New York, 1889.

    Chapter VII forms good supplemental reading on the establishment of state and local school supervision.

*Brown, S. W. *The Secularization of American Education.* 160 pp. Teachers College Contributions to Education, No. 49. New York, 1912.

    An important work on the subject. Chapters IX and X form especially good supplemental reading for this chapter.

*Brubacher, John S. *Henry Barnard on Education.* 298 pp. New York, 1931.

    His life and work, an appraisal of his educational services, and extracts from his writings.

*Culver, R. B. *Horace Mann and Religion in the Massachusetts Public Schools.* 301 pp. New Haven, Conn., 1929. Yale Studies in Religious Education, vol. III.

    The story of the various religious contests of Horace Mann's time. A well documented history of the conflict.

Confrey, Burton. *Secularism in American Education: Its History.* 153 pp. Catholic Education Press, Washington, 1931.

    Chapter IV gives a brief history (16 pp.) of the struggle as it relates to the public schools.

Fairlie, J. A. *The Centralization of Administration in New York State.* Columbia University Studies, New York, 1898.

    Chapter II deals with education, giving a history of the legislation for control.

*Hall, A. J. *Religious Education in the Public Schools of the State and City of New York.* 111 pp. University Chicago Press, 1914.

    A historical study of changes and developments.

Harris, Wm. T. "Horace Mann"; in *Educational Review*, vol. XII, pp. 105–19. (Sept., 1896.) Same in *Proceedings of the National Education Association*, 1896, pp. 52–63; and in *Report of the United States Commissioner of Education*, 1895–96, part I, pp. 887–97.

*Hinsdale, B. A. *Horace Mann, and the Common School Revival in the United States.* 326 pp. New York, 1898.

    A very good and a very readable sketch of the work and influence of Mann.

Hoyt, C. O., and Ford, R. C. *John D. Pierce.* 162 pp. Ypsilanti, Michigan, 1905.

A study of education in the Northwest, and of the founding of the Michigan school system.

*Martin, Geo. H. "Horace Mann and the Educational Revival in Massachusetts"; in *Educational Review*, vol. 5, pp. 434–50. (May, 1893.)

A good brief sketch.

*Martin, Geo. H. *The Evolution of the Massachusetts Public School System.* 284 pp. New York, 1894.

Chapter IV describes the work of Horace Mann and the revival in Massachusetts.

*Monroe, Paul. *Cyclopedia of Education.* New York, 1911–13. 5 volumes.

The following articles form good supplemental references:
 1. "Barnard, Henry"; vol. I, pp. 324–25.
 2. "Bible in the Schools"; vol. I, pp. 370–77.
 3. "Mann, Horace"; vol. IV, pp. 118–20.
 4. The historical portion of the articles on state school systems, such as Indiana, New York, etc.
 5. "Superintendent of Schools," vol. V, pp. 463–64.

*Monroe, W. S. *The Educational Labors of Henry Barnard.* 32 pp. Syracuse, New York, 1893.

A good brief sketch, with bibliography of his writings.

*Norton, A. O. *Horace Mann.* New York, 1931.

His life and work, with extracts from his writings.

Rawles, W. A. *Centralizing Tendencies in the Administration of Indiana.* 336 pp. Columbia University Studies, New York, 1903.

Chapter II deals with public education, giving the history of the development of administrative control.

*Slosson, E. A. *The American Spirit in Education.* Yale Chronicles of America Series, vol. 23. New Haven, 1921.

A very well written series of biographies, covering Mann and Barnard.

*Smith, S. M. *Religious Education in Massachusetts.* 350 pp. Syracuse, N.Y., 1926.

An excellent history of the relations of the State to religious education in Massachusetts.

*Steiner, B. C. *Life of Henry Barnard.* 131 pp. Bulletin No. 8, 1919. U.S. Bureau of Education. Washington, 1919.

A very good biography, covering his life by periods, and his work, and containing much detail and many evaluations.

*Tuttle, Jos. F. Caleb Mills and Indiana Common Schools; in Barnard's *American Journal of Education*, vol. 31, pp. 135–44.

A sketch of his life and work, and an outline of his six messages to the people regarding education.

Wells, Guy F. "The First School Survey"; in *Educational Review*, vol. 50, pp. 166–74. (Sept., 1915.)

On Barnard's 1845 *Rhode Island Report.*

Winship, A. E. *Great American Educators.* 252 pp. Chicago, 1900.

Good short biographical articles on Mann and Barnard, as well as Mary Lyon, David Page, and others.

CHAPTER VIII

THE BATTLE TO EXTEND THE SYSTEM

II. PHASES OF THE BATTLE FOR STATE-SUPPORTED SCHOOLS — *continued*

6. *The battle to establish the American high school*

The elementary or common schools which we have seen had been established in the different States, by 1850, supplied an elementary or common-school education to the children of the masses of the people, and the primary schools which, as we have also seen, were added, after about 1820, carried this education downward to the needs of the beginners. In the rural schools the American school of the 3-Rs, with a few more advanced studies added, provided for all the children, from the little ones up, so long as they could advantageously partake of its instruction. Education in advance of this common school training was in semi-private institutions — the academies and colleges — in which a tuition fee was charged. The next struggle came in the attempt to extend the system upward so as to provide to pupils, free of charge, a more complete education than the common schools afforded.

The transition Academy. About the middle of the eighteenth century a tendency manifested itself, in Europe as well as in America, to establish higher schools offering a more practical curriculum than the old Latin Schools had provided. In the cities of the Middle Colonies we saw the evolution of the English Grammar School (**Rs. 55, 56**), institutions designed to meet the new needs in our new-world life. In America it became particularly evident, too, after the coming of nationality, that the old Latin grammar-school type of instruction, with its limited curriculum and exclusively college-preparatory ends, was wholly inadequate for the needs of the youth of the land. The result had been evident during the latter part of the eighteenth century in the gradual dying out of the Latin school, which had early caused some alarm (**R. 142**), and in the evolution of the tuition Academy, previously referred to briefly at the close of Chapter IV. This new educational institution arose to meet a new need in American life, and it became a representative institution,[1] in a transition period in American history (**R. 143**).

Franklin's Academy at Philadelphia (**R. 144**), which began instruction in 1751 with three organized departments — the Latin School, the English School, and the Mathematical School — and which later evolved into the University of Pennsylvania, was probably the first American academy.[2] Others claim the honor of earlier establishment, but this is the first the foundation of which is perfectly clear. The term *academy* first appears in the statutes in Maryland, in 1778, in an act providing for the sale of a free school to Lower Marlboro Academy, though the term had been used locally earlier. The first academies in New England were the Dummer Academy,[3] in South Byfield, Massachusetts, founded in 1761, and opened for instruction in 1763; the Phillips Academy at Andover, Massachusetts, founded in 1778, and opened for instruction in 1780; and Phillips Exeter, at Exeter, New Hampshire,[4] founded in 1781, and opened for instruction in 1783. Within ten years after the opening of Phillips Andover six academies had been incorporated in the State, and by 1800 seventeen had been chartered — nearly all of them in localities where there were no public grammar schools. The academy movement spread rapidly during the first half of the nine-

[1] This new type of school came to be known by a variety of names, as academy, which was most common, and institute, seminary, collegiate institute, and sometimes college. While intended primarily for boys, the seminaries were for girls, and a few academies, particularly in the West, were coeducational.

[2] It is difficult to determine just where and when the American Academy had its beginning. Opinions differ in part through lack of agreement as to what was or was not an academy. The name was at first loosely used to designate various types and grades of schools. Evolving from the old Latin Grammar School by the addition of the more practical subjects, the academy became in America a distinctively new type of secondary school. South Carolina had a school designated an academy in 1712; New Jersey had "Tennet's Log College," which was referred to as an academy, by 1739. Most writers, however, agree that Franklin's Academy, founded in 1749 and chartered in 1753, was the first true academy as we have come to understand the term. By 1790 the academy was well recognized as a part of the educational life of America.

[3] Created by a devise of a farm and home at South Byfield, Massachusetts, by Governor Dummer, in 1761, opened in 1763 under the name of Dummer Charity School, and incorporated in 1782 as Dummer Academy, it at once took front rank as a teaching institution. Under its first master Dummer educated fifteen members of Congress, two chief justices of the Supreme Court, one president of Harvard College, and four college professors.

[4] "The founding of the two Phillips academies, at Andover (1778), Massachusetts, and Exeter (1781), New Hampshire, marks the New England beginning of the academy movement. For these two schools furnished the model and inspiration of many later institutions established in the northern states, both east and west." (E. E. Brown. *The Making of Our Middle Schools*, p. 192.)

teenth century. By 1800 there were 17 academies in Massachusetts, 36 by 1820, 68 by 1830, and 134 by 1850. In New Jersey, Newark Academy had been founded in 1774, and opened in 1775 (**R. 145**). In New York State the first academy reported was in 1787.

By 1800 there were 19, by 1820 44, and by 1850 there were 231. Estimates for the State of Georgia show that 10 academies had been founded there by 1800, 31 by 1820, 138 by 1830, and close to 300 by 1840. By 1830 there were, according to Hinsdale, 950 incorporated academies in the United States, and many unincorporated ones, and by 1850, according to Inglis, when the wave of interest in their establishment reached its crest, there were, of all kinds, 1007 academies in New England, 1636

FIG. 60. A TYPICAL NEW ENGLAND ACADEMY

Pittsfield Academy, New Hampshire, where John Swett went to school

in the Middle Atlantic States, 2640 in the Southern States, 753 in the Upper Mississippi Valley States, and a total reported for the entire United States of 6085, with 12,260 teachers employed and 263,096 pupils enrolled. A phenomenal development, considering that there were but 6000 high schools as late as 1890!

The movement gained a firm hold everywhere east of the Missouri River, the States incorporating the largest number being New York with 887, Pennsylvania with 524, Massachusetts with 403, Kentucky with 330, Virginia with 317, North Carolina with 272, and Tennessee with 264. Some States, as Kentucky and Indiana,[1] provided for a system of county academies, while many States extended to them some form of state aid. In New York State they found a warm advocate in Governor De Witt Clinton, who urged (1827) that they be located at the county towns of the State to give a practical scientific education suited to the wants of farmers, merchants, and mechanics, and also to train teachers for the schools of the State. The greatest period of their development was from 1820 to 1840, though

---

[1] Boone, in his *History of Education in Indiana*, lists (pp. 57–58) 50 of the 92 counties as opening county academies (called county seminaries there) between 1826 and 1850, and he also lists (pp. 60–61) 68 private and church academies as opening between 1816 and 1851.

they continued to dominate secondary education until 1850, and were very prominent until after the Civil War.

Organization and control. The Latin Grammar School was essentially a town free school, maintained by the towns for the higher education of certain of their male children. It was aristocratic in type, and belonged to the early period of class education. With the decline in zeal for education, after about 1750, these tax-supported higher schools largely died out, and in their place private energy and benevolence in time came to be depended upon to supply the needed higher education. A number of the earlier academy foundations were from gifts (**R. 147**), or estates left by will for the purpose by some public-spirited citizen, and many others were organized by private subscriptions or as private stock companies.[1] A few were organized along denominational lines, and were under ecclesiastical control. Practically all charged a tuition fee, and most of them had dormitories and boarding halls. A number provided for some form of manual labor, whereby a portion of the expense of attending could be earned.

The organization and administration of the academies were in the hands of a board of trustees, who usually held corporate powers through a charter [2] given the academy by the State. This board commonly was a local private corporation, often was a law unto itself in matters of control, usually reported to the state school authorities, and often was constituted as a self-perpetuating body. Many of these academies became semi-state institutions through the state aid extended to them.[3] The business and financial affairs of the

---

[1] As an example, the following:

"Article I. All the subscribers to the building shall be considered as sole proprietors in common of the Academy, and shall hold their interest in it, and in all property now pertaining, or that shall hereafter pertain to it, in proportion to the amount of their respective subscriptions; and they shall be known by the name and style of the Proprietors of the Academy in Newark." (Constitution of 1792.)

[2] What the incorporators desired through a state charter were corporate powers — that is, authority to own and control property, to receive legacies and endowments, to employ teachers and enter into contracts, and to obtain tax exemption. Not infrequently teachers and students were exempted from military duties and road duties. Often the privilege of conducting a lottery for the benefit of the academy was added.

[3] "The fact that the academy usually was tax free reflected the recognition by the public that its work ranked with the church as a public benefaction. Under various names, such as institute, seminary, academy, and even college; sometimes for boys only, sometimes for girls only, and often for both; universally requiring a tuition fee; the academy set a standard for generosity and service that has influenced the whole of American society. It contributed much to the conviction in America that prosperity is built on the intellectual leadership and character of the people." (W. E. Faught. *The Early Academies.*)

academy were managed by these trustees, and the faculty was selected by them. The two Phillips academies (Andover and Exeter) stand as the best examples of the privately-endowed academies. When the decline set in, after the rise of the public free high school, only the best endowed of the academies were able to survive. A few of the academies evolved into colleges.

The new curriculum. One of the main purposes expressed in the endowment or creation of the academies was the establishment of courses which should cover a number of subjects having value aside from mere preparation for college, particularly subjects of a modern nature, useful in preparing youths for the changed conditions of society and government and business. The study of real things rather than words about things, and useful things rather than subjects merely preparatory to college, from the first became prominent features of the new courses of study. The new emphasis given to the study of English, mathematics, and book-science is noticeable. The New York Regents, in 1817, attempted to put the state-aided academy curriculum back on the old Latin grammar school basis,[1] but so loud were the protests that the legislature, in 1827, placed the "English studies" on a par with the classical (**R. 146**). This reopened the academy curriculum for further expansion, and new subjects appeared in proportion as the academies increased in numbers and importance. Of 149 new subjects for study appearing in the academies of New York, between 1787 and 1870, 23 appeared before 1826, 100 between 1826 and 1840, and 26 after 1840. Between 1825 and 1828 one half of the new subjects appeared. This also was the maximum period of development of the academies. Among the most commonly found new subjects were algebra, astronomy, botany, chemistry, general history, United States history, English literature, surveying, intellectual philosophy, declamation, debating, etc. A number of the larger academies,[2] of which Phillips Exeter is

[1] In 1817 the Regents deprived all academies of state aid that did not teach the classics and prepare pupils for college entrance, and only for pupils pursuing such classical studies. This was such a reversion to the colonial and aristocratic conception of education, and the protests were so loud, that the legislature first investigated and then ordered the rule changed and the "English studies" included.

[2] Most of the academies were small institutions, as not many boys or girls could be spared from work for "an advanced education." For example, the average number of teachers in the academies of New York State was less than three in 1827, approximately four in 1840, a little over three in 1850. Nor was the number of students large. In 1847, a year for which we have figures for both sexes, the average attendance for the State was 35 boys and 38 girls per academy.

a good example (**R. 148**), offered two parallel courses, a classical course, intended to prepare for college, and an English course, intended to prepare for the ordinary business of life.

Not being bound up with the colleges, as the earlier Latin grammar schools had largely been, the academies became primarily independent institutions, taking pupils who had completed the English education of the common school and giving them an advanced education in modern languages, the sciences, mathematics, history, and the more useful subjects of the time, with a view to "rounding out" their studies and preparing them for business life and the rising professions. They thus built upon instead of running parallel to the common school course, as the old Latin grammar school had done (see Fig. 82, p. 306), and hence clearly mark a transition from the aristocratic and somewhat exclusive college-preparatory Latin grammar school of colonial times to the more democratic high school of today. They became educational centers wherever they were established, gave good preparation for college work, and educated many who never went to college. They soon occupied a large educational domain that would have remained unfilled for a long time had it not been for them.

The academies also served a very useful purpose in supplying to the lower schools the best-educated teachers of the time. Governor Clinton strongly urged their extension because of their teacher-training value. They offered no instruction in pedagogy, except in rare instances, but because of their advanced instruction in subjects related to the work of the common school they served as the forerunners of the normal schools.

Other features of the academies. In religious matters, too, the academies also represent a transition. While they nearly always were pervaded by a genuine religious spirit (**R. 77**) and religious exercises formed a part of their daily routine, they usually were kept free from the doctrines of any particular church. Bible reading, church attendance, and attendance at the chapel exercises of the school usually were insisted upon, but sectarian teaching was excluded (**R. 149**). The foundation grant of one of the earliest, the Phillips Academy, at Andover, Massachusetts, states well this broader religious purpose. The aim of the Academy was to be

to lay the foundation of a public free school or ACADEMY for the purposes of instructing Youth, not only in English and Latin Grammar,

Writing, Arithmetic, and those Sciences wherein they are commonly taught; but more especially to learn them the GREAT END AND REAL BUSINESS OF LIVING... it is again declared that the *first* and *principle* object of this Institution is the promotion of TRUE PIETY and VIRTUE; the *second*, instruction in the English, Latin, and Greek Languages, together with Writing, Arithmetic, Music, and the Art of Speaking; the *third*, practical Geometry, Logic, and Geography; and the *fourth*, such other liberal Arts and Sciences or Languages as opportunity and ability may hereafter admit, and as the TRUSTEES shall direct.

Though this breathes a deep religious spirit it does not evidence a narrow denominationalism, and this was a characteristic of the academies. They bridged over the transition from the ecclesiasticism of the Latin grammar schools of colonial times to the secularized high school of the present.

The old Latin grammar school, too, had been maintained exclusively for boys. Girls had been excluded as "Improper & inconsistent wth such a Grammar Schoole as ye law injoines, and is ye Designe of this Settlem^t." The new academies soon reversed this situation. Almost from the first, even in Massachusetts, academies began to be established for girls [1] as well as boys, and in time many became coeducational. In New York State alone 32 academies were incorporated, between 1819 and 1853, with the prefix "Female" to their title. In this respect, also, these institutions formed a transition to the modern coeducational high school. The course of instruction offered (**R. 150**) was as liberal and "modern" as that provided for the boys. The higher education of women in the United States clearly dates from the establishment of the academies, and particularly the Female Seminaries, which were founded in numbers in many States. Particularly in the Southern States was the Female Seminary popular during the period before the Civil War. One of the earliest of the Southern Female Seminaries was Elizabeth Academy, at Old Washington, Mississippi, chartered in 1819. In Alabama, 27 academies for girls were established between 1822

---

[1] Of the Massachusetts academies, Leicester Academy, the third academy organized in the State (1784), was coeducational from the start. Westford Academy, opened in 1792, and Bradford Academy, opened in 1803, also were coeducational from the start. Ipswich Female Seminary, opened in 1805, was at first for girls only, but later became coeducational. In New York State, the attendance of girls slowly increased until 1847, when the number attending for the first time exceeded that of the boys. The western county academies were practically all coeducational institutions.

and 1860. Troy (New York) Seminary,[1] founded by Emma Willard, in 1821; Mt. Holyoke (Massachusetts) Seminary, founded by Mary Lyon (**R. 151**), in 1836; and Hartford Female Seminary, founded by Catherine Elizabeth Beecher, in 1828, though not the first institutions for girls, were nevertheless important pioneers in the higher education of women.

In one other way the academies made a distinct contribution, and that was in building and equipment for teaching. The little one-room structure near the Meeting House, which had characterized the Latin grammar school, was replaced by a larger building, with a public hall for meetings and rhetorical exercises, while maps, charts, globes, libraries, and "philosophical apparatus" became part of the teaching equipment. In this respect, as well, the academy formed a transition institution to the modern high school.

The demand for public higher schools. The different movements tending toward the building up of free public school systems in the cities and States, which we have described in the two preceding chapters, and which became clearly defined in the Northern States after 1825, came just at the time when the Academy had reached its maximum development. The settlement of the question of general taxation for education, the elimination of the rate-bill by the cities and later by the States, the establishment of the American common school as the result of a long native evolution (Fig. 46, p. 140), and the complete establishment of public control over the entire elementary-school system, all tended to bring the semi-private tuition academy into question. The effect on the old Latin grammar school, too, had been disastrous (**R. 152**), leading to a virtual abandonment of the town grammar school, outside of Boston, and many asked why not extend the public school system upward to provide the necessary higher education for all in one common state-supported school.

The existence of a number of colleges, basing their entrance requirements on the completion of the classical course of the academy, and the establishment of a few embryo state universities in the new States of the West and the South, naturally raised the further ques-

---

[1] The Troy school was not the first school for girls that Mrs. Willard had established. After two years of teaching in early academies, she had established a seminary for girls, in 1807, at Middlebury, Vermont. As many of her students came from New York State, Governor De Witt Clinton urged her to remove her school to Waterford, New York, which she did in 1819. In 1821 it was moved again to Troy and incorporated as Troy Female Seminary, the city voting $4000 in tax and the citizens subscribing another sum to secure the school.

tion of why there should be this gap in the public school system. The increase of wealth in the cities tended to increase the number who passed through the elementary course and could profit by more extended training; the academies had popularized the idea of more advanced education; while the new manufacturing and commercial activities of the time called for more knowledge than the elementary schools afforded, and of a different type from that demanded for entrance by the small colleges of the time.

The demand for an upward extension of the public school, which would provide academy instruction for the poor as well as the rich, and in one common public higher school, now made itself felt.   As the colonial Latin grammar school had represented the educational needs of a society based on classes, and the academies had represented a transition period and marked the growth of a middle class, so the rising democracy of the second quarter of the nineteenth century now demanded and obtained the democratic high school, supported by the public and equally open to all, to meet the educational needs of a new society built on the basis of a new and aggressive democracy. Where, too, the academy had represented in a way a missionary effort — that of a few providing something for the good of the people — the high school on the other hand represented a cooperative effort on the part of the people to provide something for themselves.

FIG. 61. THE FIRST HIGH SCHOOL IN THE UNITED STATES

Established in Boston, in 1821

The first American high school. The first high school in the United States was established in Boston, in 1821.   For three years it was known as the "English Classical School," but in 1824 the school appears in the records as the "English High School."   The name seems to be Scotch in origin, having been suggested by the description of the High School at Edinburgh, by Professor Griscom, in an article in the *North American Review*, then published in Boston, in January, 1824. In 1826 Boston also opened the first high school for girls, on the monitorial plan (**R. 154**), but abolished it in 1828, due to its great popularity,[1] and instead extended the course of study for girls in the elementary schools.

The matter of establishing an English high school was first considered in 1820, and a committee was appointed to consider the matter further. This committee reported (**R. 153**), in January, 1821, among other things, that:

> The mode of education now adopted, and the branches of knowledge that are taught at our English grammar [elementary] schools are not sufficiently extensive nor otherwise calculated to bring the powers of the mind into operation nor to qualify a youth to fill usefully and respectably many of the stations, both public and private, in which he may be placed. A parent who wishes to give a child an education that shall fit him for active life, and shall serve as a foundation for eminence in his profession, whether mercantile or mechanical, is under the necessity of giving him a different education from any which our public schools can now furnish. Hence many children are separated from their parents and sent to private academies in the vicinity, to acquire that instruction which cannot be obtained at the public seminaries.

The report recommended the establishment of a new type of higher school. Though there was some public objection to the establishment of such a school, the report was approved; the course of study as recommended was adopted (**R. 153**); and the school was opened in May, 1821, as a three-year high school. Boys to be admitted were required to be at least twelve years of age, instead of nine, as in the Latin grammar school (see Fig. 82, p. 306), and to "be well acquainted with reading, writing, English grammar in all its branches, and arithmetic as far as simple proportion." Three years later English literature and geography were added. The teachers were required to have been educated at some university. No other language than English was to be taught; English, declamation, science, mathematics and its applications, history, and logic were the principal studies. The course of instruction was definitely built upon that of the English reading and writing and grammar

---

[1] The school opened with 130 pupils, selected out of 286 candidates examined, one half from private and one half from public schools. Before the end of the second year "the school had become so popular, the applicants for admission so numerous, so many parents were disappointed that their children were not received," and the increasing demand for larger and better accommodations, which would involve increased expenditure, led the School Committee, on the suggestion of the mayor (Josiah Quincy), to abolish the school.

schools, instead of paralleling these. It was in consequence clearly American in nature and purpose, rejecting entirely the English parallel-class-education idea of the Latin grammar school and the academy. The aim of the school, too, as stated in the report of the committee, was quite practical. The aims and curricula of both the

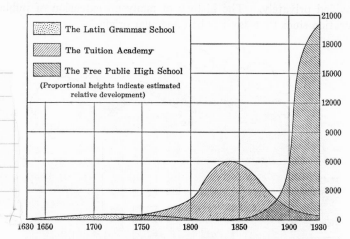

The Latin Grammar School

The Tuition Academy

The Free Public High School

(Proportional heights indicate estimated relative development)

FIG. 62. THE DEVELOPMENT OF SECONDARY SCHOOLS IN THE UNITED STATES

The transitional character of the Academy is well shown in this diagram

English High School and the Latin Grammar School were well contrasted in a statement published in 1833 by the school committee (**R. 156**), and the aim was restated in the *Regulations of the School Committee* for the school, adopted in 1833, which read:

It was instituted in 1821, with the design of furnishing the young men of the city who are not intended for a collegiate course of study, and who have enjoyed the usual advantages of the other public schools, with the means of completing a good English education to fit them for active life or qualify them for eminence in private or public station.

Josiah Quincy, who was mayor of Boston at the time of the establishment of the school, gives further corroborative evidence, in his *Municipal History of the Town and City of Boston*, as to the purpose in establishing the new high school. He says:

In 1820 an English Classical School was established, having for its object to enable the mercantile and mechanical classes to obtain an education adapted for those children, whom their parents wished to qualify for active life, and thus relieve them from the necessity of incurring the expense incident to private academies.

The free public high school thus arose,[1] to provide at public expense what the public schools had failed to provide, and had been provided privately. The history of many an extension of public education since that day has had a similar origin.

FIG. 63. THE FIRST HIGH SCHOOL IN NEW YORK CITY

Opened in 1825. The building was erected by a sale of stock, the stockholders having prior rights of entering their children or wards.

This same conception of the aim and purpose of the new high school is well expressed in the *First Annual Report of the High School Society* of New York City, which opened a public high school there in 1825. This document reads:

It should never be forgotten, that the grand object of this institution is to prepare the boys for such advancement, and such pursuits in life, as they are destined to after leaving it. All who enter the school do not intend to remain for the same period of time — and many who leave it expect to enter immediately upon the active business of life. It is

[1] While the original development took place in Boston, and the new type of public high school was created there, many improvements were made in the idea by other towns and in other States, so that the Boston development was typical for New England only in the earlier developmental stage.

very plain that these circumstances must require corresponding classifications of scholars and of studies.

Some pursuits are nevertheless common to all. All the scholars in this department attend to Spelling, Writing, Arithmetic, Geography, Elocution, Composition, Drawing, Philosophy, Natural History, and Book-Keeping. Philosophy and Natural History are taught chiefly by lectures and by questions; and these branches, together with Elocution and Composition, are severally attended to one day in every week.

The Massachusetts Law of 1827. Though Portland, Maine, established a high school in 1821; Worcester, Massachusetts, in 1824; and New Bedford, Plymouth, and Salem, Massachusetts, in 1827; copying the Boston idea, the real beginning of the American high school as a distinct institution dates from the Massachusetts Law of 1827, enacted through the influence of James G. Carter. This law formed the basis of all subsequent legislation in Massachusetts, and deeply influenced development in other States. The law (**R. 155**) is significant in that it required a high school in every town having 500 families or over, in which should be taught United States history, bookkeeping, algebra, geometry, and surveying, while in every town having 4000 inhabitants or over, instruction in Greek, Latin, history, rhetoric, and logic must be added. A heavy penalty was attached for failure to comply with the law. In 1835 the law was amended so as to permit any smaller town to form a high school as well.

This Boston and Massachusetts legislation clearly initiated the public high school movement in the United States. It was there that the new type of higher school was founded, there that its curriculum was outlined, there that its standards were established, and there that it developed earliest and best. With three exceptions [1] the high schools of the United States, says Inglis,

> owe the basis of their aim, theory, and practice to the high school first created and earliest developed in Massachusetts. As in most other educational matters, Massachusetts led the way in the older Latin grammar school education and in the newer type of secondary education — the public high school. It is all the more to her glory that no direct influence from other countries has been traced in regard to the high school system. The American high school was an institution peculiarly adapted to the needs and wants of the American people, and is an everlasting tribute to the democracy of Massachusetts and America.

These exceptions were the New York City school, which showed Scottish influence; the Central High School of Philadelphia, which was influenced by German practices; and the Baltimore City College, which showed English influence.

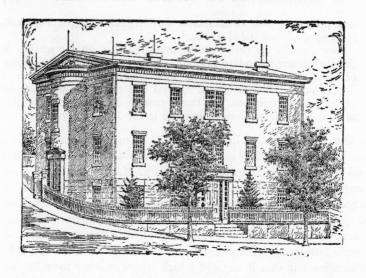

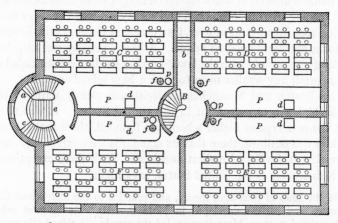

FIG. 64. THE FIRST HIGH SCHOOL AT PROVIDENCE, RHODE ISLAND

Established by city ordinance in 1838. In 1843 a superintendent of schools was employed, this building dedicated, and the high school opened, with the superintendent acting as its principal. The floor plan shows how completely it was a teacher-and-textbook type of school. Almost all high-school buildings erected before 1860 were of this type.

Among the early high schools established before 1850, the dates of which seem certain, may be mentioned the following fifty-five schools.

1821.	Boston, Mass.		Philadelphia, Pa.
	Portland, Maine		Taunton, Mass.
1824.	Worcester, Mass. (Girls)	1839.	Baltimore City College
1825.	New York City (abold. 1833)		Buffalo, N.Y.
1826.	Boston H. S. for Girls (abold. 1828)		Charleston, S.Car.
			Roxbury, Mass.
1827.	New Bedford, Mass. (abold. 1829; re-estbd. 1837)	1840.	Middletown, Conn.
		1841.	Cohasset, Mass.
	Plymouth, Mass.		Springfield, Mass.
	Salem, Mass.	1842.	Binghamton, N.Y.
1829.	Burlington, Vt.	1843.	Brookline, Mass.
1831.	Lowell, Mass.		New Orleans, La.
	Newburyport, Mass.		Providence, R.I.
1834.	Rochester, N.Y.	1844.	Detroit, Mich.
1835.	Augusta, Me.	1845.	Chelsea, Mass.
	Brunswick, Me.	1846.	Cleveland, Ohio
	Medford, Mass.		Columbus, Ohio
	Northampton, Mass.	1847.	Cincinnati, Ohio
	Waltham, Mass.		Hartford, Conn.
1836.	Ipswich, Mass.	1848.	Charlestown, Mass.
	Marblehead, Mass.		Manchester, Mass.
	Scituate, Mass.		New York City
1837.	Harrisburg, Pa.	1849.	Fall River, Mass.
	Lanesborough, Mass.		Fitchburg, Mass.
	Leominster, Mass.		Lancaster, Pa.
	Newton, Mass.		Lawrence, Mass.
	Pittston, Me.		Lynn, Mass.
1838.	Cambridge, Mass.		Toledo, Ohio
	Gloucester, Mass.		

The struggle to establish and maintain high schools. The development of the American high school, even in its home, was slow. Up to 1840 not much more than two dozen high schools, at the most, had been established in Massachusetts, and not more than an equal number in the other States. The development of the cities was as yet only beginning,[1] the academy was the dominant institution, the district system for common schools stood in the way of any higher development, the cost of maintenance was an important factor, and the same opposition to an extension of taxation to include high schools was manifested as was earlier shown toward the establishment of common schools. There was much doubt, often expressed

[1] There were as yet but 44 cities of 8000 inhabitants or over in the entire country, and 91.5 per cent of the people still lived on the farm or in villages.

in high places, as to the expediency of their establishment and maintenance.[1] The friends of the academy naturally did not like to see it displaced as a "people's college." The early state legislation, as had been the case with the common schools, was nearly always permissive and not mandatory. Massachusetts forms a notable exception in this regard. The support for the schools had to come practically entirely from increased local taxation, and this made the struggle to establish and maintain high schools in any State for a long time a series of local struggles. Years of propaganda and patient effort were required, and, after the establishment of a high school in a community, constant watchfulness was necessary to prevent its abandonment. Many of the early schools ran for a time, then were discontinued for a period, and later were reestablished. In an address given at the dedication of a new building at Norwich, Connecticut, in 1856, one of the founders of the school thus describes these early struggles to establish and maintain high schools:

... The lower schools up to the grade of the grammar school were well sustained. Men were to be found in all our communities who had been themselves educated up to that point, and understood, practically, the importance of such schools, in sufficient numbers to control popular sentiment, and secure for them ample appropriations and steady support. But the studies of the high school, Algebra, Geometry, Chemistry, Natural Philosophy, Ancient History, Latin, Greek, French and German, were a perfect *terra incognita* to the great mass of the people. While the High School was a new thing and while a few enlightened citizens had the control of it, in numerous instances it was carried to a high state of perfection. But after a time the burden of taxation would begin to be felt. Men would discuss the high salaries paid to the accomplished teachers which such schools demand, and would ask, "To what purpose is this waste?" Demagogues, keen-scented as wolves, would snuff the prey. "What do we want of a High School to teach rich men's children?" they would shout. "It is a shame to tax the poor man to pay a man $1800 to teach the children to make x's and pot-hooks and gabble parleyvous." The work would go bravely on; and on election day, amid great excitement, a new school committee would be chosen, in favor of retrenchment and popular rights. In a single day the fruit of years of labor would be destroyed.

[1] In 1874, President Porter of Yale expressed the opinion that "the expenditure of money for high schools to prepare boys for college was a doubtful experiment." In 1872, 70 per cent of the students entering the eastern colleges were graduates of the academies; fifty years later 90 per cent were graduates of the high schools.

The struggle to establish and maintain high schools in Massachusetts and New York preceded the development in most other States, because there the common school had been established and fixed in the public mind earlier. In consequence, the struggle to extend and complete the public school system came there earlier also. The development was likewise more peaceful there, and came more rapidly.

FIG. 65. THE CHICAGO HIGH SCHOOL OF 1856

The first high school in Illinois. Illustrative of the type of architecture of the period. There were four classrooms to each floor, except the third, where two of the classrooms were thrown together to form an assembly hall.

In Massachusetts this was in large part a result of the educational awakening started by James G. Carter and Horace Mann. In New York it was due to the early support of Governor De Witt Clinton, and the later encouragement and state aid which came from the Regents of the University of the State of New York. Maine, Vermont, and New Hampshire were like Massachusetts in spirit, and followed closely its example. In Rhode Island and New Jersey, due to old conditions, and in Connecticut, due to the great decline in education there after 1800, the high school developed much more slowly, and it was not until after 1865 that any marked development took place in these States. The democratic West soon adopted the idea, and established high schools as soon as cities developed and the needs of the population warranted. The high schools at Cleveland and Columbus date from 1846, Cincinnati from 1847, Toledo from 1849, Evansville from 1850, St. Louis from 1853, and Chicago and San Francisco from 1856. The courses of study required in two of these schools, Cincinnati (**R. 157**) and Chicago (**R. 158**), are reproduced in the *Readings*. In the South the main high school development dates from relatively recent times.

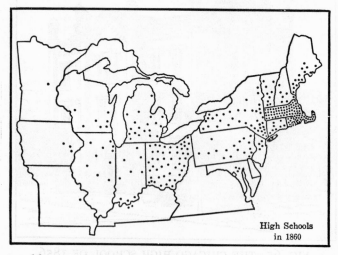

FIG. 66. HIGH SCHOOLS IN THE UNITED STATES BY 1860

Based on the table given in the *Report of the United States Commissioner of Education*, 1904, vol. II, pp. 1782–1989. This table is only approximately correct, as exact information is difficult to obtain. This table gives 321 high schools by 1860, and all but 35 of these were in the States shown in the above map. There were two schools in California and three in Texas, and the remainder not shown were in the Southern States. Of the 321 high schools reported, over half (167) were in the three States of Massachusetts (78), New York (41), and Ohio (48). Compare the distribution of high schools shown on this map with the distribution of New England people shown on the map on page 107.

Establishing the high school by court decisions. In many States, legislation providing for the establishment of high schools was more difficult to secure than in New England and New York, and often when secured was afterward attacked in the courts. In most of the States shown on the map in Figure 66, west of New England and

New York, the constitutionality of the establishment of the high school or of taxation therefor was at some time attacked in the courts and decided in favor of the schools.

One of the clearest cases of this came in Michigan, in 1872, and the verdict of the Supreme Court of that State was so positive that it influenced all subsequent decisions in other States. The case is commonly known as the Kalamazoo case (**R. 159**). The city of Kalamazoo, in 1872, voted to establish a high school and employ a superintendent of schools, and levied additional school taxes to cover the expense. A citizen by the name of Stuart brought suit to prevent the collection of the additional taxes. The case was carried to the Supreme Court of the State, and the decision was written by Chief Justice Cooley. After stating the case in hand, the contention of the plaintiff that high schools were not comprehended under the heading "common schools," and that the district board should supervise the schools, and after reviewing the educational history of the State, the court concluded:

> If these facts do not demonstrate clearly and conclusively a general state policy, beginning in 1817 and continuing until after the adoption of the present state constitution, in the direction of free schools in which education, and at their option the elements of classical education, might be brought within the reach of all the children of the State, then, as it seems to us, nothing can demonstrate it. We might follow the subject further and show that the subsequent legislation has all concurred with this policy, but it would be a waste of time and labor. We content ourselves with the statement that neither in our state policy, in our constitution, nor in our laws, do we find the primary school districts restricted in the branches of knowledge which their officers may cause to be taught, or the grade of instruction that may be given, if their voters consent in regular form to bear the expense and raise the taxes for the purpose.

> Having reached this conclusion, we shall spend no time upon the objection that the district in question had no authority to appoint a superintendent of schools, and that the duties of the superintendency should be performed by the district board. We think the power to make the appointment was incident to the full control which by law the board had over the schools of the district, and that the board and the people of the district have been wisely left by the legislature to follow their own judgment in the premises.

In almost all the Upper Mississippi Valley States this decision has deeply influenced development. In more than one State a Supreme Court decision which established the high school has been clearly based on this Michigan decision. It ranks, therefore, along with the Massachusetts law of 1827 as one of the important milestones in the establishment of the American public high school.

Gradually the high school has been accepted as a part of the state common school system [1] by all our States, and the funds and taxation originally provided for the common schools have been extended to cover the high school as well. The new States of the West have based their legislation on what the Eastern and Central States earlier fought out, though often the Western States have provided separate and additional support for their high schools. California is perhaps our best example of such separate support.

7. *The state university crowns the system*

The earlier colleges — Harvard, William and Mary, Yale — had been created by the religious-state governments of the earlier colonial period, and continued to retain some state connections for a time after the coming of nationality. As it early became evident that a democracy demands intelligence on the part of its citizens, that the leaders of democracy are not likely to be too highly educated, and that the character of collegiate instruction must ultimately influence national development, efforts were accordingly made to change the old colleges or create new ones, the final outcome of which was the creation of state universities in all the new and in most of the older States. The evolution of the state university, as the crowning head of the free public school system of the State, represents the last phase which we shall trace of the struggle of democracy to create a system of schools suited to its peculiar needs.

The colonial colleges. The close of the colonial period found the Colonies possessed of nine colleges. These, with the dates of their foundation, the Colony founding them, and the religious denomination they chiefly represented were:

| 1636. Harvard College | Massachusetts | Puritan |
| 1693. William and Mary | Virginia | Anglican |

[1] After the battle to establish general taxation for education had been fought and won, the term "common schools" was slowly extended, in the laws and in the thinking of our people, and usually without the formality of amending the constitutional statement, to include the entire school system below the university, including special schools. Our people have in time clearly conceived of the elementary and secondary school as constituting one common school system, with equal opportunities for all, and they have likewise conceived it to be the business of the State to keep the paths of intellectual opportunity open.

1701. Yale College	Connecticut	Congregational
1746. Princeton	New Jersey	Presbyterian
1753–55. Academy and College	Pennsylvania	Non-denominational
1754. King's College (Columbia)	New York	Anglican
1764. Brown	Rhode Island	Baptist
1766. Rutgers	New Jersey	Reformed Dutch
1769. Dartmouth	New Hampshire	Congregational

The religious purpose had been dominant in the founding of each institution, with the exception of Pennsylvania, though there was a gradual shading-off in strict denominational control and insistence upon religious conformity in the foundations after 1750. Still the prime purpose in the founding of each was to train up a learned and godly body of ministers, the earlier congregations, at least, "dreading to leave an illiterate ministry to the churches when our present ministers shall lie in the dust." In a pamphlet, published in 1754, President Clap of Yale declared that "Colleges are *Societies of Ministers*, for training up Persons for the Work of the *Ministry*," and that "The great design of founding this School (Yale), was to Educate Ministers in our *own Way*." The shading-off in insistence on religious conformity is well shown in the advertisement published in the New York papers (**R. 59**) announcing the opening of King's College,[1] in 1754, on an Anglican foundation, but in which it was stated that:

> IV. The chief Thing that is aimed at in this College, is, to teach and engage the Children *to know God in Jesus Christ*, and to love and serve him in all *Sobriety, Godliness*, and *Richness* of Life, with a perfect Heart and a Willing Mind: and to train them up in all Virtuous Habits, and all such useful Knowledge as may render them creditable to their Families and Friends, Ornaments to their Country, and useful to the Public Weal in their generation.
>
> And as to any particular Tenets, every one is left to judge freely for himself, and to be required to attend only such Places of Worship on the Lord's Day as their Parents or Guardians shall think fit to order or permit.

---

[1] The religious purpose was still prominent, if not dominant, as may be seen from the prayer of President Johnson, at the laying of the cornerstone of the college, August 23, 1756.

"May God Almighty grant that this College, happily founded, may ever be enriched with His blessing; that it may be increased and flourish, and be carried on to its entire perfection, to the glory of His name, and the adornment of His true religion and good literature, and to the greatest advantage of the public weal, to all posterities forevermore. *Amen.*"

These colonial institutions had all been small. For the first fifty years of Harvard's history the attendance at the college seldom exceeded twenty, and the President did all the teaching. The first assistant teacher (tutor) was not appointed until 1699, and the first professor not until 1721, when a professorship of divinity was endowed. By 1800 the instruction was conducted by the President and three professors — divinity, mathematics, and "Oriental languages" — assisted by a few tutors who received only class fees, and the graduating classes seldom exceeded forty. The course was four years in length, and all students studied the same subjects. The first three years were given largely to the so-called "Oriental languages" — Hebrew, Greek, and Latin. In addition, Freshmen studied arithmetic; Sophomores, algebra, geometry, and trigonometry; and Juniors, natural (book) science; and all were given much training in oratory, and some general history was added. The Senior year was given mainly to ethics, philosophy, and Christian evidences. The instruction in the eight other older colleges, before 1800, was not materially different.

National interest in higher education. One of Washington's most cherished ideas, and one warmly advocated by many leading citizens of the time, was that the new government should found a National University at the seat of the Federal Government (**R. 160**),

> where the youth from all parts of the United States might receive the polish of erudition in the arts, sciences, and belles-lettres... and where, during... the juvenal period of life, when friendships are formed, and habits established, that stick by one, the youth or young men from different parts of the United States would be assembled together, and would by degrees discover that there was not that cause for those jealousies and prejudices which one part of the Union had imbibed against another part.

In the Constitutional Convention of 1787, Washington, Madison, Pickering, and others desired to have a provision inserted for the creation and maintenance of a national university at the seat of government, but the general opinion was that the federal power to do so was ample without specific mention. The desirability of creating such an institution seems to have been taken for granted, and the proposal received much favorable comment in the newspapers of the time. Washington was deeply interested in the plan, and signified his willingness to make a substantial donation toward inaugurating it. In his first message to Congress, in 1790, and again later, he called the matter to the attention of Congress, as did Presidents Adams, Madison, Monroe, and the second Adams; a square of land was at one time set aside at the National Capital for the new institution, and was officially designated as University Square; and Washington, in his will (1799), left a substantial sum [1] to the Government of the United States, in trust, to start the endowment of the new university. For reasons hard to understand nothing ever came of the idea, and nothing is known today as to what became of the money which Washington left.

Immediately after the close of the Revolutionary War settlers began to move to the new territory along the Ohio, and when the sale of 1,500,000 acres of land in south central Ohio was made by Congress, in 1787, to "The Ohio Company," a New England organization, the company was granted section 16 for schools, section 29 for religion,[2] and, upon its request, two whole townships (72 sections — 46,080 acres) "for the purposes of a university." In 1788, at the time of the sale of 1,000,000 acres of land near Cincinnati, another township (36 sections) was granted "for the purpose of establishing an academy in the district," which district had also been settled by New England people. The former of these grants formed the original endowment of Ohio University, at Athens, and the latter the endowment of Miami University, at Oxford — the first state universities in the new West. The grant of two or more whole townships of land "for a seminary of learning," or "state university," begun by Congress as a land-selling proposition in the case of Ohio, was continued with the admission of each new State afterward, and these township grants for a seminary of learning formed the beginning of the state universities which were created in all the new Western and Southern States. Out of these "seminary township" grants arose the University of Alabama in 1819, Indiana University

[1] Washington left 50 shares (par value, $500) of the stock of the Potomac River Company, which he had previously offered in 1795. Samuel Blodget, a leader of the time, raised $30,000 addition by public subscription to start the project, and also added the profits from his volume, *Economia*. In 1805 Blodget memorialized Congress, asking for action, but nothing was done. Had Congress kept faith with Washington, as did the legislature of Virginia to which an equal amount was left, the project would have been undertaken. Compounded annually at 6 per cent, the bequest of Washington would, by 1931, have amounted to $42,600,000, and Blodget's $30,000 to $68,550,000 additional — a total of $111,150,000.

[2] This grant followed New England and New York precedents, and was agreed to by the old Continental Congress. After the new Constitution took effect, in 1789, Congress made no more section grants for religion.

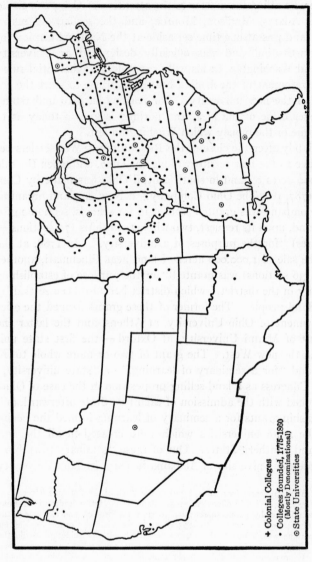

FIG. 67. COLLEGES AND UNIVERSITIES ESTABLISHED BY 1860. Of the 246 colleges shown on the map, but 17 were state institutions, and but two or three others had any state connections.

Compiled from data given in the *Reports of the United States Commissioner of Education.*

+ Colonial Colleges
• Colleges founded, 1775-1860
  (Mostly Denominational)
⊙ State Universities

in 1820 (**Rs. 79, 161**) the University of Michigan in 1835, and many other state universities in the West and South.

Growth of colleges by 1860. Fifteen additional colleges had been founded before 1800, and it has been estimated that by that date the two dozen American colleges then existing did not have all told over one hundred professors and instructors, not less than one thousand nor more than two thousand students, or property worth over one million dollars. This was an average of 4 professors and tutors, 40 to 80 students, and $40,000 worth of property. It would be a small high school today that did not have more in teaching staff, student body, and property value than these averages (**R. 79**). Even as late as 1839–40 the entering class at Harvard had but 76 students, and but 87 for the year 1849–50. Williams, these same years had 24 and 27, and Amherst 38 and 53. Princeton, as late as 1854, had but 6 professors, 2 assistant professors, 4 tutors, and 247 students. The other colleges of the time were no better supplied with students or faculty (**R. 170**), and the living conditions at them were exceedingly simple (**Rs. 162-164**). No one of the twenty-four colleges established by 1800 admitted women in any way to its privileges.

After about 1820, with the firmer establishment of the Nation, the awakening of a new national consciousness, the development of larger national wealth, and a court decision (p. 272) which safeguarded the endowments, interest in the founding of new colleges perceptibly quickened, as may be seen from the table on page 270, and between 1820 and 1880 came the great period of denominational effort. To this period belong, among many others, such important present-day colleges as Amherst (1821) in Massachusetts, Lafayette (1826) and Haverford (1830) in Pennsylvania (**R. 162**), Western Reserve (1826) (**R. 163**) and Oberlin (1833) (**R. 164**) in Ohio, Wesleyan (1831) in Connecticut, Rochester (1851) in New York, and Northwestern (1855) in Illinois. The map on page 268, shows the colleges established by 1860, from which it will be seen how large a part the denominational colleges played in the early history of higher education in the United States. Over 500 colleges and universities in the United States have been founded in response to the religious educational impulse which called for some type of collegiate affiliation with the churches.[1] While these early institutions were small and

[1] Endowments and gifts from non-state sources still bear the larger part of the burden for the maintenance of higher education in the United States. For the last year for which statistics are available, private resources carried 60 per cent of the total cost of higher education in the United States.

poor,[1] as were all colleges before the Civil War, and life in them often represented a struggle, they nevertheless were characterized by a seriousness of purpose that the modern college hardly knows, and they represented large hopes for the future (**R. 79**). The picture left us by Gladden (**R. 170**) of Williams College in the late fifties, under the presidency of Mark Hopkins, doubtless is a good description of the better colleges of that time.

Up to about 1870 the provision of higher education, as had been the case earlier with the provision of secondary education by the academies, had been left largely to private effort. There were, to be sure, a few state universities before 1870, though usually these were not particularly different from the denominational colleges around them, and often they maintained a nondenominational character only by preserving a proper balance between the different denominations in the employment of their faculties. Speaking generally, higher education in the United States, before 1870,

Before 1780	10
1780–89	7
1790–99	7
1800–09	9
1810–19	5
1820–29	22
1830–39	38
1840–49	42
1850–59	92
1860–69	73
1870–79	61
1880–89	74
1890–99	54
Total	494

COLLEGES FOUNDED UP TO 1900

(After a table by Dexter, corrected by U.S. Comr. Educ., data. Only approximately correct.)

was provided very largely in the tuitional colleges of the different religious denominations rather than by the State. Of the 246 colleges founded by the close of the year 1860, as shown on the map, but 17 were state institutions, and but two or three others had any state connections.

The new national attitude toward the colleges. After the coming of nationality there gradually grew up a widespread dissatisfaction with the colleges as then conducted (**R. 165**), because they were aristocratic in tendency, because they devoted themselves so exclusively to the needs of a class, and because they failed to answer the

[1] Two illustrations will serve here. Oberlin, in Ohio, began in 1833 with practically nothing, and up to the close of the Civil War the same condition continued. By 1908 the permanent endowment was approximately $350,000, of which 51 per cent had come as direct gifts, 24 per cent as bequests, and 25 per cent as the result of solicitations. By 1923 the total endowment was $2,934,254, with an equal valuation in property.

Carleton College, in Minnesota, began in 1867 with $20,000 subscribed by the citizens of Northfield, and $10,000 received from the Congregational Churches of the State. By 1915 the endowment funds were nearly one million dollars, and today exceed a million and a half, with nearly three million dollars' worth of property.

needs of the States in the matter of higher education. Due to their religious origin, and the common requirement that the president and trustees must be members of some particular denomination, they were naturally regarded as representing the interests of some one sect or faction within the State rather than the interests of the State itself. With the rise of the new democratic spirit after about 1820 there came a demand, felt least in New England, more in New York and the Central States, and most in the South and the new States in the West, for institutions of higher learning which should represent the State (**R. 165**). It was argued that colleges were important instrumentalities for moulding the future, that the kind of education given in them must ultimately influence the welfare of the State, and that higher education cannot be regarded as a private matter. The type of education given in these higher institutions, it was argued, "will appear on the bench, at the bar, in the pulpit, and in the senate, and will unavoidably affect our civil and religious principles." For these reasons, as well as to crown our state school system and to provide higher educational advantages for its leaders, it was argued that the State should exercise control over the colleges.

This new national spirit manifested itself in a number of ways. In New York we see it in the reorganization of King's College (1787), the rechristening of the institution as Columbia, and the placing of it under at least the nominal supervision of the governing educational body of the State. In 1810 the Massachusetts legislature began encroachments on Harvard, which finally led, in 1865, to Harvard's giving up all state connection. In Pennsylvania an attempt was made to bring the university into closer connection with the State, but this failed. Repeated efforts also were made to transform William and Mary into a state university for Virginia, but without success. The outstanding case came in 1816, when the legislature of New Hampshire tried to transform Dartmouth College into a state institution. This act was unsuccessfully contested in the state courts, and the case was finally carried to the Supreme Court of the United States, before which Daniel Webster made an able and an eloquent presentation (**R. 167**) of the rights of the college. There it was decided, in 1819, that the charter of a college was a contract,[1] the obligation of which a legislature could not impair (**R. 166**).

---

[1] Between 1758 and 1763 four appeals were made to the colonial legislature of Connecticut for a modification of the Yale charter of 1701. In 1765 President Clapp made a reply to the memorialists, and it is interesting to note that he took substantially the same ground, based on authorities, that the Supreme Court took later in the Dartmouth College case.

Effect of the Dartmouth College decision. The effect of this decision manifested itself in two different ways. On the one hand it guaranteed the perpetuity of endowments,[1] and the great period of private and denominational effort (see table, p. 270) now followed. On the other hand, since the States could not change charters and transform old establishments, they began to turn to the creation of new state universities of their own. Virginia created its state university [2] the same year as the Dartmouth case decision, and opened it for instruction in 1825. The University of North Carolina, which had been established in 1789, and which began to give instruction in 1795, was brought under full control by the State in 1821. What later became the University of Tennessee (East Tennessee College) opened for instruction in 1820. The University of Vermont, originally chartered in 1791, was rechartered as a state university in 1838, though its state connection has always been somewhat nominal. The University of Indiana was established in 1820, and opened for instruction in 1824 (**R. 161**). Alabama provided for a state university in its first constitution, in 1819, chartered it in 1820, and the institution opened for instruction in 1831. Michigan, in framing its first constitution preparatory to entering the Union, in 1835, made careful provisions for the safeguarding of the state university and for establishing it as an integral part of its state school system, as Indiana had done in 1816. Wisconsin provided for the creation of a state university in 1836, and embodied the idea in its first constitution when it entered the Union in 1848, and Missouri provided for a state university in 1839, Mississippi in 1844, Iowa in 1847, and Florida in 1856. The state university is today found in every

[1] It would be hard to overestimate the importance of the Dartmouth College decision. Chancellor Kent, writing with reference to it in his *Commentaries*, said:

"It did more than any single act proceeding from the authority of the United States to throw an impregnable barrier around all rights and franchises derived from the grant of government, and to give solidity and inviolability to the literary, charitable, religious, and commercial institutions of the country."

[2] Probably no other institution of learning has wielded more influence on higher education in the South than has the University of Virginia. The fundamental philosophy of Jefferson found expression in its early organization. Its student body came to be made up of men from every section, but especially the South. Its stamp was impressed on nearly all the other schools and colleges established in the South after its creation. It became a model in form of administration, standards of scholarship, methods of instruction, and fundamental policies. A host of its graduates entered law and medicine, particularly in the South; and large numbers of its sons entered the national service. What Harvard and Yale have been to New England and the North, the University of Virginia was, in the nineteenth century, to the South.

"new" State and in some of the "original" States, and practically every new Western and Southern State followed the patterns set by Indiana, Michigan, and Wisconsin and made careful provision for the establishment and maintenance of a state university in its first state constitution.

The American educational ladder now complete. There was thus quietly added another new section to the American educational ladder, and the free public school system was extended farther upward. The colleges thus fitted their work onto that of the recently evolved English high school, and the American educational ladder was now complete (R. 168). With the abolition of the rate-bill, which by 1860 had been done everywhere by the cities, and which still existed in the rural and town schools in but five of the then thirty-three States, this educational ladder was finally open to all American children as their educational birthright.[1] The two requisites for the climb were money enough to obtain freedom from work in order to attend, and brains and perseverance enough to retain a place in the classes.

Though the great period of state university foundation came after 1850, and the great period of state university expansion after

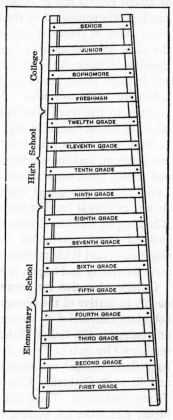

FIG. 68. THE AMERICAN EDUCATIONAL LADDER

Compare this with the figure on page 352, and the democratic nature of the American school system will be apparent.

[1] "This country gave me, as it gives to every boy and girl, a chance. It gave me schooling, independence of action, opportunity for service and honor. In no other land could a boy from a country village, without inheritance or influential friends, look forward with unbounded hope. My whole life has taught me what America means. I am indebted to my country beyond any human power to repay." (Herbert Hoover, in his speech of acceptance of the Republican nomination for President, August, 1928.)

1885, the beginnings were clearly marked early in our national history. Of the sixteen States having state universities by 1860 (see Fig. 67), all except Florida had established them before 1850. For a long time small, poorly supported by the States, much like the church colleges about them in character and often inferior in quality, one by one the state universities have freed themselves alike from denominational restrictions on the one hand and political control on the other, and have set about rendering the service to the State which a state university ought to render. Michigan, the first of our state universities to free itself, take its proper place, and set an example for others to follow, opened in 1841 with two professors and six students. In 1843–44 it was a little institution of three professors, one tutor, one assistant, and one visiting lecturer, had but fifty-three students, and offered but a single course of study, consisting chiefly of Greek, Latin, mathematics, and intellectual and moral science (**R. 169**). As late as 1852 it had but seventy-two students, but by 1860, when it had largely freed itself from the incubus of Baptist Latin, Congregational Greek, Methodist intellectual philosophy, Presbyterian astronomy, and Whig mathematics, and its remarkable growth as a state university had begun, it enrolled five hundred and nineteen.

College education for women. A change in the colleges, thoroughly indicative of the democracy of the West, was the opening of collegiate instruction to women. In 1800 women could not enter any college in the United States. In 1821 Emma Willard opened a seminary [1] for girls at Troy, New York; in 1837 Mt. Holyoke Seminary (later college) was opened by Mary Lyon in Massachusetts; and in 1828 Catherine Elizabeth Beecher founded the Hartford Female Seminary. These three institutions mark the beginnings of higher education for women, being the precursors of the Vassars, and Smiths, and Wellesleys founded in after years. Another early institution that later became a college was Georgia Female College (now Western Female College) at Macon, Georgia, which was

[1] A sixteenth child in a family of seventeen, educated chiefly by her father and mother, who at sixteen began teaching in the district schools of Connecticut. In 1807, at the age of twenty, she established a seminary for girls at Middlebury, Vermont. As many of her students came from New York State, she moved the seminary, at the urging of Governor Clinton, to Waterford, New York, in 1819, and incorporated it, hoping for an appropriation in aid from the legislature, which Governor Clinton had recommended. This means failing, the city of Troy raised $4000 by tax and more by private subscription, and the institution was then moved again to Troy and named Troy Female Seminary. This institution "became the Vassar College of New York State a half century ahead of the establishment of the institution at Poughkeepsie."

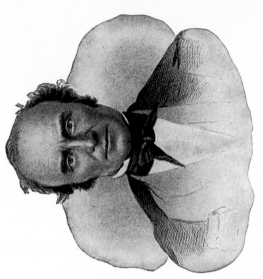

MARY LYON
(1797–1849)
Founder of Mt. Holyoke College
for Girls

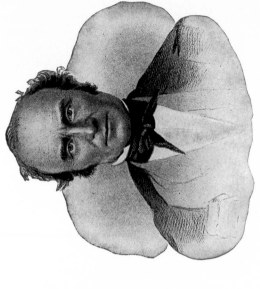

JAMES G. CARTER
(1795–1849)
Teacher, Legislator, Publicist
"Father of the Massachusetts School System"

chartered in 1836, but was not opened for some time afterward. By 1840 there were but seven institutions of all kinds for the higher education of women, but by 1860 the number had increased to sixty-one. Perhaps half of these later developed into colleges for women.

After the Civil War, during which so many women filled places formerly held by men, and especially in teaching, the colleges began to open their doors some-what generally to women students. Today eighty per cent of the non-Catholic colleges are open to women, while many special colleges for them also exist.

FIG. 69.
EMMA WILLARD
(1787–1870)

Mt. Holyoke Seminary in Massachu-setts (opened in 1837), Greensboro Col-lege for Women in North Carolina (1847), Rockford Seminary in Illinois (1849), Gen-essee College (1850) in New York, Mary Sharp College (1851) at Winchester, Tennessee, and Elmira College (1855) and Vassar College (1865), both in New York, were among the earliest of the larger women's colleges, while Oberlin [1] College (1833) and Antioch College (1853), both in Ohio, and the state university of Iowa (1856), were among the first institutions to open their instruc-tion equally to men and women. Every State west of the Mississippi River, except Missouri, made its state university coeducational from its first opening, and of those east of the same river all but three have since followed the lead of Indiana (1868) and Michigan, Illinois, and California (1870) in opening their doors freely to women students. The democratic spirit of the people west of the Allegheny Mountains has demanded, as the price of support, equal advantages for both their male and female children. Of eastern institutions, Boston University was coeducational from the beginning (1873), while Cornell opened its doors to women in 1872, and Tufts in 1892.

III. RISE OF PROFESSIONAL AND TECHNICAL EDUCATION

The beginnings of professional instruction. The colonial colleges, as has been pointed out, were largely training schools for the min-

[1] Four women entered the Freshman class at Oberlin when it opened, in 1833, and in 1841 three women were granted the A.B. degree. These were the first arts degrees granted women anywhere in the United States.

istry, and this long continued to be their one professional purpose. It was largely because of this that so many of the early leaders in education — Stowe, Peirce, Lewis, Mills, Hall, and Bateman, among others — were men who had been trained for the ministry. It was not until 1812 that theology was separated off in a school by itself at Princeton, 1819 at Harvard, and 1822 at Yale.

The first professional instruction to be added by the early universities was medicine, a medical school being established at Pennsylvania as early as 1765, King's in 1767, Harvard in 1782, Dartmouth in 1798, the University of Maryland department of medicine and the College of Physicians and Surgeons at New York both being established in 1807, and at Yale in 1813. Out of the instruction in medicine came chemistry,[1] the mother of modern science instruction, the first professors of this subject being at William and Mary in 1774, Princeton in 1795, Columbia in 1802, and Yale in 1803. The first law school in the United States was a private one conducted by a judge in his office, at Litchfield, Connecticut, from 1784 to 1833, and to this many students went for practical training. The first permanent instruction in law by a university came with the establishment of the law faculty of the University of Maryland, in 1812, and the opening of a law school at Harvard in 1817, Yale in 1824, and the University of Virginia in 1826. The medical and law schools of colonial times were the offices of practicing physicians and lawyers. Of the 3000 physicians in practice in the United States at the close of the Revolution, but 51 had taken degrees in America, and less than 350 anywhere else. There were no lawyers holding degrees. The first college of dentistry was opened in Baltimore in 1839, and the second at Cincinnati in 1845. The first college of pharmacy was opened at Philadelphia in 1822. These subjects, now so common in our state universities, are all of relatively recent development.

The beginnings of technical education. The founding of the United States Military Academy, at West Point (1802) is commonly regarded as the beginning of technical education with us, though the beginning more properly dates from 1824, when there was founded, at Troy, New York, the first of our technical schools to get under way as a technical college — The Rensselaer School. The

[1] All early instruction was book and demonstration instruction. The first chemical laboratory in America to be opened for the instruction of students was at Harvard, in 1846.

name of the school was later changed to Rensselaer Polytechnic Institute.[1] As our college development dates from Harvard, so does our technical instruction in reality date from Rensselaer. Each began a tradition, the one in literature and the arts and the other in applied science, that has been of inestimable importance in our national life. Since the courses at Rensselaer, during the first ten years of its life (**R. 171**), dealt with both the factory and the farm, it was, aside from the Fellenberg manual-labor movement, which we shall describe further on, our first agricultural college as well as our first college of technology. Though instruction in science had been offered in a number of colleges previous to 1824, and by that date there were many educators who believed that a change from or an important addition to the old Harvard-Yale type curriculum was desirable, Rensselaer was the first permanent institution to organize the work on a high plane. Within a decade it had become the first institution of its kind in America, and offered graduate work in the sciences to many who came to it from the older colleges,[2] being for American youth, up to the time of the Civil War, what Germany and its universities became after that time. In 1850, the majority of the naturalists and engineers who were teaching or practicing [3] in the United States were Rensselaer graduates, and most of those who laid the foundations of technical instruction in other institutions, from Massachusetts to Iowa, also were its graduates. After the Civil War, too, it attracted men for some time from the newer technical colleges, which had sprung up as a result of the Morrill land grant act of 1862, who came to it for graduate research work

[1] This institution was founded by a grant of land and funds made by Stephen Van Rensselaer, Patroon of Rensselaerwick. Interested in agriculture and applied science, he conceived of an institution that would instruct in and provide teachers for "agriculture, domestic economy, the arts, and manufactures." Reasons of economy soon compelled the dropping of domestic economy and courses for women, and the first head of the school, Amos Eaton, who had studied science with Silliman at Yale, soon dropped the idea of training teachers and transformed the institution into a high grade technical school.

[2] In the earlier years it drew students constantly from Amherst, Bowdoin, Columbia, Dartmouth, Harvard, Pennsylvania, Princeton, Yale, Union, Wesleyan, and Williams. From institutions where there were teachers interested in science, as Yale, there was a constant stream of students.

[3] Prior to 1840 Rensselaer had graduated 151 men. Of the first 1000 cadets graduated from West Point, 150 had become engineers, many of whom became prominent in railroad work.

"Without these, to man the new departments and to direct the construction and operation of railroads and factories, the Industrial Revolution would have been postponed twenty-five years. Those aspects of life which today seem most characteristic of America can therefore be traced in many instances to the foundation of Stephen Van Rensselaer." (R. P. Baker. *An Experiment in American Education*, p. 26.)

in the applied sciences. Cornell University, at its founding in 1868, drew on Rensselaer in both engineering and geology, as did a number of the other earlier land-grant colleges.

Harvard organized instruction in the sciences in 1847 in the form of the Lawrence Scientific School, as did Yale in the Sheffield Scientific School the same year. The Massachusetts Institute of Technology opened in 1865, Worcester Polytechnic Institute in

FIG. 70. TWO PIONEERS IN THE ESTABLISHMENT OF
TECHNICAL EDUCATION

STEPHEN VAN RENSSELAER   JUSTIN S. MORRILL
        (1764–1839)   (1810–1898)
Founder of Rensselaer Polytechnic   Sponsor of the Land Grant
                                            College Act

1871, and Case School of Applied Science in 1881. Michigan laid the cornerstone of the first building for its college of engineering in 1855, but Illinois and Minnesota did not begin their technical courses until 1868, Wisconsin until 1870, or Purdue University until 1874.

The new land-grant colleges. After about 1838 there appeared a new and rising interest in agricultural instruction.[1] In 1841, and again in 1848, memorials were presented to Congress asking for the

[1] This rising interest was in part due to the rise of the Manual Labor movement, and in part to the organization of county agricultural societies. In 1836 the New York legislature passed "an act to incorporate the New York State Agricultural School," but made no appropriation to start it and the school failed. In 1837 the Franklin Institute presented a petition to the Pennsylvania legislature praying for the establishment of a state school of practical arts. The legislature was besieged with memorials favoring, but did not act. Between 1838 and 1848 many memorials were presented to Congress urging the establishment of a national school of applied science, after the plan of West Point.

establishment of colleges of "agriculture, mechanics, road making, and architecture" in the States. In 1847 a committee of the New York legislature recommended the establishment of a school in that State to teach "agriculture and mechanic arts." The new constitution of Michigan, of 1850, had provided that the legislature "shall, as soon as practicable, provide for the establishment of an agricultural school," and that year the legislature of the State petitioned Congress for a grant of public land to found a college of agriculture, and was seconded by Illinois [1] in 1854. A state educational convention in Virginia, in 1857, in its "Address to the People" lists a state school of agriculture as one of the needs of the State. In 1858 Michigan renewed its petition. In 1854 Pennsylvania established a state agricultural school,[2] which opened in 1859, and Michigan did the same in 1855, the school opening in 1857. In 1856 Congress ordered an investigation, and in 1859 a bill, sponsored by Justin P. Morrill of Vermont, passed Congress making a grant of 20,000 acres of public land to each State, for each Senator and Representative the State had in Congress, to endow a college of agriculture and mechanic arts. This was the Fellenberg manual-labor-seminary idea in a new form, but with the manual-labor-support of students omitted. It was stated in the act that the leading purpose of these colleges

shall be, without excluding other scientific and classical studies, and including military tactics, to teach such branches of learning as are related to agriculture and the mechanic arts in such manner as the legislatures of the States may respectively prescribe, in order to promote the liberal and practical education of the industrial classes in the several pursuits and professions of life.

President Buchanan vetoed the bill because, among other reasons:

5. This bill will seriously interfere with existing colleges in the different States, in many of which agriculture is taught as a science and in

[1] The Illinois resolution of 1854 demanded "the passage of a law by Congress donating to each State in the Union an amount of public lands not less in value than five hundred thousand dollars, for the liberal endowment of a system of industrial universities, one in each State in the Union, for the more liberal and practical education of our industrial classes and their teachers."

[2] At a meeting of the State Agricultural Society of Pennsylvania, at Harrisburg, in 1853, measures were taken for the establishment of an Agricultural School. As a result, a Farmers' High School was incorporated early in 1854. In 1855 one hundred acres of land were donated in Center County and $20,000 in money raised to begin the School. In 1857 the legislature voted $50,000, on condition that a like sum be obtained from other sources, which was done, and in 1859 the School opened with 123 pupils. So successful was the school that two years later, the legislature changed the name to the Agricultural College of Pennsylvania. The Michigan school opened in 1857.

all of which it ought to be so taught. These institutions of learning have grown up with the growth of the country, under the fostering care of the States and the munificence of individuals, to meet the advancing demands for education. They have proved great blessings to the people. Many, indeed most, are poor, and sustain themselves with difficulty. What the effect would be on these institutions by creating an indefinite number of rival colleges sustained by the endowment of the Federal Government it is not difficult to determine.

In 1862 a similar bill, except that the grant was increased from 20,000 to 30,000 acres for each Senator and Representative, and that military science and tactics was added as a third required study, was passed by Congress and signed by President Lincoln.[1] This bill had the same sponsorship, and is commonly known as the First Morrill Act. A total of 11,367,832 acres of public land was given to the States to endow institutions for the teaching of the new subjects — an area one half as large as the State of Indiana — and fifty-one States and Territories, counting Porto Rico, Alaska, and Hawaii, now receive money grants from the National Government to help carry on this work. Eighteen States added the land-grant to the endowment of their existing state universities and combined the two institutions, three of the original States (originally five) gave the grant to private institutions already established within the State, and the remainder established separate agricultural and mechanical colleges.

The financial returns from the land-grants were disappointing,[2] but the educational returns have been very large. Probably no aid for education given by the National Government to the States has proved so fruitful as have these grants of land, and subsequently of money, for instruction in agriculture and the mechanic arts. New and vigorous colleges have been created (Cornell, Purdue, and the state universities of Ohio and Illinois are examples); small and feeble state universities have been awakened into new life (Vermont and

[1] For the text of the veto message of President Buchanan, the Morrill Act of 1862, the Experimental Stations Act of 1887, and the Maintenance Act (commonly known as the second Morrill Act) of 1890, see Cubberley, E. P., and Elliott, E. C., *State and County School Administration; Source Book*, pp. 83–99. The Macmillan Company, New York, 1915.

[2] A total of 10,548,295 acres of public land were granted under the Act, of which New York State received approximately one tenth. The funds produced total approximately twenty million dollars, and of this New York (Cornell University) obtained, by good management, almost one third. There are lands still unsold, mostly western, that may add, if sold at appraised price, about thirteen million more. The market for public land was glutted, as President Buchanan predicted, and land sold as low as thirty cents an acre. Some States received almost nothing for their land.

Wisconsin are examples); agriculture and engineering have been developed as new learned professions; and the States have been stimulated to make larger and rapidly increasing appropriations for their universities, until today the state universities largely overshadow all but the best endowed of the old denominational colleges.   The far-reaching educational importance of the Morrill Act of 1862, so named for the Senator who framed and sponsored it, is not likely to be overestimated.

The American free public school system now established.   By the close of the second quarter of the nineteenth century, certainly by 1860, we find the American public school system fully established, in principle at least, in all our Northern States.   Much yet remained to be done to carry into full effect what had been established in principle, but everywhere democracy had won its fight, and the American public school, supported by general taxation, freed from the pauper-school taint, free and equally open to all, under the direction of representatives of the people, free from sectarian control, and complete from the primary school through the high school, and in the Western States through the university as well, may be considered as established permanently in American public policy.   The establishment of the free public high school and the state university represent the crowning achievements of those who struggled to found a state-supported educational system fitted to the needs of great democratic States.   Probably no other influences have done more to unify the American people, reconcile diverse points of view, eliminate state jealousies, set ideals for our people, and train leaders for the service of the States and of the Nation than the academies, high schools, and colleges scattered over our land.   They have educated but a small percentage of our people, to be sure, but they have trained most of the leaders who have guided our democracy since its birth.

QUESTIONS FOR DISCUSSION

1. Show how the American academy was a natural development in our national life.
2. Show how the American high school was a natural development after the academy.
3. Show the thoroughly democratic nature of the new high schools.
4. Show why the high school could be opposed by men who had accepted tax-supported elementary schools.   Why have we abandoned such reasoning now?

5. Explain the difference, and illustrate from the history of our educational development, between establishing a thing in principle and carrying it into full effect.

6. Show why it was natural that higher education should have been left largely to denominational effort before 1860.

7. Was the early argument as to the influence of higher education on the State a true argument? Why?

8. What would have been the probable results had the Dartmouth College case been decided the other way?

9. Explain why it required so long to get the state universities started on their real development.

10. What would have been the effect educationally had we followed President Buchanan's reasoning?

11. Show how the opening of collegiate instruction to women was a phase of the new democratic movement.

12. Show how college education has been a unifying force in our national life.

SELECTED READINGS

In the accompanying volume of *Readings* the following selections, related to the subject matter of this chapter, are reproduced:

142. Adams: Effect of the Academy on the Latin Grammar School.
*143. Grizzell: The Academy a Representative Institution.
144. Trustees: The Aims of Franklin's Academy.
*145. N. Y. Gazetteer: Opening of Newark Academy.
*146. Miller: What was taught in the New York Academies.
147. Massachusetts: An Act to incorporate an Academy.
*148. Bell: The Phillips Exeter Curriculum in 1818.
149. Adams: School Life at Phillips Andover in 1780.
150. Hartford Seminary: Course of Study in 1831.
*151. Annals: The Founding of Mt. Holyoke Female Seminary.
*152. Carter: Effect of growth of the Academies.
*153. School Committee: Founding of the First High School.
*154. Advertisement: The First High School for Girls.
*155. Massachusetts: The High School Law of 1827.
156. School Committee: The Boston Secondary School System in 1823.
157. Barnard's Jr.: The Woodward High School, Cincinnati, 1856.
*158. Wells: The Public High School, Chicago, 1856.
*159. Michigan: The Kalamazoo Decision.
160. Documents: Early Efforts to create a National University.
*161. Advertisement: The opening of " Indiana Seminary."
*162. Annals: Early Days at Haverford College.
*163. Annals: Early Days at Western Reserve College.
*164. Annals: Early Days at Oberlin College.
*165. Brown: Public Dissatisfaction with the Old Colleges.
*166. U. S. Supreme Court: The Dartmouth College Case.
*167. Goodrich: Webster's Closing Argument in the Case.

*168. Coffman: The State Universities and Public Education.
*169. Michigan: Program of Studies at University of, 1843-44.
*170. Gladden: Williams College in the Late Fifties.
 171. New York: Act incorporating Rensselaer Polytechnic Institute.

QUESTIONS ON THE READINGS

1. Was the apprehension of Gov. Adams (142) warranted, as shown by subsequent developments? Why was the Massachusetts regulation as to founding of new academies sound?

2. State, briefly, the transition character of the academy (143), and its place in our educational development.

3. Just what was originally in mind in the establishment of Franklin's Academy (144)?

4. Compare the attitude toward religious instruction and life at the new Newark Academy (145) and the new King's college (59).

5. Compare the curricula of the New York academies (146) and those of Phillips Andover Academy (147), as to subjects and scope.

6. Compare the curriculum at Phillips Exeter (148) with the Colonial English Grammar Schools of the time (55, 56).

7. Show the continuance of early colonial grammar school practices in the life at Phillips Andover (149).

8. How did the course of study for girls at the Hartford Female Seminary (150) differ from that at Phillips Exeter (148) for boys?

9. Restate the ideal for Mt. Holyoke (151).

10. Compare Adams (142) and Carter (152) on the effect of the growth of the academies. Was there cause for alarm?

11. Do the fears of Adams (142) and Carter (152) enter into the motives for the establishment of the first high school (153), or was it imitative rather of the private English Grammar School (55, 56)? Or were there other motives?

12. Place the course of study for the new high school (153) with reference to the English Grammar School (55, 56), Phillips Exeter (148), and the Hartford Seminary (150).

13. Place the instruction offered the girls (154) at Boston.

14. Just what did the Massachusetts Law of 1827 (155) provide? Compare it with the Law of 1647 (16).

15. Draw a diagram to show the years and scope of the Boston school system (156) of 1823.

16. Compare the Cincinnati course of study (157) with that of the Boston high school (153), and that at Phillips Exeter (148).

17. Compare the Cincinnati (157) and Chicago (158) courses.

18. What do you see in the Kalamazoo decision (159) that made it of such great influence later in other States?

19. Write a 250 word history of the National University idea, based on the documents (160).

20. From the course of instruction advertised (161), what was the nature of the University of Indiana at the time it began?

21. How did the instruction offered (**161**) compare with that of the first year at King's College (**59**)?

22. Characterize the instruction, spirit, and living conditions in the new colleges (**162, 163, 164**) of a century ago.

23. What was this public dissatisfaction (**165**) expressive of? What did it signify in terms of the past and the future?

24. Show, from the reasoning of the Court (**166**), the importance of this case.

25. Was Webster's concluding statement (**167**) that his case was the case of every (non-state) college in the land correct? Why?

26. Show the truth of Coffman's statement (**168**) that the state universities are an expression of the spirit of the pioneers who settled west of the Appalachians.

27. Compare the instruction at the University of Michigan (**169**) in 1843–44 with a good present-day high school.

28. What were the strong points of the Williams (**170**) of Gladden's day?

29. Contrast the aims and purposes of Rensselaer (**171**) with those of the colleges of the time.

TOPICS FOR INVESTIGATION AND REPORT

1. Development and work of the Academy. (Brown; Gifford; Grizzell; Miller.)
2. The county academy system of Indiana.
3. The academy curriculum.
4. The female academy. (Barnard; Bradford; Fowler; Goodsell; Taylor; Woody.)
5. The early American high school. (Brown; Gifford; Grizzell; Inglis.)
6. The Kalamazoo decision, and its importance. (Brown; Inglis.)
7. The Dartmouth College decision, and its importance. (Beveridge.)
8. The National University idea. (Hinsdale.)
9. The new state universities, before c. 1860. (Brown; Dexter; Thwing.)
10. Instruction in science before c. 1860. (Barnard; Baker.)
11. The opening of colleges to and for women. (Taylor; Thwing; Woody.)
12. The movement for agricultural schools before 1860.
13. Establishment of the land-grant colleges. (James; Parker.)
14. Jefferson and the University of Virginia.
15. The beginnings of technical education. (Baker; James.)
16. The early beginnings of science instruction at Yale.
17. The Lawrence Scientific School at Harvard.
18. The expansion of the college curriculum between 1820 and 1875.
19. Life and work of Emma Willard. (Fowler; Goodsell.)

SELECTED REFERENCES

*Baker, Ray P. *A Chapter in American Education.* 170 pp. New York, 1924.

The story of Rensselaer Polytechnic Institute, 1824–1924.

Barnard, Henry, Editor. *The American Journal of Education.* 31 vols.

Consult *Analytical Index* to; 128 pp. Published by United States Bureau of Education, Washington, 1892.

Beveridge, Albert. *The Life of John Marshall*, vol. IV, ch. V. Boston, 1919.
A 62 pp. history of the Dartmouth College case.

Bradford, Gamaliel. "Mary Lyon"; in *Atlantic Monthly*, vol. CXXII, pp. 785–95. (Dec., 1918.)
An interesting and sympathetic sketch of her work.

*Brown, E. E. *The Making of Our Middle Schools*. 547 pp. New York, 1903.
A standard history. Chapters IX to XII describe the academies, and chapters XIII and XIV the rise of the high schools.

Brown, E. E. "Historic Development of Secondary Schools in the United States"; in *School and Society*, vol. III, pp. 227–31. (Feb. 12, 1916.)

*Brown, E. E. *Origin of the American State Universities*. 45 pp. University of California Publications on Education, vol. III, No. 1, University Press, Berkeley, California, 1903.
A very good sketch of the early colonial colleges, and the rise of the demand for state control. Good bibliography.

Coon, C. L. *North Carolina Schools and Academies, 1790–1840*. 846 pp. Raleigh, 1915. Publications North Carolina Historical Commission.
A mine of documentary information on the early schools and academies of the State.

Davis, C. O. *Public Secondary Education*. 270 pp. Chicago, 1917.
Chapters VII to IX give a very good detailed account of the rise of the academy and the high school in Michigan.

*Dexter, E. G. *A History of Education in the United States*. 656 pp. New York, 1904.
Chapter VI on the growth of the academies is a brief statement, with good statistical data. Chapter XV is a detailed history of college development, and Chapter XVI of professional schools. Chapter XXI is a good history of the education of girls and women in both public schools and colleges.

Draper, A. S. "The Rise of High Schools"; in his *American Education*, pp. 147–56. Boston, 1909.
An interesting general sketch of the rise and change in the character of the secondary school.

Fowler, Henry. "Educational Services of Emma Willard"; in *Barnard's American Journal of Education*, vol. VI, pp. 125–68.
Many details as to her work.

*Gifford, W. J. *Historical Development of the New York State High School System*. 202 pp. Albany, 1922.
An excellent study of educational development from colonial times on, covering academies and high schools.

Goodsell, W. "The Education of Women"; in I. L. Kandel's *Twenty-Five Years of American Education*, ch. XIII. New York, 1924.

*Goodsell, W. *Pioneers of Women's Education*. New York, 1932.
Good on the work of the early founders, and the obstacles they had to contend against.

*Griffin, O. B. *The Evolution of the Connecticut State School System*. 261

pp. Teachers College Contributions to Education, No. 293. New York, 1928.

A careful historical study. Has special reference to the development of the high school in the State.

*Grizzell, E. D. *The Origin and Development of the New England High School System before 1865.* 428 pp. New York, 1923.

An important research, arranged by periods and States.

Hinsdale, B. A. "Early Views and Plans relating to a National University"; in *Report of the United States Commissioner of Education, 1892–93,* vol. II, pp. 1293–1312.

A very good history of the idea, with extracts from documents.

*Inglis, A. J. *The Rise of the High School in Massachusetts.* 166 pp. Teachers College Contributions to Education, No. 45, New York, 1911.

An interesting and excellent description of the rise and curriculum of the high school in this State.

*Inglis, A. J. *Principles of Secondary Education.* 741 pp. Boston, 1918.

Chapter V, pp. 161–202, on the development of secondary education in America, forms excellent supplemental reading on the evolution of the high school.

James, Edw. J. *Origin of the Land Grant Act of 1862.* Urbana, 1910.

*Knight, Edgar W. *Public Education in the South.* 482 pp. Boston, 1822.

Chapter IV is very good on the Academy movement, with special reference to the South.

Mann, C. R. *The American Spirit in Education.* 63 pp. Bulletin No. 30, 1919, U. S. Bureau of Education.

A good brief sketch of the rise of technical education in the United States.

*Miller, G. F. *The Academy System of the State of New York.* 180 pp. Albany, 1922.

A careful and a very useful study of the rise and development of the academy in New York.

*Monroe, Paul. *Cyclopedia of Education.* New York, 1911–13. 5 vols.

The following articles form good supplemental references:
1. "Academy"; vol. I, pp. 19–23.
2. "High Schools in the United States"; vol. III, pp. 263–65.
3. "Women, Higher Education of"; vol. V, pp. 795–810.
4. Articles on the various colleges, and their founders.

Parker, Wm. B. *The Life and Public Services of Justin Smith Morrill.* 378 pp. Boston, 1924.

One chapter is devoted to his work for and promotion of the land-grant colleges.

*Taylor, Jas. M. "College Education for Girls in America"; in *Educational Review,* vol. 44, pp. 217–33, 325–47. (Oct. and Nov., 1912.)

A good brief historical article.

*Taylor, Jas. M. *Before Vassar Opened.* 287 pp. Boston, 1914.

A valuable contribution to the history of the higher education of women in America. The first two chapters contain the preceding article.

Ten Brook, A. *American State Universities and the University of Michigan.* 410 pp. Cincinnati, 1875.

A history of the origin and development of our state universities, as illustrated by the University of Michigan. An old classic.

Thompson, Wm. O. "The Small College; its work in the past"; in *Proceedings of the National Education Association*, 1900, pp. 61–67.

The work of the small denominational colleges.

*Thwing, Chas. F. *A History of Higher Education in America.* 501 pp. New York, 1906.

A very important volume. Contains detailed histories of the early colleges, traces the rise of the state universities, courses of study, education of women, etc.

*Thwing, Chas. F. *A History of Education in the United States since the Civil War.* 348 pp. Boston, 1910.

Chapter V on the "Course of Study," and Chapter VII on "Changes in Collegiate Conditions," contain interesting descriptions of the changes of the past half-century.

Woody, Thos. *A History of Women's Education in the United States.* 2 vols., 1338 pp. Science Press, Lancaster, 1929.

Deals extensively with the rise of female seminaries and colleges, and the entrance of women into teaching.

CHAPTER IX

CHARACTER OF THE SCHOOLS ESTABLISHED

SLOWLY, as we have seen, and after a series of conflicts, we gradually evolved a series of purely native American school systems to replace our earlier English inheritance. These extended from the primary school through the American-created English grammar school and the English high school. In a few Southern and Western States — notably Virginia, the Carolinas, Georgia, Ohio, Indiana, and Michigan — an embryo state university was early added at the top. In this chapter we shall examine briefly the character of the early schools thus established, note the effect of the separation from the mother country on textbooks and character and purpose, and seek to determine about what development had taken place in our city and state school systems before the outbreak of the Civil War for a time materially checked our educational progress.

The American school of the 3-R's. Toward the close of Chapter III we traced the rise of a distinctively American consciousness after 1750, and the beginnings of the evolution of distinctively American-type schools. This movement was checked by the War for Independence, but after about 1820 came out again in full force. Even before that time certain type plans had been evolved which gave clear indications of the lines along which development was eventually to take place. As schools before that time existed in their best form in New England, and as New England people carried the public school idea with them wherever they went, we naturally turn first to New England to see what types of schools were established there after the coming of nationality.

From the first the teaching of reading and writing had been a common requirement in all the New England Colonies, excepting Rhode Island, and some arithmetic, though often quite small in amount, also was gradually added. The necessities of the rural districts, where separate teachers for writing and ciphering were not possible, forced a combination of the teaching of these three subjects, thus forming the American school of the 3-R's. These subjects, with slight additions, the Massachusetts law of 1789 fixed as a general requirement for all schools of what then was Massachusetts.[1] The dame school covered the needs of the A-B-C-darians, and inducted the youngsters into the mysteries connected with the beginnings of learning to read, while the regular winter school (often divided into two parts) conducted by men teachers, and the summer school by women teachers (**R. 172a**), continued the instruction in these three subjects as long as the boys and girls were able to profit by it. With the short winter term, the frequent changes in teachers, the slow individual method of instruction, and the English textbooks by Dilworth in English and Arithmetic to fall back upon (**R. 37**), the learning process was so long-drawn-out that these three subjects, with the spelling of words and religious instruction, filled up all the time that could be devoted to learning by most children (**Rs. 51, 172b**).

FIG. 71. A SUMMER SCHOOL
From *Bolles Spelling Book*, 1831

These arts, too, were sufficient for almost all the ordinary needs of life, as their possession, in the early period of our national history, served to distinguish the educated man or woman from the uneducated.

I. NEW TEXTBOOKS CHANGE THE OLD INSTRUCTION

Almost immediately after the close of the Revolutionary War a long series of native American schoolbooks began to appear. In part this was due to the War having cut off the previous English supply, and thus stimulated authorship,[2] and in part to a desire to

[1] The law of 1789, which applied to Maine and New Hampshire as well as Massachusetts, required all towns having 50 families to support an English school for at least six months a year, which might be in one or more sessions or terms, in which should be taught reading, writing, orthography, the English language, arithmetic, and decent behavior. Towns of 100 families or over were to provide twelve months of schooling.

[2] There had been two American Spellers, published in late Colonial times, but neither had made much headway against Dilworth, and both were completely superseded by Webster. These two were:

1. *The Youth's Instructor in the English Tongue,* or the Art of Spelling Improved, in Three Parts, with a Greater Variety of very Useful Material than any other Book of this Kind and Bigness extant. (Boston, 1757.)

2. *The Pennsylvania Spelling Book, or Youth's Friendly Instructor and Monitor,* by Anthony Berezet. (Philadelphia, 3rd Ed., 1782.)

create distinctive American texts for American schools. These new books not only replaced those of English origin previously used, particularly Dilworth, but their publication also helped materially to expand the course of instruction by reducing new subjects of study to textbook form. The more important of these new textbooks will be briefly described.

FIG. 72. FRONTISPIECE TO NOAH WEBSTER'S "AMERICAN SPELLING BOOK"

This is from the 1827 Edition, reduced one third in size.

Spellers and Readers. The publication of Noah Webster's "bluebacked" *American Spelling Book*, in 1783, when he was but twenty-five years of age — a combined speller and reader — marked an epoch in the teaching of spelling and reading. Its publication at that time, says Reeder, "was an event in the history of education in this country compared to which an entire series of schoolbooks at the present time is not a circumstance." It was after the plan of Dilworth, but was thoroughly American in content and character (Rs. 174, 50) and was put up in better teaching form. It contained an easy standardized pronunciation, substituted moral reading lessons[1] for the English prayers, and American historical and geographical names for similar English names in Dilworth.[2] It at once superseded the expiring *New England Primer* in most of the cities, replaced Dilworth as a speller and reader, and did more than

[1] "Webster's *Spelling Book* held its place in the schools of Farmington for seventy-eight years until it was voted out in 1874, and the school boy no longer reads of the Boy that stole Apples, or of the Milk-maid who prematurely counted her chickens, of Poor Tray, The Partial Judge, and all the wholesome lessons in morality which it contained." (Julius Gay. "Webster's Speller and Readers in Farmington"; in *Connecticut School Document*, No. XIII, 1892.)

[2] Webster thus describes how he came to write the books he published:

"In the year 1782, while the American army was lying on the bank of the Hudson, I kept a classical school in Goshen, Orange County, New York. I there compiled two small elementary books for teaching the English language. The country was then impoverished, intercourse with Great Britain was interrupted, school books were scarce and hardly attainable, and there was no certain prospect of peace."

any other single force to create a unified American language for the new Nation (**R. 174**).

Spelling and word analysis now became and long continued to be one of the most popular subjects in the schools, and inter-school "spelling matches" became a favorite social amusement of both the old and the young. So great was the sale of the book that the author was able to support his family during the twenty years (1807–27) he was at work on his *Dictionary of the English Language* entirely from the royalties from the *Speller*, though the copyright returns to him were less than a cent a copy. In 1828 its sales were 350,000 copies, and at the time of his death (1843) the sales were approximately a million copies a year. During the thirty-five-year period from 1855 to 1890, when the copyright was controlled by D. Appleton and Company, of New York, its sales still averaged 865,419 copies a year. In 1890 the American Book Company took over the copyright, and the book may still be obtained from them.[1] The book passed through almost countless editions,[2] and the total sales up to 1880 were, at that time, estimated to have exceeded 80,000,000 copies. This was the first distinctively American textbook, and the most popular of all our early schoolbooks.

The publication of Webster's *Speller* was followed by a long line of spellers and readers, the most famous of which was Webster's *An American Selection,* or *Third Part.*[3] This was the first school reader, in the modern sense, published in America.[4] The title-page

---

[1] "That this little book has been the banner textbook of the century in America, no one will question. It is the only common school textbook that saw the opening of the century and is still in the hands of hundreds of thousands of school children at its close. Although it has long since disappeared from the city schools, and the more advanced rural schools, it is still used among the rural schools of the South and West." (R. R. Reeder. *Historical Development of School Readers,* p. 35.)

[2] Webster's *Speller* was revised frequently, and in the process much changed and improved. The book was sold under several names and printed through license in different places, but due to the color of the paper used on the cover it came to be known as Webster's Blue-back Speller. An edition of 1831 consisted of 168 pages, 14 of which were introductory, 60 contained words taken from the dictionary, 29 pages contained the names of persons, places, etc., 47 pages were reading matter, 8 contained fables with pictures, and 4 contained numbers, abbreviations, characters used in writing, and a census of the United States. It contained 5800 words arranged for spelling.

[3] Commonly known as Webster's "Third Part," the *Speller* being the "First Part," and his *Grammatical Institute* the "Second Part" of his three-book series on the English language. Each was the first of its kind from American authorship, and each marked out new lines for others to follow.

[4] "Webster's *Third Part,* coming after the War of Independence, was largely made up of the patriotic orations of Hancock, Warren, Ames, Livingston, and other American orators, with the Fourth of July oration of Joel Barlow at the North Church in Hartford,

stated well the scope and purpose of the volume, as did Bingham's *American Preceptor* and Lindley Murray's *English Reader* (1800), all three of which are reproduced as **R. 175**. *The Columbian Primer* (1802), a modernized and secularized imitation (see Fig. 59) of the old *New England Primer;* the *Franklin Primer* (1802), "containing a new and uſeful ſelection of Moral Leſſons adorned with a great variety of elegant cuts calculated to ſtrike a laſting impreſſion on the Tender Minds of Children"; and Caleb Bingham's [1] *American Preceptor* (1794) and *Columbian Orator* (1806) were other very successful early

textbooks for teaching reading. The *Preceptor* was a graded reader and soon largely replaced Webster's *Reader's Assistant*, while the *Orator*, a more advanced "Second Part," displaced the Bible as an advanced reading book in the schools. The *Orator*, too, was one of the earliest of a long list of books containing selections from poetry and prose for reading and declamation.[2] A number of other and similar books soon appeared in succession to the above, such as those by Cobb, Parley, Pickett, and Pierpont. These books, like Webster's (**R. 173**), suited well the new demo-

FIG. 73. MAKING THE PRELIMINARY BOW TO THE AUDIENCE

From Lovell's *The Young Speaker*, 1844

cratic spirit of the times, and became very popular. Selections from English poetry and the patriotic orations of Revolutionary leaders predominated. Many were illustrated with cuts, showing how to bow, stand, make gestures suitable to different types of declamation, etc. The speeches of John Adams, Ames, Hancock, Livingston, Warren, and in particular Patrick Henry's "Give me Liberty or give me Death" were

It would hardly be read with much enthusiasm by the boy of today, but at the beginning of the century every boy was taught to consider himself a possible President of the United States, and school declamations were thought a useful preparation for the future statesman." (Julius Gay. "Webster's Speller and Readers in Farmington"; in *Connecticut School Document*, No. XIII, 1892.)

[1] These books by Bingham proved more popular than Webster's "Third Part." By 1829 the *Preceptor* had passed through 68 editions and 640,000 copies of it had been printed, while 23 editions and 200,000 copies of the *Orator* had been printed and sold.

[2] In the preface to the *Orator*, a 300-page volume, Bingham says that it is "a new selection of lessons for reading and speaking in American schools"; that preference has been given to works of American genius; that no place has been given to romantic fiction; and that "tales of love have not gained admission"... "Nor is there to be found a word or a sentiment which would raise a blush on the cheek of modesty." The book contained many patriotic selections, some poetry, literary extracts, and rules for elocution.

soon being declaimed in the schoolhouses all over the land.   All of the above-mentioned textbooks were essentially New England productions, they continued to be used there for a long time, and they were carried westward by New England people in the "great migration" and used in the new schools they established.

FIG. 74. NOAH WEBSTER
(1758–1843)

In 1836, just as the common school in the then West was getting started, and the Western Literary Institute was near the height of its labors, there appeared, at Cincinnati, the first two books of one of the most remarkable series of graded readers that ever has been issued anywhere.   These were the First and Second Readers, by William H. McGuffey.[1] The year following the Third and Fourth Readers of the series appeared, and, in 1841, a Fifth Reader. Ten years afterward the five Readers were expanded into a series of six, and these were revised five times. For sixty years, three generations, the McGuffey Readers were the most widely used reading books,[2] outside of New Eng-

FIG. 75.
WILLIAM H. McGUFFEY
(1800–73)

[1] William Holmes McGuffey was born in Washington County, Pennsylvania, in 1800, of Scotch parentage. The family moved to Ohio, where he was prepared for college by a minister. In 1826 he was graduated from Washington College, Pennsylvania, and at once elected to the chair of Ancient Languages at Miami University, at Oxford, Ohio. In 1832 he was ordained as a minister, and took a pastorate. In 1836 he became president of Cincinnati College, took part in the work of the Western Literary Institute, and helped in the passage of general school law of 1838. From 1839 to 1843 he was president of Ohio University, at Athens; in 1843 he returned to Cincinnati to work in the new Woodward high school, and in 1845 he became professor of natural philosophy at the University of Virginia, where he remained until his death in 1873. During his lifetime, in addition to all his other work, he is said to have preached three thousand sermons.

[2] The series of readers was compiled for a royalty of 10 per cent until $1000 had been paid, after which the Readers became the absolute property of the publishers. For each

land. Probably half of the school children of America during this period drew their inspiration and formulated their codes of morals and conduct [1] from this remarkable series of Readers (**R. 176**). That this graded series of Readers helped to establish the graded school, with its class organization, there can be little question.

FIG. 76. WARREN COLBURN
(1793–1833)

Arithmetics. The English Dilworth's *The Schoolmaster's Assist. ant* (**R. 37**), "being a compendium of Arithmetic, both practical and theoretical, in five parts," which was much used by schoolmasters in colonial times, and which went through many American editions before 1800, did much to popularize the study of arithmetic, even though the subject remained largely a college study. In 1788, Nicholas Pike's *Arithmetic* appeared. It was a voluminous work of five hundred and twelve pages, and offered "a new and complete system of arithmetic for the use of citizens of the United States." The preface to the third edition stated that the book was "used as a classical book in all the Newengland Universities." It was too advanced for the schools, and an abridged edition was offered later. It still remained a difficult subject to teach. A number of briefer American arithmetics soon followed and, in 1821, with the publication of Warren Colburn's *First Lessons in Arithmetic on the Plan of Pestalozzi*, another famous American textbook, [2] one that

revision McGuffey was paid a fee, and after the Civil War, so successful had the books been, that the publishers paid McGuffey a voluntary annuity until he died. The president of The American Book Company, which now controls the plates, estimates the combined sales of the Readers, Primer, and Speller, between 1836 and 1920, at 122,000,000 copies. For the year 1889, for which exact figures are available, the sales were 2,172,413 copies.

[1] The testimony of hundreds of older persons is to this effect. Mark Sullivan, in his *Our Times*, vol. II, devotes a chapter (II) to McGuffey's Readers, and reproduced a number of letters as to the lasting influence of the volumes and the deep impress they made on the thoughts and ideals of the youth of the time.

[2] Colburn was a graduate of Harvard, who taught a few years, and helped form the American Institute of Instruction. Most of his later life he was a factory manager. Though acknowledging his debt to Pestalozzi for certain fundamental ideas as to method, he after all wrote the book himself and out of his experience as a teacher. He needed it himself.

must be ranked with Webster's *Speller* and the McGuffey *Readers*, appeared.   The book contained hundreds of simple problems, to be solved mentally, and arithmetic, especially mental arithmetic, now became one of the great subjects of the common schools.   Colburn changed what had previously been a difficult subject into a simple one, and made it an easy one for teachers to teach and for pupils to learn.

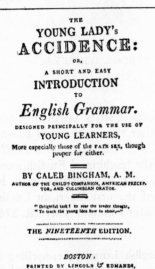

FIG. 77. AN EARLY ENGLISH GRAMMAR

Title-page of the 1813 edition of Caleb Bingham's *Young Lady's Accidence*, and a page of the text.

In 1835 there appeared, at Cincinnati, another western textbook that was destined for wide use and a long life — Ray's *Arithmetic*.[1] This work was a combination of the written methods of Pike and the mental methods of Colburn, and the text, in its different revisions, enjoyed a long run in the schools west of the Alleghenies.

and thought it was needed in the schools.   More than two million copies of this little Arithmetic of about 100 pages were sold during the fifty years following its publication. In 1856, twenty-five years after it appeared, its sales were approximately fifty thousand copies in England and one hundred thousand in the United States.   It was translated into a number of languages, and the Boston Public Library has a copy on raised type for the blind.

[1] Joseph Ray (1807-57) was educated at Franklin College, New Athens, later becoming principal of the new Woodward high school at Cincinnati.   He was the author of a number of arithmetics and algebras, noted for their good organization and clear statement of fundamental principles.

FIG. 78. TWO EARLY TEXTBOOK WRITERS
JEDEDIAH MORSE   LINDLEY MURRAY
(1761–1826)   (1745–1826)

Language study. Other new subjects of study began to appear
here and there almost immediately after the beginning of the national period. The English Dilworth's *A New Guide to the English
Tongue* had made the beginnings of the teaching of English word-
usage, and in 1784, the year following the publication of his
American Speller, Noah Webster issued the first American English
Grammar, commonly known as Webster's Second Part (**R. 174**),
and bearing the title:

> A Grammatical Institute of the English Language; comprising an
> Easy, Concise, and Systematic Method of Education. Designed for
> the use of English Schools in America. In three Parts. Part Second,
> Containing a plain and Comprehensive Grammar, grounded on the true
> Principles and Idioms of the Language.

This book marked the downfall of Dilworth, but it soon in turn
was largely superseded by two other books, published in close succession. One was Caleb Bingham's *The Young Lady's Accidence*,[1]
which first appeared in 1786 or 1787, and the other was Lindley
Murray's *English Grammar*,[2] which was first published in 1795.
Murray's text, particularly in the abridged form, was extensively

[1] Caleb Bingham (1754–1817) was a graduate of Dartmouth (1782), who in 1784 opened
a school for girls in Boston, and in 1788 took charge of one of the Reading Schools of that
city. He was one of the original promoters of a public library in Boston.

[2] Lindley Murray (1745–1826) was of Quaker stock, was educated in the schools of the
Society of Friends, and for a time taught in a boarding school at Burlington, N.J., and
later taught in England, where he died. He is chiefly noted for his four books on English
Grammar, and three school readers, all published between 1795 and 1800.

used for a long time and went through many editions. Bingham's book marked the beginnings of instruction in grammar in the Boston schools. These three books became very popular, were extensively used and imitated, and firmly fixed the new study of English Grammar as a common-school subject.

Geography and history. In 1784, the Reverend Jedediah Morse [1] published his *American Universal Geography*, with special emphasis on the interests of the United States [2] (**R. 177**), and in 1795 a much abridged school edition under the title of *Elements of Geography*. This latter was a little 16mo volume of 144 pages of descriptive matter, with two small black-and-white maps and no illustrations. The title-page of the fourth edition (1801) and a page of the text, with the map of the world, which together give a good idea as to the nature and scope of the book, are reproduced as **R. 178**. This little volume was extensively used in the schools. The same year that Morse issued his *Elements* another small descriptive school geography, Nathaniel Dwight's *A Short but Comprehensive System of the Geography of the World*, was issued at Hartford. It was a 12mo book of 214 pages, built on the question and answer form, and with no maps or illustrations. The Morse volume was the better of the two. Another early school geography to attain popularity was *Rudiments of Geography*, by William C. Woodbridge, published at Hartford in 1821, which went through many editions. It was descriptive in type, contained a number of illustrations, and had an accompanying *Atlas*. These three textbooks found a place for them-

FIG. 79. AN EARLY AMERICAN SCHOOL GEOGRAPHY (1795)

---

[1] Jedediah Morse (1761–1826) was graduated from Woodstock Academy in Connecticut, and from Yale (1783), and served for one year as a tutor there. Later he became pastor of the First Congregational Church at Charlestown, Mass.

[2] Morse, in the Preface to his *Geography*, said:

"Till within a few years we have seldom pretended to write, and hardly to think for ourselves. We have humbly received from Great Britain our laws, our manners, our books, and our modes of thinking, and our youth have been educated rather as the subjects of a British king than as citizens of a free and independent republic. But the scene is now changed. The revolution has been favorable to science in general; particularly to that of the geography of our own country. In the following sheets the author has endeavored to bring this valuable branch of knowledge home to the common schools...."

selves in the schools of the time, and helped to add another subject of study which, though opposed at first, in time became very
popular.

In 1821 a *History of the United States*, by B. Davenport, was published at Philadelphia. It contained 81 pages of questions and answers covering American history, arranged in catechetical form
(**R. 178**), to which was added the Declaration of Independence, the
Federal Constitution, and a Table of Chronology. In 1822 Samuel
Goodrich [1] published *A History of the United States*. The book was
descriptive in type and well adapted to school use, and at once
leaped into popular favor. Within the next ten years one hundred
and fifty thousand copies had been sold, and in 1836 the forty-fourth
edition was issued in a revised and enlarged form. Shortly afterward Noah Webster's *History of the United States* appeared to contest the popularity of the preceding two. Webster's volume contained an introduction to the study of the Constitution of the United
States, and his book marked the beginning of the study of Civics in
our grammar schools.

The elementary school subjects fixed.   These early school textbooks, together with a long list of imitators, firmly fixed reading,
spelling, word analysis, declamation, and ciphering as the fundamental subjects for the evolving American common school, with
arithmetic, grammar, geography, history of the United States, and
civics as additional subjects in the city schools. These new textbooks also opened up entirely new possibilities of instruction in the
evolving American common school, making it possible greatly to
expand and to enrich the teaching of the few older subjects, while
the new subjects thus introduced made possible more advanced instruction and the upward extension and lengthening of the common
school course.[2]

A race now began between arithmetic and the new subject of English grammar — a race unhappily too long continued — to see which

---

[1] Samuel Goodrich (1793–1860) was the author of 84 school textbooks and reading books
for children, including primers, readers, histories, spelling books, and elementary science
books. He is better known by his *nom de plume* of "Peter Parley."

[2] A good example here is arithmetic. "An Observer," writing in the *Annals of Education*
in 1830, says: "No other branch has been admitted with so much reluctance, notwithstanding its utility, as arithmetic... Until a few years ago it was excluded from many schools
during the day, being permitted to be taught only in the evening schools." After about
1825, with the publication of Colburn's text, this attitude changed rapidly. English grammar had a somewhat similar experience.

subject should take the place of first importance in the school.   Fact-geography and fact-history also became important older-pupil subjects.   Sewing and knitting also became common subjects of in-

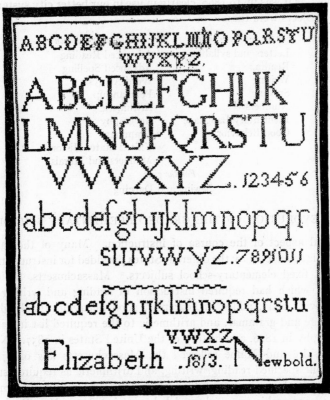

FIG. 80. A "SAMPLER"

A sampler worked on linen, in the possession of the author, which was made in a girl's school near Bristol, Pennsylvania, in 1813.

struction for the girls, and, as the culmination of such instruction, each girl made a "Sampler," of which the copy shown in Fig. 80 is a good example. These were made on linen, though in the girls' "boarding-schools" elaborate work on silk sometimes was executed. The name "Sampler" came from the expected future use in showing the proper form of letters to be used in marking the household linen.   Much attention also was paid to manners, morals, and good behavior. These represented the secularized successor of the old religious instruction of colonial times.

By 1830, certainly, we have the full curriculum of our elementary schools, as it was up to 1860, clearly in use in our better city systems. The subjects were these:

For the younger children	*For the older children*
Letters and syllables	Advanced Reading
Reading	Advanced Spelling
Writing	Word Analysis
Spelling	Penmanship
Numbers	Arithmetic
Elementary Language	Geography
Good Behavior	Grammar
	United States History
	Manners and Morals

For the girls
Sewing and Darning

II. EVOLUTION OF THE GRADED ELEMENTARY SCHOOL

Legal aspect of the course of instruction. Many of the early school laws enacted by the different States provided for instruction in certain fixed elementary-school subjects. Massachusetts, for example, which had required instruction in reading and writing in the law of 1647, added orthography, good behavior, the English language and grammar, and arithmetic to the required list in 1789, geography in 1826, and history of the United States in 1857. New Hampshire and Maine followed the Massachusetts law of 1789. Vermont specified reading, writing, and arithmetic as required subjects in its law of 1797, and added spelling, geography, grammar, United States history, and good behavior in 1827. New England people, moving westward into the Northwest Territory, carried these school requirements and the early textbooks with them, and the early schools set up in Ohio and Michigan were copies of those in the old home. Ohio, in its first school law of 1825, specified reading, writing, and arithmetic for all schools, and in 1831 permitted the cities and towns to organize instruction in other subjects. In 1848 geography and grammar were ordered added for all schools. Michigan, in the law of 1827, virtually adopted the Massachusetts plan for schools. Spelling, good behavior, and declamation were commonly added, even when not mentioned in the legal requirements.

Early city courses of study; Providence. The early courses of study adopted for the cities of the time reveal these same studies in the schools, as well as the beginnings of the classification of the pupils on the basis of the difficulty of the subjects. For example, the course of study and the textbooks adopted for the schools of Providence, Rhode Island, in 1800, read:

> The principal part of the Instruction will consist in Spelling, Accenting & Reading both Prose and Verse with propriety and accuracy, and a General Knowledge of English Grammar and Composition: Also writing a good hand according to the most approved Rules, and Arithmetic through all the previous Rules, and Vulgar and Decimal Fractions, including Tare and Tret, Fellowship, Exchange, Interest, &c.
>
> The books to be used in carrying on the above Instruction are *Alden's Spelling Book*, 1st and 2nd part, the *Young Ladies' Accidence*, by Caleb Bingham, *The American Preceptor*, *Morse's Geography*, abridged, the *Holy Bible* in select portions, and such other Books as shall hereafter be adopted and appointed by the Committee. The Book for teaching Arithmetic shall be agreed on by the Masters.
>
> The Scholars shall be put into separate Classes, according to their several improvements, each Sex by themselves.

This constituted the entire printed course of study for Providence in that day, and was typical of the time. Compared with the hundreds of printed pages of directions which we have today, the simplicity of such a course of study is evident. Though ungraded in character, the beginning of a grading of schools nevertheless is evident. This was the so-called "common school." It presupposed that the children should have learned their letters and the beginnings of reading privately, or in some dame school, before entering the public school. This requirement was common (see page 137) before the coming of Infant or Primary schools, about 1825.

In 1820, a committee was appointed by the Providence school authorities to revise "the Rules and Regulations for the Government of the Public Schools" (**R. 179**). As these related chiefly to the instruction provided, the Committee asked each "preceptor" for a statement as to how he conducted his particular school, and what subjects he taught and what books he used. Figure 81 (p. 302) is a facsimile reproduction of that part of one of the replies which related to instruction and the texts used. From the reply it is seen that the subjects of instruction taught by this teacher were reading, writing, spelling, arithmetic, and geography. The textbooks

Providence, June 7. 1820

To the Hon. School Committee

Sir,

In obedience to your request, I will state, that it is my practice to have the bell ring a few minutes before the appointed hour; then to allow about fifteen minutes for the scholars to assemble. In the morning when the school is settled, the first class of masters read in Morse's Geography abridged, and spell, and also to parse, or recite some useful lesson: the remainder of the forenoon they spend generally in the study of arithmetick.

The first class of misses read and parse in the sacred extract, give the definition of words, &c. The rest of the forenoon they spend in the study of Arithmetick.

The second class of masters and misses read in Alden's Speaker, spell, give the definition of words, and spend the residue of the forenoon in reciting lessons in grammar and the study of Arithmetick.

Their third and fourth classes of misses and masters then read in the New Testament; the chapter which they have previously studied: the remainder of the forenoon they spend in studying and spelling a page in Alden's Spellingbook.

The fifth class of misses and masters, use only Alden's spellingbook; they are kept principally to spelling.

The third, fourth and fifth Classes of misses and masters, have the same page for a spelling lesson in said spellingbook during the day.

The sixth class of Masters and misses spell in Alden's spellingbook first part. We make use of Daboll's Arithmetick.

During the intermission we prepare all the writingbooks.

In the afternoon, when the scholars are assembled and seated, while we are mending the pens, the first and second classes study the lesson given them for the next morning; and all the other classes the same spelling lesson which they had in the morning: The writing books are then served, and the afternoon is spent in writing and spelling, and exercising the small children who do not write.

We spend much time in the important branch of orthography.

I am aware, that in some instances too much has been undertaken, or too many branches taught for the advantage of the School at large: . . . . .

With sentiments of esteem,
I am yours,
John Dexter

FIG. 81. HOW AND WHAT A PROVIDENCE TEACHER
TAUGHT, IN 1820

Facsimile of a letter; Report of the *Providence School Committee*, 1899-1900. p. 37.

used were *Morse's Abridged Geography, Alden's Spelling Book* and *Speaker*, the *Testament*, and *Daboll's Arithmetic*. These were the common-school subjects of that time.[1]

John Howland, founder of the Providence schools and for long a member of the School Committee there, writing to a friend, in 1824, said that the instruction in Providence remained as prescribed in 1800, except that grammar and geography had recently been added. Of these new subjects, he said:

> Up to this time I had never seen a grammar — a sorry confession for a school committeeman, some may think — but observing that *The Young Lady's Accidence* was in use in the Boston schools, I sent to the principal bookseller in that town, and purchased one hundred copies for the use of ours.
>
> The introduction of grammar was quite an advance in the system of education, as it was not taught at all except in the better class of private schools. The same was true of geography, which had never been taught before. I sent to Boston and purchased as many as were wanted for our schools. Dr. Morse, of Charlestown, had published the first volume of his geography, and that was the work we adopted. Many thought it an unnecessary study, and some in private objected to it because it would take off their attention from arithmetic. But it met with no public opposition.

Early courses in New York City. The schools of the Free School Society in New York City were at first (1806–22) organized to cover only the work of the 3-R's and religion. An abstract of "the employment and progressive improvement of the scholars for the last year," contained in the *Fourteenth Annual Report* of the Society, for the year 1819, shows that of the 1051 children then in the schools, 1044 were "known to attend public worship on the Sabbath," as required by the rules, and that the studies pursued by them were as follows:

297 Children have been taught to form letters in sand.
615 have been advanced from letters in sand, to monosyllabic reading on boards.
686 from reading on boards, to *Murray's First Book*.
335 from *Murray's First Book*, to writing on slates.

[1] "An Observer," writing in the *Annals of Education* in 1830, says:
"Spelling, reading, writing, and arithmetic are taught now in nearly every school. Geography and grammar have, within a few years, been introduced very extensively, but in many places not without great opposition. Even arithmetic has been opposed, though with less violence. Some approved religious catechism was taught formerly at the close of each week, but since the introduction of Sunday Schools the practice has been gradually disappearing."

218 from writing on slates, to writing on paper.
341 to reading in the *Bible*.
277 to addition and subtraction.
153 to multiplication and division.
 60 to the compounds of the first four rules.
 20 to reduction.
 24 to the rule of three.

This shows the common American ungraded 3-R's school, taking children from the very beginnings, and advancing them individually and by subjects, as their progress warranted. Such schools were very common in our cities and villages in the early period.

On August 2, 1822, a committee of the New York Society was appointed to consider and report "on the propriety of instructing some of the oldest, most orderly, and meritorious of our scholars in some of the higher branches of an English Education, say Grammar, Geography, History, Mathematics, &c." This was done soon thereafter by changing the schools for a time to a pay basis, as described on page 199, and the price list there given shows that the subjects taught at that time were:

Alphabet	Grammar	Bookkeeping
Spelling	Geography	Mensuration
Writing	History	Astronomy
Reading	Composition	
Arithmetic	Needlework	

In the First Annual Report of the School Visitors for Brooklyn (1830–31), 348 pupils are reported as attending "more or less" the winter term, and of these 44 were under 6 and 48 over 16 years of age. All studied reading and spelling, from 120 to 130 studied writing, 155 arithmetic, 110 geography, 57 grammar, and 23 history.

The beginnings of school grading in Boston. Boston offers a good illustration of the beginnings of school grading, out of many that might be cited. In 1789 the Town Meeting ordered three writing schools and three reading schools established in the town, for the instruction of children between the ages of seven and fourteen, who had previously learned to read and spell,[1] boys to be admitted all

[1] "No one in the first class shall be recommended by the examining committee to be received into the English grammar schools unless he or she can spell correctly, read fluently in the New Testament, and has learned the several branches taught in the second class, and each of the scholars, before being recommended, shall be able to read deliberately and audibly so as to be heard in any part of the grammar school." (Wrightman. *Annals of the Primary School Committee of Boston*, 1821, p. 288.)

the year round, and girls only from April 20 to October 20 each year (**R. 180**).   The subjects to be taught in these schools were:

The writing school	*The reading school*
Writing	Spelling
Arithmetic	Accentuation
	Reading of prose and verse
	English Grammar and Composition

By 1823 the study of geography had been added to the instruction in the reading schools, and a little later United States history also was added.   Each school building contained two rooms, with from 180 to 200 seats each, and was divided between the two departments.   The upper room was occupied by the reading school, and the lower by the writing school.   In each room there usually were three teachers, carrying on recitations at the same time.   The pupils were interchanged, thus attending two schools and two sets of teachers each day.

Children were admitted to these schools from the Primary Schools for beginners, first established (p. 138) in 1818, each of which was an ungraded rural school in type — that is, each teacher conducted a separate school organization, and usually occupied a separate one-room building.   While the course of instruction had been divided into six steps (see Fig. 82), each teacher taught the pupils in all the six.   She began with the A-B-C-darians, and ended with the class being fitted for admission to the grammar school.[1]   A good picture of the instruction in these schools, as late as 1857, has been left us by Superintendent Philbrick (**R. 181**).

In addition to the division of the schools horizontally into Primary Schools and English Grammar Schools, and the subdivision of the latter vertically into writing and reading schools, a beginning of classification and the grading of pupils had been made, by 1823, by the further subdivision of the reading school into four classes, as follows:

---

[1] "The Primary Schools of Boston each contain (1833) about 400 children, embracing a large proportion of all those in the city, between the ages of four and seven.   They are designed to teach spelling, reading, and the elements of arithmetic, in order to prepare the children for the English Grammar Schools, in which a complete knowledge is given of the ordinary branches of a common school education.

In the Primary Schools, therefore, is laid the foundation of all the education given to the mass of our citizens; and on the health and knowledge and habits here acquired depends, in great measure, the future happiness or misery, the useful or injurious influence, of those who constitute the families, and elect the government, and control the laws of our city."   (*Report of Primary School Committee on Improvements*, Boston, 1833.)

Lowest class: Reading, spelling, accentuation.
Second class: Same, and grammar memorized.
Third class: Same, and grammar learned.
Highest class: Same, and geography.

This made four classes for the seven-year course, with a three-year primary school beneath, divided into six classes, and clearly represents the beginnings of a graded system of schools. It is a ten-year elementary-school course, beginning at the age of four In 1848 the reading or English grammar schools were further divided horizontally by putting a teacher in charge of each class, and in 1856 the same plan was extended downward to the primary schools. Figure 82 shows the organization of the Boston schools by 1823, as described in a volume, *The System of Education pursued at the Free Schools in Boston*, published that year (**R. 156**).

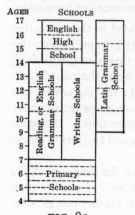

FIG. 82
THE BOSTON SCHOOL
SYSTEM IN 1823

The dotted cross-lines indicate class divisions, though not under separate teachers.

Evolution of the graded school at Providence. One of the clearest cases of the evolution of the American ungraded common school into the American graded elementary school — clear because of the presence of excellent records — is afforded by the city of Providence, Rhode Island, the schools in which began in 1800. The evolution there can be best presented by the use of a tabular statement taken from the courses of study adopted at different dates, which show the following:

1800	1820	1828
Common Schools	*Common Schools*	*Primary Schools*
(8-)	(6-)	(4-7)
Reading	Reading	Reading
Spelling	Spelling	Spelling
Accentuation	Punctuation	
Writing	Writing	*Writing Schools*
Arithmetic	Arithmetic	(7-)
Grammar	Grammar	Reading
Composition		Spelling
Geography		Writing
Bible		Arithmetic
		Grammar
		Geography
		Bookkeeping
		Epistolary Composition

1838	1840	1848
Primary Schools (4–7)	*Primary Schools* (4–7)	*Primary Schools* (5–7½)
Reading	Reading	Reading
Spelling	Spelling	Spelling
		Arithmetic
		Music
Grammar or Writing Schools (7–)	*Grammar Schools* (7–14)	*Intermediate Schools* (7½–10)
Reading	Reading	Reading
Spelling	Spelling	Spelling
Writing	Writing	Writing
Arithmetic	Arithmetic	Arithmetic
Grammar	Grammar	Music
Geography	Geography	Geography
Bookkeeping	Bookkeeping	
Epistolary Composition	U.S. History Composition Practical Ethics Constitution U.S.	
	High School (14–17)	*Grammar Schools* (10–14)
High School	List of 20 high-school subjects	Reading
The branches of a good English education		Writing
		Arithmetic
		Geography
		Grammar
		Composition
		U.S. History
		Declamation
		General History
		High School (14–17) Same as in 1840

Great variety in early forms of school organization. This creation of schools of different grades took place largely as new buildings were needed and erected, and represented the first step in the evolution of the present class-grade organization of our schools. With each additional building in the same district the children were put into better classified schools. This same division of schools for purposes of grading, as new building facilities were provided, took place generally over the United States between about 1820 and about 1860, though with quite different results and nomenclature, as the following twenty-eight selected cities will show. The numbers in parentheses indicate the number of years assigned to each school.

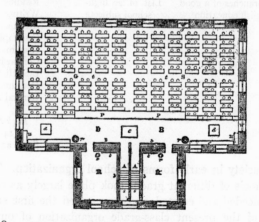

FIG. 83. EXTERIOR AND INTERIOR OF A PROVIDENCE GRAMMAR SCHOOL

This was the typical grammar-school building of about 1840. Each floor seated 228 pupils, and was conducted as a separate school. Boys and girls were here seated on opposite sides of the central aisle, though the usual plan was to give one floor to each sex. In Boston the upper floor was used by the writing school, and the lower floor by the reading school, each floor seating about 200 pupils. Two small recitation rooms are here shown leading off the main room, for the use of the assistant teachers, which was the common arrangement.

Portland, Me.	Primary, Intermediate, Grammar, High.
Concord, N.H.	Primary, Intermediate, Grammar, High.
Portsmouth, N.H.	Primary, Master's School, High.
Fall River, Mass.	Primary, Intermediate, Grammar, High.
Lawrence, Mass.	Primary, Middle, High.
Worcester, Mass.	Subprimary, Primary, Intermediate-Primary, Secondary, Grammar (3), High.
Hartford, Conn.	Primary, Secondary, Intermediate, Grammar; enter High School at 12.
New Haven, Conn.	Common Schools, enter High School at 13.
Providence, R.I.	Primary (2½), Intermediate (2½), Grammar (4), High (4).
New York City	Primary (5), Grammar (6), College (4).
Kingston, N.Y.	Primary, Junior, Senior, Academic.
Oswego, N.Y.	Primary (3), Junior (3), Senior (3), High (4).
Rochester, N.Y.	Primary (2), Intermediate (2), Grammar (3), High (4).
Syracuse, N.Y.	Primary (3), Junior (3), Senior (3), High (3).
Troy, N.Y.	Primary (3), Intermediate (3), Grammar (3), High (4).
Harrisburg, Pa.	Primary (4), Secondary (4), High (4).
Philadelphia, Pa.	Primary, Secondary, Grammar, High.
Newark, N.J.	Primary (3), Grammar (3), High (4).
New Brunswick, N.J.	Primary (4), Grammar (4), High (3).
Cleveland, Ohio	Primary, Intermediate, Senior, High.
Dayton, Ohio	Primary (3), Secondary (2), Intermediate (3), High.
Toledo, Ohio	Primary (2), Secondary (2), Intermediate (2), Grammar (2), High (3).
Indianapolis, Ind.	Primary (4), Intermediate (4), High (4).
Louisville, Ky.	Primary (4), Intermediate (3), Grammar (3), High (4).
Springfield, Ill.	Primary, Secondary, Intermediate, Grammar, High.
Detroit, Mich.[1]	Primary (2), Second grade (2), Senior (3), High (3).
Madison, Wis.	Primary (2), Intermediate (2), Grammar (2), Senior Grammar (2), High (2).
New Orleans, La.	Primary (2), Grammar, High.

At first these divisions, due largely to local building set-ups, were quite definitely separated, and promotion from one division to another commonly was based on the passing of formal examinations, but with the institution of common supervision the lines of demarcation tended to disappear, so that with time the names came to have only a historical significance.[1]

Division of each school into recitation groups.   The next step in the evolution of the graded system was the division of each school into classes.   This also began early, certainly by 1810, and was

[1] Detroit offers a good example of the early creation of detached schools, and their later consolidation to form a union elementary school.   When schools were first created there, there were three types of detached one-room schools, a primary school of two years, a "second-grade" school of two years, and a "senior" school of three years.   This was the condition from 1842 to 1849, when, despite much objection, "union schools" were begun.   In these the three schools were united to form a seven-year elementary school.   It took until 1862 to carry the plan into full effect.

fully accomplished [1] in the cities by 1840. It began by the employment of assistant teachers, known as "ushers," to help the "master," and usually the provision of small recitation rooms, off the main large room, for their use in hearing recitations. This step in the evolution of the graded system is well shown in the drawing of a Providence grammar-school building, given on p. 308, which is thoroughly typical of the period. Due to its later construction, however, the two schoolrooms in this building were smaller than was the case in earlier constructions. The New York school building

FIG. 84. AN "USHER" AND HIS CLASS

The usher, or assistant teacher, is here shown with a class in one of the small recitation rooms, off the large schoolroom. From Pierpont's *The Young Reader*, Boston, 1831.

of 1843, shown on page 139, was provided with 252 seats and three small recitation rooms. Boston buildings, in 1823, carried seats for approximately 300 pupils, and each room had a master and two ushers, but by 1848 the number had there been reduced to approximately 180 seats. Each grammar school in Providence contained two separate and distinct and duplicate schools (see Fig. 83), as was

[1] "Many of the common schools have, within the last year, been graded and the males and misses placed in separate compartments, under appropriate teachers. The results of this plan have been so favorable that the Trustees would recommend the same measures to be carried out in those schools where the males and females are collected together in the same room... A proper classification of these pupils may hereafter be called for." (*Annual Report of the Trustees and Visitors of the Common Schools of Cincinnati*, 1838, p. 3.)

a common early practice. Each school was under the control of a master and one male or two female assistants. Each little group of teachers in charge of a room was independent of the other, there being no principal for the building. Sometimes, as in Boston (**R. 182**), even the ushers were independent of the master. Only for janitor service, heating, and repairs was the building considered as one school.

Division of each school into class grades. The third and final step in the evolution of the graded system was to build larger schools with smaller classrooms, or to subdivide the larger rooms; change the separate and independent and duplicate school on each floor, which had been the common plan for so long, into parts of one school building organization; sort and grade the pupils, and outline the instruction by years; and the class system was at hand. This process began here and there in the decade of the thirties,[1] and was largely accomplished in the cities by 1860. In the smaller places it came later, but usually was accomplished by or before 1875. In the rural districts class grading was not introduced until the last quarter of the nineteenth century.

The great impetus to the establishment of this graded-class organization came from Horace Mann's *Seventh Annual Report*, in 1844, on the graded school system of Prussia (**R. 183**). The report awakened much interest as well as much opposition (see page 225). One Boston schoolmaster, however, agreed with Mann. This was John D. Philbrick,[2] principal of the Quincy Grammar School, who reorganized his school, in 1847, after the German model as described by Mann. This is considered to have been the first fully graded public school in the United States. The following year a new Quincy School was erected in Boston, and for this Philbrick worked out an entirely new type of schoolhouse architecture, which he described as follows:

---

[1] Henry Barnard, in his *First Annual Report* to the Connecticut Legislature, in 1839, wrote that then "there was hardly an instance of the gradation of schools (in Connecticut) by which the evils of crowding children of different ages, of both sexes, in every variety of study and schoolbook, under a single teacher, were avoided."

[2] John D. Philbrick (1818–86) was a notable New England educator. Graduating from Dartmouth in 1842, he was a teacher in the high schools of Roxbury and Boston from 1842 to 1847, principal of the Quincy grammar school from 1847 to 1852, principal of the state normal school at New Britain, Connecticut, from 1852 to 1854, state superintendent of schools for Connecticut from 1854 to 1856, and superintendent of the Boston schools from 1856 to 1878.

1. It was a very large school. Up to this time a grammar school with 400 pupils was considered very large. This new building had 660 seats, exclusive of the assembly hall, or 55 seats per classroom.

2. It contained a separate schoolroom for each teacher, 12 in all, and, of course, recitation rooms were not needed.

3. It contained a separate desk and chair for each pupil, this being probably the first grammar schoolhouse, here or elsewhere, into which this feature was introduced.

4. It contained a clothes room attached to each classroom.

5. It contained an assembly hall large enough to seat comfortably all the pupils that could be accommodated in its schoolrooms, and even more.

6. It was four stories high — the first of this height — the assembly hall covering all of the fourth floor. Each floor below carried four classrooms.

This building formed a new architectural type which was extensively copied, in Boston and elsewhere, and this new building, with

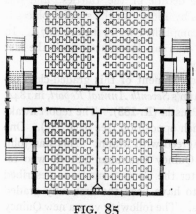

FIG. 85

FIRST, SECOND, AND THIRD FLOOR PLANS OF THE QUINCY SCHOOL, BOSTON, MASS.

The fourth floor was an assembly hall, containing a platform and 48 long benches.

its twelve classrooms, assembly hall, and a principal's office, was thought by many to represent such an advance that little improvement would ever be made on it. For the next fifty years it was the standard type of elementary school building [1] erected in our cities. More than any other single influence it stimulated the introduction of the graded classroom form of school organization. The next step in Boston came in 1854, when the separate control of the Infant or Primary Schools (see page 139) was abolished, and the principal of the new type of grammar school was also made supervising principal for the primary schools of his district.

The transition to the graded system a natural evolution. The

[1] This was in large part due to the fact that this type of building was so well adapted to a drill-and-content type of course of study, which from about 1850 to about 1900 was the dominant one.

transition to the graded system, it is seen, came naturally and easily. For half a century the course of instruction in the evolving common or English grammar schools had been in the process of expansion, due in part to the preparation of better and longer textbooks, but largely through the addition of new subjects of study. The school term had gradually been lengthened, the years of school provided had been increased in number, the school course had been differentiated into various divisions or schools, the master and his assistants had from the first divided up the work in each room on a rough age-and-grade classification basis, and the entire evolution, up to about 1840 to 1850, had prepared the way for a simple reorganization of the work which would divide the schools into seven, or eight, or nine grades, and give each teacher one grade to handle. The new Quincy school at Boston showed how this could be done. By the time of the beginnings of state and city school supervision the school systems of the cities only awaited the touch of an educational organizer to transform them from a series of differentiated and largely independent schools into a series of graded schools that could be organized into a unified system, with a graded course of study, and unified supervision provided over all. The waste in maintaining two or more duplicate schools in the same building, each covering the same three to six years of school work, when by reconstructing the building and re-sorting the pupils the work of each teacher could be made more specialized and the pupils be better taught, was certain to become obvious as soon as school supervision by teachers began to supersede school organization by laymen.

As new buildings were erected with smaller classrooms, and as the large classrooms in old buildings were divided and the schools reorganized, the graded system, with a teacher in charge of each class, and a much smaller class at that (55 to 75 were common sizes at first), came in as a perfectly natural evolution and as a matter of course. There was no change in subject-matter, as that had become fixed long before. There was no material lengthening of the course, as a combined course of seven to nine years, as we have previously shown, had become common before grading had been fully carried out. There also was no change in method or purpose, except as the coming, about this time, of some Pestalozzian ideas, described in the next chapter, tended to improve all method, and except as the elimination of sectarianism and the establishment of state-supported schools tended to give a clearer consciousness as to the citizenship-aim in instruction. Nor was there any general adopting, except in the matter of the class-grade organization, of non-native educational ideas from abroad. We merely evolved, as the result of something like a half-century of gradual educational development, the common and purely native American elementary school which we have known for so long. As shown in the last tabulation, given on page 309, this school varied from seven to nine years in length, with eight and nine years as the common numbers. The primary classes, in part due to the pressure of numbers, gradually ceased to take pupils earlier than five, and later earlier than six, outside of New England, and the present eight-year elementary school (nine in New England), with a teacher for each grade, was evolved. On top of this grade-class organization the English high school, also a purely native American creation, was superimposed, making an eleven- or twelve- or thirteen-year course of public school instruction, which was tax-supported, state controlled, freed from sectarianism and the pauper taint, and equally open to all the children of the State (**R. 93**). This evolution is shown somewhat roughly in Figure 46 (p. 140), and was fully accomplished by 1860 in all Northern States.

The high school fitted onto the graded system. In the process of this evolution the high school also was made thoroughly democratic. When the new English high schools were established they were everywhere built on top of the common or grammar-school course, the evolution of which we have just described. The Latin grammar schools, though, as shown in the case of Boston (Fig. 82), as well as the Classical Course in a few cities having both courses in one school, took pupils at an earlier age. In general this was confined to New England, though San Francisco, as late as the sixties, admitted pupils to its Latin high school at ten, and to its English high school at twelve. By 1860 this differentiation had been almost entirely abandoned as undemocratic and undesirable (**R. 93**), and high-school courses had been based on the completion of the common-school course of study. This eliminated the last vestiges of the European class educational system with which we began, and put in its place the democratic educational ladder (Fig. 68, p. 273) which has for so long characterized education in the United States.

By 1860 the English high school, now beginning to develop in all the States, had clearly begun to take over the work in English, modern languages, history, mathematics, and the physical sciences previously taught in the academies, and to offer, free from tuition, the subjects of study and courses of instruction which for so long had been found only in these institutions (**Rs. 56, 146, 148**). Still more, the colleges were gradually forced to accept these new subjects as equal to the old Latin and Greek for admission, as is seen from the following table, giving where and when each new subject was first accepted for admission to the A.B. college course.

	Subject	Date	College first accepting
Old subjects	Latin	1640	Harvard
	Greek	1640	Harvard
	Arithmetic	1802	Harvard
	Geography	1807	Harvard
	English Grammar	1819	Princeton
	Algebra	1820	Harvard
	Geometry	1844	Harvard
	Ancient History	1847	Harvard and Michigan
New subjects	Modern (U.S.) History	1869	Michigan
	Physical Geography	1870	Michigan and Harvard
	English Composition	1870	Princeton
	Physical Science	1872	Harvard
	English Literature	1874	Harvard
	Modern Languages	1875	Harvard

III. THE GREAT DAY OF THE DISTRICT SYSTEM

While the preceding section of this chapter has dealt entirely with the organization of the developing school systems of the rising cities, it must be remembered that, as late as 1840, there were but 44 cities in the entire United States (85 by 1850) that contained 8000 or more inhabitants, and that but 8.5 per cent of our people (12.5 per cent by 1850) lived in cities. We were still predominately a rural and an agricultural people, and the ungraded school of the 3-R's was the school of the time. Even in the cities, as we have seen, many of the schools were at first of the ungraded rural-school type. The consolidation of the various ward schools into a unified city school system came only with the advent of city school supervision.

The second and third quarters of the nineteenth century cover the great day of the district system. By 1830 to 1835 the district form of organization was everywhere in control and at the height of its powers. By 1840 to 1850 its serious defects as a plan for school organization and administration had become evident in the cities, and the process of unification there was under way. Even in the rural districts the defects of the plan, as pointed out so forcefully earlier by Carter, Mann, and Barnard, had begun to be apparent by 1850, and some legislation limiting district rights and authority had been enacted, but it was not much before about 1880 to 1890 that a tendency to abolish the system became clearly in evidence.

The cities were the first to curb and subordinate the districts and perfect a unified school system, and we shall accordingly consider city school organization first.

The district system in the cities. In many of our cities, especially to the westward, no such unified system of school administration as that described for Providence or Boston existed. Instead, the district system of school administration was introduced into the different wards of the city. [1] As the people in each ward felt willing to provide school facilities for their children they were permitted by law to call a meeting, organize a school district in the ward, vote to erect a school building, employ teachers, and vote to tax themselves to maintain the school. Some wards thus had public schools and others did not, but each ward so organizing was allowed to elect its own board of school trustees and to control and supervise its school. In many of our older cities outside of New England, particularly those which at first were settled by New England people, the first schools began under the same form of organization as the regular rural district schools. It was the one way to secure action in the progressive wards of unprogressive cities.

The different cities thus came to contain a number of what were virtually country school districts, each maintaining an ungraded and independent district school. As the city grew, these ungraded and independent schools increased in number and size. Later the situation became impossible, the city was unified by law for education as it previously had been for city government, a city board of education was created and given control of the scattered schools, and this board in turn employed a new supervisory officer, now becoming known as a city superintendent of schools, to unify and to supervise the schools. The early educational history of a number

---

[1] Even in Boston the Infant or Primary Schools were organized, in 1818, on the district system plan, with three trustees for each school, and so continued up to their unification with the city school system in 1856.

of our cities is the history of the formation of a number of such independent district schools in the different wards of the city, and their later unification into one city school system. It is from this that the old term "ward schools" has come down to us, as well as ward representation on the city school board and too frequently ward politics in the management of the schools as well.

Examples of city-district consolidations. The cities of Buffalo, Detroit, Chicago, and Cleveland illustrate this process very well.

The first schoolhouse in Buffalo was built privately, in 1806, and burned in 1813. In 1818 the first tax for a school in Buffalo was levied to rebuild this school.

By 1832 six one-teacher school districts had been organized in the city, and by 1837 there were seven. The city by that time had something like 15,000 inhabitants. That year the first superintendent of city schools in the United States was appointed, to unify and to supervise these seven schools. On the full establishment of the free-school system, in 1839, the

FIG. 86. THE FIRST FREE PUBLIC SCHOOL IN DETROIT

A one-room school, opened in the Second Ward, in 1838

number of districts was increased to fifteen, to supply deficiencies, and a school was ordered established in each, with a central high school for instruction in the higher English branches.

The city of Detroit is another example, of a somewhat more extreme type. Here the district system stood in the way of school organization, and had to be overthrown before any substantial progress could be made. Private and church schools had existed there from as early as 1816, and one of the early statutes of the first University of Michigania provided (1817) for the organization of a primary school in the then French city. The first public school, though, was not organized until the second ward took action, in 1838. Other wards not being willing to tax themselves for schools, little further progress was made until 1841. In that year an investigation showed that there were 27 schools of all kinds in the city, instructing a total of 714 pupils, and 1850 children of school age without any instruction whatever. Detroit was at that time a city of approximately 10,000 inhabitants. The result was a campaign for public schools, and a petition to amend the city charter to permit the organization of a city board of education to provide schools generally throughout the city. This was bitterly opposed, but the proposal carried at a city election and, in 1842, the legislature, following the best eastern practices of the time, abolished the district system in Detroit and provided for the organization of a unified system of schools for the city, under a city board of education. In 1844 the first high school west of Buffalo, New Orleans (1843) excepted, was established.

FIG. 87. CHICAGO AS IT WAS IN 1832

The year the first public school was opened there

Chicago is a third illustration of much the same type as Buffalo. A private school was opened there as early as 1816, but the first public school was not established until 1832. The town was incorporated in 1833, and in 1835 a special law for Chicago established the Massachusetts district system in the city. By 1837 there were 5 schools and 828 children, and by 1844 there were 8 schools and 816 children, the enrollments of the 8 schools being 97, 75, 130, 70, 131, 130, 110, and 75 children respectively. By 1853 there were 7 school districts, employing 34 teachers, and enrolling 3086 children, or an average of 91 children to the teacher. The schools at that time still were ungraded, and practically independent in methods, textbooks, and plan. They also were very insufficient in numbers, as they had been provided only in parts of the city where the demand for schools was strong enough to insure the voting of taxes. Thousands of children were being turned away because of lack of school facilities. In 1853 the city council appointed a city superintendent of schools to unify the work done in the districts. He at once graded and reorganized the instruction, and introduced uniform records and textbooks. In 1856 a high school (see Fig. 65) for the city was created (**R. 158**). In 1857 the legislature abolished the district system in the city, and created a city board of education to take charge of the schools. This established one city school system for the city. In 1861 the first graded course of study in Illinois was provided for the schools of Chicago.

In Cleveland, the fourth illustration, a private school was opened as early as 1800, and another in 1802, but the first schoolhouse was not built until 1815. The adjoining sketch, drawn from memory by one of the original twenty-four pupils, shows the building. This

building, 24 × 30 in size, was made possible by contributions of from $2.50 to $20 each by twenty-six of the early residents. In 1817 the village trustees refunded to them what they had contributed, and the building became Cleveland's first public school building. The schools themselves, however, remained private tuition schools, with a charity school added in 1834.

FIG. 88. CLEVELAND'S FIRST SCHOOL, 1815

In 1837, the city council enacted an ordinance establishing public schools for the then city of about 6000 inhabitants. Rented rooms were still used, and the boys and girls were taught separately. In 1839 the council purchased two school sites, and in 1840 erected two buildings. In this latter year about 1000 pupils were enrolled. In 1846 a high school for boys was opened in a church basement, and a department for girls was organized the next year. Excepting the high school at Detroit, which dates from 1844, and one at New Orleans, dating from 1843, there were no other high schools west of the Alleghenies. In 1853 a superintendent of schools was employed to bring order and organization into the rapidly growing system, as Cleveland by that time had become a city of about 18,000 inhabitants. Excepting San Francisco (1852) and Cincinnati (1850), no other city school superintendents had been provided for west of the Alleghenies, and but sixteen cities to the eastward had provided for such an officer.

Many other cities have had a similar educational administrative history, but practically everywhere the district system was early abolished, and to its early abolition and to the early unification of the school system the great educational progress of the cities during the past half-century is largely due.

Rural district management. As was stated at the beginning of this section, the district system was the natural system in the early days of state school organization and control. At a time when popula-

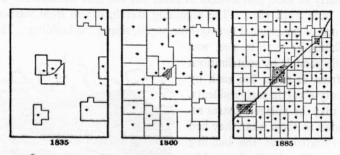

1835   1860   1885

FIG. 89. HOW THE DISTRICT SYSTEM ORGANIZED A COUNTY

From Cubberley's *Rural Life and Education*

tion was sparse, intercourse limited, communication difficult, supervision practically absent, and isolation the rule, the district system rendered its greatest service. It provided schools suited to the wants and needs of country people, and where and as fast as the people were willing to support them. The system was well adapted, too, to the earlier ideas as to the nature and purpose of education. Schools then were purely local affairs, and the imparting of a limited amount of information was almost their sole purpose. Knowledge then was power, and the schools were conducted on a knowledge basis, undisturbed by any ideas as to psychological procedure, social needs, or by the civic and economic problems of the present. The system, too, was well adapted to a deep-seated conviction of the time as to the sacredness of local government and an unshaken confidence in a localized administration of all civic affairs (**R. 184**).

Each community lived largely for its own ends, and was largely a law unto itself. Freedom and liberty were conceived of, as expressed by one of our poets, as:

> The right of every freeborn man
> To do as he darned pleases.

Naturally, under such conditions, every little community felt itself competent to select and examine its teachers, adopt its own course of study, determine the methods of instruction, supervise and criticize the teacher, and determine all such matters as boarding-around arrangements, tax rate, and length of term. The three district trustees, with the people in district meeting, exercised very important functions in guiding the Ship of State,[1] and to many a man in the districts the office of school trustee was the most important office within the gift of the American people to which he might ever hope to aspire.

Merits and defects of the district unit. One of the chief merits of the district system of school administration, and one for which it has been greatly extolled, was that the school district meeting served as a forensic center for the new democratic life of the time. The victory of Andrew Jackson was a victory for democracy which was felt even in remote rural districts. The school district has been and still is the smallest unit of local self-government in our political system, and the one small unit to which much power is still given. It corresponds to the parish in the management of church affairs, or to the early New England town meeting under the old régime. As a unit of local government it once doubtless did much to educate the people in civic spirit and patriotism, and trained them in the simple forms of parliamentary procedure. There they learned to speak and to defend their rights — real or imaginary — as well as to present their grievances and pay off old scores. At a time when general education at public expense hung in the balance, the district system doubtless did much toward awakening a conception of the need for and the benefits of popular education.

[1] For example, the school trustees at Lancaster, Ohio, in 1826, refused to permit the use of the schoolhouse for a meeting to discuss railroads, replying to the petitioners:

"You are welcome to use the schoolhouse to debate all proper questions in, but such things as railroads are impossibilities and rank infidelity. There is nothing in the word of God about them. If God designed that His intelligent creatures should travel at the frightful speed of fifteen miles an hour by steam, He would have clearly foretold through His holy prophets. It is a device to lead immortal souls down to hell."

FIG. 90. THE OLD-TIME DISTRICT SCHOOL

From a drawing by a former pupil in one, William Ladd Taylor, and reproduced by courtesy of the Curtis Publishing Company.

A spelling class is "toeing a crack" in the floor, and the teacher is pronouncing words from Webster's "old blue-backed spelling book." Note the quill pens on the teacher's desk, and the wide range in the age of the pupils.

On the other hand, the system awakened an exaggerated idea as to district importance,[1] an idea as to district perfection which rendered it impervious to criticism, a deep jealousy of larger and

[1] An example of the absurdity of district-system legislation may be had from New York, where the rural districts joined hands to enact a law (1852) whereby a large share of the public money was to be divided *according to the number of the districts*, thus virtually putting a premium on their multiplication without reference to size or need.

more prosperous districts, frequently a banding together to keep others from enjoying what the poorer ones could not enjoy, and usually persistent and bitter opposition to any attempt at reform (**R. 185**). What Guizot so well termed "the energy of local liberty" was a common manifestation. Mr. Martin's description of the workings of the district system in Massachusetts, before its abolition there (1882), could be matched by descriptions from any of the older States (**R. 186**).

Even by 1850 the tendency in the States had become marked to limit the powers of the district meeting, and to take away powers from the trustees and transfer them to the county and state superintendents which were then being created, or to determine the matter once for all by constitutional requirement or uniform state law. In most States the district meeting was shorn of such powers as the right to designate the teacher, select the textbooks, or make out the course of study, and the trustees were early shorn of their power to examine and certificate the teacher they selected. The length of term, the rate of tax that must be levied, and the subjects that must be taught were early specified in the laws. In about this form the district system has continued to the present, though a number of States have abandoned it for a better system of school administration. The earliest States to do so were Indiana, in 1852; Massachusetts, in 1882; New Hampshire, in 1885; Georgia, in 1887; Florida, in 1889; Maine and Ohio, in 1892; New Jersey, in 1894; and Vermont and Rhode Island, in 1904. Since 1900 a number of other States have taken similar action, and we can now confidently look forward to the time, in the not too distant future, when the district system of school management, with its three governing trustees, will entirely disappear and be replaced by a larger unit and a more rational and intelligent form of school control.

IV. THE TEACHERS
THEIR METHODS AND THEIR EQUIPMENT

Character of the early teachers. Our schools, like our clothing during this early period, were largely of the homespun variety. Not only were the subjects of instruction those of the natively evolving American school, but our teachers and school officers were of the same native type. The professional teacher and school officer had not as yet appeared. The first American state normal school opened at Lexington, Massachusetts, in 1839, but as late as 1860 there were but twelve such state schools in the entire United States, and these twelve were confined to nine Northern States. Teachers' institutes, first definitely organized by Henry Barnard in Connecticut, in 1839, had been introduced into but fifteen other States

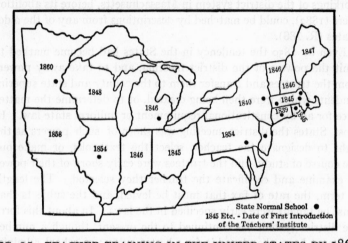

FIG. 91. TEACHER TRAINING IN THE UNITED STATES BY 1860

A few private training schools also existed, though less than half a dozen in all. Again compare this development with the spread of New England people, as shown in the figure on page 107.

by 1860, and these all in the northeastern quarter of the United States. These institutes were hailed as a quick and cheap means for giving some little training [1] to those who desired to teach

[1] Ohio offers a good illustration of the development of the Teachers Institute. Begun voluntarily in 1846, the next year the county commissioners of eleven counties were permitted to help pay lecturers, and in 1848 the law was made applicable to the whole State. In 1849 the county aid was fixed at $100, provided the teachers raised $50. Statistics for the first ten years are:

Year	Institutes	Attendance
1845	2	240
1846	9	997
1847	13	569
1848	19	1500
1849	20	1600
1850	25	2000
1851	41	3251
1852	31	2824
1853	38	3738
1854	41	2198

(**R. 187**), and as offering a substitute, for a time at least, for the more expensive normal school then being developed in Massachusetts.

Only a few books of a professional nature, aside from the *School Journals* which began to appear in the twenties and thirties (p. 343) had as yet been published. Samuel R. Hall's *Lectures on School-keeping*, published in 1829, was the first professional book published in America designed particularly for the guidance of the teacher.[1] Jacob Abbott's *The Teacher: or Moral Influences Employed in the Instruction and Government of the Young*, published in 1833, was another early book for teachers, which went through 25 editions by 1860. David Page's *Theory and Practice of Teaching*, first issued in 1847, was another of the earliest, as well as one of the most successful of all professional books. Our best teachers were graduates of the academies and the rising high schools, and the masters in the larger cities of the East were nearly always well-educated men, judged by the standards of the time, but the great mass of the teachers had little education beyond that of the schools they themselves taught. Many of the teachers were incompetent adventurers, migratory, odd in their ways, crude in their manners, and often questionable as to character. Terms were short, wages low and paid in part through "boarding-around" arrangements,[2] classes often inordinately large, and professional standards, outside a few cities, were almost completely absent (**R. 187**). The best were kept out and the most poorly prepared were brought in by these conditions. In place of the written examination in many subjects or the professional training now quite generally demanded for a teacher's certificate,

[1] So far as New England was concerned it was the first professional book, though three others had preceded it, all published in Philadelphia. The first was in German, by a Pennsylvania German schoolmaster by the name of Christopher Dock (1698–1771). It was entitled *Schulordnung*, was written in 1750, and published in 1770.

The other two were by Joseph Neef, a one-time worker with Pestalozzi in Switzerland, who came to Philadelphia in 1806, and published there his *Sketch of a Plan and Method of Education, founded on the Analysis of the Human Faculties and Natural Reason* in 1808, and his *Method of Instructing Children Rationally in the Arts of Writing and Reading*, in 1813. The circulation of these books was local, though Neef's books were carried westward later when he taught at Louisville, Kentucky, and New Harmony, Indiana.

[2] This was a means of pay at a time when little tax money was available. It meant that the teacher "boarded around" among the different families of the district, staying with each a number of weeks proportional to the number of children each family sent to school. The practice continued well up to the time of the Civil War, and later even in some States. The teacher lived with the family, helped with the work, and shared their fare. The conditions at times must have been exceedingly trying.

in the earlier period [1] teachers were given a short personal examination "in regard to moral character, learning, and ability to teach school." Not being satisfied with such requirements, the cities were early permitted to conduct separate examinations for the teachers they employed. It was customary in rural districts to hold both a summer and a winter term, and to contract separately for each (**R. 172**). Women frequently taught in the summer, but the teachers in the winter were practically always men. The rate-bill was in rather general use (**R. 189**), and this in turn tended to defeat the purpose for which the schools, such as they were, were established.

The cities then, as since, drew the best of the teachers, both in training and character. In the rural districts the teachers were men who worked on the farms or at day labor in the summer, and frequently left much to be desired.[2] Contracts and rules of the time not infrequently required that the teacher conduct himself properly and "refrain from all spirituous liquors while engaged in this school, and not to enter the school house when intoxicated, nor to lose time through such intemperance." On the contrary, many schoolmasters of the time were excellent drill masters and kind of heart, and well merited George Arnold's description:

> He taught his scholars the rule of three,
>   Writing, and reading, and history too;
> He took the little ones up on his knee,
> For a kind old heart in his breast had he,
>   And the wants of the littlest child he knew.

The required studies were reading, writing, spelling, and arithmetic everywhere, with geography and grammar generally added by 1845. Composition, United States history, and simple bookkeeping were usually included for the town schools. These subjects the teacher obligated himself in his contract to teach "to all

[1] For example, the New York Act of 1812, establishing common schools in the State, required the local school trustees to examine all applicants to teach, and every teacher was required to hold a certificate, signed by at least two of the local authorities, certifying "that he is duly qualified to teach a common school, and is of good moral character." One teacher of notoriously bad character is reported to have held a certificate which read "is of good moral character during school hours."

[2] Knight quotes an extract from a Virginia newspaper of 1843 which says that many of the teachers of the time were "invalids, some were slaves to drunkenness, some too lazy to work, most of them ignorant of the art of teaching, and a terror to their pupils," and that their "chief recommendation was their cheapness," and that their "chief capacity to instruct is predicated by their incapacity for any other employment." (Knight, E. W. *Education in the United States*, p. 352.)

the youth of the district that may be placed under his care, so far as he may be able [1] and they may be able to learn," and they constituted the instruction of the school.   Teaching was conducted on the individual basis, and progress through the schools was on the same basis.   The master remained at his desk throughout the day, and called the pupils up one by one to repeat the lesson learned, to examine slates, or to give needed help or explanation.   The teaching and questioning was directed to one pupil only, the rest of the

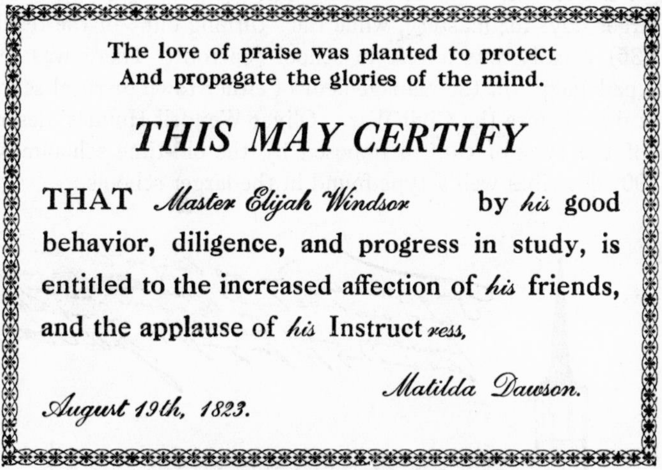

**The love of praise was planted to protect
And propagate the glories of the mind.**

THIS MAY CERTIFY

THAT *Master Elijah Windsor*   by *his* good behavior, diligence, and progress in study, is entitled to the increased affection of *his* friends, and the applause of *his* Instruct*ress,*

Matilda Dawson.

August 19th, 1823.

FIG. 92. A REWARD OF MERIT

pupils not participating in the instruction given.   Even later, when a class was called up, the master usually took the pupils one by one for questioning.

The common school subjects were taught by methods quite different from those now in use.   Oral instruction, the word method in teaching reading, language lessons, instructions about realities, elementary science, geography built on the child's environment instead of the pages of a book, arithmetic by analysis instead of sums by rule, music, drawing, reasoning instead of memorizing, and

[1] Taylor, in describing the early teachers of Pennsylvania, says:
"The first teachers were poorly qualified, and were acquainted with arithmetic no further than long division.   No geography, grammar, or mental arithmetic was taught (in Lycoming County) before 1848."   (Taylor, William S.   *The Development of Professional Education of Teachers in Pennsylvania*, p. 24.)

teaching that comes from the full mind of the teacher rather than from the pages of a book — with all of which we are now so familiar — were hardly known in the forties in the best of our schools, or before 1860 outside of the more progressive cities. At the close of the term it was customary to give the pupils merit cards, reading somewhat as shown in Fig. 92.

It was also made the duty of the teacher "to keep strict rules and good order," and the ability to discipline the school was an important part of the teacher's qualifications. The teacher often had to fight the larger boys for mastery, while the "turning out" of the teacher (**R. 235**) usually was a test in school control.[1] There was little "soft pedagogy" in the management of either town or rural schools in the days before the Civil War. Oliver Wendell Holmes' description of the type of control imposed by the old-time schoolmaster (**R. 190**) describes well a type found in the larger schools.

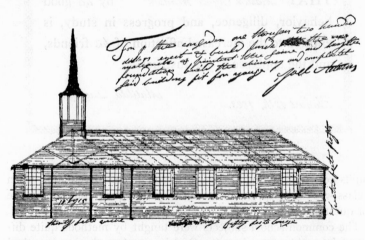

FIG. 93. EARLY SCHOOL ARCHITECTURE AND CONTRACTING

An early Rhode Island schoolhouse contract

The schoolhouses and their equipment. Up to the time Henry Barnard began to write on schoolhouse construction (about 1840), no one had given any particular attention to the subject. Schoolhouses were "home-made" (**R. 191**), and, outside of the few large

[1] Edward Eggleston, in *The Hoosier Schoolmaster*, very accurately portrays the difficulties that beset the district school teacher in this earlier period, and gives an excellent account of "turning out the teacher."

cities, were largely built without plans or specifications. For one of the early schoolhouses built in Providence, Rhode Island, the entire contract consisted of a very rough pen-and-ink sketch (Fig. 93), on a single sheet of paper, showing windows, rafters, steeple, and length and breadth, and across this the contractor had written:

> For the confider one thoufan two hundred dollars erect & build finde the matearels & paintent the fame and lay the foundations build the chimney and compleated faid building fit for youse

and signed his name. Many schoolhouses in the towns and rural districts were built in a similar manner until well after the close of the Civil War. In the rural districts "a weather-boarded box" or an old log schoolhouse, with two or three windows on each side, a few wooden benches, an unjacketed stove in the middle of the room, and often desti-tute of "facilities for preserv-ing modesty and decency," an-swered all needs. Many build-ings were in a wretched state of repair, and often schools could not proceed for lack of fuel,

FIG. 94. ONE OF THE "WEATHER-BOARDED BOXES"

which then generally was a quota-tax on the parents sending chil-dren to the school [1] (**R. 191**). Even in many of the cities the build-ing conditions were very bad (**R. 192**) until well toward the middle of the century. In the cities a very ornate school architecture came in after the building of high schools began, but few high-school buildings erected before 1860 contained any rooms beside class reci-tation rooms, an office, and an assembly hall (see Figs. 64 and 65). The instruction was still almost entirely book instruction, and little else than recitation rooms was needed.

The school furniture consisted of long home-made benches in the rural schools, and double desks in the cities. The Quincy School,

---

[1] In the First Annual Report of the School Visitors of Brooklyn, Conn. (covering the year 1830–31), 348 pupils were reported as attending school "more or less" the winter term, but that "half the schools" had been put to serious inconvenience for lack of fuel. Several schoolhouses were reported as in a bad state of repair, and most of them as being badly constructed. "In none of the schools was there any apparatus, except in one a painted ball to illustrate the shape and motions of the earth, and in one other school such a ball and a *blackboard*."

built in Boston in 1848, introduced a new type of school architecture in that the building contained a small classroom for each teacher — twelve in all, with seats for fifty-five pupils in each — an assembly room, a coat and cloak room off each classroom, and "a separate desk and chair for each pupil, this being the first grammar schoolhouse," wrote the principal thirty years later, "here or elsewhere, so far as I know, into which this feature was introduced."

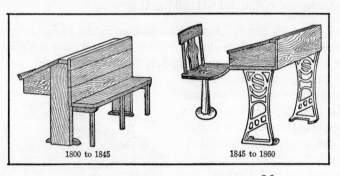

1800 to 1845   1845 to 1860

FIG. 95. SCHOOL DESKS BEFORE 1860

These represent the best types of city school furniture in general use at the time.

Blackboards were not in use until about 1820, and globes and maps were not common till later. The early geographies contained almost no maps (**R. 178**), and the early histories few illustrations. Steel pens did not replace the use of quills until near the middle of the nineteenth century.

Purposes in instruction. The knowledge aim dominated all instruction. Knowledge was the important thing, as it was rather firmly believed then that knowledge and virtue were somewhat synonymous terms. The fundamental subjects of the common-school course were drilled upon, and the trustees or the school committee, when they visited the school, examined the pupils as to their ability to read and spell, inspected the copybooks, and quizzed the pupils as to their knowledge of the rules of arithmetic and grammar, and the location of towns and rivers and capes. Competitive spelling and reading contests were common, to write a good and ornate hand was a matter of note, while the solving of arithmetical puzzles, parsing and diagramming of sentences, and locating geographical points were accomplishments which marked the higher stages of a common-school education.   Arithmetic and English grammar became firmly fixed as the great subjects of the common-school course of study, and the momentum these two subjects accumulated in the early days of public education is as yet far from spent.

> **EXAMPLE: Fifteen Christians and 15 Turks bound at sea in one ship in a terrible storm, and the pilot declaring a necessity of casting one half of these persons into the sea, that the rest might be saved, they all agreed that the persons to be cast away should be set out by lot in this manner, viz., the 30 persons should be placed in a round form like a ring and then, beginning to count at one of the passengers and proceeding regularly every ninth person should be cast into the sea until of the 30 persons there remained only 15.   The question is, how these 30 persons ought to be placed that the lot might infallibly fall upon the 15 Turks, and not upon any of the 15 Christians.**

FIG. 96.   ONE OF THE ARITHMETICAL PUZZLES [1]

Yet despite the limited school curriculum, the long hours of instruction, the great emphasis on drill, and the overemphasis of fact teaching, the pupils of the period, even in the better schools of the time, did not equal the pupils of today in their ability to write, spell, cipher, define, locate places, or solve problems involving ability to reason.   The Boston Examination of 1845, and the Springfield Tests of 1846, alike reveal that the fundamental school subjects are better taught in our schools today, despite the shorter school hours and the crowded school curriculum, than they were three generations ago.   Man is ever prone to magnify the "glories of the past."

Two celebrated tests.   In 1845, the yearly examining committee for the public schools of Boston took its appointment seriously, in so far as the nineteen Grammar and Writing Schools were concerned, and made a careful survey of the proficiency of the pupils through the means of a series of written examinations, which were given to the pupils of highest class of each of the nineteen schools.[2]

---

[1] From an arithmetic of the Early National Period.

[2] This committee prepared a series of questions, gave the tests, tabulated the answers, and published a detailed report of 125 pages, including the questions used and representative answer papers.   The report, questions, and answers have been reproduced in Caldwell and Courtis's *Then and Now in Education, 1845-1923.*

There were questions in history, geography, arithmetic, grammar, defining, natural philosophy, and astronomy.   The questions and the answers have been preserved, and in 1919 the examination was repeated in the eighth grade of the Boston schools, and later in the eighth grade in numerous other cities, but with this significant difference: in 1845 in Boston the only pupils examined were those picked by the masters as superior, comprising, as the Examining Committee reports, "the flower of the Boston Schools," [1] whereas in 1919 all eighth-grade pupils were given the tests and the results made by all entered into the comparison.   The outstanding conclusions from the repetition of the tests are that present-day children "tend to make lower scores on pure memory and abstract-skill questions, and higher scores on thought and meaningful questions." In spelling present-day eighth-grade pupils make only one fourth to one third the errors made by the pupils of 1845.   The 1919 results in parsing and punctuation were high.   In natural philosophy, the 1919 children did much better without instruction than did the 1845 children after study of the subject from a textbook.   In arithmetical problems the 1919 children did not do so well.[2]

In 1846 a written examination was given at Springfield, Massachusetts, in arithmetic, geography, spelling, and penmanship to the 86 pupils who at that time formed the ninth grade of the Springfield schools,[3] and some forty years later the complete set of papers was found preserved in the attic of the high-school building.   In 1906,

---

[1] Of 1251 pupils in the ninth grade in 1845, the largest number taking any test was 530, while most of the tests were taken by much smaller numbers.

[2] The following statements are quoted from this 1845 survey of Boston's schools:

"1. It is very difficult to believe that, in the Boston schools, there should be so many children in the first classes [eighth grades] unable to answer such questions, that there should be so many who try to answer and answer imperfectly, that there should be so many absurd answers, so many errors in spelling, in grammar, and in punctuation.

"2. There is another sad reflection suggested by these answers.   They show, beyond all doubt, that a large proportion of the scholars of our first classes [eighth grades], boys and girls of fourteen or fifteen years of age, when called upon to write simple sentences, to express their thoughts on common subjects, without the aid of a dictionary or a master, cannot write without such errors in grammar, in spelling, and in punctuation as we should blush to see in a letter from a son or daughter of their age.   And most of these children are about finishing their school career: they are going out into life."

[3] The schools of Springfield were then among the best in the State.   The school year was longer then than in 1906 — 44 weeks as against 40.   The school day also was longer — 6 hours as against 5 — or a yearly total of 1320 hours as against 1000 hours in 1906.   Springfield was the first town in Massachusetts to choose a man as superintendent (1840) who was not on the school board.   The average age of the pupils in the ninth grade was about the same.   The course of study was quite definite, with reading, writing, spelling, arithmetic, and geography about all that was taught below the high school.

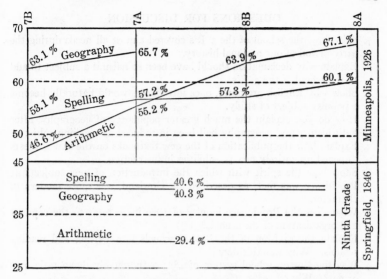

FIG. 97. THE SPRINGFIELD TESTS, THEN AND NOW

Results as obtained in Minneapolis in 1926, compared with Springfield in 1846, as shown by the percentage of correct answers.

the same questions were given to 245 ninth-grade pupils in the Springfield schools, and the results published in pamphlet form. Since then these same tests have been given in schools all over the United States, with much the same results as in Springfield, which were:

Subject	Per cent correct, 1845	Per cent correct, 1906
Spelling (20 words)	40.6	51.2
Arithmetic (8 problems)	29.4	65.5
Geography (12 questions)	40.3	53.4
Penmanship		Better

Summing up the results and changes (**R. 193**), the author of the pamphlet *The Springfield Tests, 1846–1906*, Mr. Riley, well says:

> The 3-R's — reading, 'riting, and 'rithmetic — are not being neglected in the present-day schools, but the public school system has passed irrevocably beyond the stage where its only office was to impart a little skill in these branches.

QUESTIONS FOR DISCUSSION

1. Show how the school of the 3-R's covered almost all needs during the early period of our national history.

2. Explain why declamation should have been so natural a subject to add to the school of the 3-R's.

3. Show why English grammar, once introduced, would naturally become a popular subject of study.

4. How do you explain the much greater popularity of geography, after both history and geography had been introduced as teaching subjects?

5. Explain how the publication of the new textbooks on the new subjects "opened up entirely new possibilities in instruction."

6. Show how the spirit with which the introduction of new subjects at Providence was met, as described by Howland, was quite modern in character.

7. What does the Providence inquiry of 1820 indicate as to the conduct and organization of the schools?

8. Explain the division of the Boston schools into writing and reading schools. Why was this done?

9. Was the Boston school system of 1823 a thoroughly democratic one, or not? Why?

10. Show how the absence of any professional supervision naturally tended to the independence of teachers and schools in the early period of our history.

11. Enumerate the chief steps, or stages, in the evolution of the present class-grade organization of schools.

12. Show how the erection of the Quincy School in Boston marked the close of one type of school organization and the introduction of another.

13. Why should the new high schools have been fitted on to the grammar-school course, instead of beginning as the Latin grammar schools did at an earlier period?

14. What does the list of college entrance subjects given indicate as to the change in character of the colleges?

15. Why was it a natural condition to find the district system in the cities during their early history?

16. Show how city boards of education were a natural evolution out of city-council control of the early schools, and then how a city superintendent of schools came as a further natural evolution.

17. About what percentage of the school children of Buffalo could have been cared for in the seven public schools of 1837?

18. Picture the results in Chicago or Detroit or Buffalo today if the schools of the city were still managed under the district system.

19. Explain, historically, why so many cities in the older States have special city boards of examination for teachers' credentials, instead of accepting the certificates issued by county or state authorities.

20. Describe the early Teachers Institutes, as organized by Barnard, and explain their early popularity.

21. Characterize the district school of the thirties to the sixties as to teacher, pupils, organization, and importance.
22. How do you explain such simple planning and contracting, as is shown in Figure 92, whereas today both are very technical and detailed?
23. Characterize the examination of a school by the visiting committee or the district trustees, as described on page 330.
24. Show how natural it was that the knowledge aim should have dominated instruction during the 1830 to 1860 period.
25. How do you explain the results of the Boston and the Springfield tests, when the curriculum of that day was simple and concentrated, the school hours long, and drill emphasized?
26. What about the contention of the older generation that the schools turned out better scholars then than now?

SELECTED READINGS

In the accompanying volume of *Readings* the following selections related to the subject matter of this chapter are reproduced:

*172. Ohio: Teacher Contracts for Spring and Summer Terms.
 173. Webster: Description of His Schools and Textbooks.
*174. Scudder: Noah Webster's Grammatical Institute.
 175. Title Pages: Three Early School Readers.
*176. Anon.: The McGuffey Readers.
*177. Morse: Preface to his "American Universal Geography."
 178. Sample Pages: Early Textbooks in History and Geography.
*179. Report: The Schools of Providence in 1820.
*180. Bingham: The Schools of Boston about 1790–1815.
 181. Philbrick: The Primary Schools of Boston, in 1857.
*182. Report: The English Schools of Boston in 1830.
 183. Mann: Prussian School Classification.
*184. Rawles: The District System in Indiana.
*185. Cubberley: Merits and Defects of the District System.
*186. Martin: The District System in Action.
 187. Miller: The Teachers' Institute in New York State.
*188. Address, 1831: The Poor Quality of the Schools.
*189. Lewis: Schools in Ohio in 1837.
*190. Holmes: The Old Time School and Schoolmaster.
*191. Williams: An Ohio School and Schoolhouse of 1820.
*192. Reports: Poor Quality of the Early School Rooms.
*193. Riley: The Springfield Tests.

QUESTIONS ON THE READINGS

 1. Contrast the spring and summer schools (172) as to quality of instruction and purpose.
 2. How would a school of the type described by Webster (173) put in a six-hour day?

3. Characterize the pioneer work of Noah Webster (174) and Jedediah Morse (177) as American textbook writers, and the national importance of their work.

4. If copies of any of the early school readers (175), Webster textbooks, the McGuffey Readers (176), or Davenport's History and Morse's Geography (178) are available, examine them and report on their contents.

5. Just what type of schools did Providence have (179) in 1820?

6. Make a chart showing the organization, studies, and textbooks in use in the schools of Boston in Bingham's day (180).

7. How did the Primary Schools of Boston (181) differ from the primary grades of today?

8. From readings 156 and 182, describe the English schools of Boston.

9. Show how Mann's description (183) set a new standard for accomplishment for American schools.

10. Just what kind of schools did the district system provide for the people of Indiana (184) in 1837?

11. What elements, in the development of the district system (185), persist and cause rural people to cling to the system so tenaciously today?

12. Can you add another illustration (186) of the district system in action?

13. At what stage in the development of a state school system would the early teachers' institutes (187) be valuable? Would they be useful today?

14. Do any of the deficiencies pointed out in the New York Address (188) exist today?

15. Show that the Ohio conditions of 1837, as described by Lewis (189) were typical of the early stages in the development of a state school system, and were phases of the battle for tax support.

16. Characterize the type of discipline described in 190.

17. Do we have any comparable school conditions as are described in readings 191 and 192 anywhere today?

18. How do you explain the presence of such schoolrooms in leading cities of the time as are described in reading 192? Could you find such conditions in cities anywhere today?

19. Have we continued to improve instruction since Riley wrote (193) at as rapid a rate as before? Illustrate.

TOPICS FOR INVESTIGATION AND REPORT

1. The nature and influence of Webster's Speller and Readers.
2. A comparative study of the early Readers mentioned.
3. A comparative study of the early Arithmetics mentioned. (Monroe.)
4. A comparative study of the early Grammars mentioned.
5. A comparative study of the early Geographies mentioned.
6. A comparative study of the early Histories mentioned.
7. McGuffey and his series of Readers. (Sullivan.)
8. Caleb Bingham and his work in Boston. (Fowle.)

9. John Howland and his work for the schools of Providence. (Carroll.)
10. Early city courses of study. (Barnard.)
11. Early school buildings: plans and types. (Barnard; Johnson.)
12. Development of the course of study at Boston. (Fitzpatrick.)
13. The work of John D. Philbrick at Boston. (Barnard, vol. II; Bunker.)
14. Subjects taught in the early high schools. (Barnard.)
15. Early standards for certificating teachers. (Barnard.)
16. History and character of the teachers' institutes. (Barnard.)
17. Educational opportunities for girls before 1850.
18. Professional books and magazines before 1850.
19. The Boston examination of 1845. (Caldwell and Curtis.)
20. The Springfield Tests. (Riley; Hedgepeth.)
21. The Springfield and Norwich Tests compared. (Riley; Tirrell.)
22. Character of the early instruction in reading, arithmetic, geography, spelling, or other subject before 1850. (Barnard; Breslich; Caldwell and Curtis; Johnson; Lyman; Monroe; Reeder.)

SELECTED REFERENCES

Arrowood, C. F. "The Backwoods School in American Fiction; in *School and Society*, vol. XXVIII, pp. 373–83. (Sept. 29, 1928.)
> A very interesting article on early American education.

Barnard, Henry, Editor. *The American Journal of Education.* 31 vols. Consult *Analytical Index* to; 128 pp. Published by United States Bureau of Education, Washington, 1892.

Breslich, E. R. "Arithmetic 100 Years Ago"; in *Elementary School Journal*, vol. XXV, pp. 664–75. (May, 1925.)
> Describes, with eight plates from an old M.S. Arithmetic.

Bunker, Frank. *Reorganization of the Public School System.* 186 pp. Bulletin 8, 1916, United States Bureau of Education.
> Chapter II deals with the rise of the graded school.

*Caldwell, O. W., and Curtis, S. A. *Then and Now in Education; 1845–1923.* 400 pp. World Book Co., Yonkers, 1924.
> Describes the Boston examination of 1845, evaluates the school efficiency of that day, and reproduces the full reports and examination questions, with representative answers, made by the Boston examining committees of 1845. Also sample pages from the 1845 textbooks. Further reproduces the 1919 tests, record sheets, and directions for using them.

*Carroll, Charles. *Public Education in Rhode Island.* 500 pp. Providence, 1918.
> Good on early schools, and work of John Howland.

Dodd, William E. *Expansion and Conflict.* Boston, 1915.
> Chapter XI describes cultural conditions in ante-bellum days.

Eggleston, Edw. *The Hoosier Schoolmaster.* New York, 1892.
> Probably the best account of the district school of the early period, the pupils, and the teacher.

Fitzpatrick, E. A. *The Educational Views and Influences of De Witt Clinton.* 157 pp. Teachers College Contributions to Education, No. 44. New York, 1911.

> Describes the schools of 1830.

Fitzpatrick, Frank A. "The Development of the Course of Study"; in *Educational Review*, vol. XLIX, pp. 1–19. (Jan., 1915.)

> Takes Boston as a type and treats the subject historically.

*Fowle, William B. "Caleb Bingham and the Public Schools of Boston"; in Barnard's *American Journal of Education*, vol. V, pp. 325–49.

> His work, textbooks used, and teaching methods.

Hedgepeth, V. W. B. "Spelling and Arithmetic in 1846 and Today"; in *School Review*, vol. XIV, pp. 352–56. (May, 1906.)

> The Springfield test at Goshen, Indiana. One of the many comparative studies.

*Johnson, Clifton. *Old-Time Schools and School Books.* 380 pp. New York, 1904.

> Chapter IV describes the district schools of the first half of the nineteenth century and succeeding chapters the textbooks used. A valuable book.

*Keller, Jacob W. "Warren Colburn's Mental Arithmetic"; in *Pedagogical Seminary*, vol. XXX, pp. 162–71. (June, 1923.)

> Good on book, and the sources of Colburn's idea.

Knight, Edgar W. *Public Education in the South.* Boston, 1922.

> Chapter VIII good on practices in the South before 1860.

*Knight, E. W. *Education in the United States.* 588 pp. Ginn, Boston, 1929.

> Chapters XII on Teachers and Teaching, and XIV on Later Practices, contain much supplemental matter on the early teachers and early school practices and conditions.

*Lyman, R. L. *English Grammar in American Schools before 1850.* Bulletin 12, 1921. United States Bureau of Education. 170 pp.

Maddox, W. A. *The Free School Idea in Virginia before the Civil War.* Teachers College Contributions to Education, No. 93. New York, 1918.

> Chapter VIII deals with the low qualifications for teachers.

Martin, G. H. "Boston Schools 100 Years Ago"; in *New England Magazine*, vol. XXVI, pp. 628–42. (July, 1902.)

> A very general article.

McManis, John T. "History in the Elementary Schools, 1825–1850"; in *Educational Bimonthly*, vol. VI, pp. 322–32. (April, 1912.)

> Historical.

*Moehlman, A. B. *Public Education in Detroit.* 263 pp. Bloomington (Ill.), 1925.

> A good history of the development of a city school system.

*Monroe, W. S. *Development of Arithmetic as a School Subject.* 170 pp. Bulletin No. 10, United States Bureau of Education, Washington, 1917.

> An excellent collection of illustrative material on early arithmetic teaching.

*Murray, David. *History of Education in New Jersey.* 344 pp. Circular of Information No. 1, United States Bureau of Education, Washington, 1899.

   Chapter VIII very good on the character of the schools during the colonial period and up to the middle of the nineteenth century.

Nelson, A. H.   "The Little Red Schoolhouse"; in *Educational Review,* vol. XXIII, pp. 304–17. (April, 1902.)

   Description of a rural school taught in Maine in the winter of 1858–59, which was characteristic of many rural school positions before 1870.

Powers, S. R.   *History of the Teaching of Chemistry in the Secondary Schools of the United States before 1850.* Publ. University Minnesota, 1920.

*Providence, Rhode Island.   *Centennial Report of the School Committee,* 1899–1900. Providence, 1901.

   Contains many valuable historical documents.

*Reeder, Rudolph R.   *The Historical Development of School Readers and Methods of Teaching Reading.*   Columbia University Contributions to Philosophy, Psychology, and Education, vol. VIII, No. 2. New York, 1900.

*Riley, J. L.   *The Springfield Tests, 1846–1906.* 51 pp. Holden Patent Book Cover Co., Springfield, Mass., 1908.

   A reprint of the results of the two examinations, showing the comparative results of the pupils in spelling, arithmetic, writing, and geography.

Smith, Sherman M.   *The Relation of the State to Religious Education in Massachusetts.*   350 pp. Syracuse, 1926.

   This volume contains many details as to instruction, textbooks, and teachers in the schools of Massachusetts in Horace Mann's day.

*Sullivan, Mark.   *Our Times,* vol. II. New York, 1927.

   Contains a good chapter on the McGuffey Readers.

*Tirrell, Henry A.   "The Norwich Tests, 1862–1909"; in *School Review,* vol. XVIII, pp. 326–32. (May, 1910.)

   A comparative study, similar to the one at Springfield, and equally conclusive as to arithmetic, geography, history, and grammar.

CHAPTER X

NEW IDEAS FROM ABROAD

I. ENGLISH ORIGINS AND EARLY INDEPENDENCE

Early influences largely English. As will have been seen from a study of the earlier chapters, the chief source from which our early educational ideas came was England. Throughout all the colonial period, and well into our national period also, we were English in our history, traditions, and development. Though the Dutch and Swedish parochial schools were introduced into New Amsterdam, though many French Huguenots settled along the Carolina coast, and though the German parochial school was firmly planted in Pennsylvania, these really influenced American development but little. The Dutch, Swedish, and French were rapidly absorbed and largely lost their identity after the English occupation, while the Germans became isolated and influenced development but little outside of eastern Pennsylvania and parts of the Ohio valley. The great source of all our early educational traditions, types of schools, textbooks, and educational attitudes was England, and education was established and for a time conducted here much after the fashion of the practices in the mother country. In New England it was the English Puritan with his Calvinistic viewpoint, and to the southward it was the Anglican churchman interpreting the Englishman's "no-business-of-the-State" attitude as to education.

The dame school, the tutor in the home, private and parochial pay schools, apprenticeship training, the pauper-school idea, the Latin grammar school, and the college — all were typical English institutions brought over by the early colonists and established here. For a century and a half the textbooks, and many of the teachers, were also imported from England. After the coming of nationality, the creation of distinctively American textbooks, and the evolution of more American-type schools, we still continued to draw our new educational ideas and creations from the old mother land. The Sunday School, the Charity School, the Philanthropic Society idea, the Lancastrian Monitorial Schools, and the Infant-School idea all came directly from England and were fitted into and onto the slowly evolving native American school. Even the Academy idea goes back in part to the Puritan academies of England.

Early French influences. After the French had extended aid to us in the War for Independence there was a tendency, for a time, to imitate French examples. The University of the State of New York, a governing body controlling all higher educational activities in the State,[1] established in 1784 and organized in its permanent form in 1787, shows unmistakably the influence of the chief educational ideas of the French revolutionists. The French, on the other hand, drew some inspiration from us. Jefferson had tried, unsuccessfully, in 1779, to secure the establishment of a complete system of public education for Virginia (**R. 67**). His proposed system comprehended the establishment of free elementary schools scattered throughout the State, secondary schools, and a state college (William and Mary) as the culmination of the State's educational system. Jefferson's plan was translated into French about the time (1784) that he arrived in France as American ambassador. The Du Pont de Nemours Plan for National Education (1800) embodied the essentials of Jefferson's plan.

Jefferson's plan was too advanced for acceptance at the time. Later (1819), he secured the establishment of the University of Virginia, which today stands as a monument to his memory.[2]

The College of New Orleans, created in 1805 with provision for academies for the counties, and the elementary school system organ-

---

[1] The University of the State of New York is a clear copy of Diderot's *Plan of a University*, prepared in 1776 for Catherine II of Russia. While the plan was never carried out in Russia, it was printed and much discussed in France. The plan was later (1808) adopted in its main outlines by Napoleon in forming the University of France. The Catholepistemiad, or University of Michigania, formed in 1817, embodied much the same idea.

[2] Jefferson's interest in the new university was deep and lasting. He helped secure the enactment of the law creating the institution, fought for its location at Charlottesville, drew plans for its buildings, supervised their erection, rode down from his hill-top home almost daily to oversee the work, and helped select the first faculty and plan the internal organization of the institution.

Concerning it, he wrote to a friend:

"I have only this single anxiety in this world. It is a bantling of forty years' birth and nursing, and if I can see it on its legs, I will sing, with serenity and pleasure, my *nunc dimittis*."

Among his papers he left instructions for the inscription which he wished engraved on his tombstone, as follows:

Here lies Thomas Jefferson
Author of the Declaration of Independence
Of the Statute of Virginia for Religious Freedom
And Father of the University of Virginia.

ized for the State in 1806, were clearly modeled after Napoleon's law of 1802, organizing instruction throughout France. Only the college was ever put into operation. The early constitutional provisions regarding education in Indiana (**R. 70**), providing for a system of free education "ascending in regular gradation from township schools to state university," probably owed their formulation to the influence in the constitutional convention of the French refugees then living in Vincennes. The founding of the University of Michigan, in 1817, at a time when the population was half French, with the absurd name of *Catholepistemiad*, and its whimsical organization (**R. 194**), embodied the same French idea [1] of a state organization of education extending from the elementary school to the university.[2] We have comparatively little, though, that can be traced back to French sources, partly because we were so soon estranged from France by the unfriendly actions of Napoleon, and partly because France had, before the estrangement, done so little in education that we could imitate.

Our early isolation and independence. Up to the close of the first third of the nineteenth century we remained isolated and followed purely native lines of development, modified, as we have seen, by new ideas brought over from England and a few ideas as to organization from France. We were a young and a very independent nation, traveling but little, reading but little, and depending almost entirely upon our own ideas and resources. Schools were being evolved along purely native lines, and adapted to the needs of a new nation on a new continent which it was busily engaged in reducing to civilization. Still more, our early textbook writers, notably Webster and Morse, had definitely aimed to free American schools from any dependence

---

[1] "When the Catholepistemiad was founded, the great Napoleon was only in the second year of his exile. His marvelous career was still fresh in the minds of admiring Americans, whose warm and wondering regard for the great man was much enhanced by certain recollections of our own war with Great Britain, then just closed..." Those who sponsored the law "must have understood the system organized under the name of the University of France, and certainly this act looks very much like an attempt to copy it in Michigan." (Ten-Brook, A. *American State Universities and the University of Michigan*, p. 98.)

[2] To illustrate, Statute 3 of the new University made provision for instructing the pupils in the primary schools in reading, writing, English grammar, and declamation. Statutes 4, 5, and 6 established primary schools in Detroit, Mackinaw, and Monroe. Statute 12 adopted textbooks for these schools — Murray's Reader, Speller, and Grammar, and Walker's Elocution, and Dictionary. Statute 7 provided a course of instruction for the pupils in the classical academies. Statute 8 established a classical academy in Detroit. Statute 15 established a college at Detroit under the name of the "First College of Michigania."

THOMAS JEFFERSON

(1743–1826)

Author of
The Declaration of American Independence
Of the Statute of Virginia for Religious Freedom
Father of the University of Virginia

JEAN JACQUES ROUSSEAU

(1712–1778)

on England, as they did not want to risk the danger of American children "imbibing from such books the monarchical ideas and the national prejudices of the English" (**R. 177**).

Our teachers and schoolmasters were of the same native homespun variety, as were our early leaders as well. They were all alike innocent of such a thing as normal training, had read no professional literature, had attended few if any teachers' institutes, and knew little as to what even their neighbors, much less what peoples in other States and lands, were doing in the matter of organizing and directing schools. New ideas were spread by teachers moving about rather than by other means. As an evidence of this, it was almost twenty years after Warren Colburn's famous *Intellectual Arithmetic* was published in Boston (1821) before it began to be used in New Jersey, "when those who had studied it in New England," according to Murray, "became teachers there." Yet this was the great book of its day, and shaped all subsequent teaching of the subject.

Educational journalism begins. It was not until the twenties that our educational literature began, and not until the decade between 1835 and 1845 that we really began to learn, for the first time, of what had been and was being done on the continent of Europe in the matter of organizing instruction. The earliest educational journals published in the United States, which continued to be issued for one year or more, were:

1. *The Academician*, New York, 1818–20. Semimonthly. Twenty-five numbers. Edited by Albert and John W. Pickett.
2. *The American Journal of Education*, Boston, 1826–31. Five volumes. Edited by William Russell.
3. *Teachers' Guide and Parents' Assistant*, Portland, Me., 1826–28. Semimonthly. Edited by J. L. Parkhurst. Consolidated with no. 2 in March, 1828.
4. *American Annals of Education and Instruction*, Boston, 1831–39. Edited by W. C. Woodbridge.
5. *Common School Assistant*, Albany, N. Y., 1836–40. Five volumes. Edited by J. Orville Taylor.
6. *Western Academician and Journal of Education and Science*, Cincinnati, 1837–38. Edited by John W. Pickett.
7. *Journal of Education*, Detroit (vol. I) and Marshall, Ill. (vol. II), 1838–40. Two volumes. Edited by John D. Pierce.
8. *Connecticut Common School Journal*, Hartford, 1838–42. Four volumes. Edited by Henry Barnard.
9. *Common School Journal*, Boston, 1839–52. Ten volumes edited by

Horace Mann (1839–48), and four volumes by Wm. B. Fowle (1849–52). Semimonthly.

10. *District School Journal for the State of New York*, Albany, 1840–52. Various editors.

11. *Journal of Rhode Island Institute of Instruction*, 1845–49. Three volumes. Edited by Henry Barnard.

12. Barnard's *American Journal of Education*, Hartford, 1855–81. Thirty-one large volumes. Edited by Henry Barnard. A monumental work.

The circulation of these various journals was not large or extended, and for a time was confined almost altogether to New York and New England, but they gradually reached the leaders of the time and slowly but positively influenced public opinion. We find their pages filled with notes of progress, and letters and articles on Infant Schools, Pestalozzian methods, Fellenberg and the manual-labor movement, Lancastrian Schools, and extracts from or reprints of the reports made by Cousin and Stowe. Their great service was that of spreading information as to what was being done, both at home and abroad, and in extending the work of propaganda for the maintenance of schools.[1] With the beginnings of Barnard's *American Journal of Education*, in 1855, an educational journal was brought out which interpreted for American educators the best results of educational practice in all lands and times, and greatly extended the vision and enlarged the point of view of the American schoolman.

II. WORK AND INFLUENCE OF PESTALOZZI

The inspiration of Pestalozzi. One of the greatest books of the eighteenth century, the *Émile* of Jean-Jacques Rousseau, a French Swiss by birth then living in Paris, appeared in 1762. In this Rousseau vigorously attacked the formalism of the age in religion, manners, and education. The book described the education of the boy, Émile, by a new plan, that of rejecting the formal teaching of the schools and permitting him to grow up and be educated according to nature. The volume was extensively read, and made a deep impression throughout all Europe, but was particularly influential among the thinkers of Switzerland. Gathering up the current idea of his age that the "state of nature" was the ideal one, and the one

[1] The state journals edited by Mann and Barnard in particular did notable work. Of the Massachusetts *Common School Journal* Mann wrote that "it was born, not because it was wanted, but because it was needed."

in which men had been intended to live; that the organization of society had created inequalities which prevented man from realizing his real self; and that human duty called for a return to the "state of nature," whatever that might be; Rousseau stated them in terms of the education of the boy, Émile. Despite its many exaggerations, much faulty reasoning, and many imperfections, the book had a tremendous influence on Europe in laying bare the defects and abuses of the formal and ecclesiastical education of the time. Though Rousseau's enthusiasm took the form of theory run mad, and the educational plan he proposed was largely impossible, he nevertheless popularized education. He also contributed much to changing the point of view in instruction from subject-matter to the child to be taught, and the nature of instruction from formal religious doctrine, preparatory for life hereafter, to the study of the life and universe amid which man lives here. The iconoclastic nature of Rousseau's volume may be inferred from its opening sentence, where he says: "Everything is good as it comes from the hand of the author of nature; everything degenerates in the hands of man."

Among those most deeply influenced by Rousseau's book was a young German Swiss by the name of Johann Heinrich Pestalozzi, who was born (1746) and brought up in Zurich. Inspired by Rousseau's writings, he spent the early part of his life trying to render service to the poor, and the latter part in working out for himself a theory and method of instruction based on the natural development of the child. Trying to educate his own child according to Rousseau's plan, he not only discovered its impracticability but also that the only way to improve on it was to study the children themselves. Accordingly he opened a school and home on his farm at Neuhof, in 1774. Here he took in fifty abandoned children, to whom he taught reading, writing, and arithmetic, gave them moral discourses, and trained them in gardening, farming, and cheese-making. It was an attempt to regenerate beggars by means of education, which Pestalozzi firmly believed could be done. At the end of two years he had spent all the money he and his wife possessed, and the school closed in failure — a blessing in disguise — though with Pestalozzi's faith in the power of education unshaken. Of this experiment he wrote: "For years I have lived in the midst of fifty little beggars, sharing in my poverty my bread with them, living like a beggar myself in order to teach beggars to live like men."

Turning next to writing, while continuing to farm, Pestalozzi now tried to express his faith in education in printed form. His *Leonard and Gertrude* (1781) was a wonderfully beautiful story of Swiss peasant life, and of the genius and sympathy and love of a woman amid degrading surroundings. From a wretched place the village of Bonnal, under Pestalozzi's pen, was transformed by the power of education.[1] The book was a great success from the first, and for it Pestalozzi was made a "citizen" of the French Republic, along with Washington, Madison, Kosciusko, Wilberforce, and Tom Paine. He continued to farm and to think, though nearly starving, until 1798, when the opportunity for which he was really fitted came.

Pestalozzi's educational experiments. In 1798 "The Helvetic Republic" was proclaimed, an event which divided Pestalozzi's life into two parts. Up to this time he had been interested wholly in the philanthropic aspect of education, believing that the poor could be regenerated through education and labor. From this time on he interested himself in the teaching aspect of the problem, in the working out and formulation of a teaching method based on the natural development of the child, and in training others to teach. Much to the disgust of the authorities of the new Swiss Government, citizen Pestalozzi applied for service as a schoolteacher. The opportunity to render such service soon came.

That autumn the French troops invaded Switzerland, and, in putting down the stubborn resistance of the three German cantons, they shot down a large number of the people. Orphans to the number of 169 were left in the little town of Stanz, and citizen Pestalozzi was given charge of them. For six months he was father, mother, teacher, and nurse. Then, worn out himself, the orphanage was changed into a hospital. A little later he became a schoolmaster in Burgdorf; was dismissed; became a teacher in another school; and finally, in 1800, opened a school himself in an old castle there. He provided separate teachers for drawing and singing, geography and history, language and arithmetic, and gymnastics. The year following the school was enlarged into a teachers' training school, the

[1] "The picture shown in *Leonard and Gertrude* is very crude. Everywhere is visible the rough hand of the painter, a strong, untiring hand, painting an eternal image, of which this in paper and print is the merest sketch.... Read it and see how puerile it is, how too obvious are its moralities. Read it a second time, and note how earnest it is, how exact and accurate are its peasant scenes. Read it yet again, and recognize in it the outpouring of a rare soul, working, pleading, ready to be despised, for fellow souls." (J. P. Monroe. *The Educational Ideal*, p. 182.)

PESTALOZZI MONUMENT AT YVERDON

A picture of this monument occupies a prominent place in every
schoolroom in Switzerland

government extending him aid in return for giving Swiss teachers one month of training as teachers in his school. Here he wrote and published *How Gertrude Teaches her Children*, which explained his methods and forms his most important pedagogical work; a *Guide for Teaching Spelling and Reading;* and a *Book for Mothers*, devoted to a description of "object teaching." In 1803, the castle being needed

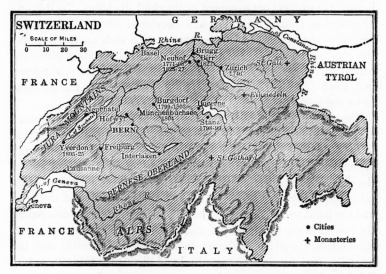

FIG. 98. THE SCENE OF PESTALOZZI'S LABORS

by the government, Pestalozzi moved first to Münchenbuchsee, near Hofwyl, opening his institute temporarily in an old convent there. For a few months, in 1804, he was associated with Emanuel von Fellenberg, at Hofwyl, but late in 1804 he moved to Yverdon, where he re-established the Institute, and where the next twenty years of his life were spent and his greatest success achieved.

The contribution of Pestalozzi. The great contribution of Pestalozzi lay in that, following the lead of Rousseau, he rejected the teaching of mere words and facts, which had characterized all elementary education up to near the close of the eighteenth century, and tried instead to reduce the educational process to a well-organized routine, based on the natural and orderly development of the instincts, capacities, and powers of the growing child. Taking Rousseau's idea of a return to nature, he tried to apply it to the education of children.

This led to his rejection of what he called the "empty chattering of mere words" and "outward show" in the instruction in reading and the catechism, and the introduction in their place of real studies, based on observation, experimentation, and reasoning. "Sense impression" became his watchword.[1] As he expressed it, he "tried to organize and psychologize the educational process" by harmonizing it with the natural development of the child (**R. 195**). To this end he carefully studied children, and developed his methods experimentally as a result of his observation. To such an extreme was this idea carried at Burgdorf and Yverdon that all results of preceding educators and writers were rejected, for fear that error might creep in. Read nothing, discover everything, and prove all things, came to be the working guides of himself and his teachers.

The development of man he believed to be organic, and to proceed according to law. It was the work of the teacher to discover these laws of development and to assist nature in securing "a natural, symmetrical, and harmonious development" of all the "faculties" of the child. Real education must develop the child as a whole — mentally, physically, morally — and called for the training of the head and the hand and the heart. The only proper means for developing the powers of the child was use, and hence education must guide and stimulate self-activity, be based on intuition and exercise, and the sense impressions must be organized and directed. Education, too, if it is to follow the organic development of the child, must observe the proper progress of child development and be graded, so that each step of the process shall grow out of the preceding and grow into the following stage. To accomplish these ends the training must be all-round and harmonious; much liberty must be allowed the child in learning; education must proceed largely by doing instead of by words; the method of learning must be largely analytical; real objects and ideas must precede symbols and words; and finally the organization and correlation of what is learned must be looked after by the teacher.

Still more, Pestalozzi possessed a deep and abiding faith, new at the time, in the power of education as a means of regenerating

[1] "When I now look back and ask myself: What have I specially done for the very being of education, I find that I have fixed the highest supreme principle of instruction in the recognition of *sense impression as the absolute foundation of all knowledge*. Apart from all special teaching I have sought to discover the *nature of teaching itself*, and the prototype, by which nature herself has determined the instruction of our race." (Pestalozzi. *How Gertrude Teaches her Children*, x, § 1.)

society. He had begun his work by trying to "teach beggars to live like men," and his belief in the potency of education in working this transformation, so touchingly expressed in his *Leonard and Gertrude*, never left him. He believed that each human being could be raised through the influence of education to the level of an intellectually free and morally independent life, and that every human being was entitled to the right to attain such freedom and independence. The way to this lay through the full use of his developing powers, under the guidance of a teacher, and not through a process of repeating words and learning by heart. Not only the intellectual qualities of perception, judgment, and reasoning need exercise, but the moral powers as well. To provide such exercise and direction was the work of the school.

Pestalozzi also resented the brutal discipline which for ages had characterized all school instruction, believed it by its very nature immoral, and tried to substitute for this a strict but loving discipline — a "thinking love," he calls it — and to make the school as nearly as possible like a gentle and refined home. To a Swiss father, who on visiting his school exclaimed, "Why, this is not a school, but a family," Pestalozzi answered that such a statement was the greatest praise he could have given him.

The consequences of these ideas. The educational consequences of these new ideas were very large. They in time gave aim and purpose to the elementary school of the nineteenth century, transforming it from an instrument of the Church for church ends, to an instrument of society to be used for its own regeneration and the advancement of the welfare of all.[1] The introduction of the study of natural objects in place of words, and much talking about what was seen and studied instead of parrot-like reproductions of the words of a book, revolutionized both the methods and the subject-matter of instruction in the developing elementary school. Observation and investigation tended to supersede mere memorizing; class discussion and thinking to supersede the reciting of the words of the book; thinking about what was being done to supersede routine learning; and class instruction to supersede the wasteful individual teaching which had for so

---

[1] "What he did was to emphasize the new purpose in education, but vaguely perceived, where held at all, by others; to make clear the new meaning of education which existed in rather a nebulous state in the public mind; to formulate an entirely new method, based on new principles, both of which were to receive a further development in subsequent times, and to pass under his name; and finally, to give an entirely new spirit to the schoolroom." (Monroe, Paul. *Text Book in the History of Education*, p. 600.)

long characterized all school work. It meant the reorganization of the work of elementary education on a modern basis, with class organization and group instruction.

The work of Pestalozzi also meant the introduction of new subject-matter for instruction, the organization of new teaching subjects for the elementary school, and the redirection of the elementary education of children. Observation led to the development of elementary-science study, and the study of home geography; talking about what was observed led to the study of language usage, as distinct from the older study of grammar; and counting and measuring led to the study of number, and hence to a new type of primary arithmetic. The reading of the school also changed both in character and purpose. In other words, in place of an elementary education based on reading, a little writing and spelling, and the catechism, all of a memoriter type with religious ends in view, a new primary school, much more secular in character, was created by the work of Pestalozzi. This new school was based on the study of real objects, learning through sense impressions, the individual expression of ideas, child activity, and the development of the child's powers in an orderly way. In fact, "the development of the faculties" of the child became a by-word with Pestalozzi and his followers.

Pestalozzi's deep abiding faith in the power of education to regenerate society was highly influential in Switzerland, throughout Western Europe, and later in America in showing how to deal with orphans, vagrants, and those suffering from physical defects or in need of reformation, by providing for such a combination of intellectual and industrial training.

The spread and influence of Pestalozzi's work. So famous did the work of Pestalozzi become that his schools at Burgdorf and Yverdon came to be "show places," even in a land filled with natural wonders. Observers and students came from all over Europe to see and to teach in his school. In particular the educators of Prussia were attracted by his work, and, earlier than other nations, saw the far-reaching significance of his discoveries. Herbart visited his school as early as 1799, when but a young man of twenty-three, and wrote a very sympathetic description of his new methods. Froebel spent the years 1808 to 1810 as a teacher at Yverdon, when he was a young man of twenty-six to eight. "It soon became evident to me," wrote Froebel, "that 'Pestalozzi' was to be the watchword of my life."

Many Swiss teachers were trained by Pestalozzi, and these spread his work and ideas over Switzerland. Particularly in German Switzerland did his ideas take root and reorganize education. Of his Swiss followers one of the most influential was Emanuel Fellenberg, who, adopting Pestalozzi's idea of combined intellectual and industrial training, developed a combined intellectual and manual-labor school at Hofwyl, near Berne, which he conducted very successfully from 1806 to 1844. By 1829, when his work was first made known to American educators through the articles of William Woodbridge, his school included:

1. A farm of about six hundred acres.
2. Workshops for manufacturing clothing and tools.
3. A printing and lithographing establishment.
4. A literary institution for the education of the well-to-do.
5. A lower school which trained for handicrafts and middle-class occupations.
6. An agricultural school for the education of the poor as farm laborers, and as teachers for the rural schools.

Fellenberg's work was widely copied in Switzerland, Germany, England, and the United States, and contained the germ-idea of our modern agricultural, manual, and reformatory education.

Pestalozzi's ideas in Prussia. It was in Prussia that Pestalozzi's ideas made the deepest impression, and there that they were most successfully transplanted and carried out. As early as 1803 an envoy, sent by the Prussian king, reported favorably on the methods used by Pestalozzi, and in 1804 Pestalozzian methods were authorized for the primary schools of Prussia. In 1807–08, after the severe defeat inflicted on Prussia by Napoleon, the German philosopher Fichte, who had taught in Zurich and knew Pestalozzi, exploited Pestalozzi's work in Berlin, and emphasized the importance of reorganizing the work of the common schools of Prussia, as a phase of the work of national regeneration, along the lines laid down by him. To popular education, Fichte declared,[1] must the nation turn to develop new strength to face the future. As a result the civil service was put on an efficiency basis; the two-class school system, shown in the accom-

---

[1] "He set all his hopes for Germany on a new national system of education. One German State was to lead the way in establishing it, making use of the same right of coercion to which it resorted in compelling its subjects to serve in the army, and for the exercise of which certainly no better justification could be found than the common good aimed at in national education." (Paulsen, Fr., *German Education, Past and Present*, p. 240.)

panying drawing, was reorganized and freed from clerical control; and the basis of the strong military state which set Europe afire in 1914 was laid.

The Prussian Government now (1808) sent seventeen teachers to Switzerland to spend three years, at the expense of the Government, in studying Pestalozzi's ideas and methods, and they were particularly enjoined that they were not sent primarily to get the mechanical side of this method, but to

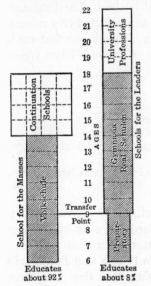

> warm yourselves at the sacred fire which burns in the heart of this man, so full of strength and love, whose work has remained so far below what he originally desired, below the essential ideas of his life, of which the method is only a feeble product.
>
> You will have reached perfection when you have clearly seen that education is an art, and the most sublime and holy of all, and in what connection it is with the great art of the education of nations.

FIG. 99. GERMAN STATE SCHOOL SYSTEMS BEFORE 1914

Compare with Fig. 68, p. 273, and note the difference between a European two-class school system and the American democratic educational ladder.

On their return these, and others, spread Pestalozzian ideas throughout Prussia, and so effective was their work, and so readily did the Prussian people catch the spirit of Pestalozzi's endeavors, that at the Berlin celebration of the centennial of his birth, in 1846, the German educator Diesterweg, often called "der deutsche Pestalozzi," said:

> By these men and these means, men trained in the Institution at Yverdon under Pestalozzi, the study of his publications, and the applications of his methods in the model and normal schools of Prussia, after 1808, was the present Prussian, or rather Prussian-Pestalozzian school system established, for he is entitled to at least one-half the fame of the German popular schools.

Pestalozzianism in England. Pestalozzi's ideas were also carried to England, but in no such satisfactory manner as to the German States. Where German lands received both the method and the spirit, the English obtained largely the form. The introduction into England was due chiefly to the Reverend Charles Mayo and his sister Elizabeth, but England was at that time so deeply immersed in monitorial instruction that the country was not in a frame of mind to profit greatly from the new ideas. Mayo spent the years 1819–22 at Yverdon (**R. 196**), when Pestalozzi's institute was in its decline, rent by dissensions, and rapidly approaching its end. On his return to England he opened a private Pestalozzian school for children of the wealthy. His sister shortly afterward published a Pestalozzian manual for teachers, called *Lessons on Objects*, but missed the spirit of Pestalozzi's work. The lessons were formal, scientific, far too detailed and analytical, and much beyond the comprehension of children.

For example, if common salt were the "object" for the lesson, the children would be expected to learn its chemical composition, its uses, how and where found in nature, how mined and refined, that its crystalline form is cubical, that it varies in color from white to bluish and reddish, that it is transparent to translucent, that it is soluble in water and saline in taste, that it imparts a yellow color to a flame, etc., without more contact with a piece of real salt than seeing the "specimen" passed around by the teacher. "Object teaching" soon became the great educational fad in England, and was later brought to the United States. The effect of this instruction was to "formalize" the Pestalozzian movement in England, and in consequence much of the finer spirit and significance of Pestalozzi's work was lost.

The Mayos were prominent in the Infant-School movement, which made such great headway in England after about 1820, and in 1836 they helped organize "The Home and Colonial Infant Society" to spread the idea at home and abroad. This Society adopted a somewhat more liberal interpretation of Pestalozzian methods than the Mayos had introduced, though still more formalized than that Pestalozzi had developed. It established a Model Infant School and a Training College for teachers, and later had an important influence in introducing the English type of formalized Pestalozzianism into the schools of the United States.

After Pestalozzi's institution had become celebrated, and visitors and commissions from many countries had visited him and it, and after governments had vied with one another in introducing Pestalozzian methods and reforms, the vogue of the Pestalozzian ideas became very extended and many excellent private schools were founded on the Pestalozzian model.

III. EARLY AMERICAN TRAVELERS AND OFFICIAL REPORTS

Early American travelers. Our first contact with the educational thought and practices of continental Europe came through some half-dozen Americans who studied at the Prussian university of Göttingen, then almost unknown outside of German lands, before 1820. Our first contact with the work of Pestalozzi in Switzerland came through Joseph Neef, one of Pestalozzi's teachers, who came to America and taught a private school in Philadelphia for a time between 1806 and 1809, and who later wandered westward to Louisville, and for a short time taught in a little communistic colony at New Harmony, Indiana. In 1808 he published, at Philadelphia, his *Sketch of a Plan and Method of Education Founded on an Analysis of the Human Faculties and Natural Reason*, and in 1813 his *Method of Instructing Children Rationally in the Arts of Writing and Reading*. So little had been done, though, in developing public education with us before 1815, south of New England and New York, that Neef's work remained almost unknown, outside of a small local circle of interested persons, while those who had studied at Göttingen influenced educational development, even in the colleges of the time, but very little.[1]

Griscom and Woodbridge. Our first real contact with continental European ideas and accomplishments in education came in 1819, through the publication in this country of *A Year in Europe*, written by Professor John Griscom, of New York, who had spent the year 1818–19 in visiting the schools, colleges, and charitable institutions of Great Britain, Holland, France, Switzerland, and Italy. His description of his visit to Pestalozzi awakened some interest (**R. 197**), and his volume was read by the leading thinkers of the day.[2] After

---

[1] Neef's *Sketch of a Plan and Method of Education*, published at Philadelphia in 1808, was the first strictly pedagogical work published in English in the United States. It dealt with the aims and methods of education. In 1813 he published, also at Philadelphia, his *Method of Instructing Children Rationally in the Arts of Writing and Reading*. These books, good though they were, seem scarcely to have been known to the northward.

[2] "When you see John Griscom," wrote a gentleman in Virginia to his friend in Philadelphia, shortly after the publication of the book, "tell him that Mr. Thos. Jefferson said that his book gave him the most satisfactory view of the literary and public institutions of England, and France, and Switzerland, that he had ever read. He read it with great care, and obtained some useful hints in relation to his university from it." (*Memoirs of John Griscom*, New York, 1859, p. 152.)

his return he became an active propagandist for Pestalozzian ideas and methods. Our city and state school systems, though, were as yet hardly under way, Lancastrianism was at its height, and Griscom's work influenced our common-school development scarcely at all. Griscom's description of the high school at Edinburgh, though, probably gave the name to the new school at Boston (p. 253) and to the American secondary school as well.

FIG. 100. TWO EARLY AMERICAN TRAVELERS
JOHN GRISCOM   WILLIAM C. WOODBRIDGE
(1774–1852)   (1794–1845)

The chief influence of the book proved to be along the lines of reformatory and charitable education, in which we were just making a beginning. Griscom told what had been done along these lines in Europe. This information was welcomed by the few Americans interested in such development, and came as a valuable contribution at the time.

Another early American traveler was William C. Woodbridge, of New England, who spent the year 1820 and the years 1825–29 in Europe. It was he who, through his enthusiastic "Letters," published in Russell's *American Journal of Education*, and elsewhere, first really brought the work of the Swiss reformers — Pestalozzi and Fellenberg — to the attention of American teachers (**R. 198**). After his return he published two textbooks on geography (1824, 1833 — see page 297), based on Pestalozzian methods, and it was he who inspired Lowell Mason to offer his services, in 1836, to introduce music into the schools of Boston. This was probably the first teaching of music in the schools of the United States, so successful with us up to that time had been the Calvinistic idea of the repression as irreligious of all joyful and artistic instincts. Even this start was a failure, and it was a quarter of a century later before music and drawing became generally recognized as subjects of study, even in the better city schools.

Still another early American traveler was Henry E. Dwight, whose *Travels in the North of Germany, 1825–26*, told of the new teachers' seminaries which had been established in Prussia. He urged better preparation for teachers in Connecticut, and held that with properly prepared teachers "the intellectual character of the mass of inhabitants would in one generation not only become superior to that of

every other people, but it would become the wonder and admiration of our country." There is little evidence, however, that his book was generally read or that it exerted any special influence.

Cousin's Report on German education. The first document describing European schools which made any deep impression on those then engaged in organizing our American state school systems was an English translation of the famous *Report on the Condition of Public Instruction in Germany, and particularly Prussia*, made to the French Government by Victor Cousin, in 1831, and publicly printed the next year. This *Report* was reprinted in London, in 1834, and the first half of it, explaining the administrative organization of Prussian education and the Prussian system of people's schools, was reprinted in New York City,[1] in 1835. Most of the early educational journals, listed on page 343, reprinted this report, in whole or in part.

FIG. 101

VICTOR COUSIN

(1792–1867)

After the overthrow of the old restored monarchy in France, in 1830, a new government was set up, supported by the leading thinkers of the time. One of the most important measures to which atten-

[1] Cousin's *Report on Primary Education in Prussia.*

"Mrs. Austin's translation of this *Report* is republished by Wiley and Long, of New York, with a Preface by J. Orville Taylor. It is an account of the best school system in the world, by the first philosopher of the age." (Advertisement in *American Annals of Education*, April, 1835.)

tion was at once turned was the creation of a state school system for France. Cousin was sent to Prussia to study what was then the best state school system in Europe, and so convincing was his *Report* that, despite bitter national antipathies, it carried conviction throughout France and was deeply influential in securing the creation of the first French national schools, in 1833. The church control of the school committees was broken, the examination of teachers was required, thirty new normal schools to train teachers were established, state aid for primary and infant schools was provided, freedom of religious instruction was guaranteed, recommendation was changed to obligation, and both state and local supervision were instituted. The modern state school system of France dates from the Law of 1833, and this from Cousin's *Report*.

Influence of Cousin's Report in the United States. The translation of Cousin's *Report* into English and the publication of half of it in the United States came just as our new state school systems were beginning to take form, and just as the battle for state control was in full swing. It was the first complete and comprehensive report on European schools that became available to the English reader, and its convincing description of the strong Prussian state school organization, under a state minister, and with state control over so many matters, was everywhere of value in this country (**R. 199**). It gave support to the demands of the few leaders of the time who were struggling to reduce the rampant district system to some semblance of order, and who were trying to organize the thousands of little community school systems in each State into one state school system, under some form of centralized control. Though actually influencing legislation in but one or two of our States, the two main ideas gained from it were the importance of some form of centralized state control, and the training of teachers in state normal schools. These influences were evident chiefly in Michigan and Massachusetts.

The publication of the *Report* came just as Michigan was organizing to enter the Union as a State, and two leaders there — John D. Pierce (1797–1882), a minister who was a graduate of Brown University and who later became the first head of the state school system,[1] and General Isaac E. Crary (1804–54), chairman of the com-

[1] Pierce was a descendant of one of New England's oldest families, which settled at Watertown, Massachusetts, in 1637. He was graduated from Brown in 1813, taught, and was principal of an academy, became a Congregational minister, and in 1831 went westward and settled at Marshall, Michigan. From 1836 to 1841 he was Superintendent of Public Instruction for Michigan.

mittee on education in the constitutional convention [1] — obtained a copy of it and were deeply impressed by Cousin's statements.[2] They discussed together "the fundamental principles which were deemed important for the convention to adopt," and it was agreed by them that education "should be made a distinct branch of the government, and that the constitution ought to provide for an officer who should have the whole matter in charge and thus keep its importance perpetually before the public mind." Largely as a result of their efforts Michigan was the first State to take the 16th section school lands, given by the National Government for schools (p. 92), from the control of the townships and place them under the control of the State, and likewise the first State to create the appointive office (a pure Prussian imitation) of State Superintendent of Public Instruction.[3] The first constitution also made very definite provision for a state system of schools and a state university. That Cousin's *Report* influenced the class-organization or class-work of the Michigan schools, or the schools of any other State for that matter, is a contention recently advanced which the facts scarcely warrant. It was Mann's *Seventh Report* that did this.

In Massachusetts Cousin's *Report* came just in time to give useful support to Brooks, Carter, Mann, and the few others interested who were trying there to secure the establishment of the first American state normal school. The normal-school idea in America, though, as we shall point out in the following chapter, was of native American growth, and had clearly taken form before Prussian normal schools were known of in this country. The descriptions of the Prussian training schools for teachers only awakened new support and helped

[1] Crary also was of Puritan stock, born in Connecticut, a graduate of Trinity College, and a leader in early Michigan affairs.

[2] "About this time Cousin's report of the Prussian school system came into my hands, and it was read with much interest. Sitting one pleasant afternoon upon a log on the hill north of where the court house at Marshall now stands, Gen. Crary and myself discussed for a long time the fundamental principles which were deemed important for the convention to adopt in laying the foundations of our State. The subject of education was a theme of special interest. It was agreed, if possible, that it should be made a distinct branch of the government, and that the constitution ought to provide for an officer who should have the whole matter in charge and thus keep its importance perpetually before the public mind." (John D. Pierce, in *Michigan Pioneer and Historical Collections*, vol. XVII, p. 245.)

[3] A later superintendent of public instruction in Michigan, writing in 1852 on the history of the system, said that "the system of public instruction which was intended to be established by the framers of the constitution, the conception of the office, its province, its powers, and duties were derived from Prussia."

along more rapidly a movement which was then well under way as a purely native development.

Stowe's Report on Elementary Education in Europe. In 1829 there was formed at Cincinnati the "Western Academic Institute and Board of Education" (**R. 101**), and for a decade this was practically the only active organization for education in the State of Ohio. It was a private propaganda organization, and included in its membership such men as Lyman Beecher, Samuel Lewis, Professor Calvin E. Stowe, John W. Pickett, and William H. McGuffey. Money was raised, an agent (Lewis) was sent to visit the schools of the State, reports as to conditions were prepared, and delegations were sent to the legislature to urge action. When Professor Stowe started for Europe, in 1836, to buy a library for the Lane Theological Seminary, with which he was connected, the "Institute" induced the legislature of Ohio to commission him to examine and report on the systems of elementary instruction found there. The result was his celebrated *Report on Elementary Education in Europe*, made to the legislature in 1837.

This was the first report on European educational conditions by an American which attracted general attention. In it he contrasted educational conditions in Ohio with those of Prussia and Würtemberg, with particular reference to the organization and thoroughness of the instruction, and the maintenance of institutions for imparting to prospective teachers some knowledge of the science and art of teaching. The meager legal requirements in Ohio of instruction in reading and writing and arithmetic, with school trustees frequently forbidding instruction in any higher branches; the untrained and poorly educated teachers, and the absence in the State of any means of training teachers; he contrasted with the enriched elementary-school curriculum, the Pestalozzian methods, and the well-informed and trained teachers of Prussia and Würtemberg. The *Report* commanded the admiration of legislators and educators, was widely read, extensively quoted and commended in the educational journals of the time, and "not a little of the advancement in common schools," says Barnard, "during the next twenty years may be traced to this Report." The legislature of Ohio ordered ten thousand copies of it printed, and a copy sent to every school district in the State. It was later ordered reprinted and circulated by vote of the legislatures of Pennsylvania, Massachusetts, Michigan, North Carolina, and Virginia.

In his summary Professor Stowe held that the Prussian scheme was thoroughly practicable for Ohio (**R. 200**), and that it could be carried out there as it had been for years in Prussia "in the best district schools that have ever been organized." To show how much influence this *Report* had with legislatures in Ohio it might be added that it was not until 1848 that grammar and geography were added to the narrow elementary-school curriculum, not until 1853 that the rate-bill was abandoned and the schools made free, and almost three quarters of a century before the first state normal school was established by the State.

Barnard, Bache, Julius, and Smith. In the years 1835–37 Henry Barnard visited the schools of the different countries of Europe, and from this visit dates his interest in introducing into our state school systems the best of European organization and practices — an inter-

est he retained all his active life. He made no special report at the time of his visit, but through the pages of the educational journals which he edited, for the next forty years, he continued to set before his readers interesting descriptions of educational organization and practices in other States and lands. He also gathered together the important parts of all these reports and issued them in book form, in 1854, under the title *National Education in Europe*.

In 1836 the trustees of the newly founded Girard College, at Philadelphia, an institution for the education of orphans, sent Professor Alexander Dallas Bache [1] "to visit all establishments in Europe resembling Girard College." On his return, in 1839, his *Report on Education in Europe* was printed. In this he devoted about two hundred pages to an enthusiastic description of Pestalozzian methods as he had seen them in the schools of Holland, and also described the German *Gymnasium*.

[1] Bache, a great-grandson of Benjamin Franklin, was graduated from the U.S. Military Academy at West Point in 1826, and for two years was an instructor there. From 1828 to 1836 he was a professor at the University of Pennsylvania, when he was elected president of Girard College and sent to Europe for two years that he might study the educational systems of the old world. Stephen Girard, dying in 1831, bequeathed $2,000,000 for the establishment of a college for orphans in Philadelphia, and it was this institution that Bache helped to organize.

In 1835 a Dr. H. Julius, of Hamburg, crossed the ocean with the Reverend Charles Brooks, of Hingham, Massachusetts, and during the forty-one days of the passage from Liverpool to New York, described to him the Prussian system of elementary schools. Through Brooks's efforts Dr. Julius was invited to give an account of the Prussian system of education before the committee on education of the Massachusetts legislature, but "his delineations, though clear and judicious, were so brief as led to no action." What he had to say was printed by the State, and later on reprinted by New York State. There is no evidence that what Dr. Julius said had much influence, except with the Reverend Mr. Brooks, but upon him the Prussian idea of institutions for training teachers made a deep impression, as we shall see a little further on.

In 1839, in response to a request of Governor Campbell of Virginia, Dr. Benjamin F. Smith, of Danville, Virginia, who had lived in Prussia and was familiar with the work of Russell, Stowe, and Cousin, prepared a *Report* on the Prussian School System which was submitted to the Virginia legislature by the Governor in support of his recommendation for action as to education. Dr. Smith based his *Report* "on notes taken on the spot, and the observations of others under similar circumstances, particularly Professor Stowe of Cincinnati." Dr. Smith's *Report* was a significant document (**R. 201**), and deserves to rank with the other early American reports on European school systems. In particular, he attempted to apply the Prussian educational principles to the needs of an American republican State. His recommendations as to Virginia were sound, but the legislature was not stimulated to action.

Mann's Famous Seventh Report. In 1843 Horace Mann spent some months visiting schools in Great Britain, Belgium, Holland, the German States, and France, and on his return devoted his *Seventh Report* (1843), a report of nearly two hundred pages, to a description and appraisal of what he had seen,[1] but with particular reference to

---

[1] Of this *Report* Hinsdale writes:

"Read half a century after it was written, the *Seventh Report* impresses the reader as being the work of an open-minded man, who is making a hurried examination of educational institutions that were before known to him only at second hand. The matter is copious; facts and ideas fairly crowd the pages. The writer is evidently anxious to discover and report the e ct truth. He wants to show his countrymen the schools just as he sees them. He has no prejudices against things that are foreign. The writer not only has a first-hand interest in the subject, but is also conscious that he is writing things new and strange to his audience.... We are so familiar with these things now that we may

the studies taught, classification of pupils, methods of teaching, teachers, discipline, and the training of teachers (**R. 202**).

Mr. Mann ranked the schools of the different countries he visited in the following order: Prussia, Saxony, the western and southern German States, Holland, Scotland, Ireland, France, Belgium, and, lowest of all, England. The lack of a national system of education in England, in which the whole people participated, he felt was full of admonition to the people of Massachusetts, as it was a condition toward which they were drifting before the work of Carter and the organization of the State Board of Education. The schools of the German States, with their Pestalozzian methods and subject-matter, trained and well-informed teachers, oral instruction, mild discipline, class organization, normal schools for teachers, and intelligent supervision, particularly won his enthusiastic approval. "There are many things abroad which we at home should do well to imitate," he wrote, "things, some of which are here as yet matters of speculation and theory, but which, there, have long been in operation and are now producing a harvest of rich and abundant blessings." [1]

His controversy with the Boston schoolmasters. This *Report* might have exerted no greater influence than other previous *Reports*, and possibly even less, had it not been the last straw to the Boston school principals, many of whom had appropriated to themselves the Secretary's previous sharp criticism of school conditions in Massachusetts. There had been no comparisons made in the *Report* between the schools of Massachusetts and those of Prussia and Saxony, or of Boston with Hamburg or Dresden, but the Boston masters, many of whom shared the opposition that the creation of the State Board of Education had awakened, and stung by such expressions in the *Report* as "ignorance of teachers," and "sleepy supervision," felt called upon to attack the *Report* in a very personal and offensive manner. A committee of the Principals' Association accordingly issued a book of 144 pages, attacking and replying to the *Report* of Mr. Mann. Two months later Mr. Mann replied, in a volume of

wonder at Mr. Mann's enthusiasm over them; but we must remember that a half century has wrought great changes in American schools, changes that in some measure have grown out of the very document we are reading." (*Horace Mann*, p. 171.)

[1] "Mr. Mann was never happier than when, before an audience or at a writing table, he set himself to deal with some great human question — a question that involved politics, education, morality, and religion; and in the impressive review of the Old and New Worlds, with which the *Seventh Report* closes, he is seen at his best." (Hinsdale, B. A. *Horace Mann*, p. 174.)

176 pages, in which he not only vindicated himself and what he had written, and pointed out the difficulties with which he had to contend arising from unintelligent criticism, but, feeling that the attack on him had been unprovoked and uncalled for, he retaliated on his assailants with terrible severity. Though he objected to severe punishment for children, he apparently had no objection to giving a sound drubbing to a body of schoolmasters. Some of the masters later replied to Mr. Mann's reply, and he again responded to them in kind. This ended the controversy, public opinion being too thoroughly against the schoolmasters to warrant its further continuance (**R. 129**).

The result of this unexpected public debate was to attract very much more attention to Mr. Mann's *Seventh Report* than would otherwise have been given to it, to fix the attention of the public generally on the need for educational improvement, and to add to Mr. Mann's importance in the history of American education. In particular it gave support to the recently established normal schools, and to the efforts of a few to improve instruction by the adoption of a better classification of pupils and Pestalozzian methods and subject-matter. The result was that Mr. Mann's report on European school practices proved to be the most influential of all the *Reports* on education in Europe.

The Fellenberg manual-labor movement. The one European idea which we did adopt almost bodily, because we had no previous development of the kind, and because we found it so well suited to early democratic conditions among a people of little wealth, was the Pestalozzian idea, worked out by Fellenberg and his followers at Hofwyl, in Switzerland, of combining manual labor with schooling. Early in our national history the interest in farming was strong, the first farmers' journals were established, and there soon arose a demand for special schools for farmers' sons. The advantages, both pecuniary and educational, of combining schooling and farming made a strong appeal in the days when money was scarce and opportunities limited, and such schools, drawing their inspiration from the very successful school of Fellenberg, were founded first in Connecticut in 1819, Maine in 1821, Massachusetts in 1824, Kentucky in 1826, New York in 1827, Pennsylvania (**R. 203**) in 1829, New Jersey in 1830, Virginia in 1831, Georgia (**R. 204**) and Tennessee in 1832, and North Carolina in 1834. The purpose in each was to unite training in agriculture with the studies of the school, and thus give to farmers' boys a double type of training. The idea was soon extended to the rapidly rising mechanical pursuits, and manual-labor institutions of a mechanical type also arose. The Oneida School of Science and Industry,[1] the Genesee Manual-Labor School, the Aurora Manual-Labor Seminary, and the Rensselaer School (page 277), all in New York (**R. 171**), and the Worcester Manual-Labor High School in Massachusetts, were among the most important of these early institutions. The Andover Theological Seminary also adopted the plan, and by 1835 the manual-labor-school idea had been tried in a dozen States, extending from Maine to Illinois. Many of the institutions thus founded became colleges later on, as, for example: the Rensselaer and Worcester schools, both of which evolved into Polytechnic Institutes; Western Reserve College (**R. 163**), and the Institute that later evolved into Oberlin College,[2] in Ohio (**R. 164**); the Indiana Baptist Manual-Labor Institute, which later became Franklin College; the Wabash Manual-Labor Seminary, in Indiana, which later became Wabash College; the Knox Manual-Labor College, in Illinois, which later became Knox College; the Virginia Baptist Seminary, which later became Richmond College; and Davidson College and Wake Forest College in North Carolina. In 1831 the short-lived "Manual Labor Society for Promoting Manual Labor in Literary Institutions" was formed in New York to promote the idea.[3] This Society also added gymnastics to its program, and

[1] The following note relating to this school appeared in the *Annals of Education*, of February, 1831:

"The Oneida Institute is established at Whitesborough, N.Y., and is a Manual Labour Seminary. Forty-two young men earned, during the year, a sum equal to the amount of their board, which, at a little more than a dollar a week, amounts to $2000. All the other expenses for instruction, room-rent, fuel, and contingencies, amount to $28 a year. The accommodations now are limited, and it is said in the Report of the Trustees that five hundred applicants, during the year, were refused admission for want of room. The Trustees now propose erecting buildings to accommodate one hundred pupils."

[2] "We have lately received a notice of another institution with the same general object in view, in a select colony about to be established under the name of Oberlin, in Lorain County, Ohio. It is intended, ultimately, to embrace all grades of instruction from the infant school to the theological seminary, with the great object of preparing teachers and pastors for the great basin of the Mississippi. Its plan is founded on sound principles of education. It is also to embrace the plan of manual labor, and from the favorable circumstances of its situation and privileges, its founders feel themselves authorized to state that a donation of $150, expended in establishing the literary and manual labor departments, will secure the education of one student annually for active usefulness, without any more labor than his own welfare demands." (*American Annals of Education*, September, 1833, p. 429.)

[3] In June, 1831, an enthusiastic meeting of manual-labor advocates was held in New York, and the Society for Promoting Manual Labor in Literary Institutions was formed.

the early recognition of the value of physical training in the schools of the United States is in part due to the interest awakened in it by the work of this Society. In 1833 the governor of Indiana recommended to the legislature the establishment of manual-labor academies to train teachers for the schools of the State, and in 1836 a resolution was offered in the United States Senate proposing "a grant of public lands to one or more colleges in each of the new States for educating the poor upon the manual-labor system."

While the manual-labor idea awakened much interest for a time (**R. 205**), it was, however, short-lived in this country. It was at its height about 1830, but the movement soon collapsed. The rise of cities and wealth and social classes was against the idea, and the opening up of cheap and rich farms to the westward, with the change of the East from agriculture to manufacturing, turned the agricultural aspect of the movement aside for a generation. When it reappeared again in the Central West it came in the form of a new demand for colleges to teach agriculture and mechanic arts, but with the manual-labor idea omitted.

General result of these foreign influences. The general result of these various observations by travelers and official *Reports*, extending over nearly a quarter of a century in time; and the work of the new educational journals, particularly the publication work of Henry Barnard; was to give to American educators some knowledge of different and better school organizations elsewhere. In particular they gave strong support to the movement, already well under way, to organize the many local school systems into state school systems, subjecting them to state oversight and control; further stimulated the movement, already well begun, to grade and classify the schools in a more satisfactory manner, and to reduce class size to a more workable unit; helped to inaugurate a movement for the introduction of Pestalozzian methods to replace the wasteful individual and the mechanical Lancastrian plans, which had for so long been in use; and gave material assistance to the few leaders in Massachusetts and New York who were urging the establishment by the State of professional training for teachers for the educational service. The distinctively state school organization provided for in the Michigan

Theodore J. Weld, who had been connected with the Oneida Manual-Labor Institute, was appointed general agent for the Society, and he made a tour in the interests of the plan, but without success. Practical tests of the plan proved it much less satisfactory than its advocates claimed, and the promotion movement soon collapsed.

constitution of 1835, and the creation of the first state normal schools in the United States in Massachusetts, in 1838, are in part directly traceable to the influence of German practice, as described in these *Reports*. The one idea we for a time tried to copy and adapt to our needs was the Fellenberg manual-labor school for combining instruction in agriculture with the study of books. The later introduction of a form of Pestalozzian procedure into our normal schools and city school systems, and later into all our schools, to which we turn in a subsequent chapter, also is traceable in part to the interest awakened in better classroom practice by the descriptions of Pestalozzian instruction in other lands.

That we at this time adopted the German *Volksschule*, as has occasionally been asserted, an examination of the evidence will show was hardly the case. Not only did we not adopt its curriculum, or spirit, or method of instruction, but we did not adopt even the Prussian graded system. The *Volksschule* is a definite eight-year school, an end in itself and leading to the continuation school, while we worked out and have ever since retained seven-year, eight-year, and nine-year elementary schools, in different parts of the United States, each leading directly to the secondary school above. That the elementary school we developed was in general an eight-year school, as in the German *Volksschule*, was due to the school age of children and to a perfectly natural native development, rather than to any copying of foreign models. Our own development had been proceeding naturally and steadily toward the lines we eventually followed, long before we knew of Prussian work. The great thing we got from the study of Prussian schools was not a borrowing or imitation of any part or feature, but rather a marked stimulus to a further and faster development along lines which were already well under way. Even the better grading of pupils in smaller class groups, as described by Mann and put into effect first by Philbrick at the Quincy School in Boston, was but a "next step" in a purely native development.

QUESTIONS FOR DISCUSSION

1. Explain why we remained isolated educationally for so long.
2. Is there any evidence that the common tendency of new democracies to reject world experience and knowledge influenced us also?
3. State the essential defects in the educational plan of Rousseau.

4. State the change in the nature of the instruction from that of the church schools to that of Pestalozzi.
5. Compare Pestalozzi's ideas as to child development with modern ideas.
6. Explain the educational significance of "self-activity," "sense impression," and "harmonious development."
7. How far was Pestalozzi right as to the power of education to give men intellectual and moral freedom?
8. What do you understand Pestalozzi to have meant by "the development of the faculties"?
9. State how the work of Pestalozzi was important in showing the world how to deal with orphans and defectives.
10. Show how the germs of agricultural and technical education lay in the work of Fellenberg.
11. Contrast the German and the American school systems, as shown in the figures on pages 273 and 352.
12. How do you explain the fact that the Germans got the spirit of Pestalozzi's work so much better than did the English?
13. Show why Neef influenced American development so little.
14. Point out the Prussian influences and characteristics in the early organization of education in Michigan.
15. How do you explain the failure of Stowe's report to exert a greater influence on practice in Ohio? Elsewhere?
16. How do you explain our failure to take up Pestalozzian ideas in instruction more rapidly?
17. Explain the reasons for the popularity of the manual-labor idea, about 1825 to 1830, and its failure to maintain this popularity.

SELECTED READINGS

In the accompanying volume of *Readings* the following selections, related to the subject matter of this chapter, are reproduced:

194. Statute: The University of Michigania.
*195. Pestalozzi: Explanation of His Work.
*196. Mayo: On Pestalozzi.
*197. Griscom: A Visit to Pestalozzi at Yverdon.
*198. Woodbridge: An Estimate of Pestalozzi's Work.
199. Cousin: Report on Education in Prussia.
*200. Stowe: Report on Elementary Education in Europe.
*201. Smith: Report on Education in Prussia.
*202. Mann: Seventh Report.
*203. Report: The Manual Labor Academy of Pennsylvania.
*204. Annals: Manual Labor Schools in Georgia.
*205. Annals: Editorial on Manual Labor Schools.

QUESTIONS ON THE READINGS

1. State, in a few words, the type of institution created (**194**) for Michigan, in 1817.
2. Just what did Pestalozzi attempt (**195**) to accomplish?

3. What do the tributes of Mayo (**196**) and Woodbridge (**199**) reveal as to the character of Pestalozzi, and his influence?
4. Compare the accounts as to purpose and instruction as given by Pestalozzi (**195**) and Griscom (**197**).
5. Just what did Cousin recommend (**199**) as to (*a*) control and administration, and (*b*) schools to be created?
6. Assuming that Stowe was right as to applicability to Ohio (**200**), how do you explain the very long delay in putting such a plan into effect?
7. What did Smith (**201**) regard as the strong points of European schools?
8. Have we today, as a Nation, conceived of education as did Mann (**202**) in his summary? Justify your answer.
9. As you read the descriptions of the manual-labor schools (**203, 204, 205**), what is your impression of the type of education they offered?

TOPICS FOR INVESTIGATION AND REPORT

1. Character of early educational journalism.
   a. *The Academician.*
   b. Russell's *American Journal.*
   c. Woodbridge's *Annals.*
   d. Mann's *Common School Journal.*
   e. Barnard's *Connecticut School Journal.*
   f. Barnard's *American Journal of Education.*
2. The educational contributions of Pestalozzi.
3. Fellenberg's school at Hofwyl. (Barnard.)
4. *Leonard and Gertrude.* Read and characterize.
5. The English system of Object Teaching.
6. The Manual Labor idea in the United States. (Anderson; Barnard; Monroe.)
7. Mr. Mann's *Seventh Report.*
8. Pestalozzi Institute at Yverdon.
9. Cousin's *Report*, and its influence in America.
10. Griscom's *A Year in Europe.*
11. Woodbridge's *Letters.*
12. Stowe's *Report on Education in Europe.*
13. Bache's *Report on Education in Europe.*
14. Beginnings of Technical Education in the United States. (Anderson; Bennett.)
15. Work of Joseph Neef in America.

SELECTED REFERENCES

*Anderson, L. F. *Pestalozzi.* New York, 1932.
   A very good statement of his work and influence.

*Anderson, L. F. "The Manual Labor School Movement"; in *Educational Review*, vol. XLVI; pp. 369–88. (Nov., 1913.)
   A very good historical article on the Fellenberg movement in the United States.

*Arrowood, C. F. *Thomas Jefferson and Education in a Republic.* 184 pp. New York, 1930.

An appraisal of his services, and reproductions from his educational writings.

Barnard, Henry, Editor. *The American Journal of Education.* 31 vols. Consult *Analytical Index* to; 128 pp. Published by United States Bureau of Education, Washington, 1892.

*Barnard, Henry. *National Education in Europe, 1854.* C. W. Bardeen, Syracuse.

Reprints of extracts from many of the early Reports.

*Barnard, Henry. *Pestalozzi and his Educational System.* 745 pp. C. W. Bardeen, Syracuse, 1906.

His life, educational principles, and methods, with sketches of several of his assistants. A standard volume of source material regarding the work of Pestalozzi and the Pestalozzian movement, both in Europe and America.

Bennett, Chas. A. *History of Manual and Industrial Education up to 1870.* 461 pp. Peoria, 1916.

A good account, dealing with early beginnings.

Davis, S. E. *Educational Periodicals during the 19th Century.* Bulletin 28, 1919, U.S. Bureau of Education.

Early influences, and descriptive list, arranged chronologically.

Good, H. G. "Early Educational Legislation in Ohio"; in *School and Society*, vol. x, pp. 597–604. (Nov. 22, 1919.)

Considers Prussian influence on early Ohio legislation.

Griscom, John. "Fellenberg and Hofwyl"; in *Barnard's Journal*, vol. XXXI, pp. 269–80.

An extract from Griscom's *A Year in Europe.*

*Guimps, Roger de. *Pestalozzi; his Aim and Work.* 320 pp. C. W. Bardeen, Syracuse, 1894.

A standard biography, written in a very interesting style, and from the personal point of view.

*Hinsdale, B. A. "Notes on the History of Foreign Influence upon Education in the United States"; in *Report of the United States Commissioner of Education*, 1897–98, vol. I, pp. 591–629.

Very good on English, French, and German influence, and contains much valuable material.

*Holman, H. *Pestalozzi, his Life and Work.* New York, 1908.

A very useful volume for the general student.

Hoyt, C. O., and Ford, C. *John D. Pierce; A Study of Education in the Northwest.* 162 pp. Ypsilanti, Mich., 1905.

Work of Pierce and Crary, and the founding of the Michigan public school system.

Jones, A. J. "Are our Schools Prussian in Origin?" in *Educational Review*, vol. LVI, pp. 271–93. (Nov., 1918.)

Concludes that Prussian influences were very important after 1830.

*Knight, Edgar W. *Reports on European Education.* New York, 1930.

Descriptive of early European influences, and contains much source material.

*Krüsi, Hermann, Jr. *Life and Work of Pestalozzi.* 248 pp. 1875.

A valuable work, by the Oswego teacher.

*Monroe, Paul. *Cyclopedia of Education.* The Macmillan Co., New York, 1911–13.

The following articles are specially important:
1. "Fellenberg, P. E."; vol. II, pp. 590–91.
2. "Pestalozzi, J. H."; vol. IV, pp. 655–59.

*Monroe-Judd Controversy, as to Prussian origin:
1. Judd: "Prussia and Our Schools"; in *New Republic*, April 20, 1918. (Vol. XIV.)
2. Monroe: "Further Consideration of Prussia and Our Schools," in *School and Society*, June 15, 1918. (Vol. VII.)
3. Judd: "Shall We Continue to Imitate Prussia?"; in *School and Society*, June 29, 1918. (Vol. VIII.)
4. Monroe: Shall We Continue to Advocate Reforms by False Arguments?" in *School and Society*, Sept. 7, 1918. (Vol. VIII.)

A somewhat partisan controversy, Judd contending that there is a strong Prussian origin, and Monroe that our schools are a native product. The article by Good favors Monroe, and the article by Jones favors Judd's point of view.

*Parker, S. C. *History of Modern Elementary Education.* 506 pp. Boston, 1912.

Chapter XIII is very good on the Pestalozzian movement in Europe and America, and Chapter XIV on Pestalozzian industrial education for juvenile reform.

*Pestalozzi, J. H. *Leonard and Gertrude.* Translated and abridged by Eva Channing. 181 pp. Boston, 1888.

A charming story; one which every teacher ought to read.

Pestalozzi, J. H. *How Gertrude Teaches her Children.* 256 pp. Syracuse, 1894.

This volume contains the essentials of Pestalozzi's ideas and methods, and shows how his methods were developed. Written in a somewhat uninteresting style.

Pine, John. "The Origin of the University of the State of New York"; in *Educational Review*, vol. XXXVII, pp. 284–92. (March, 1909.)

Pinloche, A. *Pestalozzi and the Foundation of the Modern Elementary School.* 306 pp. New York, 1901.

A rather technical evaluation of his work and influence.

*Quick, R. H. *Essays on Educational Reformers.* 566 pp. 2d revised edition. New York, 1890.

Contains a very well-written chapter on Pestalozzi and his ideas.

Snedden, D. S. *American Juvenile Reform Schools.* 206 pp. Teachers College Contributions to Education, No. 12, New York, 1907.

Contains a brief historical statement, and an excellent account of recent tendencies.

Ten Brook, Andrew. *American State Universities and the University of Michigan.* 410 pp. Cincinnati, 1875.

Good on early conditions as to culture and education in the West, and on the beginnings of the University of Michigan.

CHAPTER XI

THE BEGINNINGS OF TEACHER–TRAINING

I. THE RISE OF THE NORMAL SCHOOL

Beginnings of the teacher-training idea. The first training class for teachers organized in the world was a small local school organized by Father Démia, at Lyons, France, in 1672. Stimulated into activity by the results of the Protestant Revolts, he had begun schools in his parish to teach reading and the catechism to the children of his parishioners. Not being satisfied with the volunteer teachers he could obtain, he organized them into a class that he might impart to them the ideas he had as to teaching. The first real normal school was that founded at Rheims, France, in 1685, by Abbé de la Salle, to educate and train teachers for the schools of the order he had founded — "The Brothers of the Christian Schools" — to give free religious primary education to the children of the working classes of France. He later founded a second school of the kind in Paris, and called each institution a "Seminary for Schoolmasters." In addition to imparting a general education of the type of the time and a thorough grounding in religion, his student teachers were trained to teach in practice-schools, under the direction of experienced teachers.

The beginning of teacher-training in German lands was Francke's *Seminarium Praeceptorum*, established at Halle, Prussia, in 1697. In 1738 Julius Hecker, one of Francke's teachers, established the first regular seminary for teachers in Prussia, and in 1748 he established a private *Lehrerseminar* in Berlin. In these two institutions he first showed the German people the possibilities of special training for teachers. Between 1750 and 1794 a dozen seminaries for the training of elementary-school teachers were established in Prussia and other German States. By the close of the eighteenth century there were about thirty institutions, of all kinds, in the different German States which had added teacher-training to their academic work. It was not, however, until 1809 that the Prussian Government established normal schools to train teachers for its elementary or peoples' schools. The work of Pestalozzi (page 344) had arrested the attention of the government, and after the crushing blow delivered by Napoleon the leaders of the State turned to public education as a means of national regeneration. To prepare teachers for the work they created the best Teachers' Seminaries the world had so far known.

In 1808, as a part of the reorganization of higher education in France by Napoleon, the *École Normale Supérieure* (higher normal school) of France was created, and between 1831 and 1833 thirty new normal schools were established by the new French government. Pestalozzi had trained teachers in his methods of instruction at Burgdorf and Yverdon, from 1800 to 1825, but the Swiss did little with the idea until later. Both the Lancastrian and the Bell monitorial systems of education in England, which developed about the beginning of the nineteenth century, had trained their monitors for teachers, but the first "Training College" for teachers in England, established to impart a modified type of Pestalozzian method, dates from 1835.

Of all this development, excepting the work of Pestalozzi, we in America were ignorant until about 1830. By that time we were so well on the way toward the creation of native American training schools that the knowledge of what Prussia and France had done, which came in then through the *Letters* of Woodbridge and the *Reports* of Bache, Cousin, Julius, and Stowe (Chapter X), merely stimulated a few enthusiastic workers to help carry more rapidly into effect the establishment of the first training schools for American teachers.

The Independent American development. As early as the founding of Franklin's *Academy* at Philadelphia (page 246) which began instruction in 1751, one of the purposes specified in its establishment was "that others of the lesser sort might be trained as teachers" (**R. 144**). In an article in the *Massachusetts Magazine*, for June, 1789, on "The Importance of Studying the English Language Grammatically," the author recommends the establishment of institutions to prepare "young gentlemen for schoolkeeping." In a commencement address at Yale College, in 1816, on "The State of Education in Connecticut," by Denison Olmstead, a plan for "an academy for schoolmasters" was outlined and urged, to prepare intending teachers for "the organization and government of a school."

REV. SAMUEL R. HALL
(1795–1877)
Principal of the First Private
Normal School
Concord, Vt.

CYRUS PEIRCE
(1790–1860)
Principal of the First American
State Normal School
Lexington, Mass.

THE FIRST NORMAL SCHOOL PRINCIPALS IN THE UNITED STATES

In 1818 a Lancastrian Model School was established in New York City, and Governor Clinton first called the attention of the Legislature of New York to the desirability of preparing teachers for the common schools (**R. 213**).   As early as 1820 James G. Carter (page 221), often called the "Father of the Massachusetts School System and of Normal Schools," published a pamphlet in which he suggested "an institution for the training of teachers."   In 1823 two papers appeared, one by William Russell,[1] and the other by Professor James L. Kingsley of Yale,[2] both of which urged the establishment of such schools.   In 1825 two more papers appeared, one by James G. Carter and the other by T. H. Gallaudet (**R. 206**), both of which outlined plans for state institutions to train teachers for the schools.   To these four papers Mr. Barnard traces much of the early interest in teacher-training in the United States.   In 1825, also, Walter R. Johnson, of Germantown, Pennsylvania, in a pamphlet urged the establishment of schools similar to those in Prussia to train teachers, and the acting president of the College of New Jersey, in an address, made the same recommendation.[3]   During 1824–25 Carter published numerous newspaper articles[4] and public appeals for the establishment of a teacher-training institution (**R. 207**).   In 1827 he showed his faith in such schools by opening one himself, at Lancaster, Massachusetts, and petitioning the legislature of the State for aid.   This was probably the second school of its kind in America.   Carter definitely anticipated the general structure of the present-day normal school, as he stressed the desirability of experimental and practice facilities as well as academic training.

[1] Russell, then a teacher in an academy at New Haven, issued a pamphlet in which he held that the instructors in the common schools too often barely knew enough "to keep the teacher at a decent distance from his scholars."   He proposed a seminary for teachers, with certification on graduation, and held that "the effects of such an improvement on education seem almost incalculable."

[2] Kingsley's article was printed in the *North American Review*.   He urged that teachers be trained to give new vigor to the schools, and declared that the teachers had little knowledge beyond what they were called upon to teach.   The prevailing method of employment he held to be "a very imperfect check on the intrusion of ignorance."

[3] "We have our theological seminaries" he said, "our medical and law schools, which receive the graduates of our college and fit them for their prospective professions, and whenever the profession of teaching shall be duly honored and appreciated, it is not doubted but that it will receive similar attention and be favoured with equal advantages."

[4] These appeared in the *Boston Patriot*, and attracted much attention.   He pointed out the waste caused by poorly prepared teachers, held that mere knowledge was no guarantee of the ability to impart it, and contended that schools to prepare prospective teachers to teach should be established and maintained by the State as a part of the state school system.

In 1829, William Woodbridge, then just returned from four years in Europe, was planning, with Gallaudet, the establishment of a teachers' seminary, after the Prussian model, in Hartford. While the seminary did not materialize, Woodbridge never lost interest in the idea, and in 1831, as editor of the newly established *Annals*, he remarked that "in those of the countries of Europe where education has taken its rank as a science, it is almost as singular to question the importance of a preparatory seminary for teachers, as of a medical school for physicians."

From this time on many articles, widely scattered in place of publication, appeared urging that something be done by the States in the matter,[1] various scattered efforts (**R. 212 a-e**) were made to begin teacher-training, and here and there legislative proposals [2] for the creation of some type of school to train teachers appeared.[3] Some of the early manual-labor seminaries also, for a time, made efforts to train teachers for the schools.[4] The general enlightenment of the people having been conceived as essential to the

[1] After about 1830 we find numerous references to the need of teacher-training in the literature of the day, as, for example, the following resolution adopted by the State Convention of Teachers and Friends of Education, held at Utica, New York, in January, 1831.

"*Resolved:* That this Convention recommend to the teachers and principals of academies, high schools, and other institutions of the same rank, the establishment of Departments for qualifying Teachers, and supplying the same with suitable apparatus."

[2] By a resolution of the House of Representatives of the State of Pennsylvania, adopted in December, 1832, the Committee on Education of that body was directed to inquire into the expediency of establishing, at the expense of the State, a Manual Labor Academy for the instruction of teachers for the public schools. Later the Committee recommended the adoption of the plan, claiming that the expense of education could thereby be reduced one half. An act was submitted to establish such a school, near Harrisburg, to accommodate 200 pupils, and provide a two-year course, for which the graduates were to be obligated to teach at least one year in the schools of the State. No legislative action was taken on the proposal, however.

[3] In 1832, President Joseph Caldwell, of the University of North Carolina, in a pamphlet entitled *Letters on Popular Education, Addressed to the People of North Carolina*, strongly advocated "an institution for preparing schoolmasters for their profession, upon the most improved methods of instruction," and contended that teaching was "an act not to be comprehended and established in the habits of an individual without much time, education, and discipline."

In 1838, and again in 1839, the Directors of the North Carolina Literary Fund urged the legislature to establish a normal school to train teachers.

[4] The original object of the Rensselaer School, at Troy, New York, founded in 1825 by the Honorable Stephen Van Rensselaer, and for some time largely supported by him, was stated in the act of incorporation to be "to qualify teachers for instructing youth in villages and common-school districts, belonging to the class of farmers and mechanics, by lectures or otherwise, in the application of the most important principles of experimental chemistry, natural history, natural philosophy, and practical mathematics, to agriculture, domestic economy, the arts, and manufactures, thus giving instruction in the application of science to the common purposes of life." After a decade the teacher-training aspect of its work was given up.

protection and preservation of republican institutions, it was n\
felt to be important, as Governor Clinton expressed it, that th\
"mind and morals of the rising and perhaps the destinies of all future
generations, be not entrusted to the guardianship of incompetence."

Our first teacher-training school. Excepting only the Lancastrian
Model Schools (1818), the first teacher-training school in America
was established privately, in 1823, by the Reverend Samuel R. Hall,
who opened a tuition school for training teachers at Concord,
Vermont,[1] as an adjunct to his ministerial duties (**R. 209**). He was
led to do this by reason of his own observation and experience as to
the need for such a school.[2] This he continued there until 1830; at
Andover, Massachusetts, until 1837; and at Plymouth, New Hampshire, until 1840 (**R. 208**). He offered a three years' course (**R. 210**),
based on a common-school education, which reviewed the common-
school branches; studied much mathematics, some book chemistry
and natural philosophy, logic, astronomy, evidences of Christianity,
moral and intellectual philosophy; and, in the third term of the third
year, took up a new study which he called the "Art of Teaching."
Observation of teaching was offered in the school, and practice in
teaching was obtained by teaching during the winter in the rural
schools. It was the typical academy training of the time, with the
Art of Teaching added. Without a professional book to guide him,

[1] One hundred years afterward the State of Vermont erected a stone shaft on the site
of this first normal school, bearing a bronze tablet which reads:

THE STATE OF VERMONT
Erects this Tablet August 15, 1923
on the site of the
FIRST NORMAL SCHOOL IN AMERICA
Opened March 11, 1823, by its Founder
REVEREND SAMUEL READ HALL, LL.D.
Originator of America's System
of Teacher Training
Author of the First Text-Book on Teaching
Published in America
Pioneer in the Use of the Blackboard
as a Schoolroom Appliance

[2] "The first public statements in this country in favor of a special course for training
teachers seem to have grown out of a study of conditions in the common schools, and they
began to be made before there was much evidence of foreign influence. The first course
offered in Massachusetts seems to have been planned deliberately for the purpose of meeting a definite need in the schools of that State, and without any thought of copying from
any European country. A comparison of this course with the German course most widely
advertised in this country fails to show any evidence of copying from Germany. The
people had become accustomed to the course offered in the academies, and the evidence
indicates that a modified form of it constituted the first course ever offered in this country
by a state institution for the training of teachers." (Napier, T. H. *Trends in Curricula
for Training Teachers*, p. 54.)

and relying only on his experience in teaching, Hall tried to tell his pupils how to organize and manage a school. To make clear his ideas he wrote out a series of *Lectures on Schoolkeeping*, which some friends induced him to publish. This appeared in 1829, and was the first professional book in English and intended primarily for teachers (see page 376) to be issued in America. It was a success from the first (**R. 211**), illustrating the rising professional interest of the time. The acting superintendent of common schools of New York ordered ten thousand copies of it for distribution throughout the State, and a committee on education in Kentucky recommended that the same be done for that State.

The academies begin teacher-training. The Lancastrian higher schools in New York and elsewhere had, by 1810, evolved classes for educating monitors as teachers, and as early as 1818 Governor De-Witt Clinton had called the attention of the legislature (**R. 213**) to the need of supplying the schools of New York State with trained monitorial teachers. After his return to the governorship he urged the legislature, in 1826, to establish "a seminary for the education of teachers in the monitorial system of instruction." In 1827, he recommended the creation of "a central school in each county for the education of teachers." Again, in 1828, he recommended the establishment of county monitorial high schools, "a measure so well calculated to raise the character of our schoolmasters and to double the power of our artisans by giving them a scientific education" (**R. 213**).

Still earlier (1821) the Board of Regents of the State of New York had declared that it was to the academies of the State "that we must look for a supply of teachers for the common school," and the committee of the legislature, to whom Governor Clinton's recommendations had been referred, thought as had the Regents (**R. 214**). The result was the New York Law of 1827, appropriating state aid [1] to the academies "to promote the education of teachers." In the *Annual Report* of the Regents for 1828 we find the statement that

the academies have become, in the opinion of the Regents, what it has always been desirable they should be, fit Seminaries for imparting in-

---

[1] The Law of 1827, however, did nothing more than increase the state fund for aiding schools, apparently assuming that "training of teachers" consisted chiefly in increased educational opportunity. The law left the training of teachers as it "had been before; it was still voluntary, incidental, and unorganized."

struction in the higher branches of English education, and especially for qualifying teachers of Common Schools.

In the *Report* for 1831 two academies report "Principles of Teaching" as a new subject of study, and by 1835 five were offering instruction in this new subject. In 1834 the New York Legislature enacted "the first law in this country making provision for the professional education of teachers for common schools" (**R. 214**). After providing for state aid to one academy in each of the eight judicial districts of the State, the law reads:

§ 2. The trustees of academies to which any distribution of money shall be made by virtue of this act shall cause the same to be expended in educating teachers of common schools in such manner and under such regulations as said Regents shall prescribe.

Excepting the Lancastrian monitorial schools, and the private schools of Hall and Carter, this was the first form of the normal-school idea in the United States. In this form the training of teachers was continued in New York State until the establishment of the first

FIG. 103. DAVID P. PAGE
(1810–48)

First Principal of the State Normal School at Albany, New York

State Normal School, at Albany, in 1844, with the young and vigorous David P. Page as principal.[1] The school met with deep and bitter opposition,[2] as had been the case in Massachusetts, and in 1849 teacher-training in the academies was re-established, and continued to exist in the high schools of the State until 1933.

[1] David Perkins Page (1810–48) was born in New Hampshire, and was graduated from Hampdon Academy. At nineteen he began teaching, and at twenty-two was elected vice-principal of the new high school at Newburyport, Massachusetts. He actively aided Mann in his work in Massachusetts, and when the first state normal school was created by New York he was selected as its principal on the recommendation of Mann and Barnard. His *Theory and Practice of Teaching*, published in 1847, became deservedly popular. By the end of the copyright period (1889) over 100,000 copies had been sold, and shortly thereafter new editions were issued by three American publishers.

[2] While the school survived, Page wore himself out in traveling about the State and explaining its purpose. "The newspapers ridiculed and denounced it. They invented all kinds of falsehoods about Mr. Page, and in many ways misrepresented the school and its work. The politicians were against it, and the teachers of the state had no love for the school or its Massachusetts principal." The legislature tried to abolish it, but Page's "speeches turned the tide, and public sentiment favored the school."

The training of teachers in the academies now became common everywhere. Among the older and more important ones, Phillips Andover, for example, introduced an English course primarily to train teachers in 1830, with the Reverend Samuel R. Hall as director, and many other New England academies did the same. To the south and westward also many academies added instruction intended primarily for teachers, and several offered instruction for teachers on the manual-labor part-time plan. In Indiana, Governor Noble, in 1833, recommended to the legislature, "that seminaries be fitted to instruct and prepare teachers," and suggested that state aid be granted to one or more such institutions "for the preparation of young men as teachers for the township schools on the manual labor system."

The training offered was almost entirely academic, as it was in the first state normal schools as well, there being as yet no professional body of knowledge to teach. There was as yet no organized psychology; child study had not been thought of; and there was no organized history of education, applied psychology, philosophy of education, or methodology of instruction.[1] Principles of teaching and school management, taught by lectures and almost entirely out of the personal experience of the principal of the school, was about all of professional instruction there was to give. This subject constituted one study, and the remainder of the time was given to reviews of the common-school subjects and to advanced academic studies. Hall's course at Andover (**R. 210**), from which Horace Mann drew many ideas and much in inspiration, was typical of the time.

Our first state normal schools. The publication of the Reports by Cousin (1835) and Stowe (1837), with their descriptions of the teacher-training seminaries of Prussia, together with the contact of Dr. Julius and the Reverend Charles Brooks (1835), united to give valuable support to the efforts of Carter, Mann, and a few others in Massachusetts who were laboring to inaugurate such schools there. Carter, in particular, had been at work on the idea for a decade and

[1] The first real history of education, that of Karl Georg von Raumer, did not appear in Germany until 1843, when the first two volumes were published, the third appearing in 1847, and the fourth in 1853. Barnard later translated and published much of this work for the benefit of American educators. The foundations of a new psychology were laid in Germany between 1850 and 1875. The first kindergarten in America was established in 1855, while Herbartian ideas as to the aim and method of education did not become known in Germany before about 1870 and in the United States before about 1885.

a half, and on his election to the legislature, in 1835, he began a reform campaign that resulted in the creation of the State Board of
Education in 1837 (see page 211), and the first American state
normal schools in 1838. The recently organized (1830) American
Institute of Instruction, which embraced in its membership the
educational leaders of New England, presented a strongly worded
petition (**R. 215**) to the Massachusetts legislature in 1837, urging
the immediate establishment of "a seminary for the instruction of
suitable teachers for our common schools,"
and this association ably backed Carter in
his fight. Though the law gave no name
to these new institutions, they soon settled
down to that of Normal Schools — a distinctively French term.

While Carter worked with the legislature, Brooks worked with the people, traveling over two thousand miles in his chaise
and at his own expense throughout Massachusetts,[1] during the years 1835–38, explaining the Prussian system of teacher-
training and the Massachusetts need for
such, and everywhere awakening interest
in the idea by his enthusiastic portrayal.
Finally a merchant of Boston, Mr. Edmund Dwight, authorized Mr. Mann to
say to the legislature that he personally

FIG. 104. THE
REVEREND CHARLES
BROOKS
(1795–1872)

Prominent in the establishment of the first State Normal
Schools.

would give $10,000 for the project, if the State of Massachusetts
would give a similar amount (**R. 216 a**). A bill to this effect was
put through by Carter, then chairman of the committee on education in the State Senate, and the new State Board of Education

---

[1] Of the Reverend Brooks' travels, the following, from the *Annals of Education* for February, 1837, is a typical note:

"A Convention of the friends of Common Education was held at Plymouth, Mass., on
the evenings of the sixth and seventh of December last. The first evening was spent in
hearing, from the Reverend Charles Brooks, of Hingham, an account of the Prussian system of instruction. The second evening was also spent by Mr. B. in pointing out the
application of the Prussian system of education to the 'Old Colony.' Mr. B. afterward
offered the following resolution, which was adopted, after spirited debate:

"'*Resolved*, That a committee of seven be appointed, who shall address a circular to
each town in the County, and the town of Cohasset, asking them to appoint each three
delegates, who shall meet in convention in Halifax, and devise methods of securing to
Plymouth County a Seminary for the education of Teachers.'"

was authorized to expend the money "in qualifying teachers for the common schools of Massachusetts" (**R. 216 b**). No schools were created and no plans were laid down, everything being left to Mr. Mann and the State Board of Education to decide. After mature deliberation it was determined not to follow the New York plan of aiding academies (**R. 214**), and particularly the monitorial plan of teacher-training, but instead to create special state schools for the purpose, as had been done in France and in German lands.

FIG. 105. WHERE THE FIRST STATE NORMAL SCHOOL IN
AMERICA OPENED

On July 3, 1839, the first state normal school in the United States was opened in the town hall at Lexington, Massachusetts, with one instructor, and three girl students.[1] At the close of the first quarter there were but twelve students, twenty-five at the close of the first year, at the end of three years there were but thirty-one, and at the end of seventeen years but thirty-five.[2] The course of instruction was one year in length, but could be extended to two years (**R. 217**).

[1] That night the new principal, Cyrus Pierce, wrote in his diary:
"Lexington, July 3rd, 1839. This day the Normal School, the first in the country, commenced. Three pupils — Misses Hawkins, Smith, and Damon — were examined by the Board of Visitors and admitted."

[2] In 1856, the attendance at the four schools then existing was reported as:

	MALES	FEMALES	TOTALS
1. Framingham	—	35	35
2. Westfield	18	90	108
3. Bridgewater	24	44	68
4. Salem	—	121	121

It was much the same as Hall's earlier one (**R. 210**), but the distinctive feature of the school was the addition of a small Model School, in which the students observed and taught.

The opening of this first school was not particularly auspicious. Ignorance, bigotry, and economy were arrayed against the undertaking. Few knew what such a school was to be. Many teachers regarded its creation as derogatory to them. Many academies did not especially welcome its competition. Not a note of congratulation welcomed the new principal [1] to his post. Only a few zealots in the cause of reform looked upon its opening with favor. Much depended on the new principal,[2] and of him Henry Barnard later wrote: "Had it not been for Mr. Cyrus Peirce, I considered that the cause of normal schools would have failed, or have been postponed for an indefinite period." As it was the new schools had to weather schoolmaster opposition and legislative storms for more than a decade before they became firmly established as parts of the school system of the State. Fortunately, the new schools had some strong friends, who rallied to their support (**R. 219**), and helped Mann win the battle for their preservation.

It is indeed fortunate that this new institution was created and its period of trial carried through in Massachusetts, under the care of so able an advocate and protector as Mr. Mann. Massachusetts was without doubt the only State in the Union where state normal schools could have been established at so early a date,[3] or where, if

---

[1] Cyrus Peirce (1790–1859) was a graduate of Harvard (1810), had served in the ministry for seven years, and then taught four years at Andover and nine years at Nantucket. He was selected by Horace Mann to head the new movement, and he proved to have qualifications even beyond Mr. Mann's expectations. "He not only knew how to teach with precision," wrote Mrs. Mann later, "but he evoked from his pupils such a force of conscience as insured thorough study and assimilation. When Mr. Mann first visited his school at Nantucket he was charmed by the evidence of power that the whole management and all the recitations of the school evinced."

[2] Writing of his work to Henry Barnard, in 1851, Cyrus Peirce said:

"You ask me what I aimed to accomplish and would aim to accomplish now, with my past experience before me, in a normal school. I answer briefly that it was my aim, and it would be my aim again, to make better teachers, and especially better teachers for our common schools... teachers who would know more of the nature of children, of youthful development, more of the subjects to be taught, and more of the methods of teaching them.... In short, I was desirous of putting our schools in the hands of those who would make them places in which children could learn, not only to read and write and spell and cipher, but where they would have all their faculties trained in such harmony as would result in the highest formation of character."

[3] Speaking at the semi-centennial celebration of the founding of the State Normal School at Worcester, on June 14, 1924, Professor Bagley well stated the nation-wide influence of Massachusetts' pioneer work when he said:

established, they would have been allowed to remain. Much, too, was due to Cyrus **Peirce**, this "Arnold of America," who put so much of his own life blood into the new undertaking (**R. 220**). From 1840, when the legislative attack [1] on the new schools was launched (**R. 219**), to March, 1842, when the State definitely adopted the new schools, was a trying time for all concerned. In April, 1842, in a pathetic letter to Mann (**R. 221**), Pierce, worn out with the work and the responsibility, begged to be released.

FIG. 106. THE FIRST STATE NORMAL SCHOOL BUILDING
IN AMERICA

At Bridgewater, Massachusetts. Dedicated by Horace Mann, in 1846.

On September 5th, 1839, the State Board of Education opened another normal school at Barre,[2] and a third at Bridgewater, in 1840.

"What the state normal schools have done for Massachusetts, they have done in part for other States. But only in part. The record of this Commonwealth, I am sure, has never been surpassed. In the record of the Massachusetts public schools is to be found the clearest and most convincing evidence of the fundamental service that good normal schools may render the state and the nation."

[1] "The period from 1839 to 1845 may well be termed the period of experiment and controversy. Opponents of both the State Board of Education and the normal schools were numerous and active. Two committee reports recommending the abolition of both the Board and the normal schools were made to the General Court in 1840, the first by a committee on retrenchment and the second by the Committee on Education. Debate on these reports brought to the legislature numerous memorials in defense of normal schools and the Board (**R. 219**). At the end of the probationary three-year period the success of the normal schools, though moderate, had been such that the legislature appropriated $6000 annually to carry them on for another three-year period." (Wright, Frank W., in *Elementary School Journal*, January, 1930.)

[2] The amount of money available was so inadequate for the purpose that the Board appealed to the towns to co-operate, asking them to provide buildings and maintenance, while the Board paid salaries. Charles Brooks solicited funds for Bridgewater, and the school was located there permanently. Lexington was moved to West Newton in 1844, and then to Framingham in 1849, where it has since remained. Barre moved to Westfield in 1846, where it also has since been located. In 1854, Salem donated a site and building for a fourth school.

Speaking at the dedication of the first building for normal-school purposes erected in the United States, at Bridgewater, in 1846, Mr. Mann revealed (**R. 222**) the deep interest he felt in the establishment of normal schools.

Further development and change in character.   The new idea as embodied in these schools awakened deep interest on the part of the leading educators of the time, and in 1852 a petition was submitted to Congress asking that it endow, from the proceeds of the public lands, "one Free Normal School for the education of Female Teachers in every State of the Union" (**R. 223**), but Congress was not interested and nothing came of the proposal.   The matter was thus left to each State, to handle as it saw fit.   The States which established normal schools, before 1860, and their order of establishment were:

1839. Massachusetts (1st).	1854. Massachusetts (4th).
1839. Massachusetts (2d).	1854. Rhode Island.
1840. Massachusetts (3d).	1855. New Jersey.
1844. New York.	1857. Illinois.
1849. Connecticut.	1859. Pennsylvania.
1849. Michigan.	1860. Minnesota.

The city of St. Louis also, in 1857, established a city normal school, the first of its kind in the United States.   The year 1860 thus found the United States with twelve state and one city normal schools, in ten States (see map, page 324), and six private schools [1] organized for the same purpose.   By 1865 the number had increased to twenty-two state schools,[2] and thereafter, for reasons which we will next describe, the development of both public and private normal schools was rapid.   Their development, compared with the growth of the United States, is shown in Figure 107.   Teacher-training also

[1] One of the earliest, as well as one of the most important of these private normal schools was the one founded in 1855 at Lebanon, Ohio, by Alfred Holbrook (1816–1909), son of Josiah Holbrook, founder of the Lyceum Movement.   The institution was chartered in 1855 as the South Western Ohio Normal School, in 1870 the name was changed to National Normal School, and in 1881 to National Normal University.   It opened with 257 students the first year, and came to enroll 2000 a year.   Holbrook was principal for fifty years, and the school was largely an expression of his personality.   Many noted later leaders got their start at Lebanon.   Its great period was between about 1880 and 1895.

[2] The entrance requirements of the early state normal schools were very simple, as the following extract from the 1873 catalogue of the Indiana State Normal School will show:

"Pupils, if females, must be sixteen years of age; if males, eighteen.   If residents of Indiana, they must promise to teach, if practicable, in the common schools of the state a period equal to twice that spent as pupils in the Normal School.   They must pass a fair examination in reading, spelling, geography, and in arithmetic through percentage.   They must write a legible hand, and be able to analyze and parse simple sentences."

changed markedly in character, after about 1860, with the rise of a new methodology of instruction, which we shall next describe.

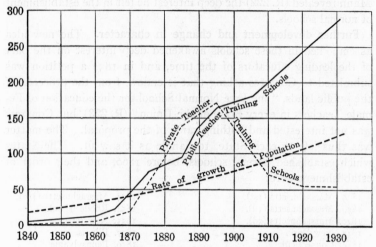

FIG. 107. GROWTH OF PUBLIC AND PRIVATE NORMAL
SCHOOLS IN THE UNITED STATES

High-school training classes not included.

II. THE INTRODUCTION OF PESTALOZZIAN METHODS

Early beginnings. Although much had been made of the new Pestalozzian procedures in German lands and in England, and here and there some enthusiast for the new ideas had tried to introduce them with us, nevertheless it may be said that up to about 1860 there had been no general adoption in the United States of Pestalozzian ideas as to instruction, aside from primary arithmetic. Much had been written about his work in Switzerland, and the various *Reports* by American travelers abroad had extolled the Pestalozzian-Prussian elementary-school instruction, but American teachers mostly continued to follow the methods and practices of earlier times. The introduction of Infant Schools, after 1818, had done something to bring about a more rational conception as to the educational process (page 137), particularly as to teaching reading and numbers, and the publication of Warren Colburn's *First Lessons in Arithmetic on the Plan of Pestalozzi*, in 1821, had gradually substituted mental arithmetic for ciphering sums in the lower grades of our schools.   Neef had taught a Pestalozzian school at Philadelphia from 1809 to 1813, and published two books there on Pestalozzian method, but his influence was local and soon lost, due to his departure for the then West.   The new educational journals (page 343) and the many magazine articles also had done much to familiarize schoolmen with the ideas and practices of the Swiss reformer.

As early as 1839 Henry Barnard had distributed among the teachers of Connecticut a pamphlet on Pestalozzi, and in 1847 and 1849 he distributed two other pamphlets on his work and method of instruction.   Horace Mann's *Seventh Report* (**R. 202**) for 1843 had dealt largely with Prussian schools, and had done something to familiarize Massachusetts schoolmasters with the newer teaching procedures.   In Massachusetts, Pestalozzian methods were introduced at first into a few private schools, and in 1848 Pestalozzian object teaching was introduced into the state normal school at Westfield.   From 1848 to 1854 Arnold Guyot, a Swiss, who had recently come to America, acted as an Agent of the Massachusetts State Board of Education and State Institute Lecturer on the teaching of home and observational geography, and from 1855 to 1857 Hermann Krüsi, Jr., a son of one of Pestalozzi's teachers, who had come to America three years before, held a similar position for drawing and arithmetic.   Louis Agassiz, the distinguished naturalist and teacher of science, who had come from Switzerland to Harvard to a professorship in zoölogy and geology in 1848, also joined in giving science lectures for teachers.   Still, notwithstanding these promising efforts, the work remained local and exerted little influence on school practice elsewhere, and up to about 1860 it may be said that Pestalozzian ideas, though adopted here and there, had as yet made no deep impression in the United States.

The Oswego Movement marks the real introduction.   The real introduction of Pestalozzian ideas and methods is due to the energy and initiative of Edward A. Sheldon, of Oswego, New York, and so thoroughly did he do the work that in a few years everyone was talking in terms of Pestalozzian procedure, and the ideas and methods he introduced soon spread all over the country.

Mr. Sheldon began, much as had Pestalozzi himself, by establishing, in 1848, at the age of twenty-five, a school in Oswego for poor and neglected children.   Following English terminology it was called a "ragged school," and was composed of "120 rude and untrained Irish boys and girls between the ages of 5 and 21." In 1851 Mr. Sheldon was elected superintendent of the schools of Syracuse, but in 1853, at the age of thirty, he was recalled to Oswego to become its first school superintendent.[1] Himself a careful student, familiar with the pedagogical literature of the day, he first reorganized the schools from the ungraded district type which he found there to a graded series of schools (page 309). He next wrote a new course of study which eliminated much of the textbook memorizing, and began to give his teachers training in teaching by better methods.[2]

In the summer of 1859 Mr. Sheldon saw, in the museum at Toronto, Canada, a full set of the models, objects, method-materials, and publications of the English Home and Colonial Infant Society, which, it will be remembered (page 353), had adopted the formal type of Pestalozzian work introduced into England by the Mayos. His interest now fully awakened, he set about reshaping the training of his teachers after the plans of the English Society. The necessary books and apparatus were imported from England in 1860, the course of study was remade to shift the emphasis in teaching from the acquisition of knowledge to the stimulation of observation and inquiry, and the next year the Board of Education of Oswego dignified the work he was doing by creating a city normal school[3] to train

[1] Sheldon's entry into school work was almost an accident. He first went into business, but in 1848, when he was twenty-five, the firm he was connected with failed, and he found it necessary to find employment. He first thought of entering Auburn Theological Seminary and preparing for the ministry, but was induced to head a school for illiterate and destitute children, privately financed. In 1850 he became principal of a private school in Oswego; in 1851 he became superintendent of the schools at Syracuse, at a salary of $600 a year; and in 1853, on the organization of the free school system of Oswego, he was recalled as superintendent at $800 salary. The need for better teachers at Oswego gradually opened the way for the development of a city training school.

[2] "In the above plan of studies the object is not so much to impart information as to educate the senses; arouse, quicken, and develop the perceptive and conceptive faculties, teach the children to observe, and to awaken a spirit of inquiry. To this end the pupils must be encouraged to do most of the talking and acting. They must be allowed to draw their own conclusions, and if wrong *led* to correct them. The books should be used only for reference and as models for the lessons to be given. Every lesson should be previously and carefully prepared by the teacher, so that she may go before the class with a feeling of ease and confidence." (*Course of Study*, Oswego Schools, 1859–60.)

[3] Confronted by the impossibility of accomplishing his purpose without trained teachers, Mr. Sheldon proposed to the board of education that a city training school be established, to which "graduates from our own and other high schools, or persons of equal scholastic attainments" be admitted to a special course for primary teachers which would be "strictly professional" in character. "One half of the time was to be given to a discussion of educational principles and their application to teaching the elementary branches, and the other half to teaching under criticism." The board of education approved the proposal, and the Oswego school was begun.

DR. EDWARD A. SHELDON

(1823–1897)

Superintendent of Schools, Oswego, N.Y.
Principal of the Oswego State Normal School

PROFESSOR HERMANN KRÜSI

(1817–1902)

Born at Yverdon, Son of Pestalozzi's
assistant. For a quarter of a
century a teacher at Oswego

TWO LEADERS IN THE INTRODUCTION OF PESTALOZZIAN IDEAS

teachers in the new methods for the schools of the city.   The
Board also (1861) obtained permission for Miss Margaret E. M.
Jones, a teacher in the English Training College of the Society, to
come to Oswego and establish the work.[1] On her return to England in 1862, Hermann Krüsi, Jr., who had taught in the Home
and Colonial Infant Society Training College in England for five
years, and who had been in the United States for ten years, teaching
in a private school and acting as institute lecturer on drawing and
arithmetic for the Massachusetts Board of Education, was secured
to continue the training Miss Jones had started.[2]

The English formalized Pestalozzian methods were soon firmly
established in the Oswego schools (**R. 224**), and so well was the work
there advertised, and so important did the movement become, that
it for a time completely overshadowed the Swiss and German type
of Pestalozzian instruction which had been introduced earlier into
Massachusetts, and here and there into schools in other States. In
1862 a committee of prominent educators accepted an invitation to
visit and examine the Oswego schools, and they made a favorable
report on the work.   In 1863 Mr. Sheldon explained his work before the National Teachers' Association, making a complete statement of his understanding of the purposes of education and of the
advantages of object teaching in forwarding those purposes.[3] After
this, "object teaching" held a place of first importance on the program of this and other teachers' associations for at least a decade.

---

[1] Mr. Sheldon wrote to the English Home and Colonial Infant and Juvenile Society to ascertain if a teacher could be obtained for a year to start the work properly. A reply came
that Miss Jones, a teacher of eighteen years' experience in their school, could be obtained
for a salary of $1000 and all living expenses. The Board was staggered, as the salary of
the superintendent was but $800. The Board finally agreed on Mr. Sheldon's promise
that it "should not cost the taxpayers one cent." By contributions from the teachers,
charging a tuition fee, and saving the cost of one teacher, he met the agreement.

[2] Hermann Krüsi was born at Yverdon, in 1817. His father was a teacher with Pestalozzi
there. He studied in Germany, became familiar with the Prussian schools, and assisted
his father in the conduct of a private Swiss normal school from 1841 to 1846. He then
taught for a year with the Mayos near London, and for three years in the Home and Colonial School in London. Returning to Switzerland in 1852, he was induced to come to
the United States to accept a position in a private normal school at Lancaster, Massachusetts, conducted by William Russell. From 1855 to 1857 he was an institute lecturer for
the Massachusetts State Board of Education; from 1857 to 1859 he was a teacher at the
new State Normal School at Trenton, New Jersey; then three years more as a lecturer
in Massachusetts; and in 1862 he went to Oswego, where he remained until he retired in
1887. He died in Alameda, California, in 1903.

[3] *Proceedings of the National Teachers' Association*, 1863, pp. 93–102 (object teaching); pp.
387–90 (training of teachers).

In 1864 the National Teachers' Association, after listening to a discussion *pro* and *con*, appointed a committee to investigate the system, and this committee reported favorably the following year.[1]   In 1863 the State of New York granted $3000 a year aid to the Oswego school, and in 1866 took it over as a second State Normal School.

Visitors now came in numbers to see this new type of teaching, students came from afar to study the new methods, "oral instruction" and "object teaching" became for a time the great new ideas in education, and Oswego graduates were sought by city school systems and new normal schools all over the United States.   For at least two decades Oswego was distinctively the training school for normal school instructors, critic teachers, and city school supervisors, and the "striking personalities" which Mr. Sheldon gathered and held together (**R. 225**) for years, and the enthusiasm for the new work which his teachers imparted to others, gave his school a deserved national reputation.[2]   As a recent writer has well said, "he shaped a coherent course of study (**R. 226**) and turned out a large group of teachers who thought teaching, on Oswego lines, the greatest thing in the world."   What the so-called "Oswego Movement" in our educational history really meant may be shown most easily by indicating the changes in the nature of instruction which came as a result of it.

Oral and objective teaching.   In the first place, it meant a very great change in the character of the teaching process itself.   As we have seen, colonial and early national education was characterized by individual reciting.   The pupil did his work at his seat, and the teacher heard him read or looked over his work or the sums on his slate or paper.   The next advance step was to class organization, which we traced in Chapter IX, but the teacher or the assistant teacher still heard recitations from subject matter which the children had learned, that is memorized, from a book.   Many of the early geographies and histories had even been constructed on the plan of

[1] S. S. Green, chairman.   "Object Teaching"; in *Proceedings of the National Teachers' Association*, 1865, pp. 245–70.   Several thousand copies of this *Report* were ordered printed and circulated throughout the country.

[2] "Mention should also be made of the educational contacts made through lectures and institute work on the part of the instructors and its graduates; by the textbooks, manuals, and materials printed by the same groups; and by the publicity and information given by the frequent appearance of articles in newspapers and educational journals.   There can be little doubt, in the face of the facts presented in this study, that there was justification for Oswego being called a Mecca of American elementary education."   (Dearborn, Ned H. *The Oswego Movement in American Education*, p. 102.)

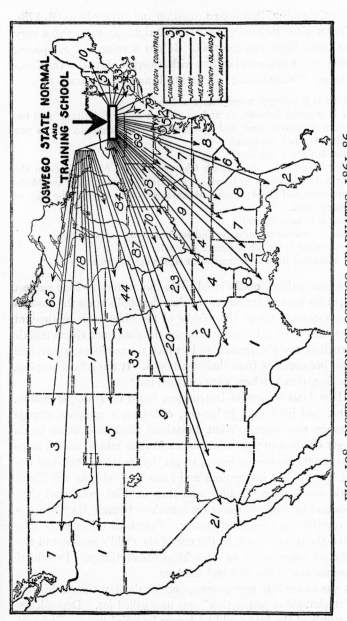

FIG. 108. DISTRIBUTION OF OSWEGO GRADUATES, 1861–86

During this first quarter-century, a total of 897 out of 1373 graduates found places outside of the State of New York, whereas but 175 of the graduates came from outside. (After Dearborn, p. 101.)

the older Catechism, that is on a question and answer basis (**R. 178**). The *System of Geography* by Nathaniel Dwight, an early and a very popular book, illustrates the plan. It was a volume of 215 pages, beginning with Europe and ending with America, and all of the Catechism type. The following, relating to France, is illustrative:

Q. What is the situation and extent of France?
A. It is situated between 42 and 51 degrees of north latitude, and between 5 degrees west and 8 degrees of east longitude. It is 600 miles long and 500 broad.
Q. How is France bounded?
A. It is bounded by the English Channel and the Netherlands on the north; by Germany, Switzerland, and Italy on the east; by the Mediterranean and the Pyrenean Mountains, south; and by the Bay of Biscay, west.
Q. How is France divided?
A. Into 21 provinces formerly, and lately into 83 departments.
Q. From what is the name France derived?
A. It is derived from a German word signifying *free men*.

There was nothing for the child to do but memorize such subject matter, or for the teacher but to see that the pupils knew the answers to the questions. Up to the middle of the nineteenth century, at least, and much later in many schools, the dominant characteristic of instruction was the recitation, in which the pupils merely recited what had been learned from their textbooks. It was school-keeping, not teaching, that teachers were engaged in.

The Pestalozzian form of instruction, based on sense-perception, reasoning, and individual judgment, called for a complete change in classroom procedure. What Pestalozzi tried most of all to do was to get children to use their senses and their minds, to look carefully, to count, to observe forms, to get, by means of their five important senses, clear impressions and ideas as to objects and life in the world about them (**R. 196**), and then to think over what they had seen and be able to answer his questions because they had observed carefully and reasoned clearly. Pestalozzi thus clearly subordinated the printed book to the use of the child's senses, and the repetition of mere words to clear ideas about things. Pestalozzi thus became one of the first real teachers.

This was an entirely new process, and for the first time in history a real "technique of instruction" was now called for. Dependence on the words of the text could no longer be relied upon. The oral instruction of a class group, using real objects, called for teaching skill. The class must be kept naturally interested and under control, the essential elements to be taught must be kept clearly in the mind of the teacher, the teacher must raise the right kind of questions, in the right order, to carry the class thinking along to the right conclusions, and, since so much of this type of instruction was not down in books, it called for a much more extended knowledge of the subject on the part of the teacher than the old type of school-keeping had done. The teacher must now both know and be able to organize and direct. Class lessons must be thought out in advance, and teacher-preparation in itself meant a great change in teaching procedure. Emancipated from dependence on the words of a text, and able to stand before a class full of a subject and able to question freely, teachers became conscious of a new strength and a professional skill unknown in the days of textbook reciting. It is not to be wondered that the teachers leaving Oswego went out feeling that teaching, by the Oswego methods, was the greatest thing in the world.

Language instruction. From such teaching oral language lessons, once so rare and now so common, naturally followed as a matter of course. Pupils trained to observe and think naturally come to be able to express. Boys and girls who are full of a subject have little difficulty in telling what they have seen or know. Free exercise in oral expression — oral language work — thus entered the school. Pestalozzi made it one of the great features of his teaching. Stowe and Mann, in their *Reports*, had called attention to it as an important element of the instruction in the Prussian people's school. Some start had been made in introducing such instruction into the schools of Massachusetts, but it was left to Oswego to demonstrate clearly the importance of oral language in the instruction of children. Oral language work thus came in as a new subject for instruction in the primary grades, and, to a degree, oral and written language work tended to replace the former great emphasis on English grammar in the upper grades of the elementary school.

From oral language work, once made a feature of instruction, the teaching of correct speech-usage came naturally to the front, and usage, rather than learning the rules of grammar, came to be depended upon as the chief means for teaching English. Virtually a new subject of instruction was thus added to the elementary-school course as a result of the oral and objective teaching introduced into our schools between 1860 and 1875.

Object teaching leads to elementary science. Another new and most valuable subject of instruction also came in now as an outgrowth of oral and objective teaching, and this was the study of nature. The first step in the process was the object-lesson idea, popularized in England after 1830 by Miss Mayo's book, and in this country after 1860 by the work at Oswego. Thousands of lessons (**R. 227**) were written out on all forms of natural objects, many far too technical and too scientific to be of much interest or value to children, and these were taught by the teachers.

Under the influence of William T. Harris, who became superintendent of schools in St. Louis in 1867, an important change was made from the scattered object lessons on all sorts of scientific subjects to a much more logically organized study of the different sciences. He published, in 1871, an extremely well-organized course of study for the orderly study of the different sciences, and one thoroughly characteristic of his logical, metaphysical mind.[1] Due in part to his high standing as a school superintendent, and in part to his course of study being a marked improvement over the English-Oswego object-lesson work, this type of course of study was widely copied, became very popular in our schools for the next generation, and did much to introduce science instruction into our schools. Oral lessons in physiology were also introduced into all the grades, and this subject, due to its importance, soon tended to separate itself off as a new study.

The next step, and a relatively recent one, was the development of the modern nature-study idea. By this is meant, for the lower grades at least, "a simple observational study of common natural objects and processes for the sake of personal acquaintance with the things which appeal to human interest directly, and independently of relations to organized science," and to include object lessons, observation, picnics, stories told and read, awakening a love of nature, and finally a more serious study of selected simple phases of agriculture, geology, and the physical and biological sciences. Thus,

[1] Superintendent Harris first considered the place of the sciences in modern civilization, then outlined a course of instruction extending from the first to the eighth grade and adapted to the seasons, and concluded with a discussion of teaching method in science. The document appeared in his *Annual Report* to the St. Louis School Board for 1871, and again for 1879. It was reprinted in the *Annual Report* of Superintendent Philbrick, of Boston, for 1877. This *Report* is a classic document in the history of education in the United States.

by a process of evolution, we have obtained another new and very important study — two, if we count physiology and the more recent development of health instruction as a separate subject — as an outgrowth of the objective and oral instruction which goes back in its origin to Pestalozzi and the *Émile* of Rousseau.

Instruction in geography revolutionized.   Oral and objective teaching also led to great changes in the character of instruction in geography.   The old geography was fact-geography — astronomical, physical, natural, and political — and some of the earlier, briefer compends, as we have pointed out, were of the question and answer type.   The early work by Morse (**R. 177**) fixed the type of text and the nature of the instruction.   Definitions, all kinds of political and statistical data, boundaries, capitals, products, exports and imports, and similar more or less useless information, filled the texts.   This was learned and recited by the pupils, and the teacher's task was to see that it was memorized.   Such geography has been called ship-captain or mail-clerk geography.

Objective and oral teaching, applied to geography, wrought a vast change in the character of the instruction.   Following Rousseau's idea of "back-to-nature" and Pestalozzi's plans for instruction, the new study of home geography was developed, and from the immediate surroundings geographical instruction was extended to the region thereabout.   This called for observation out-of-doors, the study of type forms, and the substitution of the physical and human aspects of geography for the political and statistical.   The German, Karl Ritter,[1] developed this new type of geography, between 1817 and 1859, and especially home geography after the ideas of Pestalozzi.

In 1848 the Massachusetts State Board of Education brought to this country a Swiss by the name of Arnold Guyot,[2] who had been a

---

[1] In 1809 Ritter, then a young man of 28, visited Pestalozzi at Yverdon, spending several weeks there.   Of this visit he writes:

"I have seen more than the paradise of Switzerland, I have seen Pestalozzi, I have learned to know his heart and his genius.   Never have I felt so impressed with the sanctity of my vocation as when I was with this noble son of Switzerland.

"I left Yverdon resolved to fulfill my promise made to Pestalozzi to carry his method into geography.... Pestalozzi did not know as much geography as a child in our primary schools, but, none the less, have I learned that science from him, for it was in listening to him that I felt awaken within me the instinct of the natural methods; he showed me the way."   (Guimps, Baron de. *Pestalozzi, His Aim and Work*, p. 167.)

[2] Arnold Henry Guyot was a Swiss-American geographer.   He studied at the College of Neuchâtel and the University of Berlin, taking his degree at Berlin in 1835.   He was a pupil of Karl Ritter.   From 1839 to 1848 he was professor of history and physical geog-

pupil under Ritter, and who for the next six years was an institute lecturer and state inspector for Massachusetts, and later did similar work in New Jersey. He addressed thousands of teachers on the needed reforms and proper methods, and later, through his beautifully illustrated textbooks and a detailed method-guide for teachers, all published about 1866, tended to fix the new type of instruction among the more progressive teachers of the time. An Oswego teacher helped him prepare his books, the aims of which he stated to be "to fill the young with vivid pictures of nature in such regions

of the globe as may be considered great geographical types." The work of Colonel Francis W. Parker in training teachers, his *How to Teach Geography* (1889), and the textbooks by Frye (1895), continued the work of Guyot, improving on it and bringing geographical teaching down to its modern form. We thus have a direct line of descent from Rousseau through Pestalozzi, Ritter, Guyot, Parker, and Frye to modern practices.

FIG. 109
ARNOLD HENRY GUYOT
(1807–84)

Mental arithmetic. Before Pestalozzi, arithmetic had meant ciphering, and either commercial counting or the solution of complicated problems. Pestalozzi replaced ciphering with simple and rapid mental calculations. Counting beans, boys, sticks, lines, mountain peaks, and holes in the lace curtains or flowers on the wall-paper of the castle, formed the basis for his arithmetic. The number chart shown here was for long a prominent feature in all Pestalozzian schools, the purpose being to keep before the pupil's perception the number combinations from one to ten (**R. 228**). Concrete number ideas, and not words about numbers, were what Pestalozzi was trying to teach. He held that the mental processes of the pupil were the most important part of arithmetical study, and that the quickness,

raphy at Neuchâtel. Then he came to America, and from 1848 to 1854 he was lecturer on geography to the normal schools and teachers' institutes of Massachusetts. In 1855 he was appointed professor of physical geography at Princeton, where he remained until his death there in 1884. He prepared and published the best series of geographies issued up to his time. A bronze tablet on a Swiss glacial boulder, on the Princeton campus, records his service as a teacher.

accuracy, judging, and reasoning developed by such work was of prime importance in the education of children. He accordingly discarded sand-tables, paper, and slates for ciphering, and trained the pupils to solve mentally rather complicated problems with whole numbers and fractions. Visitors to his school were astonished at the skill displayed by the children in the use of the four fundamental

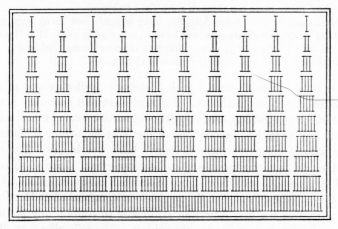

FIG. 110. A PESTALOZZIAN NUMBER CHART

operations in arithmetic. Mental arithmetic being a very practical subject, Pestalozzian ideas and plans were soon adopted generally in the schools of Switzerland, Holland, the German States, and England. After the close of Pestalozzi's school in Switzerland, in 1825, Reiner, who had taught arithmetic there, went to England and became a teacher in the Training College of the Home and Colonial Infant Society.

Pestalozzian mental arithmetic was the first of the new subjects to reach us, coming through Warren Colburn's *First Lessons in Arithmetic on the Plan of Pestalozzi*, published in Boston, in 1821. The publication of this book marked our first adoption of Pestalozzian ideas in teaching,[1] and was the only phase of Pestalozzianism

---

[1] Colburn had obtained his knowledge of Pestalozzi's principles wholly from the writings of American travelers, as he had never seen him or his work. While a student at Harvard he had taught winter schools, and for about two and a half years after his graduation (1820) he taught a select school in Boston, after which, until his death in 1833, he was superintendent of manufacturing plants at Waltham and Lowell. He acknowledged his indebtedness to the system of Pestalozzi for assistance in arranging his number combinations, but the qualities that made the book such a success were his own work.

to be widely adopted before 1860. The book contained a multitude of simple problems, to be solved mentally, and many of these were stated in particularly attractive form. The following extracts are illustrative:

How many hands have a boy and a clock?
Four rivers ran through the Garden of Eden, and one through Babylon; how many more ran through Eden than Babylon?
Judas, one of the twelve Apostles, hung himself; how many were left?
Miss Fanny Woodbury was born in 1791, and died in 1814; Miss Hannah Adams lived to be 53 years older; how old was Hannah Adams?
At \$2.50 a yard, what will $2\frac{1}{2}$ yards of cloth cost?

This book must be ranked with Webster's *Speller* as one of the greatest American textbooks. For more than half a century it was one of the most widely used school books in America. Mental arithmetic, by 1850, had become one of the most important subjects of the school, and everywhere Colburn's book was in use. The sale of the book was enormous, and its influence great. Like all successful textbooks, it set a new standard and had many imitators. One of these, Barnard's *A Treatise on Arithmetic*, published at Hartford, in 1830, was the first American arithmetic to contain any pictures to aid beginners in mastering the subject. The following is an illustration from this book.

5. One stage has four horses. How many horses have two stages?

6. Then 2 times 4, or *twice* 4 are how many?

The Grube idea. In 1842 a German, by the name of Grube, tried to improve on the teaching of arithmetic thus developed by applying to it another Pestalozzian principle, namely, that of reducing each subject to its elements, and then making a thorough study of each element before proceeding to the next. His idea had all the characteristics of logical German thoroughness, carried to typical German extreme. Fortunately, the method was not exploited in this country until 1870, when it was explained in a paper by Louis Soldan, then a teacher in St. Louis, a school system then under the leadership of Dr. Harris and at the front in all movements intended to improve instruction. The paper was republished in many States, from New England to California, and soon marked out a new line for the teaching of primary arithmetic. By 1885 even the rural schools of the United States had adopted the Grube idea, and it is only since about 1900 that we have turned back once more to the better ideas of Pestalozzian teaching as represented in Colburn's book and its modern successors.

The essential idea of Grube's method was intense thoroughness in teaching every element. The number one was taught for days before going to number two, and two in all possible and imaginary combinations before taking up three, and so on. The entire first year was devoted to teaching the numbers one to ten, and the second year the numbers to one hundred. The method was extremely absurd, and so clearly away from the better teaching of Colburn that one wonders how American teachers came to take up so completely for a time the Grube idea.

Writing, drawing, and music. Grube's work in organizing a subject so as to proceed by carefully graded stages from the simplest element to the more and more complex illustrated another Pestalozzian idea, viz., that the teaching process could eventually be so "mechanized" that there would be a regular A, B, C, for each type of instruction, which, once learned, would give perfection to a teacher. This idea Pestalozzi strove, unsuccessfully, to work out. In reading it led to the alphabet-syllable-word — A, B, C, ba, ca, ra; bat, cat, rat — method of teaching, long retained by us, but early discarded by the Germans for the word method, and now replaced in this country by a combined word and sound method for teaching beginners to read. In arithmetic the idea led eventually to the absurd Grube method. In object lessons it led to a detailed study and analysis of properties and characteristics, and to an absurd — for children — scientific classification of objects.

When applied to the new subjects of writing, drawing, and music, which really came in as elementary-school subjects after about 1845 in Massachusetts, and more generally only with the Oswego work after 1860, we get this Pestalozzian principle in its extreme form. For a generation the teaching of these newer subjects was formal, mechanical, lifeless, and largely ineffective because of the attempt to present the subjects logically to children, and to analyze each subject into its elements. Before children began really to write they were drilled on lines and curves and angles and movements until they were thoroughly tired of writing as a subject because it led to so little writing. In drawing, year after year was spent in studying form, with scientific instruction as to angles and geometrical figures and perspective, but without reaching color and expression. In music, similarly, much drill was put on tone studies, scales, and reading notes, but without much real singing. For a

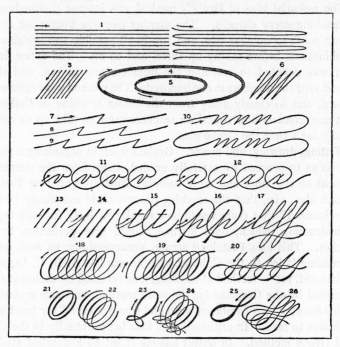

FIG. III. EARLY SPENCERIAN WRITING EXERCISES

From *Spencerian Penmanship No. 4, Revised.* Copyright, American Book Company, publishers. Reproduced by permission.

generation these methods of teaching these special subjects, largely brought over from England at the beginnings of the Oswego Movement, were the ruling methods. Since about 1900 they have been generally abandoned for the far simpler and easier procedure which leads earlier and more directly to actual writing and drawing and singing, and to a childish appreciation of the value of these special arts. The new methods are far less logical than the earlier plans, but we have long since learned from a study of the psychology of the learning process that children do not think along the same logical lines as adults.

History not developed until later.   History as a subject of study in our elementary schools came in largely as a by-product of the Civil War.   Davenport's *History of the United States* (**R. 178**) had been published in 1821 at Philadelphia, and in 1822, Goodrich's text with a similar title (page 298) appeared in Boston.   A few years later, Noah Webster's *History of the United States* appeared to contest the popularity of the preceding two.   Before the publication of these little volumes such history as had been taught had been brought in incidentally under geography and in reading.   Vermont, in 1827, was probably the first State to add history to the required list of elementary-school subjects.   Massachusetts, the same year, added the subject for the schools of the larger towns and the cities, but did not include it for all until 1857.   In most of the older Northern States history was added to the list of required subjects shortly after the close of the Civil War, though many cities had added it to their course of study at an earlier date.   The purpose from the first was to emphasize American accomplishments, with the chief stress on the memorization of facts relating to our national heroes, wars, and political struggles.   The dominant purpose was the development of patriotism and an enthusiasm for the Union.

Rousseau had declared history to be a subject of no importance for children, and Pestalozzi had done practically nothing with it. Neither had the followers of Pestalozzi anywhere, so with the introduction of Pestalozzianism at Oswego and elsewhere instruction in history was not included.   It was added generally about this time, however, but, being unaffected by the new Pestalozzian ideas as to instruction, it began to be taught by the old memory methods of its earlier ancestor, geography.   The reorganization of history instruction did not come until near the end of the nineteenth century, under the inspiration of a new German influence, to be described in a subsequent chapter.   The reorganization of reading, and the creation of a methodology for instruction in both history and literature, also date from the coming of this new influence.

The normal school finds its place.   The great change which took place in the character of elementary-school education, between about 1850 and about 1880, will now be evident.   As the people had neither the money nor the public interest necessary to expand the school system along material lines, or to add new types of schools, the great educational development of these three decades was within. New subjects of study were introduced, the teaching of the older ones was revolutionized, and a technique — a methodology — for instruction in each subject, except history and literature, was worked out. Where before the ability to organize and discipline a school had constituted the chief element in instruction, now the ability to teach scientifically took its place as the prime professional requisite. A "science and art of teaching" now arose, to be added to the older classroom management, and the new subject of Pedagogy began to take form and secure recognition.

The normal school now found its place, and Figure 107, showing its development, reveals how rapidly the movement to establish these schools gained headway after about 1865 for public normal schools, and after about 1870 for the private tuition schools. The thirteen public normal schools of 1860 increased to 61 by 1872 — 54 state, 2 county, and 7 city — and to approximately 80 by 1880. To head the practice schools of these new normal schools and introduce the new instructional techniques, the source of supply, for almost a quarter of a century, was the Oswego school. How powerful a factor the Oswego school was in the new work of teacher-training during this time the map shown in Figure 108 clearly reveals.

Among the private normal schools of this period, the National Normal University, at Lebanon, Ohio; the Valparaiso Normal School, in Indiana; and the Northern Illinois Normal School, at Dixon, are types of dozens of such private low-tuition schools, which had thousands of students and were good money-makers for their owners. These illustrate the great interest awakened by the work at Oswego and elsewhere in the effort to psychologize the educational process and to reduce teaching procedure to rule and method.

Psychology becomes the master science. The new conception of the child as a slowly developing personality, demanding subject matter and method suited to his stage of development, and the new conception of teaching as that of directing the educative process instead of hearing recitations and "keeping school," now replaced the earlier knowledge-conception of school work. Psychology soon became the guiding science of the school, and imparting to would-be teachers the methodology of instruction, in the different school subjects, the great work of the normal school.

The new normal-trained woman teacher now began to be markedly in evidence and, after 1880, the displacement of men teachers was rapid in all parts of the country. Only since 1920 has there been a slight change from the steady downward movement. This new teacher brought with her to the school a new conception of childhood, a new and a minute methodology, and a new enthusiasm, all of which were valuable additions, though for a time often

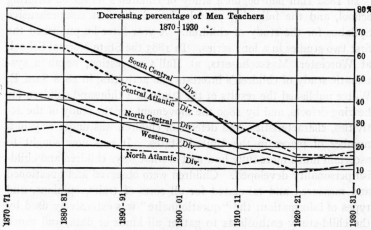

FIG. 112. THE DECREASING PERCENTAGE OF MEN TEACHERS

carried to a ridiculous extreme. Problems had to be analyzed just so, pupils must answer just so, and thinking must proceed in approved order and be stated in proper form. Each problem to be solved must first be analyzed in correct English into a correct statement, short-cut though correct replies were not allowed, while such errors as the multiplication of children by dimes or the division of dollars by horses were almost unpardonable. The spirit of instruction was often lost in a too strict observance of the form. These defects and excesses, almost always the accompaniment of any new movement which strongly influences the course of educational development, in time largely disappeared, and methodology fell into its proper place as a part, but not the whole, of the science of education.

The child-study movement. A little later, the eighties and early nineties, the natural successor of the normal-school-methodology movement — child study [1] — made its appearance, and for a time almost monopolized the educational field. Though carried on in all parts of the United States, the work of G. Stanley Hall (1844–1924) and his students, at Clark University, formed the leading center of the movement, and the *Pedagogical Seminary* was founded (1891) to disseminate the results.

In 1880 Hall had begun a study of children's minds on entering school, and the following year he issued the first comprehensive Syllabus for the study of children. A year later he published the first two studies in a long series. In 1885 the State Normal School, at Worcester, Massachusetts, at Hall's suggestion, began a systematic study of children's interests and activities; in 1888 Sara E. Wiltze published the results of the study of a thousand children for hearing defects, and by 1890 the movement for the study of the activities, characteristics, and defects of children was under way in a number of places in the United States. It was now sought to ascertain much more fully how and in what ways children and childish personality developed. Children were observed and questioned and measured and tabulated for all sorts of traits, opinions, and types of information; the "questionnaire" was extensively used by the child-study enthusiasts to gather all kinds of data, and much useful as well as much worthless information was gathered as to child nature and ideas. By 1900, however, this new movement had been largely assimilated into educational psychology, and also had found its place in the developing science of education.

QUESTIONS FOR DISCUSSION

1. How do you explain the long-continued objection to the establishment of teacher-training schools, when the evidence as to the success of the Prussian teacher seminaries seemed so clear?
2. Contrast the proposals of Governor Clinton and James G. Carter as to nature and purpose of training schools.
3. Contrast the New York academy plan and the Massachusetts special state school plan for training teachers.

---

[1] The beginnings of this new movement practically date from the work of Hall in America and the publication in Germany, in 1881, of *The Mind of the Child*, by Professor W. Preyer, of the University of Jena. This two-volume work was translated and published in the United States in 1888, and a one-volume abridged edition in 1893.

Still earlier, in 1877, the Massachusetts State Board of Health had published a study of physical measurements of thirteen girls and twelve boys, and in 1879 Boaz and Porter published the results of extensive measurements of school children.

G. STANLEY HALL
(1844–1924)
President of Clark University
(1888–1919)

4. Why should the schoolmasters of Massachusetts have opposed the creation of the new normal schools?

5. Why is it probable that the state normal school could hardly either have arisen or survived, at the time it did, in any other State, than Massachusetts?

6. Why was it a natural development that St. Louis, in 1856, should have established the first city normal school in the United States?

7. Enumerate a number of happenings to prove that Massachusetts, from about 1840 to about 1855, was clearly in the lead in interest in education.

8. How do you explain the large and immediate success of Mr. Sheldon?

9. Contrast "oral and objective teaching" with the former "individual instruction."

10. Show the complete change in classroom procedure this involved.

11. Show how Pestalozzian ideas necessitated a "technique of instruction."

12. Show how psychology and the methodology of instruction now became the important subjects of the normal school.

13. How do you explain the slow rate at which the Pestalozzian ideas as to language and arithmetical instruction have influenced the teaching of these subjects in the school?

14. How do you explain the decline in importance of the once-popular mental arithmetic?

15. How do you explain the small interest in history as a school subject until after the Civil War?

16. How do you explain the decrease in men teachers after the rise of the normal school?

17. Show how Child Study was a natural development from the Pestalozzian psychology and methodology.

18. Using the map given in Figure 108, estimate the importance of the Oswego Normal School as a national force during the period of its maximum greatness.

SELECTED READINGS

In the accompanying volume of *Readings* the following selections, related to the subject matter of this chapter, are reproduced:

*206. Gallaudet: Seminaries for Teachers.
*207. Carter: A State Institution to Train Teachers.
*208. Stone: The First Normal School in America.
*209. Hall: Contract with the Congregation at Concord.
*210. Hall: Normal Training Course at Andover.
*211. Hall: Lectures on Schoolkeeping.
*212. News Notes: Early Attempts to Provide Trained Teachers.
*213. Clinton: Recommendations for Teacher Training Schools.
*214. Miller: The Legislature and Regents Favor Academies.
 215. American Institute: Memorial for a Normal School.
*216. Massachusetts: Creation of the First State Normal Schools.

217. Massachusetts: Instruction in the New Normal Schools.
218. Everett: Purpose of the New Normal Schools.
*219. Salem: Defense of Mann and the Normal Schools.
*220. Gordy: How Cyrus Peirce labored.
*221. Pierce: Letter to Mann asking Release.
*222. Mann: Importance of the Normal School Idea.
223. Anon: Memorial for National System of Normal Schools.
*224. Report: The Pestalozzian Methods at Oswego.
225. Sheldon: The Oswego City Normal School Faculty.
226. Sheldon: The Oswego State Normal School Course.
227. Sheldon: A Typical Object Lesson.
228. Sheldon: A Lesson on Number.

QUESTIONS ON THE READINGS

1. State, briefly, Gallaudet's argument (206).
2. Just what kind of a state school did Carter propose (207)?
3. Characterize the life work (208) of Hall.
4. Characterize Hall's contract (209) and his work at Concord.
5. Compare Hall's course (210) with that of a high school or academy of the time (148, 150, 158).
6. Evaluate Hall's book (211) as to its helpfulness to teachers. Compare it with Page's *Principles and Practices of Teaching* (page 377), or some more modern book on *School Management*.
7. What do the early attempts to train teachers (212) reveal as to general interest in the problem?
8. Explain Governor Clinton's insistence on the type of teacher-training institution (213) he recommended.
9. What reasons can you advance for the Regents and legislature preferring (214) another type of institution?
10. Contrast the two plans (213, 214) as to education and training.
11. What are the strong points in the Memorial (215) presented?
12. Show that the Massachusetts law of 1838 (216) was but the merest entering wedge.
13. Contrast the instruction in the new normals (217) with that provided earlier by Hall (210).
14. Contrast Governor Everett's statement of purpose of the normal school (218) with that of such a school today.
15. Would you say that Mann made a good selection in Peirce (220, 221)?
16. Do you think Mann overestimated (222) the importance of what he had helped to create?
17. What do you think of the memorial (223) for a national system of training schools? Why should Congress ignore the pleas so completely?
18. Contrast the new Pestalozzian procedures at Oswego (224) with earlier teaching methods.
19. Contrast Sheldon's course of instruction (226) with that of Hall (210), and that of the Massachusetts schools (217).

20. How would we teach such a lesson on flowers (227) today?
21. How would we teach such a lesson on number (228) today?

TOPICS FOR INVESTIGATION AND REPORT

1. Training of Teachers in the Lancastrian Model Schools.
2. Early work of Carter, Hall, and Brooks in establishing normal schools. (Barnard, Wright and Gardner.)
3. Work of Cyrus Pierce at Lexington. (Barnard; Gordy; Norton.)
4. The Academies as training schools in New York State. (Miller; Fitzpatrick.)
5. David Page and the Albany normal school.
6. Founding and early work of the first State normals in Connecticut, Illinois, Indiana, Michigan, New Jersey.
7. The legislative fight of 1840 on the normal schools of Massachusetts. (Hinsdale; Norton.)
8. Work of the Home and Colonial Infant Society. (Barnard; Mayo.)
9. Work of Henry D. Sheldon at Oswego. (Dearborn; Hollis; Monroe)
10. The object teaching controversy of the sixties, and the Reports on the Oswego school. (Dearborn; National Teachers' Association.)
11. The Pestalozzian movement in the United States. (Monroe.)
12. Work and influence of William T. Harris at St. Louis. (Barnard.)
13. Arnold Guyot, and his textbooks.
14. Work of the National Normal School at Lebanon, Ohio.
15. The child study movement and G. Stanley Hall.

SELECTED REFERENCES

Barnard, Henry, Editor. *The American Journal of Education*, 31 vols. Consult *Analytical Index* to; 128 pp. Published by United States Bureau of Education, Washington, 1892.

See volumes especially for articles on Brooks, Carter, Guyot, Krüsi, Hall, Peirce, Page, Sheldon, normal schools, object teaching, etc.

Barnard, Henry, Editor. *On Normal Schools*. Vol. I, United States; vol. II, Europe. Hartford, 1851. Reprinted by Colorado State Teachers College, Greeley, 1929.

Very valuable, as they contain many historical documents of importance.

*Dearborn, Ned H. *The Oswego Movement in American Education*. 189 pp. Teachers College Contributions to Education, No. 183. New York, 1925.

An important volume. Contains important bibliography, and a number of valuable documents.

Fitzpatrick, Edw. A. *Educational Views and Influence of DeWitt Clinton*. 157 pp. Teachers College Contributions to Education, No. 44. New York, 1911.

Contains a few pages on his interest in teacher-training.

*Gordy, J. P.   *Rise and Growth of the Normal School Idea in the United States.*   145 pp.   Circular of Information, U.S. Bureau of Education, No. 8, 1891.
> An important historical contribution.

Hall, Saml. R.   *Lectures on Schoolkeeping.*   1829, 1929.   (See Wright and Gardner, further on.)

Hinsdale, B. A.   *Horace Mann and the Common School Revival.*   326 pp.   New York, 1898.
> Chapter VI describes Mann's relation to the normal school movement.

*Hollis, A. P.   *The Oswego Movement.*   136 pp.   Boston, 1898.
> The contribution of the Oswego Normal School to educational progress in the United States, through its work in introducing Pestalozzian methods.

Jones, L. H.   "E. A. Sheldon"; in *Educational Review,* vol. XIV, pp. 428–32.   (Dec., 1897.)
> An appreciative sketch.

Knight, E. W.   *Education in the United States.*   Boston, 1929.
> Chapters XI and XII deal with the rise of teacher-training in the United States.

Krüsi, Hermann.   *Recollections of my Life.*
> Reminiscences of an interesting and a fruitful life.

*Mangum, V. L.   *The American Normal School; Its Rise and Development in Massachusetts.*   Baltimore, 1928.
> A comprehensive study of the struggle, and the importance of the Massachusetts pioneer work.

*Miller, Geo. F.   *The Academy System of the State of New York.*   180 pp.   Albany, 1922.
> Chapter VI deals with the early attempts of the academies to train teachers for the common schools.

Monroe, Paul, Editor.   *Cyclopedia of Education.*   5 vols.   New York, 1911–13.
> Contains a number of brief articles on men and movements.

Monroe, Walter S.   *Development of Arithmetic as a School Subject.*   170 pp.   U.S. Bureau of Education, Bulletin No. 10, 1917.
> Contains an informing chapter on Colburn's relation to the development of arithmetical instruction.

Monroe, Will S.   "Joseph Neef and Pestalozzianism in America"; in *Education,* vol. XIV, pp. 479–91.   (March, 1894.)

*Monroe, Will S.   *History of the Pestalozzian Movement in the United States.*   244 pp.   Syracuse, 1907.
> Good on early movements at Oswego and St. Louis.   Good bibliography.

Norton, Arthur O.   *The First State Normal School in America.*   299 pp.   Harvard Documents in the History of Education, vol. I.   Cambridge, 1926.
> The *Journals* of Cyrus Peirce and Mary Swift, with related documents, and a good historical introduction, with legislative documents reproduced.

*Parker, S. C.   *History of Modern Elementary Education.*   506 pp.   Boston, 1912.
> Chapter XV is very good on Pestalozzian object teaching and oral instruction, and Chapter XVI on Pestalozzian formalism and degenerate object teaching.

*Reisner, Edw. H. *Francis W. Parker*. New York, 1932.

A very good statement as to his work and influence.

Sheldon, E. A. *Autobiography*.

Written about 1895, but not published until 1911.

Stone, Mason S. "The First Normal School in America"; in *Teachers College Record*, vol. XXIV, pp. 263-71.

On Hall's school at Concord. Reproduces a half-page advertisement of the proposed opening of the school, with date of May 14, 1823.

*Woody, Thos. *History of the Education of Women in the United States*. 2 vols. Lancaster, Pa., 1929.

Volume I, chapter X, is good on the entrance of women into the teaching profession.

Wright, A. D., and Gardner, G. E. *Hall's Lectures on Schoolkeeping*. Hanover, N.H., 1929. 192 pp.

An exact reproduction of the first (1829) edition of Hall's book, with an account of his life and works, and a bibliography.

*Wright, Frank W. "The Evolution of the Normal Schools"; in *Elementary School Journal*, vol. XX, pp. 363-71. (January, 1930.)

Sketches the early history, opposition, and gradual establishment of the normal schools.

Reisner, Edward H. *Nationalism and Education since 1789.* New York, 1922.
   A very good statement as to life were and influence.

Sheldon, E. A. *Autobiography.*
   Written about 1885, but . . .

Stone, Mason S . . . . . . "The First Normal School in America," in . . . .

CHAPTER XII

THE CIVIL WAR CHECKS DEVELOPMENT

I. ANTE-BELLUM DEVELOPMENT IN THE SOUTH

The "awakening" felt at the South. As was stated in Chapter IV, no general progress in the development of public education had been made in the South previous to the time of the great awakening under the leadership of Carter, Mann, Barnard, and others in the Northern States. After the close of the War for Independence and the establishment of the new Federal Union, the Southern States, as well as the Northern, were impoverished, and education of any type remained at a low level. Life in the South, as in the new West, was for decades largely a life of hardships and dangers and privations, and the teachings of the life of practical everyday experience answered well as a substitute for that of the school of books. Education of the more formal type continued to be looked upon, as it had been for so long outside of New England and areas settled by New England stock, as a family or a church affair with which the State was only remotely connected. The private pay school met the needs of the land-holding and propertied classes, and the free school, where provided at all, was looked upon as a charity maintained for certain of the indigents of society. Here and there, as was pointed out in Chapters IV and VI, certain hopeful beginnings had been made, though the absence of any strong motive for the maintenance of any general system of public instruction made educational development of necessity slow and local in character.

That the progress in the development of state systems of education, after the movement for tax-supported schools got under way in this country, was less rapid in the South than at the North or the West is explainable as due in part to differences in the early traditions and attitudes of the people, as was set forth in Chapter IV; to the more rural and agricultural character of the Southern States; and also to the absence of industrial development at the South, with the consequent lack of cities and manufacturing and the peculiar social and educational problems of such localities. The presence of the institution of slavery also tended to retard the growth of an educational consciousness in the Southern States, and class and sectional struggles prevented the organization of schools.

The educational awakening in the North, however, had begun to be felt in the South by the middle of the nineteenth century; public opinion on the subject of state education was being formed; educational conventions were being held in a number of the States to consider conditions and needs; progressive governors were beginning to call the attention of legislatures to constitutional provisions, and to urge action; and a somewhat general movement looking toward the erection of a series of state free school systems may be said to have been well under way in a number of the Southern States by 1860. Throughout the South generally the new impulses to action were being felt when the outbreak of the War between the States for a time put an end to further educational development. The history of education in the Southern States doubtless would have been quite a different story had it not been for this gigantic struggle, primarily over the question of slavery, and the appalling sequel of reconstruction days.

A brief digest of the important educational legislation enacted in the different Southern States before the outbreak of the Civil War will reveal the conditions existing and the progress that was under way at that time. If the reader will remember that "the great awakening" at the North took place in the decades of the thirties and the forties, he will see that this same movement was being felt in the South as well, though a little later in time.

1. *In the original States*

Delaware. For a summary of early educational efforts in Delaware, see page 101. The first free school law was enacted in 1821. This act created a county-district system, provided for county school superintendents, and state aid from the income of the school fund, created in 1796, was to be given to each district equal in amount to that raised locally, up to $300 a year. By 1833, 133 school districts had been organized in the State. The school fund income being insufficient, it was supplemented by a lottery in 1835, and the Surplus Revenue distribution of 1837, though this same year the required district tax was reduced to $25. The burden of taxation proving heavy, an educational convention in 1843 went on record as opposing compulsory school taxation. In 1852 the schools of Wilmington were given independence and allowed to develop as they wished, while the district system in the counties continued as best it could. Nothing more was done until 1861, when a new law raised the required district taxation to $30 in Sussex County, $75 in New Castle County, and $100 in Kent County, and further permitted district taxation up to $400 a year for maintenance and to $500 for buildings.   At this point the school law remained until 1875, when new legislation laid the foundations for the present school system.

Maryland.   For a summary of the State's educational history up to 1827, when the first general law of 1825 was repealed, see page 101. Little more was attempted, and outside of Baltimore there was no school system up to the time of the Civil War.   The new constitution of 1864 made the first mention of education, and the law of 1865 provided for a centralized and effective system of administration, with a state board of education, state school superintendent, county superintendents, a state school tax, and a tax to create a permanent school fund.   In 1867 a new constitution, and in 1868 a new and less centralized school law, laid the basis for the present school system.

Virginia.   For a summary of early educational legislation, see page 102.   By 1843 it was estimated that one half the indigent children of the State were receiving three months' schooling a year, under the provisions of the pauper school law of 1818.   There was much educational agitation for a better school system after 1837, with governors repeatedly recommending action.   Governor Campbell, in 1838 recommending action, reported that there were 200,000 children of school age in the State, 40,000 of whom were indigents, and but 20,000 in schools, and in 1839 he again urged action and submitted a prepared report on the Prussian schools (**R. 201**).   The Census of 1840 confirmed these figures,[1] and a storm of protest arose that found expression in a number of educational conventions, held from 1841 to 1845, which adopted memorials urging the creation of a state system of schools, with general taxation, and submitted bills for the consideration of the legislature (**R. 229**). Governor McDowell, in 1843, urged action in vigorous language, but without effect,[2] and the legislature of 1845–46 recommended against the district free school and in favor of retaining the indigent system.[3]   In

[1] The Census of 1840 reported Virginia as having 58,732 adult illiterates, or about one adult in thirteen.   New Jersey, Kentucky, and Alabama ranked higher than Virginia in percentage of illiteracy.   North Carolina, with a district system just begun, reported one fourth of its adult population as illiterate.   Ohio and New York had 35,000 adult illiterates, and Kentucky 40,000, while Massachusetts reported but 4500, and Connecticut only 526. A storm of protest found expression in the Clarksburg and Lexington conventions of 1841, which, sweeping eastward, through meetings at practically every courthouse, culminated in the two important educational conventions at Richmond in 1841 and 1845.

[2] Commenting on the results under the law of 1818, he said:

"If sixty days' tuition to one half of the indigent children of the State is the grand result which our present system is able to accomplish after so many years of persevering effort to enlarge and perfect its capacity, it is little more than a costly and delusive *nullity* which ought to be abolished and a better one established in its place."

[3] The Committee of Schools and Colleges of the House of Delegates, after considering the proposed bills, reported:

"That it is inexpedient to adopt the district free school recommended by the Educational Convention, and that the present system for the education of the indigent should be pre-

1846 a new school law was enacted, under which county commissioners were to lay off the counties into school districts, to levy a county school tax to provide a free school for all white children, to examine and license teachers, and to inaugurate teachers' meetings. The law was optional, however, and was adopted by only nine counties, while the pauper law of 1818 continued as the main school law of the State. In 1849 an attempt was made to provide every county with some kind of a school system by requiring each county to choose which one of several school systems authorized in the past it would adopt and try to develop. For the large majority of the counties this meant the continuation of the ineffective law of 1818.[1]   The Constitution of 1851 provided for a state capitation tax to be added to the Literary Fund income, and this provision was continued in the new Constitution of 1864.

Important educational conventions met at Richmond in 1856 and 1857 and memorials to the legislature were formulated, but no new legislative action resulted.   By 1860 there was a superintendent and a board of school commissioners in every county, with some attempt at an educational system (R. 230), and about 50,000 poor children were being given an average of 77 days' schooling, in 3197 primary schools, at a cost of approximately $190,000 for tuition and books.   Many academies for advanced instruction had been established, and, in 1850, 9068 students in 317 academies, with 547 teachers, were reported.   The new Constitution of 1869, and the new school law of 1870, laid the foundation of the present state school system.

North Carolina.   For a summary of early legislation up to the first school law of 1839, see page 103.   From 1840 to 1852 was an experimental period, with a gradual increase in the number of counties voluntarily adopting the two laws of 1839 and 1840.   By 1846 all counties had adopted these laws.   In 1849 the county superintendency was created, and in 1852 the state superintendency, thus remedying a previous lack of central control.   The first state appointee, Calvin H. Wiley,[2] held office from 1852 to 1866, when the office was abolished,

served and amended, [but] that any county or corporation should be empowered to adopt such a system of primary schools as a majority of the voters of such counties or corporations may elect; and that any tax imposed in addition to the quota of the Literary Fund shall be made obligatory upon the same." (*House Journal*, 1845–46.)

[1] Concerning the operation of this law, Governor Wise, in 1857, declared:

"The truth is that the pauper children do not partake of this bounty in any considerable proportion at all.   The poor little girls without fly-flap bonnets and the little shoeless boys do not go to school, because the shame of poverty keeps them away from that *charity* which points its finger at their indigence.   The fact is that the larger number of parents whose children take the bounty, are those who are able to pay the tuition.   The poor are driven away from the fund, and it is used as a mere auxiliary for those who have enough of their own to educate their children; and the application of the fund in the present mode has, in many instances, the injurious effect of relaxing their efforts to establish and keep up efficient schools.   The pretext then that this bread is needed to feed the poor, is but the art of misapplying the funds for education."

[2] Calvin H. Wiley was born on a farm in North Carolina in 1819, of Scotch-Irish Presbyterian stock.   He was prepared for college by David Caldwell in one of those "log college" academies that did such effective work in the South.   Graduating from the University

and the history of education in the State for that period is almost the biography of Wiley.[1]   The greatest hindrance to development was the lack of trained teachers. From 1850 to 1859 the Normal College, which later (1859) became Trinity College, rendered valuable aid, its graduates (1850) being certificated to teach.   A State Teachers' Association and a state educational magazine were established in 1856.   By 1858 a four months' school term was maintained, and by 1860 the State had

6 colleges for males, 13 colleges for females, 350 academies and select schools, and about 3000 primary schools with an enrollment of about 150,000 children. At the outbreak of the Civil War North Carolina had the best school system of any slaveholding State, with higher salaries for teachers and a longer school term than any other Southern State before 1860, or again before 1900.   The Civil War checked development, though the temptation to use the $2,000,000 school fund for war needs was resisted, and the schools were kept open throughout the conflict.[2] The loss of the school fund as a result of the fortunes of war caused the schools to close in 1865, and they were not reopened until

FIG. 113. CALVIN H. WILEY
(1819–87)

1870.   The new constitutions of 1868 and 1876 laid the foundations of the present school system.

of North Carolina in 1840, he studied law and became a lawyer and a noted editor.   Entering the legislature in 1850, he sponsored a bill to create the office of state superintendent of schools, which was enacted, and the legislature elected him to the office in January, 1853.   He held the office until it was abolished, in 1866.   He died in 1887.

[1] "Considering the obstacles which confronted him, Wiley's educational achievements will challenge a most favorable comparison with the work of any educational leader of the *ante-bellum* period.   Before the outbreak of the Civil War his leadership was widely recognized and his services were greatly in demand in other States.   Virginia, South Carolina, and Georgia sought to copy the educational example of North Carolina, and Wiley was invited to appear before the legislature of Georgia for the purpose of aiding that State in improving its school system."   (Knight, E. W.   *Public Education in the South*, p. 237.)

[2] Wiley, in his last *Report*, well said:

"To the lasting credit of North Carolina, her public schools survived the terrible shock of the cruel war.... The common schools lived and discharged their useful mission through all the gloom and trials of the conflict, and when the last gun was fired, and veteran armies once hostile were meeting and embracing in peace upon our soil, the doors were still kept open, and they numbered their pupils by scores of thousands."

South Carolina. Though the law of 1811 (**R. 76**) had tensible beginnings of a state free school system (see pa organization, due to a shortage of funds and the preference giv and the children of the poor by the law, remained virtuall) school system throughout all the *ante-bellum* period. The sa tions and habit of thinking which retarded development in .irginia operated in South Carolina with even more force. Though a number of early governors, between 1817 and 1835, urged the legislature to improve conditions, no action was taken by that body. In 1835, Governor George McDuffie, in a vigorous message (**R. 231**), urged the legislature to action and repeated his recommendation the following year, but the only result was an amendment of the law of 1811 prescribing penalties for negligence on the part of school officials, and the appointment of a legislative committee to consider the subject. This committee reported in 1836, and recommended that "none but poor orphans and children of indigent and necessitous parents should be educated at the expense of the State." A number of subsequent governors took a broader view and urged the creation of a real state school system, as did an educational convention at Columbia (1851), but without result. In 1845 the governor recommended the creation of a state superintendent of schools to supervise the education being provided, but the legislature regarded the expense as too great to comply with the recommendation.[1] A state legislative committee, reporting in 1847, urged more liberal provisions for general education (**R. 232**), but again without results. In 1852 the legislative appropriation for schools was increased from $37,000 to $74,000, but no other action was taken until after the Civil War, though there was continued agitation from 1855 to 1860. In 1854 the city of Charleston petitioned to be permitted to establish a tax-supported free school system, which was granted, and this system began work in 1856. In 1858 the city established a girls' high school, with a normal department to train teachers. Outside of Charleston, the 1811 system virtually continued up to 1860, rendering such service as it could (**R. 233**). The new constitution of 1868 made the first constitutional mention of education and provided for the first state superintendent, and a school law was enacted in 1870, but the real beginnings of the state school system date from about 1877.

Georgia. The early interest in education in this State was chiefly in academies and a state university. The University of Georgia was chartered as early as 1784, and opened for instruction in 1801. By 1820 thirty-one academies had been chartered. In 1817 a fund for free schools was created, but in 1822 the income from the fund was designated for the tuition of poor children, as the academy fund had been in 1820. In 1837 the academy fund and the common-school fund were

[1] "Impressed by the sound views presented in the message, and concurring in these views almost entirely, the committee yet feel constrained by both the condition of the treasury, and the present circumstances of the people, to withhold the legislation which they would otherwise have proposed for your deliberation." (Report of a legislative committee, 1845.)

consolidated, one third of the United States Surplus Revenue distribution to South Carolina was added, and a common-school system established. In 1838, county courts were allowed to levy a county tax for schools. In 1840, however, both the 1837 and the 1838 laws were repealed. In 1843, county courts were permitted to levy a tax sufficient to educate the children of the poor, and a typical Pennsylvania pauper school system was provided for in the law. The law, however, was never put into full effect. The officers charged with its operation neglected their duties, not over three fourths of the children of the poor being reported, and not over half of these were sent to school. As late as 1850 no returns were received from fifteen counties, and during one year of the intervening period only fifty-three out of ninety-three counties applied for any state apportionment for schools.

Between 1845 and 1858 several attempts were made to inaugurate a state school system, and two important educational conventions were held which memorialized the legislature,[1] but all efforts ended in failure except that in the year 1858 the word "poor" was eliminated from the school law, and that same time $100,000 a year from the income derived from the Western and Atlantic railroad was set aside for aid to schools. In 1859, figures showed that there were 130,000 children in the State entitled to participate in the poor fund, and that 72,000 of these were being taught. The teachers as a rule provided the building and received seven cents per pupil per day for the instruction they offered. While there was promise of good development by the time the Civil War put an end to all educational progress, the principle of general public education for all children had not been accepted, but was a later outcome.

2. *New States, in order of admission*

Kentucky. Admitted as a State in 1792. For early legislative attempts, see page 103. No general interest in education before 1820. In 1821, first provision for aid to common schools and a fund created, but this proved abortive, as legislature used the fund for other purposes. This same year a legislative committee was appointed, which reported in 1822, recommending a general system of education in common schools and academies, after the New York plan, with a central university. No action. In 1830 was passed the first general law for schools, establishing a district system, with local taxation, but this proved a dead letter due to lack of interest in education and unwillingness to bear taxation. In 1838, real interest manifested itself with the enactment of a law providing for district organization, county school commissioners, a state board of education, a state superintendent of schools, and local taxation. At that time it was estimated that one half the children of the State had never been to school, and one third of the adult

---

[1] The memorial of the Atlanta convention asked for "schools to which the children of the poorest citizen shall be sent, without submitting parent or child to the jeer of pauperism, and school houses that shall awaken a feeling of pride in every neighborhood.... We must have *free public schools* in every school district in Georgia."

population was illiterate. A state school fund also was established and $850,000 of the Surplus Revenue of 1837 was put into it. It required, however, fifteen years to overcome opposition and to get this law into operation in every county. Louisville schools date from 1819, were made free during 1829–30, and permanently after 1840.

In 1840, the State refused to pay interest on the new school fund, and in 1845 the school bonds were destroyed by legislative action. In 1848 the debt of the State to the school fund was acknowledged (page 187), in 1849 the first state school tax of 2 cents was levied, and the new constitution of 1850 made the first mention of education. The law of 1850 made the interest on the school fund a first charge on the treasury, and in 1855 the state school tax was raised by vote of the people from 2 cents to 5 cents. By 1853 a school existed in each county, for the first time. The yearly income from all state sources was but 60 cents per census pupil at this time, and by 1863 it had risen to $1.10. The Civil War interrupted this system and left the State with depleted resources. In 1867, agitation for education began anew; in 1869, the state school tax was increased from 5 cents to 20 cents; and a new school law of 1870 laid the basis of the present school system.

Tennessee. Admitted as a State, in 1796. Although different governors had urged action, the beginnings of education date from the law of 1830, which formed the basis of all *ante-bellum* legislation. This law established the district system, and provided for district trustees and county commissioners, but made no provision for the support of schools other than apportionments from the income of the school fund (created in 1827), donations, and fees. The schools were to be for all, with no distinctions between rich and poor, and free. For the time and the region the law was commendable. Its defect was lack of support, as the income from the school fund was sufficient to maintain the schools but a few weeks each year; this was supplemented, however, by a rate-bill.[1] Reports for 1839 showed 185,000 children in school.

In 1835 a new constitution was adopted in which provision for education was made for the first time. An act of that year provided for the appointment of a county officer to examine teachers and oversee the district schools, and designated the Secretary of State as *ex-officio* superintendent of public instruction. An economy wave of 1844 reduced supervision, and for the next ten years the poorly organized district was little more than a name. An educational convention held at Knoxville, in 1847, recommended the creation of an effective state school system, with general taxation for education, and this recommendation was transmitted to the legislature with the endorsement of the governor, but the bill to carry the recommendation into effect failed of passage In 1853 Governor Andrew Johnson urged action, and in

[1] A three months' school was supposed to be maintained, the rate-bill being used as the means of supplementing the meager state support. However, the local school officials were authorized to exempt from the rate "such poor persons within the district as they shall think proper."

1854 a property tax of 2½ cents, and a capitation tax of 25 cents, were levied to aid in the maintenance of schools. The examination and certification of teachers were next added. The law, though, was "an effort rather than an accomplishment; a promise rather than a fulfillment," as the legislation proved too advanced except for a few cities, and the results were disappointing. In 1856 a bill to create a normal school failed, on third reading, due to sectional jealousies over its location. With the outbreak of the Civil War the schools were closed, and no further attempt at public education was made until 1867. The law then enacted also proved too advanced for an impoverished State, and the real beginnings of the present school system were not made until 1873.

Louisiana. Admitted as a State in 1812. In 1821 a parish (county) tax for academies was authorized, in return for the education of indigent children therein. In 1833, the beginnings of state supervision were made by an act designating the Secretary of State to act *ex-officio* as state school superintendent. Though governors repeatedly recommended the abandonment of the subsidized parochial school system and the establishment of a public school system, no action could be obtained from the legislature. In 1841, New Orleans was given authority to establish a complete system of public schools, with a city superintendent and support by taxation, and a good city school system soon developed there, with the first city school superintendent (1841) to be appointed in the South.

A new constitution in 1845 made the first provision for a state school system by including an article providing for the state school fund, a state superintendent of public instruction, general property taxation, and a general system of free public schools throughout the State, thus putting an end to the old system of subsidized private schools. The constitution of 1852 practically repeated the provisions of that of 1845. The free-school law of 1847, the first to be enacted by the State, carried the mandate of the constitution into effect by providing for a state superintendent of schools, levying a mill state school tax, a capitation tax, providing for local school directors, parish (county) superintendents to license and supervise teachers, and for local taxation for school buildings. By 1850 there were 692 organized school districts in the State, maintaining 618 schools, with 22,000 children enrolled. In a few communities high schools were reported as being organized. In 1850 the office of parish superintendent was abolished, which greatly crippled the system, and a provision whereby parents could obtain their children's quota of public money and use it to pay private teachers and governesses [1] also greatly weakened the system. As a result private schools flourished, while the public schools declined in efficiency. At the outbreak of the Civil War, fully half the pupils of school age outside of New

---

[1] On this point the 1859 *Report* of the state superintendent of schools said:
"Under the present law every planter has a school at his house and draws the pro rata share out of the public treasury. The poor children have not the benefit of these schools."

Orleans were attending public schools, and as late as 1862 the Confederate legislature appropriated $485,000 for public schools. The war, military control, and the reconstruction constitutions of 1864 and 1868 practically ended this state school system; the present system dates from the constitution of 1867.

Mississippi. Admitted as a State in 1817. Though a Literary Fund had been established in 1821, with county commissioners to apply the income to the education of poor children, the law was virtually repealed in 1824, and in 1833 any plan for state education was abandoned and the income from the Fund devoted wholly to the education of indigents. During the early forties there was much agitation for a law for public schools, and in 1844 and 1846 the governor made earnest pleas for legislation. The result was the law of 1846, the first law enacted in the State looking to the general establishment of public schools. This provided for district schools, permissive local taxation, and the licensing of teachers. In 1848, the governor appealed for a better law, but instead the legislature enacted four special school laws, applying to six, five, seven, and fourteen different counties, while the remainder of the counties continued under the law of 1846. During the remainder of the *ante-bellum* period the evil of local and privileged legislation continued.[1] Statistics for 1860 showed 1116 common schools in the State, 1215 teachers employed, and 31,000 pupils enrolled, with about three fifths of the cost of instruction coming from tuition fees. The Civil War ended these efforts, and the present school system dates from the new constitution of 1868 and the law of 1870.

Alabama. Admitted as a State in 1819, with a constitution making rather good provisions for education. The law of 1823 provided for school districts, local trustees, hiring and examination of teachers, and reports as to pupils, but with emphasis on the education of the children of the poor at the expense of the district or county; other children to pay a tuition fee. In 1826, a special law permitted Mobile to organize schools for the city,[2] and to levy a tax for their support. In 1840, it was provided that the state bank should pay over $200,000 a year to aid schools, but the bank failed shortly thereafter and, as the 16th section lands had been neglected, there was little support left for schools. During the forties and fifties there were some efforts made to improve conditions, and the legislature gave some consideration to plans, but without funds and with no state aid but little could be done. In the 1851-52 session of the legislature a bill was pushed to provide for a state superintendent of schools, but it failed of passage. At that time there were

---

[1] The effect of these special acts was virtually to repeal the law of 1846 providing for a general system of common schools for the State. The special-act counties were no longer required to make reports to the State office, with the result that by 1849 only one fourth of the counties reported, and in 1851 only three counties. Just what was the condition of education in the State became hard to tell.

[2] For a good brief history of the school system in Mobile, 1826-65, see Chapter IV of S. B. Weeks's *History of Public School Education in Alabama*.

approximately 100,000 children of school age in the State, with but 29,000 in 1152 public schools, employing 1195 teachers. Hundreds of communities had no schools whatever.

In 1854, in response to an awakened public sentiment, the first real school law was enacted. This law created an educational fund, provided for a state superintendent, county school commissioners, local trustees, examination and certification of teachers, county taxation, and made a state appropriation of $100,000 a year for schools. The first state school superintendent, Calvin F. Perry, in 1855 reported that three fourths of the children in the State were without instruction, the schoolhouses miserable in character, and the county and township organization very defective (R. 234). In 1856 a revision of the law improved the system, that same year the Alabama Educational Association was formed, and in 1857 the *Alabama Educational Journal* was established. A new public-school sentiment had been awakened, the counties were rapidly being organized for educational work, and public funds were being increased and doubled by subscriptions. The war was a disturbing influence, but the people desired to continue the schools and many were kept open throughout most of the war period.[1] A new constitution in 1867 made very definite provision for a highly centralized state school system, but the present school system dates from the constitution of 1875 and the law of 1876. Another new constitution in 1901 continued most of the educational provisions of the constitution of 1875.

Missouri. Admitted as a State in 1820. The constitution of 1820 directed the legislature to preserve the school lands, apply the income to the support of schools, to establish at least one school in each township "where the poor may be taught gratis," and "as soon as may be" to establish a state university. In 1824 the first school law was enacted, a form of optional district system, with a school district tax if two thirds of the voters demanded it. Little was done under this law. In 1835 a "Committee for Literary Purposes" — virtually an *ex-officio* state board of education — was provided for, and in 1839 the office of state superintendent of common schools was created (abandoned in 1841), county school commissioners were provided for, and a three months' school term ordered. The first public school in St. Louis, virtually the first free public school in the State, was opened in 1838. The census of 1840 showed that most of the existing schools were private, there being but 642 primary schools in the State, St. Louis included, and but 526 pupils educated wholly at the public charge. By 1842 but 28 of the 77 counties then organized had schools. By 1850 there were 1570 public schools, though nearly one half the support came from tui-

---

[1] The schools were kept open until the appointment of a provisional governor in July, 1865. The records and papers of the state superintendent's office were carted about the country in boxes, to prevent their destruction, during most of the time after 1863. The people seemed determined to keep the schools open wherever possible as long as could be done.

tion fees. In 1844 the state university was created, and opened for instruction in 1847, but it had a struggling existence for two decades as the first state support for the institution was not voted until 1867.

In 1853, the office of the state superintendent of schools was re-established, and the first high school in Missouri was opened in St. Louis. By 1854 the schools of that city were well established as a public school system, having at that time thirteen primary schools, fourteen grammar schools, and one high school, with 75 teachers employed and 4193 pupils enrolled. By 1858, every county had been organized into the public school system, and by 1861 there were 5670 teachers employed and the expenses of the system were approximately $850,000, one fourth of which came from rate-bills. The coming of the war put an end to this school system, and the legislature of 1861 abolished the office of state superintendent and suspended the appropriations for schools. During the war the schools of the State were virtually closed. The present school system dates from the constitutions of 1865 and 1875, and the school law of 1875.

Arkansas. Admitted as a State in 1836, with good constitutional provisions for education. Education had made a good start under territorial administration, and some type of school, mostly private, was to be found in nearly every township of the few organized counties.[1] The first general school law was enacted in 1843, providing for a state board of education, county school commissioners, local trustees, and a four months' school in every township, but making no provision for support beyond the income from the 16th section lands, private contributions, and tuition fees, but indigents were to be admitted free. In 1846, a state appropriation of $250,000 was made to help carry the law into effect, but the money seems not to have reached the schools. In 1853, a more advanced law was enacted, which provided for an *ex-officio* state superintendent and some centralization of authority, but it proved ineffective due to lack of tax support. The first *Superintendent's Report* of 1854 presented a gloomy picture of counties without schools, public indifference, and lack of tax support. By 1856, returns from half the counties revealed the same unsatisfactory conditions, with an estimate of about twenty-five schools in the State maintained wholly from common-school funds. By 1860, reports show approximately 750 common schools in operation, about 2000 children in school, and about 100 academies in the State. Up to the time of the Civil War education in Arkansas was generally regarded as a domestic or religious affair, and consequently little need was felt for taxation for school support. The war for a time put an end to schools. A good new school law was enacted in 1867, but it was rendered inoperative by the reconstruction policy of Congress. The present school system dates from the legislative act of 1875 and the new constitution of 1874.

[1] A number of these were of the "Old Field" school type, and were taught by well-educated men. Others were under the direction of the county courts, and were supported by funds derived from the school lands and tuition fees.

Florida. Organized as a Territory in 1819. In 1831 the Florida Educational Society was organized to diffuse information as to education, and the following year a common school was established at St. Augustine. In 1839 a permissive law provided for the organization of boards of township trustees, and the application of any income from school lands for the support of schools. In 1843 the county sheriffs were made *ex-officio* commissioners for the care of the school lands. In 1845 Florida entered the Union as a State,[1] with the county judges directed to act *ex-officio* as school superintendents. The first real school law dates from 1849. This provided for an *ex-officio* state superintendent of schools, directed that the income from the school fund should be used for the education of indigents, and permitted county taxation for schools, though but two counties levied such a tax. In 1852 Tallahassee began a tax-supported school system, and by the late fifties a growing sentiment for schools began to be evident. The lack of tax support remained the chief weakness of the schools up to the Civil War, and hence but little was accomplished. The present school system dates from 1869, and any real progress from about 1880.

Texas. Seceded from Mexico in 1836, and adopted a constitution which provided for a state superintendent of schools and declared it to be the duty of the legislature, "as soon as circumstances will permit, to provide by law for a general system of education." By a law of 1839 "three leagues of land" were given to each county [2] for the establishment of primary schools or academies, and fifty leagues were set aside for the support of two colleges or universities in the Republic. In 1840 county school commissioners were created to organize school districts, examine and certificate teachers, and to inspect schools. In 1845 Texas entered the Union as a State, with a constitution which made rather advanced provisions for education. Among other things it affirmed the school lands previously granted, and directed that one tenth of the annual tax revenue of the State be appropriated for the support of free schools. The law of 1854 established the school system of the State, and the first school was opened that year at San Antonio. The law provided for a district system, county commissioners, and an *ex-officio* state superintendent. Support was to come from state aid, local subscriptions, and the rate-bill, with permission to trustees to pay the money to private schools and teachers. By 1860 there were 1218 schools in the State employing 1274 teachers, and enrolling about 37,000 pupils. They could hardly be called free schools, as tuition fees formed the larger por-

---

[1] The constitution of the new State provided for the creation of a perpetual fund for the support of schools, and the seminary of learning, and the proper appropriation of the income thereof, but it did not enjoin on the legislature the establishment of a general system of education.

[2] This Act of the Republic of Texas, under date of January 26, 1839, granted three leagues of public land to each county for elementary schools, and also set apart fifty leagues of public land for the endowment of two colleges or universities, thereafter to be created. These provisions form the basis of the large school-land fund of the present State.

tion of their means of support. The Civil War checked this development, and the present system dates from 1866.

West Virginia. Organized as a separate Territory in 1861, and admitted as a State in 1863. The early history of education here is that of Virginia, from which it was carved, though much less was done in organizing education in the western counties than in Virginia proper. Even as late as 1860 but three counties in West Virginia had organized schools under the optional Virginia law of 1846. By 1862, a total of 65 academies had been chartered in the State. The city school systems of Sheperdstown date from 1846, Wheeling 1849, and a few other city systems were organized prior to 1860, but most of the town and city schools of the State date from 1864, when the schools of Charlestown and Fairmount were organized, or even later. The Clarksburg convention of 1841 was evidence of a rising interest in education, and the new state constitution of 1862 made detailed provision for a good state school system which was given form in the law of 1863. The second constitution of 1872 continued the provisions of the constitution of 1862, as did the new school law of 1873. Up to about 1880 was a period of establishment, as support was meager, many questioning the value of much that was proposed.

II. GENERAL CHARACTER OF THE ANTE-BELLUM SOUTHERN SCHOOLS

Awakening slower at the South. From the résumé of progress in the different Southern States which has just been given, it will be seen that response to the new interest in public education was slower at the South than at the North, but that an awakening was taking place there, after about 1840, that held much in promise as to the future. From the thirties to the fifties we note, in most of the States, that governors were calling the attention of their legislatures to the need for general educational provisions for the children of the State, but that legislatures were hard to convince and slow to act. The Sunday-School movement had been of help in arousing a desire for education in Virginia, and the Lancastrian plan, after which schools had been opened here and there in the cities of the South, also had acted as a leaven among the people. The educational revival in the North in the thirties and forties also seems to have served to awaken new interest in the educational problem on the part of the leaders in the South, and there is evidence that Horace Mann was repeatedly consulted as to educational practice and procedures. In a number of Southern cities — Wheeling, **Charleston, Mobile, Tallahassee** — good tax-supported school systems had been established, and the number of such was increasing when the Civil War put an end to educational progress.

Reasons therefor. There were many reasons why the awakening was much slower in the South than in the North. In the first place, there was the century-long tradition that education was primarily a family and a religious affair, and that the State's interest extended only as a charity for orphans and the children of the poor. Not only had voluntary associations for long assisted in caring for and educating these classes, but the States had also given what little educational funds they had to private and sectarian agencies as well as to public schools. The same arguments that education might be made too common and prove a mistaken effort were advanced at the South as at the North. Many regarded the whole idea of public education as visionary and impractical, and likely, if carried out, to break down those social barriers which had for so long existed between the different classes of the population. The institution of slavery, too, was a retarding influence of the first magnitude.

The great and important reasons for the slower development at the South, however, were that the region was essentially rural and but sparsely settled; farming and farm life was still, aside from cotton culture, in large part in the self-subsistence stage; there were but few cities of any size to serve as centers of intellectual influence and ferment; there were few industries or railroads, and only meager facilities for intercommunication; the need for formal education was but little felt, except by a small class which provided it for its own children; and the people generally were slow to respond to new social movements. Despite the wealth in land and slaves there was little free capital, and not much could be obtained from the proceeds of taxation. There were many charming homes and delightful social intercourse prevailed among the propertied classes, but the South, in remaining somewhat isolated, had not kept up with the advancing Nation. There was also a more or less general opposition to taxation, particularly if the proceeds were to be used for the education of the children of someone else. In so far as school organization had been developed, too, it was largely after the optional district-system type and with but little central control.

These backward conditions were beginning in the fifties, however, to give way to new conceptions. The numerous educational conventions, with their memorials to the legislatures; the "letters to

the press" from prominent citizens asking for schools; the "addresses" to the public of propaganda organizations; the building of
railroads into the South, with the consequent opening up of communication; the rise of a few city school systems, and the example
of a few States which showed what could be done; and the telling
statistics as to illiteracy which the Federal Census reports of 1840
and 1850 contained — all these and other forces were causing the
people of the different States to give fresh consideration to the question when the outbreak of the Civil War for a time put an end to
further educational progress in the South.

Character of the Southern schools. The general character of the
schools in the Southern States was not particularly different from
that of schools of the same type in the North, except that the Northern schools as a rule got well started toward better educational
conditions, teachers, and instruction from one to two and three
decades earlier, varying in different States, than did those at the
South. In the Northern States, too, there was the early uplifting
influence of a large number of developing city public-school systems
— a force largely lacking in the South. Taxation for education
evolved in the North, also, a generation before it became general in
the South.

In the rural schools of the South, reading, writing, spelling, and
arithmetic seem to have been about the only studies taught to any
extent before about 1850. These were the studies upon which teachers were examined for certification, when any examination at all
was required. The textbooks used up to that date were much the
same as at the North, with special partiality to Webster's blue-
backed *Speller*, McGuffey's *Readers*, Murray's *English Reader*, and
Colburn's *Arithmetic*, though numerous other books were used in
these staple subjects of the school. Geography and history were
late in finding a place in the elementary curriculum of the South,
though the geographies by Morse and Jesse Olney, and the histories
of Goodrich and Webster, were in use here and there. Grammar
found only a small place for itself, outside a few cities, in the *ante-
bellum* schools, though Murray's *English Grammar* was reported as
in use in "half the counties of Virginia" in 1840, and here and there
elsewhere in other States of the region. After about 1845 a distinct
tendency was manifested in the South to prepare their own textbooks, rather than use those published in the North, largely due to a

feeling that the North was not fair to the South in the matter of slavery.

"Incompetent teachers, wasteful methods of teaching, harsh discipline, poor physical equipment, crude methods of administration, and lack of organization and professional supervision" were the common defects of the Southern schools during the *ante-bellum* period. The teachers frequently were of the poorest type,[1] and the individual methods of teaching employed only added to their general inefficiency. Discipline was hard and often cruel,[2] there were many rules and penalties, and frequent use was made of dunce-blocks and fools' caps. Ability to teach meant primarily the ability to maintain

FIG. 114. A "FIELD SCHOOL" INTERIOR

the upper hand in a school often containing boys as large and as strong as the teacher. The latter practically always had to meet the test of "turning out the teacher" (**R. 235**), and physical strength as well as resourcefulness were demanded. High moral or professional qualifications were neither required nor expected.

The "Old Field" schools. A class of schools and teachers common throughout the South, particularly before 1850, were what were known as "Old Field" schools and teachers. The term originated from the practice of allowing long-cultivated fields to lie idle for a time "to sweeten." Rude schoolhouses often appeared on the cleared but vacant land,

---

[1] Governor Henagan, in a message to the Legislature of South Carolina, in 1840, said:

"The men who take charge of our public schools, and accept so miserable a pittance as the reward of their labors, are they who cannot get employment on any other terms. Necessity forces them to make the offer of their services, and necessity forces the commissioners to accept them. It is now in South Carolina a reproach to be a teacher of a free school, as it is regarded as *prima-facie* evidence of want of qualification."

[2] The following extract from an editorial in the Fredericksburg *Virginia Herald*, of November 28, 1830, is illustrative:

"What are the beatitudes of a scholastic paradise? To be fagged, flogged, thumped, and coerced to mental labor and constrained in personal liberty. This may be all very proper and salutary (so is physic), but it is not happiness, and there is very, very rarely an instance of a boy, while he is in one of these prisons of the body and treadmills of the mind who is not always wishing to get out of school and go home."

and took their name from the location.   Beyond rude benches facing the walls and a high desk for the teacher, there were no necessary furnishings.   A teacher coming into the community was given the use of the building, or of some outhouse on a plantation, for school purposes, and the educational institution thus set up went by the name of an Old Field school.

These schools were of all types, though mostly not unlike those of rural schools of elementary grade elsewhere.   In a historical sketch of education in Wythe County, Virginia,[1] the teachers in these schools were described as follows:

> Some of the teachers of these old field schools were invalids, some were slaves to drunkenness, most of them were entirely ignorant of the art of teaching and a terror to their pupils.   There were a few who possessed culture, intelligence, morality, and ability.

A good description of one of these Old Field schools has been left by a former pupil of one of them in a volume,[2] published in 1856, dealing with the school system of South Carolina (**R. 236**).

Academies and colleges.   Not infrequently these Old Field schools were termed Academies, and at times were incorporated as such in order that they might appoint trustees and draw public money for their support.   The South had been prominent in the academy movement, and it was but natural that many schools, not real academies in themselves, should take the name.   There were, however, in practically all the Southern States a large number of real academies (page 247) which rendered good service in the days before the war.   They offered preparation for the numerous colleges of the South, and at the same time sought to give a practical training to those who were not to attend college.   Their teachers often were well equipped for their work, discipline was rigid, and the training given was of a very satisfactory grade.   The academies did much, also, to stimulate a better preparation for teaching in the common schools of the time, and after the so-called revival period of the thirties and forties the academies came to be looked to in the South, as in the North, as sources of supply of the better-educated teachers, and a distinct movement was on, before the outbreak of the war, to

[1] By Major W. G. Repass, county superintendent of schools for Wythe County; in *Virginia State School Report*, 1885, Part III, p. 288.

[2] *The Free School System of South Carolina*, Columbia, 1856.   Author unknown.

use these institutions as training schools for teachers for the new elementary schools then being created in the Southern States.

In the matter of state universities, the South also was prominent at an early date. Georgia had been the first of all the States, in 1784, to provide for a state university, though it did not open it for instruction until 1801. North Carolina had followed Georgia five years later in creating its state university (1789), and in opening the institution for students in 1795 had been the first State to begin such instruction. Both these institutions made noteworthy contri-

FIG. 115. THE UNIVERSITY OF GEORGIA AS IT WAS BEFORE THE CIVIL WAR

Founded in 1784, and opened for instruction in 1801

butions to collegiate education during the period before the Civil War. The University of Virginia, founded in 1819 and opened for students in 1825, was for long celebrated for the high quality of instruction it offered. South Carolina founded its state university in 1801, and opened it for instruction in 1805; Tennessee laid the foundations of a state university in 1807, and began instruction in 1820; Alabama chartered its state university in 1820, and began classes in 1831; Missouri founded its state university in 1839, and began instruction in 1847; and Mississippi provided for a state university in 1844, which began instruction in 1848. These new universities were all relatively small in faculty, student body, and resources in the *ante-bellum* days, but they represented substantial hopes for the future.

III. GENERAL EFFECT OF THE CIVIL WAR ON
EDUCATION

Development at the North and the South. The coming of the Civil War, more or less evident for a decade before the storm broke, checked educational development at the North and put an almost complete stop to that of the South. It was a major disaster to the peaceful evolution of the Nation, and a terrible material and social calamity to the South. The growth of democracy and the industrial revolution had greatly altered the thinking of the North and the West, developed a conception of nationality to replace that of a confederacy of States (**R. 238**), and created a new world in which the institution of slavery was an anachronism. The South, in remaining rural and agricultural, clung to the conception of State's rights and state sovereignty, saw no way to do without slavery, and felt forced to defend the special type of civilization which it had built up.[1] Caught in the grasp of evolutionary forces it did not understand and could neither control nor stop, and its statesmen failing to recognize the new national life rapidly becoming dominant, its people finally came to hope for a solution through a peaceful secession and the right to live their own type of life (**R. 237**). The forces that had created nationality were not willing that this should be, and the result was the greatest civil war in history, with economic and political disaster for the South. The war itself absorbed the energies of the people, both North and South, and it was a decade after its close before any marked signs of educational expansion and development were evident in the North, and a third of a century before there was a real educational awakening at the South.

The second quarter of the nineteenth century had been, at the North, essentially a period of the establishment of the American free public school in the minds of the people and in the laws of the States. By 1850 the main lines for future development had been laid down, and the main battles had been won. The people had

[1] "What all the South had in common, what made a man a Southerner in the general sense — a distinction from a Northerner on the one hand, or a Virginian, Carolinian, Georgian on the other — the ideal of Southern life in general terms that were common — were country life, broad acres, generous hospitality, and an aristocratic system." (Stephenson, N. W. *The Day of the Confederacy*, p. 31.)

definitely decided that they intended to establish and maintain a series of state systems of free, publicly controlled, tax-supported, non-sectarian common schools, and that these common-school systems should provide whatever educational advantages the needs of the States might seem to demand. Many minor points still remained to be decided, and many local struggles still remained to be fought out, but the main lines of future development had been firmly established. In some of the Southern States a similar line of thinking was beginning to be in evidence, but it had not as yet been able to express itself in forceful legislation.

Northern development checked. After about 1850 a number of additions to and extensions of the public-education idea began to be noted — evidences of a desire on the part of those who had fought out the battle of taxation for education to extend the school systems they had created, and to make of them more useful instruments for state and national service.

Evening schools, probably first begun in New York City, about 1833, in Louisville, 1834, and in Baltimore, in 1840, began to be added by a number of northern cities to their school systems, and the first evening high school was opened in Cincinnati, in 1856. The first general state law for evening schools was enacted by Ohio in 1839, followed by Massachusetts in 1847.

Music, which had early found a place for itself in the female seminaries, began to be taught in Boston in 1837, and in Providence by or before 1848, and was beginning to find favor as a school subject here and there in the Eastern cities, but the development was largely checked for the next three decades.

Drawing, after certain temporary attempts at instruction in the subject in Boston as early as 1821 and 1836, had been placed on the list of optional grammar-school studies in 1848, largely as a result of Mann's *Seventh Report* in which he had described the German instruction in the subject. The celebrated painter, Rembrandt Peale, had offered instruction in drawing in the Philadelphia high school from 1840 to 1844, and other teachers had continued the work; Cincinnati began instruction in drawing in the high school, in 1847; Baltimore employed an architect of the city to teach drawing in its high school in 1848; and Cleveland made the beginnings of drawing instruction in a few schools in 1849. Henry Barnard, during the time of his labors in Connecticut, had also tried unsuccessfully to introduce instruction in drawing into the schools of that State. These early efforts, however, were somewhat sporadic and in part temporary and optional; there was no real interest in the work; [1] and the real beginning of instruction in drawing and design in the schools of the United States belongs to Massachusetts and was due to new impulses coming from abroad (Chapter XIII).

In 1840, Rhode Island, and in 1842, Massachusetts, enacted the first child-labor laws to be passed by American States. In 1852 the first compulsory school-attendance law was enacted by Massachusetts, followed by New York in 1853; after this latter date there were no further enactments until Vermont in 1867, and New Hampshire and Michigan in 1871.

City school supervision, which seemed well started by 1850, was so checked by the Civil War that but four additional cities created the office of city superintendent of schools between 1855 and 1870. High-school development also was retarded for a time.

The school term, however, was being lengthened steadily, increasing sums were being spent on the schools, and educational opportunity was being broadened, and these efforts continued at the North despite the war, as the annexed table shows. Taking into account all public and private schooling of whatever grade, the United States Bureau of Education estimated that each individual in our population received, during his lifetime, at the dates given, an average of the number of days and months (of 20 school days each) of schooling shown in the adjoining table. We had also, by 1860, made marked progress in opening up education of all grades to girls as well as boys, though in many places the girls were still taught in separate classrooms or schools.

Year	Total Number of Days	Months
1800	82	4 m. 2 d.
1840	208	10 m. 8 d.
1850	450	22 m. 10 d.
1860	434	21 m. 14 d.
1870	582	29 m. 2 d.
1880	690	34 m. 10 d.
1890	770	38 m. 10 d.
1900	934	41 m. 14 d.
1910	1080	54 m. 0 d.
1920	1226	61 m. 6 d.
1930	1591	79 m. 11 d.

A new type of internal development at the North. Up to about 1880 at the North, and 1890 to 1900 at the South, however, educational development and expansion came but slowly; expenses were kept down, school buildings were kept simple and along established lines, few

[1] There was no real interest because it met as yet no national need, which did not develop for two to three decades later.

new features were added to the curriculum, and few new school supervisory officers were employed. Then came the wonderful development in public education which has characterized the past thirty-five to forty years.

In the meantime our educational system was being developed in another way. Up to 1835 certainly, and in most places for from one to two decades longer, all development was a purely native develop-

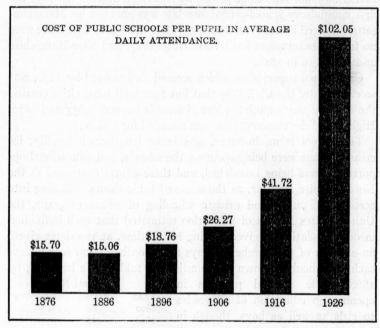

COST OF PUBLIC SCHOOLS PER PUPIL IN AVERAGE
DAILY ATTENDANCE.

1876	1886	1896	1906	1916	1926
$15.70	$15.06	$18.76	$26.27	$41.72	$102.05

FIG. 116. PER PUPIL COSTS, 1876–1926

From F. M. Phillips's *A Graphic View of our Schools*

ment. After about 1835 to 1840 we began to be touched by new influences from the outside, through new citizens and returning travelers who described for us the work of Pestalozzi and his disciples in Switzerland and the Pestalozzian organization of instruction in England, Holland, and the German States. After 1860 we began seriously to introduce among our teachers a new method of instruction, based on the psychological foundations worked out by Pesta-lozzi and his successors (Chapter XI). The period from about 1860 to about 1880 or 1890 was the period of the introduction and organization of teaching method, when we made up in internal organization what we lacked in external development. The grading of schools was continued, the size of classes was reduced, the quality of teaching was steadily improved, and better administrative organization was effected. The normal school was adopted and found its place, a science and an art of teaching arose, psychology became the guiding science of the school, and a philosophy for the educative process was formulated and stated. Teachers were stimulated to read and think, to understand better their tasks, and to conceive of the education of the child in an entirely new way. In this work of internal development two leaders, Dr. William T. Harris and Colonel Francis W. Parker, whose work will be mentioned more in detail in the following chapter, were prominent.

IV. THE POST-WAR RECONSTRUCTION PERIOD

The task that faced the South. The South had staked her all in defense of a theory of life and government, and had lost (**R. 238**). As the final outcome of the war had been evident for some time before its actual close, the leaders both in the North and the South had been thinking of the period of reconstruction which must follow. For the South it meant virtually starting life over again, with depleted man power, a country ravaged by conflict, slaves valued at $2,000,000,000 freed, and a land whose wealth had been largely swept away. In addition, one of its chief assets, some four million blacks, were now to be freed and turned into a tremendous liability. Its school funds, invested mostly in bank stocks and railways, had largely been destroyed as a result of the fortunes of war. Its public and private schools had closed, and many of its colleges had been ruined and their endowments lost.

In addition, each Southern State was faced by the necessity of revising its constitution and its laws to change the black man and his family from a chattel to a citizen. Fleming [1] has well expressed the situation confronting the South when he says:

> The new laws must meet many needs; family life, morals, and conduct must be regulated; the former slave must be given a status in court in order that he might testify and be protected in person and property;

[1] Fleming, W. L., *The Sequel of Appomattox*, pp. 90, 115.

the old, the infirm, and the orphans must be cared for; the white race must be protected from lawless blacks and the blacks from unscrupulous and violent whites; the negro must have an opportunity for education; and the roving blacks must be forced to get homes, settle down, and go to work....

These laws were a measure of the extent to which the average southern white would go in "accepting the situation" so far as the blacks were concerned. On the whole the recognition of negro rights made in these laws, and made at a time when the whites believed that they were free to handle the situation, was remarkably fair. The negroes lately released from slavery were admitted to the same rights as the whites as to legal protection of life, liberty, and property, as to education, and as to the family relation, limited only by the clear recognition of the principles of political inferiority and social separation. Unfortunately, this legislation was not to be put to the test of practical experience.

The task faced by the South was one of enormous proportions, and one calling for the best intelligence and the most devoted service the remaining leaders could provide. It was a tremendous undertaking for a people whose property had been largely swept away and whose school funds were mostly lost.

Robert E. Lee well expressed the best Southern feeling when he wrote, in 1866, to his friend Leyburn:

So greatly have those interests [educational] been disturbed at the South, and so much does its future condition depend upon the rising generation, that I consider the proper education of its youth one of the most important objects now to be attained, and one from which the greatest benefits may be expected. Nothing will compensate us for the depression of the standard of our moral and intellectual culture, and each State should take the most energetic measures to revive the schools and colleges, and, if possible, to increase the facilities for instruction and to elevate the standard of learning.

Unfortunately, the problem early became complicated by a bitter quarrel between the President and Congress as to reconstruction procedure, and the equities of the case were soon lost in the rancor of a struggle so intense and so prolonged that it left its blight on the subsequent life of the Nation. The Southern man of brains and character, who knew the colored people and the problem, was eliminated, and an attempt was made to reconstruct the Southern States by military control, negro legislatures, and Northern officials who had little or no grasp [1] of the situation (**R. 239**).

---

[1] A Northern leader, who lived at the time, well said:

"In the day when the supreme need was for such a handling of the business of emancipation as should enlist the interests of the southern people in their former slaves, and bind

The presidential plan. Before the war closed President Lincoln had inaugurated a plan for restoring the Southern States to normal relations with the Union by utilizing the intelligence and good-will in service of the best of the whites in the different States, and to this end he had established provisional governments in Arkansas, Louisiana, and Tennessee, and had recognized the new State of West Virginia. After his death, President Johnson attempted to carry on with the same plan, and appointed provisional governors for North Carolina, South Carolina, Georgia, Florida, Mississippi, and Texas. Each State was required to organize a provisional government and call a constitutional convention, which was to frame a new constitution, ratify the Thirteenth Amendment to the Federal Constitution abolishing slavery, declare the ordinance of secession null and void, repudiate the war debts, elect new state officers, select senators and representatives, and thus become ready for readmission to the Union. This was done by the different States, with certain minor exceptions, and they were ready for readmission, but Congress refused to receive them.

The new constitutions of Arkansas, Louisiana, and Maryland of 1864, Missouri and Florida of 1865, and Texas of 1866, made better provisions for public education than these States had known before, and a new educational interest appeared in many of the Southern States which, for the time, was quite remarkable. The governor of Arkansas, in a message to the legislature, asked that provision be made for the education of every child in the State, to be enforced by proper penalties, to which the legislature of 1866–67 responded with a good law. The Alabama law of 1867 provided for the creation of a state school system, "open to every child between the ages of six and twenty-one." Tennessee provided for a legislative committee to study the school systems of other States, increased the *ante-bellum* state school tax, and enacted a law which contemplated schools for both races. In Mississippi the planters were urged to establish schools on their plantations for the new freedmen. The Texas constitution of 1866 provided for schools for both blacks and whites. The Georgia law of 1866 made provision for a general system of schools. The Southern leaders were recognizing the changes

the two races together in friendship, the whole policy seemed to be directed toward the fomenting of antipathies between the races, and the employment of the blacks for the humiliation of the whites." (Washington Gladden. *Recollections*, p. 155.)

which the war had brought about, and started to create new conditions. Had they been allowed to do so, the history of education in the South for a generation to come might have presented an entirely different picture from what it did.

The congressional plan. Congress, however, had different ideas, and it set up the claim that Congress alone had power to determine the conditions for readmission to the Union. The first fruit of such action was the Fourteenth Amendment, which gave to the new freedmen equal civil and political rights and disqualified, for any state or federal office, all who had been in rebellion after having taken the oath to support the Constitution of the United States. Every Southern State, except Tennessee, rejected this amendment, as it would disqualify for office most of the leading whites and would put the governments in the hands of the Negroes.[1]

Early in March, 1867, the radicals in Congress triumphed over the moderate Republicans and Democrats, and passed, over the veto of the President, the first so-called reconstruction act. This abandoned the presidential plan, set up military law for the South, and reduced it to five military districts under army control. This condition was to continue until the "rebel States" formed constitutions which recognized the new status, said constitutions to be formed by conventions elected by male citizens of voting age without regard to "race, color, or previous condition of servitude," with disfranchisement for all who had been in rebellion. The States were then to elect officers and representatives, ratify the Fourteenth Amendment, and apply for readmission to the Union. A supplemental act, passed three weeks later, directed the commanders of the military districts to register the legal voters and call elections for the constitutional conventions. Of these conventions,[2] writes Knight:

---

[1] The death of Lincoln, for which the South was not to blame, changed the whole picture by releasing a bitter attack of anti-Southern sentiment at the North which blasted all hope of prompt reconciliation, and which left the Southern people angry and sullen. More, it had removed from the head of the Nation, at the hour when he was most needed, the man best qualified for its leadership. The South had lost its best friend. It is said that General Ewell, when he heard the news, burst into tears at the thought of the fate of the South.

[2] For example, the Virginia convention of 105 delegates included 13 scalawags, 34 carpetbaggers, 22 native Negroes, and 33 conservatives. The South Carolina convention of 124 delegates was composed of 76 Negroes and 48 whites. Of the 76 Negroes, 27 were from out of the State. Of the 48 whites, 4 were conservatives, and 25 were carpet-baggers. As to property, 23 of the whites and 59 of the Negroes paid no taxes. The Alabama convention of 100 delegates consisted of 42 scalawags, 18 Negroes, 38 carpet-baggers, and 2 conservatives.

The composition of these bodies was altogether unlike anything ever before seen in the South. They consisted of scalawags, or native whites who were out of sympathy with the South and who favored the congressional plan of restoration; carpetbaggers, northern men who went South after the war, who favored the plan of Congress, and who were later charged with exploiting the people and seeking private gain; ignorant negroes; and a few conservative whites.

The debates in these constitutional conventions, in so far as education was concerned, centered about equal rights and mixed schools. These were not desired by either race, nor were they to the ultimate advantage of either race, yet mixed schools were provided for in a number of the new constitutions,[1] with the result that the white children did not attend the schools when created.

The new legislation. The new constitutions were more or less similar in regard to the Article on Education, and were largely based on Northern models.[2] A full set of school officers was provided for, more comprehensive and mandatory provisions as to schools were included, the old *ante-bellum* school funds were to be recognized, and fairly satisfactory articles as to taxation and support usually were included. The school laws which later were enacted to carry out these new constitutional provisions also represented a distinct advance in most cases, though usually following rather closely earlier laws of the States, but they were far less discretionary than these. Many of the laws were unenforcible, however, owing to the poverty of the people, the uncertain political conditions, the mixed-school conception of public education, and the ignorance and corrupt practices of those in charge of government.[3] The presence of the Negro and his new political status, coupled with the lack of

[1] Separate schools for the two races were, however, provided for in the new constitutions of Georgia, Alabama, Tennessee, Arkansas, and Texas, while the constitution of North Carolina was silent on the question, but the school law of 1869 provided for separate schools there also. Mississippi had also been silent, but there the school law of 1870 ordered the schools open to all youth of the State.

[2] "On paper these schemes were often admirable. Usually they were modeled after the system in the State from which some influential carpet-bagger came, and, under normal conditions, if honestly and judiciously administered, they would have answered their ostensible purpose and would have done much to raise the intellectual level of the population. Conditions, however, were not normal. Under existing conditions the communities could not support the schemes of education which had been projected." (Thompson, H. *The New South*, p. 159.)

[3] Generally speaking, the new legislation was most successful where the conservative white element had been most prominent in formulating it, as in Virginia, where the new law of 1869 was built on the old law of 1839, and least successful where the radical and ignorant elements were most fully in control.

taxable resources, made the maintenance of any system of public schools, for a long time to come, a most difficult matter. Lack of teachers, partisan strife, and fraud and extravagance in government also contributed their quotas. The gift of the ballot to a race wholly unprepared to use it intelligently likewise was a factor that kept passionate political feeling at a white heat. The general result was a wasting of resources and a deadening of public interest in education.

The cost of reconstruction. In 1877, President Hayes withdrew the troops from the South and ended military rule. The Southern white people were now free to take control once more of their own affairs, and the next two decades were given over largely to a reconstruction of governmental organization and to the development of new wealth on which the support of education might be based. Many of the Southern States adopted new constitutions, after 1875, which were more in harmony with Southern wishes, and new school laws also were enacted.

The cost to the South of the eight years of reconstruction, from 1868 to 1877, was enormous. Some writers assert that the loss was greater than that of the war itself. The property and wealth that had escaped destruction during the conflict was largely dissipated in the reconstruction process. School funds that remained were spent,[1] treasuries were looted, huge debts were piled up by the negro and carpet-bagger governments, the state universities were largely ruined,[2] and industry and agriculture were largely set back in their development. The building of schools and the provision of state systems of education were compelled to wait until new material resources could be built up and public confidence restored. As a result, speaking generally, education in the South was possibly at a lower ebb in 1890 than it was in 1860. To the mistakes of the reconstruction period many of the educational problems of the region today can trace their origin. (**R. 240**).

There was also a great social cost. In the bitter days of reconstruction the pleasantest side of Southern life came to an end. The

[1] As for example in Louisiana, where the negro legislature appropriated the fund to pay their appropriations and salaries. Also North Carolina, where the remains of the old Literary Fund saved from the destruction of the war was squandered during the reconstruction period.

[2] For example, in the University of South Carolina, over which the legislature presided, a corn-field Negro, barefooted, illiterate, sat in the chair and drew the salary of the professor of Greek.

good feeling produced by the magnanimity of Grant at Appomattox disappeared, to be replaced by intense rancor. The old plantation families were largely bankrupt, and the struggles with Negroes, Northern officials, and missionaries largely took the charm and grace out of the Southern temperament. Hospitality markedly declined, life narrowed and adjusted itself to a strict economy, and the old pleasing individuality tended to disappear. The moral, social, and intellectual results of the war and its aftermath left a permanent mark on Southern character.

Freedmen's Aid Societies. What to do with the Negroes who appeared within the Union lines during the war became a grave question to the Union commanders, and what to do with the blacks found on abandoned plantations in large areas taken over from the South after 1863 became an even more serious problem. In either case the colored man and his family came under Union jurisdiction in a helpless, frightened, and destitute condition. While the different Union commanders did what they could, Northern societies were soon organized to take over the burden, partially at least, and later the Federal Government undertook to do something to alleviate conditions. While all plans at the start were vague, the relief of physical suffering naturally came first. The second thought was for education, and the call soon came for books and teachers.

The first society established primarily for freedmen's aid was the Boston Educational Commission, later known as the New England Freedmen's Aid Society, organized in February, 1862. The National Freedmen's Relief Association was organized three weeks later in New York, and in March, 1862, the Pennsylvania Freedmen's Relief Commission of Philadelphia came into being. Each of these was a nation-wide organization. Other organizations along state lines were formed in Rhode Island, Maine, and New Hampshire, and throughout the Middle West. In 1863 a combination of five of the larger of these societies — those centering at Boston, New York, Philadelphia, Cincinnati, and Chicago — was effected at Washington, and became known as the United States Commission for the Relief of the National Freedmen, the purpose being to "supply the immediate and pressing physical wants of the freed people, provide them with homes and employment, organize them into communities, and furnish them with such instruction as their case demands to prepare them for the privileges and duties of Christian freemen." This Commission was displaced in March, 1865, by the American Freedmen's Aid Union, with approximately the same aims, and later in the same year this gave way to the American Freedmen's Aid Commission, which was a union of most of the important Eastern and Western societies, for more effective relief work. At the first meeting of this last-formed organization it was decided to send at once two thousand teachers to the Negroes, to prevent their ill-treatment and to secure rights of citizenship for them. At a convention held in Cleveland in May, 1866, of practically all co-operating societies, the name was further changed to the American Freedmen's Union Commission, and the principle of "no distinction of race or color" was definitely laid down. By 1867 this Commission had ten branches in different sections of the North, working unitedly in a common cause, but early in 1869, with peace established, the Commission and most of its branches discontinued work, leaving the task to the individual Southern States or to other religious and philanthropic agencies.

The different churches also carried on an extensive system of freedmen's aid, the Methodists, Presbyterians, Congregationalists, and Baptists being especially prominent. These either joined in the work of the American Missionary Society, or set up Freedmen's Aid or Missionary Societies of their own, and spent their efforts on physical relief and the establishment of schools and churches.

In the meantime Congress also began work on the problem by creating a Bureau of Refugees, Freedmen, and Abandoned Lands, in February, 1865, placing it under the War Department, to have "the supervision and management of all subjects relating to refugees and freedmen." In 1866 the work was extended and placed under General Howard, as chief Commissioner, with power to appoint assistant commissioners in the different military districts. One of the chief objects of the reorganized Bureau came to be that of providing schools for the Negroes and the introduction of school teachers from the North. The Bureau co-operated largely with the voluntary benevolent associations mentioned above, appointed state superintendents for the different States, and encouraged the founding of schools for and by the new freedmen. The general work of the Bureau came to an end, however, in 1870, when the last congressional appropriation was exhausted, though the school work continued for a few years beyond that date.   The *Report on Schools for Freedmen* for 1870 states that there were then 2677 day and night schools, with 3300 teachers, of whom 1800 were colored, and 149,581 pupils in attendance.   During the five years of its existence the Bureau spent over six and a half million dollars in relief and rescue work and education, a good proportion of which was for schools.[1]

The establishment of the Peabody Fund, in 1867, served to give a new turn to the Southern educational movement.

Peabody Education Fund.   During the period of deep discouragement that followed the close of the war, one of the most cheering and helpful influences that the South experienced came through the work of The Peabody Education Fund.   In 1867, George Peabody, a citizen of Massachusetts, but at that time a resident of London, established a trust fund (**R. 241**) which, with a subsequent donation in 1869, totaled approximately $3,500,000 for the promotion of education in the Southern States, or, as he expressed it, "those portions of our beloved and common country which have suffered from the destructive

FIG. 117
GEORGE PEABODY
(1795–1869)

ravages, and not less disastrous consequences, of civil war."[2] This trust is usually considered as having been the first of our great educational foundations.[3]   Sixteen trustees were named to manage the Fund, and they chose the Reverend Barnas Sears, fifth president of Brown University, as General Agent of the Fund, a position he held until his death in 1880.   He was succeeded by Professor J. L. M. Curry, a Southern Colonel, a native of Georgia, and at the time of his appointment President of Howard College,

[1] For an interesting account of the work of the Freedmen's Bureau, see an article by W. E. B. DuBois, in the *Atlantic Monthly*, vol. 87, p. 354.

[2] The Honorable R. C. Winthrop, for long chairman of the Board of Trustees of the Fund, pronounced the gift "the earliest manifestation of a spirit of reconciliation toward those from whom we have been so unhappily alienated and against whom we of the North had been so recently arrayed in arms."

[3] For this generous gift, Congress adopted a "resolution of thanks," approved March 16, 1867, and made it the duty of the President of the United States "to cause a Gold Medal to be struck, with suitable devices and inscriptions, which, together with a copy of this resolution, shall be presented to Mr. Peabody, in the name of the People of the United States."

Alabama, who continued to direct the work [1] until his death [2] in 1903, when the trust was dissolved. As a Southerner, he could speak more freely and more effectively to the people than his predecessor could do.

The conditions of the trust were so liberal and so elastic that the trustees were able to use it in many different ways to help the Southern people to create educational advantages they needed and

FIG. 118. THE TWO AGENTS OF THE PEABODY FUND

BARNAS SEARS   JABES LAMAR MONROE CURRY
(1802–1880)   (1825–1903)

did not possess. First, public school systems in the larger towns and cities were inaugurated, and then maintained until the local authorities could take over their support. In a similar manner, state school organizations were assisted until the legislatures could maintain them — a task largely completed by 1875. The Fund also promoted rural school consolidation, and aided in the advancement of rural education by paying the salaries of state supervisors in this field. Model demonstration schools, and normal schools for Negroes, also

[1] For a good statement of the work of Curry, and of the Peabody Fund during his period of management, see *Report of the U.S. Commissioner of Education*, 1903, vol. I, pp. 521–52, which contains a collection of addresses under the title of "J. L. M. Curry and His Services to Education in the South." He devoted his energies largely to the awakening of public sentiment for schools, and to this end he addressed public meetings and legislatures "from the Potomac to the Rio Grande."

[2] "The chief work of this noble life was to develop an irresistible public opinion in a democracy for the accomplishment of permanent ends. In short, through such work as his in one generation of grim purpose and intellectual audacity, the South has lost its economic distinctness and has become a part of American life and American destiny, and the North has learned to love, and trust, its brothers whom it did not know and therefore could not understand." (Address of Dr. Edward A. Alderman, at the memorial service for Dr. J. L. Curry, Charlottesville, 1903.)

were prominent features in the work. In 1875 the Fund created a normal school at Nashville to train teachers, and began the granting of scholarships to Southern teachers for study there. By 1903, state normal schools had been sufficiently developed in the South that the trustees decided to distribute the Fund, as they were permitted to do after thirty years, and gave $1,500,000 of the money to endow the Peabody College for Teachers, at Nashville, for more advanced teacher-training. After a few other grants to colleges in the South for schools of education, the remainder of the Fund, $350,000, was given to the John F. Slater Fund. During the forty-six years of its existence the Peabody Education Fund gave in grants, from income, $3,650,556 for the advancement of education in the South, and this amount almost entirely in co-operation with local authorities in support of some worth-while educational effort. Mr. Peabody had wisely provided that the income should never be appropriated on the basis of population or of comparative community destitution, but on the sound principle of helping communities to help themselves. The wholesome influence of the

FIG. 119
JOHN F. SLATER
(1815–84)

grants was enhanced by the absence of any element of charity in their distribution.

The Slater Fund. In 1882, John F. Slater, a cotton and woolen-goods manufacturer of Connecticut and Rhode Island, created a somewhat similar flexible trust to which he gave $1,000,000 "for the uplifting of the lately emancipated people of the Southern States and their posterity, by conferring on them the blessings of Christian education." This was the second of our great educational foundations, and became known as the "John F. Slater Fund." Under the direction of Dr. Atticus G. Haywood, a preacher of distinction in the Southern Methodist Episcopal Church, who became the Agent of the Fund, much was done to acquaint the people of the North with the needs and the point of view of the South, and to establish the Fund firmly as an aid to the South. The income from this Fund has been used mainly for the support of normal schools and industrial education for the negro race, as grants for the partial support of schools, for the salaries of industrial and training teachers in such schools, and for aid to teachers in training in the many county normal schools which it established.

The definite results of these two Funds are to be found in the history of education in practically all the Southern States. Dr. Sears in particular worked to establish in the minds of the people that public education was a necessary function of government, and the final establishment of complete state systems of education in the South, after the ravages of reconstruction were over, was greatly facilitated by the policy adopted in granting aid and by the personal efforts of the officers of the two Funds. Hostility to the idea of educating the children of the negro race also was diminished by the work of these Funds. These gifts coming from Northern men, coupled with the tactful work of the Trustees and their Agents, contributed not a little also to eliminate sectional feelings and to establish a new bond of fellowship between North and South.

National attempts to aid the South. The prostrate condition of the Southern States and the illiteracy of the new citizenship alike seemed to many Northern people too heavy a load for the Southern people and philanthropy to carry, and to demand some form of national assistance for education, while the statistics of illiteracy, chiefly among the blacks, which the National Census of 1870 revealed, formed strong arguments for such action. The Hoar Bill of 1870, sponsored by Representative George F. Hoar of Massachusetts, gave concrete form to the discussion in that it proposed the creation of a national system of compulsory education, the establishment of a national permanent school fund from the proceeds of national land sales, and the distribution of the income to the States for educational purposes. For the first ten years the aid was to be distributed in proportion to the illiteracy in each State, as shown by the Federal Census. Although the bill awakened much interest throughout the North, and was strongly endorsed, its proponents were never able to secure its enactment.

The Federal Census of 1880 revealed equally alarming conditions as to illiteracy, and the Blair Bills of 1884–87, sponsored by Senator Henry W. Blair of New Hampshire, and in a way a corollary of the Hoar Bill, proposed similar aid in temporary form.[1] The enactment

---

[1] The first year the grant was to be $15,000,000, and to decrease $1,000,000 a year until ten payments had been made and then to stop. The apportionment was to be in proportion to the illiteracy of the States, and 79 per cent of the amount would have gone to the former slave-holding States.

of these bills was urged by many influential organizations; they were passed three times by the Senate, and were favored by a majority of the House; but so bitter had become the reconstruction conflict that the House leaders were always able to kill them in committee. The bills also awakened strong resentment in the South; many Southern people felt that they would do more harm than good. They would have built schoolhouses and paid teachers, but no supply of competent teachers could be had. The nature of the Blair Bills, as well as some of the reasons for their failure, were set forth in an address given by Senator Blair before the Department of Superintendence of the National Education Association in 1887 (**R. 242**).

That such a grant of national aid would have been just and generous to the South, as well as good business from the Northern point of view; that it would have contributed more than it cost toward restoring peace and amity between the two sections; that it would have materially aided the South in recovering from the devastating effects of the war; and that it would have laid the foundations for an extensive system of national aid for education, which probably would have been well developed by now, is generally recognized.

The slow progress at the South. Despite all the efforts made, public education at the South has been slow in getting under way. The best progress was made in the larger towns and cities which had been stimulated by the Peabody Fund, but outside these places the status of public education was for a long time deplorably low. The reasons for this state of affairs were at bottom economic, as the value of all property had shrunk and but little new wealth had been created. There was little to tax for the support of so vast an undertaking. The mixed-school issue, and after its final settlement by the general establishment of separate schools for the two races, the cost for the maintenance of two distinct school systems, likewise acted as a strong retarding influence. The South, too, was still essentially rural and but sparsely populated, and in large areas the blacks outnumbered the whites. There could be little change in these conditions until there could be a creation of new wealth, of a new middle class, and until new native leaders could arise. All this required time, and the result was that for from two to two and a half decades following the close of reconstruction there was but little progress in the development of public schools in the States of the Confederacy, outside of the cities and the larger towns. Up to about

1900 the general run of schools in the South were poor indeed.[1] About that time new influences and new leaders started an awakening which was comparable to that caused by the work of Horace Mann and Barnard in the North sixty years before, and to which we shall recur in a later chapter.

QUESTIONS FOR DISCUSSION

1. What place does permissive and optional legislation play in the development of a new undertaking? Illustrate from the history of some of the Southern States.
2. Was the lack of trained teachers at the South before the War worse than at the North a quarter of a century earlier, or not?
3. Compare the legislative urging of governors in Virginia and South Carolina with similar earlier urgings in Pennsylvania and New Jersey.
4. Compare the work of Breckinridge and other leaders in Kentucky with the struggle for support in Indiana.
5. Compare the creation of city school systems, by special legislative acts, in a few Southern cities with similar legislation (and cases) in the Northern States at an earlier date.
6. What does the fact that optional legislation for schools was ever availed of in so few counties, in a number of the Southern States, indicate as to sentiment for education there? Have we any analogous conditions in the Northern States?
7. How do you explain the early interest in land endowments for schools made by Texas?
8. Give four or five reasons why educational development at the South lagged behind that of the North.
9. Show the influence of the "state's rights" conception at the South in preventing the larger conception of nationality.
10. Show the effect of a larger number of cities and a greater city population at the North in the development of better educational conditions. Illustrate by cases.
11. Did the North, at an earlier period, have any equivalent of the "Old Field" schools?
12. Was "turning out the teacher" a northern as well as a southern practice? Illustrate from literature.

[1] For example, in 1900, the annual amount raised for school support per adult ranged from $2.65 in Alabama and North Carolina to $6.37 in Texas, while the average for the whole United States was $10.93. The school term varied from 70 days in North Carolina to 119 days in Louisiana and Virginia, with an average of less than 100 days for the entire South, against an average for the whole United States of 145 days. The average annual salary of teachers in the South decreased from $175 in 1860 to $159 in 1900, whereas the average for the whole United States in 1900 was $310. No Southern State had enacted a compulsory-attendance law before 1900, and less than 60 per cent of the school population enrolled and less than 40 per cent was in average daily attendance.

13. Compare New York State and the South in the matter of the academies and teacher-training.
14. How do you explain the earlier development of state universities at the South?
15. Explain what you understand to be meant by the statement that "the North and West had developed a conception of nationality to replace that of a confederacy of States."
16. Was such an evolutionary development what Washington and other early leaders had hoped for? Illustrate.
17. Illustrate, from the facts given in the text, how educational development at the North was checked for a couple of decades as a result of the coming of the Civil War.
18. Chart the table given on page 429 to see what kind of a curve results.
19. Contrast the general development of education in the South and the North by 1860.
20. Show how the congressional reconstruction policy tended to destroy interest in educational development at the South, as well as to make such development more difficult later on.
21. Show the many advantages of intelligently organized giving, as exhibited in the management of the Peabody and Slater Funds, over miscellaneous charity, as illustrated by the earlier missionary efforts.
22. Do you think that the North should have aided the South in developing its schools after the close of the Civil War? Why?
23. Show how natural it was that the Civil War should have checked expansion and material development, and forced the schools to a development within.

SELECTED READINGS

In the accompanying volume of *Readings* the following selections, related to the subject matter of this chapter, are reproduced:

*229. Maddox: The Work of Propaganda in Virginia.
*230. Maddox: Education in Virginia on the Eve of the Civil War.
*231. McDuffie: A Governor addresses the Legislature.
*232. South Carolina: Report of a Special Legislative Committee.
*233. Anon.: The Pauper School System Evaluated.
*234. Perry: Educational Conditions in Alabama in 1856.
*235. Sims: Turning Out the Teacher.
 236. Anon.: An "Old Field" School in South Carolina.
*237. Bradford: Differing Attitudes of the North and the South.
*238. Winton: Slavery was our Greatest Enemy.
*239. Jones: Northern Efforts for Schools in the South.
*240. Gladden: Foolishness of the Reconstruction Policy.
 241. Peabody: Letter to Trustees creating the Fund.
*242. Blair: The Blair Bills, and the Outcome.

QUESTIONS ON THE READINGS

1. Compare the propaganda work in Virginia (**229**) with that in Pennsylvania (**99, 103**) and New Jersey (**122**) as to time and popular sentiment represented.
2. How far had Virginia education developed by 1860 (**230**)?
3. Compare the message of Governor McDuffie (**231**) with that of Northern governors (**104, 118**) at about the same time.
4. What does the South Carolina legislative report (**232**) reveal as to the status and type of education there by 1847?
5. What were the points of strength and weakness (**233**) of the pauper school system? Would these same points probably have been true of the pauper system of Pennsylvania and New Jersey? Why?
6. At about what time would Superintendent Perry's description of educational conditions in Alabama (**234**) have been true, if at all, of Indiana or Illinois?
7. Does Eggleston, in *The Hoosier Schoolmaster*, describe anything like that described by Sims (**235**)?
8. Did the new West, in the early period, have an equivalent to the "Old Field" Schools (**236**)? Did New England?
9. From **237**, do you think that the "inevitable conflict" could have been prevented by any ordinary compromises? Which was the more comfortable type of civilization in which to live? Why?
10. Show that Winton's conclusions (**238**) are in accord with sound economic thought.
11. Show that the blunders made by Northern agencies (**239**) were those natural to such an effort.
12. Evaluate the reconstruction policy (**240**) as it applied to education in the South.
13. Characterize the spirit and the attitude toward the South as shown in the Peabody letter (**241**).
14. What do you make out to have been the causes and fears that defeated the Hoar and Blair bills (**242**)?
15. How do you explain the general and continued opposition of Congress to the development of anything tending toward national education?

TOPICS FOR INVESTIGATION AND REPORT

1. Efforts, before 1860, to develop a system of public instruction in any Southern State.
2. Collegiate opportunities in the South by 1860.
3. Character of the instruction provided at the University of Georgia, North Carolina, or Virginia before the Civil War.
4. The type of internal development that took place, between about 1860 and about 1880, in the school systems of a few Northern cities.
5. Reconstruction of the Southern colleges.

6. Northern missionary effort in the reconstruction of education in the South after the war.
7. The wasting of the educational funds that remained by reconstruction legislatures and officers.
8. A picture of educational reconstruction in any selected Southern State.
9. The Peabody Education Fund and its work.
10. The Slater Fund and its work.
11. The struggle, in Congress and out, to pass the Blair bills, and the nature of the opposition.
12. The more recent work of the Julius Rosenwald Fund.

SELECTED REFERENCES

Bowers, C. M. *The Tragic Era.* 566 pp. Boston, 1929.

A long but very readable account of the struggle between the President and Congress, and the sad story of reconstruction in the South. Covers the period from 1865 to 1876.

Cochran, Thos. E. *History of Public School Education in Florida.* Marion, Alabama, 1924.

Coulter, E. M. *College Life in the Old South.* New York, 1928.

A good account of college life in the Old South, with the University of Georgia taken as the type.

*Curry, J. L. M. *History of the Peabody Education Fund.*

*Dunning, W. A. "The Undoing of Reconstruction"; in *Atlantic Monthly*, vol. LXXXVIII, pp. 437–49. (October, 1901.)

Tells how the Southern people regained control of affairs after reconstruction.

Eby, Fr. *The Development of Education in Texas.* New York, 1925.

*Fleming, W. L. *The Sequel of Appomattox.* 322 pp. Chronicles of America Series, Yale University Press, 1919.

Good chapters on reunion, carpet-bag and negro rule, church, schools, and the resumption of local control. Good bibliography.

Harris, T. H. *The Story of Public Education in Louisiana.* New York, 1924.

Heatwole, C. J. *History of Education in Virginia.* New York, 1916.

A good study of a single State.

Hendrick, B. J. *The Training of an American.* Boston, 1928.

College life in the South in the seventies, as described through the life and letters of Walter H. Page.

*Knight, E. W. *The Influence of Reconstruction on Education in the South.* Teachers College Contributions to Education, no. 60. New York, 1913.

*Knight, E. W. *Public Education in the South.* 482 pp. Boston, 1922.

An excellent piece of historical work. Chapters VII–XII deal in detail with the period covered by this chapter.

Knight, E. W. *Public Education in North Carolina.* 384 pp. Boston, 1916.

Chapter X deals with *ante-bellum* practices, and other chapters deal with other aspects of southern education as presented in this chapter.

Knight, E. W. "Reconstruction and Education in Virginia"; in *South Atlantic Quarterly*, January and April, 1916. Also same for South Carolina, in same magazine for October, 1919, and January, 1920.

Two studies of the period of reconstruction and the educational outcomes in particular States.

Lingley, C. R. *Since the Civil War.* Rev. ed., New York, 1926.

Chapter I good on the reconstruction period.

*Maddox, Wm. A. *The Free School Idea in Virginia before the Civil War.* 225 pp. Teachers College Contributions to Education, no. 93. New York, 1918.

An excellent study of education in one State before the Civil War, with a very complete bibliography.

Noble, S. G. *Forty Years of the Public Schools of Mississippi.* 142 pp. Teachers College Contributions to Education, no. 94. New York, 1918.

Covers the period from 1870 to 1910, with special reference to the education of the Negro.

Sims, J. M. *The Story of My Life.* New York, 1885.

A good account of school practices in the South in *ante-bellum* days, but with special reference to South Carolina.

*Thompson, H. *The New South.* 250 pp. Chronicles of America Series, Yale University Press, 1919.

Very good on the rebuilding of the South after the end of the reconstruction period. Chapter VIII gives a good brief sketch of educational progress.

United States Bureau of Education. *Circulars of Information*, 1888-1903.

A series of studies, relating largely to the history of higher education in the Southern States, and covering: Alabama, Arkansas, Florida, Georgia, Louisiana, Mississippi, North Carolina, South Carolina, Tennessee, and Texas.

Weeks, S. B. *History of Public School Education in Arkansas.* 128 pp. United States Bureau of Education, Bulletin no. 27. Washington, 1912.

Weeks, S. B. *History of Public School Education in Alabama.* 209 pp. United States Bureau of Education, Bulletin no. 12. Washington, 1915.

Weeks, S. B. *History of Public School Education in Delaware.* 181 pp. United States Bureau of Education, Bulletin no. 18. Washington, 1917.

A series of excellent state histories of public education.

Weeks, S. B. "Calvin Henderson Wiley, and the Organization of Common Schools in North Carolina"; in *Report of United States Commissioner of Education*, 1896-97, vol. II, pp. 1379-1474.

CHAPTER XIII

MORE NEW IDEAS FROM ABROAD

I. NEW IDEAS FROM HERBARTIAN SOURCES

Where Pestalozzi left the educational problem. Pestalozzi had done a work of the greatest importance in reorganizing and re-directing the education of children, but after all his work had been based wholly on observation and experimentation, and without at-tempting to measure it up with any guiding scientific principle. Still more, there were then no guiding scientific principles with which he could measure what he had done. His unwearied patience, his intense personal sufferings, and his self-sacrifice for childhood were wonderful. The story of his life forms one of the most touching chapters in the history of education, and his sufferings and successes gave reality to his statement that after all "the essential principle of education is not teaching; it is love." His elaboration of the thought of Rousseau that education was an individual development, a drawing out and not a pouring in; that the basis of all education exists in the nature of man; and that the method of education is to be sought and not constructed, were his great contributions. These ideas led him to emphasize sense perception and expression; to formulate the rule that in teaching we must proceed from the simple to the complex, and from the concrete to the abstract; and to con-struct a "faculty psychology" which conceived of education as "a harmonious development" of the different "faculties" of the mind. It was at this point that Pestalozzi left the problem, and in this form that we received it by way of England in the sixties.

The work of Herbart. Taking up the problem as Pestalozzi left it, a German by the name of Johann Friedrich Herbart [1] (1776–1841) carried it forward by organizing a truer psychology for the whole

---

[1] "Philosophers before Herbart (Wolff, Kant, and his disciples) adhered to Aristotle's principle, but slightly modified, that the soul is the dwelling-place of higher and lower capacities, entirely separate from each other. According to this theory, mental processes lying open to the observation of experience were classified into smaller and larger divisions, according to their similitude. All phenomena of one kind were regarded as effects of a single capacity, originally inherent in the soul. Three chief capacities were assumed — knowledge, feeling, and will, each of which was again separated into its sub-capacities, the result being a system which was nothing more than a classification of so-called capacities. Given these ⌐s the material for their work, the old school of teachers set before itself a corresponding di-

educational process (**R. 243**), by erecting a new aim in instruction, by formulating new steps in method, and by showing the place and the importance of properly organized instruction in history and litera- ture in the education of the child. Though the two men were en- tirely different in type, and worked along entirely different lines, the connection between Herbart and Pestalozzi was, nevertheless, close. Herbart had visited Pestalozzi at Burgdorf, in 1799, just after graduating from Jena and while acting as a tutor for three Swiss boys, and had written a very sympathetic description of his school and his theory of instruction. Herbart was one of the first of the Germans to understand and appreciate "the genial and noble Pestalozzi."

The two men, however, approached the educational problem from entirely different angles. Pestalozzi gave nearly all his long life to teaching and human service, while Herbart taught only as a travel- ing private tutor for three years, and later a class of twenty children in his university practice school. Pestalozzi was a social reformer, a visionary, and an impractical enthusiast, but was possessed of a remarkable intuitive insight into child nature. Herbart, on the other hand, was a well-trained scholarly thinker, who spent the most of his life in the peaceful occupation of a professor of philosophy in a German university. The son of a well-educated public official, Herbart was himself educated at the *Gymnasium* of Oldenburg and the University of Jena. After spending three years as a tutor, he became, at the age of twenty-six, an under teacher at the University of Göttingen. At the age of thirty-three he was called to become pro- fessor of philosophy at Königsburg, and from the age of fifty-seven to his death at sixty-five he was again a professor at Göttingen. It was while at Königsburg, between 1810 and 1832, and as an appendix to his work as professor of philosophy, that he organized a small practice school, conducted a Pedagogical Seminar, and worked out his educational theory and method. His work was a careful, schol- arly attempt at the organization of education as a science, carried out amid the peace and quiet which a university atmosphere almost alone affords. He addressed himself chiefly to three things: (1) the aim, (2) the content, and (3) the method of instruction.

versity of aims, each of which was to be reached by a separate road, and imagined an all- round perfection of the single capacity would follow from its concentration on one object. Herbart proved not only the falsity of this theory, but also that, were it true, education in its noblest conception would be but an empty word." (H. M. and E. Felkin.)

The aim and the content of education. Locke had set up as the aim of education the ideal of a physically sound gentleman. Rousseau had declared his aim to be to prepare his boy for life by developing naturally his inborn capacities. Pestalozzi had sought to regenerate society by means of education, and to prepare children for society by a "harmonious training" of their "faculties." Herbart rejected alike the conventional-social education of Locke, the natural and unsocial education of Rousseau, and the "faculty-psychology" conception of education of Pestalozzi. Instead he conceived of the mind as a unity, rather than divided into "faculties," and the aim of education as broadly social rather than personal (**R. 243**). The purpose of education, he said, was to prepare men to live properly in organized society, and hence the chief aim in education was not conventional fitness, natural development, mere knowledge, nor personal mental power, but personal character and social morality. This being the case, the educator should analyze the interests and occupations and social responsibilities of men as they are grouped in organized society, and, from such analyses, deduce the means and the method of instruction. Man's interests, he said, come from two main sources — his contact with the things in his environment (real things, sense-impressions), and from his relations with human beings (social intercourse). His social responsibilities and duties are determined by the nature of the social organization of which he forms a part (**R. 243**).

Pestalozzi had provided fairly well for the first group of contacts, through his instruction in objects, home geography, numbers, and geometric form. For the second group of contacts Pestalozzi had developed only oral language, and to this Herbart now added the two important studies of literature and history, and history with the emphasis on the social rather than the political side. Two new elementary school subjects were thus developed, each important in revealing to man his place in the social whole. History in particular Herbart conceived to be a study of the first importance for revealing proper human relationships, and leading men to social and national "good-will."

The chief purpose of education Herbart held to be to develop personal character and to prepare for social usefulness. These virtues, he held, proceeded from enough of the right kind of knowledge, properly interpreted to the pupil so that clear ideas as to relationships might be formed. To impart this knowledge interest must be awakened, and to arouse interest in the many kinds of knowledge needed, a "many-sided" development must take place. From full knowledge, and with proper instruction by the teacher, clear ideas or concepts might be formed, and clear ideas ought to lead to right action, and right action to personal character — the aim of all instruction. Herbart was the first writer on education to place the great emphasis on proper instruction, and to exalt teaching and proper teaching-procedure instead of mere knowledge or intellectual discipline. He thus conceived of the educational process as a science in itself, having a definite content and method, and worthy of special study by those who desire to teach.

Herbartian method. With these ideas as to the aim and content of instruction, Herbart worked out a theory of the instructional process and a method of instruction (**R. 244**). Interest he held to be of first importance as a prerequisite to good instruction. If given spontaneously, well and good; but, if necessary, forced interest must be resorted to. Skill in instruction is in part to be determined by the ability of the teacher to secure interest without resorting to force on the one hand or sugar-coating of the subject on the other. Taking Pestalozzi's idea that the purpose of the teacher was to give pupils new experiences through contacts with real things, without assuming that the pupils already had such, Herbart elaborated the process by which new knowledge is assimilated in terms of what one already knows, and from his elaboration of this principle the doctrine of apperception — that is, the apperceiving or comprehending of new knowledge in terms of the old — has been fixed as an important principle in educational psychology. Good instruction, then, involves first putting the child into a proper frame of mind to apperceive the new knowledge, and hence this becomes a cornerstone of all good teaching method.

Herbart did not always rely on such methods, holding that the "committing to memory" of certain necessary facts often was necessary, but he held that the mere memorizing of isolated facts, which had characterized school instruction for ages, had little value for either educational or moral ends. The teaching of mere facts often was very necessary, but such instruction called for a methodical organization of the facts by the teacher, so as to make their learning contribute to some definite purpose. This called for a purpose in instruction; the organization of the facts necessary to be taught so as to select the most useful ones; the connection of these so as to establish the principle which was the purpose of the instruction; and training in systematic thinking by applying the principle to new problems of the type being studied. The carrying out of such ideas meant the careful organization of the teaching process and teaching method, to secure certain predetermined ends in child development, instead of mere miscellaneous memorizing and school-keeping.

Of Herbart's contribution his English translators [1] write:

> The immeasurable service Herbart rendered to education by the new light he threw on the laws of mind, indicates his distinct advance in one direction on his predecessors. Comenius and Pestalozzi, insisting that education should follow the course of the child's natural development and be based on the psychological laws of human nature, had advanced far in the same direction. But the knowledge of those laws in their day was too vague to allow of any but the most general expression of the vital truth they saw and proclaimed. Herbart himself made no pretension to possess a complete science of mind; no one was more penetrated than he by the conviction that this science was in its earliest beginning, leaving an immeasurable field for future investigators. But his wide knowledge, his power of analytic and abstract thought, and incorruptible love of truth enabled him to gain a more accurate insight into the origin and process of mental activity, and with it the possibility of marking out a systematic course of education, which in the employment of definite means would attain sure results and compass its appointed end. Such a course of education, together with its means and their employment, is developed in the *General Principles of the Science of Education*. The system of education it contains is, as the title of the book sets forth, deduced from its aim — morality, which Herbart presents as the highest aim of humanity, and consequently of education...

The Herbartian movement in Germany. Herbart died in 1841, without having awakened any general interest in his ideas, and they remained virtually unnoticed until 1865. In that year a professor at Leipzig, Tuiskon Ziller (1817–83), published a book setting forth Herbart's idea of instruction as a moral force. This attracted much attention, and led to the formation (1868) of a scientific society for the study of Herbart's ideas. Ziller and his followers now elaborated Herbart's ideas, advanced the theory of culture-epochs in child development, the theory of concentration in studies, and elaborated the four steps in the process of instruction, as described

[1] Henry M. and Emmie Felkin; in Translators' Introduction to Herbart's *Science of Education*. London, 1891.

by Herbart, into the five formal steps of the modern Herbartian school.

In 1874 a pedagogical seminary and practice school was organized at the University of Jena, and in 1885 this came under the direction of Professor William Rein, a pupil of Ziller's, who developed the practice school according to the ideas of Ziller. A detailed course of study for this school, filling two large volumes, was worked out, and the practice lessons given were thoroughly planned beforehand and the methods employed were subjected to a searching analysis after the lesson had been given.

Herbartian ideas reach the United States. Between 1885 and 1890 a number of Americans, many of them graduates of the state normal school at Normal, Illinois, studied in Jena, and returning brought back to the United States this Ziller-Rein-Jena brand of Herbartian ideas and practices. Charles De Garmo's *Essentials of Methods*, published in 1889, marked the beginning of the introduction of these ideas into this country. In 1892 Charles A. McMurry published his *General Method*, and in 1897, with his brother, Frank, published the *Method in the Recitation*. These three books probably have done more to popularize Herbartian ideas and introduce them into the normal schools and colleges of the United States than all other influences combined. Another important influence was the "National Herbart Society," founded in 1892 by students returning from Jena, in imitation of the similar German society. For the first few years of its existence its publications were devoted to a discussion of interest, apperception, correlation, recitation methods, moral education, the culture-epoch theory, training for citizenship, the social function of history and geography, and similar subjects. This Society is still rendering good service under the name of the "National Society for the Study of Education," though its earlier Herbartian character now has disappeared.[1]

Herbartian ideas took like wildfire over the United States, but particularly in the normal schools of the Upper Mississippi Valley. Methods of instruction in history and literature, and a new psychology, were now added to the normal school professional instruc-

[1] National Herbart Society, 1895-99; five *Yearbooks*. National Society for the Scientific Study of Education, 1900-08; First to Eighth *Yearbooks*. National Society for the Study of Education, 1909 to date; *Yearbooks* from Ninth on; *Thirty-Second Yearbook* in 1932. All *Yearbooks* in two parts, or volumes, since 1900. These volumes contain some of our most important educational literature.

JOHANN FRIEDRICH HERBART
(1776–1841)
Organizer of the Psychology of Instruction

FRIEDRICH WILHELM FROEBEL
(1782–1852)
Founder of the Kindergarten

tion. Though this psychology has since been outgrown, it has been very useful in shaping pedagogical thought. New courses of study for the training schools were now worked out, in which the elementary-school subjects were divided into drill subjects, content subjects, and motor-activity or expression subjects (see page 518). Apperception, correlation, social purpose, moral education, and recitation methods became new words to conjure with. From the normal schools these ideas spread rapidly to the better city school systems of the time, and soon found their way into courses of study everywhere. Practice schools and the model lessons in dozens of normal schools were remodeled after the pattern of those at Jena, and for a decade Herbartian ideas and child study vied with one another for the place of first importance in educational thinking. The Herbartian wave of the nineties resembled the Pestalozzian enthusiasm of the sixties. Each for a time furnished the new ideas in education, each introduced elements of importance into our elementary-school instruction, each deeply influenced the training of teachers in our normal schools by giving a new turn to the instruction there, and each gradually settled down into its proper place in our educational practice and history.

To the Herbartians we are indebted in particular for important new conceptions as to the teaching of history and literature, which have modified all our subsequent procedure; for the introduction of history teaching in some form into all the elementary-school grades; for the emphasis on a new social point of view in the teaching of history and geography; the emphasis on the moral aim in instruction; a new and a truer educational psychology; and a better organization of the technique of classroom instruction. With the introduction of normal child activities, which came from another source about this same time, our elementary-school curriculum as we now have it was practically complete, and the elementary school of 1850 had been completely made over to form the elementary school of 1900.

II. THE KINDERGARTEN AND PLAY

To another German, Friedrich Froebel (1782–1852), we are indebted, directly or indirectly, for three other additions to elementary education — the kindergarten, the play idea, and handwork activities.

Origin of the kindergarten. Of German parentage, the son of a rural clergyman, early estranged from his parents, retiring and introspective by nature, having led a most unhappy childhood, and apprenticed to a forester without his wishes being consulted, at twenty-three Froebel decided to become a school teacher and visited Pestalozzi in Switzerland. Two years later he became the tutor of three boys, and then spent the years 1808–10 as a student and teacher in Pestalozzi's institute at Yverdon. During his years there Froebel was deeply impressed with the great value of music and play in the education of children, and of all that he carried away from Pestalozzi's institution these ideas were most persistent. After serving in a variety of occupations — student, soldier against Napoleon, and curator in a museum of mineralogy — he finally opened a little private school, in 1816, which he conducted for a decade along Pestalozzian lines. In this the play idea, music, and the self-activity of the pupils were uppermost. The school was a failure, financially, but while conducting it Froebel thought out and published (1826) his most important pedagogical work — *The Education of Man.*

Gradually Froebel became convinced that the most needed reform in education concerned the early years of childhood. His own youth had been most unhappy, and to this phase of education he now addressed himself. After a period as a teacher in Switzerland he returned to Germany and opened a school for little children in which plays, games, songs, and occupations involving self-activity were the dominating characteristics, and in 1840 he hit upon the name *Kindergarten* for it. In 1843 his *Mutter-und Kose-Lieder*, a book of fifty songs and games, was published.

Spread of the kindergarten idea. After a series of unsuccessful efforts to bring his new idea to the attention of educators, Froebel, himself a rather feminine type, became discouraged and resolved to address himself henceforth to women, as they seemed much more capable of understanding him, and to the training of teachers in the new ideas. Froebel was fortunate in securing as one of his most ardent disciples, just before his death, the Baroness Bertha von Marenholtz Bülow-Wendhausen (1810–93), who did more than any other person to make his educational ideas known (**R. 245**). Meeting, in 1849, the man mentioned to her as "an old fool," she understood him, and spent the remainder of her life in bringing to the attention of the world the work of this unworldly man who did not know how to make it known for himself. In 1851 the Prussian Government, fearing some revolutionary designs in the new idea, forbade kindergartens in Prussia, so the Baroness went to London and lectured there on Froebel's ideas, organizing kindergartens in the English "ragged schools." She later expounded Froebelian ideas in Paris, Italy, Switzerland, Holland, Belgium, and (after 1860, when the prohibition was removed) in Germany. In 1870 she founded a kindergarten training college in Dresden. Many of her writings have been translated into English, and published in the United States.

In this country the kindergarten idea has met with a cordial reception. The first kindergarten in the United States was a German kindergarten, established at Watertown, Wisconsin, in 1855, by Mrs. Carl Schurz, a pupil of Froebel. During the next fifteen years some ten other kindergartens were organized in German-speaking communities. The first English-speaking kindergarten was opened privately in Boston, in 1860, by Miss Elizabeth Peabody.[1] In 1868 a private training school for kindergarteners was opened in Boston, largely through Miss Peabody's influence, by Madame Matilde Kriege and her daughter, who had recently arrived from Germany. In 1872 Miss Marie Boelte opened a similar teacher-training school in New York City. Another recent arrival, Emma Marwedel (1818–93), whose kindergarten in Hamburg Miss Peabody had visited, conducted the first teacher-training classes in Washington from 1872 to 1876, in Los Angeles from 1876 to 1878, in Oakland and Berkeley from 1878 to 1880, and in San Francisco[2] from 1880 to about 1890. In 1873, a pupil of Marie Boelte, Miss Susan Blow, accepted the invitation of Superintendent William T. Harris, of St.

[1] Elizabeth Palmer Peabody (1804–94) was born at Billerica, Massachusetts. Her mother, a very talented woman, conducted a private school, at which she and her two sisters were educated. One of her sisters became Mrs. Nathaniel Hawthorne, and the other Mrs. Horace Mann. She began as a teacher in Boston at the age of eighteen. In 1859 she became acquainted with the educational ideas of Froebel, and the year following she opened the first kindergarten for English speaking children in America. In 1867 she went to Europe to study the kindergarten at first hand, and induced several experienced German kindergarteners, among them Emma Marwedel and Matilde Kriege, to come to America.

[2] Miss Marwedel was, for two decades, an important force in the development of kindergartens in California, and particularly in San Francisco. An oil painting of Miss Marwedel hangs in the library of the School of Education at Stanford University, and a photograph of this is found in Swift's monograph. The painting owes its origin to Mrs. Stanford, who for long helped maintain the kindergarten organization in San Francisco. Kindergartens there did not pass from the philanthropic and charitable to the city-maintained stage until about 1910.

Louis, to go there and open the first public school kindergarten in the United States. St. Louis, then perhaps the most prominent city school system in the country, soon became a center from which public kindergarten ideas were diffused. The first kindergarten in Chicago was opened in 1874, in Boston in 1877, and Cincinnati in 1879, and by 1880 some three hundred kindergartens and ten kindergarten training schools, mostly private undertakings, had been opened in the cities of thirty of the States of the Union. By 1890 philanthropic kindergarten associations to provide and support kindergartens had been organized in most of the larger cities, and after that date our city schools rapidly began to adopt the kindergarten as a part of the public school system,[1] and thus add, at the bottom, one more rung to our educational ladder. Today there are approximately three quarters of a million children enrolled in public and private kindergartens, and they are to be found as a part of the public school system in nearly all cities,[2] while training in kindergarten principles and practices is now given by most of our state normal schools.

The kindergarten idea. The dominant idea in the kindergarten is natural but directed self-activity, focused upon educational, social, and moral ends. Froebel believed in the continuity of a child's life from infancy onward, and that self-activity, determined by the child's interests and desires and intelligently directed, was essential to the unfolding of the child's inborn capacities. His conception of self-activity was quite different from that of Pestalozzi (**R. 246**), and a distinct advance over what Pestalozzi had thought out. He saw, more clearly than any one before him had done, the unutilized wealth of the child's world, that the child's chief characteristic is self-activity, the desirability of the child finding himself through play, and that the work of the school during these early years was to supplement the family by drawing out the child and awakening the ideal side of his nature. To these ends doing, self-activity, and ex-

[1] The kindergarten in the United States has passed through three distinct stages of development. At first it was a philanthropic agency relieving impoverished conditions under which the children of immigrants and of the poor in cities lived. Later the parents of children in the upper stages of economic and social life saw its value and urged its adoption by the public school. Finally it was adopted into the public school system and made available for all children.

[2] In 1930, a little over three quarters of a million children were enrolled in kindergartens with all but about five per cent of the number in public schools. This was one third of the four- and five-year-old children reported by the 1930 Census as living in cities. In the decade 1920–30, kindergarten enrollment increased one third.

pression became fundamental to the kindergarten, and movement, gesture, directed play, song, color, the story, and the human activities a part of kindergarten technique. Nature study and school gardening were given a prominent place, and motor activity much called into play. Advancing far beyond Pestalozzi's principle of sense impressions, which, as we have seen under object lessons, was largely passive learning, Froebel insisted on motor activity and learning by doing (**R. 246**).

Froebel, as well as Herbart, also saw the social importance of education, and that man must realize himself not independently amid nature, as Rousseau had said, but as a social animal in co-operation with his fellowmen. Hence he made his schoolroom a miniature of society, a place where courtesy and helpfulness and social co-operation were prominent features. This social and at times reverent atmosphere of the kindergarten has always been a marked characteristic of its work. To bring out social ideas many dramatic games, such as shoemaker, carpenter, smith, and farmer, were devised and set to music. The "story" by the teacher was made prominent, and this was retold in language, acted, sung, and often worked out constructively in clay, blocks, or paper. Other games to develop skill were worked out, and use was made of sand, clay, paper, cardboard, and color. The "gifts" and "occupations" which Froebel devised were intended to develop constructive and æsthetic power, and to provide for connection and development they were arranged into an organized series of playthings. Individual development as its aim, motor expression as its method, and social co-operation as its means were the characteristic ideas of this new school for little children.

Since Froebel's day we have learned much about children that was then unknown, especially as to the muscular and nervous organization and development of children, and with this new knowledge the tendency has been to enlarge the "gifts" and change their nature, to introduce new "occupations," elaborate the kindergarten program of daily exercises, to give the kindergarten more of an out-of-door character, and to develop much more of an activity program for it. As a result, the kindergarten of today is quite a different institution from what it was a third of a century ago.

The Montessori method. Another recent development of the kindergarten idea, which a couple of decades ago created quite a furore in many countries, is the scheme of child-training devised by Dr. Maria Montessori, at Rome.[1] Designed primarily for the training of mentally-deficient children, the method has been extended to use with normal children. The essentials of the system are the strong emphasis on sense training, both formal and incidental in type, and the great stress laid on the freedom of the child and individual treatment. Many Montessori schools have been opened in different parts of the United States, and the method for a time was heralded as a great improvement over the kindergarten. A more critical examination of the basic ideas has led, however, to their somewhat general rejection by most American educators, and it seems probable that Montessori schools will have their largest usefulness with sub-normal children or those whose development is retarded. Based on an outgrown faculty psychology, a plan for sense training of doubtful psychological validity, and involving a too early start in the formal arts of learning, the method has been generally decided to be distinctly inferior to the modern Americanized kindergarten. Its best features have been drawn from the work of Séguin, and the method probably always will have its greatest value for sub-normal children.

The contribution of the kindergarten. Wholly aside from the specific training given children during the year, year and a half, or two years of training, the addition of the kindergarten to American education has been a force of very large significance and usefulness. The idea that the child is primarily an active and not a learning animal has been given new emphasis, and that education comes chiefly by doing has been given new force. The idea that a child's chief business is play, so different from our early Calvinistic conception, has been of large educational value. The elimination of book education and harsh discipline in the kindergarten has been an idea that has slowly but gradually extended upward into the lower grades of the elementary school. The play and game idea brought in by the kindergarten has also been exceedingly useful in slowly changing the character of the physical training exercises of the upper grades

[1] Madame Montessori was, for some years prior to 1900, an assistant at the Psychiatric Clinic in the University of Rome. There she came to study defective children, and became a close student of the methods of Séguin and Itard. From this she began the teaching of this type of children, devising for their instruction a large amount of sense training material. Next followed lectures to teachers on her work, followed by its application to normal children in some infant schools which she organized in some model tenements in Rome. These schools she termed Children's Houses — *Casa dei Bambini.*

and of the high school from the stiff *Turnen* and military type of bodily exercises, brought in by the Germans after their great migration to America began, to the free play and competitive games which we now have quite generally developed. Within the past two decades the kindergarten has been so closely united with the work of the lower two grades of the primary school that the character of the old primary school has been greatly changed.

Today, largely as a result of the spreading of the kindergarten spirit, we are coming to recognize play and games at something like their real social, moral, and educational values, wholly aside from their benefits as concern physical welfare, and to schedule play as a regular subject in our school programs. Music, too, has attained new emphasis since the coming of the kindergarten, and methods of teaching music more in harmony with kindergarten ideas have been introduced into the upper grades of our schools.

III. INSTRUCTION IN THE MANUAL ACTIVITIES

Extension of Froebel's idea to handwork. Froebel not only introduced constructive work — paper folding, weaving, needlework, and work with sand and clay and color — into the kindergarten, but he also proposed to extend and develop such work for the upper years of schooling in a school for hand training, which he outlined but did not establish (**R. 247**). His proposed plan included the elements of the so-called manual-training idea, developed later, and he justified such instruction on the same educational grounds that we advance today. It was not to teach a boy a trade, as Rousseau had advocated, or to train children in sense-perception, as Pestalozzi had employed all his manual activities, but as a form of educational expression, and for the purpose of developing creative power within the child. The idea was advocated by a number of thinkers, about 1850 to 1860, but the movement finally took its rise in Finland, Sweden, and Russia, rather than in German lands.

The first country to organize such work as a part of its school instruction was Finland, where, as early as 1858, Uno Cygnaeus [1] (1810–88) outlined a course for manual training involving bench and

[1] Uno Cygnaeus (1810–88) was the founder of the present school system of Finland. Commissioned by his government to investigate the people's schools of France, Germany, and Switzerland, he became acquainted with the work of Pestalozzi and Froebel, from which he derived the inspiration for the handwork he introduced into the schools of Finland in the reorganization of 1866.

metal work, wood-carving, and basket-weaving. Of this work Cygnaeus wrote:

> The idea of the introduction of handwork came to me from the study of the writings of Pestalozzi and Froebel; I have therefore derived it from Germany.

In 1866 Finland made some form of manual work compulsory for boys in all its rural schools, and in its training colleges for male teachers.

In 1872 the government of Sweden decided to introduce sloyd work into its schools, partly to counteract the bad physical and moral effects of city congestion, and partly to revivify the declining home industries of the people which were suffering from factory competition. A sloyd school was established at Näas, in 1872, to train teachers, and in this a few of our early manual-training teachers studied. In 1875 a second sloyd training school was instituted. In 1877 the work was added to the Folk School instruction of Sweden, largely as a result of contact with the work in Finland and the Froebel philosophy.[1] At first the old native sloyd occupations were followed, such as carpentering, turning, wood-carving, brush-making, book-binding, and work in copper and iron, but later the industrial element gave way to a well-organized course in educational tool work for boys from twelve to fifteen years of age, after the Finnish plan.

Manual training reaches the United States. The first general introduction of the United States to this new form of instruction came as a result of the exhibit made by the Russian Government, at the Centennial Exhibition in 1876, of the work in wood and iron done by the pupils at the Imperial Technical School at Moscow. This was a heavy type of work especially adapted to secondary school and collegiate instruction, and which had been worked out at Moscow as a substitute for the older and inefficient apprenticeship system.

It so happened that President John D. Runkle (1822-1902), of the recently opened (1865) Massachusetts Institute of Technology, was looking for some system of training through the use of tools that might be added to the college course, and at the Centennial Exhibi-

---

[1] Otto Saloman, director of the school at Näas, visited Finland and made the acquaintance of Cygnaeus. He was so much impressed with the presentation of Froebel's views on the educational importance of handwork that he began at once to shift the emphasis in the sloyd of Sweden from economic to educational ends.

tion he found it in the Russian exhibit. The fact that another and a better exhibit was also made there by the new Sibley College of Cornell University, which included "a steam engine, power-lathes, face-plates, and various tools of precision, admirably finished, and each a model of its kind" (R. 248), entirely escaped President Runkle's eye, yet the Cornell exhibit was as original in concept as the Moscow exhibit, and better adapted for use in American college instruction, as later events proved to be the case (R. 248). His Report on the Russian exhibit [1] led to the adoption of the idea by the Massachusetts Institute.[2] It was Runkle's discovery of and his plan for using the Russian system in college instruction, together with his enthusiastic *Report* on the idea, which marks the beginning of the manual-training movement in the United States. His Report also set going a whole series of new questions as to the character and nature of education.

It so happened, also, that some experimentation in the use of shop work in instruction had been carried on at Washington University, at St. Louis, for some time by Calvin M. Woodward (1837-1914), Professor of Mathematics and Mechanics and Dean of the Polytechnic School. Runkle's report on the Russian exhibit greatly encouraged him and formed "the special inspiration" of an address on "Manual Education" which he made in St. Louis, in 1878, and which led to the founding, by a group of St. Louis business men in 1880, of the St. Louis Manual Training (High) School, the first of its type in the United States.[3]

[1] "Russia, for the first time, has built up a school for instruction — not construction, but instruction — in the use of tools. We think that they make this instruction just as systematic as our instruction is in mathematics, chemistry, drawing, or any other subject. The instruction is given to classes." The system, he added, did not train for any particular trade, which he believed to be impracticable, but rather "it cultivated skill in the elements which underlie all industrial pursuits." (J. D. Runkle, in *Report to New England Manufacturers' Association*, October, 1876.)

[2] The course of study for this earliest adaptation of the Russian idea to college instruction was as follows, for the first two years at the Massachusetts Institute of Technology:

FRESHMAN YEAR	HOURS PER WEEK	SOPHOMORE YEAR	HOURS PER WEEK
Shop Instruction	12	Shop Instruction	12
Freehand Drawing	3	Mechanical Drawing	6
Algebra, 1st half	3	Algebra, 1st half	3
Plane Geometry, 2d	3	Solid Geometry, 2d	3
Rhetoric and Composition	3	English Literature	2
		French	3

[3] This school was a completely equipped high school, giving instruction in various lines of shopwork and mechanical drawing, as well as the regular secondary school subjects, with

This school at once formed a type for the organization of such schools elsewhere. Privately supported schools of this type were organized in Chicago, Philadelphia, Toledo, Cincinnati, and Cleveland before 1886, and the first public manual-training high schools were established in Baltimore in 1884, Philadelphia in 1885, and

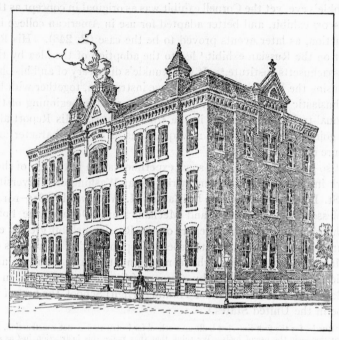

FIG. 120. THE FIRST MANUAL-TRAINING HIGH SCHOOL

Erected in 1879; opened in 1880. Connected with Washington University, St. Louis Missouri.

Omaha in 1886. The shopwork, based on the "Russian system," included wood-turning, joinery, pattern-making, forging, foundry and machine work. Hampton Institute, after 1870, and Tuskeegee Institute, after 1881 (R. 308), developed and applied the same type of technique for teaching trades to Negroes.

The first high school to provide sewing, cooking, dressmaking, and millinery for girls was the one at Toledo, established in 1886, though

the exception of the classics. The work of this school attracted wide attention, and its success led to the organization of similar schools elsewhere.

private classes had been organized earlier in these subjects in a number of cities. Indianapolis included full courses in cooking, dressmaking, millinery, and art in its manual-training high school, organized in 1889. This type of high school has developed rapidly with us, and today the tendency is strong to introduce such courses into all our high schools, making of them what are known as cosmopolitan high schools.

Manual work in the elementary school. The introduction of manual work into the elementary schools came a little later and a little more slowly, but now is very general. As early as 1880 the Workingmen's School, founded by the Ethical Culture Society of New York, had provided a kindergarten and had extended the kindergarten constructive-work idea upward, in the form of simple woodworking, into its elementary school. This same year Emily Huntington helped organize the Kitchen Garden Association, the aim of which was to extend the kindergarten idea upward by using pots and pans and brooms for the cubes and spheres and colored pasteboards of the kindergarten. In 1876 Juliet Corson founded

FIG. 121
REDIRECTED MANUAL TRAINING

A boy at Portland, Oregon, mending his shoe, instead of making a mortise-joint.

a cooking school in New York City for girls of school age.[1] In the public schools, experimental classes in elementary school woodworking were tried in one school in Boston, as early as 1882, the expense being borne by Mrs. Quincy A. Shaw. In 1888 the city took over these classes. In 1886 Mr. Gustav Larson was brought to Boston from Sweden to introduce Swedish sloyd, and a teacher-

---

[1] The movement for instruction in cooking to girls of school age had started earlier in England, and the idea was transplanted and adapted to American needs. After about 1880, with the changed conditions in the home then becoming evident, cooking made rapid progress as a school subject.

training school which has been very influential was established there in 1889. In 1876 Massachusetts permitted cities to provide instruction in sewing, and Springfield introduced such instruction in 1884, and elementary school instruction in knifework in 1886. In 1882 Montclair, New Jersey, introduced manual training into its elementary schools, and in 1885 the State of New Jersey first offered state aid to induce the extension of the idea. In 1885 Philadelphia added cooking and sewing to its elementary schools, having done so in the girls' high school five years earlier. In 1888 the City of New York added drawing, sewing, cooking, and woodworking to its elementary school course of study. By 1890 approximately forty cities, nearly all of them in the North Atlantic group of States, had introduced work in manual training into their elementary schools, and from these beginnings the movement has extended to practically all cities and to many towns and rural communities.

The educational discussion. From about 1885 to 1888 the manual-training idea was under heavy fire, the papers at the meeting of the Department of Superintendence of the National Education Association, in 1887 and 1888, being a culmination of the discussion. The new work was then advocated on the grounds of formal discipline — that it trained the reasoning, exercised the powers of observation, and strengthened the will. The "exercises," true to such a conception, were formal, arranged in a psychological order, and uniform for all. With the breakdown of the "faculty psychology," and the abandonment in large part of the doctrine of formal discipline in the training of the mind, the whole manual-training work has had to be reshaped. As the writings of Pestalozzi, Herbart, and Froebel were studied more closely, and with the new light on child development gained from child-study and the newer psychology, manual training came to be conceived of in its proper light as a means of individual expression, and to be extended to new forms, materials, colors, and new practical and artistic ends.

Today the instruction in manual work in all its forms, elementary and secondary, has been further changed to make it an educational instrument for interpreting the fields of art and industry in terms of their social significance and usefulness. In the United States, more than any other Nation, the work has been individualized and applied in many new directions — clay, leather, metal, cement — and used as a very important instrument for self-expression and the development of individual thinking.   In the secondary field, it has resulted in the creation of a type of manual-arts high school that has no counterpart in European countries.

IV. THE ADDITION OF ART AND SCIENCE STUDY

Rising interest in the study of art and science.   A very prominent feature of our educational development, since about the middle of the nineteenth century, has been the general introduction into the schools of the study of drawing and science.   It is no exaggeration of the importance of this development to say that the addition of drawing and art has been of the greatest value to us as a Nation, and that no addition of new subject-matter and no change in the direction and purpose of education has been of greater importance for the welfare of mankind, or more significant of new world conditions, than has been the emphasis recently placed, in all divisions of state school systems, on instruction in the principles and the applications of science.

England's pioneer work in drawing and design.   Though a few beginnings in art instruction had been made in the high schools of a few cities in the forties (see page 428), the real beginnings of such instruction in the schools of the United States date from the work of Massachusetts, two decades later.   The inspiration for this development came from England, where instruction in art and design had been under development for three decades before the Massachusetts beginning.   After the close of the Napoleonic wars England rapidly developed into the world's leading industrial Nation.   As early as 1830 the House of Commons had appointed a committee

to inquire into the best means of extending a knowledge of the arts, and of the principles of design, among the people (especially the manufacturing population) of the country; also to inquire into the constitution, management, and efforts of institutions connected with the arts.

After six years of investigation, the committee recommended the creation of a "Normal School of Design, with a Museum and Lectures," which was done.   The school opened in June, 1837, the stated purpose being

to afford the manufacturers an opportunity of acquiring a competent knowledge of the fine arts, in so far as these are connected with manufacture, and that steps ought to be taken to limit the students to these interests.

In 1840 an appropriation was made to start two other schools in the larger cities of England, and by 1850 some twenty such schools had been developed in England and Ireland.

In 1851 a great World's Fair was held in the Crystal Palace in London, and at this exhibition England made an elaborate exhibit of what the manufacturers of the country had been able to do in applying art and science to trade and industry. The exhibits revealed, to an astonished Europe and America, the great industrial advantages to arise from intelligent and directed instruction in drawing, design, and the principles and applications of science. Following up these advantages, Parliament created, in 1853, a State Department of Science and Art, and a National Training School was established at South Kensington. This latter almost at once became a noted art center.

The Massachusetts development. Massachusetts manufacturers, returning from the London Exhibition of 1851, at once began an agitation for instruction in drawing and design in the schools of that State. Massachusetts had by this time become an important cotton and paper manufacturing center, and the need for artistic designing for the prints produced there was large. There was much discussion of the matter, and in 1860 the legislature of that State listed drawing as a permissive school subject, and in 1870 drawing was made a required subject in all the larger towns and cities.[1] Boston had previously, in 1864, made drawing a required subject in the upper grades, and in 1868 made it such for all grades from the intermediate to the normal school. In 1870, the State of Massachusetts brought Walter Smith, from the South Kensington Art School, to Massachusetts as the first state supervisor of drawing and art, a position he held for the next thirteen years, and in 1873 the Massachusetts Normal Art School was created to train teachers of drawing and art for the schools of the State.

From these beginnings in Massachusetts, which owed their inspiration to English development, instruction in drawing and de-

---

[1] The Massachusetts law of 1870 read:

Sec. 1. This section included "drawing among the branches of learning which are required to be taught in the public schools."

"Sec. 2. Any city or town may, and every city or town having more than 10,000 inhabitants shall, annually make provision for giving free instruction in industrial or mechanical drawing to persons over 15 years of age, either in day or evening schools, under the direction of the school committee."

"Approved, May 18, 1870."

sign has spread to the schools of the entire United States. Between 1870 and 1907 drawing had been made a required study by legislative act in twelve States, and had been approved as a study by local action by city and town school systems in thirty-one other States. Today some type of instruction in drawing is given in all our cities and towns, and in most of our rural schools. Thus another subject was added to our school curriculum.

The beginnings of science instruction in the United States. Book instruction in such sciences as astronomy, natural philosophy, chemistry, and zoology came in very early in the nineteenth century, particularly in the academies, but the first laboratory instruction in science [1] — chemistry, at Harvard — was not begun until 1846, and our real interest in science teaching dates from after the rise of the land-grant colleges (page 278). The academies and the early high schools had both offered book instruction in a number of the sciences,[2] and this tendency the rising high schools inherited and expanded. By 1850 some lecture-table demonstration had become common in the better academies and high schools, and after about 1870 laboratory instruction for students began to find a place for itself.

The Oswego movement had brought "object lessons" on scientific objects (page 385) into elementary-school instruction, though for a couple of decades teachers were not able to do much in elementary science instruction for the reason that their own training had not included science. In 1871, Superintendent William T. Harris, of St. Louis, worked out and published the outlines of a course of study in science [3] instruction for grades one to seven. This course of study was reprinted in a number of cities, and did much to show

---

[1] Chemistry was the first science to develop, being the mother of science instruction. The first American university to provide laboratory instruction in chemistry was Harvard, in 1846. The science instruction in most of our universities, up to at least 1850, was book instruction. The first high school laboratories for instruction in science date from about 1870.

[2] Astronomy, botany, chemistry, and natural philosophy had been prominent studies in the academies. Between 1825 and 1840 was the great period for the introduction of science studies. The first American high school (Boston, 1821) offered instruction in geography, navigation and surveying, astronomy, and natural philosophy. The Fellenberg manual labor movement also attracted some attention to science study.

[3] This course of instruction in science appeared first in Superintendent Harris's *Annual Report of the Board of Education* of St. Louis for 1871, and again in 1879. In 1877, Superintendent Philbrick, of Boston, reproduced the outline in full in his *Annual Report* to the school board of Boston. It was reprinted in 1887, and a new edition in 1894, by C. W. Bardeen, of Syracuse, New York.

what might be done and to give instruction in the elements of science a place in the work of our elementary schools.

The challenge of Herbert Spencer. By the middle of the nineteenth century the scientific and industrial changes had so modified the conditions of living in all progressive nations that the growing controversy between the partisans of the older classical training and the newer scientific studies as to their relative worth or importance, both for intellectual discipline and as preparation for intelligent living, had become quite sharp. The psychology upon which the theory of the discipline of the powers of the mind by classical studies was largely based was attacked, and the contention was advanced that the content of studies was of more importance in education than was method and drill. The advocates of the scientific studies con-

FIG. 122
HERBERT SPENCER
(1820–1903)

tended that a study of the classics no longer provided a suitable preparation for intelligent living, and the question of the relative worth of the older and newer studies elicited more and more discussion as the century advanced.

In 1859, one of England's greatest scholars, Herbert Spencer, brought the whole question to a sharp issue by the publication of a remarkably incisive essay on "What Knowledge is of Most Worth?" In this essay he declared that the purpose of education was "to prepare for complete living," and that the only way to judge of an educational program was first to classify, in the order of their importance,

the leading activities and needs of life,[1] and then measure the instructional program by how fully it offers such a preparation. Doing so (**R. 249**), and applying such a test, he concluded that of all subjects a knowledge of science (**R. 250**) "was always most useful for preparation for life," and therefore the type of knowledge of

---

[1] Spencer's classification of life activities and needs, in the order of their importance, was:

1. Those ministering directly to self-preservation.
2. Those which secure for one the necessities of life.
3. Those which help in the rearing and disciplining of offspring.
4. Those involved in maintaining one's political and social relations.
5. Those which fill up the leisure part of life, and gratify taste and feelings.

most worth.   In three other Essays — Intellectual Education; Moral Education; Physical Education;[1] he recommended a complete change in the type of training which had dominated English education since the days of the Renaissance.   Still more, instead of a few being educated for a life of learning and leisure, he urged general instruction in science that all might receive training and help for the daily duties of life.

These *Essays* attracted wide attention, not only in England but in the United States as well.   They were a statement, in clear and forceful English, of the best ideas of the educational reformers for three centuries.   Though his work was not specially original, we must nevertheless class Herbert Spencer as one of the great writers on educational aims and purposes, and his *Essays* as of great influence in reshaping educational thought and practice.   Out of the extended discussion which followed their publication, both in England and the United States, came a new and a greatly enlarged estimate as to the importance of the study of science in all divisions of the school.

V. THE ELEMENTARY SCHOOL NOW REORGANIZED AND COMPLETE

The new and expanded elementary school course.   Excepting instruction in agriculture, which came in recently as an outgrowth of nature study, and in response to an economic demand, the elementary course of study of 1900 contained all the elements of this course today.   The changes and additions, and the variations in relative emphasis and in teachers' methods in each subject, are shown in the chart on page 473.   It was a vastly changed course of study, though, from that of 1850, both as to content and methods.   The beginning of these changes goes back to the work of Pestalozzi, though his contributions and those of Herbart, Froebel, and their disciples and followers are so interwoven in the educational practice of today that it is in most cases impossible to trace them or separate them out one from the other.   Our elementary-school instruction of today remains, as before, a sturdy native development, but deeply influenced, since 1860, by the best ideas of the great European theorists and reformers.

[1] The four essays were published in book form, in 1861, under the title of *Education; Intellectual, Moral, and Physical*.   The first essay served as an introduction to the other three.

The interrelation between the movement for the study of the sciences and the other movements for the improvement of instruction, which we have described in this chapter, was close. Pestalozzi had emphasized instruction in geography and the study of nature; Froebel had given a prominent place to nature study and school gardening; the manual-arts work tended to reveal industrial processes and relationships; and the emphasis on the content rather than drill was in harmony with the theories of the modern reformers.

The place of Harris and Parker. In the great reorganization and redirection of elementary education, which took place between 1860 and 1900 in response to these new ideas, probably no two Americans were more influential than Dr. William T. Harris and Colonel Francis W. Parker.

Dr. Harris [1] was America's first great educational philosopher. By reason of his long and intelligent study of psychology, history, and the philosophy of education, he developed an insight into educational problems such as was enjoyed by none of his predecessors and by few of his contemporaries. Going to St. Louis at the age of twenty-two, he passed successively from a teacher to that of principal of a grammar school, assistant superintendent, and superintendent of city schools. During his administration the St. Louis schools occupied a very prominent place (**R. 251**) in American education. His thirteen *Annual Reports* as city superintendent of schools established his reputation as an educational thinker and constructive school executive; his Report as chairman of the Committee of Fifteen of the National Education Association on the Correlation of Studies (1895) was an important contribution to our educational literature; and his *Annual Reports* as United States Commissioner of Education, from 1889 to 1906, commanded the respect of educators at home and abroad. In the debates at meetings of the National Education Association and the Department of Superintendence he was for long the leader of a group of almost equally able men (**R. 252**). In his contributions to education he strove to

[1] Born at Killingly, Connecticut, Harris prepared for college and attended Yale for two years, but left that he might have more freedom for the pursuit of studies he was more interested in. At first he taught shorthand and tutored, but he soon entered the St. Louis school system and quickly rose to the head of it. Resigning in 1880, he first went to Europe, and then settled in Concord, Massachusetts, becoming one of the founders of the Concord School of Philosophy and Literature. In 1889 he was appointed United States Commissioner of Education by President Harrison, a position he held for seventeen years and until within two years of his death, at the age of seventy-three.

DR. WILLIAM T. HARRIS

(1835–1908)

Teacher and Principal of Schools, St. Louis, 1857–1867
Superintendent of Schools, St. Louis, 1867–1880
U.S. Commissioner of Education, 1889–1906

COL. FRANCIS W. PARKER

(1837–1902)

Supt. of Schools, Quincy, Mass., 1875–1880
Asst. Supt. of Schools, Boston, 1880–1883
Prin. Cook County Normal School, Chicago, 1883–1899

TWO AMERICAN EDUCATORS, PROMINENT IN THE REORGANIZATION

1775	1825	1850	1875	1900
READING	READING *	READING	READING	READING *
	Declamation	DECLAMATION	Literary Selections	LITERATURE *
Spelling	SPELLING *	SPELLING	SPELLING	Spelling
Writing	Writing	WRITING	PENMANSHIP *	Writing *
Catechism	Good Behavior	Manners	Conduct	....
BIBLE	Manners & Morals *	Conduct		
Arithmetic	ARITHMETIC *	MENTAL ARITH.	PRIMARY ARITH.	ARITHMETIC
		CIPHERING	ADVANCED ARITH.	
	Bookkeeping	Bookkeeping	....	ORAL LANGUAGE
	GRAMMAR	Elem. Language	Oral Language *	Grammar
	Geography	GRAMMAR	GRAMMAR	Home Geography
		Geography	Home Geography	TEXT GEOGRAPHY*
		History U.S.	TEXT GEOGRAPHY *	History Stories *
			U.S. HISTORY	TEXT HISTORY *
			Constitution	
		Object Lessons	Object Lessons *	Nature Study *
			Elementary Science *	Elem. Science
			Drawing *	Drawing *
	Sewing and Knitting		Music *	Music *
			Physical Exercises	Play
				Physical Training *
		....	....	Sewing
				Cooking
				Manual Training

CAPITALS = Most important subjects.   Italics = Subjects of medium importance.   Roman = Least important subjects.
* = New methods of teaching now employed.

FIG. 123. THE EVOLUTION OF THE ELEMENTARY-SCHOOL CURRICULUM, AND OF METHODS OF TEACHING

show the futility of the old psychology, with its "faculties of the mind," and to substitute a newer one; to establish the "faith of the Nation in the school as a social institution of first importance; and to place the subject of education on an enduring foundation." He subjected the whole field to critical analysis, interpreting and justifying the school, and assigning to it its proper place in the scheme of institutional life.

Another important contributor to the reorganization and redirection of American education during this same period was Colonel Francis W. Parker.[1] After a few years of teaching, he spent the years 1872 to 1875 in study in Germany. On his return he was superintendent of schools at Quincy, Massachusetts, from 1875 to 1880, and from 1883 to 1899 was principal of the Cook County Normal School, at Chicago. It was he who introduced Germanized Pestalozzian-Ritter methods of teaching geography; he who strongly advocated the Herbartian plan for concentration of instruction about a central core, which he worked out for geography;[2] he who insisted so strongly on the Froebelian principle of self-expression as the best way to develop the thinking process; he who emphasized the Spencerian idea that science was of fundamental importance in the education of the child; and he who saw educational problems so clearly from the standpoint of the child that he, and the pupils he trained, did much to bring about the reorganization in elementary education which had been worked out by 1900. (R. 253).

More than any other person of his time, his work in the improvement of elementary teaching and in advancing the claims of childhood acted as a ferment which stimulated teachers and school officers to activity. Especially was his work effective in the West, where the teachers were younger and their minds more open than in the East.

---

[1] Born at Bedford, New Hampshire, and educated in New England, Parker taught district schools in New Hampshire from the time he was sixteen until he was twenty-one. Then (1858) he became principal of schools at Carrollton, Illinois, but on the outbreak of the Civil War he entered the army and rose to the rank of colonel. From 1865 to 1868 he was again a school principal at Manchester, New Hampshire; from 1868 to 1872 an instructor in a normal school at Dayton, Ohio; and from 1872 to 1875 a student at the University of Berlin. On his return he was for five years superintendent of schools at Quincy, Massachusetts, then three years as assistant superintendent at Boston, and in 1883 he became principal of the Cook County (Chicago) normal school, a position he held until 1899. Then he was elected principal of the Chicago Institute which, a year before his death, became the School of Education of the University of Chicago.

[2] *How to Study Geography.* A practical exposition of methods and devices in teaching geography which apply the principles and plans of Ritter and Guyot. By Francis W. Parker. International Education Series. New York, 1889. (R. 253).

During the twenty-five years of his major period of activity the kindergarten made steady headway, manual training began to be introduced, science study was adopted as an elementary-school subject, physical education was seen to be fundamental and vital, and a new life and a new spirit came to characterize the teacher in the elementary school. He was concerned not only with the freedom of the child, but with that of the teacher as well. His vigorous personality and his enthusiasm attracted students to the Cook County Normal School from all parts of the country, though in largest numbers from the Middle West, and the enthusiastic and well informed teachers he trained did much to bring about the progress made since his day. Since his time the most influential constructive critic of the elementary school has been Professor John Dewey, to whom we shall refer a little later on.

QUESTIONS FOR DISCUSSION

1. Explain what is meant by the statements that Herbart rejected:
    (a) The conventional social idea of Locke.
    (b) The unsocial ideal of Rousseau.
    (c) The "faculty-psychology" conception of Pestalozzi.
2. Explain what is meant by saying that Herbart conceived of education as broadly social rather than personal.
3. Show in what ways and to what extent Herbart:
    (a) Enlarged our conception of the educational process.
    (b) Improved the instruction content and process.
4. In what ways did Herbart's conception of character development offer more promise than did the older faculty psychology?
5. Explain why Herbartian ideas took so much more quickly in the United States than did Pestalozzianism.
6. State the essentials of the kindergarten idea, and the psychology behind it.
7. State the contribution of the kindergarten idea to American education.
8. Show how the extension of Froebel's ideas as to self-activity to include the manual-training activities was a natural extension of thinking.
9. Show the connection between the sense impression ideas of Pestalozzi, the self-activity of Froebel, and the manual activities of the modern elementary school.
10. Show how a faculty psychology and set and uniform manual-training exercises stood and fell together.
11. What advantages did sloyd work appear to have over the earlier manual training?
12. Explain why scientific ideas came into the schools so slowly up to about 1860, and rapidly after that time.

13. Does the reasoning of Herbert Spencer appeal to you as sound?   If not, why not?
14. Show how the argument of Spencer for the study of science was also an argument for a more general diffusion of educational advantages.
15. What forces had come into American life, after about 1860, that caused Spencer's *Essays* to make a far greater appeal than would have been the case before that time.
16. State the new method in instruction indicated by the * for each subject in the table on page 473.
17. What is meant by correlation and concentration in studies?
18. Why did the adaptations made in the kindergarten adapt it better to American needs and lead to its general adoption?
19. State the educational contribution of William T. Harris.
20. State the educational contribution of Francis W. Parker.

SELECTED READINGS

In the accompanying volume of *Readings* the following selections, related to the subject matter of this chapter, are reproduced:

243. Felkin: Application of Herbart's Ideas to Instruction.
244. Felkin: Herbart's Psychological Ideas Applied.
*245. Marenholtz-Bülow: Froebel's Educational Views.
*246. Hailmann: Pestalozzi and Froebel on Self-activity.
247. Froebel: Handwork in the Scheme of Education.
*248. White: The Prior Development of Manual Instruction at Cornell.
*249. Spencer: What Knowledge is of Most Worth?
*250. Spencer: Conclusions as to the Importance of Science.
*251. Whiteside: William T. Harris as a School Superintendent.
252. Butler: William T. Harris as an Educational Leader.
*253. Jackman: Colonel Parker's Services for Education.

QUESTIONS ON THE READINGS

1. State the essentials of Herbart's educational ideas (**243, 244**), and the nature of the advances he made over his predecessors.
2. State the essentials of Froebel's educational ideas, as explained by the Baroness von Marenholtz-Bülow (**245**).
3. Show how Froebel advanced over Pestalozzi in his conception of self-activity as an educative impulse (**246**).
4. Show how the theory for the Swedish handwork was founded directly on the conceptions Froebel expressed (**247**) but did not work out.
5. How do you explain the great Moscow influence (**248**), rather than that of Cornell?
6 Would you add anything else to Spencer's requirements to prepare for complete living (**249**)?   What?   Why?
7. How do you explain science being "written against in our theologies and frowned upon from our pulpits" (**250**), when it is of such importance as Spencer concludes?

8. Evaluate Harris as a school superintendent in terms of present-day standards (251).
9. What ones of the list of leaders of a generation ago, mentioned by Butler (252), do you know anything of as to their place in the history of education in the United States?
10. Show that Parker was a many-sided leader in the progressive school movement of his time (253).

TOPICS FOR INVESTIGATION AND REPORT

1. Early work, leaders in, and publications of the American Herbart Society. (Publications.)
2. Early leaders in the kindergarten movement in the United States. (Parker; Swift; Vandewalker.)
3. The philanthropic stage in the kindergarten with us. (Swift.)
4. The work of Baroness von Marenholtz-Bülow.
5. The work of Elizabeth Peabody in Boston.
6. The work of Emma Marwedel in San Francisco. (Swift.)
7. The N.E.A. discussion over education through manual activities. (*Proceedings.*)
8. The founding and work of Hampton Institute.
9. The beginnings of sloyd work in the United States.
10. The discussion awakened by Spencer's *Essays.*
11. The change in geography teaching during the last century.
12. The change in the teaching of reading during the last century.
13. Change in the character of the kindergarten since its introduction.
14. Change in the character of manual-training instruction since its introduction.
15. The work of William T. Harris as a school superintendent at St. Louis.
16. The work of Francis W. Parker at Quincy and at the Cook County Normal School.
17. Early History of Manual Training in the United States. (Anderson; Bennett; Coates.)
18. Early History of Art Instruction in the United States. (Bennett.)

SELECTED REFERENCES

Anderson, L. F. *History of Manual and Industrial School Education.* 251 pp. New York, 1926.

Chapter VII deals with the leading personages of this chapter. Part II gives a good brief history of industrial education in the United States. Good bibliographies.

Barnard, Henry, Editor. *The American Journal of Education*, 31 vols. Consult *Analytical Index* to; 128 pp. Published by United States Bureau of Education, Washington, 1892.

Bennett, Charles A. *History of Manual and Industrial Education Up to 1870.* 461 pp. Peoria, Illinois, 1926.

A comprehensive and well-written account, dealing with early beginnings. Chapter XI good on early history of art instruction.

*Bowen, H. C. *Froebel and Education through Self-Activity.* 209 pp. New York, 1893.

An excellent historical account.

Coates, C. P. *History of the Manual Training School of Washington University.* 86 pp. United States Bureau of Education, Bulletin 3, 1923. Washington, 1923.

A good history of the founding and work of what became the St. Louis Manual Training School.

Compayré, G. *Herbert Spencer and Scientific Education.* New York, 1907.

A good treatment of his work and importance.

*De Garmo, Charles. *Herbart and the Herbartians.* 268 pp. New York, 1895.

Traces the development of the movement in Germany and America.

Dewey, John and Evelyn. *Schools of Tomorrow.* 316 pp. New York, 1915.

Chapter X gives a good criticism of the new Montessori work, and compares it with the more psychologically sound kindergarten.

*Elementary School Teacher, June, 1902.

Parker Memorial Number.

Graves, F. P. *Great Educators of Three Centuries.* New York, 1912.

Contains good chapters on Herbart and Froebel.

Harris, William T. "Twenty Years of Progress in Education"; in *Proceedings of the National Education Association,* 1892, pp. 56–61.

Jackman, W. S. "Colonel Francis Wayland Parker"; in *Proceedings of the National Education Association,* 1902, pp. 399–409.

*Monroe, Paul. *Cyclopedia of Education.* The Macmillan Co., New York, 1911–13.

The following articles are particularly important:
1. "Froebel, F."; vol. II, pp. 713–23.
2. "Herbart, J. F."; vol. III, pp. 250–53.
3. "Kindergarten, The"; vol. III, 598–606.
4. "Manual Training"; vol. IV, pp. 124–28.
5. "Parker, F. W."; vol. IV, pp. 606–07.
6. "Spencer, Herbert," vol. V, pp. 400–01.

Also see articles on Arithmetic, Geography, Manual Training, etc.

Monroe, Walter S. *Development of Arithmetic as a School Subject.* 170 pp. United States Bureau of Education, Bulletin no. 10, Washington, 1917.

An excellent collection of very interesting illustrative material. The chapters deal with colonial arithmetic, the ciphering-book period, Colburn's Pestalozzian arithmetic, influence of Colburn, and recent tendencies. The volume also gives the table of contents of the most important early arithmetics.

*Moore, E. C. *Fifty Years of American Education.* 96 pp. Boston, 1917.

A summary of the progress of education in the United States from 1867 to 1917.

*Parker, S. C. *History of Modern Elementary Education.* 506 pp. Boston, 1912.

Chapters XVII and XVIII are very detailed and readable accounts of the Herbartian and Froebelian movements in education.

Phillips, C. A. "Development of Methods in Teaching Modern Elementary Geography"; in *Elementary School Teacher*, vol. x, pp. 427–39, 501–15.

Quick, Herbert. *Essays on Educational Reformers.*

Chapters XVII on Froebel and XIX on Spencer are very readable.

*Reeder, R. R. *Historical Development of School Readers.* 92 pp. Columbia University *Contributions to Philosophy, Psychology, and Education,* vol. VIII, no. 2. New York, 1900.

A good description of early readers, and of the evolution of modern methods of teaching reading.

*Reisner, Edward H. *Francis W. Parker.* New York, 1931.

A well-written and sympathetic account of his work.

*Reisner, Edward H. *The Evolution of the Common School.* 590 pp. New York, 1930.

Pages 411–85 are good on the work and place of Froebel and Herbart.

Smith, D. E. "The Development of American Arithmetic"; in *Educational Review*, vol. LII, pp. 109–18. (Sept., 1916.)

Historical sketch of influences and results.

Sutton, W. S. *Problems of Modern Education.* 1913.

Contributions of William T. Harris to the development of education in the United States.

Swift, F. H. *Emma Marwedel, Pioneer of the Kindergarten in California.* University of California, *Publications in Education*, vol. VI, no. 3, pp. 139–216. Berkeley, 1931.

An excellent, well-illustrated and documented biographical sketch.

Tigert, J. J. "An Appreciation of William T. Harris"; in *Proceedings of the National Education Association*, 1927, pp. 179–84.

*Vandewalker, N. C. *The Kindergarten in American Education.* 274 pp. New York, 1908.

A very important historical account of the kindergarten movement in the United States.

Whitford, W. G. "A Brief History of Art Education in the United States"; in *Elementary School Journal*, vol. XXIV, pp. 109–15. (October, 1923.)

CHAPTER XIV

NEW MODIFYING FORCES

WE HAVE now traced the evolution of the American public school from the beginnings of education at public expense down through the educational reorganization which took place within the school between 1860 and 1900, and have shown how the native American elementary school was modified and expanded and changed in character as the result of new educational ideas which came to us from abroad. Since 1860, too, but particularly since about 1885 to 1890, our schools have also been profoundly modified in character and changed in direction by forces other than educational, and to these we next turn. In doing so we shall need to go back and pick up the beginnings of these new forces, trace briefly their development, and point out their far-reaching influence on our educational aims and procedure. The two great new forces to which we refer were foreign immigration and the industrial revolution. These two combined produced vast social changes which in turn have necessitated important changes in our educational aims and practices.

I. CHANGES IN THE CHARACTER OF OUR PEOPLE

Our original stock. In previous chapters it has been shown that in all our early educational traditions and procedure we were essentially English. The Dutch parochial school had been established in a few towns in New Amsterdam, but most of these had lapsed or been superseded by English schools after New Amsterdam passed to the control of the English. Some Lutheran Swedes had settled along the Delaware and established there their type of schools, but in time these were assimilated by the English around them and they, too, became English-speaking schools. Only in Pennsylvania was there any marked grouping of non-English-speaking peoples. We were in origin, and by the time of the American Revolution certainly had become, an English-type colony, speaking the English language, following English customs and observances, adopting English law and English habits in morality and Sunday observances, and such schools as existed were, always excepting the Germans of Pennsylvania, almost entirely English-speaking schools.

Some conception as to the character of our original population may be obtained from the records of the first Federal Census, taken in 1790. It was not customary then, as it is now, to note down the country in which each person was born and the nationality of the parents, but an analysis has been made of the names of all persons appearing on the lists of this first census to determine their original nationality. The result is shown, for the white population, in the accompanying drawing. This shows that 83.5 per cent of the population possessed names indicating pure English origin, and that 91.8 per cent had names which pointed to their having come from the British Isles. The next largest name-nationality was the German, with 5.6 per cent, and these were found chiefly in Pennsylvania, where they consti-

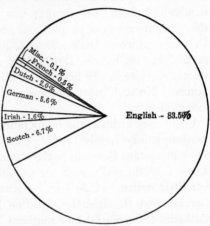

Misc. - 0.1%
French - 0.5%
Dutch - 2.0%
German - 5.6%
Irish - 1.6%
Scotch - 6.7%
English - 83.5%

FIG. 124. NATIONALITY OF THE WHITE POPULATION, AS SHOWN BY THE FAMILY NAMES IN THE CENSUS OF 1790

tuted 26.1 per cent of the total population. Next were those having Dutch names, who constituted 2 per cent of the whole population, and 16.1 per cent of the population of New York. No other nationality constituted over one half of one per cent of the total. The New England States then were almost as English as England itself, 93 to 96 per cent of the names being pure English, and 98.5 to 99.8 per cent being from the British Isles.

The stream of immigrants begins. Up to 1820 the annual immigration into the United States was quite small, mostly English in character, and no records as to it were taken by the Government. In 1820, the first year for which records were kept, the number coming was only 8385, and it was not until 1825 that the number of immigrants reached fifty thousand, and not until 1842 that it reached one hundred thousand. Excepting only two years during our Civil War, the immigration to the United States, since 1845 and up to 1930, has never been less than one hundred thousand. Between 1847 and 1857 inclusive, the number coming was in no year less than two hundred thousand, and in 1854 the number was 427,833. Between 1903 and 1914 the numbers ranged from three quarters of a million to one and one quarter millions each year, and the total immigration from 1820 to 1927 was 36,386,381. Compared with this vast movement of peoples to a new world the migrations of the Germanic tribes — Angles, Saxons, Jutes, Goths, Visigoths, Ostrogoths, Vandals, Sueves, Danes, Burgundians, Huns — into the old Roman Empire in the fourth and fifth centuries pale into insignificance. No such great movement of peoples was ever known before in history.

Up to 1825 at least, the immigrants coming to the United States continued to be largely English, Scotch, and Protestant Irish, with a few Protestant Germans to the Eastern cities and to Pennsylvania. These fitted in easily with the existing population, and awakened but little notice and no fear. Between 1820 and 1840 both the German and the Irish immigration increased rapidly, and Irish Catholics from central and southern Ireland began to replace the northern Protestant Irish of the earlier migration. It was during the period from 1830 to 1850 that the Catholic parochial-school question first began to appear in cities of the North Atlantic group of States, and the controversy over the secularization of American education was brought to the front.

The north and west of Europe migrations. For a long time the Irish had been coming in increasing numbers to what they termed "the States," but the climax of the movement came in 1846–48, when the potato crop of Ireland was almost a complete failure. Driven out by famine and by the oppressive system of landlordism which prevailed,[1] great numbers of Irish immigrants now came to the United States to find a new home. They settled chiefly in the cities of the North Atlantic group of States. Between 1845 and 1855 a

---

[1] "There were four principal causes which induced the transplanting of the race: rebellion, famine, restrictive legislation, and absentee landlordism.... Long before the great Irish famine of 1846–47 America appeared like a mirage, and wondering peasants in their dire distress exaggerated its opulence and opportunities. They braved the perils of the sea in overcrowded ships and trusted to luck in the great new world." (Orth, S. P. *Our Foreigners,* chap. V.)

million and a quarter came, and again, in 1882, following another famine, Irish immigration reached another high point. In all, over four millions of Irish have come to us since 1820, and they still constitute ten per cent of all our foreign-born people. Unlike the other North and West of Europe peoples, Ireland had a high degree of illiteracy. The census of 1841 showed that fifty-three per cent of the people of Ireland over five years of age were unable to read and write. Less than one half of those who came in the early migration, and scarcely one quarter of those who came later, could read and write, and the coming of such large numbers of people, poor and uneducated, who would ultimately become citizens and voters, awakened a solicitude for our political future among the people of the northeastern part of the United States which materially aided in the establishment there of public education and the development of state oversight and control.

About this time the United States also began to receive large numbers of Germans. Up to 1830 the number of this nationality arriving had been negligible, as the government at home had been satisfactory. After 1835, however, with the growing narrowness of the German state governments, German immigration began a constant increase, and after the unsuccessful German revolutions of 1848 great numbers of liberty-loving Germans, chiefly from the South German States, left the Fatherland and came to this country. During the decade from 1846 to 1855 over a million and a quarter came, settling in the cities [1] of the eastern part of the United States and the cities and farming regions of the upper Mississippi Valley. After the establishment of the Imperial German Government, in 1870, and the definite embarkation of this Government on an aggressive military policy, large numbers of Germans left the Empire and came to us, approximately two millions arriving between 1881 and 1895. In all, a total of about five and a quarter million Germans, the best and most liberty-loving of the German people, have come to this country since 1820.

Unlike the Irish who came earlier, the Germans were a picked

---

[1] The growing western cities had a place for the skilled artisans and the small tradesmen among these immigrants, and the cities also formed a natural gathering place for the intellectuals among them. In 1830 the Germans formed only 5 per cent of Cincinnati, but by 1840 they formed 23 per cent and by 1869 the percentage had risen to 34. Milwaukee became known as "the American Athens." St. Louis became a center of German influence and liberalism felt throughout the Mississippi Valley.

and a well-educated class, the earlier ones having left Germany largely because of political and religious oppression, and the later ones largely to escape forced military service. The early Germans usually came in groups, formed settlements by themselves, held themselves aloof, and for a time constituted a segregated intellectual aristocracy among our people.[1] They too awakened considerable alarm, as they, for a time, showed but little disposition to become a part of our national life.

During the middle years of the nineteenth century large numbers of English came, in all a total of about three and a half millions having arrived since 1820. After 1840 Scandinavians, attracted by the free farms of the Northwest, also began to appear, though they did not reach the great period of their migration until the decade of the eighties. In all nearly two million Scandinavians have come to our shores.

While these different peoples frequently settled in groups and for a time retained their foreign language, manners, and customs, they have not been particularly difficult to assimilate. Of all these early immigrants the Germans have shown the greatest resistance to the assimilative process. All except the Irish came from countries which embraced the Protestant Reformation (see map, Fig. 1, page 7), where general education prevailed, and where progressive methods in agriculture, trade, and manufacturing had begun to supersede primitive methods. All were from race stock not very different from our own, and all possessed courage, initiative, intelligence, adaptability, and self-reliance to a great degree. The willingness, good-nature, and executive qualities of the Irish; the intellectual thoroughness of the German; the respect for law and order of the English; and the thrift, sobriety, and industry of the Scandinavians have been good additions to our national life.

Change in character of our immigration. After about 1882 the character of our immigration changed in a very remarkable manner. Immigration from the North and West of Europe began to decline

[1] "There were several causes, working in close conjunction, that impelled these thousands to leave Germany. Economic disturbances turned the thoughts of the hungry and the harrassed to the land of plenty across the sea. But a potent cause of the great migration in the thirties and the forties was the universal social and political discontent which followed in the wake of the Napoleonic Wars.... The desire to immigrate spread like a fever. Whole villages sold out and, with their pastor or their physician at their head, shipped for America. ... In the glow of their first enthusiasm many of the intellectuals believed they could establish a German State in America." (Orth, S. P. *Our Foreigners*, chap. VI.)

rather abruptly, and in its place immigration from the South and East of Europe set in. This soon developed into a great stream. Practically no Italians came to us before 1870, but by 1890 they were coming at the rate of twenty thousand a year, and during the five-year period 1906–10 as many as 1,186,100 arrived. After 1880, in addition, people from all parts of that medley of races which formerly constituted the Austro-Hungarian Empire — Poles, Bohemians, Moravians, Slovaks, Slovenes, Ruthenians, Dalmatians, Croatians, Bosnians, Magyars, and Austrians; Serbs, Bulgars, Roumanians, Montenegrins, and Albanians from the Balkans; Slavs, Poles, and Jews from Russia; and Japanese and Koreans from the Far East, began to come in numbers. After 1900, Finns and Lithuanians from the North, driven out by Russian persecution; and Greeks, Syrians, Armenians, and Turks from the South,

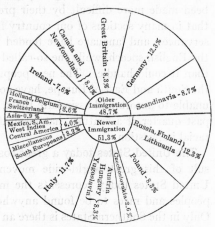

FIG. 125. FOREIGN-BORN IN THE UNITED STATES, AS SHOWN BY THE CENSUS OF 1930

also came in shiploads to our shores. French Canadians also have crossed the border in large numbers and crowded into the mill-towns of New England. As a result we had, in 1930, almost thirteen and a half millions of foreign-born people in our population, of whom practically forty-five per cent had come from the South and East of Europe. Of the immigration since 1900 almost eighty per cent has come from there. In addition to these thirteen and a half millions of foreign-born, an additional nine and a half million were native-born but the children of foreign parents, and of another six million one parent was foreign-born.

These Southern and Eastern Europeans were of a very different type from the North and West Europeans who preceded them. Largely illiterate, docile, often lacking in initiative, and almost wholly without the Anglo-Saxon conceptions of righteousness, liberty, law, order, public decency, and government, their coming has served to dilute tremendously our national stock and to weaken and corrupt our political life. Settling largely in the cities of the North, the agricultural regions of the Middle and the Far West, and the mining districts of the mountain regions, they have created serious problems in housing and living, moral and sanitary conditions, and honest and decent government, while popular education has everywhere been made more difficult by their presence. The result has been that in many sections of our country foreign manners, customs, observances, and language have tended to supplant native ways and the English speech, while the so-called "melting-pot" has had more than it could handle. The new peoples, and especially those from the South and East of Europe, have come so fast that we have been unable to absorb and assimilate them, and our national life, for the past quarter of a century, has been afflicted with a serious case of racial indigestion.

The United States today a great cosmopolitan mixture. The result of this great world-wide movement of peoples is that the United States today represents the most cosmopolitan mixture of peoples and races to be found anywhere on the face of the earth. Only in the Southern States is there an absence of a large percentage of foreign-born, and there the problem of the Negro and his education takes the place of the foreign-born educational problem.

How great the American mixture is we scarcely realize until we take stock of our neighbors. We buy our groceries of Knudsen and Larsen, our meats of Klieber and Engelmeier, our bread of Rudolf Krause, Petar Petarovich delivers our milk, Giuseppe Battali removes our garbage, Swen Swensen delivers our ice, Takahira Matsui is our cook, and Nicholas Androvsky has recently taken the place of Pancho Garcia as our gardener. We occasionally take dinner at a café managed by Schiavetti and Montagnini, we buy our haberdashery of Moses Ickelheimer, Isaac Rosenstein is our tailor, Azniv Arakelian sells us our cigars, and Thirmutis Poulis supplies our wants in ice cream and candies. Timothy Mehegan represents our ward in the city council, Patrick O'Grady is the policeman on our beat, Nellie O'Brien teaches our little girl at school, Nels Petersen is our postman, Vladimir Constantinovitch is our street-sweeper, Lazar Obichan reads our electric meter, Lorenzo Guercio sells potted plants and flowers on the corner, Mahmoud Bey peddles second-grade fruit past our door, and Alexis Grablowsky mends and presses our suits and cleans our hats in a little shop two blocks down the street. The service garage, run by Pestarino and Pozzi, looks after our car, Emil Frankfurter is the cashier at our bank, Kleanthis Vassardakis shines shoes in our office building, and Wilhelmina Weinstein is our office stenographer. The military poster of World War days, calling attention to the draft registration of those 18 to 45, was repeated in fifteen different languages on the sheet. The casualty list in the morning paper as the original edition of this book was written announced that, among others, such representative American citizens as Rudolph Kochensparger, Robert Emmet O'Hanlon, Ralph Mc-Gregor, John Jones, Rastus Brown, Pietro Sturla, Rafael Gonzales, Dominico Sebatino, Ignace Olzanski, Diego Lemos, and Manthos Zakis had, the preceding day, made the supreme sacrifice on the battle-fields of France in defense of the civilization of the world. If our earlier statesmen were concerned at the coming of the Irish and the Germans, well may we be alarmed at the deluge of diverse peoples which has poured into this Nation during the past fifty years.[1]

Finally, alarmed at the conditions that might result from the unrestricted immigration of European peoples to America after the World War, Congress, in 1924, enacted the first of the real restricting laws — the Johnson Immigration Law, limiting the future intake to two per cent, for each nationality, of those already here as shown by the Census of 1890. In 1929 further restrictions were made, based on the "national origins" of the 1920 population. The effect of these laws has been to restrict immigration to a possible maximum of a little less than 150,000 a year, sorted by nationalities and selected on a basis of physical and mental fitness. Due, however, to this nation having no registration and identification laws, such as are common in all Continental European countries, probably a still larger number is "bootlegged" over the border each year, and these an unselected lot at that.

[1] The way these newer peoples have sought educational advantages and found their way through our colleges is well revealed by an election of 30 seniors to Phi Beta Kappa in January, 1930, at Columbia College, New York City. The list included: Louis Barillet, John Dropkin, E. E. P. Friedenmuth von Helms, Bernard Friedlander, Edward Yuen Hsu, Isador Kagno, M. V. Mikolainis, James O'Connell, Seymour Rosin, E. R. Schlesinger, Arthur Shapiro, H. B. Shookhoff, Harry Slobodin, A. H. Vander Veer, and Isador Ziferstein. Phi Beta Kappa is an honorary society to which only those of outstanding records for scholarship are elected.

Assimilation and amalgamation. The problem which has faced
and still faces the United States is that of assimilating these thousands of foreigners into our national life and citizenship. We must
do this or lose our national character. The German tried to solve
the problem with his subject peoples by coercion, and failed; the
French and English hold their colonials by kind, considerate, and
good government; we have until recently either neglected the problem entirely or have trusted to our schools to handle the children
and to our labor unions to initiate the adults. As a result, the census
of 1910 showed that we still had among us ten millions of foreign-
born who professed no allegiance to the land of their adoption, and
a larger percentage of this number could neither read nor write English. Still worse, many of the number lived in foreign settlements
or foreign quarters in our cities, where they could get along without
even speaking the English language, and their children not infrequently were sent to a non-English-speaking parochial school. Of
the 11,726,506 immigrants who came to us during the four years preceding the outbreak of the World War, 26.5 per cent were unable to
read and write any language, and not over 12 per cent could speak
English. The World War finally opened the eyes of our people to
the danger of having groups of non-assimilated peoples living
among us, and a determined effort was made, after the close of the
War, to Americanize those who were here. By 1930 the number of
aliens living in the United States had been reduced to approximately
two fifths the number of twenty years before.[1]

In view of the large migrations of diverse peoples to us since 1845
we were fortunate, indeed, that before that time we had settled in
the affirmative the question of general education at public expense;
that we had provided for English schools, even for the Germans of
Pennsylvania; and that we had definitely eliminated the sectarian
school from our program for public education. A common English
language, our common law and political institutions, our common
democratic life, our newspaper habit, our free social intercourse, our
common free schools, our ease of communication, our tolerance of

---

[1] The 1930 Census still showed that there were over four millions of illiterates, ten years
of age or over, in our total population; that in many of our cities an illiteracy of 5 to 7 per
cent was common, with up to 10 per cent found in some of our northern manufacturing cities;
and that an illiteracy of 20 to 25 per cent among the foreign-born was frequent. Of our
over thirteen millions of foreign-born, but 58.8 per cent had been naturalized by 1930, and
only 9.3 per cent additional had taken out their first citizenship papers. Twelve and a half
millions of these were over 25 years of age, which included a million and a half illiterates.

other peoples, and the general absence of a priesthood bent on holding nationalities together for religious ends — all these have helped us in the assimilation of other races. On the other hand, the process has been retarded by the coming of such numbers, by city congregation and segregation, by the coming of so many male adults without their wives and children, by the work of the Germans in trying to preserve their language and racial habits and *Kultur*, and by the work of the Catholic and Lutheran churches in endeavoring to hold nationalities together.[1]

The greatest success in assimilating the new peoples who have come to us has been made by the school and the labor unions, but up to recent years the school has reached only the children of those classes bringing their families with them and who have not been attracted by the foreign-language parochial school. With these children the results have in general been remarkable, and the schools have proved to be our greatest agency for unifying the diverse elements of our population. Even under the best circumstances, though, it requires time to so assimilate the foreign-born that they come to have our conceptions of law and order and government, and come to act in harmony with the spirit and purpose of our American national ideals. After this end has been attained, which usually requires two or three generations, the amalgamation of the descendants of these peoples into our evolving American racial stock may take place through intermarriage and the mixture of blood. Assimilation is a blending of civilizations and customs to create that homogeneity necessary for citizenship and national feeling, and may be promoted by education and social institutions and wise legislation; amalgamation is a blending of races and bloods, and is a process of centuries. Through the assimilation of all our diverse elements we are preparing the way for that future amalgamation of racial elements which will in time produce the American race.

II. THE INDUSTRIAL REVOLUTION

Industrial changes since 1850. In Chapter V, under the heading "Rise of Manufacturing" (page 144), we traced somewhat briefly

[1] Compared with a highly organized and centralized nation, such as France, Germany, Italy, or Japan, we seem feeble in our ability to organize and push forward a constructive program for national development. Many of the tools and methods they have used so effectively are entirely lacking with us.

the beginnings of manufacturing in the United States, and pointed out how the application of steam, the perfecting of inventions, and the development of transportation revolutionized the industrial methods of our people of the northeastern part of the United States, between 1820 and 1850. We also pointed out how these industrial changes and the rise of the factory system meant the beginnings of the breaking up of home and village industry, vast changes in farm life (R. 254), the inauguration of a cityward movement of the population, the rise of entirely new educational and social problems, the ultimate concentration of manufacturing in large establishments, and the consequent rise of the city to a very important place in our national life (R. 255).

The changes which had been accomplished by 1850, though, or even by 1860, were but the beginnings of a vast change in the nature of our national life which has since gone forward with ever-increasing rapidity, and has extended to all parts of the Nation. As a result the United States stands today as the greatest manufacturing country of the whole world. There are few things connected with the wonderful development of our country since 1850 which stand out more prominently than the amazing rapidity with which we have gone to the front as a manufacturing nation. Awakening to the wonderful possibilities which the vast native resources in iron, coal, timber, and mineral wealth of the country gave us; utilizing the best European, and especially the best English manufacturing experience; and applying new technical knowledge, which in 1860 we had scarcely begun to teach — Yankee ingenuity and energy and brains have since pushed American products to the front by leaps and bounds. In textiles, in iron and steel products, and in high-grade tools and machinery in particular, our American products successfully compete throughout the world. In coal production, the lumber industry, and in agriculture the United States today is near the front. The packing and exporting of meats and meat products has also become a great national industry, and American refrigerated beef and bacon and hams are sent to all quarters of the globe. In hundreds of specialized industries, such as the manufacture of furniture, desks, typewriters, office conveniences, automobiles, motorcycles, bicycles, farm tractors, reapers and threshers, locomotives, printing-presses, sewing machines, surgical instruments, edge tools, electrical goods, plumbing supplies, refrigerators, phonographs, radios, moving pictures, rifles, explosives, cotton goods, and shoes, American manufactured articles supply not only the home market, but are exported all over the world. Scarcely a year has passed, during the last fifty at least, that American inventive genius and energy and labor combined have not wrested from other nations a world-lead in some new article of manufacture, and the result of the World War promises to be that the leadership in many new lines will pass to us. Particularly do we promise to gain in such large and important lines as the manufacture of dyes and chemicals, in which for so long the Germans had the lead.

Vast changes since Lincoln's day. We can perhaps get a better idea of the tremendous industrial development of the United States since 1860 if we try to picture to ourselves the things with which Lincoln was unacquainted. When he died, in 1865, the world was relatively simple and undeveloped, and business methods were old-fashioned compared with what we know today. If Lincoln were to return now and walk down the streets of Washington, he would be astonished at the things he would see. The beautiful city which would now meet his gaze, and the large and beautiful buildings in which the government business is now carried on, would alike be a matter of wonder to him. Buildings more than three or four stories high would be new, as the steel-frame and the reinforced concrete building were alike unknown in 1865. The large plate-glass show windows of the stores, the electroliers along the curb, the moving-picture establishments, the electric elevators in the buildings, the beautiful shops, and especially the big department stores would be things in his day unknown. The smooth-paved streets and cement sidewalks would be new to him. The fast-moving electric street-cars and the thousands of motor-vehicles would fill him with wonder. The air-plane overhead he would not understand at all. Entering the White House, the sanitary plumbing, air conditioning, steam heating, electric lights, electric fans, electric refrigerator, tele-phones, typewriters, teletypes, modern office furniture and filing devices, the Edison phonograph and dictaphone, and the fountain pen would have to be explained to him. In his day plumbing was in its beginnings, coal-oil lamps and gas-jets were just coming into use, and the steel pen had but recently superseded the quill. There were stenographers then, but all letters and papers were still written out by hand. As for communication, messenger boys with written notes ran everywhere on foot, and the transaction of all kinds of business was exceedingly slow. The telegraph had recently been installed, but it still required two weeks to get news from England, and two months from Manila or Valparaiso.

The steel rail, the steel bridge, fast vestibuled trains, high-powered locomotives, transcontinental railways, dining-cars, refrigerator cars, artificial ice, friction matches, repeating rifles, machine guns, smokeless powder, submarines, air planes, tanks, dynamite, TNT, money orders, special-delivery stamps, weather reports and flags, the parcels post, air-mail, gasoline engines, electric motors, type-setting machines, chemical fire engines, self-winding watches, player-pianos, phonographs, moving pictures, the cable, the wireless, the traction engine, the cream separator, the twine binder, the cater-pillar tractor — these and hundreds of other inventions in common use, which now simplify life and add to our convenience and pleas-ure, were all alike unknown. The cause and mode of transmission of the great diseases which decimated armies and cities — plague, cholera, malaria, yellow fever, typhoid fever, typhus, and dysentery — were all unknown. Anæsthetics, sanitary plumbing, paved streets, sleeping-cars, and through railways were just coming in when Lincoln died, while such terms as "bacteria," "eugenics," "evolu-tion," "sanitation" and "aviation" were seldom used or entirely unknown. Much of what everyone ate or wore was still manufac-tured in the home, the apprenticeship system still ruled in almost all lines, and every youngster still had "chores" to do and enough physical and manual activity to answer all human needs. Life was still relatively simple, agriculture was still the great industry of the people, and 77.8 per cent of the people of the Nation still lived on the farms. But 16.1 per cent had settled in cities of 8000 or more inhabitants, and there were but 141 of these in the entire United States. Even in these cities the character of living was far simpler than in a Western town of six hundred people today.

Changes in the nature of living. Since 1865 vast and far-reaching changes have taken place in the nature and character of our living, with the result that we live today, in many respects, in an entirely new world. During the past hundred years steam and steel, and during the past forty years electricity and medical science, have wrought an alteration in human living greater than was wrought in all the time from the Crusades up to a hundred years ago.

Along with the far-reaching industrial transformation has come a tremendous increase in the sum of our common human knowledge. The applications of science have become so numerous, books and magazines have so multiplied and cheapened, trade and industry become so specialized, all kinds of life have been so increased in complexity, and the inter-relationships of mankind have been so extended and have grown so intricate, that what one needs to know today has been greatly increased over what was the case half to three

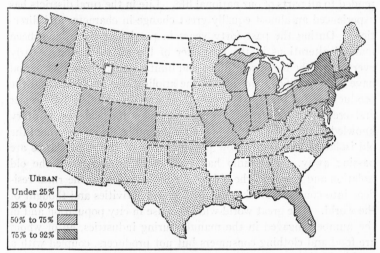

FIG. 126. URBAN AND RURAL POPULATION DISTRIBUTION IN 1930

Average for the United States, 56.2% per cent

quarters of a century ago. Once the ability to read and write and cipher distinguished the educated from the uneducated man; today the man who knows only these simple arts is an uneducated man, hardly fitted to meet the struggle for existence in which he is placed, and certainly not fitted to participate in the complex industrial, social, and political life of which he now forms a part.

Since 1860 cities have greatly increased in number and in the complexity of their life. From 141 cities of 8000 inhabitants or over in 1860, there are over 1200 such cities today, and over 16,600 incorporated towns and cities of all sizes. Over one half our people today (56.2 per cent in 1930) live in incorporated towns or cities, as against one sixth three quarters of a century ago. Great numbers of people of all kinds have congregated together in the cities, as the industrial life of the Nation has developed, and within recent decades entire new cities have been built and developed to supply the needs of the workers in some one or two lines or a group of related industries.[1]

Rural life also greatly changed. The effects of the industrial revolution have not been confined to the cities alone, but have extended to all parts of our national life. Life in the rural districts has experienced an almost equally great change in character and direction. During the past forty years in particular there have been marked alterations in the character of life on the farm. Nearly everywhere the harsh conditions and limitations of the earlier period have been modified, everywhere the applications of science and the products of the press have made their way and rendered life easier and created new interests, everywhere new medical and sanitary knowledge have made rural life more desirable, and everywhere the old isolation and the narrow provincialism of the rural classes are passing away. The radio has completely broken down the old isolation and removed the old loneliness by bringing the rural resident into constant touch with the life and activities and thought of the world. The great world-wide increase in city population and in the number engaged in the manufacturing industries, all of whom are food and clothing consumers but not producers, coupled with a world-wide increase in the standard of living and the per capita food and clothing consumption of the people, have created much greater demands for fruits, grains, meats, hides, cotton, and wool than heretofore. The general introduction of scientific processes and methods and machinery, the development of farming on a large scale, and the opening of world-wide markets due to the perfecting of means of transportation, have alike combined to change farming from a self-subsistence industry and make of it an important business undertaking. Near our large cities, intensive truck gardening has been extensively developed, and in this our foreign-born have been particularly successful. New agricultural regions have been opened, new grains and fruits introduced into old regions, entirely

[1] Gary, Indiana, is a good illustration, where a city of 100,426 inhabitants (1930) was laid out by the United States Steel Corporation, a quarter of a century ago, on the sand wastes of the south shore of Lake Michigan.

new demands in food consumption developed, new methods of marketing and preserving demonstrated, and new bookkeeping methods employed. Largely as a result of the work of the new agricultural colleges, agricultural education has been placed on a firm foundation, and practical and helpful assistance has been extended to farmers all over the United States.

Within recent years a marked change in the character of the farming population itself has taken place. In the richest agricul-

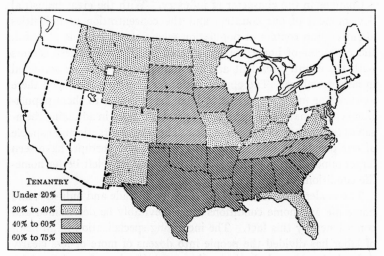

FIG. 127. FARM TENANTRY IN 1930

Average for the United States, 56 per cent

tural sections of our country the earlier sturdy type of American farmer is everywhere giving way to the tenant farmer, because he is leasing his farm and moving to the town or city to live more comfortably and to give his children better educational and social advantages. From twenty-five to forty per cent of the farms in the North Central States, and from sixty to seventy-five per cent of the farms in the South, are today let out to tenant farmers. Still more, the foreign-born tenant is rapidly displacing the native-born, and Italians, Austro-Huns, Poles, Slavs, Bulgars, Serbs, Armenians, and Japanese, and in the South Italians and Negroes, are today replacing the well-to-do native farmer of an earlier period, and it is probable that the movement of these new peoples to the farms is as yet only in its beginnings. Capable agriculturists, thrifty and economical, they pass successively from farm laborer to tenant, and from tenant to owner. The agricultural consequences of these changes in the character of our rural population may not be very significant, but the educational and social consequences are very important and very far-reaching (**R. 260**).

III. EFFECT OF THESE CHANGES ON THE HOME

Changes in the character of industry. With the great industrial development of our country, and the concentration of industries about certain centers of population where cheap labor is plentiful, the character of home life has altered greatly. To these centers both the country resident and the immigrant have been attracted in large numbers. The opportunities for gaining a livelihood there at easier or more remunerative labor have drawn to these population-centers many who have found great difficulty in adjusting themselves to the new and peculiar life. The most energetic and capable of our people, as well as the most vicious and corrupt, have seen larger opportunity for success in the city and have left better home-life conditions to join the city throngs.

The modern city is essentially a center of trade and industry, and home life and home conditions must inevitably be determined and conditioned by this fact. The increasing specialization in all fields of labor has divided the people into dozens of more or less clearly defined classes, and the increasing centralization of trade and industry has concentrated business in the hands of a relatively small number of people. All standards of business efficiency indicate that this should be the case, but as a result of it the small merchant and employer are fast giving way to large mercantile and commercial concerns. No longer can a man save up a few thousand dollars and start in business for himself with much chance of success. The employee tends to remain an employee; the wage-earner tends to remain a wage-earner. New discoveries and improved machinery and methods have greatly increased the complexity of the industrial process in all lines of work, and the worker in every field of trade and industry tends more and more to become a cog in the machine, and to lose sight of his part in the industrial processes and his place in our industrial and civic and national life (**R. 260**).

The effect of such conditions on the family has been very noticeable, and in some respects very unfortunate. Under the older village and rural-life conditions a large family was an asset, as every boy and girl could help about the house and farm from an early age. In doing this they received much valuable education and training. City life, though, has changed a large family from an asset to a serious liability, and the result is shown in the large number of small or childless families found there. Only among the foreign-born and in rural communities does one any longer find large families common. The native American, and the more thoughtful citizen generally, tends today to limit the size of his family to the few children he can clothe and educate according to his standard of life.

Changes in the character of home life. As a result of the changes of living incident to the change from an agricultural to an industrial society, and the rapid development of city-life conditions, the home life has greatly altered in character. Once it was a center where the rudiments of almost all the trades and industries of life were practiced, and where both boy and girl obtained many valuable life experiences. In the villages, blacksmiths, wagon-makers, cabinet-makers, harness-makers, shoemakers, millers, and saw-mill workers carried on most of the fundamental trades. In their small establishments the complete industrial processes were carried through, and could be seen and learned. In the homes girls were taught to sew, make hats and clothing, cook, bake, wash, iron, mend, and clean the house. On the farm the boy learned to plant, cultivate, and reap the crops, care for and feed the horses and stock, watch and learn to read the signs of the weather, mend wagons and harness, make simple repairs, and go to town on errands. The boy in town as well had the daily "chores" to attend to (**R. 256**).

These conditions, within the past half-century, have largely passed away. Since about 1890 the process of change has been particularly rapid. The farm is no longer the center of industry it used to be. Purchases at city stores supply much that formerly required hand labor. Both the farmer and his wife have been freed from much that used to constitute the drudgery of life, and have been given much new time to read and think and travel. In the villages the small artisans and their apprentices have almost completely disappeared. Wagons now come from South Bend, furniture is made largely in Grand Rapids, harness comes largely from New York State, and shoes from the cities of eastern Massachusetts, while flour is ground in large mills in a few industrial centers. Even bread and cakes, that used everywhere to be made in the homes, are now supplied, cheaper and better, by large baking companies which are city or national in scope. The telephone, the delivery wagon, the elevator, gas and electricity, running water, the bakery and delicatessen shop, the steam laundry, and the large department store have taken from children their "chores" and from their parents much hard labor (**R. 260**). As a result homes in our cities have come to be little more than places where families eat and sleep and children grow up. The old family home has disappeared in the tenement and the apartment house, with a resulting change of vast consequences to the children (**R. 256**) as well as the adults.

There are many compensating advantages, it must be remembered, for the losses the home has sustained. Children grow up under much more sanitary conditions than formerly, are better cared for, have far greater educational advantages provided for them, learn much more from their surroundings, are not so overworked, and have opportunities which children did not have in an earlier day. Still, a boy or girl under modern living conditions has so little of the old-fashioned home-life, so little useful manual activity, and acquires so much information through the eye and the ear and the senses and so little by actual doing, that the problem of providing a proper environment and education for town and city children, and of utilizing their excess leisure time in profitable activities, has become one of the most serious as well as one of the most difficult social and educational problems now before us. Under the new conditions of living, the older conventual type of training pupils in docility and obedience, too, has had to be superseded by a training to assume initiative and responsibility (**R. 257**).

The home, nevertheless, has gained. Despite the concentration of industry and business in the hands of a small percentage of our people, the virtual abolition of apprenticeship, the concentration of manufacturing in large establishments where specialized labor is the rule, and the prevalence of much poverty and wretchedness among certain classes of our people, society as a whole is by no means the worse for the change, and in particular the poor have not been growing poorer. The drudgery and wasteful toil of life have been greatly mitigated. People have leisure for personal enjoyment previously unknown. The radio, the automobile, and the "movies" have brought information, recreation, and enjoyment to millions of people who in previous times knew only work, and whose pleasures consisted chiefly of neighborhood gossip, church attendance, and drink. Wages have increased faster than the cost of living, the advantages of education have been multiplied and extended, health conditions in home and shop and town are better than ever known before, far more is done for people by the corporations and the State than formerly, and the standard of comfort for those even in the humblest circumstances has advanced beyond all previous conception. The poorest workman today can enjoy in his home lighting undreamed of in the days of tallow candles, warmth beyond the power of the old smoky soft-coal grate, kitchen conveniences and an ease in kitchen work that our New England forefathers probably would have thought sinful, and sanitary conditions and conveniences beyond the reach of the wealthiest even half a century ago. If the owner of the poorest tenement house in our cities today were to install the kind of plumbing which was good enough for George Washington, we would lock him up in jail. The family as a unit has gained tremendously by the changes of the past forty to fifty years; the losses have come to the children, and to society and government.

Weakening of the old educative influences. As an accompaniment of the far-reaching nature of these recent changes in the character of our living and of our population, there has followed a general weakening of the old social customs and traditions which once exercised so strong a restraining and educative influence on the young. Children formerly, much more than now, were taught reverence, courtesy, respect, proper demeanor, obedience, honesty, fidelity, and virtue, and both boys and girls were trained in useful employments. The Church, too, was a much more potent factor in the lives of both old and young than it is today. The young were trained to go to Sunday School and Church, and Sunday was observed as a day of rest and religious devotion. The minister was generally respected and looked up to by both parents and children. A religious sanction for conduct was often set forth. Communities were small and homogeneous in character, and everyone's actions were everyone's business. The community code of conduct and community sentiment exercised strong restraints. The positive convictions of the older members served to check the tendencies toward waywardness in both boys and girls, while the number of opportunities to go wrong were much fewer than they are today. Along certain lines these early restraining influences were highly educative, served to keep many a boy and girl in the path of rectitude, and helped to train them for an honest and a respectable life. As these old restraining influences have given way, new tasks have been thrown upon the school (**Rs. 258, 260**).

Changes that have taken place. In some of our smaller and older communities these conditions still in part persist, though much modified by the character of present-day life, but in the cities, towns, and the newer parts of the country these older educative influences and traditions have largely broken down, or have entirely ceased to exist. The little homogeneous communities, with their limited outlook and local spirit, have been changed in character by the coming of a much more cosmopolitan population, semi-urban conditions, and a much freer and easier life. The Church has lost much of its hold and influence over the young, and frequently the parents give it only nominal allegiance. Thousands of children are growing up today without any kind of religious training, and the former general knowledge of Biblical history and characters has largely passed away. New sects and religions, as well as new nationalities and races of people, have come among us, and within a generation the character of Sunday observance has greatly changed. The attitude of the people generally toward the old problems has been materially altered. Parents everywhere are less strict than they used to be. The discipline of the young in obedience and proper demeanor is no longer fashionable, and the attitude of thousands of communities today, as expressed in their life, their newspapers, their city government, and their general failure to enforce obedience to law, is really opposed to righteousness and good citizenship. The coming of the automobile, the radio, and the moving picture have tended to increase the burden of proper guidance of the young.[1]

[1] "We observe a disposition to leave to the schools increasing responsibility for education, both formal and informal. Careful inspection will reveal the fact that the school has lessened neither its interest nor its efficiency in administering the systematic program of instruction. As the nonschool interests have multiplied and intensified they have become powerful influences in youthful character development and they should therefore be fully conscious of the larger responsibility that has come with this larger influence. The Department of Superintendence appeals to these nonschool agencies such as the home, the industrial organization, the radio, and the movietone to recognize their opportunities and their obligations and to join hands co-operatively with the schools in developing the type of manhood and womanhood that may prove equal to the increasing moral, social, and industrial strain thrust upon the youth of today by a suddenly developed age of power, speed, wealth, and newborn liberties." (*Resolution*, Department of Superintendence, N.E.A., 1930.)

The home, altogether too often, is unintelligent and neglectful in the handling of children, and not infrequently it has abdicated entirely and turned the whole matter of the education and discipline of the young over to the public school [1] to handle (**R. 259**).

The effect of all these changes in our mode of living is written large on our national life. The social and industrial revolutions which we have experienced have been far-reaching in their consequences. The home and life conditions of an earlier period are gone, never to return (**R. 256**). This country has passed through that stage of its national development (**R. 260**). Instead, we now form a part of a new and vastly more complex world civilization, in competition with the best brains of all mankind, with a great and an ever-increasing specialization of human effort taking place on all sides, and with new and ever more difficult social, commercial, industrial, educational, and human-life problems awaiting solution. We have given up our earlier isolation and independence — social, political, and industrial — and have become dependent even for some of the necessities of life upon the commerce of remote regions and distant peoples. For us the world has become both larger and smaller than it used to be, and its parts are linked up with our future welfare to an extent never known before. The Spanish War did much to destroy our earlier isolation and independence; the great World War has cast us upon the middle of the world stage.

IV. EFFECT OF THESE CHANGES ON THE SCHOOL

New national needs make new demands. It is impossible to understand the present complexity of American public education, and the many new lines of educational effort being put into practice in our schools, except in the light of the great social and industrial

[1] "A second reason for what I regard as the unsatisfactory form and content of our present-day education is to be found in the excessive and impossible burden which is put upon the school by the collapse of the family and the church as co-operating educational agencies. Sound and complete education is a product of three factors — the home, the school and the church. No one of these can assume the task of either of the others, much less that of both of them, and succeed. Where instances of particularly well-trained young men and young women have come to my notice in recent years, I have taken pains to seek out an explanation. Invariably this explanation has been found in the fact that family influence and family discipline were playing their proper part, and that to the school was left only that which the well-organized and well-conducted school can reasonably and properly do. If parents are to turn over the entire training of their children to school teachers and to abdicate their own just authority and responsibility, we are faced by a situation, which to speak mildly, is alarming." (Nicholas Murray Butler, Convocation Address, University of the State of New York, 1929.)

and home-life changes of the past half-century which we have just traced.[1] It is these vast and far-reaching social and industrial and home-life changes which have been behind the changes in direction which our public schools have taken during the past quarter of a century, and which underlie the most pressing problems in educational readjustment of the present. It is as true today as when public schools began that the nature of the national need must determine the character of the education provided. As civilization increases in complexity, education must broaden its activities, often change in part its direction, and increase in efficiency.

Our schools are essentially time- and labor-saving devices, created by us to serve democracy's needs. To convey to the next generation the knowledge and accumulated experience of the past, important as this may be, we now see is neither the only nor the chief function of public education. Instead, our schools, within the past quarter-century, have been asked to prepare their children more definitely for personal usefulness in life, and the future citizen more directly for the tomorrow of our complex national and international existence. Instead of mere teaching institutions, engaged in imparting book-information and imposing discipline, our schools have been asked to grasp the significance of their social relationships, to transform themselves more fully into institutions for the improvement of democracy, and to prepare the young who attend them for greater social efficiency by teaching more that is directly useful and by training them better for citizenship in a democracy [2] such as ours (Rs. 259, 260).

A new lengthening of the period of dependence. As modern city-life conditions have come more and more to surround both boys and girls, depriving them of the training and education which earlier

[1] "The scope of American life is staggering. Its content is almost hopelessly complicated. The American scene is a welter of interrelated forces, institutions, ideals, cultures, prejudices, conventions, protests, and what not. The school curriculum is the only great organized agency which can muster sufficient potential to prepare the younger generation to understand it." (Harold Rugg, *Twenty-Sixth Yearbook, National Society for the Study of Education*, Part I, p. xi.)

[2] "We reaffirm our belief that the increased demands on the public schools for a more extensive and a more intensive educational program make the increased cost of public education inevitable; that through the vision, scientific knowledge, technical skill, and business ability produced by such an education the resources of the country are developed; that no people ever became poorer by thus preparing themselves for the effective use of their capital, time, energy, resources, and money; and that it is largely because of adequate expenditures for education that our unprecedented wealth-producing power has been gained." (Resolution, Department of Superintendence, N.E.A., 1930.)

farm and village life once gave, the school has been called to take upon itself the task of giving training in those industrial experiences and social activities which once formed so important a part of the education of American youths. With the breakdown of the old home and village industries,[1] the passing of the old "chores," and the coming of the factory system and city-life conditions, it has come to be desirable that children should not engage in productive labor. On the contrary, all recent thinking and legislation have been opposed to their doing so. Both the interests of organized labor and the interests of the Nation have set against child-labor. Even from an economic point of view, all studies which have been made as to the money-value of an education have shown the importance of children remaining in school as long as they are able to use with advantage the educational opportunities provided. It has at last come to be a generally accepted principle that it is better for children and for society that they should remain in school until they are at least sixteen years of age. As a result, child life everywhere has recently experienced a new lengthening of the period of dependence and training, and all national interests now indicate that the period devoted to preparing for life's work should, for most children, be further lengthened rather than shortened (**R. 260**).

Everywhere the right of the State to compel communities to maintain not only the old common school, but special types of schools and advanced training, has been asserted and sustained by the courts. Conversely, the corollary to this assertion of authority, the right of the State to compel children to partake of the educational advantages provided, has also been asserted and sustained by the courts.

New social and national problems. As our social life has become broader and more complex, a longer period of guidance has become necessary to prepare for proper participation in it. As our industrial life has become more diversified, its parts narrower, and its processes more concealed, new and more extended training has been

[1] "Large-scale production, extreme division of labor, and the all-conquering march of the machine, have practically driven out the apprenticeship system through which, in a simpler age, young helpers were taught, not simply the technique of some simple process, but the 'arts and mysteries of a craft' as well. The journeyman and the artisan have given way to an army of machine workers, performing over and over one small process at one machine, turning out one small part of the finished article, and knowing nothing about the business beyond their limited and narrow task." (*Report of the Commission on National Aid to Vocational Education*, vol. I, pp. 19-20.)

called for to prepare the worker for his task, to reveal to him something of the intricacy and interdependence of our modern social and industrial life, and to point out to him the necessity of each man's part in the social and industrial whole. With the ever-increasing subdivision and specialization of labor, the danger from class subdivision has been constantly increasing, and more and more has been thrown upon the school the task of instilling into all a social and political consciousness that will lead to unity amid our great

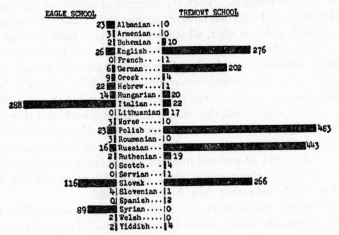

EAGLE SCHOOL		TREMONT SCHOOL
23	Albanian	0
3	Armenian	0
2	Bohemian	10
26	English	276
0	French	1
6	German	202
9	Greek	4
22	Hebrew	1
14	Hungarian	20
288	Italian	22
0	Lithuanian	17
3	Norse	0
23	Polish	483
3	Roumanian	0
16	Russian	443
2	Ruthenian	19
0	Scotch	4
0	Servian	1
116	Slovak	266
4	Slovenian	1
0	Spanish	2
89	Syrian	0
2	Welsh	0
2	Yiddish	4

FIG. 128. DISTRIBUTION BY NATIONALITIES OF PUPILS IN TWO ELEMENTARY SCHOOLS IN CLEVELAND

From Miller's *The School and the Immigrant Child*, p. 34. Reproduced by permission.

diversity, and to united action for the preservation and improvement of our democratic institutions. As large numbers of the foreign-born have come to our shores, and particularly from countries where general education is not common and where the Anglo-Saxon conception of law, order, government, and public and private decency does not prevail, a new and still greater burden has been placed on all the educative forces of society to try to impart to these new peoples, and their children, something of the method and the meaning of our democratic life. As the children of these new classes have crowded into our public schools, our school systems have been compelled to pay more attention to the needs of these new elements in our population, and to direct their attention less exclusively to satisfying the needs of the well-to-do classes of society. Education has in consequence recently turned away still more from its earlier aristocratic nature, and has become more and more democratic in character. It is only as schools serve as instruments for the perpetuation and improvement of our democratic life that the general education of all at public expense can be justified (**Rs. 259, 260**).

Beginnings of the change. The period following 1860, as was pointed out in Chapter XII, was a period of internal reorganization of our elementary education. As has been shown, the school then became more clearly conscious of itself, and reorganized its teaching work along lines dictated by the new psychology of instruction which had come to us from abroad. The thorough adoption of this new psychological point of view covered the period from 1860 up to about 1900. Beginning back about 1880 to 1885, however, our schools began to experience a new but steady change in purpose and direction along the lines of the new social and democratic forces, though it is only since about 1900 that any marked and rapid changes have set in.

The old limited book-subject curriculum, both elementary and secondary, could no longer meet the changing character of our national life, and new studies began to be introduced. Drawing, clay modeling, color work, nature-study, sewing, cooking, and manual training were introduced here and there into city elementary schools, and the sciences and the manual and home arts into the high schools. This was done despite the objections of many conservative teachers and citizens, and much ridicule from the public press. Many spoke sneeringly of the new subjects as representing the "fads and frills" of education, but they slowly made a place for themselves and have ever since remained. The cities, as in practically all other educational advances, were the leaders in introducing these new subjects and in attempting to transform their schools from mere disciplinary institutions, where drill was given in the mastery of the rudiments of knowledge, into institutions of democracy calculated to train for useful service in the office, the shop, and the home, and intended to prepare young people for intelligent participation in the increasingly complex social, political, and industrial life of our democratic society (**Rs. 259, 260**).

At first these new studies were introduced as experiments, and came in as new drill and disciplinary studies. Their introduction was generally defended on disciplinary grounds. An attempt also was made to organize a definite psychological procedure for instruction in each, as had recently been done for the older fundamental subjects. In consequence these new subjects for a time made but slow headway, and the results obtained were not always what had been expected. Only when they came to be organized as expression subjects did they become useful and effective teaching instruments.

The work of John Dewey. The foremost interpreter, in educational terms, of the great social and industrial changes through which we have passed, and the one who has done more since 1895 to think out and state for us an educational philosophy suited to the changed and changing conditions in our national life, is John Dewey (1859–——), for many years head of the School of Education at the University of Chicago, but more recently Professor of Philosophy at Columbia University.[1] His work, both experimental and theoretical, has tended both to psychologize and socialize American education; to give to it a practical content, along scientific and industrial lines; and to interpret to the child the new social conditions of modern society by connecting the activities of the school closely with those of real life (**R. 260**). Believing that the public school is the chief remedy for the ills of society, he has tried to change the work of the school so as to make it a miniature of society itself. Social efficiency, and not mere knowledge, he conceives to be the end, and this social efficiency is to be produced through participation in the activities of an institution of society, the school. The different parts of the school system thus become a unified institution, in which children are taught how to live amid the complexities of modern social life.

Education, therefore, in Dewey's conception, involves not merely learning, but play, construction, use of tools, contact with nature, expression, and activity, and the school should be a place where children are working rather than listening, learning life by living life, and becoming acquainted with social institutions and industrial processes by studying them. The work of the school is in large

[1] Born at Burlington, Vermont, in 1859: A.B., University of Vermont, 1879; Ph.D., Johns Hopkins, 1884, instructor and assistant professor of philosophy, University of Michigan, 1884–88; professor, University of Minnesota, 1888–89; same, Michigan, 1889–94; head of department of philosophy and education, University of Chicago, 1894–1904, and director of the School of Education, 1902–04; professor of philosophy, Columbia University, 1904–30, and professor emeritus in 1930.

JOHN DEWEY
(1859–   )
Professor of Philosophy and Education, University of Chicago
(1894–1904)
Professor of Philosophy, Columbia University
(1904–1930)

part to reduce the complexity of modern life to such terms as children can understand, and to introduce the child to modern life through simplified experiences. Its primary business may be said to be to train children in co-operative and mutually helpful living. The virtues of a school, as Dewey points out (**R. 260**), are learning by doing; the use of muscles, sight and feeling, as well as hearing; and the employment of energy, originality, and initiative. The virtues of the school in the past were the colorless, negative virtues of obedience, docility, and submission. Mere obedience and the careful performance of imposed tasks he holds to be not only a poor preparation for social and industrial efficiency, but a poor preparation for democratic society and government as well. Responsibility for good government, with us, rests with all, and the school should prepare for the political life of tomorrow by training its pupils to meet responsibilities, developing initiative, awakening social insight, and causing each to shoulder a fair share of the work of government in the school (**R. 258**). Russell has carried these conceptions further in his statement of the needs of education in an industrial age (**R. 275**).

Remarkable progress since 1898. The Spanish-American War of 1898 served to awaken us as a Nation and to shake us out of our earlier national isolation and contentment. Among other things it revealed to us something of the position we should probably be called upon to occupy in world affairs. Both it and the Russo-Japanese War which followed served particularly to concentrate attention on the advantages of general education, as it was "the man behind the gun" who won in each war. For the two decades following the Spanish-American War our country experienced an unprecedented period of industrial development and national prosperity, while the immigration of peoples further removed from our racial stock reached a maximum. The specialization of labor and the introduction of labor-saving machinery took place to an extent before unknown; city conditions became even more complex and potentially more dangerous; villages grew more urban, and a more cosmopolitan attitude began to pervade our whole life; the national feeling was intensified; and the national and state governments were called upon to do many things for the benefit of the people never attempted before (**R. 275**).

In consequence, since 1898, public education has awakened a

public interest before unknown. Since 1900 the Southern States have experienced the greatest educational awakening in their history — an awakening to be compared with that of Mann in Massachusetts and Barnard in Connecticut and Rhode Island. Everywhere state educational commissions and city school surveys have evidenced a new critical attitude on the part of the public. Much new educational legislation has been enacted; permission has been changed to obligation; minimum requirements have been laid down by the States in many new directions; and new subjects of instruction have been added by law. Courses of study have been entirely made over, and new types of textbooks have appeared. The democratic American high school has been transformed into a truly national institution. A complete new system of industrial education, national in scope, has been developed. New normal schools have been founded, and higher requirements have been ordered for those desiring to teach. College departments of education have increased from eleven in 1891 (first permanent chair in 1873) to something like five hundred today. Private gifts to colleges and universities have exceeded anything known before in any land. School taxes have been increased, old school funds have been more carefully guarded, and new constitutional provisions as to education have been added. Compulsory education has begun to be a reality, and child-labor laws to be enforced. A new interest in child-welfare and child-hygiene has arisen, evidencing a commendable desire to look after the bodies as well as the minds of our children. The education of the defective and the delinquent, and the education of the foreign-born everywhere, have received new attention. In recent years a new and an extensive national interest in agricultural, industrial, vocational, and household education has become clearly evident. However much we may have lost interest in the old problems of faith and religion, the American people has come to believe thoroughly in education as the best means for the preservation and advancement of the national welfare. In the chapters which follow the changes and additions and expansions which have accompanied the educational evolution of the past quarter-century will be set forth in some detail.

QUESTIONS FOR DISCUSSION

1. Show how the fact that all the earlier immigrants, except the Irish, came from lands which had accepted the Protestant Reformation ideas as to education made their assimilation easier.

2. Explain why the recent South and East of Europe immigration has served to dilute our national stock, and weaken and corrupt our political life.

3. Show how we have left the problem of adult assimilation largely to the labor unions and the political boss.

4. Canada allowed Quebec to retain its French language on entering the Union of Canada, with bad results. Show what might have been the result had we allowed Pennsylvania to remain a German-language State.

5. Why is it much more dangerous when any foreign element collects in colonies than if it scatters?

6. Show why the extensive changes in home life since 1860 have necessitated a different type of education, and changed the large family from an asset to a liability.

7. What are the effects of the foreign-born tenant farmer on rural social life and the rural school?

8. It is often stated that the coming of so many foreign-born to America has tended to decrease the size of native American families. Why should it?

9. Show how the vast industrial and commercial development has tended to limit individual opportunities, and made broader education for all necessary.

10. Show how the elimination of waste and drudgery and disease has also made larger educational opportunities desirable.

11. How do you account for the change in the character of home training and discipline?

12. Would schools have advanced in importance as they have done had the industrial revolution not taken place? Why?

13. Why is more extended education called for as "industrial life becomes more diversified, its parts narrower, and its processes more concealed"?

14. Point out the social significance of the educational work of John Dewey.

15. Explain why the social and national changes since the Spanish American War should have led especially to the expansion of the high school.

16. Point out the value, in the new order of society, of each group of school subjects listed on page 518.

SELECTED READINGS

In the accompanying volume of *Readings* the following selections, related to the subject matter of this chapter, are reproduced:

*254. Wagenen: Changes in Farm Life in Half a Century.

*255. Rugg: The Dynamic American Scene.

*256. Dewey: Life under the Old Home Conditions.
*257. Hoover: The New Strains of Modern Life.
*258. Dewey: New Conceptions in Pupil Training.
*259. Rugg: The Task of the School.
*260. Dewey: Resulting Modifications of the School.
*261. Rugg: The Work of Parker and Dewey Contrasted.

QUESTIONS ON THE READINGS

1. Compare the rapidity of the changes described (254) with changes two to three centuries ago.
2. Contrast farming as a mode of life (254), and as a business undertaking, and the resulting change in the nature of education the children receive.
3. Enumerate factors that have tended to make the American scene (255) so dynamic.
4. Show that Dewey reconstructs a good picture (256) of village and rural life of sixty or more years ago.
5. Show that health and physical training work in the schools are a direct resultant of the new strains (257) of modern life.
6. Show how Dewey's conception of pupil training (258) is today carried out in the schools.
7. Is there a danger today that the public has all too completely accepted Rugg's conception (259) of the task of the school?
8. Illustrate the modifications described by Dewey (260) from the curricula and scope of the modern high school.
9. Which type of person usually comes first, the worker or the organizing thinker (261)? Why?

TOPICS FOR INVESTIGATION AND REPORT

1. Effect of the Industrial Revolution on child life.
2. Discipline as affected by the changed conditions.
3. Curriculum revision to meet the new needs.

SELECTED REFERENCES

Betts, Geo. H. *Social Principles of Education.* 318 pp. New York, 1912.
    Chapter V, on institutional modes of experience, forms quite simple collateral reading for this chapter.

Bogart, E. L. *The Economic History of the United States.* 522 pp. New York, 1908.
    Part IV gives a very good sketch of agricultural and industrial development since 1860.

*Commons, John. *Races and Immigrants in America.* 242 pp. New York, 1907.
    A very readable volume. Chapters I to IV and IX are especially valuable as supplemental to this chapter.

*Dewey, John. *School and Society.* 130 pp. University of Chicago Press. 1899.

Lecture I, on the School and Social Progress, is an excellent statement of the problem.

Draper, A. S. "The Adaptation of Schools to Industry and Efficiency," in *Proceedings of the National Education Association*, 1908, pp. 65–78.

A good article on elementary-school waste, and the lack of balance and adaptation to national needs of elementary-school programs of study.

Ellis, A. C. *The Money Value of Education.* 52 pp. Illustrated by charts. United States Bureau of Education, Bulletin no. 22, Washington, 1917.

A document showing the relation of education to individual success.

Ellwood, C. A. *Sociology and Modern Social Problems.* 394 pp. 2d ed.; New York, 1913.

Chapter VIII, on the problem of the modern family; Chapter X, on the immigration problem; and Chapter XII, on the problem of the modern city, form good supplemental reading along the lines of part of this chapter.

*Fletcher, H. J. "Our Divided Country"; in *Atlantic Monthly*, vol. 117, pp. 223–33. (Feb. 1916.)

An excellent article on the problem of the assimilation of our foreign-born.

*Garis, R. L. *Immigration Restriction.* 376 pp. New York, 1927.

The need for and methods of restricting.

Gibbins, H. de B. *Economic and Industrial Progress of the Century.* 594 pp. London, 1901.

A well-written volume on the progress made by the world during the nineteenth century.

*Hyde, Wm. deW. "Social Mission of the Public School"; in *Educational Review*, vol. 12, pp. 221–35. (Oct. 1896.)

An old, but a very good article.

Jenks, J. W., and Lauck, W. J. *The Immigration Problem.* 655 pp. New York, 1922.

A good general treatise, with race descriptions and characterizations.

*Orth, S. P. *Our Foreigners.* 255 pp. Yale Press, 1920. Chronicles of America, vol. 35.

A very good statement of what we have received, and the influences that caused the different races to come to our shores.

Roberts, Peter. *Immigrant Races in North America.* 109 pp. New York, 1910.

A brief and important volume, classifying and describing our immigrant people.

Rosenstein, David. "Contributions of Education to Ethnic Fusion in the United States"; in *School and Society*, vol. 13, pp. 673–82 (June 18, 1921).

*Ross, E. A. *The Old World in the New.* 327 pp. New York, 1914.

An excellent work, classifying and describing the larger immigrant groups. Chapters 9–11, on the economic, social, and political effects of immigration, particularly good and useful.

*Ross, E. A. "The Value Rank of the American People"; in *Independent*, for Nov. 10, 1904. Also in his *Foundations of Sociology*, chap. XI.

   Characteristics; education; decimation; dilution.

*Rossiter, Wm. S. "Who are Americans?"; in *Atlantic Monthly*, vol. 126, pp. 270–80. (August, 1920).

   A good article. Says 65 per cent of English stock in 1910.

Smith, W. R. *Introduction to Educational Sociology*. 412 pp. Boston, 1917.

   Chapter IV, on the family, good on the losses and new demands.

*Suzzallo, Henry. "Education as a Social Study"; in *School Review*, vol. 16, pp. 330–40. (May, 1908.)

   An excellent article on education and democracy.

Stephenson, G. M. *A History of American Immigration, 1820–1924*. 316 pp. New York, 1926.

*Thompson, H. *The Age of Invention*. 265 pp. Yale Press, 1921. Chronicles of America Series, vol. 37.

   The great inventions that have caused the industrial revolution.

Warne, F. J. *The Immigrant Invasion*. 335 pp. New York, 1913.

   An illustrated and very interesting description of the older and newer immigrants.

CHAPTER XV
NEW EDUCATIONAL CONCEPTIONS AND ADJUSTMENTS

I. NEW CONCEPTIONS OF THE EDUCATIONAL PROCESS

The old knowledge conception. Our earlier school work was carried on on the unexpressed assumption that children were alike in needs and capacities, and that the training necessary for citizenship and life consisted in their acquiring certain book-knowledge which the school sought to impart. While some children were able to remain longer in school than were others, and consequently could climb higher on the educational ladder, the type of training while ascending the ladder was practically the same for all. Only in the high school were some options allowed. The knowledge aim, as we have seen, everywhere dominated instruction. Knowledge and civic virtue came to be regarded as somewhat synonymous, and disciplinary drill was the main purpose of the teaching process.

It was but natural, with the rise of democratic government and state-supported school systems, that we at first should have conceived of knowledge as power, and as almost certain to lead to virtue. The new state school was erected primarily to promote literacy and citizenship, and this was to be done by insuring to the people the elements of learning, thus preparing them for participation in the functions of government. There was, too, an early assumption that the training needed for citizenship and life consisted in the pupils acquiring certain book-knowledge which it was the business of the school to impart. Early taking deep root with our people, the knowledge conception for a long time everywhere dominated our school instruction, and its end is not yet.

The disciplinary conception. Closely allied with the knowledge conception of education was the psychological conception, evolved between 1860 and 1890, which was based on the assumption that the mind could be trained by a uniform procedure of mental discipline and drill. By means of selected subject-matter, now to be psychologically organized and presented, teachers would be able to drill the attention, will, memory, imagination, feelings, judgment, reasoning, ability in observation and sense discrimination, and other "powers of the mind," and thus awaken the egoistic and social feelings, stimulate the higher sentiments, and develop the moral character of the children so taught. By such means the citizenship-aim of education would be realized. The mind of the child was conceived of as consisting of a number of more or less water-tight compartments, or "faculties," the drilling of which was the business of the school. Imparting information, drilling for mastery, and controlling the school were the work of the teacher; the work of the supervisor consisted largely in testing the pupils to see that the teaching had been well done.[1]

Courses of instruction were now much more minutely outlined than before; the work for each grade was quite definitely laid down; the kind, amount, and order of subject-matter to be learned, by all pupils in all parts of the city, and regardless of age, past experience, future prospects, or physical or mental condition, was uniformly prescribed for all; and the examination test at the end of the term became the almost uniform proof that what had been outlined had or had not been mastered. Such courses of study and such conceptions of the educational process came to be the prevailing type between about 1870 and 1890, and are still found here and there in cities and villages which have not been touched by the newer conceptions of education (R. 262).

Education as development. Quite a different conception as to the nature of child development and the purpose of education appeared when we began to turn from these older theories to the theory that the function of the school was primarily to assist in the process of developing the inborn capacities of children. Under this conception each child in the school came to be regarded as a bundle of possibilities to be developed, or repressed, and not as a reservoir to be filled. In part this was a Pestalozzian conception, emphasized for us by Sheldon and his followers, but in large part it was an outcome of the child study movement of the eighties (page 402) which had called new attention to the child as an individual. Knowledge

---

[1] This conception of the educative process was based on a now-abandoned psychology that conceived of the mind as a group of separate faculties — as memory, judgment, will, etc., each of which could be trained through exercise. Studies were taken up and mastered that the mind of the pupil might be "disciplined" to do other pieces of work later on. It was assumed that training in one kind of work would "carry-over" to another.

now came to be conceived of as life experience and inner conviction, and not as the memorization of the accumulated knowledge of the past — as a tool to do something with, and not as a finished product in itself. The whole conception of the school then changed from a place where children prepare for life by learning certain traditional things, to a place where children are daily brought into contact with such real life experiences as will best prepare them for the larger problems of life that lie just ahead.

Principals and teachers in a school system working according to such a philosophy of the educative process naturally came to occupy quite different positions from those of principals and teachers in school systems working according to the older educational conceptions. Instead of recitation hearers and drill masters, they came to stand as stimuli to pupil activities. It became their work to propose problems, and then to guide the pupils in thinking and studying them through. They became friendly critics by whose help young people learned to think clearly and to reason more accurately.

Newer conceptions of educational work. From the discussion in the preceding chapter, regarding changed social, industrial, and national conditions, the reader will have seen why the older knowledge conception of education ultimately must give way to newer and sounder ideas as to the nature and purpose of public education. To meet the newer conditions of our national life not only must the direction of educational effort be changed, but also the education of different classes of children must take somewhat different directions. Still more, new classes of children, hitherto largely neglected, must now be provided for (**R. 263**).

Beginning here and there, back in the decade of the eighties, and becoming a clearly defined movement after about 1900, new courses of study and new teaching directions appeared which indicated that those responsible for the conduct of the school systems were actuated by new conceptions as to the nature and purpose of the educational process. Recognizing that the needs of society and the community were ever changing and growing, and that the needs of pupils, both by classes and individually varied much, the courses which were then outlined came to include alternatives and options, and to permit variations in the work done in different rooms and schools. The excess of drill which had characterized earlier school work came to be replaced by lessons in subjects involving expression and appreciation, such as art, music, manual work, domestic training, play, and humane education; the kindergarten and the kindergarten spirit began to effect changes in the character of the work of the receiving class and of the first grade or two of the elementary school; the discipline of the school everywhere became milder, and pupil-co-operation schemes for training in self-control arose; science as an important element in modern living began to receive emphasis; subjects which prepared better for efficient participation in the work of democratic society, such as hygiene, community civics, industrial studies, and thrift, were added; the social relationships of the class-room and school were directed, through studies in conduct and manners, toward the preparation of more socially efficient men and women; and the commercial and industrial life of the community began to be utilized to give point to the instruction in manual training, local history, civics, geography, and other related studies.

The main duty of the teacher, under these newer courses, came to be that of guiding and directing the normal processes of thought and action on the part of the pupils, of extending their appreciation in new directions, of connecting the work of the school with life in a better way, of widening the horizons of the thinking and the ambitious among the children, and of stimulating them to develop for themselves larger and better ideals for life and service. Instead of being fixed and largely finished products, this new type of courses of study remained plastic, to be changed in any direction and at any time that the best interests of the children might seem to require.

The new center of gravity. The most marked change between this newer type of course of study and the older type was the shifting of the center of gravity from that of the subject-matter of instruction to that of the child to be taught (**R. 263**). The children of a particular community who presented themselves for education, and not the more or less traditional subject-matter of instruction, now came to be the real educational problem. Viewed from the angle of child needs and child welfare the school became a new institution. It came to be seen that facts possess but little real importance until they have been put to use.[1] Child welfare and social

---

[1] "Knowledge that is worthy of being called knowledge, training of the intellect that is sure to amount to anything, is obtained only by participating intimately and actively in activities of social life.

"This is Pestalozzi's great positive contribution. It represents an insight gained in his own personal experience; for as an abstract thinker he was weak. It not only goes beyond Rousseau, but it puts what is true in Rousseau upon a sound basis." (John Dewey. *Schools of Tomorrow*, p. 63.)

welfare were perceived to be closely intertwined. To train children for and to introduce them into membership in the little community of which they form a part, and from this to extend their sense of membership outward to the life of the State, the Nation, and to world civilization; to awaken guiding moral impulses; to fill them with the spirit of service; and to train them for effective self-direction — these became the great tasks of the modern school.

The teacher in the new type of school. The teacher under the earlier type of school was essentially a drill master and a disciplinarian. It was his business to see that his pupils learned what was set before them, and to keep order. In the period between 1860 and 1900 it came to be conceived of as the teacher's chief function so to impart the selected subject-matter of instruction as to introduce it to the mind of the child by the most approved psychological procedure. The function of the teacher, though rendered much more important, still remained that of an instructor rather than that of a guide to instruction.

While retaining both of these earlier aims as important — drill where drill is needed, and proper psychological procedure in the teaching process — the newer conceptions as to school work went beyond either of these earlier aims. Both principals and teachers came to be expected to think over their work of instruction in the light of their local problems, with a view to adapting and adjusting the school work to the particular needs and capacities of the pupils to be instructed. Both a science and an art of education were now called for, and teaching now became a finer art and a still more difficult psychological process than before (**R. 264**). Individual results, as well as group results, now were aimed at. The teacher proposed problems to the pupils, and then guided them in examining and studying them. Problems involving life-situations became of greatest value. In each case the solving became the main thing; not the memorizing of some one else's solution.

Both principals and teachers now came to stand as stimuli to individual activity, as whetstones upon which those stimulated could bring their thinking to a keener edge, and as critics by whose help young people might develop their ability to reason accurately and well. The aim of instruction became that of fitting young people, by any means suited to their needs and capacities, to meet the responsibilities of life; to train them to stand on their own feet; to develop in them the ability to do their own thinking; and to prepare them for civic and social efficiency in the national life of tomorrow.

The spirit of the modern school.   Such, in brief, are the actuating motives which have come to underlie the work of the efficiently directed modern school.   The school often falls far short of such ideals in the results it is able to achieve, but such at least, consciously or unconsciously, are the actuating motives of its work.   Its aim is not mere knowledge, except as knowledge will be useful; not mental discipline, of the drill sort, but a discipline of the whole life; not a head full of facts, but a head full of ideas; not rules of conduct learned, but the ability to conduct one's self properly; not a pupil knowing civics, but one who can think over civic questions; and not so much a learned as a well-trained output.

Through community civics, studies in science and industry, studies of community life, the study of community health problems, studies of home needs, domestic science, manual training, drawing, music, thrift training, manners and conduct, play and games, as well as through a reorganization and redirection of the work in the older subjects — arithmetic, geography, language study, literature, history — the modern school aims to train pupils for greater social usefulness and to give them a more intelligent grasp of the social and industrial, as well as the moral and civic, structure of our modern democratic life.[1]

The studies which have come to characterize the modern elementary school may now be classified under the following headings:

DRILL SUBJECTS	CONTENT SUBJECTS	EXPRESSION SUBJECTS
Reading	Literature	Kindergarten Work
Writing	Geography	Music
Spelling	History	Drawing
Language	Social Studies	Manual Arts
Arithmetic	Manners and Conduct	Domestic Arts
	Science	Plays and Games
	Agriculture	School Gardening
		Vocational Subjects

[1] In the century since about 1825 or 1830, as America developed its institutions, her people have been constantly confronted by new issues and problems that have called for intelligent consideration.   Problems of immigration and assimilation, problems of city living, problems of industry and trade, problems of transportation, problems of the conservation of human and natural resources, problems of the distribution of taxation and wealth, problems of hygiene and living, problems of the intelligent use of leisure time, problems of peace and world affairs — these are types that call for training for social and civic usefulness.

The order of arrangement is not only almost the order of the historical introduction of the different subjects into the elementary school,
but the three groups also represent the three great periods of our
elementary school development (**R. 265**). The drill subjects characterized the earlier school; the content subjects, excepting the last,
the period of development between 1860 and 1890; and the expression subjects the modern elementary school development.

One main purpose in the introduction of the newer studies has
been the attempt to interpret to the young people of today the vast
changes in living which the industrial and social revolutions of the
nineteenth and early twentieth century have produced (**Rs. 255,
256**). During the past half-century the school has been transformed from a disciplinary institution into an instrument of democracy calculated to train young people for intelligent living in the
complex and difficult world in which they now find themselves (**Rs.
259, 260**). Its efficiency as an instrument of democracy is determined by how well it fulfills this function.

II. NECESSARY ADJUSTMENTS AND DIFFERENTIATIONS

The average or uniform course of study. The earlier school, as
has been stated, dealt with children as though they were approximately alike in ability to partake of what the school had to give. In
time, as differences between groups of children as to mental capacity
began to be evident to schoolmasters, an attempt to meet these
group differences was made through adjustments in the operation
of the school course of study so as to adapt it better to the needs of
different groups. Intelligence measurements had not yet been
developed, and the large individual-trait differences that we now
know to exist had not been revealed.

Up to relatively recently, one may say, all our school work has
been adjusted to meet the needs of the so-called "average child."
As children of average capacity usually do reasonably well under
uniform courses of study constructed with average needs in view,
the results for a long time were not noticeably bad. Teachers tried
hard to bring all their pupils "up to grade." Those who could not
master the subject-matter were in time promoted anyway, while
the bright pupils marked time. The teacher naturally labored most
with those who had the most difficulty with their studies. The
next figure shows the results of such instruction in a city where

the courses of study and the promotional plans were arranged and carried out to meet the average needs of the great mass of the city's children. The great bulk of the pupils, it will be seen, made normal progress, while approximately equal percentages were ahead and behind their grade. In an average school of 42 pupils in that city, 6 would be ahead of grade, 29 on grade, and 7 below grade. This represents what may still be said to be an average and a tolerably satisfactory condition. In many school systems the percentage of retarded pupils is much higher, and the number who are ahead is much lower than in the school system here shown.

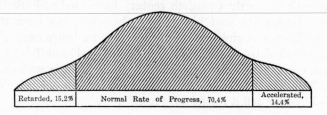

Retarded, 15.2%   Normal Rate of Progress, 70.4%   Accelerated, 14.4%

FIG. 129. PROMOTIONAL RESULTS IN A CITY FOLLOWING
A COURSE OF STUDY ADJUSTED TO THE AVERAGE
CAPACITY OF THE PUPILS

From Cubberley's *Public School Administration,* p. 435

Children whom average courses do not fit. For some of the children, though, it was found that some or all of the school work either was too difficult, or was entirely unsuited to their needs. As a result they failed to make proper progress, and gradually dropped farther and farther behind. In the city shown in the diagram, 15.2 per cent of the children were in this class. One often finds such children two, three, or four years over-age for their grades, and accomplishing little in school that is of value to them (**R. 262**). On the other hand, for some children the work was entirely too easy. Such children could do their school work in short time and without half trying, and in consequence fell into habits of idleness by not being worked to capacity. Often, too, these more capable children were held back by teachers, in part because their capacity was not recognized, and in part to keep their grade progress nearer to their age progress. The result was that they were actually retarded, even though they were "up to grade."

The effect of uniform and average courses of study on both classes of children was found to be distinctly bad. On the one hand, the pupils who were held for years in the lower grades instead of advancing, too large for their seats, often unfit associates for the smaller children, and usually accomplishing little because the school work was too difficult for them or was not suited to their needs, and they were being prepared by the school to join the ranks of the inefficient and unsuccessful and dissatisfied in our working world. When one considers with what a meager life-equipment these young people eventually leave school, and what a poor preparation they have for social efficiency or intelligent citizenship, the bad results of unsuitable school work becomes evident. If the school could do better by these children it was its duty as a social institution, it was in time seen, to do so. To learn to succeed is one of the purposes of going to school. On the other hand, bright children should not be held back when they ought to be put into more advanced work, better suited to their needs and more likely to awaken their interest and enthusiasm. To learn to dawdle and loaf is not the purpose of education.

We thus came to see that we really had at least three well-recognized groups or types of children in our schools with which to deal — the below-average, the average, and the above-average. While these three classes had in a way for a long time been recognized, it is only relatively recently that we have begun to pay any particular attention to the needs of the two non-average groups. For a long time we continued to educate the average child, hoping to bring the slower pupil up by a little extra attention, and letting the bright child rather shift for himself.

Flexible grading and promotion plans. The earliest and most common attempt to remedy conditions arising from the discovery that uniform courses of study were not fully adjusted to the needs of all was along the lines of coaching the backward children by an assistant teacher. This plan goes back to the days of the usher, or assistant teacher (p. 318), and in its modern form was employed by Colonel Parker at Quincy, Massachusetts, in the late seventies, and still later was more fully applied at Batavia, New York.[1] The Ba-

[1] The plan was inaugurated by Superintendent John Kennedy, at Batavia, New York, some three decades ago and is described in some detail in his *The Batavia System of Individual Instruction*, 299 pp., Syracuse, 1914. The Batavia plan is one of our oldest attempts to overcome promotional difficulties, while retaining the semi-annual promotional plan for all.

tavia form became known, and about twenty-five years ago was tried in many parts of the United States, but it met with only limited favor. The plan is well shown in the drawing below. The idea was to use the assistant teacher to coach the laggards and bring them up to grade, so that all might be promoted together.

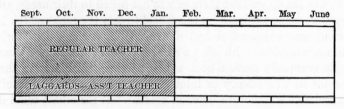

FIG. 130. THE BATAVIA PLAN

Showing a half-year's progress for all pupils under this plan. The coaching of the slow pupils by the assistant teacher makes this equality of progress possible. In North Denver this plan was reversed, the assistant teacher working with the brighter pupils. From Cubberley's *Public School Administration*, p. 448.

The next plan tried was that of breaking up the yearly grade system, which we had evolved, so as to make promotion easier and more frequent. The essential feature of this plan consisted in providing semi-annual, or even quarterly [1] promotions, so that children might be advanced one half or one quarter of a year's work, or be set back that amount as conditions might seem to indicate as desirable. This provided two grades, an A and B, for each school year, and pupils failing of promotion need repeat only a half-year instead of a whole year of school work. Both of these ideas were put into use after about 1875 to 1880, and the semi-annual promotion has since become an established institution in our American schools.

Since about 1900 the problem has been approached from a different angle, by the organization of what are variously known as *supplementary classes, over-age classes, or ungraded classes*, one or more such classes being provided for in each large city school building.

[1] William T. Harris was a pioneer here. In a "Bird's Eye View of the St. Louis Public School System in 1880," we read, under Classification:

"An important innovation in the stereotyped organization, as found in many school systems, has been made in St. Louis, with a view to facilitate grading and classification. In order to meet the wants of the pupils frequent reclassification is made, in such a manner as to allow the bright and rapid pupils to advance into the classes above. This promotion and reclassification occurs as often as once in ten weeks, whereas, according to the old plan, such classification takes place only at the end of the school year."

To such classes are sent the over-aged, the "left-overs," those behind due to illness or absence, those who need special coaching to enable them to understand some school subject or to make up some deficiency, or those ahead and about ready to jump a grade. Such pupils may remain in these classes all day, or only during the time they are receiving extra teaching, and for only a few weeks or for quite a long time. For pupils for whom such classes are adapted they render the double service of instructing them better and of relieving the regular class teacher of their care. Their purpose is not only to make the graded system more flexible, and thus break up somewhat the so-called "lock-step" of the public school, but also to meet the needs of both the dull and the bright children, by providing special instruction better adapted to their stage of progress than is the regular instruction of the average school grade. As a matter of experience the brighter children usually receive but little direct help from such classes, as they are used almost entirely for the dull or retarded pupils. The average pupils who remain with the grade teacher receive better instruction because the more time-consuming cases have been removed from the room.

Parallel courses of study. None of these plans, however, make any specific provision for the advancement of the pupils capable of going ahead much faster then the average. Since about 1895 the wants of this class have been somewhat recognized, here and there, and a number of different plans have been evolved and put into operation, in different parts of the United States, the purpose of which has been to provide better for the needs of the brighter pupils in the school. Two addresses [1] by President Eliot, of Harvard, in 1892, one before the Department of Superintendence of the National Educational Association in February, on "Shortening and Enriching the Grammar School Course," and the other before the National Educational Association, in July, on "Undesirable and Desirable Uniformity in Schools" (**R. 266**), were influential. While the contents of these two addresses would not be considered particularly illuminating today, they nevertheless did much to stimu-

---

[1] In the first address President Eliot listed five needs for a better teaching program: (1) better teachers, (2) better school curricula, (3) elimination of waste in both elementary and secondary schools, (4) cutting down retardation, and (5) a lengthened school day. "The chief objects of this address are," he concluded, "first, to point out a serious difficulty which is embarrassing the whole course of American education; and, secondly, to indicate briefly a few of the directions in which labor may be wisely spent in improving our school system, to the general end that the pupils may receive a better training in a shorter time."

late thinking as to the desirability of providing better for the needs of the more capable children. The uniformity in grading and promotion he condemned as "suppressing individual differences instead of developing them and leaving individual capacities undiscovered and untrained, thus robbing the individual of happiness and serviceableness, and society of the fruits it might have enjoyed from the special endowments of thousands of its members."

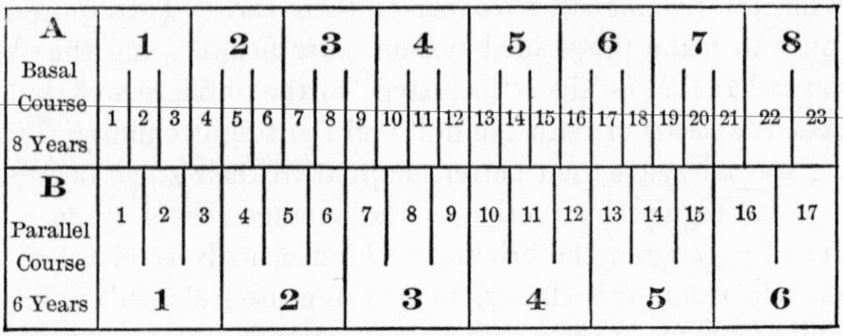

A Basal Course 8 Years	1			2			3			4			5			6			7			8	
	1	2	3	4	5	6	7	8	9	10	11	12	13	14	15	16	17	18	19	20	21	22	23
B Parallel Course 6 Years	1	2	3	4	5	6	7	8	9	10	11	12	13	14	15	16	17
	1		2		3		4		5		6

FIG. 131. THE NEW CAMBRIDGE PLAN

Two parallel elementary-school courses, with one third more work assigned for each year in Course B than in Course A. From Cubberley's *Public School Administration*, p. 452.

The Cambridge, Massachusetts, plan, shown in the above drawing, is a 1910 revision of a still earlier plan inaugurated there to meet such needs as President Eliot had described.[1] The essential features of it are two parallel courses of study, one of eight years for the average pupil, and a parallel course of six years in length for the gifted pupil, with natural transfer points which make it possible for a pupil to take any amount of time from six to eight, or even more, years to complete the course. The Cambridge plan is typical of a number of somewhat similar parallel-course plans which have been evolved, the purpose of all of which has been to enable the more capable pupils to advance more rapidly. They make, however, no provision for the slow pupil, aside from repetition of the work of the grade.

Differentiated courses of study. About 1898 an experiment was

[1] Previous to 1910 the work of the first three grades had been the same for all pupils, with a chance to do the remaining six years in anywhere from four to six. In 1910 the nine-year elementary course was reduced to eight years and the new plan substituted. Statistics kept at the three high schools showed that, under the old plan, those who completed the elementary course in the shortest time did the best work in the high school.

begun at Baltimore, by Superintendent James H. Van Sickle (1852–1926), and about the same time a somewhat similar one was tried for a short time at Santa Barbara, California, both of which were very important viewed from the standpoint of the best interests of our democratic life. Each was an attempt to provide, through a one-class school system, something of that effectiveness in the training of leaders for which the European two-class school systems have for long been noted.[1] Similar experiments have since been tried and are still in use in a number of places.

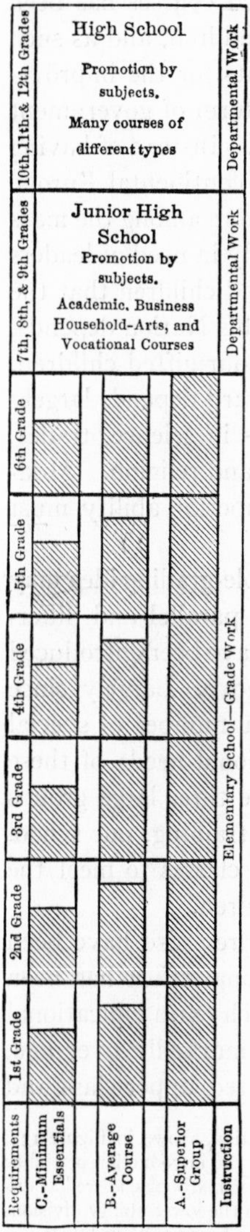

The essential idea underlying each was that children are different not only in mental capacity but in future possibilities as well; that they fall roughly into three groups — the slow, the average, and the gifted; that a course of study for each group should be worked out which is up to but not beyond the capacities of the pupils of each group to accomplish; that transfer from one group to the other, in either direction, should be easy; that during the first six years of school life the courses should vary in the amount of work done, but not in the time consumed; and that, after this preliminary sorting period, the largest possible opportunities should be given to the gifted group to move rapidly, take extra studies, and enjoy extra educational advantages, the other groups at the same

FIG. 132. THE DIFFERENTIATED-COURSE PLAN

The accompanying figure shows the plan as followed in Santa Barbara, California. From Cubberley's *Public School Administration*, p. 454. The Baltimore plan was essentially the same.

[Figure content:]

	1st Grade	2nd Grade	3rd Grade	4th Grade	5th Grade	6th Grade	7th, 8th, & 9th Grades	10th, 11th, & 12th Grades
Requirements							**Junior High School** Promotion by subjects. Academic, Business, Household-Arts, and Vocational Courses	**High School** Promotion by subjects. Many courses of different types
C.–Minimum Essentials								
B.–Average Course								
A.–Superior Group								
Instruction	Elementary School—Grade Work						Departmental Work	Departmental Work

---

[1] In the Baltimore plan, so-called central schools, taught by a departmental plan of instruction and with an enriched curriculum, were provided for the more gifted children, while the average or slow children continued through seventh and eighth grades in the grade schools.

time not being neglected. The adjoining diagram shows the nature of these plans.[1]

The prime idea underlying these differentiated courses has been that of providing better advantages for gifted children, and as such they are among the most interesting experiments for the improvement of democracy that have been made. No form of government is so dependent on intelligence as is a democracy. Instead of having leaders trained for us in separate schools, as in continental Europe (see Fig. 99, page 352), they must with us come from among the mass of our citizenship. A democracy, too, is especially in need of leaders to guide the mass, and it is from among its gifted children that the leaders must be drawn. The future welfare of this Nation depends, in no small degree, upon the right education of our gifted children. The degree to which our civilization moves forward depends largely upon the work of creative thinkers and leaders in science, trades, industry, government, education, art, morality, and religion. Moderate ability can follow, or can imitate, but superior ability must point the way.

Differentiated classes and schools. The flexible-grading idea may be said to have become common by 1890, and parallel and differentiated courses of study for elementary pupils have been introduced almost entirely since 1900, and largely since 1910. Largely since 1910, too, we have seen the establishment of a number of special types of classes or schools to meet the educational needs of these different classes of children. Realizing that the three large groups could not include all classes in need of special training, our school systems have begun the organization of special classes to meet the peculiar needs of small percentages of their children.

In a few places special classes for gifted children also have been organized, though most of the special educational effort has been placed at the other end of the scale.[2] Among such extra educational efforts may be mentioned classes for children markedly over age, these children often being advanced into selected upper-class and

[1] A further improvement of the differentiated plan of instruction, shown in Figure 132, has been made in Detroit and Los Angeles, since 1920, through the introduction of ability grouping within the different groups. This has called for different textbooks, as well as different courses of study and methods of teaching, as the pupils in the lower-ability divisions could not read and understand books that upper-ability divisions found to their liking.

[2] As yet, but little has been done for the gifted children — the most seriously retarded of all children in our schools. Yet one gifted child may be worth more to society than two thousand of the sub-normals upon whom we spend so much money and effort.

high-school work because of their age, and regardless of their failure to be promoted; classes for stutterers and stammerers,[1] to correct speech defects as early as possible; open-air classes, for tubercular and anæmic children; special classes for non-English-speaking children, to teach them the use of the language; ship schools, in the ports, to train boys for the sea, and at the same time impart to them a general elementary school training; industrial classes, where certain types of industrial work are substituted for academic branches less useful and particularly difficult for such types of children; special art and music schools, where pupils showing special aptitude for drawing or music may receive special attention; and home schools, where girls of upper grammar-school age may receive special preparation for home-keeping.

A better manufacturing establishment. The effect of the introduction of these specialized classes has been to reduce waste, speed up the rate of production, and increase the value of the output of our schools. The condition of our schools before about 1900, and to a certain degree this condition still persists, was that of a manufacturing establishment running at a low grade of efficiency. The waste of material was great and the output small and costly — in part because the workmen in the establishment were not supplied with enough of the right kind of tools; in part because the supervision emphasized wrong points in manufacture; but largely because the establishment was not equipped with enough pieces of special-type machinery, located in special shops or units of the manufacturing plant, to enable it to work up the waste material and meet modern manufacturing conditions. Since about 1900, through the introduction of flexible promotions, parallel courses of study, differentiated courses, and special-type classes and schools, we have been engaged in improving the business by speeding it up, supplying it with new and specialized machinery, saving wastes, and increasing the rate and the value to society of the output. The public schools of the United States are, in a sense, a manufactory, doing a two-billion dollar business each year in trying to prepare future citizens for use-

---

[1] *Classes for stutterers and stammerers.* Pupils suffering from speech defects are sent to small special classes, under teachers specially trained for such service, and by slow and careful speech-training are educated to speak properly. From one to two per cent of all school-children would be helped by such special-class speech training. Such classes are common in European cities, and have been established in a number of American cities, since the first one was founded in New York, in 1909.

fulness and efficiency in life. As such we have recently been engaged in revising our manufacturing specifications and in applying to the conduct of the business some of the same principles of specialized production and manufacturing efficiency which control in other parts of the manufacturing world.

III. MORE FUNDAMENTAL REORGANIZATIONS

In addition to the differentiated courses of study and classes just described, the past two decades have witnessed a number of still more fundamental reorganizations of the school which are of far-reaching importance, and which in themselves reveal the progressive character of recent American educational thinking.

The Dalton Laboratory Plan. All of the plans for adjusting school instruction to the needs of different groups of pupils, so far described, have involved the retention of the class organization. Within the past two decades two other plans, which more or less sacrifice the class organization, have been evolved which call for brief comment. These are the so-called Dalton plan, and the Winnetka plan.

The Dalton plan was first introduced into a public school system in the high school at Dalton, Massachusetts,[1] in 1919. In its essentials the plan uses the regular curriculum, but frees the pupil to work in his own way while doing the regular work of the school. It is primarily a plan for individual instruction, and permits the pupil to determine for himself how and when he will do the work in the allotted time. The course of study for the year is divided into as many "jobs" as there are months in the school year, and each "job" is further subdivided into twenty "units." For each unit, work sheets are made out to show the pupil what is to be done, and how to attack each "unit" of the job. Each pupil has a "job card" on which to record and measure his progress, and from which he can see at a glance where he stands on each "job." At the end of each month all the "jobs" for that month must be completed. In essence, it is an administrative device under which the pupils manage their time and plan their work, on an individual basis, so as to master fixed quotas of subject matter within definite periods of time. Its essential defect, according to its opponents, is that it

[1] In the thinking of the originator of the plan, Miss Helen Parkhurst, its inception goes back to 1911. The plan has made an especially strong appeal to the English, a people that have always emphasized individual initiative and effort, and it has found a place for itself there in over 2000 schools. Some 200 schools in the United States have used the plan.

follows a fixed curriculum too closely and conceives of school work as primarily the mastery of knowledge for use in adult life. While applicable to any part of school work above the third grade, its largest usefulness has been found to be with pupils of secondary school age.[1]

The Winnetka plan. The so-called Winnetka individual system was begun by Superintendent Carleton Washburne at Winnetka, Illinois, in 1919. The curriculum at Winnetka is divided into two main parts. One part deals with those older common knowledges or skills — reading, spelling, writing, counting, language usage — that it is assumed everyone needs, and the other part provides for the newer group activities and self-expression subjects (R. 267). Assuming that all children need the common essentials, and knowing that children vary much in learning ability, it is the time required for mastery, rather than the course of study material (as in Figure 132), that varies. Pupils here move at their own gait, but the common essentials must be mastered. Time thus varies, rather than quality of work. For the second part of the curriculum, on the other hand, there are no fixed standards; here all differences in pupil ability are allowed for (R. 267).

To administer such a curriculum, the day is divided into four parts and the school into two schools, as in the Gary plan, described further on (see Figure 133). Pupils do part one of the curriculum (the common essentials) under individual instruction, and in this work grade lines are all broken down. The work in the essentials is laid off into "units," much as in the Dalton plan. Each pupil checks his progress on a work sheet as he goes along, and when he is 100 per cent perfect he passes to other work. No child ever "fails" and no child ever "skips a grade" here; for the group-activity part of the program, on the other hand, there are no definite goals, nor are the children tested on what they do. The absence of definite standards for the group activities is as important a feature of the plan as is the presence of definite standards for the common essentials, while the absence of a definite fixed time for mastery of

[1] "The Dalton plan is a philosophy of learning and teaching rather than a detailed method to be adopted *in toto* by any single school. Each school seeking to break the lock-step of the class by individualizing instruction must expect to solve its problems in terms of its local situation. As a result, it is inevitable that so-called Dalton schools should present notable differences in the application of the general principles of individual instruction." (Ralph I. Underhill, in *School and Society*, vol. 22, p. 337)

the latter enables the authorities to adjust the instruction better to pupil needs.[1]

As expressed by Superintendent Washburne:

The underlying philosophy of the Winnetka curriculum demands that every normal child master the knowledges and skills he is going to need in life; that every child be given a chance to live happily and richly as a child; that every child be given an opportunity to develop fully his own individuality; and that all children be brought to the fullest possible realization that in the world's good is one's own, and in one's own good is the world's.

The Gary idea. Another educational reorganization, or rather the construction of a school system from the foundations along new lines, is represented by the school system built up at Gary, Indiana, by Superintendent Will Wirt, between about 1908 and 1915. This represents one of the most original pieces of constructive thinking ever attempted in American education,[2] and one that, in its various adaptations, has profoundly modified school organization in this country (R. 268).

At Gary the schools run on a four-quarter plan, each quarter of twelve weeks' duration; the school plant is a play-ground, garden, workshop, social center, library, and a traditional-type school all combined in one; the elementary-school and the high-school work are both given under the same roof; some of the high-school subjects begin as early as the fifth grade; specialization in the instruction and, in consequence, departmental instruction run through the schools; classes in special out-door activities and shop work are carried on at the same time as indoor classes, thus doubling the capacity of the school plant; the school day is eight hours long, with the school plant open also all day Saturday; continuation schools and social and recreational centers are conducted in the same plant in the evenings; and play and vocational work are important features of

[1] "Time has been the one measurable factor in education until recently. Consequently, we have laid out our educational system in terms of time units. These have been constant, while the achievement of the pupils within the time units has varied according to individual ability. But with the development of the achievement test it is becoming possible to reverse the order. We now make units of achievement the constant factor, varying the time to fit the individual capacities of the children." (Washburne, C. W., in *Journal of Educational Research*, March, 1922, p. 195.)

[2] The Gary plan (see Burris) in a way arose as a means of facing a school situation created by the rapid growth of a new city, where every department of the city needed funds for development. By building larger school buildings, with many special rooms, each building was made to care for a double shift of pupils, thus reducing materially the initial per capita cost for school plant.

the instruction in all schools. Each school is, in effect, a world in itself, busily engaged in the work and play and government of the world, and so well do such activities and a highly flexible curriculum meet the needs of all classes that the need for most of the promotional machinery and special-type classes and schools found elsewhere is here eliminated.

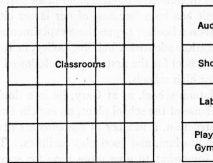

FIG. 133. THE GARY SCHOOL BUILDING PLAN

After Flexner and Bachman

The most characteristic features of the Gary idea are its greatly enriched curriculum, its equipment for work, its double school organization, and the maximum use of the school facilities. The curriculum provides four distinct types of training: (1) the drill and content subjects, such as the 3 Rs, history, geography, and English usage; (2) special work in science, many forms of shop work, and the domestic arts; (3) health and physical education, and play; and (4) auditorium work and social activities. Half of a Gary school building, as Figure 133 shows, is devoted to these special activities, and half to classroom instruction. The double school organization, that is two schools, an X school and a Y school, is a feature of the Gary plan that has been widely copied. When the X school is using the classrooms for the drill and content studies, the Y school is using the shops, laboratories, auditorium, and playgrounds, and *vice versa*. (See footnote, page 532.)

The platoon school. The Gary plan for a time attracted much attention, and between about 1910 and 1920 hundreds of visitors each year went to Gary to see the schools in operation there. A number of modifications of the idea have been worked out by different city school systems, and features of the plan have been copied here and there. The most widely accepted of these modifications is known as the Platoon School. Embodying many of the desirable features of the Gary school, but planned primarily for the elementary-school grades and involving somewhat less of buildings and equipment than at Gary, the platoon school has been adopted as the form of school organization by hundreds of cities, and in all parts of the United States. Detroit has been foremost of our larger cities in the development of platoon schools. Begun there experimentally in 1917, the board of education adopted a building policy, in 1919, that called for the platoon school for the first six years, followed by three-year junior and senior high schools.

The essentials of the platoon school, as at Gary, lie in a double school organization,[1] better use of the school plant, an enriched curriculum, departmental instruction, a number of schoolrooms fitted up as special rooms, an auditorium, and good play facilities. The school day is lengthened somewhat to give more time for special instruction, though the time actually spent in the classroom is decreased.

The "Progressive School." Within recent years much has been said as to progressive education, and so-called progressive schools have been established in many places. While these "new schools" have varied much in nature and scope, and while some have gone to extremes, they nevertheless have been but an application of the progressive ideas as to the nature of children and the learning process which found expression first in the work of Pestalozzi and Froebel, and later in this country in the work of Parker (R. 253) and Dewey (R. 258), and which have gradually taken root in the minds and practices of progressive teachers and schools. The progressives have tried to transform the school from a place of confinement to a place of interested activity, intellectual work from memorizing to creative thinking, and the school from a formal institution to a child's home. Certain characteristics of these progressive schools (R. 269) will be found today in an increasing number of public and

---

[1] Roughly, the organization of the two schools would be about as follows:

Periods	X School	Y School
8.45–10.15	Class Work	Special Work
10.15–11.45	Special Work	Class Work
11.45–12.45	Noon Intermission	
12.45–2.15	Class Work	Special Work
2.15–3.45	Special Work	Class Work

12 sections, or classes

2 platoons

6 home rooms

Each home room accommodates two sections of the
same grade

6 special rooms

Auditorium, Gymnasium, Library, Music, Art,
Social Studies

6-hour day

4 periods of 1½ hours each

3 activity periods during each 1½ hour period

Pupils alternate in their programs, one 1½ hour
period in home room, then one 1½ hour period in
special room, or vice-versa, throughout the day.

One section taught in each special room, except
Auditorium, which carries two sections at a time.

FIG. 134. A TWELVE-SECTION PLATOON SCHOOL
ORGANIZATION

(After Case.) This represents a small city or town school of 12 classes.

private schools, from kindergarten to university, all over the United States. Practically all of the experimental schools, mentioned in the next section of this chapter under curriculum construction, have been progressive in type. The school of Mrs. Johnson, at Fairhope, Alabama, was markedly both a "progressive school" and an experimental school. One writer (**R. 269**) sums up the new movement in the following words:

> The new school movement is at once a protest and a vision. It has effectively challenged the authority, the repression, and the barrenness of an educational procedure which was at odds with nature and which in practice defeated many of its own purposes. It has created schools in which teachers and pupils work together happily, under conditions mentally wholesome, in a richly stimulating environment, living in the fullest sense the life of today to be ready for tomorrow.

The course of our evolution. What has been presented so far in this chapter reveals a fairly constant evolution in our conception of the nature and purpose of education, and in our attempts to adjust the school instructional and promotional machinery to the differing needs of the different types of pupils the school contains. Especially is it evident that there has been a progressive recognition of the presence of large individual differences among, first groups of pupils, and later pupils within the groups, and the importance of dealing intelligently with these differences. The change from the old uniform knowledge-type course of study which was described at the beginning of the chapter, to the differentiated and individualized instructional plans of our most progressive school systems of today, has been large indeed. The change has been of far-reaching importance for children, and that it has been toward an individualization and improvement of instruction there can be little doubt.

All these changes are significant of the great shift in direction which has come over American education since the decade of the eighties. Then everyone was talking about subject-matter, psychological procedure, and the "faculties" of the mind, and uniformity in educational output was the prevailing educational conception. The fifty years which have since elapsed, with the consequent social and industrial and political changes through which our Nation has passed, have witnessed a complete alteration in attitude, and the child to be educated has been brought to the front in our educational thinking. Today child welfare, rather than subject-matter, occupies the center of the stage, while our educational practice is directed by a truer psychology than the decade of the eighties knew.

QUESTIONS FOR DISCUSSION

1. Explain what you understand is meant by a "faculty psychology," and show the educational consequences of such a conception.
2. Do the same for the disciplinary conception.
3. Point out the great contribution of Pestalozzi by his conception of education as development.
4. Contrast the earlier book-knowledge conception of education and the newer child-to-be-educated conception.
5. Contrast the knowledge-as-experience conception with the knowledge-as-memorized-learning conception of education.
6. Contrast the training and work of a teacher in these two types of schools.
7. State the dominating ideas of the modern school.
8. What is meant by pupil-co-operation schemes for training in self-control?
9. Show how the three classifications of the subjects in the modern curriculum (p. 518) represent the historical order of the appearance of the subjects.
10. State the advantages and disadvantages of "average courses" of study.
11. In what way are over-age and retarded children being prepared to join the ranks of the unsuccessful and dissatisfied of our working world?
12. Does a uniform literary-type course of study tend to awaken ambitions which can never be fulfilled? Why?
13. Do differentiated courses and schools tend to prevent such disappointments, and if so, how?
14. Show that a considerable amount of the increased cost of the modern school has been due to the attempt to make a "better manufacturing establishment" of it.
15. Show that this increased cost has been or has not been justified: (a) from the point of view of democracy, (b) from the point of view of results.
16. Indicate the educational consequences of accepting the idea that all children are to be given as good an education as their needs require.
17. State your evaluation of the Dalton plan.
18. State your evaluation of the Winnetka plan.
19. State your evaluation of the Gary plan.
20. State your evaluation of the platoon plan.
21. Show that there has been a steady evolution in administrative organization over the past three quarters of a century, with the aim of better adapting the school organization to pupil needs.

SELECTED READINGS

In the accompanying volume of *Readings* the following selections, related to the subject matter of this chapter, are reproduced:

*262. Spaulding: A Knowledge-type Curriculum.
*263. Dewey: New Classes of Pupils to be Provided for.
*264. Cubberley: Teaching as an Art.
*265. Cubberley: Three Great Periods of Elementary School Development.
266. Eliot: Desirable and Undesirable Uniformity in Schools.
*267. Washbourne: Philosophy of the Winnetka Curriculum.
268. Flexner-Bachman: Merits of the Gary Plan.
*269. Snyder: What is Progressive Education?

QUESTIONS ON THE READINGS

1. What characteristics of this selection (262) determine it a knowledge-type curriculum?
2. Show how these conclusions (263) mean an expanded, more differentiated, and more costly school system.
3. List the characteristics that differentiate knowledge from art (264).
4. List, with the theory of education held, the school curriculum that characterized each of these great periods of development (265).
5. Show how Eliot was a pioneer (266) in his thinking, and the extent to which his ideas are accepted today.
6. State why you accept or reject the Winnetka philosophy (267).
7. To what extent have these merits (268) been absorbed into the platoon plan school?
8. From what preceding educational reformers do the progressives (269) most clearly derive their ideas?

TOPICS FOR INVESTIGATION AND REPORT

1. Changing conceptions of the educative process.
2. Changing conceptions of school grading and classification.
3. The Dalton plan.
4. The Winnetka plan.
5. The Gary plan.
6. The platoon school plan.

SELECTED REFERENCES

Ayers, L. P. *Laggards in the Schools.* 236 pp. New York, 1909.
   An important early study of the retardation and elimination of pupils.

Bourne, R. S. *The Gary Schools.* 200 pp., illustrated. Boston, 1916.
   A well-rounded description of the organization and work of these schools.

*Bunker, F. F. *Reorganization of the Public School System.* 186 pp. United States Bureau of Education, Bulletin no. 8, Washington, 1916.

A very full and a very important discussion of the question. Reviews the arguments and describes practices. Chapters VII and VIII give a good idea of the changes required, and the new purposes in instruction.

Burris, W. P. *The Public School System of Gary, Indiana.* United States Bureau of Education, Bulletin no. 18, Washington, 1914.

A good and easily available description, giving plans, programs, and illustrations of the work done.

*Cubberley, E. P. "Desirable Reorganizations in American Education"; in *School and Society,* vol. II, pp. 397–402. (Sept., 1915.)

Presents briefly the desirable administrative reorganizations needed.

*Case, R. D. *The Platoon School in America.* 283 pp. Stanford University Press, 1931.

Chapter II presents a good history of the development of the idea.

Department of Superintendence, N.E.A. *The Junior High School Curriculum; Fifth Yearbook.* 560 pp. Washington, 1927.

A very exhaustive study of the junior high school, with special reference to curricula.

*Dewey, John. *School and Society.* 125 pp. University of Chicago Press, 1899.

Three lectures which presented early the need for educational reorganization.

*Dewey, John and Evelyn. *Schools of Tomorrow.* 316 pp. New York, 1915.

A very interesting and a very well-written book, describing a number of reorganization experiments being carried out. Chapter II describes the experiment of Mrs. Johnson at Fairhope, Alabama; Chapter III the reorganized elementary school at the University of Missouri; and Chapters VII and X the work at Gary, Indiana.

Eells, W. C. *The Junior College.* 833 pp. Boston, 1931.

Our most comprehensive treatise on the history and work of this new expansion of our educational system.

Flexner, A. and Bachman, F. P. *The Gary Schools; A General Account,* 264 pp. New York, 1918.

A general description of the Gary school system, with a summary of the results of the survey made.

*Hardy, E. L. "The Reorganization of our Educational System"; in *School and Society,* vol. V, pp. 728–32. (June 23, 1917.)

Proposes a new 4-4-4-4 plan of reorganization, based on psychological and biological grounds. An able and thought-provoking paper.

Johnson, F. W. "The Dalton Plan"; in *Teachers College Record,* vol. XXVI, pp. 464–72. (February, 1925.)

What the plan is, how it operates, and its weak points.

*Moore, E. C. *What is Education?* 354 pp. Boston, 1915.

The first two essays, on "What is Education," and "What is Knowledge," form good supplemental reading for the first two sections of this chapter.

National Society. *Minimum Essentials in Elementary School Subjects.* *Yearbooks* of the National Society for the Study of Education. 1st Report, 152 pp. *Fourteenth Yearbook*, Part I, 1915. 2d Report, 192 pp. *Sixteenth Yearbook*, Part I, 1917.

Two rather long reports, dealing with the reduction of the subject-matter of instruction in the common-school subjects.

*National Society. *Adapting the School to Individual Differences.* *Twenty-Fourth Yearbook*, Part II, of the National Society for the Study of Education, 1925. 362 pp.

The most complete study of typical attempts to adjust schools to individual differences, the problems involved, and an appraisal. Good bibliography.

Parkhurst, Helen. *Education on the Dalton Plan.* 278 pp. New York, 1922.

The plan explained by its founder.

*Pechstein, L. A., and McGregor, A. L. *Psychology of the Junior High School Pupil.* 280 pp. Boston, 1924.

A good statement of what the junior high school is, and what special needs of the pupil it aims to meet.

*Spain, Charles L. "The Platoon School; Its Advantages"; in *Elementary School Journal*, vol. XXVI, pp. 733-44. (June, 1926.)

A very good brief summary statement.

CHAPTER XVI

CURRICULUM AND SCHOOL REORGANIZATION

I. CURRICULUM REORGANIZATION

The overcrowded curriculum. From the diagram given on page 473, showing the evolution of the elementary-school curriculum, it must be evident that, if the school subjects of 1825 or 1850 occupied all the time of the six-hour-day school of that period, the new subjects which had been added by 1875, and even more so by 1900, must have seriously overburdened the course of study, even after making all due allowance for better-trained teachers, longer school terms, and better text-books and teaching appliances. The newer expression subjects (page 518) also require better teaching preparation and more careful supervision than did the old book subjects. To the 1900 list should now be added school gardening, agriculture, play as a regular school subject, often directed school-assembly work, and a much greater emphasis on the social and industrial aspects of all our school work.

It will be evident, from a glance at the chart given on page 473, that by 1875 it had become the established practice in curriculum making to add new subjects of study in response to the new and changing demands of that period, but the old subjects were retained and taught much as before. New interests began to clamor for a place in the curriculum, and to push their way in — peacefully if possible, and by legislation if necessary. The result soon was that our elementary-school courses of study became badly crowded and that teachers, especially in the upper grades, could no longer be expected to be qualified to teach satisfactorily all the subjects of the elementary-school course. Nor was there time any longer in which to teach all the subjects in the old way, even admitting that the teacher was properly prepared to do so.

Two camps opposed each other during the period from about 1880 to 1910. One camp, representing the older point of view, advocated the *status quo*, and desired standardization, uniformity, and organized methods of teaching.   The other camp formed about such leaders as William T. Harris, Francis W. Parker, Charles W. Eliot, James M. Greenwood, and John Dewey, and advocated flexibility, more individualized instruction, and an enrichment of the curriculum based on the normal activities of the child (**R. 270**). The attack at first centered naturally around a reform of the administrative procedures of the graded school, with a struggle for more flexible promotional plans, "double-track" grading, and differential courses of study.   These movements for reform resulted in a number of administrative improvements, the main lines of which we have described in the preceding chapter, but they dealt but slightly, if at all, with a reform of the content and objectives of the curriculum itself.

Early attempts at solving the problem.   With the increase of new studies, the "over-burdening of the curriculum" had become a real live issue by 1890, and various attempts have since been made to solve the problem.   In many places the introduction of the expression subjects was fought [1] by calling them "fads and frills," and for a time they were kept out.   This line of attack has now been given up except by a few of the older generation.   It has been seen that abuse and ridicule are not arguments, while it has become increasingly evident that these same expression studies are not only valuable educational instruments in themselves, but also supply a real need under our changed conditions of living.

One of the earliest proposals for solving the overburdened-curriculum difficulty was that we *concentrate* instruction about a few main subjects, and then *correlate* the other school work about these central subjects.   Colonel Francis W. Parker (page 474) was the leading advocate of this idea, and his book on the teaching of geography (1889) was to show how this could be done about geography as the central core.

Eliminating useless subject-matter.   Another plan proposed, and one that has proved very useful, has been to cut out parts of many of the subjects taught and to confine instruction to what is left. This has been done extensively.   For example, we do not now teach a third as much arithmetic or grammar as we used to do; the facts

---

[1] Colonel Parker, for example, fought vigorously to retain drawing and clay modeling in the schools of Chicago against a vicious newspaper campaign against these "fads and frills" of education, with headlines of "Mud, Mud, Mud," "Mud Pies in the Schools," and similar unintelligent publicity

in geography and the dates and battles of history are made much less prominent than they used to be; and bone and muscle and nerve physiology and the memorization of the Constitution have been displaced by hygiene and community civics. The tendency has been

In the midst of a meadow,
  Well stored with grass,
I've taken just two acres,
  To tether my ass:
Then how long must the cord be,
  That feeding all round;
He mayn't graze less or more, than
  Two acres of ground.

When first the marriage knot was ty'd,
  Between my wife and me;
My age was to that of my bride,
  As three times three to three;
But now when ten and half ten years,
  We man and wife have been,
Her age to mine exactly bears
  As eight is to sixteen;
Now tell, I pray, from what I've said,
  What were our ages when we wed?

FIG. 135. TWO OF THE PUZZLES WE NO LONGER TEACH

to eliminate the puzzles and little-used information, and to cut out all that is not useful for modern-life needs. We thus not only simplify the teaching of the subject but make room for other subjects as well.

The Herbartians have been of much help here, as they have urged the teaching of "type studies," instead of hundreds of isolated facts. For example, in geography, a study of such types as coal-mining, a seaport, a railroad-center, the cotton industry, sheep and wool, shipping, transportation, and the interdependence of people should take the place of learning great numbers of isolated facts. In history, instruction in such type studies as the internal development of our Nation, the development of the West, the growth of political parties, the rise of slavery, the evolution of transportation, the Monroe Doctrine, and the dominance of cotton in our early history and the effect of the invention of the cotton gin, should replace the chronological study of American annals. The same idea has been applied to science instruction, literature, civics, hygiene, and other studies. The work of Charles, Frank, and Lida McMurry has been very helpful along these lines.

The "project" idea. Another very important attempt at the solution of the problem has been along the line of abandoning largely the old subject-classification, and teaching "projects" instead. The work of John Dewey, in the experimental elementary school he conducted for some years (1896–1900) at Chicago, was pioneer work along this line. Making motor expression, social participation, and the industries of life the ideas around which instruction centered, and making the school reproduce the typical conditions of social life, he constructed a course of study based largely on occupations, projects, and social demands, and continually calling for expression rather than receptivity. In his school the work of the teacher was largely that of planning, guiding, and interposing "pedagogical interference" to direct the activities of the children along lines that would be helpful and educationally profitable. The old formal school subjects, with set times for classes, were replaced by studies, projects, and activities into which were introduced number, speech, reading, writing, drawing, manual work, history, and geography, as needed to understand or work out the project of the day or week. The school resembled a combination of a kindergarten and a series of workshops more than an ordinary school (**R. 273**).

Reforming the curriculum through National Committees. In 1888 President Charles W. Eliot, then president of Harvard University, read a paper before the Department of Superintendence of the National Educational Association on "Can School Programs be Shortened and Enriched?" (**R. 277**), and in the next two years he and others led an agitation for educational reform which led to the appointment of three committees by the National Educational Association, the reports of which were widely read and materially influenced subsequent thinking. These were:

APPOINTED	COMMITTEE	REPORTED
1891	Committee of Ten on Secondary School Studies	1893
1893	Committee of Fifteen on Elementary Education	1895
1895	Committee on College Entrance Requirements	1899

The Committee of Ten, under the chairmanship of President Eliot and composed largely of college professors,[1] dealt largely with the

[1] The Committee of Ten consisted of 5 college presidents, 1 college professor, 2 head-masters of private schools, 1 principal of a public school, and the United States Commissioner of Education. The 90 members of the 9 conference subject groups they organized contained 47 college professors and presidents, 21 head-masters of private schools, 14 public high school principals, 2 superintendents of schools, 4 normal school instructors, and 2 representing other services.

teaching of the subjects of the secondary school, the need for uniformity in content, standardization of requirements, time allotment, and admission to college. The effect of its Report was to supersede a program of short courses in many subjects, of the old academy type, by one of relatively few subjects, and it soon led to considerable uniformity in secondary school courses throughout the United States.

The Committee of Fifteen, under the chairmanship of Superintendent Maxwell, of New York City, dealt with the organization of a school system, the co-ordination of studies, and the preparation of teachers. Half of the space of the Report, devoted to the co-ordination, concentration, and correlation of the elementary school subjects, was from the pen of Dr. Harris. During the nineties these were great terms to conjure with.

The Committee on College Entrance, under the chairmanship of Dr. Nightengale, superintendent of high schools in Chicago, dealt with the length of the course, the age at which the various studies should begin, and the standardization of units of credit. The chief influence of its Report, as of that of the Committee of Ten, was to fix, for a time, the domination of the college-entrance idea on the high schools of the United States.

These committees were dominated by subject-matter specialists, possessed of a profound faith in the value of mental discipline. No study of pupil abilities, social needs, interest, capacities, or differential training found a place in their deliberations. The basis of their recommendations throughout was that of individual judgment. It was twenty years afterward before any use was made of investigations as to curriculum content, or any experimental work was made as to grade placement and the organization of the materials of the curriculum. As the committees supported one another, their views became accepted and the reconstructed curriculum which followed soon became crystalized and difficult to change. There was much vigorous dissent from teachers, but for a long time it was not influential (**R. 271**). A change came only as we turned from college presidents and professors, subject-matter specialists, and private-school executives, whose interests were in mind training, scholarship as such, and knowledge for knowledge's sake, and who compiled their reports by arm-chair philosophic methods, to students of educational practices who applied the experimental and quantitative method to the solution of educational problems and built their report on the results of experimental research (**R. 272**).

The Committee on the Economy of Time. A new method of studying curriculum problems was inaugurated with the work of the Committee on Economy of Time, appointed by the National Educational Association in 1911. Its personnel, made up of students of education [1] and organized under the chairmanship of Superintendent H. B. Wilson, then of Berkeley, California, marked it off sharply from those committees previously mentioned. The purpose of this new committee was stated to be to effect an economy of time in the school through the employment of scientific methods in the determination of socially worthwhile instructional materials, their proper grade placement, their organization to fit the life-needs of pupils, and the elimination of subject matter no longer of real worth. In personnel, as well as in methods of procedure, this committee marked a turning point in curriculum study in this country. The committee made four *Reports* (**R. 272**), as listed below, and these formed the basis for the annual programs of the National Society for the Study of Education for the years from 1915 to 1919. The *Reports* were:

I. 1915 — Minimum Essentials; *Fourteenth Yearbook*, Part I, 152 pp.
II. 1917 — Minimum Essentials; *Sixteenth Yearbook*, Part I, 192 pp.
III. 1918 — Minimum Essentials; *Seventeenth Yearbook*, Part I, 122 pp.
IV. 1919 — Principles of Method; *Eighteenth Yearbook*, Part II, 123 pp.

Beginning with the construction of tests to determine instructional efficiency, and an inventory of current curricula and textbooks to determine existing content and possible eliminations, the committee passed to a study of human activities to determine what were socially worthwhile knowledges and skills, and finally to a study of the chief institutions and problems of contemporary American life and the trends in the development of human society. The work closed by putting together the results of the by then numerous scientific studies of the learning process, and applying them to teaching methods and the selection of instructional materials. The work of this committee was very important in that it formulated a new

[1] Three of the seven members were professors of education or of educational psychology — Bobbitt, Henmon, and Thompson; three were superintendents of large city school systems — Hunter, Spaulding, and Wilson; and one — Woodley — was a college president.

method, based on scientific procedures,[1] for use in curriculum construction. Parallel with the work of this committee was the rise of the new school-survey movement, which also supported the committee's work, as practically all school surveys, from the one made in Portland in 1913 on, made a critical evaluation of the school curriculum a feature of the survey report. By 1920 the scientific movement was culminating in numerous new studies,[2] more scientific procedures in the school surveys, new school textbooks embodying the new results and the indicated new procedures, and the rise of research departments in connection with city school systems,[3] one phase of the work of which was curriculum revision.

The Department of Superintendence studies. Following the completion of the reports of the Committee on Economy of Time, the Department of Superintendence of the National Education Association inaugurated a series of nation-wide co-operative studies, working through a National Commission and the research staff of the Association at Washington. The results of these studies appeared in six *Yearbooks*, between 1924 and 1929, as follows:

Second Yearbook, 1924; The Elementary School Curriculum. 296 pp.
Third Yearbook, 1925, Research in Constructing the Elementary School Curriculum. 424 pp.
Fourth Yearbook, 1926; The Nation at Work on the Public School Curriculum. 520 pp.
Fifth Yearbook, 1927; The Junior High School Curriculum. 562 pp.
Sixth Yearbook, 1928; Development of the High School Curriculum. 584 pp.
Seventh Yearbook, 1929; Articulation of the Units of American Education. 616 pp.

These six *Reports* contained a large amount of material of a type very useful to curriculum builders. The *Yearbooks* dealt with present practices, machinery and organization for revising, curricu-

---

[1] "Under the leadership of Thorndike, Judd, Cubberley, Strayer, Terman, Whipple, Freeman, Gray, and others, the quantitative method began to be applied to the solution of educational problems. The fact-finding era was launched; it was the day of the question blank and the school survey. Learning was being experimentally investigated in the laboratory; 'tests' had entered the classroom." (Rugg, H. *Twenty-Sixth Yearbook, National Society for the Study of Education*, Part I, p. 67.)

[2] The most important of the studies of this period were:
  1. The National Committee on Mathematical Requirements (1920–23).
  2. The Classical Investigation (1921–25).
  3. The Modern Language Study (1924–   ).
  4. The Preliminary Study of History, and Related Subjects (1925–   ).

[3] The first city to make a beginning in the establishment of research work was Rochester, N.Y., in 1911, when a municipal expert was employed to advise the board of education on accounting and finance, and in 1913 a Bureau of School Efficiency was established. Baltimore had created a Bureau of Educational Research in 1912. By 1914, fifteen cities had begun this service, by 1920 there were fifty-three, and by 1925 one hundred and six.

lum problems and their scientific solution, summarized researches as to curriculum content by subjects for each of the three divisions of the school, and made a detailed study of articulation of the different divisions of the school with one another (**R. 272**). Such a mass of scientific data relating to the problems of curriculum construction had never before been brought together; still more, so recent has been the scientific study of the instructional problem, it would not have been possible to assemble such a collection at an earlier date.

City curriculum study. These nation-wide studies were paralleled and followed by the work of individual cities which set up research departments and, enlisting the aid of committees of teachers, and sometimes also of citizens, began the work of city curriculum revision. The conspicuous early leaders in this movement were Winnetka, Illinois, under the leadership of Superintendent Carleton Washbourne, and Denver, Colorado, under Superintendent Jesse H. Newlon. Washbourne and a group of classroom teachers, organized (1920) as the Winnetka Research Seminar, began a series of studies as to the basic needs in the teaching of reading, spelling, geography, history, and language teaching, with measurements of the speed and accuracy of adults in common-school procedures. The Denver study, begun in 1922, which required a number of years and cost a considerable sum of money, has been notable for the experimentation with new subject-matter, in both the elementary and the secondary school, and the employment of outside specialists to assist in the study. The culmination at Denver came, in 1925, in the creation of a Curriculum Department, under a Director, for the continuous study of curriculum problems (**R. 274**).

Within the past decade the curriculum-revision movement has spread to other cities in all parts of the United States,[1] and the results of these efforts at curriculum revision, as expressed in printed curricula, undoubtedly have been better adapted to individual city needs than were the older courses of study as prepared by the board of education in the earlier periods, and later by the superintendent of schools, and often merely by copying what others had done.

[1] Denver and Pueblo, Colorado; Houston, Texas; St. Louis, Missouri; Los Angeles, Long Beach, Berkeley, Oakland, California; Detroit, Michigan; Sioux City and Burlington, Iowa; Dayton and Youngstown, Ohio; Melrose, Massachusetts; and Baltimore County, Maryland, are examples of cities where city-wide studies, at a cost of thousands of dollars, have been carried through. In Denver, approximately $100,000 was spent on course of study revision (1922-26).

Curriculum studies covering a three- to a five-year period have been embarked on and carried through. More important even than the final results, as expressed in printed courses of study, have been the by-products of this new work. New interest has been awakened in professional thinking, new leaders have been developed among the classroom teachers, a new desire for the study of professional literature has become in evidence, a deeper insight as to aims and purposes in instruction has been imparted, and a new spirit of co-operation between teachers and administrative officers has resulted. Able better to interpret the school to the public, the public has taken a new interest in both the teachers and the school.

Curriculum study in experimental schools. Not even a brief account of recent curriculum study in the United States would be complete without at least some reference to the work done by a number of experimental schools. Beginning with the work of Colonel Francis W. Parker at the Cook County Normal School,[1] and the Chicago Institute (1883–1901), the John Dewey Laboratory School [2] (1896-1904) (**R. 273**), and the Horace Mann School (1887) and the Speyer School (1899) at Teachers College,[3] Columbia University, a number of notable experimental schools have been established and these have made their contributions to the curriculum problem. The experimental elementary school begun at the University of Missouri by Professor J. L. Meriam, in 1904, which divided the day's work equally among four activities — play, stories, observation, and hand work — and built its instruction around these four, was a notable early attempt at a solution of the problem. Another early school was that established by Mrs. Marietta L. Johnson (1907)

[1] "From the beginning Colonel Parker was compelled to fight both the enmity of partisan politicians who hampered him at every stage of his work, and the conservatism of school principals and teachers. By the most unfair and unreasonable examination of his Practice School they tried to injure him and his reputation. Nevertheless, he built up in the Cook County Normal School a faculty of experimentalists, of fearless innovators, real students of childhood, and a practice school which proved an influential object lesson for both teachers and the general public. The school became a national pedagogical center." (Harold Rugg, in *Twenty-Sixth Yearbook, National Society for the Study of Education*, p. 88.)

[2] In 1904, Dewey said of the Laboratory School, then become a part of the School of Education of the University of Chicago, that it had been operated "especially for the purpose of scientific investigation and research into the problems connected with the psychology and sociology of education. Its aim was to further the application of scientific concepts and methods to the conduct of school work."

[3] From the beginning, the Horace Mann group aimed at the improvement of instruction "through the existing subjects of study," while the Speyer School was frankly experimental, and in addition was probably the first experimental school that combined a social settlement with its work.

at Fairhope, Alabama. There the elementary-school course of study was organized under the headings of physical exercise, nature study, music, hand work, field geography, descriptive geography, reading, story-telling, sense culture, number, dramatization, and games. Two other schools of importance have been the experimental school at the University of Iowa (1915), under the direction of Professor Ernest Horn, and the Lincoln School [1] of Teachers College (1917), under the direction of Professors Otis W. Caldwell and Jesse H. Newlon. The work of Dr. Judd, at the University of Chicago school, a successor of the work of Parker and Dewey, has occupied a somewhat middle ground. [2]

All of these schools have attempted to improve the content and the method of public school education through experimentation with children under actual school conditions, and to create a curriculum based largely on child activity, creative self-expression, and spontaneity to replace the older curriculum based largely on ideas of mental discipline, conformity, and the docile acceptance of what was taught (R. 273). The aim of all these reformers has been disciplined initiative on the part of the pupils, rather than "chaotic freedom on the one hand or regimented conformity" on the other. One of the important by-products of their work, and one of no small importance at that, has been the demonstration of what they are doing to the thousands of teachers and interested laymen who have visited them.

The curriculum problem. Any set of curricula is an attempt to provide teachers with specifications for the manufacture of our future citizenship. With the best of curricula, however, there is always a certain lag between the instruction given in the schools and the needs of American life. The problem is to reduce this lag to the smallest possible dimensions [3] (R. 276).

[1] It is of interest to the student of the history of education, says Rugg, to note the close relationship between the Cook County Normal School group, the School of Education of the University of Chicago, both of which were Parker institutions, and the first staff of The Lincoln School at Teachers College. A number of the same individuals, were on the staffs at one time of the three schools.

[2] This school, under Dr. Judd's direction, has sought to improve the school curriculum and methods of teaching by assuming a middle position between the rigid formality of the old school and the "chaotic freedom" of some of the modern progressives. This has been attempted through revitalizing the content of the school by means of scientific research as to both subject-matter and method, and by organizing a large amount of spontaneous activity on the part of the pupils.

[3] "In a hundred years the school has lagged behind. It has never caught up with the momentum of industry, business, community life, or politics. Only rarely has it succeeded in

FIG. 136. PROBLEMS OF THE COMING INDUSTRIAL AGE, AND THEIR EDUCATIONAL IMPLICATIONS

(By Dean William F. Russell, in his *Annual Report* as Dean of Teachers College, 1930.)

	WHAT USED TO BE — AGRARIAN AGE *Colonial New England* *Illinois when Lincoln was a boy* *Iowa in the days of Vandermark's Folly*	WHAT WE HAVE PASSED THROUGH — INDUSTRIAL REVOLUTION I *Massachusetts in 1830* *Middle West, 1850–90*	WHAT WE SEEM TO BE COMING TO — INDUSTRIAL REVOLUTION II *Present time and future*	POSSIBLE IMPLICATIONS FOR THE SCHOOLMASTER
Employment	EMPLOYMENT FOR EVERYBODY Free land "Anyone who truly wants to work can get a job" "Young man! Go West!"	TECHNOLOGICAL UNEMPLOYMENT EMPLOYMENT FOR THOSE WHO CAN GET IT Differentiation of processes Decay of apprenticeship Still free land in West	ALL OF THE WORKERS IDLE *SOME OF THE TIME* SOME OF THE WORKERS IDLE *ALL OF THE TIME* BECAUSE OF (a) Increasing technological unemployment (b) Mergers (c) Emphasis on the younger worker (d) Closed frontier	GREATER IMPORTANCE OF GENERAL AND PREVOCATIONAL EDUCATION INDIVIDUAL VERSATILITY OF GREAT IMPORTANCE VOCATIONAL EDUCATION MUST NOT BE TOO NARROW MUST TEACH IMPORTANCE OF SAVINGS ADULT EDUCATION HIGHLY IMPORTANT
Interdependence	FAMILY OR SMALL COMMUNITY RELATIVELY SELF-SUFFICIENT Little recourse to trade Barter Personal relationships	INCREASING INTERDEPENDENCE Trade — but few commodities	ALMOST COMPLETE INTERDEPENDENCE Great variety of commodities Everything expressed in money value Impersonal relations We buy: ready-made clothes — baker's bread — canned food	INCREASED IMPORTANCE OF SOCIAL STUDIES
Women	WORK — A FAMILY ENTER-	FACTORY LABOR OF WOMEN	MORE THAN ONE WAGE-	IMPORTANCE OF VOCATIONAL

Standard of Living	SIMPLE STANDARD OF LIVING "A pain economy"	LOW STANDARD OF LIVING. POVERTY AMONG WORKERS Accumulation of wealth	HIGH STANDARD OF LIVING IN SOME WAYS "A pleasure economy" Salesmanship Advertising Dissipation of natural resources Automobiles Radios Washing-machines etc.	STUDY OF SPENDING AND SAVING CONSUMPTION vs. CONSERVATION LUXURIES vs. NECESSITIES
Control	LAISSEZ FAIRE POLICY Personal initiative and enterprise	BEGINNINGS OF SOCIAL LEGISLATION Health and morals Hours of labor Conditions of work	INCREASING GOVERNMENT CONTROL BY Information Advice Direction	NEW SCIENCE OF GOVERNMENT HOW TO DEVELOP CO-OPERATIVE POWERS OF INDIVIDUAL
Administration	INDEPENDENCE OF INDIVIDUAL	BOSS AND WORKER Strikes Boycotts Lockouts Collective bargaining	CO-OPERATIVE CONTROL SCIENTIFIC MANAGEMENT GOVERNMENT CONTROL Increasingly impersonal	STUDY OF ART AND SCIENCE OF ADMINISTRATION
Tempo	LEISURELY TEMPO LONG HOURS— LOW PRODUCTIVITY RHYTHM OF THE SEASONS	INCREASING TEMPO LONG HOURS— INCREASED PRODUCTIVITY REGIMENTATION OF LIFE Whistles Time clocks	QUICK TEMPO SHORT HOURS— HIGH PRODUCTIVITY PERIODIC SHUTDOWNS MUCH { IDLENESS OR LEISURE } When is a vacation unemployment?	MUCH ATTENTION TO PROBLEMS OF THE USE OF LEISURE PROVISION FOR THE "RAINY DAY" PROBLEMS OF HYGIENE — PHYSICAL AND MENTAL

From time to time, in the progress of a Nation, the rate of progress is accelerated by some mighty force, and then attention is directed anew to the extent of the lag between school instruction and the needs of our national life. The World War was such a force, and probably the greatest modifying force that has ever come to stir the schools into new activity and advancement. The changes in the living and thinking of our people as a result of the conflict have been enormous and far-reaching in their effects. The War ushered in a new world, with new social and moral, and new economic and industrial problems. Still more, the full effects of the changes initiated by the World War have not as yet been realized, and just what some of the future changes will be we cannot as yet predict. We see, though, that the Industrial Revolution is still under way, that vast changes in living are still ahead of us, and that the educational implications for the schoolmaster are large indeed (**R. 275**). Dean Russell has summarized the changes, past and future, well in the chart which we here reproduce as Figure 136.

To give to our youth an intelligent understanding of this new and exceedingly complicated social and industrial world which has been ushered in we now see to be one of the main functions of the school (**R. 276**). Contemporary American civilization and its needs, both today and in the years to come, we now realize to be of greater importance as a subject of study than is the civilization of the past, important as this past has been. To carry these new conceptions as to the function of the school over into the instruction of the classroom has called not only for extensive curriculum revision and reorganization, but for a redirection of the work of the school as well (**R. 276**). These new conceptions, in turn, have called for new thinking as to what we teach and why we teach it on the part of all concerned, from the superintendent of schools down to the classroom teacher; they have also called for certain important reorganizations and expansions in the structure of the school itself (**R. 275**).

II. REORGANIZATION OF FORM AND SCOPE

The 8-4 school as evolved by 1890. Our common-school system was an outgrowth of a great democratic movement, beginning

dealing with contemporary issues and conditions; never has it anticipated social needs. The masters of the American mind have fashioned the public school as the great conserving agency, and the halo of the past has oriented those who have made the content of our school curriculum. Rarely have educational leaders affirmed for the school a preparatory and prophetic function." (Harold Rugg, *Twenty-Sixth Yearbook, National Society for the Study of Education*, Part I, p. 4.)

in the early part of the nineteenth century, which created common tax-supported schools for democracy's ends. The college, on the other hand, has its roots back in the Middle Ages, and originally was founded to pass on to a small privileged class the inherited learning of the ages. In between the two there arose with us the academy, and this later was superseded by the public tax-supported high school. This, when created, unlike the common practice with higher schools in Europe (see Fig. 99, p. 352) was superimposed by democracy on the common school which had previously grown up. As was shown in the tabulation for twenty-eight cities, given on page 309, the parts of our school system at first possessed no fixed limits or length of course. Sometimes we found a three-year high school superimposed on anywhere from a six-to a nine-year elementary-school course of study, and sometimes a four-year school superimposed on schools of varying length below. In time the nine-year elementary school became common in the New England States, the seven-year elementary school in the Southern States, and the eight-year elementary school elsewhere, with a three-year and later a four-year high-school course superimposed on top of each.

By 1890, the 8–4 plan of organization, shown in the chart (Fig. 46) on page 140, had become common everywhere, except in the South, the nine-year elementary school in New England being largely due to the admission of children to the lowest grade at five, instead of six. The high school was thus dovetailed in between the common school on the one side and the college on the other, as is shown in the left-hand plan given in Figure 138, page 559. A perfect educational ladder was thus provided by democracy, leading from the kindergarten at the bottom to the graduate or professional schools at the top. This all came about so naturally as the result of a slow native evolution, and seemed to fit so well the educational needs of the time, that no one for a time questioned the arrangement.

First questioning of the arrangement. In 1888 President Charles W. Eliot, of Harvard University, read a paper before the Department of Superintendence of the National Educational Association on "Can School Programs be Shortened and Enriched?" (**R. 277**) and in 1892 followed this by another before the same Department on "Shortening and Enriching the Grammar School Course." In July, 1892, he read a third paper before the summer meeting of the National Educational Association on "Undesirable and De-

CHARLES WILLIAM ELIOT
(1834–1926)
President of Harvard University
(1869–1909)

sirable Uniformity in Schools" (**R. 266**). These three papers started
a discussion of a new educational problem — that of the respective
purposes and places in our educational system of the common elementary school, the high school, and the college. The discussion
centered about the questions of shortening the instruction in the old
drill subjects, the addition of new and more advanced studies in
the upper grades of the elementary school, the specialization of the
work of teachers there by the introduction of a departmental type
of teaching for the sixth, seventh, and eighth school grades, and the
shortening of the whole course of instruction so that boys might
begin their professional study and life-work at an earlier age. These
topics were much discussed for a decade and a half, and much careful thinking was given to them.

As a result, many schools, between about 1890 and 1905, reorganized the instruction in the upper grades by changing from
the grade-teacher plan to a departmental type of instruction.[1] A
few new subjects, such as elementary algebra and geometry, elementary science, and Latin or a modern language were introduced,
here and there, as new studies for selected classes in the upper
grades, but usually there was no differentiation in courses, and no
changes in the relation of the elementary school to the high school.
The public school system still remained an 8–4 school system, with
at best the five lower grades taught by the grade plan and the three
upper by the departmental plan. The chief result of the discussion, though by no means a small one in itself, was to specialize
more the work of the teachers in the upper elementary-school
grades, with a resulting improvement in the quality of the instruction.

A new direction given the discussion. In 1901 Professor John
Dewey, and in 1902 President Harper, at the meetings of conferences
of academies and high schools at the University of Chicago, gave
the discussion a new direction by questioning the organization of
public education as then developed. President Harper proposed to
condense and shorten the elementary school to six years, and then

[1] The following will show the change in arrangement that may be assumed to have been
made in the upper grades:

GRADE PLAN, FOUR ROOMS	DEPARTMENTAL PLAN, FOUR ROOMS
1 teacher of 6B grade	1 teacher of mathematics and drawing
1 teacher of 6A grade	1 teacher of history and geography
1 teacher of 7B and 7A grades	1 teacher of language and literature
1 teacher of 8B and 8A grades	1 teacher of science and music.

extend the high school to an equal length of time. For such a change he advanced many educational arguments.[1] This proposal, too, brought forth much educational discussion. John Dewey, in particular, pointed out the advantages of such a proposed reorganization, and the proper place and work of both the elementary and the secondary school (**R. 278**). A number of committees to consider the proposals were appointed by different educational associations, a number of reports were prepared and printed, and many articles on the question appeared in the educational magazines. The fact that, in 1900, two of the most progressive nations, France and Japan, had revised their national systems of education and virtually limited elementary education to six years, was quoted; and the educational exhibits at the St. Louis Exposition, in 1904, made it conspicuously evident that the United States was almost the only important nation to prolong elementary education to eight or nine years. In the Philippines, too, we had just organized a school system built on a four-year elementary schoool.

In 1908, a committee of the National Education Association reported in favor of a six-year course of study for elementary schools,[2] and an equal division of the twelve-year school system between the elementary and the secondary school.

General result of the discussion. The result of a decade of discussion which followed this new proposal was a rather general acceptance, at least by those who had participated actively in it, of the idea of shortening the drill and fundamental-knowledge instruction of the elementary school to six years, and the organization of all the instruction of the following eight years — the seventh and eighth grades, the four years of the high-school period, and the first two years of the college course — into some organized form of secondary education, as is done in most European countries. It gradually came to be felt that such an arrangement would not only provide for better instruction, but that it would be based on better psychological grounds than the 8–4 plan. Under the plans pro-

---

[1] For President Harper's proposals, and the arguments for and against, see *The School Review*, vol. XI, pp. 1–3. (January, 1903.)

[2] "There is nearly unanimity of opinion that much time is wasted in elementary education, and a large majority claim that the time should be shortened. That there are too many odds and ends, topics and subjects, is a common criticism, the teaching and the lack of knowledge of ends aimed at having their share...

" A majority favor a change of the high-school period, the preference being for from twelve to eighteen." (*Proceedings*, N. E. A., 1908, p. 468.

posed the first two years of the college course would become more closely connected with the secondary school — perhaps an integral part of it — and the university of the future would in consequence become a group of professional schools beginning at the present junior year. The general result would be the enrichment of instruction, the provision of larger educational opportunities at home for the more ambitious pupils, while the capable student would be able to finish college by the time he was twenty, get his professional preparation made by twenty-three or twenty-four, and thus enter upon his professional life at least two years earlier than was then the case. The following statement made in 1909 by Professor Alexis F. Lange, an early advocate of such a reorganization, was expressive of the general result arrived at as the outcome of the discussion carried on between 1902 and 1909:

> The question is no longer, Shall the high school live unto itself; but, How shall it live with its neighbors on either side?... Education must become more continuous, not mechanically, but organically. The sixteen or more grades of our school system must come to stand approximately for as many adaptations to unbroken growth. The educational edifice erected by the nineteenth century still resembles too closely an irregular pyramid of three boxes, the tops and bottoms of which are perforated in order that the more acrobatic pupils may vault from the known to the unknown, and their teachers above and below may exchange maledictions. The twentieth century cannot accept this arrangement as final. The structure, as seen from the outside, may well remain intact; but the provisional tops and bottoms inside must be refitted, if not removed. Now, one essential in preparing for this task is to realize that adolescence begins at least two years earlier and ends about two years later than the inherited accidental high-school period. Divested of artificial meanings, secondary education is seen to cover not less than eight grades, instead of four.

Up to about 1909 or 1910 the question of educational reorganization remained largely an academic question, though being increasingly subjected to critical analysis by practical school men to see if the reorganizations proposed could be carried out in practice. Along with this study of the problem of educational reorganization a number of other practical school problems, such as the acceleration of capable children, retardation and its causes, flexible grading, promotional schemes, courses of study eliminations, and parallel and differentiated courses of study to meet varying social and individual needs, also began to receive a hitherto unknown attention.

Within the next decade not only these problems, but the earlier question of educational reorganization as well, were put in a new light through the development and use of the new standard tests and the new ability to measure and grade intelligence. The desirability of some form of educational reorganization now stood forth clearer than ever before.

The 6-3-3 plan evolved. The result of these two decades of discussion following President Eliot's papers, the careful thought given to the practical administrative problems just mentioned above, the new light on our educational work obtained through the use of new measuring tests, and a growing consciousness that the problem of educational reorganization was a real one, with educational, social, and psychological bearings of far-reaching importance, all combined to change the problem from an academic into a very practical issue. From the educational point of view the problem became — Can any reorganization better fit the school to attract and retain a larger percentage of the older boys and girls who drop out, and can a more flexible organization be devised to meet the needs alike of the slow, the gifted, and the peculiar? From a social point of view the problem became — Can the instruction, by any reorganization, be adapted better to the needs of the different social classes, and thus meet better the social and industrial demands of our modern world? From the psychological point of view the problem became — Can we adjust our school work better to the natural growth and mental-development periods of child life? From the democratic point of view the problem remained almost as stated by President Eliot — Can we by any rearrangement meet better the needs of the gifted children, and thus permit them to progress more rapidly through the school?

After the problem of reorganization had shaped itself in these ways, as a result of the long discussion, a number of important experiments in educational reorganization began, the most important of which were the organization at Berkeley [1] (California), in 1909, and at Los Angeles in 1910, of what were then termed intermediate schools, but since have taken the name of junior high schools. Columbus, Ohio, made a similar organization during the school

[1] The theory of the Berkeley and the Los Angeles reorganizations, which were the pioneers in the junior high school development, is well set forth in the monograph by F. F. Bunker, *The Reorganization of Public School Systems*, Bulletin 8, 1916, United States Bureau of Education, 186 pp.

year 1909–10. In each case the seventh, eighth, and ninth grades were regrouped to form a new school. This form of reorganization soon was adopted by many California cities, and has since spread all over the United States. By 1930 there were approximately four thousand junior high schools in the United States, enrolling over a million and a quarter of pupils. It substituted a 6–3–3 type of organization for the old 8–4 type.

Advantages of such educational reorganization. The junior high school thus evolved represents a distinctly new creation in American education, intermediate in type between the elementary school on the one hand and the secondary school on the other, and designed to meet the special biological, psychological, social, and moral needs of young people in their early teens. The 6–3–3 plan not only makes better provision for meeting varying educational and social needs, but can be defended as psychologically more sound than the 8–4 plan. The age of twelve, rather than the age of fourteen, is the dividing place between the pre-adolescent and the adolescent stages of development, and the place where methods and types of instruction should change. By a rearrangement by means of which each division of the school system is made to serve a distinct educational, social, and psychological purpose, and has a distinct outline of work shaped to meet such ends, the school is made into a much more useful social institution (**R. 279**). Eight years, beginning at six, carry the child beyond the period necessary for acquiring the tools of knowledge, and beyond the natural division of his life which comes at the dawn of adolescence.

Instead of being kept under grade teachers, grinding on the tools of knowledge long past the period of interest in such work, the child at twelve passes to a school organized by subjects, taught by teachers with better preparation in specialized lines, and better adapted to utilize that curiosity, eagerness, plasticity, impressionability, and ambition toward adult goals which characterize the years from twelve to fifteen or sixteen. In such a school general courses, offering a survey of the fields of human knowledge, and some opportunity to determine individual aptitudes, should be the characteristics of the instruction. There should also be some options and differentiations in courses to meet the needs of different types of children.

With such an introductory training, pupils are better fitted to enter and carry the work of the regular high school which follows, or to turn to the trade and vocational courses and become intelligent workers in our modern industrial society. With such an educational reorganization it should be the ambition of every community to see that every normal pupil, before the compulsory school-years have passed, shall have completed the six-year elementary course and some line of study in the three-year junior high school.[1]

Further expansion above; the Junior College. The high school, within the past two decades, has experienced the most rapid expan-

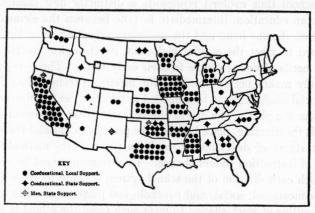

FIG. 137. PUBLIC JUNIOR COLLEGES BY 1930

From W. C. Eells's *The Junior College*, p. 30. In addition to the 171 public junior colleges, there were in 1930, 279 private and denominational junior colleges, located mostly in the East and South.

sion of any part of the public school system. Certainly one reason for this expansion has been the somewhat general organization of junior high schools. Wherever they have been introduced there has been a marked gain in numbers, not only in those continuing through the junior high school grades, but also in those entering the high school. New provisions for secondary education usually have

[1] The purpose of the junior high school organization has been well stated by Superintendent R. G. Jones, of Cleveland, as follows:

1. To make a better adaptation of the curriculum to the needs of the early adolescent period.

2. To bridge the gap between the elementary school and the high school so that the percentage of failures in the early years of the high school will be materially lessened.

3. To provide a vocational try-out in an attempt to discover abilities and adaptabilities.

4. To attempt to keep pupils in school beyond the compulsory school age.

5. To give an opportunity for earlier development of leadership than was possible under the old style of school organization.

had to be made, new high schools have had to be opened, and often differentiated types of high schools have been developed as well. This remarkable high school expansion has resulted, in turn, in a remarkable increase in college attendance. Still more, there has come a strong demand, more evident as yet in the West and the Middle West than in the East, but certain to be felt there as well in time, that the public school system should be extended upward to include the first two years of collegiate work (**R. 280**).

With the enrichment of courses of study and the moving of subjects down in the school program, it has been seen possible ultimately to effect a shortening of the period of general education to approximately the age of twenty, at the completion of the fourteenth school year, thus enabling young people to begin professional preparation and get their start in life two years earlier than under the present plan. As a result we have seen the rise of a new unit of public education, best developed as yet in the West and South, known as the Junior College, covering the Freshman and Sophomore years of college work, and thus adding the thirteenth and the fourteenth years of instruction to the public school system. The final result has been the reorganization of public education after a Kn–6–3–3–2 form, the essential features of which are shown by the right-hand diagram given in Figure 138. The first public junior college to continue to the present time was the Joliet Junior College, in Illinois (1902), which owed its inspiration to President Harper.[1] By 1904 there were six public junior colleges, and eighteen semi-public institutions, located in different parts of the United States. By 1930 the numbers had increased to 171 public and 279 private junior colleges.

There have been four ways in which these new institutions have developed. In some cases, existing high schools have been expanded upward to cover the two additional years; in other cases new junior colleges have been created *de novo;* in other cases four-year colleges have discontinued their last two years and concentrated their effort on the junior college years; and, in still other cases, universities have segregated their first two years of work and reorganized it as a junior

[1] "The public junior college was established in Joliet, Illinois, in 1902. Joliet takes no particular credit for it, but concedes it to the man of vision, Dr. William R. Harper, the first president of the University of Chicago." (Brown, J. S. *The Growth and Development of the Junior Colleges in the United States,* p. 27. United States Bureau of Education, Bulletin 19, 1922.)

college division. In these new institutions, says Eells,[1] "a college course worthy of the highest respect can be given today which will be equal to, if not in many respects superior to, the average college course of a half-century ago."

The completed reorganization. The essential features of the final plan, as shown in Figure 138, are (1) the reorganization of the first six years into a school for literacy and citizenship, and for attaining the use of the fundamental tools of learning; (2) the organization of the last two years of the elementary school and the first year of the high school into a new school, known as the junior high school, to be provided for in separate buildings, taught by a departmental plan of instruction, and to offer more advanced studies than the usual grade-school does, with some variations in courses to meet different pupil needs; (3) the formal high school to constitute the three upper years; and (4) the first two years of college work to be closely related, and in a sense complementary, to the work of the high school. Where possible the first two years of college work may be added to the high school, or closely connected with it by a separate organization known as a junior college. When so connected, as is done in a number of California cities, the plan becomes a 6-3-5 plan. The university then should consist of a large number of professional schools, beginning with the junior year, or so-called senior college. This plan, as will be seen from the diagram, can be made to meet the needs of different social classes with different educational destinations, can so shorten college and professional preparation that our youth may complete their professional preparation some two years earlier than at present and begin their life-work at an earlier age, can be adapted easily to the needs of the new vocational education, and can be fitted to continuation schools which will carry the youth along to the age of eighteen in vocational lines.

Significance of the reorganization movement. It has been the effort to readjust the work of our inherited educational system to meet the changed conditions in our national life — social, industrial, political, religious, economic, scientific — brought about by the industrial revolution of the latter part of the nineteenth century and

[1] Eells, Walter C. *The Junior College.* 833 pp. Houghton Mifflin Company, Boston, 1931. The one comprehensive volume on the subject. Chapter III gives a good historical sketch of this division of our educational system.

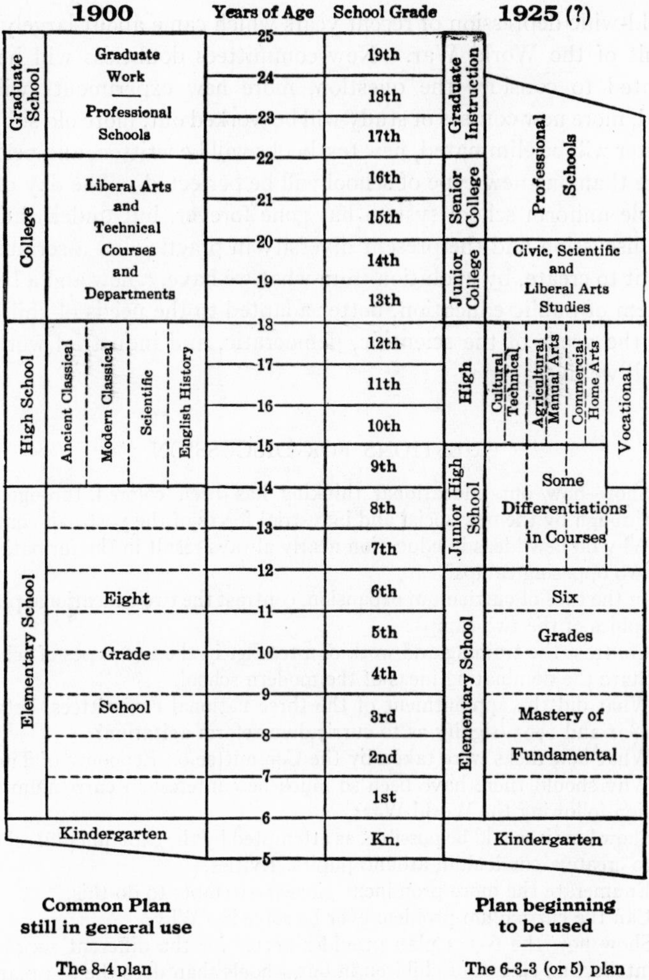

FIG. 138. THE REORGANIZATION OF AMERICAN EDUCATION

the earlier part of the twentieth, which has been behind all the discussion and the efforts at educational reorganization since President Eliot started the discussion over forty years ago.   The question is as yet by no means settled, and further, the need for educational reorganizations is certain to be given new emphasis by reason of the new need for economy in our national life brought about by the world-wide depression of recent years which came about largely as a result of the World War. New committees doubtless will be appointed to consider the question, more new experiments will be tried, more new courses of study will be worked out, more old subject-matter will be eliminated, new textbooks will be written, and perhaps more than one new type of school will be perfected. The day of the simple uniform school system has gone forever, but underneath all the discussion and the present diversity in practice lies a serious attempt to create, by evolution from what we have, a new and a better system of public education, better adapted to the needs of child life and the needs of the scientific, democratic, and industrial world in which we live.

QUESTIONS FOR DISCUSSION

1. Show how our educational thinking has been colored through and through by the new social and industrial forces of the past half century.
2. Why do new ideas in education nearly always result in the formation of two opposing camps?
3. In the case of curriculum expansion, contrast the two educational philosophies of the two camps.
4. Contrast the training and work of a teacher in the two types of schools.
5. State the dominating ideas of the modern school.
6. What did the appointment of the three national committees, between 1891 and 1895, signify as to curriculum reform agitation?
7. What new tacks were taken by the Committee on Economy of Time?
8. Why should there have been so much new interest in curriculum revision following the World War?
9. Show how it would be possible, as attempted by the experimental schools, to create a curriculum around pupil activities.
10. Enumerate the more prominent pioneer attempts to do this.
11. Can the curriculum problem ever be solved? Why?
12. Show how the 6–3–3 plan provides better for the different social and intellectual classes of children in our schools than does the 8–4 plan.
13. Show how, with the 6–3–3 plan, it could be made possible to put all children of fair ability through the ninth grade before the end of the compulsory education period.
14. Evaluate the statement of Professor Lange.
15. In what ways may the junior high school minister better to the special needs of the early adolescent?
16. Enumerate the educational advantages of the junior college.

SELECTED READINGS

In the accompanying volume of *Readings* the following selections, related to the subject matter of this chapter, are reproduced:

270. DeGarmo: The Problem of the Curriculum, Historically.
*271. Rugg: Curriculum Making by National Committees.
*272. Rugg: Reports of the Committee on Economy of Time.
*273. Dewey: The Experimental School at Chicago.
274. Newlon: Curriculum Revision a Continuous Process.
*275. Russell: Education for the Industrial Era.
*276. Rugg: The Task of the Curriculum Makers.
277. Eliot: Can School Programs be Shortened and Enriched?
*278. Dewey: Place and Work of the Elementary and Secondary Schools.
279. Judd: Special Function of the Junior High School.
*280. Eells: The Junior College; Fad or Fixture?

QUESTIONS ON THE READINGS

1. Show the relation between our national development (**270**) and an expanding curriculum.
2. Contrast the favorable and the unfavorable results of the work of the National Committees (**271**).
3. Why was such work as the Committee on Economy of Time (**272**) not possible when the three National Committees did their work?
4. Show how the work of Dewey (**273**) represented both a new procedure and a new conception of the problem.
5. If Newlon is correct (**274**), is teacher participation then made more necessary than before? Why?
6. Can the school ever hope to catch up, in its curriculum and teaching, with so rapidly advancing an industrial civilization (**275**)? What can we do about it?
7. Are our teachers, as a body, conscious of such a curriculum problem as is set forth in **276**? What can be done to make them conscious? Is the problem theirs, or the superintendent's, or the school board's?
8. Show the pioneer thinking of President Eliot in **277**.
9. Show the pioneer thinking of Professor Dewey in **278**.
10. Using Judd's statement (**279**) as a basis, contrast the teaching and the purpose of the elementary school and the junior high school.
11. State the arguments you would advance to prove that the junior college (**280**) is either a fad or a fixture.

TOPICS FOR INVESTIGATION AND REPORT

1. Personnel and work of the Committee of Ten.
2. Personnel and work of the Committee of Fifteen.
3. Personnel and work of the Committee on College Entrance Requirements.
4. Work of the Committee on Economy of Time.

5. The Department of Superintendence *Yearbooks*.
6. The work of experimental schools.
7. Special function of the junior high school.
8. Special function of the junior college.

SELECTED REFERENCES

Department of Superintendence, N.E.A., *Yearbooks*. (See page 545 for list.)
> Six *Yearbooks*, each a large and an important study.

*Dewey, John. "The Situation as Regards the Course of Study"; in *Proceedings*, N.E.A., 1901, pp. 332–48. Also in *Educational Review*, vol. XXII, pp. 26–49.
> A good early statement of the obstacles to progress, and the need of substituting some better plan for the tentative and empirical experimentation which characterized progress during the 19th century.

Dewey, John and Evelyn. *Schools of Tomorrow*. 316 pp. New York, 1915.
> Chapter IV describes a number of early attempts to reorganize the curriculum in experimental schools.

*Eells, W. C. *The Junior College*. 833 pp. Boston, 1931.
> A very complete description, with a good historical statement.

*Hardy, E. L. "The Reorganization of our Educational System"; in *School and Society*, vol. v, pp. 728–32. (June 23, 1917.)
> A good early statement of reasons for a 4–4–4–4 organization.

*Judd, Charles H. "The Curriculum; a Paramount Issue"; in *Proceedings, Department of Superintendence, N.E.A.*, 1925, pp. 173–79.
> A good statement of the new forces that have forced revision.

National Society for the Study of Education; *Yearbooks*. (See page 544 for list of Reports of Committee on Economy of Time.)

*Rugg, Harold. "A Century of Curriculum Construction in American Schools"; in *Twenty-Sixth Yearbook*, National Society for the Study of Education, Part I, pp. 3–116.
> A splendid historical treatment of the forces that have shaped the curricula of American schools.

Seashore, C. E. "Education for Democracy and the Junior College"; in *School and Society*, vol. xxv, pp. 469–78. (April 23, 1927.)

CHAPTER XVII

PUBLIC SCHOOL EXTENSIONS

'1 ne many new forces — social, economic, national, and international — which have so materially affected the life of our Nation since the close of the Spanish-American War, and the entirely different conceptions as to the nature and scope and purpose of public education which we as a people have in time come to accept, have alike combined to cause us to see not only the importance of some form of education for all educable youths, but also the desirability of extending educational opportunities and advantages to adults and to prospective citizens, regardless of age. The result has been the enactment of new compulsory-attendance and child-labor laws, the development of part-time and citizenship training, a new interest in the training of handicapped children, and the beginnings of an extensive system of adult education. To these extensions of the public school system we now turn.

I. COMPULSORY ATTENDANCE AND CHILD LABOR

Compulsory school-attendance legislation. In the earlier days of our educational development we dealt with school delinquents much as the Church of the time dealt with religious delinquents. They were simply left outside the pale. As the Church could not be wrong and the difficulty must of course lie with the sinner, so the school felt itself to be right and the difficulty to be with the children who found the school unattractive and did not attend. Both Church and school have since seen fit to revise this judgment, as well as their methods of dealing with the young.

Though Massachusetts and Connecticut had had colonial laws requiring school attendance,[1] these in time fell into disuse, and the first modern compulsory-attendance law was enacted by Massachusetts, in 1852. This required all children between the ages of eight and fourteen to attend school for twelve weeks each year, six weeks of which must be consecutive. A number of other States

[1] The Massachusetts laws of 1647, and the Connecticut law of 1650. See Chapter II.

and Territories in time followed Massachusetts' lead, those before 1885 being as follows:

1864.	District of Columbia	1875.	Maine
1867.	Vermont		New Jersey
1871.	New Hampshire	1876.	Wyoming Territory
	Washington Territory	1877.	Ohio
1872.	Connecticut	1879.	Wisconsin
	New Mexico Territory	1883.	Rhode Island
1873.	Nevada		Illinois
1874.	New York		Dakota Territory
	Kansas		Montana Territory
	California		

Six other Western States and Territories were added by 1890, and by 1900 nearly all the Northern and Western States had enacted some form of a school-attendance law.[1] Finally in 1918, sixty-six years after Massachusetts had initiated the new legislation, the forty-eighth State, Mississippi, enacted a compulsory school-attendance law. The problem now passed from that of securing initial legislation to that of revising and extending and strengthening existing laws.

The uneven development of legislation. The history of compulsory-attendance legislation in the States has been much the same everywhere, and everywhere laws have been enacted only after overcoming strenuous opposition (**R. 281**). At first the laws were optional in character, and not infrequently required acceptance by vote of the cities or counties concerned before becoming effective. Later the law was made state-wide in application, but the compulsory period each year was short (ten to twelve weeks) and the age limits low (nine to twelve years). After this the struggle came to extend the time, often little by little, to include the entire period during which the schools are in session; to extend the age limits downward to eight and seven and upward to fourteen, fifteen, or sixteen; to make the law apply to children attending private and parochial schools as well as public schools, and to require co-operation from such schools in the enforcement of the law; to secure proper information as to the ages of children as a basis for enforcement; to require the appointment of attendance officers and the

[1] As late as 1890, though, but one State, Connecticut, had required attendance at school during the entire period the schools were in session. All the other States had followed the Massachusetts plan, requiring attendance for from twelve to twenty weeks, only a portion of which need be consecutive.

establishment of parental schools for the proper handling of cases; to institute some state supervision of local enforcement; and to connect school-attendance enforcement with the child-labor legislation of the State through a system of working permits and state inspection of mills, stores, and factories. As a consequence the development of compulsory-attendance legislation has been very uneven in our States, and attendance laws in almost all the stages of legislative evolution may still be found. On the one hand we have such States as Massachusetts, Connecticut, New York, Michigan, and Ohio, where good laws exist and the enforcement is relatively strict, and on the other hand such States as Alabama and Mississippi, where both the law and its enforcement are still weak.

Since 1900, and due more to the activity of persons concerned with social legislation and those interested in improving the physical and moral welfare of children than to educators themselves, there has been a general revision of the compulsory education laws of our States and the enactment of much new child-welfare and anti-child-labor legislation. As a result of this the labor of young children has been greatly restricted; work in many industries has been prohibited entirely, because of the danger to life and health; compulsory education has been extended in a majority of the States to cover the full school year; poverty, or dependent parents, in many States no longer serves as an excuse for non-attendance; often those having physical or mental defects also are included in the compulsion to attend, if their wants can be provided for; the school census has been changed so as to aid the location of children of compulsory-school age; and special officers have been authorized or ordered appointed to assist school authorities in enforcing the compulsory-attendance and child-labor laws. Having taxed their citizens to provide schools, the States have now required the children to attend and partake of the advantages provided. The schools, too, have made a close study of retarded pupils, because of the close connection found to exist between retardation in school and truancy and juvenile delinquency.

One result of this legislation. One of the results of all this legislation has been to throw, during the past quarter of a century, an entirely new burden on the schools. These laws have brought into the schools not only the truant and the incorrigible, who under former conditions either left early or were expelled, but also many children of the foreign-born who have no aptitude for book learning, and many children of inferior mental qualities who do not profit by ordinary classroom procedure. Still more, they have brought into the school the crippled, tubercular, deaf, epileptic, and blind, as well as the sick, needy, and physically unfit. By steadily raising the age at which children may leave school from ten or twelve up to fourteen and sixteen, our schools have come to contain many children who, having no natural aptitude for study, would at once, unless specially handled, become a nuisance in the school and tend to demoralize schoolroom procedure. These laws have thrown upon the school a new burden in the form of public expectancy for results,[1] whereas a compulsory-education law cannot create capacity to profit from education. Under the earlier educational conditions the school, unable to handle or educate such children, expelled them or let them drop from school and no longer concerned itself about them; now the public expects the school to get results with them. Consequently, within the past twenty-five years the whole attitude of the school toward such children has undergone a change, and an attempt, not always successful, has been made to salvage them and turn back to society as many of them as possible, trained for some form of social and personal usefulness.

Enlarging the educational opportunities of the schools. With the recent tendency of our States to insist on the education of all children until they are sixteen years of age, and for all the time the schools are in session, the need for modifications in schoolroom procedure to meet the needs of the children thus brought in has recently become very pressing. The result has been not only the establishment of differentiated and parallel courses of study, and special-type schools (Chapter XV), but also, in our better organized school systems, the provision of such a number of different types of school opportunities that somewhere in the school system every boy and girl may find the type of education suited to his or her peculiar needs. Where this cannot be done locally, due to the small size

[1] "Whereas, formerly, students were from a highly selected group, now America demands that we educate the whole group; whereas in earlier days pupils represented a narrow economic, social and intellectual level, today the public schools teach children from every economic level, from every social status, from every intellectual level. It is a much more difficult problem to teach all of the children than to teach those who want to learn. The earlier school could rest content with furnishing the selected student with an opportunity for learning by hearing classes; now it is necessary to teach with consummate skill if all children are to be given the modicum of training essential to American citizenship." (Walter A. Jessup, President University of Iowa.)

of the school system, it should be done by the county or by the State. Otherwise compulsory-education laws will only force children into schools from which they will get little of value and in which they will often prove troublesome, with a resulting increase of over-age children, refractory cases, and corporal punishment, and at the same time defeat the social and citizenship aims of the schools. It may cost more to train such children properly than it does the so-called normal children, but it is cheaper for society in the long run that the schools should do it. This is something that American communities have not as yet learned.

Double nature of the problem. Accordingly our schools have undertaken to organize new types of special classes to meet these new educational needs, and also to redirect some of their older instruction. The problem is a double one — first, that of providing for the needs of the classes forced in or forced to remain; and second, that of preventing the development of delinquency among other children of the school.

For the first class the remedy has been found largely in the differentiated courses of study we have just described; the organization of elementary industrial school work; the organization of non-English-speaking and over-age classes; the liberal use of play and school gardening; training in government and self-control; and particularly the use of the newer expression studies which involve the elements underlying the trades of modern industrial society. For the second class of children, those who early exhibit a tendency to be wayward, the problem is one of weighting down the wrong path by making it hard to follow, and of lighting up the right path by giving to it the rewards and social approval of the school as an institution.

New types of schools needed. In addition to the differentiations in courses and classes, and the new types of schools and instruction, indicated above, the handling of cases showing tendencies toward truancy and waywardness and incorrigibility involves the creation of one special type of class and two types of central schools. The first may be organized in any graded school building; the second has been organized in many cities, and could be organized for a county as a whole. The third has been organized by a few cities, and the need could also be met by providing a few state schools of the type. These may be described, briefly, as follows:

1. *The disciplinary class.* A special class, usually organized in the regular school building, to which refractory children of either sex may be assigned for an indefinite period, in part to relieve the regular class-room of these troublesome cases, and in part to adjust the school work and discipline to the needs of such children. These classes are kept small, are individual in their instruction, are taught by particularly capable teachers, and often have benches, tools, and other equipment in the room for teaching some of the expression subjects. Their purpose is to handle, in an efficient and orderly manner, and to turn back if possible into the main current of the school, those who have begun to manifest difficulty in fitting into the work of the ordinary class. When this cannot be done, the pupils may later be transferred to an industrial, or other type of special class or school.

2. *The parental school.* To this school those who cannot be controlled in the disciplinary classes may be sent. Incorrigible pupils from all the schools of a county are sometimes sent to one central county parental school, or a city and county may unite in maintaining such a school. Some of these children, too, can be turned back into the regular current of the school, but a larger percentage than in the disciplinary classes will be unable to profit there. Many can best be directed into the next type of school.

3. *Central schools for peculiar boys and girls.* The sexes now are arranged for separately, pupils are gathered into these schools largely on the basis of age, and without regard to school-grade advancement, and the effort is to discover in what lines such peculiar children may be made useful to society. Such schools emphasize instruction in music, industrial art, manual and domestic activities, play, dramatics, and group-organization and constructional and pre-vocational activities. Some of the pupils later can be sent to a regular trade school, public or private, while many will pass out into life at the end of the compulsory-school period. For such children instruction which leads toward such trades or occupations as carpentry, bricklaying, plastering, cement work, plumbing, electrical work, automobile repairing, and acting as chauffeur, gardener, waiter, baker, cook, and seamstress, has been found quite satisfactory.

State industrial schools. With a few pupils all these types of specialized instruction will fail, and such will need to be committed to a state school of a reformatory type, now usually known as a State Industrial School. Of all children enrolled in public and private schools of all kinds in the United States, in 1930, approximately 1 in 350 was in a State Industrial School. In these schools the sexes, and in the Southern States the two races also, are usually kept in separate institutions.

Reformatory education is only a century old. The first juvenile reform school was founded at Birmingham, England. in 1817, and the second was the New York House of Refuge, founded in 1824. But few additional schools were founded before 1850, but by 1900 there were 90 such schools in the United States, and by 1930 we had 173 state institutions, with approximately 70,000 boys and 21,000 girls, of whom 13 per cent were colored, who had been committed to them. Many of these were illiterate,[1] and many were feeble-minded or of low mentality. With the latter class the public school was doomed to fail from the first.

The earlier institutions were almost entirely for the older and more depraved children, the commitment of some crime usually being a prerequisite to being sent to the school. Recently other state institutions have been founded to handle the more youthful and less serious offenders, and these cover much the same ground as the central city schools for peculiar and over-age children, described above. The idea in this latter type of school is cure through re-education, rather than confinement and punishment.

The next step in the state system of education for delinquents is the penitentiary for youthful first offenders. Such institutions have recently been established in a few States, and, while not usually thought of as being part of the state educational system, in reality they should be so considered and conducted.

Useful adjuncts in enforcement. In the enforcement of the compulsory-attendance laws in any State, officers will find cases in which an aged or infirm parent, or other person standing in parental relation to the child, is, to some important degree, dependent upon the labor of the child for his means of support. While much fraud may be practiced here, and every case requires careful investigation by deputies, school nurses, visiting teachers, or special charity workers, to be sure of the facts, many cases of real need nevertheless are found in the cities among the foreign-born and the very poor.

The State is thus faced with the alternative of looking after the needs of the parent or of the child. If the parent is to be favored, the child will go without needed education; if the child is given the preference, the parent will be left in dire need for support. Within

[1] Of the number committed the last year for which statistics are available, 9.4 per cent could neither read nor write, while of the number discharged, the same year, all but 0.5 per cent had been taught to read and write. The percentages of those committed that were foreign-born, native-born, and of mixed parentage were about the same as in the population as a whole.

the past fifteen years some of our States have begun to cope with this phase of the problem of compulsory school-attendance by enacting legislation to protect the right of the child to his chance for an education, by providing that, in cases of real need, the working permit shall be refused the child and he shall be sent to school until the full required attendance has been completed. When this is done, in States having mothers' pension laws, the parent is cared for under such provisions, but elsewhere an allowance, or rather a credit, is made to the parent from the poor-relief funds of the county, at least equivalent in amount to what the child could have earned at labor. The attendance-officer may also, after investigation as to need, order shoes and clothing for the child from the poor-relief funds, if necessary to enable the child to attend school. The need of the parent is thus recognized, without the future citizen of the State being compelled to forego his birthright.[1]

The school nurse and the visiting teacher. In addition to the compulsory-attendance officer, two very useful assistants in the carrying into effect of a compulsory-attendance law are the school nurse and the visiting teacher, both of whom are relatively recent additions to our school systems. The school nurse dates from 1902, and the visiting teacher from 1906–07. Beginning first in the cities, most of our States have since provided for the appointment of school nurses, and a few States have also made legal provision for the appointment of the visiting or home teacher.[2]

The visiting teacher, who stands in an intermediate position between the classroom teacher on the one hand and the social worker on the other, is capable of very large usefulness in our cities in assisting in the enforcement of the compulsory-attendance laws. In county-unit school systems and smaller cities and villages, the school nurse can give somewhat the same type of assistance. Children irregular in attendance, children falling behind in their work, cases of probable home neglect or underfeeding, and cases involving moral delinquency or requiring serious discipline may alike be referred to the visiting teacher or nurse for investigation and report.

[1] See article on "Family Allowance System as a Protector of Children," by Paul H. Douglass, in September, 1925, issue of *Annals of the American Academy of Political and Social Science.*

[2] See article by R. F. Gray on "The Home Teacher in California," in *School and Society,* vol. 12, pp. 330–34 (October 16, 1920), describing the operation of the California law of 1915 providing for the visiting teacher. See also bulletin by Gleim, describing development in the States.

The visiting teacher or nurse thus comes into close contact and often intimate relations with the home, and is able to secure a type of co-operation denied to the attendance-officer. Each irregular or difficult case becomes a special case for individual study and adjustment, and the causes underlying the trouble are ascertained and, so far as possible, removed.

Child labor and the school. Closely connected with the enforcement of compulsory attendance is the problem of child labor, and that of the issuance of working permits to children allowing them to engage in certain kinds of labor for certain limited periods. While child-labor legislation began before compulsory-attendance legislation got under way,[1] and has somewhat paralleled it in its development, effective compulsory-attendance legislation has tended to outrun effective child-labor legislation. One finds today some form of child-labor legislation as well as some form of compulsory-attendance legislation in all the States, but the stringency of the laws varies greatly, as do the means provided for their enforcement. While a number of States now have reasonably satisfactory compulsory-attendance laws, in all respects except perhaps effective means for their enforcement, a smaller number of States have as yet enacted satisfactory child-labor laws.[2] One reason for this condition is that compulsory-attendance legislation has been largely a resultant of educational effort, has dealt with the relations of home and school and the child, and usually has not met with serious opposition in its enforcement. Child-labor legislation, on the other hand, has tried to regulate the employment of children in industry, has had to face the opposition of manufacturing and mining and amusement interests, and has drawn its chief support from organized labor and humanitarian sources.

There is, however, a clearly marked tendency today to study the question carefully, to enact good state laws regulating the labor of youths of school age, to provide stringent penalties for their violation, to create state inspectors to visit places of employment to see that the laws are obeyed, and to connect the issuance of all

[1] The first child-labor law was that enacted by the English Parliament in 1802, and the first laws in the United States were those of Rhode Island in 1840 and Massachusetts in 1842.

[2] By 1924, nine States had no law prohibiting all children under fourteen from working in factories and stores; twenty-three States with a fourteen-year minimum-age limit had weakened their laws with exceptions; fourteen States permitted children to go to work without evidence of a common-school education; nineteen States did not make physical fitness a condition of employment; and eleven States allowed excessive hours of employment.

work-permits closely with the enforcement of compulsory attendance in the school. The state laws of New York and Ohio form good examples of our best child-labor legislation, while the attendance laws and the factory-inspection laws of Massachusetts and Connecticut furnish good types of combined child-labor, school-attendance, and factory-inspection regulation.

National attempts at child-labor regulation. While the rising consciousness of the evils of child labor in an industrial society first found expression in laws enacted by the States, the issue became prominent enough, by 1906, for a bill to regulate child labor to be proposed in both houses of Congress. No action was taken until 1916, when a national child-labor law was enacted prohibiting the labor of those under fourteen on articles entering into interstate commerce. This law was declared unconstitutional by the United States Supreme Court in 1918, and in 1919 Congress enacted a similar law placing a tax on such articles. In 1922 this law also was declared unconstitutional. Finally, early in 1924, Congress proposed to the States an amendment (20th) to the Federal Constitution which read:

Sec. 1. The Congress shall have power to limit, regulate, and prohibit the labor of persons under the age of eighteen.

Sec. 2. The power of the several States is unimpaired by this article except that the operation of state laws shall be suspended to the extent necessary to give effect to legislation enacted by Congress.

Though this amendment passed the House by a vote of 297 to 69, and the Senate 61 to 23, it so far has failed to secure ratification by the necessary thirty-six States,[1] though the recent financial depression and the attention given unemployment have directed new attention to this amendment, and the prospects for its final ratification are brighter now than at any time since it was proposed.

The amendment met with vigorous opposition (**Rs. 282, 283**). The lines came to be drawn with particular reference to federal regulation of industry and the extension of federal authority in the States, the child-labor amendment being only a minor factor in the struggle.[2] The alignment of interests and forces was much the same

[1] This outcome was forecast by the vote in the United States Senate, where the tabulated vote showed 30 States favoring the amendment, 7 opposing, and 11 with a split vote and hence regarded as undecided.

[2] Many of those opposing the amendment, aside from manufacturers' organizations, did so probably with the hope thereby to stop, or at least check, many of the other movements

as has been in evidence ever since the movement for education and human welfare began, early in the nineteenth century.

Part-time school laws. In 1910 New York State attacked the problem in another way by enacting a permissive part-time schooling law. In 1911, Wisconsin passed a compulsory part-time education act which, as since amended, requires that all youths between fourteen and seventeen must either attend an all-day school or be regularly employed and in attendance at a continuation school for eight hours per week and for eight months of the year. Ohio in 1913, Pennsylvania in 1915, and Indiana in 1916 enacted part-time laws, the one in Pennsylvania being the best of the three. Little more was done during the war years, but in 1919, fourteen States, in 1920 five, and in 1921 one, enacted part-time instruction laws. By 1922, twenty-one States had enacted part-time education laws that were state-wide in their application, and twenty-two other States were helping to maintain some form of such instruction. These laws apply to young people over fourteen years of age who are employed, and require attendance at some form of part-time public school instruction until the youth becomes sixteen, seventeen, or eighteen years of age, the time required being from four to eight hours per week at special daytime classes, and usually for the full number of weeks that the public schools are in session. The part-time school thus deals with boys and girls who have left the regular public school permanently, with their schooling admittedly incomplete and inadequate,[1] and is representative of democratic government at its best in that it protects them at a critical period in their lives (**R. 284**).

The courses of instruction are designed to meet the workers' needs, the subjects are arranged in short unit-courses, intensive study is provided for skilled workers, courses to teach skill to the unskilled are offered, oral and written English is emphasized, instruction in the care of health and the duties and responsibilities of citizenship is provided, individual counsel and vocational guidance are available, and

---

for child-welfare legislation and the improvement of education in the States, which, once undertaken, are certain to call for millions in new expenditures. They do not want to see the principle involved in the co-operative work of the Department of Agriculture extended to human-welfare work or to public education.

[1] In 1926 a bill was proposed in the Massachusetts legislature to merge part-time and vocational education by requiring pupils between fourteen and sixteen, out on work permits, to work half time and go to school half time, thus continuing schooling up to sixteen.

permits for work and school-enrollment certificates are combined.[1] A fully organized plan for part-time instruction in a city would provide classes to meet seasonal and irregular employment conditions, as well as alternating attendance at school and employment at work, and all would be closely related to vocational counseling and guidance, and to employment supervision. The most difficult aspect of the part-time education problem is the magnitude of the task.[2]

Extending the compulsory-education period. From the discussion which has preceded, it will be seen that entirely new conceptions as to educational needs have come to us as a people during the past quarter-century. As our civilization and political life have grown in complexity, as our place in world affairs has become larger and more difficult, as the privileges and responsibilities of citizenship have increased, as our social and industrial life has become more extended, and as production has come to be more specialized and the possibility of change from one vocation to another more limited, we have come to see that both the nature and the extent of the education offered young people in preparation for life must both change and increase. As these truths have become recognized by our people, we note the extension of state requirements for attendance at school. The leaving-age has accordingly been increased from twelve to fourteen and sixteen, and in a few States to eighteen years of age — unless the pupil has completed all or a substantial part of the elementary school course, and in some cases the secondary school course — and the required period of attendance at school each year has been increased from a few months to the full term the schools are in session.

This legislation has been enacted in the interests of the State, as well as in the interests of the child.[3] During the years nominally

[1] Mr. O. D. Evans, principal of the Boston Continuation School, states the aim or function of the part-time school as follows:

    1. Conservation and extension of the education already acquired.

    2. Provision of opportunity for pre-vocational experience to aid in the choice of a vocation.

    3. Vocational guidance and follow-up work.

    4. The establishment of an efficient employment bureau.

    5. Tying school work with the job.

[2] So far less than a quarter of a million youths have been enrolled, out of a possible two millions and a quarter.

[3] Recent studies of adult learning and of intelligence levels have thrown some doubt as to the wisdom of long school-attendance requirements for all youths. See particularly E. L. Thorndike's *Adult Learning*, chap. XIII (New York, 1928).

devoted to high school, the youth passes from boyhood or girlhood into manhood and womanhood. The habits and ways of childhood and youth give way to the thoughts and ideals of adult life. It is a period during which the character of most young people is given its "set," and without school training the new adjustments are far too frequently made also without the guidance of home, church, or society. To provide educational and social direction during this transition period has been one of the purposes of the extension of school oversight and control (**R. 284**).

When one realizes that only about seventy-five per cent of our young people between fourteen and sixteen years of age are attending school, and that only about thirty-five per cent of those between sixteen and eighteen are registered in any kind of school, one can appreciate more readily the importance of extending the school period by legislation, or of providing part-time education for those who go to work. These years are too important as formative and training years to be neglected, while the money value of the earnings during these years is small. The industries, finding the unskilled labor of these youths unprofitable,[1] either discard them, pay them small wages, or establish schools to provide them with needed additional training. Since only the large employers can or will provide additional training, and since the provision of such training puts a handicap on the industry or employer providing it, general legislation to protect youths from exploitation and the State from danger has been made necessary, and the result has been the enactment of a number of state part-time educational laws.

A vast movement slowly taking form. One who gives any serious study to the related problems of compulsory school attendance and child labor can hardly fail to see that what has so far been done represents only the beginnings of a great movement, under way in Europe as well as in the United States, looking to an improvement of the conditions surrounding human living, and especially those concerning child life. The movement is recent, and as yet not under full headway. Factory laws, compulsory-attendance laws, and

[1] It has been estimated (Cooley) that 90 per cent of the wage-earning jobs open to youths under eighteen are undesirable from the point of view of offering opportunities for personal development and preparation for any sort of skilled employment, "but," says Cooley, "I know from practical experience with thousands that when the job is hooked up with the school the number of 'dead-end' situations is vastly diminished, and the 'dead-end' jobs cease to be the very great menace they otherwise constitute." (R. L. Cooley, in *Industrial Arts Magazine*, May, 1920.)

child-labor laws represent but the beginnings. Mothers'-pension laws, the establishment of juvenile courts, laws protecting women and girls, cigarette-sale laws, poolroom laws, obscene-literature laws, juvenile-delinquency laws, and the creation of children's code and child-welfare commissions [1] in the States are other expressions of the same welfare movement on the part of the States. The creation of Child Welfare Experimental Stations at a few of our state universities, to do for babies and children what has for long been done for hogs and corn, is still another expression of the rising popular interest in child-welfare problems. The creation of the Children's Bureau (1912) and the Women's Bureau (1918) in the Federal Department of Labor, and the enactment of the Sheppard-Towner Maternity Act (1921) are expressions of the same idea on the part of the Federal Government. The recent marked attention to the whole pre-school period of child life, as expressed in nurseries, nursery schools, clinics of many kinds, provisions for handicapped children, pre-school hygiene, health centers, pre-parental education, and the work of the visiting nurse and the visiting teacher are other expressions — as yet largely voluntary in character — of a rising interest in child and adult welfare on the part of a thinking minority of our people. The organization of the recent (1930) White House Conference on Child Health and Welfare is still another evidence of a rising interest in the problem.

By the time the next generation is in control of government we may expect to see strong child-welfare divisions in connection with our State Departments of Education, or State Departments of Health, and the Federal Government giving some such attention to the study of child and adult-welfare problems as it now gives to the study of those related to the office, the factory, the mine, and the farm. The more one considers the problems of compulsory school-attendance the closer are seen to be its relations to home conditions, pre-school care, child labor, mothers' pensions, factory and tenement laws, and the question of health. The immediate problem of the school is attendance, but society must face the many problems lying back of this one.

---

[1] By the beginning of 1924, twenty-nine States and the District of Columbia had, at some time during the preceding twelve years, created official commissions for the study and revision of child-welfare laws. Among the more successful of the state commissions were those of Minnesota, North Dakota, and Virginia.

II. THE EDUCATION OF HANDICAPPED CHILDREN

A new attitude toward the handicapped. On page 527 we mentioned briefly the organization of special types of classes to meet the special needs of those suffering from minor handicaps, such as the over-aged, non-English-speaking, speech defectives, tuberculars, and peculiar children, and on page 355 we mentioned very briefly the beginnings of an interest in the special instruction of the deaf, blind, and feeble-minded in the United States. Special schools for the first-mentioned classes have been organized almost wholly within the present century, but special institutions for the more seriously handicapped children began to be organized in this country about the middle of the nineteenth century. At first the feasibility of such instruction was doubted, as throughout all history it had never been done (**R. 285**). The work in most cases began privately, and it was some time before our people came to see the possibilities of such instruction or to be willing to pay for it. The first institutions were small, and the pupils taught were commonly exhibited in public to show what could be done, and to awaken interest in the work.

Up to about 1850 only a few States had taken up the problem of the education of their defective children, but today the education of defectives forms so important a part of the state's educational system that no book on public education in the United States would be considered complete without at least a brief statement regarding the origin and development of such special schools. The change in attitude toward educating such classes has come about as a part of the changed attitude of society on many questions involving human and social welfare. We now see that it is better for the State, as well as for the unfortunates themselves, that they be cared for properly and educated, as far as can be done, for self-respect, self-support, and some form of social usefulness. An uneducated defective is a dependent on someone or on society, and finds but little real enjoyment in life; an educated defective usually becomes able to support and care for himself, and sometimes to care for others in addition. So convinced have we at last become of the value of education for defectives that our American States are now somewhat generally requiring the attendance of defectives, after certain specified ages, at a state institution or a public-school class specialized for their training.

Education of the deaf. The attempt to educate the deaf really began in 1760 in France, when a school was opened in Paris for the instruction of poor deaf mutes (**R. 285**). A few years later a school was opened in Edinburgh, and in 1778 a third in Leipzig. In England the work remained a family monopoly up to 1819. The beginnings of this work in this country were made at Hartford, Connecticut, in 1817, by the Reverend Thomas H. Gallaudet (1787–1851). The school opened with seven pupils, and enrolled thirty-three during the year.[1] In 1819 Massachusetts provided for the

education of twenty pupils at Hartford, at state expense, and New Hampshire and Vermont soon adopted the same policy. In 1823 Kentucky established the first state school for the education of the deaf, and Ohio followed in 1827. Each obtained teachers from the Hartford school. From these beginnings, the movement has grown until today all but four of our American States support one or more

FIG. 139. THE REVEREND THOMAS H. GALLAUDET TEACHING THE DEAF AND DUMB

From a *bas-relief* on the monument of Gallaudet, erected by the deaf and dumb of the United States, in the grounds of the American Asylum, at Hartford, Connecticut.

special state schools for the education of the deaf. In 1930 there were 69 state schools, 16 schools under private control, and 83 schools as parts of city school systems, for the education of the deaf in the United States, with approximately eighteen thousand pupils enrolled, and with a cost for maintenance of approximately $500 per pupil per year in state schools, and $329 in private schools. In addition, there is maintained at Washington the only institution for the higher education of the deaf in the world — Gallaudet College.

[1] Gallaudet was a graduate of Yale College (1805) and Andover Theological Seminary. Becoming interested in the deaf, through the child of a neighbor, he went to England and France to study methods. The private school proprietors in England would not divulge their method, but in France Abbé Sicard taught him all that the French then knew. The school which he organized at Hartford trained practically all the instructors for schools of the deaf in this country for half a century. As a result the manual or sign alphabet became the dominant method of instruction.

Gallaudet, in establishing his Hartford school, followed the method he saw in France, which was the sign method. Among the things which Horace Mann saw in German lands, and commented upon favorably in his famous *Seventh Report*, was a new method of teaching the deaf. This was a pure oral method, using speech and lip reading, and excluding all signs and finger spelling. Mann considered this method much superior to that used in the schools of the United States. It will be remembered that Mann's *Seventh Report* was received with anything but an open-minded attitude (page 362)

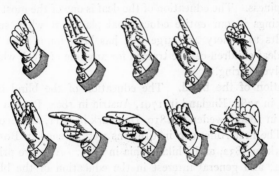

FIG. 140. THE SIGN MANUAL OF SPEECH

The first ten letters of the alphabet

and, as the teachers of the deaf did not agree with Mr. Mann, no change took place until 1867, when the Massachusetts legislature established the first oral-method school in the United States.[1] This creation awakened much opposition and discussion, but the method slowly made headway, and is today the one in general use with all normal-minded deaf.

State institutions cannot, however, conveniently receive such children before they are twelve years of age, whereas deaf children who are to learn to speak and read the lips should begin to receive instruction at the age of three or four. In 1869 the first city day-school for the oral instruction of little deaf children in the United States was organized in Boston, and very appropriately named the Horace Mann School. For the next twenty years there was much controversy as to the desirability of cities establishing such schools.

[1] This school came to be organized because of agitation in Massachusetts for a trial of the oral method. Finally, in 1867, John Clarke offered to endow a school for the deaf in that State, and the Clarke School was opened. The method of this school always has been oral.

In 1890 the "American Association to Promote the Teaching of Speech to the Deaf" was organized in New York, under the presidency of Dr. Alexander Graham Bell, and the influence of this Society and of Dr. Bell on the establishment of day schools for the oral instruction of deaf children has been both deep and lasting.[1] By 1930 there were eighty-five cities in twenty-two States which maintained, as a part of the city public school system, day schools where little deaf children were trained to speak and to read the lips, and fitted for further public school education and for social usefulness and happiness.   The education of the deaf is one of the most difficult undertakings in our entire educational plan, but when successful the results to society are large.   It has been found that normal-minded deaf children can be trained for any line of work which does not involve hearing.

Education of the blind.   The education of the blind began in France [2] in 1784, England in 1791, Austria in 1804, Prussia in 1806, Holland in 1808, Sweden in 1810, Denmark in 1811, and Scotland in 1812.   The first American institutions were opened in Boston and New York in 1832, and Philadelphia in 1833.   All were private institutions, and general interest in the education of the blind was awakened later by exhibiting the pupils trained in these institutions before legislatures and bodies of citizens.   The first book for the blind was printed at Paris, in 1786.   In 1825 a special raised alphabet for the blind was devised, which has greatly facilitated the reading process for them.[3]   In 1873 Congress began to aid the

[1] At the Eleventh Convention of American Instructors of the Deaf, in 1886, the following resolution was adopted:

"*Resolved*, that earnest and persistent efforts should be made in every school for the deaf to teach every pupil to speak and read from the lips, and that such efforts should only be abandoned when after thorough tests by experienced and competent teachers it is plainly evident that the measure of success attainable is so small as not to justify the necessary amount of labor."

At the Twelfth Convention, in 1890, the oral teachers present separated and organized the American Association to Promote the Teaching of Speech to the Deaf, with Dr. Alexander Graham Bell as president.   The Clarke School was designated as a training school for oral teachers.

[2] In 1771, at a fair in Paris, an innkeeper exhibited a group of blind men, dressed ridiculously and wearing pasteboard spectacles.   They gave a "concert," at which the people laughed as they had laughed at the peculiar efforts of the blind for centuries.   One of the spectators, Valentin Haüy, often spoken of as "the Moses of the blind," induced a bright-faced boy to quit begging and submit to instruction.   His success with this lad led to the founding, in 1784, of the first school for the blind in the world.

[3] Celebrating the centenary of the invention of Braille printing, Helen Keller wrote for the *New York Times:*

"The magic wand with which he wrought this miracle was a group of six dots, in which

American Printing House for the Blind, at Louisville, Kentucky. Partly because of this, partly because of our invention of special presses for embossing the letters, and partly because the Post-Office Department carries books for the blind free, America has printed more books and built up better libraries for the blind than has any other country. Practically all state libraries, and many city libraries, contain special libraries for the blind, and some city libraries maintain special reading rooms for them.

As with the deaf, the object in the education of the blind is to change them from dependents to self-sustaining men and women, and to promote their happiness as well. They are taught to read from books the print of which consists of a series of raised points, the alphabet of which is shown in Fig. 141. Besides learning to read, and being instructed orally from books, industrial work naturally plays an important part in their training. The chief industries in which the blind eventually find employment are basketry, weaving, hammock-making, carpet-weaving, cordage work, mattress-making, upholstering, broom- and brush-making, toy-making, and chair caning, though the wonderful results recently achieved in the re-education of blinded soldiers promises to open up many new opportunities and lines of instruction. The blind showing musical talent are educated as musicians, organists, etc., or as piano-tuners, while still others of special ability become teachers and ministers.

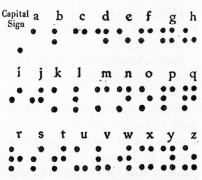

(Revised Braille, Grade 1 1/2)

FIG. 141. THE AMERICAN BRAILLE ALPHABET FOR THE BLIND

Devised in 1825, and now used all over the world. The alphabet is made by using parts of a six-point type :: A letter is capitalized by prefixing to it one lower point, with a little space before the letter, thus, for capital B, .:

the vertical line consists of three dots and the horizontal of two. The combination of these dots in various positions produces characters to each of which we assign a particular meaning, just as the seeing do to characters of print. Sixty-three combinations of these six dots may be used.... Braille's invention was as marvelous as any fairy tale. Only six dots! Yet when he touched a blank sheet of paper it became alive with words that sparkled in the darkness of the blind!"

We have recently had two United States Senators who were blind. A century ago the blind were dependents, and the adult blind lived largely in almshouses; today most of the normal-minded blind care for themselves, and some have families of their own. The United States Census Reports now show relatively few adult blind in alms-houses.

There are at present fifty-eight state or state-aided schools for the blind in the United States, and ten private schools. About twenty-five cities also maintain one or more schools for the blind as parts of the city school system. The first kindergarten for the blind was established in Germany, in 1861; and the first school for the colored blind by North Carolina, in 1869. The first public city school for the blind was established by New York in 1909. By 1913 this city had opened eleven additional classes for blind children, and two classes for children with contagious eye diseases.

Special schools for crippled children. The first attempt to educate crippled children in schools especially adapted to their needs was made in Munich, in 1832. The model school in Europe for the education of cripples was established in Copenhagen, in 1872. The work was begun privately in New York City, in 1861. In 1898 the London School Board undertook to provide classes for crippled children. In January, 1899, the city of Chicago established the first public school for crippled children in the United States. In 1898 there was organized in New York City "The Guild for Crippled Children of the Poor," and in 1900 the "Crippled Children's East Side Free School" began work. During the next six years a number of other private-aid organizations also opened schools for crippled children, and in 1906 the New York City Board of Education began the organization of such special classes in the public schools. By 1912 the city was educating, in 23 special classes, about 450 of the estimated 18,000 crippled children in the city. In 1907 Massachusetts opened the first state institution for the care and education of crippled and deformed children in the United States. Since this time a number of cities have organized special classes or schools to care better for these otherwise normal school children.

Open-air classes. This type of class has come in with the recent new interest in health education, it being designed to enable physically run-down children to continue their education and at the same time regain health and physical vitality. Such classes are held in the open air, the children are well fed and warmly clad, the hygienic conditions are closely supervised, and the instruction is carefully adjusted to the needs and capacities of the children. The first open-air school was organized in Berlin, in 1904, London opened its first open-air school in 1907, and the first in the United States was opened at Providence, in 1908. Boston and New York City opened similar schools the same year, and Chicago in 1909. The movement spread rapidly, and by 1912 forty-four American cities had organized similar special classes. The number of these is probably in excess of one hundred today.

In this country the classes have so far been confined largely to helping tubercular children, but in the European cities much more has been done than with us in caring for and improving children suffering from various forms of physical debility and subnormal vitality. With the better ventilation and less overheating of school-rooms, the need for open-air classes, except for the tubercular, is decreasing.

Education of the feeble-minded. Before the nineteenth century the feeble-minded and idiotic were the jokes of society, and no one thought of being able to do anything for them (**R. 285**). In 1811 Napoleon ordered a census of such individuals, and in 1816 the first school for their training was founded at Salzburg, in Austria. The school was unsuccessful, and closed in 1835. The real beginning of the training of the feeble-minded was made in France by Edouard Seguin (1812–1880), "The Apostle of the Idiot," in 1837, when he began a lifelong study of such people.[1] By 1845 three or four institutions for their study and training had been opened in Switzerland and Great Britain, and for a time it was thought that idiocy might be cured. Gallaudet had tried to educate such children at Hartford, about 1820, and a class for idiots was established at the Blind Asylum in Boston, in 1848. The interest aroused resulted in the creation of the Massachusetts School for Idiotic and Feeble-Minded Youth, in 1851, the first institution of its kind in the United States. By 1875 seven state and two private institutions had been established in this

[1] In 1839, Seguin, a graduate in medicine, established at Paris the first school for the training of the feeble-minded. In 1848 he came to America to reside, and took an active part in the organization of schools for the feeble-minded. Seguin, in his study of medicine, worked under the famous Dr. Itard, who had made special studies of the feeble-minded. Madame Montessori, when an assistant at the Psychiatric Clinic of the University of Rome, made a close study of the writings of Itard and Seguin. Guided by their writings, she devised a large amount of her materials for the teaching of children by her method.

country, but until about 1890 the movement for the education of the feeble-minded had made but little real headway. Within the past twenty years, as the social consequences of feeble-mindedness and idiocy have been brought to the attention of our people, a new interest in the institutional care of the worst cases, and the education within the range of their possibilities of the higher grade of feeble-minded children, has been awakened. As a result we have today fifty-six state institutions in forty States, and thirty-five private institutions in sixteen States, for the institutional care and education of the distinctively feeble-minded.

In 1867 the first city school class to train children of low-grade intelligence was organized in Germany, and all the larger cities of Germany later organized such special classes. Norway followed with a similar city organization in 1874, and England, Switzerland, and Austria about 1892. In 1893, the first American city, Providence, organized special instruction for children of low intelligence. Boston and Springfield did the same in 1898, and New York City in 1900. Since then approximately 150 American cities, up to 1930, had organized school classes for the segregation and training of the higher grades of children of low mental capacity. In the state institutions approximately fifty thousand feeble-minded persons are being cared for, and about twenty-five hundred in private institutions. The approximately 150 cities were educating, in special classes, fifty thousand children of this type in 1930. As studies show that approximately two per cent of all school children are of such low-grade intelligence that they need special classes, and that at least two persons in each thousand are definitely feeble-minded or idiotic, it will be seen that but a small percentage of those who should be educated separately or confined in institutions are as yet under proper educational or institutional care.[1]

New conceptions of the problem. The education of these children was at first largely of the old drill-subject type, but more recently

[1] A recent investigation made by the National Committee for Mental Hygiene reported 900,000 mentally deficient children who were "getting little or no benefit from the ordinary course of instruction in the public schools of the country." For these the Committee held that the States were as yet doing little "in providing the facilities for special-class instruction sorely needed by these children." The Committee found that fourteen States had as yet (1925) no laws on the subject, and that less than 50,000 mentally deficient children were being cared for. The recommendations of the Committee were better diagnosis, provision of special classes, supervision, and the placing of the whole subject of the education and training of handicapped children under the general care and oversight of the State Department of Education, that a proper state program may be carried out.

has been shifted largely to the expression-type of studies, with special emphasis on preparation, for the higher grades of such children, which will fit them into the occupations mentioned under the heading of *Central Schools for Peculiar Boys and Girls* (page 568). The different types of state institutions now provided are as shown in figure 142.

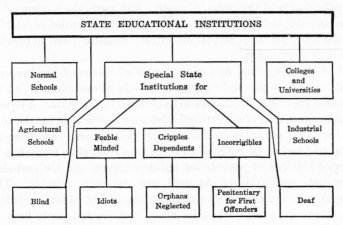

FIG. 142. EDUCATIONAL INSTITUTIONS MAINTAINED BY
THE STATE

As state educational institutions, other than public schools

With our new knowledge as to the nature and extent of idiocy, epilepsy, and feeble-mindedness, our States have, within the past fifteen years, given entirely new attention to the custodial care and education of such children. Massachusetts, New York, New Jersey, and Ohio have been among the leaders in dealing with the problem of feeble-mindedness. Large institutions have been created and equipped, custodial departments for the low-grade have been established, farm and industrial colonies have been organized, the trainable child has been provided with vocational opportunities, medical examination and treatment have become prominent, research departments for the study and classification of pupils have been added, and a few States have established separate colonies for the care of epileptics.

Created originally as schools and as a part of the common school system, there has recently been a marked change in the character of our American institutions for the feeble-minded. Since the development of the Binet-Simon scale for the measurement of intelligence, with the resulting grading of mental defectives, the earlier idea that feeble-mindedness is susceptible of cure has been given up, and the tendency has been to provide special city classes for the training of those with higher grades of intelligence, and for the State to take charge of the custodial cases. Still more, the tendency has been to enact laws making the commitment and retention in colonies of the lower grades of mental defectives mandatory, and to provide for their sterilization.

The handling, care, and education of all classes of handicapped children is thus seen to be primarily an educational problem, and a phase of the oversight and care of its children by the State. A square deal in the matter of educational advantages would call for the education of all according to abilities and possibilities, while from an economic and social point of view the education of as many handicapped children as possible for self-dependence, and the custodial care and sterilization of the unfit, are also very desirable. The largest part of the problem lies with those of low mentality, partly because so little can be done for many of them, and partly because of their very great numbers.

Significance of this work. It will have been noted that all the differentiations and extensions of educational effort which we have described in this and the two preceding chapters are recent in origin, both with us and in other parts of the world. The oldest of the special efforts here described, that of the education of the deaf, goes back less than a century, while the great development of state institutions for the education of delinquents and defectives has come since 1875. The earlier interest in defectives may, in a general way, be said to have been a phase of the great humanitarian movement which followed the Napoleonic wars, and found expression in education, poor relief, workingmen's societies, the protection of children, and anti-slavery propaganda.

Beginning about 1875 to 1880, and not becoming prominent until after about 1890 to 1900, a new interest in education and child welfare has become evident in all lands having what may be called an advanced type of civilization. The new interest is less humanitarian than the earlier, and is more an outgrowth of the changed conditions in the national life. There is a new consciousness of social needs, in part a truer Christian conception of one's duty to his fellow men, and a new feeling of need for the transformation of all possible dependents into independent members of society. The result has been a great expansion of public educational effort, as shown in the chart on page 589. In addition, with us, the new interest in providing so many new types of educational effort has arisen in large part because our American communities have come to see that, having committed themselves to the idea of educating all children, it is only fair and wise that there should be provided such a variety of schools, classes, and courses that every boy and girl may obtain in our schools, local or state, an education of such a type as each can use to the greatest personal and social advantage. The fact that we have recently come to see that many different types of schools and classes are required to provide adequately for the needs of all has been felt to be no reasonable ground for discrimination between children.

III. ADULT EDUCATION AND CITIZENSHIP

Evening schools. Providence is said to have established an evening school as early as 1810, New York in 1833, and Louisville in 1834. Baltimore organized six evening schools as early as 1840. In 1847 the new Board of Education for New York City was permitted by law to organize evening schools for males, as well as day schools, and similar permission was extended for females, in 1848, and to Brooklyn, in 1850. The first general state law for evening schools was enacted by Ohio, in 1839, and evening schools were opened in Cincinnati the following year. Massachusetts followed with a similar optional law in 1847. New York City opened the first evening school for girls in 1848, and in 1855 Cincinnati also opened evening schools for girls. The first public evening high school was opened in Cincinnati, in 1856, and similar schools were opened in New York City in 1866, Chicago and St. Louis in 1868, Philadelphia in 1869, and Boston in 1870. By 1870 there were 60 public evening high schools in the United States, and a larger number of evening elementary schools. By 1881, 32 cities were providing evening schools; by 1900, 165; by 1909, 233; and by 1916 the number had increased to 458, with 647,861 pupils enrolled. Since 1917, with the enactment of the Smith-Hughes Vocational Education Act (Chapter XIX), the number of cities providing technical evening-school instruction has materially increased the total, but accurate figures as to number are not available.

Originally evening schools were established to provide education for those unable to attend during the day, and such continued to be their important function up to about 1900. Since that time, however, the evening school, both elementary and high, has been greatly expanded and materially changed in character. With the more general enforcement of compulsory education, the urgent need for providing duplicate elementary schools for children at work during the day has in large part disappeared, as such children are now required to attend day elementary schools until they are fourteen, and in some States fifteen or sixteen years of age. In consequence, evening elementary schools are now chiefly useful, in States enforcing a good compulsory-education law, in providing the foreign-born with the elements of an English education, and in preparing would-be voters for citizenship. As this change has come, the evening schools have turned from the teaching of youth to the teaching of those of more advanced age, and grown vastly in importance. While continuing to offer cultural studies for those who have completed the elementary schools and wish, while working, to continue study, they have now largely become schools for study along scientific, technical, home arts, commercial, and industrial lines. A few use the evening high schools to prepare for entrance to college or a technical school, but the large majority attend them to attain greater efficiency in the occupations in which they are engaged. Technical, home arts, trade, and business studies are in greatest demand, and many trades-apprentices now attend regularly.[1] The enactment of the Smith-Hughes bill for aid for vocational education, and described in Chapter XIX, has resulted in a further marked expansion of the evening high school along vocational lines. Such studies as applied mathematics, navigation, mechanical drawing, machine design, engineering subjects, physics, chemistry, the various trades, automobile work, salesmanship, home economics, accounting, business management, and similar studies now hold a prominent place in evening high school work.

Adult education. Compared with England and France, the

[1] For example, in a number of New Jersey cities the employers have made apprenticeship agreements with the evening schools for the benefit of their employees. The school provides job co-ordinators for the boys, who connect the school work closely with the needs of the trades represented.

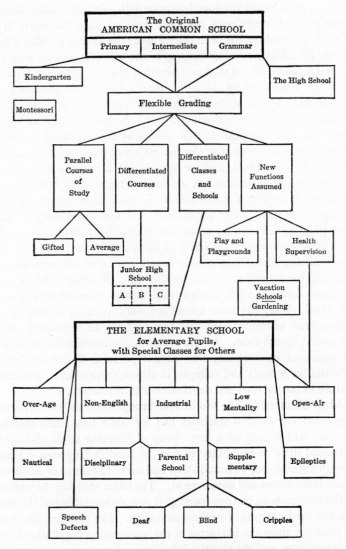

FIG. 143. EVOLUTION OF THE EXTENSIONS OF AMERICAN
PUBLIC EDUCATION

United States has as yet done but little with adult education, though a new interest in the work has been evident since the World War. What has been done has been chiefly along the lines of evening school classes for adults, evening lectures in the schoolhouses on topics of general interest, efforts at the elimination of adult illiteracy, farmers' institutes conducted by the agricultural colleges, and university extension work by the state universities. What has been done so far, though, marks but a beginning of what the coming decades are almost certain to demand as new phases of the educational service. As new national needs arise the conception of public education must broaden to meet them, and we may expect to see the scope of our systems of public instruction gradually extended to include more and more of the forms of adult education now under private or institutional auspices.[1] The importance and the desirability of carefully planned schemes for adult education, in a modern democratic form of government, is not likely to be overestimated, and adequate provision for such study is now recognized as an essential part of any plan for general education by the State (R. 286). The demand for many forms of adult educational offerings, growing rapidly since the World War, has been intensified since 1930 by reason of the wide-spread unemployment and the need for an intelligent use of the added leisure time. A wide program of education for citizens of all ages and occupations, who cannot partake of the regular instruction in schools and colleges, is almost certain to be a marked feature of our educational development in the future.

Adult illiterates. The World War brought seriously to our attention what our Census statistics had for some time been showing, that we had among us a large body of illiterate adult males who possessed little or no ability to use the English language. Many, though naturalized, we found know and care little for us or our democratic institutions and government. The chart showing the nativity of the foreign-born in 1930 (page 485) reveals something of the character of the immigrants we have among us. The two circular charts on page 591 show the character of the male voting population in the United States, and the ability of the foreign-born to use our common language, as shown by the Census of 1930. The situation disclosed

[1] Good examples of types of work, once under private or institutional control, are the many courses on such subjects as salesmanship, advertising, house decorating, and economic subjects provided, a quarter of a century ago, almost alone by the Y.M.C.A. of the United States.

by these charts, while much better than two decades ago, still is not a particularly agreeable one. Even more, the problem is worst in our large cities, where assimilation is most difficult. In the army draft for soldiers for the World War armies, eight per cent of all the young men called up could understand no English, and an almost equal additional number could understand so little as scarcely to be able to follow commands.[1] Such conditions are a serious menace to the national welfare of any Nation.

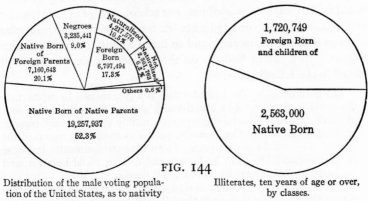

FIG. 144

Distribution of the male voting population of the United States, as to nativity

Illiterates, ten years of age or over, by classes.

(From the Census of 1930)

While providing schooling for such of the children of the foreign-born as choose to attend public rather than parochial schools, we have, through all our history, left to chance the Americanization of the adults. The outbreak of the World War, and the beginning of hostile propaganda among our people by the agents of Germany and Austria-Hungary, brought forcibly to our attention the fact that we have for long reposed in a false security. A long list of strikes among foreign-born colonies in our munition factories; "accidents" and explosions on docks and ships; the burning of barns and crops; the formation of "leagues" and "societies" interested in other than our national welfare; meetings of alien races for racial ends; the new prominence of the I.W.W.; the prominence given to the hyphen by the German-Americans, Irish-Americans, and others; the activity

[1] The National Academy of Sciences, from a study of the data as to the recruits, has estimated that about one fourth of the American army were not "functionally literate" — that is, knew so little of the English language that they were only partially literate.

of the foreign-language press, and even the traitorous nature of some of the newspapers previously regarded as American — these and many other happenings led us quickly to see that we had in the past been very negligent, and that we were facing a vast social problem involving our national security and unity and the preservation of our national ideals.

One result of this revelation was the enactment of immigration-quota laws and a strict limitation of future intake (page 487). For the first time we as a Nation realized that national safety and national welfare alike demanded that our schools engage in a systematic and organized endeavor to educate the foreign-born in the principles and ideals of our democracy, and to make English our one common tongue. In a recent bulletin on the subject the danger was well stated in the following words:

> The government of the United States is a government by representation, and its integrity and effectiveness depend upon the intelligence of all the people. This intelligence rests mainly upon the easy transfer of thought and information from one person to another by means of the spoken word and the printed page. In an illiterate community the sense of civic responsibility is at its lowest, and disease, social isolation, and industrial inefficiency are found in highest degree.
>
> It is difficult for those who can read easily to form even a bare conception of the mental limitations of the illiterate, the near-illiterate, and the non-reader. It is still harder to appreciate the material handicaps to earning a livelihood entailed by illiteracy. While illiteracy does not necessarily imply ignorance, it does predicate lack of information, comprehension, and understanding. It increases prejudice, suspicion and passion, and diminishes natural appreciation and power to co-operate, yet co-operation is the essence of modern civilization, and inability to co-operate is the basis of race hatred. So that illiteracy is clearly a topic for national solicitude, and its eradication a proper subject for governmental action.

Citizenship classes. In 1915–16, under the lead of the United States Bureau of Education, our cities made the beginnings, through their adult citizenship classes, of what now seems destined to grow into a great campaign for the better assimilation of the adult foreign-born, and the stamping-out not only of illiteracy, but of the lack of ability to use and understand the English language as well.[1] We

[1] "Restricted immigration has emphasized the necessity for education for intelligent citizenship.... It has brought home civic responsibility, and the classes contain thousands who have long been alien residents of this country and yet unable to speak English. The value of English-speaking communities is being impressed deeply on town officials." (Comment by the State Commissioner of Education, in *Connecticut School Report*, 1927.)

have in the past cared little as to whether those coming among us became naturalized or not, and we have even admitted those still owing allegiance to other Nations to important positions in local, state, and even national governmental work. We have had legal requirements for naturalization, to be sure, but no facilities have been provided to enable the foreign-born to meet these requirements. We have required the ability to "understand English," and that the applicant be "attached to the principles of the Constitution," but we have provided no pre-citizenship education, and the naturalization proceedings before judges, especially about election time, have too frequently been mere farces.

We see now that our schools must at once take on another new function, that of providing special classes and night schools, on an adequate scale, that will induct the foreign-born into the use of English as his common speech, and prepare him for naturalization by training him in the history and principles of our government, thus fitting him for proper membership in our national life by educating him along political, social, industrial, and sanitary lines. He, and she, must be educated for good citizenship if they are to remain among us.

The New York literacy law. New York State has recently taken the whole matter of illiteracy and citizenship properly in hand by the enactment (1923) of a revision of the election law — based on an amendment [1] to the state constitution (1921) — which placed with the Regents of the University of the State of New York (State Board of Education) the sole authority to prescribe rules and regulations for the issuance of certificates of literacy to all new voters — native and foreign-born — in the State. Without such a certificate of literacy no new voter (after January 1, 1922) may be registered for voting. These certificates, which must be issued through the offices of the superintendents of schools throughout the State, are to be presented as evidence to the election boards when registering. They may be based on the diploma of graduation from an eighth-grade elementary school, or any higher school in which English has

[1] This amendment was first proposed in the constitutional convention of 1894, and was under discussion afterward. It was finally adopted at the November election of 1921, by a majority of 264,211. It reads:

"After January 1, 1922, no person shall be entitled to vote by attaining majority, by naturalization, or otherwise, unless such person is also able, except for physical disability, to read and write English, and suitable laws shall be passed by the legislature to enforce this provision."

been the language of instruction; or they may be granted to those who have completed the sixth grade of the public schools, or its equivalent, or to those who successfully pass a literacy test provided by the state department of education.[1] This is a most commendable type of state legislation, and one that should be followed generally by our States. Were Congress to enact a general law requiring ability to read and write English intelligently (sixth-grade standard) for all aliens, at the time they take out their final citizenship papers, and for all persons for voting at a Federal election, a nation-wide campaign for literacy and an intelligent electorate could be waged with much better chances of success.

In different places a number of other plans have been tried, in an effort to reach the illiterates and the foreign-born, with a view to influencing the home toward American standards. Some of the plans which have proved quite effective are the home teacher, in California and elsewhere; the community-center and mothers'-aid organizations, in many places; the logging-camp schools of the Northwest; and the "Moonlight Schools" of the mountains of Kentucky.

Who constitute our illiterates. The Federal Census of 1930 showed that we still had 4,283,749 persons in the United States, ten years of age or over, who could not read or write, and that of these 1,720,749 were foreign-born or the children of foreign-born parents. Although there were 648,152 fewer illiterates in 1930 than ten years earlier, the decrease seemed hardly comparable to the wide-spread programs for the elimination of illiteracy which our schools have carried out since the close of the World War. An analysis of the figures reveals that it is the Negroes of the South, and the unassimilated foreign-born in the Northern and Western States, who constitute our illiterates,[2] and shows that illiteracy is confined to no section of the country but is still a national problem.

[1] See article by J. R. Voorhis, in *Education Review*, vol. 67, pp. 1–4 (January, 1924), which gives samples of the New York State Regents' literacy tests for the use of the ballot. Also see article by J. C. Morrison, in *Journal of Educational Research*, vol. 12, pp. 145–55 (September, 1925), which reproduces tests given.

[2] The distribution of illiterates ten years of age or over, by classes and by decades, has been:

	1880	1890	1900	1910	1920	1930
All persons	17.0%	13.3%	10.7%	7.7%	6.0%	4.3%
Native whites	8.7	6.3	4.6	3.0	2.0	1.5
Foreign-born whites and of foreign parentage	12.0	15.3	14.5	13.6	13.9	10.5
Negroes	70.0	57.1	44.5	30.4	22.9	16.3

The children, whom the school is easily able to reach, Figure 145 shows have never been much of a problem.

The solution of the problem lies in the enforcement of compulsory-attendance laws that will reach all children, the provision of evening-school classes for illiterate adults, and the enactment of continuation-school laws for illiterate minors which will require them to continue under part-time instruction for a certain number of hours per week until a sixth-grade standard of proficiency is reached. Such legislation and educational provisions have now been generally accepted as a part of the work of public education. In addition, numerous special plans and classes have been ordered established to meet the needs of certain limited classes, such as schools for the children of migratory laborers, logging-camp and cannery schools, the

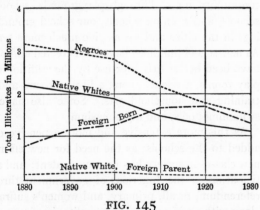

FIG. 145
WHO CONSTITUTE OUR ILLITERATES

"Moonlight Schools" of the mountains of Kentucky and elsewhere in the South,[1] and the visiting home teacher. Sometimes these classes have been placed under the special direction of the state department of education, sometimes under a state commission on immigration and housing, sometimes under a state department of labor or child welfare, and sometimes under other state agencies. Wherever placed, the work represents the interest of the State in the education of the illiterate with a view to their better assimilation into our American life.

The school as a community center. An important recent effort looking toward better training of our people for citizenship is the one to transform the public schoolhouse from a mere day school

---

[1] See *Moonlight Schools*, by Cora W. Stewart, Bulletin 20, 1913, United States Bureau of Education, for a description of these schools. Also a book by the same author and with the same title, published by E. P. Dutton & Co., New York, 1922.

for children into a usable center for the entire community life. In the eighties and the nineties the schoolhouses of our cities were used only between nine in the morning and three or four in the afternoon, and for from 150 to 180 days in the year. The remainder of the time the school plant stood idle, and boys and girls were not allowed even about the grounds. The buildings usually contained only classrooms and an office, and were not adapted to other than day-school uses. Today, everywhere, the tendency is to change these earlier conditions and to put the school plant to the largest possible community use. Through playgrounds, school gardens, vacation schools, and evening schools, our school grounds and school buildings in the cities and towns give much more service than formerly. As new school buildings have been erected and old ones rebuilt, they have been better fitted for use by the addition of an assembly hall, play rooms, a science room, a library room, and rooms for manual-training and household arts. Some also have workshops, baths, swimming-pools, and a gymnasium.

As this more extensive and more expensive equipment has been added to the schools; as the need for new efforts to assimilate the new classes in society has become evident; and as an increased participation in the functions of government through the initiative, referendum, recall, primary, and women's suffrage has come about, along with an increasing cosmopolitanism in our people; the demand has come that the public school, as the one great, active, unifying, non-racial, non-political, non-sectarian force in our national life, should take upon itself a new service and make of itself a center for the formation and education of community sentiment. As the school plant already belongs to the people, it has also been demanded that it be put to a more constant after-school use for the benefit of the community about it.

This has been done in many cities, and in a few rural communities as well. Starting almost entirely since 1900, statistics collected by the United States Bureau of Education show that hundreds of cities, and many consolidated rural schools, today carry on community-center activities in their school buildings. These activities included lectures on all kinds of human welfare topics, entertainments, adult society meetings, clubs for civic discussion, public meetings, dramatics, parties, social dancing, banquets, quiet reading and study, and the like.

The aim has been to make the public school building a center for the life of the community; to extend the work of the school into the homes, and thus influence the civic and social welfare of the people; and to broaden the popular conception of education by making it a life-long process.[1] We know that learning ability does not stop at the end of the school-age period (**R. 287**) but is a life-long process. We also know, from our studies of the elderly and the aged, how important a continuation of the learning process is in preventing an uninteresting and pessimistic old age.[1] Still more, we have recently learned how important continuation education is in maintaining the morale of the unemployed. A recent writer puts the matter well when he says:

> The public school as a community center is the answer to this national need. The community-center movement recognizes the fact that the mind matures more slowly than the body, and that education is a life-long process. While the public school is dedicated primarily to the welfare of the child, it is becoming daily more evident that the Nation's welfare requires it to be used for adults and youths as well. Notwithstanding the fact that it is our finest American invention and the most successful social enterprise undertaken, its golden age lies before it. It is now being discovered anew in its possibilities for larger service. The fact that all men desire knowledge is the fact which has justified the investment of millions in public school equipment; it is the fact which now justifies the use of this equipment for adults. In every part of the country there is a manifest tendency for the public school to develop into a house of the people to be used by them "for mutual aid in self-development." This is the significant fact at the heart of the community-center movement, and the touchstone of its value to the national welfare.

Library extension service. The public library, while frequently under the control of a different governing board, must nevertheless be regarded as a part of our system of public education, and library-

---

[1] "Comparing youth and middle age I find that there is hardly a subject in our curriculum that the average mature mind will not grasp with equal ease and with superior understanding. Take two men of equal intelligence, one forty-five and the other one twenty, both in good health and with good habits, both free from hampering worries, and turn them loose on a new subject in which they are both interested. One finds immediately that the man of age and experience has all the advantage." (Statement by President F. B. Robinson, College of the City of New York.)

[2] "Perhaps the greatest contrasts in life are noticeable in men and women after forty-five or fifty years of age because some are able at this time to make a transition from interests that are largely physical to those that are more largely mental and spiritual, while others are unable to make this transition and their old age is, therefore, uninteresting and pessimistic — one of the greatest tragedies of life." (L. R. Alderman, *Biennial Survey of Education, 1926–28*, p. 260.)

extension service as a form of educational extension. The State of New York began, in 1893, to send out assorted packages of books to communities within the State applying for them and not having local libraries. Wisconsin took up the work in 1895, and Minnesota, Iowa, California, and Ohio a little later. Today many of our States have organized some form of library extension. From the State the extension work passed to the counties, through the organization of the county free library system. California early began this type of work, and has been prominent in its development (R. 288). The extension of city library service to the high school, with the appointment of teacher librarians, and the extension of county library service to the larger consolidated schools of a county, have been further extensions of the work.

Library service involves a very important phase of public school extension, representing a form of adult continuation education of large value and usefulness. The schools must lay the foundations by teaching the tools of learning and by awakening interests and a desire to read; the library then supplies the means by which the education of one's self may be continued throughout life. To many an elderly man and woman the pleasure that comes from books obtained at the public library represents probably the largest return, after health and safety, they receive from government for the taxes they pay.[1] In but few States has the library service as yet been well developed, and nowhere has the saturation point been reached. Generally speaking, libraries do not dare to advertise their wares because they now are unable to meet the public demand.

Agricultural extension. By an Act of Congress, approved May 8, 1914, and commonly known as the Smith-Lever Co-operative Agricultural Extension Act, Congress made the beginnings of what must ultimately prove to be a very important national movement for adult education along the lines of the improvement of agriculture and rural home-life. This Act was an outcome of the Report of the Country Life Commission, appointed by President Roosevelt, in 1909, to examine into the life-needs of rural people and to suggest remedies. After analyzing the rural-life problem, this Commission recommended, among other things, that an effort be made to improve life for both men and women on our farms, with a view to making

[1] The Wisconsin Free Library Commission recently printed a grateful letter from a farmer's wife, saying that she had read eighty books to her husband the preceding winter, largely while he was engaged in milking the cows.

the country a more satisfying place in which to live. The Smith-Lever Act provided for national aid to the States for "the diffusion among the people of useful and practical information on subjects relating to agriculture and home economics, and to encourage the application of the same," the work to be under the direction of the United States Department of Agriculture and to be done by the Agricultural Colleges in each State. The work must "consist of the giving of instruction and practical demonstrations in agriculture and home economics" to persons not attending the colleges. An important part of the educational work is to be through publications. For aiding the work national aid to the States was provided, and the amount set aside was further increased, in 1928, so that the total funds now amount to $10,000 a year to each State and the Territory of Hawaii for printing and distributing information, $500,000 a year for the work of agricultural extension agents, and $4,100,000 a year for rural extension work, the two larger items to be distributed to the States in the proportion that the rural population in each State bears to the total rural population of the United States. Each State must double, from state sources, all national aid received. The far-reaching future importance of this new educational effort toward improving crops, stocks, and rural home-life among our people can hardly be overestimated. The rural teacher should know and keep in touch with this new work.

For the year 1931–32 this co-operative agricultural extension work required the services of 6179 people. Of this number 4444 were employed in the counties, of whom 2616 were county farm advisers, 1287 were employed in home demonstration work, 251 in boys' and girls' club work, and 290 in negro extension work in the Southern States. During a year it is estimated that workers under the Smith-Lever Act come into instructional contact with approximately 2,000,-000 farmers, 650,000 farm women, and 500,000 farm boys and girls in club work.

QUESTIONS FOR DISCUSSION

1. Show how the breakdown of the old apprentice system has: (a) made the educational problem more difficult, and (b) caused us to raise the compulsory school age.
2. Show how the changes to the factory system and the growth of manufacturing cities have made compulsory education more of a necessity.

3. Show how the increase of immigration has not only made compulsory attendance more necessary but also has compelled an enlargement of educational opportunity.

4. Would the class of children brought into the school by the first real enforcement of compulsory attendance laws be a more difficult class than would be found after a decade or more of enforcement? Why?

5. Would one be warranted in saying that the character of the compulsory attendance legislation of any State is an index to the popular interest in child protection? Why?

6. What changes in educational organization and in subject matter would be necessary if all unemployed youths up to eighteen were required to attend school.

7. How has the enforcement of compulsory attendance legislation created expectancies on the part of the public that the school finds it difficult to satisfy?

8. Why have the parent's needs now become a matter of state concern, whereas a generation or two ago the parent did not figure?

9. What new social and educational needs have called for the services of the Visiting Teacher?

10. If the compulsory school age is to be extended to fifteen or sixteen for all, what light is thrown on the problem of junior high school reorganization and courses of instruction by such legislation?

11. In quite recent years there has been a strong effort made to break down much of our compulsory-attendance and child-labor legislation. How do you explain this new tendency? Can it be justified?

12. Just what kind of "a vast movement is slowly taking form" (page 575)? Do you think the prediction is sound, or not? Why?

13. Assuming that the prediction is realized, what new leisure-time problems for youth face us? Will this new leisure be beneficial to the race? Why?

14. How do you account for the recent great interest in the education of delinquents and defectives, after their age-long neglect?

15. How do you explain the marked interest in the education of the feeble-minded, compared with the comparative neglect, in the public schools, of the gifted child?

16. Was the assumption that feeble-mindedness could be remedied by education a natural early assumption? Why?

17. Indicate (a) the educational, and (b) the financial consequences of accepting the idea that all children are entitled to as good an education as their powers permit and their needs require.

18. Show how illiteracy and citizenship are even more national than state problems.

19. How would a general literacy election law, enacted by Congress, help in the solution of the illiteracy problem?

20. Show how assimilation is promoted by literacy, and retarded by illiteracy.

21. Show how and why a people with one common language is safer and happier than one having many.

22. Explain how the public school is the natural center for community activities for advancing the public welfare.
23. Show that library service is a very cheap and a very effective form of adult educational service.
24. Explain why agricultural and home-life extension is important enough to warrant national aid and state supervision.
25. Would you say that the Smith-Lever Act was a form of national aid for education in the States? Why?

SELECTED READINGS

In the accompanying volume of *Readings* the following selections, related to the subject matter of the chapter, are reproduced:

*281. Northrop: Objections to Compulsory Education Laws.
*282. Crabtree: National Regulation of Child Labor a Necessity.
*283. Forbes: Child Labor has an Educational Value.
*284. Snyder: An Act in the Interests of Children.
 285. Wallin: The Education of Handicapped Children.
 286. Frank: On the Firing Line of Democracy.
*287. Thorndike: Implications from a Study of Adult Learning.
 288. Ferguson: The Library and Country Life.

QUESTIONS ON THE READINGS

1. The objections listed by Northrop (281) are perfectly natural objections. When they can be so easily and so logically answered, how do you explain their persistence in the popular mind?
2. State the advantages of uniform national regulation, as argued for by Crabtree (282).
3. Do the objections of Forbes (283) constitute a real argument against general child-labor legislation? If so, how?
4. Restate Snyder's argument (284) for state part-time education laws.
5. Explain the relatively recent interest in the education of defectives and handicapped children (285), compared with their long neglect.
6. Picture a university with a state-wide campus (286).
7. What light do Thorndike's findings (287) throw on the enactment of compulsory school-attendance laws? On types of education needed?
8. Is a state library system (288) of any more value to rural than to city people? Why?

TOPICS FOR INVESTIGATION AND REPORT

1. History of the compulsory-education movement in the United States.
2. The organization and work of some parental school.
3. History of child-labor legislation in the United States.
4. The care of defectives.
5. The Chautauqua movement.
6. Literacy laws, and their effectiveness.

7. History and development of adult education.
8. History and development of library extension service.
9. The Smith-Lever work.

SELECTED REFERENCES

American Association for Adult Education. *Annual Reports.*

*Cook, W. A. "A Brief Survey of the Development of Compulsory Education in the United States"; in *Elementary School Teacher*, vol. 12, pp. 331–35. (March, 1912.)

  A historical survey.

Deutsch, A. "A Phase of Compulsory Education"; in *School and Society*, vol. 25, pp. 73–87. (February, 1917.)

  The new New York law; conditions as to enforcement.

*Dooley, W. H. *The Education of the Ne'er-do-Well.* 164 pp. Boston, 1916.

  Special needs of this class of children; adaptations of school work; and a constructive program for their instruction.

*Draper, A. S. *American Education.* 382 pp. Boston, 1909.

  The address on "Illiteracy and Compulsory Education," pp. 61–73, forms good supplemental reading for this chapter.

*Finney, R. L. "The Child Labor Amendment in Perspective"; in *School and Society*, vol. 21, pp. 233–35. (February 21, 1925.)

  The significance of the determined opposition to the amendment.

*Fletcher, H. J. "Our Divided Country"; in *Atlantic Monthly*, vol. 117, pp. 223–32. (February, 1916.)

  An excellent article on the problem presented by our un-Americanized foreign-born.

Horn, J. L. *The Education of Exceptional Children.* 344 pp. New York, 1924.

Irwin, E. J. *An Americanization Program.* 60 pp. Bulletin 30, 1923, United States Bureau of Education.

  A good study of work being done, and of plans of organization and administration.

Journal of Adult Education. Quarterly, 1929 to date.

*Kellor, Frances A. "The Education of the Immigrant"; in *Educational Review*, vol. 48, pp. 21–36. (June, 1914.)

  A very able and interesting article, pointing out the need of action.

*Learned, W. S. *The American Public Library and the Diffusion of Knowledge.* 89 pp. New York, 1924.

  The tax-supported library, and its future as an educational institution.

*Lord, H. C. *County Library Service.* 206 pp. American Library Association, Chicago, 1925.

  The county library system as the solution of the library problem for rural communities.

*Mahoney, J. J. *Americanization in the United States.* 42 pp. Bulletin 31, 1923, United States Bureau of Education.

  Excellent on what should be and is being done.

*Monroe, J. P. "The Grievance of the Average Boy against the Average School"; in *New Demands in Education*, pp. 3–25. Doubleday, Page & Co., New York, 1912.

A good statement from the point of view of the boy.

Monroe, Paul. *Cyclopedia of Education.* 5 vols. The Macmillan Co., New York, 1911–13.

The following articles are important:
1. "Attendance, Compulsory"; vol. I, pp. 285–95.
2. "Blind, Education of"; vol. I, pp. 395–401.
3. "Crippled Children, Education of"; vol. II, pp. 230–34.
4. "Deaf, Education of"; vol. II, pp. 257–65.
5. "Deaf Blind, Education of"; vol. II, pp. 265–70.
6. "Defectives, Education of"; vol. II, pp. 275–79.
7. "Gardens, School"; vol. III, pp. 10–12.
8. "Reform Schools"; vol. V, pp. 130–33.
9. "Special Classes"; vol. V, pp. 384–86.
10. "Speech Defects"; vol. V, pp. 389–91.
11. "Vacation Schools"; vol. V, pp. 701–02.

Perrin, J. W. "The Beginnings of Compulsory Education"; in *Educational Review*, vol. 25, pp. 240–48. (March, 1903.)

Early history of, before 1750.

*Reed, A. Y. "Child Labor Legislation — A Point of View"; in *Elementary School Journal*, vol. 23, pp. 276–83. (December, 1922.)

On the importance of an educational program to provide for the needs of pupils forced into school by restrictive labor legislation.

*Rejall, A. E. "A New Literacy Test for Voters"; in *School and Society*, vol. 19, pp. 233–38. (March 1, 1924.)

Good description of the New York law, and the tests used.

Sharlip, W., and Owens, A. A. *Adult Immigration Legislation.* New York, 1925.

Peculiar problems of adult education with foreign-born, with courses and techniques.

*Snedden, D. "The Public School and Juvenile Delinquency"; in *Educational Review*, vol. 33, pp. 374–85. (April, 1907.)

An excellent article on the handling of juvenile delinquents, and the place and work of the public schools in the process.

Thorndike, E. L. *Adult Education.* New York, 1926.

An excellent study of the problem, with conclusions different from those commonly held.

Wallin, J. E. W. *The Education of Handicapped Children.* 394 pp. Boston, 1924.

A standard textbook on the education of the feeble-minded.

CHAPTER XVIII

CHILD HEALTH AND WELFARE

A new type of school building. In 1847, it will be remembered (page 311), a new type of school building was worked out at Boston, and in 1848 the new Quincy Grammar School (Fig. 85, page 312), with its smaller classrooms and an assembly room, set a new pattern and standard in grade-school architecture. This type of school building, with minor modifications, continued to be the prevailing type for more than half a century.

Beginning about 1900, a superior type of elementary-school building began to be erected, and one progressively better adapted to the newer type of educational program by that time coming into use in our more progressive cities. With the introduction of the newer-type expression studies (page 518), and the reorganization of school systems to include junior high school, platoon-type organization, and Gary-school features, the older type of school building was found unfitted for teaching needs. The newer type of school building made provision not only for classrooms in which the drill and content instruction (page 518) could be given, but also had rooms for the kindergarten, manual training and home arts, a science room, music and drawing rooms, and an auditorium. There was also added play space, and an improvement in what had preceded in lighting, heating, ventilation, and sanitary arrangements. Figure 146 gives the space distribution of a modern elementary school of today, of two stories and a basement, which may be said to be the prevailing type of newer school building now in use in our cities. This type provides a structure adapted to a modern educational program, with emphasis alike on the drill, the content, and the expression subjects, and with proper provision for an adequate health service. That many school buildings, even in our cities, are not of this type,[1] is unfortunately still too true (**R. 289**).

[1] Probably no one in the United States has studied public school buildings as intensively as have Professors Strayer and Englehardt, of Teachers College, Columbia University. By a rating sheet which they developed, based on 1000 points for a perfect score, and 600–700 for a fairly satisfactory public school building, they found the median score for the public school buildings of 334 larger cities to be 463, distributed all the way from six buildings scoring between 1 and 100, to one building scoring between 900 and 1000.

Changes in construction and architecture. Along with the changes in the character and distribution of room space, which the figure given below shows, there has also come a change in almost every type of construction standards. Wood has largely given place to brick and concrete; the lighting has been changed from two sides to one, and so banked as to distribute it better; the heating and ventilation have been greatly improved; in smoky cities the air supplied the rooms is washed; much better artificial lighting has been provided; many new forms of desks and tables have been in-

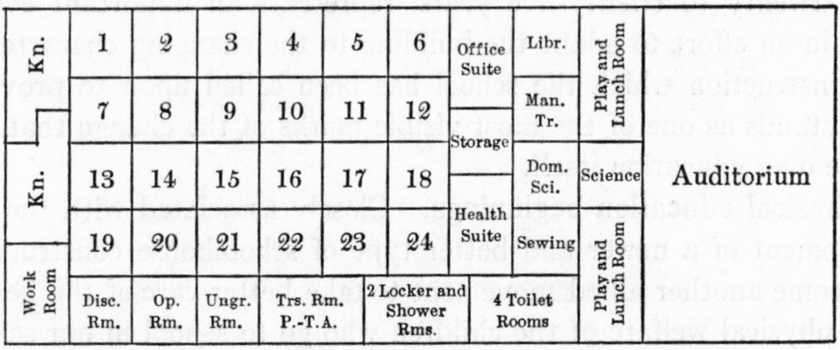

Kn.	1	2	3	4	5	6	Office Suite	Libr.	Play and Lunch Room	Auditorium
	7	8	9	10	11	12	Storage	Man. Tr.		
Kn.	13	14	15	16	17	18		Dom. Sci.	Science	
	19	20	21	22	23	24	Health Suite	Sewing	Play and Lunch Room	
Work Room	Disc. Rm.	Op. Rm.	Ungr. Rm.	Trs. Rm. P.-T.A.	2 Locker and Shower Rms.		4 Toilet Rooms			

FIG. 146. SPACE DISTRIBUTION OF AN ELEMENTARY SCHOOL OF TODAY

troduced; the cleaning is done more thoroughly, and the building is more sanitary; the drinking fountain has supplanted the drinking cup and water pail; the toilet facilities have been vastly changed in character and usefulness; and in dozens of other ways the comfort, convenience, sanitation, and attractiveness of school buildings have been enhanced. Still more, instead of crowding two- or three-story elementary-school buildings on a quarter of a city block, as used to be done quite commonly, and with almost no play space, the whole tendency of the past twenty-five years has been toward buildings of not more than two stories, outside of the largest cities, and the provision of ample play-ground space. A site of five acres for an elementary-school building, one of eight acres for a junior high school, and of twelve acres for a high school, and with an average city block as a minimum even in the larger cities, has come to be accepted as representing satisfactory modern standards.

In plan, organization, equipment, and purpose the school of today, in any of its divisions, is a vastly different institution from that of a third to a half century ago. To the ordinary citizen the change in the character of the work of the school may not be evident without an inspection, but the change in the character of the school plant is apparent even to those who give to the school only a passing glance.   The new school buildings now being erected in American communities attract attention not only by reason of the pleasing types of architecture employed, but also because of their size, equipment, and adaptability to a modern educational program.   The development which has taken place in the character of our school buildings within the past half century, and especially within the past twenty to twenty-five years, represents an important evolution in an effort to adapt the building to the changing character of the instruction which the school has been called upon to provide, and stands as one of the most visible marks of the change that has come over education itself.

Physical education beginnings.   Closely associated with the development of a newer and better type of schoolhouse construction has come another allied movement to take better care of the health and physical welfare of the children who go to school in our school buildings (**R. 289**).   The beginnings of such an interest may be said to have arisen about 1875 to 1880, with the introduction of Swedish gymnastics [1] into this country.   It was asserted then, and for a time assumed to be true, that physical training was almost the only approach to health and physical welfare, and that gymnastics and calisthenics were almost a necessity if health and strength were to be realized and maintained.   Accordingly we note (see chart, **Fig. 123**, page 473) the introduction of physical exercises into school work, with young people required to go through certain arm, leg, and trunk exercises for a few minutes at least twice a day.   This new instruction was better than nothing, but, as we know today, very far from actual needs.   There is much more to healthful living, we now know, than merely taking exercise.   Dr. John Sundwall, in an address at a Boston Conference a decade ago, well stated the problem when he said:

With the introduction and growth of physiology, biochemistry, pathology, and closely allied medical subjects, we began to realize more and more that there is no single approach to health and physical perfection. Indeed, we have learned that there are many factors which are of even

[1] There had been, to be sure, an earlier interest, in the decade of the thirties and the forties, which concerned itself with heavy German-type gymnastics and military drill, but the enthusiasm for this soon died out and it left no permanent influence.

greater importance in the maintenance of health than daily exercise. Malnutrition, focal and other infection, impaired elimination of the body's waste matter, insufficient sleep and rest, faulty habits of living, nervous instability — any of these may contribute more to a "break down" than does lack of exercise.

Although originally introduced and developed as a health measure, physical education almost from the first became lost in its particular techniques and failed to make use of the many new discoveries then being made by science and in medicine. The discovery and isolation of bacteria; the vast new knowledge beginning to come in as to the transmission and possibilities for the curbing and gradual elimination of many children's diseases; the spread of new information as to sanitary science and preventive medicine — all these new influences made little impression on the teachers and supervisors of school calisthenics. Concerning themselves largely with gymnastic drills, indoor games, and athletics, the important approaches to health and physical efficiency which medical workers were developing were not appreciated or applied by them. The rise of the play movement, about 1900, with its emphasis on free play and athletics, added further to the decline of the old physical training, although the play movement soon changed — for the older pupils — into competitive athletics with the consequent overtraining for a few and a bleacher type of exercise for the many.

Medical inspection and health supervision begin. Medical inspection of schools began in France, in 1837, though genuine medical inspection, in a modern sense, was not begun in France until 1879. The pioneer country was Sweden, where health officers were assigned to each large school as early as 1868. Norway made such appointments optional in 1885, and obligatory in 1891. Belgium began the work in 1874. Tests of eyesight were begun in Dresden in 1867, Frankfort-on-Main appointed the first German school physician in 1888. England first employed school nurses in 1887; and, in 1907, following the revelations as to low physical vitality growing out of the Boer War, adopted a mandatory medical inspection and health development act applying to England and Wales, and the year following Scotland did the same. Argentine and Chili both instituted such service in 1888, and Japan made medical inspection compulsory and universal in 1898.

In the United States the work was begun voluntarily in Boston, in 1894, following a series of epidemics, in an attempt to combat disease. The city was divided into fifty inspection districts, and fifty physicians were appointed to inspect the children in the schools each day. Chicago organized medical inspection in 1895, with nine districts and nine physicians; New York City in 1897, with one hundred and thirty-four inspectors; and Philadelphia in 1898, with fifteen. The first school nurse in the United States was employed in New York City, in 1902, and the idea at once proved to be of great value. From these larger cities the idea spread to the smaller ones, at first slowly, and then very rapidly. By 1911 as many as 411 cities had provided some form of medical inspection, and 415 school nurses were at work. Today some form of health service is found in almost every city, while a number of county-unit school systems have provided at least a traveling school nurse for the town and rural schools.[1] In 1906 Massachusetts adopted the first state medical inspection law, and by 1911 twenty States had enacted such legislation. In 1912 Minnesota organized the first "State Division of Health Supervision of Schools" in the United States, and this plan has since been followed by many other States.

This new work was welcomed as a desirable addition to the older physical training, but as the work was organized and developed it soon was realized that the attempt to detect and control disease, after it had become established, was only a first step in the process of health supervision, and that any school-health program of value had to be extended in many new directions. The school inspections brought to light an alarming number of physical defects, such as diseased teeth, nose and throat troubles, malnutrition, defective hearing and vision, heart and lung disorders, bone and joint diseases, and similar developmental infirmities. Taking average school children, although approximately 80 per cent of babies seem to be born in perfect condition, approximately 80 per cent of the school children are found to have actual or potential, and also largely curable, physical defects [2] (**R. 290**). Physical examinations to detect

[1] The Census of 1930 showed a rural population of approximately 51,000,000 people, and of these only 11 per cent were receiving any form of health supervision. Two hundred and thirty-one counties — 8 per cent of the total — had some form of rural health service under whole-time officers. In eighteen States not a single county had been organized for health supervision.

[2] Despite all the work that has been done and the much better knowledge as to healthful living which people today possess, the percentage of physical defects in school children has not experienced any great decline. In Boston, for example, where health work has been car-

hidden diseases, and a constructive health-and-physical-development program for the schools, were the natural outcomes of this new movement, and a new burden was added to the work of the school (**R. 291**). The movement came at first almost wholly from the medical profession, but it has been earnestly supported from the beginning by school officers.

Further development of the work. From mere medical inspection to detect contagious diseases, in which the health and physical welfare movement everywhere began, it was next extended to tests for eyesight and hearing, to be made by teachers or physicians, and since has been enlarged to include physical examinations to detect hidden physical defects [1] and diseases and a constructive health program for the schools.

The work now has come to include eye, ear, nose, throat, and teeth, as well as general physical examinations; the supervision of the teaching of hygiene in the schools, and to a certain extent the physical training and playground activities; and a constructive program for the development of the health and physical welfare of all children. The value of the remedial work in reducing physical defects among school children, when effective work is done, may be seen from the following:

PERCENTAGE OF PUPILS HAVING PHYSICAL DEFECTS

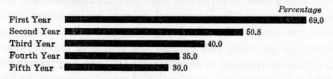

FIG. 147

RESULTS OF FIVE YEARS' WORK IN A PENNSYLVANIA CITY, AFTER THE ENACTMENT OF A STATE HEALTH WORK LAW

Properly to carry on this work has called for the organization of school clinics, and in the best modern school buildings a "health

ried on for a generation, the percentage of physical defects was 69 in 1915, and 50 in 1922. For the fourth class school districts (having less than 5000 population) of the State of Pennsylvania, the percentage in 1922 was 74 per cent. In New York State, in 1924, the average was 61.5 per cent.

[1] "These physical defects are of many types, and have arisen from various causes. Defects arising from infections and communicable diseases may also be traced to poor care during school age. These include tuberculosis, diseased tonsils, defective hearing, and organic heart disease." (Keane, C. H., *Physical Welfare of the School Child*, p. 8.)

suite" has been set apart for the use of the school physicians and nurses. There are several types of school clinics, the most common being the dental clinic, for the treatment of teeth and gums. Other clinics are for eye-testing and the accurate determination of eye defects, while others deal with ears, nose and throat, and adenoids and tonsils. Still other clinics relate to general physical condition, and include the poorly nourished. Still others deal with the mentally defective, and those seriously handicapped. In an elementary school a generalized clinic will cover many or all of the above in the pupil examinations.

Health work can now be carried on as satisfactorily in small cities and in county-unit school systems as in the larger places, and some knowledge of health needs and some ability to detect disease is every year becoming increasingly important for teachers. Child hygiene is a new study which teachers need to take up (**R. 292**).

The emphasis has now shifted from the detection of disease to its prevention, and from remedial procedures to the preservation of health. Within the past decade and a half, and particularly since the close of the World War (**R. 293**), the work has further developed to the extent that a number of our States are now inaugurating a comprehensive program of health and physical development work, embracing schoolhouse construction and sanitation; physical education, with a view to corrective work and the elimination of faulty posture and curable developmental defects; health supervision, to include the work of the school physician and school nurse, and a program for guarding and guiding the health of children; health training and instruction, to develop right attitudes and train in sound health habits; the proper organization of school programs; the health of teachers and janitors; and a teacher-training program in health and physical development work. Such a program, when organized, should extend to all children in all public, private, and parochial schools. The very fundamental change which has taken place in the nature and scope of educational hygiene, and the new aspects of the problem we now face, have been well stated by Terman and Almack (**R. 293**).

Size of the problem. That the work to be done is large may be seen from the following statistics, brought together by one of the committees of the recent White House Conference on Child Health and Protection. This committee stated that, out of 45,000,000 children in the United States, 35,000,000 are reasonably normal, while 10,000,000 are not. Of this 10,000,000:

> 6,000,000 are improperly nourished.
> 1,000,000 have speech defects.
> 1,000,000 have weak or damaged hearts.
> 675,000 present behavior problems.
> 450,000 are mentally retarded.
> 382,000 are tubercular.
> 342,000 have impaired hearing.
> 18,000 are totally deaf.
> 300,000 are crippled.
> 50,000 are partially blind.
> 14,000 are wholly blind.
> 200,000 are delinquent.
> 500,000 are dependent.

Of the 10,000,000 deficient children, more than 80 per cent are not receiving the necessary attention, though most of the deficiencies can be remedied.

An adequate program for health and physical development work is an important part of a national program for increasing the wealth of a Nation, and one that ultimately results in large financial returns. To decrease the number of those who are sick, and increase the number of those who are well, is adding to the productive capacity and the economic wealth of a people [1] just as certainly as is an increase in the number of pure-bred stock, miles of railway lines, going manufacturing concerns, or savings bank deposits. Health work in the schools, while an added expense [2] of course, is nevertheless one that pays for itself many times over, in the increased health and wealth and productive capacity of a people (**R. 289**).

Play and playground activities. Closely related to the health supervision of our schools is the play and playground work of the children, itself also a recent educational development. Probably the first playground organized in the United States especially for children was provided by the Children's Mission in Boston, in 1886.

---

[1] It is estimated that two and one half millions of us are seriously ill on any given day. Approximately six days out of every hundred of the school term are lost because of absence due to illness. In reducing this loss the schools have a great duty to perform in giving proper instruction to the pupils under their control.

[2] Keene, one of our best authorities, estimates an annual per capita cost of $5.00 to $6.00 a year for a good school health service. Then he adds:

"Expensive! Yes! It costs, per child enrolled in the schools, as much as smoking one ten-cent cigar a week, or going to a twenty-five-cent motion-picture show once a fortnight, or buying two-gallons of twenty-four-cent gasoline per month."

Two summer playgrounds were established privately in Philadelphia, in 1893, a sand garden in Providence in 1894, and a summer playground in Chicago in 1897. The first public playground was organized in Chicago in 1898. By 1911, 257 cities reported 1543 playgrounds as in operation, and 75 other cities known to have playgrounds did not report. The number has increased rapidly since 1911, and today organized play and playground directors are generally recognized necessities in the proper education of children.

At first the tendency was to provide separate grounds and management, under a city playground commission, but within the past fifteen years the tendency has been to place the direction of playgrounds under the school department of the city, and to organize and schedule play as a regular school subject. The inclination also has been marked, within recent years, to get away from the German type of *Turnen* exercises, and all highly organized types of group games; to permit of much free play and to use play not only for physical development but also to develop mental and moral qualities, and above all the ability to play the game fairly and to lose cheerfully. Still more, we now open the playgrounds, under paid teachers and playground directors, after school hours, on Saturdays and Sundays, and especially during the long summer vacation. The value of games and sports in sustaining the morale and physical stamina of the Allied armies on the Western Front was a new demonstration of the value of directed play.

Vacation schools. Another recent educational development, also along the line of child welfare, has been the organization of vacation schools. The first vacation school of which there is any record was held in the old First Church of Boston, as a private affair, in 1866. Its purpose was solely to get the children off the streets and under good influences. From 1868 to 1876 certain citizens voluntarily supported a vacation-school at Providence, which the School Committee permitted to be held in one of the school buildings. In 1894, Providence again began such schools, and in 1900 the city school authorities adopted them as a regular part of the city school system. The first city to establish vacation schools as a part of its city school organization was Newark, in 1885. In 1894, "The New York Society for Improving the Condition of the Poor" was permitted to open four vacation schools in the city, and in 1897 the vacation-school idea was adopted by the Board of Education and the schools taken over. In Cleveland, "The Ladies' Aid Society of the Old Stone Church" established the first vacation-school, in 1895, and in 1903 these volunteer schools were taken over by the city. In Chicago the Associated Charities in 1896, the University Settlement in 1897, and the Chicago Women's Clubs in 1898 opened vacation schools, and these have since been taken over by the city.

Almost everywhere, prior to 1900, vacation schools had their beginning in the voluntary effort of philanthropic organizations, being taken over later by the city school department. The early beginnings of these schools remind one of the early public school societies for the establishment of the first free schools. Within the past ten years the vacation-school idea has been accepted generally by our cities, and such schools are now maintained in hundreds of places. Begun first to take children off the streets, the idea has now changed to that of offering real instruction as well, though usually with more emphasis on the expression studies than is given in the regular winter schools. Manual training, domestic science, music, story-telling, nature-study, gardening, personal and community hygiene, local history and geography, excursions on Saturdays, play, swimming, and marching and drills occupy a large part of the instruction. The term usually is six weeks, though there was a noticeable tendency, after 1915, to extend the term to cover the entire summer vacation period, thus organizing the schools on an all-year four-quarter basis. Cleveland, Gary, Newark, and a few other places definitely provided such all-year schools. In many places the high school work has been extended as well, and either a six-weeks review school or a summer quarter has been provided.

School gardening. This is another recent activity undertaken by the school. The work began as an economic measure in Germany, in the first half of the nineteenth century, and was in time adopted quite generally by the state school systems of the different European nations, largely as a food-production measure. France and Denmark have in the past forty years made wonderful successes with such instruction. In this country the movement is little more than two decades old. The first school garden with us was the Wild Flower Garden, established at Roxbury, Massachusetts, in 1891. The gardens established, in 1897, by the National Cash Register Company, of Dayton, Ohio, for the children of its employees, were among the first real school gardens in this country. At first, school officials saw little in the idea, and practically all gardens organized before about twenty years ago were by private agencies. Only since about 1910 have the public schools become interested in the idea as an educational undertaking. After the outbreak of the World War, and the increasing world-wide scarcity of food which followed, the National Food Administration began an energetic campaign to stimulate the organization of school gardens as a food-production measure. In 1918 the United States Bureau of Education appointed a national organizer of school gardens, and an Educational Land Army of boys and girls was formed, under command of the President of the United States. The impetus thus given to the establishment of these gardens, together with the many valuable educational aspects of the work, promises to make school gardening with us, a new elementary-school subject of large importance.

School gardening comes in naturally as a phase of the vacation-school work, described above, as the gardens planted in the spring can be cared for during the summer as a part of the work of the vacation school. Wholly aside from the money-value and food-production aspects of the work, now most emphasized, the work makes a strong appeal from a purely educational point of view. To many city children it is almost the only contact they ever get with nature; to some it is a type of education in which they become deeply interested; and to many it means good and healthful exercise, under proper conditions, in the fresh air and sunshine. The nature-study value of the observation of how plants germinate, grow, and mature; the lessons in social co-operation which gardening can be made to teach; the industrial experience coming from the money value of the products raised; the efforts to excel developed by competition in production; the withdrawal of children from the games and vices of the streets; and the possibilities offered by the work for carrying over a vacation-school interest — all are features of the school gardening movement which are of much moral and social as well as educational value.

Safety education. Another recent addition to school instruction has been instruction in accident prevention, with a view to the promotion of human safety. Beginning about 1905, a few far-sighted employers began to study accidents in an attempt to reduce their number and seriousness, and between 1910 and 1920 a number of States enacted workingmen's compensation laws. In 1913 the National Safety Council [1] was organized to serve as a clearing house of information and a medium for study and research. Life and accident insurance companies also became deeply interested in the safety movement, and the very rapid increase in the number and seriousness of automobile accidents drew especial attention to the new movement. It was soon seen that mechanical safeguarding and law enforcement were not adequate to the task without a third factor, viz., safety education, and after about 1918 courses of instruction in safety education, accident prevention and care, and first-aid work began to find a place in the elementary-school curriculum, from the fourth grade up, in many city school systems, while textbooks for the use of both pupils and teachers soon became plentiful. It was soon found that the accident toll to school children could be reduced one half by simple instruction and training,[2] while the first-aid work was exceedingly valuable and had a large carry-over into the homes. Beginning as an industrial-safety movement, the school soon made of it a public-safety movement, and finally a home-safety movement as well. Another subject of instruction was thus added to our school curriculum, and incorporated into the health-and-welfare teaching of our schools.

The army-draft revelations. The appalling revelations of the army-draft medical examinations of 1917–18 came as a rude shock to the American people. In the first draft, approximately one in four of the young men between the ages of twenty-one and thirty, the time when a man should be in the prime of physical condition, was rejected for the army because of physical defects which would incapacitate him for the life of a soldier.[3] Others who were ac-

---

[1] This Council had done valuable work, both for industry and for education. The Educational Division of the Council has published a monthly magazine for school use, since 1920, entitled *Safety Education*. New York, No. 1 Park Avenue.

[2] "Not only is it true that the *saving* of life during the past sixteen years (1908–23) — the difference between actual deaths during that period and what the total would have been at the 1907 rate — is about five times our loss of life in the World War, but every two years — despite the automobile — we now save enough lives, as compared with the 1907 rate, to replace our sacrifices in France." (S. J. Williams, in *The Present Status of Safety Education*, p. 3.)

[3] The figures, based on the examination of 2,753,922 men, showed that 46.82 per cent of those examined were handicapped by one or more physical defects, and that in the case of 24.96 per cent the defects were so serious that they were rejected entirely for army service. The essentially rural States made a much better showing than the essentially urban States. Kansas, for example, showed but 35 per cent of defects, as against 65 per cent for Rhode Island. Rejection in Rhode Island reached 42 per cent.

cepted had to be placed in "developmental battalions" to bring them up to physical standard. Over all, approximately one third of those called for military service were found to be suffering from physical defects (**R. 291**), with the largest percentages rejected coming from the cities and manufacturing States, and the States having large numbers of the foreign-born.[1] This is well shown in Figure 148.

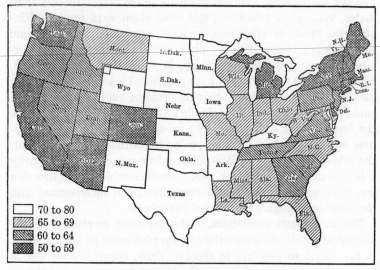

FIG. 148. PERCENTAGE OF DRAFTED MEN PASSING PHYSICAL EXAMINATION, BY STATES

After Ayres

Legend:
- 70 to 80
- 65 to 69
- 60 to 64
- 50 to 59

Such results from tests of the Nation's stamina were startling, and gave an impetus to new legislation that has since made physical training and health education a subject of much new interest (**R. 293**) to the American people. Prior to 1915 only three States — North Dakota (1899), Ohio (1904), and Idaho (1913) — had laws relating to physical education. During the war years, 1917–18, eight additional States enacted legislation requiring physical education to be given in the schools, and seventeen more States put similar laws

[1] It was found that 100,000 country boys produced 4790 more physically fit soldiers than an equal number of city boys; 100,000 whites, 1240 more soldiers than an equal number of colored; and 100,000 native-born 3500 more soldiers than an equal number of foreign-born. (L. P. Ayres, *The War with Germany*, p. 21.)

on their statute books before the close of the year 1921. Other States have followed since, and the movement now promises to become general. Thus physical education has come to the front again and, along with medical inspection and health teaching, has been made a requirement of law. Thus one of the by-products of the World War is a new and a deep interest in health and physical education, and there is every likelihood that we shall make progress in the scientific organization of the work during the next decade which might not have been made in twice the time if the War had not revealed to our people the extent and the importance of the problem.

Pre-school health-and-development work. Another by-product of the new interest in health and physical welfare has been the new attention given to babies and their mothers. As a result a new movement, under way both in this country and in Europe, has arisen, the purpose of which is to give much more attention to the pre-school years. The numerous health movements in our cities, the infant-welfare work now being developed, the classes being organized for instruction of mothers in infant hygiene, the baby-week campaigns, the child-conservation work — these and many other recent undertakings are directing new attention to the importance of the problems of maternity, infant care, and community hygiene.

The development of parental training, home teaching, infant care and welfare, and pre-parental education are parts of the health-and-welfare problem of a State. Until recently we have not concerned ourselves with these problems, conceiving of them as belonging to the home. The establishment of the Children's Bureau by the Federal Government in 1912, the passage of the Sheppard-Towner Maternity and Infancy Act in 1921 by Congress, and the creation of child hygiene and child welfare divisions by our States, are indicative of a change in attitude as to responsibility on the part of our people. Just what connection the forms of organization developed in our States to deal with these new problems ultimately will have with the school remains to be seen, but many who have thought on the problem feel that an extended (downward) kindergarten, and an extended school-health service, will in time be called upon to contribute much toward the working out and handling of these new problems. For such service the school already has a potential staff in its medical service — nurses, home-visiting teachers, teachers of home economics, and health supervisors. It may well be that, in the near future, pre-school health and welfare and guidance work may be added to the health and physical welfare program of our state school systems.[1]

Child-welfare research stations. In 1917 the State of Iowa inaugurated a new form of state welfare service for children, of large possible future significance, by the creation, in connection with its state university, of the Iowa Child Welfare Research Station. This new creation marked the beginnings of an attempt to do for child life what we have been doing for forty years and more for pigs and cattle, wheat and corn, and fruit and vegetables. The beginnings of the service were made in 1915, when the legislature enacted that any boy or girl in Iowa "under sixteen years of age who is afflicted with some deformity or suffering from some malady that probably can be remedied," and whose parents are unable to provide means for surgical and medical treatment and hospital care, might be treated free of expense in the hospitals of the university. In 1919 this age limit was removed. In 1917 the Iowa Child Welfare Research Station was established at the university — the first of its kind in this country or abroad — for scientific research in the conservation and development of normal and superior children.

The purpose of the work, as developed, is to make scientific analysis of the factors contributing to child betterment, to develop practical methods of child rearing, and "to give to parents dependable counsel to insure the continuous improvement of every child to the maximum ability consistent with its native endowment and special abilities." [2] In 1924 the State organized an Iowa Child Welfare Commission, and further extended the work of the station by authorizing this commission to call on the station for assistance in its work for delinquent, dependent, neglected, or illegitimate children. While, theoretically, the services of the station are

[1] Speaking on child welfare, a number of years ago, Herbert Hoover said: "If we would grapple with the whole child situation for one generation, our public health, economic efficiency, moral character, sanity, and the stability of our people would advance three generations in one."

[2] To this end the station has organized divisions of anthropometry, nutrition, maternity and infant hygiene, corrective speech, eugenics, sociology, and psychology; and co-operates with the university schools of public health, nursing, medicine, dentistry, the children's hospital, the psychopathic hospital, the extension division of the university, and the State Board of Health.

available to any parent in Iowa, in practice the facilities provided have proved entirely inadequate to meet the demands made upon them.[1]

Such work as this at Iowa, which has since been copied by a few other States, marks a mere beginning of a service that our States might provide, and that the Federal Government might aid in providing, which would be of the greatest value to the rising generation. Perhaps some day, when the world turns its energies

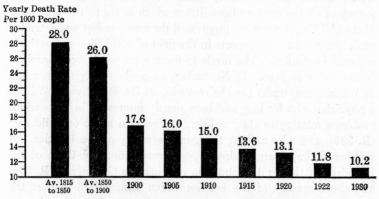

Yearly Death Rate
Per 1000 People

"Health as a rule is a purchasable commodity,
and the price is education."

FIG. 149. REDUCTION OF DEATH-RATE IN A CENTURY

from fighting and preparation for fighting, and realizes that well-developed children may be as valuable to a State as an increase in pork and butter fat or the yield of oats or barley, such child welfare stations will come to be regarded as a necessary part of a state educational service, and be supported accordingly.[2] Few other forms of service that a State can provide will do more to help teachers,

[1] On this point a recent (1924) bulletin of the station says: "The facilities are still quite inadequate to meet the many demands for the care and training of children. Many a crippled child has to wait months before it can be accommodated in the hospital where its lameness can be cured. Thousands of mothers could be assisted in the problems of child training if funds were at hand to extend the services that are now being developed. Urgent scientific problems are delayed in their solution because of the lack of trained workers and proper facilities."

[2] Yet in this State, the legislature recently increased the appropriation for the study and elimination of tuberculosis among cattle from $100,000 to $250,000, and refused to increase the appropriation for the investigation of tuberculosis among children from $5000 to $10,000

supervisors, and parents to care better for the health and the proper physical development of children of school and pre-school age.

The White House Conference. In 1929, President Hoover, who had long been interested in child-welfare work, effected the preliminary organization for what became known as The White House Conference on Child Health and Protection. A planning committee of twenty-seven men and women, whose national interests were closely related to the various phases of child health and protection, were first selected to develop plans for a comprehensive national survey of all the facts and conditions which relate to the well-being of the child. As the work progressed the membership was extended until more than 1200 experts in the field of child life were actively engaged in studies. The funds to finance the work were provided from private sources. In November, 1930, the full conference met at Washington, under the chairmanship of Dr. Ray Lyman Wilbur, a physician who for long had been deeply interested in the various problems relating to child welfare, had written much on child care (**R. 295**), and who at that time was Secretary of the Interior. A number of important addresses were made, notably those of the President of the United States in opening the Conference (**R. 294**) and the Secretary of the Interior which summarized in part the recommendations of the different committees. The more important parts of the work of the different committees, as well as a summary volume, have since been printed by a New York publishing house,[1] while "The Children's Charter" of child rights,[2] "for every child, regardless of race, or color, or situation, wherever he may live under the protection of the American flag," has been given wide circulation. The most important conference on child welfare ever conducted in this country was thus held under Federal auspices but without the Federal Government contributing in any financial way[3] to its success. The interest thus begun has since been contin-

[1] The Century Company, 353 Fourth Avenue, New York City. See list, page 626.

[2] The concluding item of this Charter reads as follows:

"XIX. To make everywhere available these minimum protections of the health and welfare of children, there should be a district, county, or community organization for health, education, or welfare, with full-time officials, co-ordinating with a state-wide program which will be responsive to a nation-wide service of general information, statistics, and scientific research."

[3] The Federal Government has given aid to the States since 1887, in increasing amounts, for agricultural research. The amount now is $90,000 a year to each State, and to Hawaii, Porto Rico, and Alaska, or a total grant of $4,590,000 a year. In addition these research stations all have the franking privilege for sending out their printed matter through the

ued by President and Mrs. Roosevelt through their deep interest in problems of child health and welfare.

As the published Reports of this Conference are read and its work becomes more generally known, and as its findings find a place for themselves in textbooks and medical practice, the influence of the work of the Conference on the future care of children, both in the school and in the home, is certain to be large.

Mental hygiene. What may be considered as the youngest child of the health-and-physical welfare movement is mental hygiene, in its application to child life. That imperfect mental reactions are an important factor in pupil retardation in school is now generally recognized. The importance of mental hygiene in school life and work has been well stated by Burnham,[1] in the following words:

> One of the greatest advances in child hygiene in recent years is the insight that mental hygiene is quite as important as bodily hygiene, and that objectively excellent methods in hygiene, important rules of health, and significant teaching all avail nothing unless right mental attitudes and right habits of healthful mental activity are developed. Thus, in connection with every school subject, every lesson in child hygiene, and every form of motor training, the dictates of common sense and the plain teachings of scientific mental hygiene are to be considered, as well as those of physical hygiene.

Proper and adequate attention to the teachings of mental hygiene, we now know, will result in an improved mental attitude, with all that that means for the social, mental, and physical health of the child. It means the reduction of school absence and retardation, and often not only more rapid progress but longer retention in school as well.

We know today the importance of good school buildings and surroundings in a mental-health program, and the very great importance of the health and energy and personality of the teacher herself (**R. 296**). After the teacher, the school nurse is of most importance in seeing that things go as they should. We now know that there should be joy and pleasure in the school work, that the ambitions of young people should be encouraged, that destructive

mails, and additional sums are spent in other ways, making a yearly total of about $5,000,000 for agricultural research. No federal grants are made for child-welfare research.

[1] Burnham, William P. *The Normal Child*, p. 3. New York, 1924.

criticism is not good, that worry and jealousies are harmful, that physical defects need attention, and that proper co-operation between home and school should be maintained if the best results from the point of view of mental hygiene are to be attained. These represent great changes in attitude from the school of the past. Only as our normal schools come to understand this new aspect of child hygiene, and make efforts to give their teachers training in understanding its requirements, shall we be able to build up in our schools that healthful atmosphere that results in the best of mental health and development (**Rs. 292, 296**).

The health of the teacher. Even a brief review of the new field of hygiene as it relates to the school, such as has been presented in this chapter, cannot fail to reveal the enormous change in conception as to the work and activities of the teacher which the past quarter of a century has witnessed. Not only is the teacher expected to know much more and to be much better trained, but a new type of teaching personality now is called for. The teacher himself, or herself, we now know should be an example of good physical and mental health, and should know how to keep himself or herself in that condition. Still more, the teacher should know how to organize and conduct the classroom work so as to stimulate good mental reactions. The success of any program for child health and physical and mental welfare is determined largely by the physical and mental health of the teacher, yet personal hygiene, which means good health-habits, is a matter to which teachers as a body give entirely too little care. The whole atmosphere of the classroom depends largely upon the physical and mental condition of the teacher. Only when she is physically and mentally well can she place before her pupils that model of vital force and good posture and wholesome attitude toward life which is essential if pupils themselves are to develop the proper attitudes toward physical and mental health and efficiency (**R. 296**). It is very probable that the physical efficiency of teachers is to play a much larger part in their selection and retention in the future than has been the case in the past. Certain it is that a course for teacher-training based only on a study of psychology, methods, and practice teaching has seen its day (**R. 292**). It is a far cry from the type of teacher who found employment half a century ago to the type that the future of American education will demand. Only as teachers become conscious of the physical and mental health aspects of what they do will the health of the Nation be made secure.

QUESTIONS FOR DISCUSSION

1. Show how an elementary-school building such as is represented in Figure 146 is "adapted to a modern teaching program," whereas the older type of grade-school building is not.

2. State something of the nature of the changes in our national life that have made a different type of education, and hence school building, necessary.

3. How do you explain the early teachers of physical education "becoming lost in their own techniques" and hence failing to develop a health program?

4. Explain the implications of Dr. Sundwall's statement for the teacher.

5. Characterize the three main stages in the development of a school health program, and show why they naturally came in this order.

6. Show how the new interest in school health work was a natural outcome of the World War experiences.

7. How do you account for the long neglect of child welfare, contrasted with the recent interest in it as seen in health work, safety education, playgrounds, clinics, etc.?

8. Is the vacation school more a phase of public school work, or of child-welfare work? Why?

9. Do you agree with the statement that a health-and-physical-development program should be made to apply to private and parochial as well as public schools? Why?

10. How do you explain the results shown in Figure 148?

11. Show how pre-school health-and-development work contributes to the success of school work later on.

12. Prove the statement that the improvement of the health of a Nation increases its economic wealth, and in consequence its ability to have, to produce, and to enjoy.

13. Why have States considered an increase in pork and butter fat more important than the creation of well-developed children?

14. It is frequently stated that the White House Conference was the most important single movement for child welfare ever made in this country. In what ways may this be true?

15. Contrast physical hygiene and mental hygiene.

16. Show the importance of a "good school atmosphere" in learning.

17. Show the importance of the physical and mental health of the teacher in classroom work.

18. Is it unreasonable to assume that "if we could have one generation of properly born, trained, educated, and healthy children," many other problems of government would vanish?

SELECTED READINGS

In the accompanying volume of *Readings* the following selections, related to the subject matter of this chapter, are reproduced:

*289. Keene: The Corner Stone of National Welfare.
*290. Hoover: Chaos in Childhood.
*291. Cumming: Disease; An Added School Burden.
*292. Wood: The Teacher and Child Health.
*293. Terman and Almack: Changes in School Hygiene since the World War.
*294. Hoover: Problems of Child Welfare.
*295. Wilbur: Give the Little Fellow a Chance.
*296. Keene: The Health of the Teacher.

QUESTIONS ON THE READINGS

1. If this cornerstone is so important (289), how do you explain not only past but present neglect?
2. What home and life conditions cause the change of the two eighty per cents (290)?
3. Is the elimination of the child defects enumerated (290) as important as the elimination of illiteracy among children? Do we so regard it?
4. How do you explain the unwillingness of cities and communities to assume the added school burden (291)?
5. What program would you outline for a teacher-training institution (292) determined to assume this added element in the selection and training of teachers?
6. Why was it natural that the early post-war programs (293) should have placed their chief emphasis on drill and physical education rather than education in health habits?
7. Contrast the school health work of today (293) with that of thirty years ago as to methods, aims, and results.
8. Contrast the importance, for our national welfare, of the problems set forth in 294, with the importance of learning arithmetic and grammar.
9. Are the new functions for the school set forth in 294 unreasonable additions, or not? Why?
10. If ill-nourished children with us are not so much the results of poverty as "the product of ill-instructed children and ignorant parents" (294), what new duties and forms of education are called for?
11. What is called for if the little fellow is to have a chance (295)?
12. What new standards might be erected, both in the selection of teachers at admission and in their subsequent training (296), that would tend to provide more efficient workers for our schools?

TOPICS FOR INVESTIGATION AND REPORT

1. The early forms of physical training.
2. The effect of the Boer, Japanese-Russian, and World Wars on our concepts of physical and health education.

3. Work of the National Safety Council.
4. The Army-draft examinations.
5. The White House Conference on Child Health and Protection.
6. The new field of mental hygiene.
7. Organization and work of some open-air classes.
8. Organization and work of some city school health department.
9. Work of a school dental clinic.
10. The work of the school nurse.
11. School feeding.
12. Health work in the schools of England and the United States compared.

SELECTED REFERENCES

*Averill, L. A. *The Hygiene of Instruction.* 386 pp. Boston, 1928.

   A study of the mental health of the school child, and instruction.

*Averill, L. A. *The Physical Welfare of the School Child.* 505 pp. Boston, 1929.

   Contains good chapters on the health of the teacher, and on mental hygiene.

Ayers, May, Williams, J. F., and Wood, T. D. *Healthful Schools.* 292 pp. Boston, 1918.

   Contains good chapters on medical inspection, play, and school feeding, as well as a good treatment of building hygiene.

*Commonwealth Fund. *Five Years in Fargo.* 207 pp. New York, 1929.
*Commonwealth Fund. *Children of the Covered Wagon.* 123 pp. New York, 1930.

   Two publications of the Commonwealth Fund of New York, detailing the results of two five-year demonstration projects, the first in the city school system of Fargo, North Dakota, and the second in the town and rural schools of Marion County, Oregon.

Dublin, L. I. "The Physical Disability of New York City's School Teachers"; in *School and Society,* vol. IV, pp. 564–69, 602–07. (Oct. 7 and 14, 1916.)

   A study of the records as to absences of 3877 city teachers.

*Gesell, A. *The Pre-School Child.* 263 pp. Boston, 1923.

   The problems of infant welfare and child hygiene, and the proper organization for such work from the standpoint of public health and education.

Hetherington, C. W. *School Program in Physical Education.* 132 pp. Yonkers, 1922.

Hoag, E. B., and Terman, L. M. *Health Work in the Schools.* 321 pp. Boston, 1914.

   Health teaching, open-air schools, health supervision, and school housekeeping.

*Keene, Charles H. *The Physical Welfare of the School Child.* 505 pp. Boston, 1929.

   A comprehensive and authoritative treatise on all phases of the school health and development program. Well written. Good bibliographies.

National Society for the Study of Education. *Yearbooks.*
   1. *Health in Education. Ninth Yearbook,* Part I, 1910. 108 pp.

2. *The Nurse in Education.* *Ninth Yearbook*, Part II, 1910. 76 pp.

3. *The Present Status of Safety Education.* *Twenty-Fifth Yearbook*, Part I, 1926. 377 pp.

4. *Pre-School and Parental Education.* *Twenty-Eighth Yearbook*, Parts I and II, 1929. 831 pp.

*Terman, L. M., and Almack, J. C. *The Hygiene of the School Child.* 505 pp. Rev. and enlarged ed., Boston, 1929.

> An excellent book. Contains much important information relating to growth, physiological differences, malnutrition, physical defects, preventive mental hygiene, and the effects of school life on children. Good chapter bibliographies.

Williams, J. F. *The Organization and Administration of Physical Education.* New York, 1922.

> On the administrative aspect of the work.

*White House Conference. Conference Publications; Century Co., New York.

1. *The White House Conference.* 365 pp.
2. *Health Protection for the Pre-School Child.* 275 pp.
3. *Parent Education.* 354 pp.
4. *Body Mechanics.* 166 pp.
5. *Communicable Disease Control.* 243 pp.
6. *Special Education; the Handicapped and the Gifted.* 604 pp.
7. *The Delinquent Child.* 499 pp.
8. *Child Labor.* 592 pp.
9. *Vocational Guidance.* 396 pp.
10. *The School Health Program.* 400 pp.
11. *Appraisement of the Child.* 344 pp.
12. *The Home and the Child.* 165 pp.

CHAPTER XIX

NEW DIRECTIONS OF EDUCATIONAL EFFORT

I. THE EXPANSION OF THE HIGH SCHOOL

Great recent development. The diagram, on page 255, showing the development of the Latin grammar school, academy, and high school; and the map on page 262, showing the high schools established by 1860, alike indicate the slow development of the free public high school in the United States. Though begun in 1821, the public high school, up to 1860, had made but little headway except in regions where New England people had gone. The Civil War checked further development for two decades, but after about 1880 to 1885 a rapid growth of the American high school began. While no accurate figures are available, there were probably about 500 high schools in the United States by 1870, about 800 by 1880 (in cities 244), while by 1890, the first year for which complete statistics were collected by the United States Bureau of Education, the number was 2526. Since then the development has been more rapid, as the following table shows:

| YEAR | FREE PUBLIC HIGH SCHOOLS | TEACHERS | STUDENTS | PER CENT OF PUPILS IN: | | APPROXIMATE PER CENT OF PUPILS OF HIGH SCHOOL AGE ENROLLED IN HIGH SCHOOLS |
				Public High Schools	Private High Schools	
1869–70	c. 500		80,227			2.0
1879–80	c. 800		110,289			3.0
1889–90	2,526	9,120	202,969	68.13	31.87	5.0
1894–95	4,712	14,122	350,099	74.74	25.26	7.5
1899–00	6,005	20,372	519,251	82.41	17.59	9.0
1904–05	7,576	28,461	679,702	86.38	13.62	10.0
1909–10	10,213	41,667	915,061	88.63	11.37	12.5
1914–15	11,674	62,519	1,328,984	89.55	10.45	20.0
1919–20	14,326	97,654	1,857,155	91.00	9.00	29.0
1924–25	c. 20,000	158,000		91.60	8.40	47.0
1929–30	c. 22,000	c. 156,000				52.0

Accurate comparable figures for recent years are not available due to the rise of the junior high school and the inclusion of data for these as part of the secondary school figures.

Unlike the development before 1860, the recent marked increase in the number of high schools has been true of all parts of our country,

West as well as East, and South as well as North. Before 1900 the development was more marked in the North; since 1900 in the South and West. The period up to 1860, and to a certain extent up to about 1880, was an experimental period. The new school had to find its work and become established, and the people had to grow accustomed to the idea of the support of higher schools as a proper function of a democratic State. By 1880 not only had we at last become convinced as to the need of extending education upward, for democratic ends, but by that time the industrial and social changes coming in our national life were making it evident that the further development and progress of our democracy would be seriously hampered unless the amount of education extended to our youths was both materially increased and changed in character. Since about 1885 to 1890 our people generally seem to have accepted the idea that a secondary school education, at public expense, should be placed within the reach of as many of our youth as is possible. After about this time legal and legislative objection to the establishment of high schools largely ceased, and many new laws providing for union schools and enlarged taxation for support appear on the statute books of our States. The result of this change in attitude of our people toward the high school is shown in the increased percentage of the total population enrolled in the secondary school (**R. 297**).

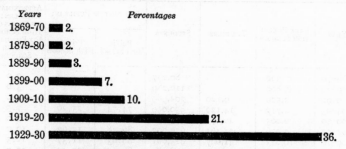

FIG. 150. NUMBER OF PUPILS ENROLLED IN PUBLIC HIGH SCHOOLS, PER THOUSAND OF TOTAL POPULATION

Change in character of the school. Along with this rapid development of the high school — in number of schools, teachers, and students, and the superseding of the old academy and the private high school by tax-supported institutions under public control —

has also come a marked change in the character of the high school itself.   The course of study, before 1860, was essentially a book-study course, usually three years in length, and the same for all students (**Rs. 157, 158**).   Reading, writing, geography, arithmetic, bookkeeping, history and Constitution of the United States, and English grammar, all of which have since been dropped back into the upper grades of the elementary school, were commonly taught in the high schools before 1860.   In add'tion, ancient and moderr history, rhetoric, logic, intellectual and moral philosophy, natural philosophy, astronomy, algebra, geometry, trigonometry, Latin, and Greek usually were included.   This list of high school subjects (**Rs. 157, 158**), as well as the floor plans of the high school buildings of the time (see floor plans for the Providence school, page 258, which are typical, and also **R. 158,** showing the Chicago high school), show that the high school was essentially a place to study and recite.

While not originally begun with the idea of preparing young people for college (see statement of purposes in establishing the high schools in Boston, page 255, and New York, page 256), this soon became one of the important purposes of our high schools, thus making of them a part of our educational ladder and the transition institution between the common school and the college.   Up to the time of the Civil War, however, but eight high school subjects (page 315) had found a place in the entrance requirements of the colleges of the time, and but six more were added up to 1875.   Since then the number has been greatly increased by adding new high school subjects to the list.   Of the fourteen accepted by 1875, but two — physical geography (1870) and physical science (1872) — were other than book and recitation subjects, and for some time both of these were taught from textbooks and without laboratory equipment.   Since 1890 laboratory science, and since 1900 manual, domestic, and agricultural subjects, have found a large place in the college-entrance list.

Development of new courses and schools.   After about 1880 the introduction of new subjects to meet the needs of new classes (**R. 298**) was so rapid that the old course of study became overcrowded, resulting in:

(a) the extension of the high school course to four years;
(b) the introduction of options and electives in the course; and
(c) the creation of a number of parallel four-year courses, such as

(1) the ancient classical course;
(2) the modern classical course;
(3) the English-history course;
(4) the scientific course;
(5) the business course;
(6) the manual-arts course;
(7) the household-arts course;
(8) the agricultural course;
(9) the teacher-training course;
(10) special vocational courses.

In addition to this multiplication of courses, in many cases separate high schools for teaching some one or more of the courses given above have also been developed, with the result that we have today:

(1) The general culture high school, being the successor, though now greatly modified both in subject matter and spirit, of the original general high school.

(2) The cosmopolitan high school, offering in one building, or group of buildings, many or all of the different courses of study mentioned above.

(3) The manual-training high school, first begun as a part of our public school system in 1884 (page 463), but now more commonly developed in connection with (2).

(4) The household-arts high school, usually provided for as a course under (2) or (3), but sometimes organized separately.

(5) The commercial high school, for training for business life. Begun as a separate course in many high schools in the seventies. After 1898 a number of commercial high schools were organized in the more important of our commercial cities, but within the past two decades the tendency has been to absorb this instruction into the cosmopolitan high school (2).

(6) The agricultural high school, first established in connection with the University of Minnesota, in 1888. By 1898 there were ten such schools in the United States. Since 1900 the development of the agricultural high schools has been more rapid than has been the case with any other previous type of high school. By 1909 there were 60 separate agricultural high schools, and agricultural courses were offered in 346 other high schools. The number of high schools today offering agricultural instruction is probably in excess of two thousand.

(7) Trade and industrial schools, of high-school grade, for vocational training. This represents our most recent development, and is treated more at length under the second division of this chapter. With national aid for such schools and courses, this type of school promises to increase very rapidly.

Experience has shown that in some places and cases it is better that one or more of the above types of special high schools exist separately, while in other cases it is better that such courses be combined in what is now commonly spoken of as the cosmopolitan American high school. In their beginnings new types of education often prosper better if organized in separate schools; after the work has been established, and accepted as a legitimate form of educational effort, it has been found wise to combine a number of different types of education in one school, thus enabling the high school to offer to each pupil a wider range of choice in studies. The American high school, unlike the secondary school of Europe, has been conceived of as pre-eminently a place for trying out young people, developing tastes, testing capacities, opening up life opportunities, and discovering along what lines pupils show enough special aptitude to warrant further education and training. The same principles that apply to the differentiation of elementary-school courses to meet individual needs, as stated in the preceding chapter, apply with even greater force to pupils between the ages of fourteen and eighteen. This involves freedom from hard and fixed courses of study, a rich and varied offering of courses from which to select, and intelligent guidance of pupils toward preparation for a life of useful service.

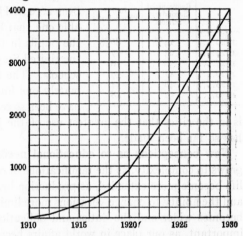

FIG. 151. NUMBER OF PUBLIC JUNIOR HIGH SCHOOLS AND DEPARTMENTS OF JUNIOR-SENIOR HIGH SCHOOLS

After Phillips

The junior high school. This new type of school, designed particularly to meet the special needs of early adolescent youth (see page 555), and now generally recognized as representing the lower division of the field of secondary education, also has shared with the high school proper in the recent rapid development which has taken place, as Figure 151 shows.

In addition to the strictly junior high schools, there are today some three thousand other public secondary schools which have re-organized their work by abandoning the older 8–4 form of organization (in the South a 7–4 form), and now form parts of a 6–3–3 school system, or a 6–5 or a 6–6 system in which the secondary school is not divided into two separate schools. That this change has taken place with great rapidity the attached tabulation shows. So rapidly has the reorganization, first begun in 1909–10, been accepted by our people as a desirable one that by 1930 over one half of the pupils in the secondary schools of the United States were in reorganized schools. The fact that only approximately one fourth of the high schools have been so reorganized shows that it is in the cities that the greatest use of the junior high school idea has so far been made.

YEAR	PER CENT OF ALL SECONDARY SCHOOL PUPILS IN:	
	Reorganized Secondary Schools	In 8–4 Plan Schools
1920....	14%	86%
1922....	23	77
1924....	30	70
1926....	41	59
1928....	46	54
1930....	52	48

New conceptions as to educational needs. As our civilization grows in complexity, as the ramifications of our social and industrial life become more extended, as production becomes more specialized and the ability to change vocations more limited, as our political life becomes wider and the duties and obligations of citizenship more important, as our place in world affairs becomes larger, and as the privileges conferred and the responsibility for proper living resting on each individual in society increase, the nature and extent of the education offered as preparation for life must correspondingly increase. An education which was entirely satisfactory to meet the needs of the simpler form of our social and industrial national life of the sixties or the eighties is utterly inadequate for the complex life of the twentieth century (**R. 299**). All this has come to be generally recognized today, and in consequence our American States are providing for the further establishment of more high schools and new types of high schools, extending the compulsory school age upward, and offering the advantages of secondary education to as many of our children as can advantageously use what the schools have to give. The ultimate outcome doubtless will be that some form of secondary school program will be made available to every normal boy and girl. City boys and girls have such opportunity now; the problem is so to reorganize rural and village education that the boys and girls who live on the farms and in the villages may also be provided with secondary school advantages adapted to their needs.

Since the outbreak of the World War a large amount of new thinking has been given to the problem of how better to adapt the secondary school to the changing needs of our complex modern society through the reorganization of the instruction offered. The discussion has centered about a determination of objectives, a reorganization of subject matter, a simplification of programs of study, and even a questioning of the values of general secondary education for all (**R. 300**). In a way this discussion as to the aims and work of the secondary school has been similar to the earlier discussion as to the overcrowded course of study of the elementary school. Some of the high marks in this discussion have been the following:

Cardinal principles of secondary education. In 1911 a committee report was made to the National Education Association on the articulation of high school and college,[1] and as an outgrowth of the discussion which ensued a new Commission on the Reorganization of Secondary Education was appointed to define the objectives and the most approved procedures for the secondary school. This new Commission reported by subjects [2] during the years 1913–18, and in 1918 issued a small but important document [3] entitled *Cardinal Principles of Secondary Education*. In this final report on the objectives of the secondary school the Commission held that education in the United States should be guided by a clear conception of the meaning of democracy; that in a democracy each member should find opportunities to develop such as would prepare him for the largest usefulness to himself and to society; and that, consequently, education in a democracy "should develop in each individual the knowledge, interests, ideals, habits, and powers whereby he will find his place and use that place to shape both himself and society toward ever nobler ideals." The Commission then proceeded to de-

---

[1] In a way the report of this Committee was a continuation of the work of the earlier (1895) Committee on College Entrance Requirements in that it dealt with number of units to be required for entrance, particular units to be required of all, and the general make-up of the high-school course. The requirements as laid down were quite definite both as to subject matter and amount. For the full report, see *Proceedings, N.E.A.*, 1911, pp. 559–65.

[2] The various reports were printed as Bulletins of the United States Bureau of Education from 1913 to 1918, there being nine reports in all. The reports began with the teaching of subject matter, and ended with reports on moral values, vocational guidance, and finally with a statement of the objectives of education itself.

[3] *Cardinal Principles of Secondary Education*. 32 pp. Bulletin 35, 1918, United States Bureau of Education.

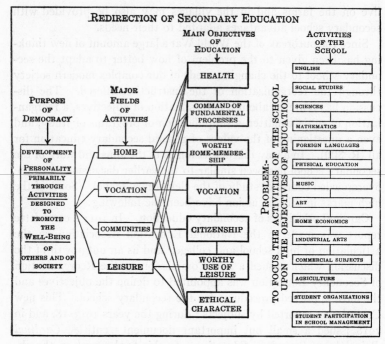

FIG. 152. REDIRECTION OF THE SECONDARY SCHOOL

Based on the *Report of the Commission on the Reorganization of Secondary Education*

termine "the main objectives that should guide education in a democracy" through an analysis of the activities of an individual in our present-day life and world.   These it determined to be:

1. Sound health-knowledge and habits.
2. Command of the fundamental processes (reading, writing, arithmetical computation, and oral and written expression).
3. Worthy home membership.
4. Education for a vocation.
5. Education for good citizenship.
6. Worthy use of leisure.
7. Ethical character.

These seven objectives were called the "cardinal principles of secondary education."

In 1924 a new book entitled *Principles of Education* appeared, written by two professors [1] then at Yale, which restated our theory of education in terms of the conceptions of modern biology and psychology and the changing needs of an economic and industrial civilization. The educative process, they said, should be centered about the desirability of knowledge, under the conditions of modern society, concerning six fundamental life needs, namely: (1) health, (2) family life, (3) economic adjustment, (4) civic life, (5) recreation, and (6) religion; and the authors then applied the results to the study of the organization and instruction in the different divisions of the school.

These two statements, along with the work of Dewey, set forth well for us the modern conceptions as to educational objectives and gave us a modern philosophy for the work of the school, and a number of attempts have been made recently to reconstruct the secondary-school curriculum better to adapt it to satisfy these objectives.

The Flexner "Modern School" proposal. In 1916 President Eliot published a paper [2] on the "Changes needed in American Secondary Education," in which he asserted that "the best part of all human knowledge has come by exact and studied observation made through the senses," and that "the most important part of education has always been the training of the senses through which the best part of knowledge comes." He accordingly urged that our high schools give much more time to scientific and technical instruction and to music and art, in place of their excessive devotion to book-subject studies, and that the school day be lengthened and the long summer vacation shortened. This was followed, in 1917, by a paper [3] on "A Modern School," by Abraham Flexner, of the General Education Board, which was in a way a constructive sequel to President Eliot's paper. In this he asserted that tradition largely determined what was taught in our high schools; showed that the great amount of time spent on Latin, literature, and mathematics did not produce results; and asserted that a modern school should make it much more important to young people to know, to care about, and to understand the physical and social world in which they live. To

---

[1] Chapman, J. C., and Counts, George S., *Principles of Education.* 645 pp. Houghton Mifflin Co., Boston, 1924.

[2] Publications of the General Education Board, New York, 1916. Occasional Papers, no. 2. 29 pp.

[3] Publications of the General Education Board, New York, 1916. Occasional Papers, no. 3. 23 pp.

this end a modern secondary-school course of study should emphasize activities in four fields:

1. *Science* — This to be the central feature of the school.
2. *Industry* — The occupations and trades of the industrial world.
3. *Civics* — History, civic institutions, and the organization of society and government.
4. *Æsthetics* — Literature, languages, music, and art.

He also contended that the subjects of the high-school course were in need of revision to eliminate useless material and to add much-needed new material.   Still further, he contended that all general education should be completed by the age of twenty, so that young people could enter on professional study or life-work by that age.

The latter paper brought forth much discussion, and some bitter criticism from the partisans of the old classical training.   Finally a school, to carry out the experiment and evolve the kind of modern instruction described, which became known as The Lincoln School, was endowed by the General Education Board, in New York City, and placed under the direction of the Teachers College at Columbia University.   The work to be done in this school will be well worth watching, as it is likely to work out important new lines in elementary-, as well as secondary-school instruction.

The Bobbitt reorganization proposals.   A still more fundamental proposal for the reorganization of the secondary-school curriculum was made by Franklin Bobbitt, in 1924, as a result of his curriculum work for Los Angeles.[1]   His fundamental assumption was contained in the statement that:

Education is primarily for adult life, not for child life.   Its fundamental responsibility is to prepare for the fifty years of adulthood, not for the twenty years of childhood and youth.

His first attempt was to determine the major objectives of education (**R. 301**), which he stated to be:

1. Social intercommunication.
2. Maintenance of physical efficiency.
3. Efficient citizenship.
4. General social contacts and relationships.
5. Leisure occupations.
6. General mental efficiency.
7. Religious attitudes and activities.

[1] Bobbitt, Franklin. *How to Make a Curriculum.*   292 pp.   Houghton Mifflin Co., Boston, 1924.

8. Parental responsibilities.
9. Unspecialized practical activities.
10. Occupational activities.

He next outlined a general training program to consist of (*a*) basic studies, to be taken by all students, and (*b*) additionals or extra studies, to be taken only by the more capable and the specially talented pupils, further subdividing the basic studies into three ability curricula for different ability-groups of pupils, as has been done for the elementary-school pupils, as shown in Figure 132, page 525. The basic studies, for all secondary-school pupils, then would be:

1. The English language: how to read, speak, and write it. English usage.
2. Literature: English and general, for appreciation.
3. Citizenship attitudes, judgments, and activities. The Social Studies: to replace formal history, in part.
4. Science: the several fields, to be selected from.
5. Everyday mathematics: practical and applied; to replace algebra and geometry, in part.
6. Physical training, physical and mental hygiene, health habits, sanitation.
7. Unspecialized practical arts, partially differentiated for boys and girls.
8. Musical training, for appreciation and judgment.
9. Art training, for appreciation and judgment.

The extras or electives would include the foreign languages, advanced mathematics, the history of English literature, music and art for technical proficiency, literary writing, dramatics, public speaking, and a few other subjects.

Vocational subjects and training would follow the completion of the basic studies.[1]

The Bobbitt proposals represent a fundamental reorganization of the secondary school, somewhat like that of the Winnetka plan for the elementary school. Such a reorganization and simplification of the instruction of the secondary school will not be easy to carry through, largely because it means a reversal of the process of differentiation of schools and multiplication of courses which we have so long been following. The plan, however, seems essentially sound.

Whether, in the process of reorganization, we shall, in any near future time, come to the limitation of cultural secondary-school

[1] See Bobbitt, pp. 68–75, for the full program, with conditions and limitations.

advantages, as proposed by Professor Monroe (**R. 300**), or a rigid selection of those who are to go on as proposed by Sir Michael Sadler (**R. 300**), and as do the English, cannot now be foretold.

II. THE DEVELOPMENT OF VOCATIONAL EDUCATION

Vocational education in Europe and the United States. For more than half a century the leading countries of Western Europe, in an effort to readjust their age-old apprenticeship system of training to modern conditions of manufacture, have given careful attention to the education of such of their children as were destined for the vocations of the industrial world. Germany, Austria, Switzerland, and France have been leaders, with Germany most prominent of all. No small part of the great progress made by that country in securing world-wide trade, before the World War, was due to the extensive and thorough system of vocational education worked out for German youths. The marked economic progress of Switzerland during the past half century has likewise been due in large part to that type of education which would enable her, by skillful artisanship, to make the most of her very

FIG. 153. THE DESTRUCTION OF THE TRADES IN MODERN INDUSTRY
Thirty-nine different persons work at manufacture of a coat.

limited resources. France has profited greatly, during the past half century also, from vocational education along the lines of agriculture and industrial art. In Denmark, agricultural education has remade the nation since the days of its humiliation and spoliation at the hands of Prussia.

In the United States but little attention was given to educating for the vocations of life until within the past twenty years, though modern manufacturing conditions had before this destroyed the old apprenticeship type of training. Endowed with enormous natural resources, not being pressed for the means of subsistence by a rapidly expanding population on a limited land area, able to draw on Europe for both cheap manual labor and technically educated workers, largely isolated and self-sufficient as a nation, lacking a merchant marine, not being thrown into severe competition for international trade, and able to sell our products to nations anxious to buy them and willing to come for them in their own ships, we did not up to recently feel any particular need for anything other than a good common-school education or a general high-school education for our workers.   The commercial course in the high school, the manual-training schools and courses, and some instruction in drawing and creative art were felt to be about all we needed to provide.

Beginnings of vocational education with us. Largely within the past twenty years, due in part to our expanding commerce and increasing competition in world trade, in part to the new educational impulses arising out of our new world position following the Spanish-American War, in part to the increasing world-wide demand for foodstuffs and manufactured articles, and in part to a growing realization of the many advantages that would accrue to us as a nation and to our workers as individuals if we were to provide better and more specific types of education for those who are to labor, we have at last turned our attention in a really serious manner to the many problems surrounding the establishment of schools of secondary grade for the vocational education of our workers.

Due to our early national importance in agriculture, and the endowment in each State of a college of agriculture by the Federal Government, in 1862 (page 279), it was natural that in this country agricultural education for pupils of high-school age should have been the first of the vocational subjects to be developed.   The first publicly supported agricultural high school, as was stated above, was founded in 1888, in connection with the University of Minnesota, and since 1900 instruction in agriculture has become an established feature of American school life.   In several of our American States, as for example Alabama, Georgia, Virginia, Oklahoma, and Massachusetts, a number of state agricultural high schools have been established by the legislature.   In other States, among them Wisconsin, Michigan, and Maryland, county high schools of agriculture have been established, and these receive state aid for support.   Many of the agricultural colleges also maintain an agricultural high school as a part of their work, and a number of cities have recently added courses in agriculture to their high schools.

After about 1908 the introduction of agricultural instruction into regular secondary schools became common,[1] and largely within the past fifteen years instruction in elementary agriculture has been added by law to the courses of instruction in the rural and village schools in many of our States.

The first trade school in the United States was established privately in New York City, in 1881, and by 1900 some half dozen schools of the trade or industrial type had been established privately in different parts of the country. Due in part to the whole idea being new, and in part to the suspicion of organized labor that such schools were not being founded for any purpose favorable to them, the development of trade education came slowly.

The fifteen years from 1902 to 1917 was a period of investigation, discussion, and growing interest. Commercial bodies and manufacturers' organizations sent school and business experts to Europe to investigate and report on the work of vocational schools in the different European nations; state commissions made investigations and reports; and much propaganda work was done by volunteer societies interested in establishing vocational education. In 1906 Massachusetts led the way by creating a State Commission on Industrial Education, with power to superintend the creation and maintenance of industrial schools for boys and girls, and appropriated state aid therefor. In 1907 Wisconsin enacted the first trade-school law, authorizing the creation of industrial schools by the cities of the State, largely independent of the regular school systems.[2] The Milwaukee School of Trades, established earlier, now was taken over and made a part of the city school system, and a number of trade schools were established in other cities. In 1909 New York similarly permitted the organization of trade schools

---

[1] The number of high schools reporting instruction in agriculture was 19 in 1900, 52 in 1905, 465 in 1910, and 609 in 1918, the first year of the Smith-Hughes Law. By 1920 the number had increased to 1375, and by 1926 to 4371. Of the 4371 schools, 3081 were regular day high schools, 197 were part-time schools, and 50 were evening schools. Another interesting change was that, in 1916, 40 per cent of the high-school students in agriculture were girls, and by 1922 the percentage had dropped to 13.

[2] This law created a state board of vocational education, to be appointed by the governor and to control all state aid for vocational courses, and local boards of industrial education in all cities and towns "establishing or maintaining industrial, commercial, continuation, and evening schools," to "take over and maintain," such schools, with power to determine tax levies therefor up to half a mill for maintenance yearly. The state superintendent of public instruction was to be *ex officio* a member of the state board, and city school superintendents *ex-officio* members of city boards, but two separate school systems were to be maintained

in cities.   Back in 1902 the Manhattan Trade School for Girls [1] had been organized privately in New York City, and the work of this school did much to awaken public interest in trade education. In 1910 it was made a part of the free public school system of the city.

The National Commission on Vocational Education.   Had we depended upon isolated state and local action it would have been at least a generation, and probably longer, before anything approaching a national system of vocational education would have been evolved. Realizing the slow rate of local action, those interested in the movement urged the creation at once of a national system of vocational schools, with national aid to the States for their maintenance.   The Davis Bill [2] of 1907, and the Page Bill [3] of 1912, were unsuccessful attempts to secure national encouragement for the movement.

In 1911, the legislature of Illinois petitioned Congress to appropriate $1 per capita of the population to each State and Territory to extend the public school system by adding instruction "in such practical, industrial, and vocational training" as "the interests of the community may seem to require."   In 1912, a Committee of the National Society for the Promotion of Industrial Education, meeting at Philadelphia, adopted a "Tentative Statement of Principles and Policies" as to vocational education,[4] which declared state aid necessary, indicated fields of work, outlined the form of administration desired, and declared for a separation of vocational and general education and for local autonomy.   For a time, everything seemed headed for the creation of a separate system of vocational schools, paralleling and largely independent of the general secondary school system which with time had been built up.   The statement of John Dewey (**R. 302**), made at the time, was influential in pointing out the evils likely to follow separate control of different parts of what

---

[1] See a very interesting article on the early history and work of this school in the *Educational Review* for September, 1905 (vol. XXX, pp. 178–88), by Mary Woolman, entitled, "The Manhattan Trade School for Girls."

[2] For text of this bill see *Report of the United States Commissioner of Education*, 1908, vol. I, pp. 85–87.   The bill proposed a national aid grant of ten cents per capita of the total population to each State and Territory for the aid of secondary schools in agriculture, mechanic art, and home economics.

[3] The Page Bill was much like the Smith-Lever Bill of 1914, described in Chapter XVII.

[4] This Statement of Principles was approved by the Board of Managers of the Society shortly afterward, and appears in the *Annual Report* of the Society for 1912, pp. 292–97. Also see Cubberley and Elliott, *State and County School Administration, Source Book*, pp. 375–79; and for the 1911 Wisconsin law see pp. 379–85.

after all was but a common system of public schools, and did much to check the movement for a separate system of industrial education. Finally Congress, in 1913, provided for a Presidential Commission to investigate the matter and to report on the desirability and feasibility of national aid for the promotion of vocational training. After a careful investigation this Commission reported, in June, 1914, and submitted a plan for gradually increasing national aid to the States to assist them in developing and maintaining what will virtually become a national system of agricultural, trade, and vocational education.

The Commission's findings. The Commission found that there were, in 1910, in round numbers, 12,500,000 persons engaged in agriculture in the United States, of whom not over one per cent had had any adequate preparation for farming; and that there were 14,-250,000 persons engaged in manufacturing and mechanical pursuits, not one per cent of whom had had any opportunity for adequate training. In the whole United States there were fewer trade schools, of all kinds, than existed in the little German kingdom of Bavaria, a State about the size of South Carolina; while the one Bavarian city of Munich, a city about the size of Pittsburgh, had more trade schools than were to be found in all the larger cities of the United States put together.[1] The Commission further found that there were 25,000,000 persons in this country, eighteen years of age or over, engaged in farming, mining, manufacturing, mechanical pursuits, and in trade and transportation, and concerning these the Report said:

If we assume that a system of vocational education, pursued through the years of the past, would have increased the wage-earning capacity of each of these persons to the extent of only ten cents a day, this would have made an increase of wages for the group of $2,500,000 a day, or $750,000,000 a year, with all that this would mean to the wealth and life of the nation.

This is a very moderate estimate, and the facts would probably show a difference between the earning power of the vocationally trained and the vocationally untrained of at least twenty-five cents a day. This would indicate a waste of wages, through lack of training, amounting to $6,250,-000 every day, or $1,875,000,000 for the year.

[1] "In the four decades which measure the period of her rise as an industrial and commercial nation, Germany has demonstrated that nations which depend upon convention, established prestige, or superior natural resources, cannot compete successfully against a nation which systematically develops the intelligence and efficiency of her laborers, and regards the farm, the shop, and the factory as laboratories for the application of science to economic processes." (*Report of the Commission on National Aid to Vocational Education*, vol. 1, p. 22.)

The Commission estimated that a million new young people were required annually by our industries, and that it would need three years of vocational education, beyond the elementary-school age, to prepare them for efficient service. This would require that three million young people of secondary-school age be continually enrolled in schools offering some form of vocational training. This is approximately equal to the number of young people today enrolled in all public and private high schools in the United States. In addition, the untrained adult workers now in farming and industry also need some form of adult or extension education to enable them to do more effective work. The Commission further pointed out that there were in this country, in 1910, 7,220,298 young people between the ages of fourteen and eighteen years, only 1,032,461 of whom were enrolled in a high school of any type, public or private, day or evening, and few of those enrolled were pursuing studies of a technical type. True to our ancient traditions, our high schools were still largely book-study schools, preparing for political activity and the learned professions, and not for the vocations in which the majority of men and working women must earn their living. Continuing, the Commission said:

> At present this vast body of over seven million youths represents on the whole an untrained army, needing vocational training to make it efficient. It has been estimated that the total cost of bringing a child from birth to the age of 18 is $4000, or $220 per year, of which about $60 per year comes from the State. If we assume that it would require on the average an additional outlay of $150 per person to prepare each properly for usefulness, so that society might realize more fully upon its vocational and civic possibilities, certainly no business man would hesitate for a moment to thus secure the protection of the sum of $4000.
>
> Since commercial prosperity depends largely upon the skill and well-being of our workers, the outlook for American commerce in competition with our more enterprising neighbors, under present conditions, is not very promising.
>
> It is even more short-sighted of the State and Nation to neglect these investments, since national success is dependent not alone on returns in dollars and cents, but in civic and social well-being.

The Commission regarded the establishment of an adequate system of national vocational education of so much importance that it declared our national prosperity was at stake (**R. 303a**).

The Smith-Hughes Bill. Bills to carry out the recommendations of the Commission were at once introduced in both branches of Congress, in the Senate by Senator Hoke Smith, in the House by Representative Hughes. President Wilson early expressed himself as favoring the proposed legislation. After some delay, due in part to the outbreak of the World War, the bill was finally passed, and approved by the President on February 23, 1917. This new American legislation was based on the best of Continental European experience. The law was purposely made very flexible and elastic. It dictated neither to the States nor to the schools, but instead offered a scheme of co-operation. The schools were left free to work out any varying kinds of vocational training, suited to the needs of the different communities and the States. The aim was to get vocational training started, with freedom for adaptation to local needs.

The law provided for the creation of a Federal Board for Vocational Education; acceptance of the law by the States; national aid to the States for the salaries of teachers in the schools created, which aid the States must duplicate, dollar for dollar; federal supervision of work and expenditure; and national studies and investigations regarding needs in agriculture, home economics, industry, trade, commerce, and courses of instruction. The courses must be given in public schools; must be for those over fourteen years of age, and be of less than college grade; and must be primarily intended for those who are preparing to enter or have entered a trade or useful industrial pursuit. Both full-time and part-time classes were provided for.

One strong feature of the new schools was that they were to be an integral part of the existing public school system, and not separate schools as had been provided for in the Davis Bill of 1907 and the Page Bill of 1912, thus preserving the unity of our public educational system.

The national aid was divided into four funds, as follows:

1. For the purpose of co-operating with the States in paying the salaries of teachers, supervisors, and directors of agricultural subjects, to be allotted to the States in the proportion which their rural population bears to the total rural population of the United States.

2. For the purpose of co-operating with the States in paying the salaries of teachers of trades, home economics, and industrial subjects, to be allotted to the States in the proportion which the urban population bears to the total urban population of the United States.

3. For the purpose of co-operating with the States in preparing teachers, supervisors, and directors of agricultural subjects and teachers of trade and industrial and home economics subjects, to be allotted to the

States in the proportion which their population bears to the total population of the United States.

4. For making or co-operating in studies, investigations, and reports as to needs and courses in agriculture, home economics, trades, industries, and commerce.

The sums appropriated by Congress increased each year for nine years, when the maximum was reached, and are as shown in the accompanying table. By the time the maximum had been reached the work had so demonstrated its usefulness that a further enlargement of the grants was made, as the table also shows. The bill has met with general acceptance everywhere,[1] and promises in a few decades to give us a national system of vocational training not surpassed in effectiveness by that of any other Nation (**R. 304**).

YEAR	FOR AGRICULTURAL EDUCATION	FOR TRADE, HOME-ECONOMICS, AND INDUSTRIAL EDUCATION	FOR TRAINING TEACHERS OF BOTH	FOR INVESTIGATIONS	TOTAL NATIONAL AID
1917–18....	$500,000	$500,000	$500,000	$200,000	$1,700,000
1918–19....	750,000	750,000	700,000	200,000	2,400,000
1919–20....	1,000,000	1,000,000	900,000	200,000	3,100,000
1920–21....	1,250,000	1,250,000	1,000,000	200,000	3,700,000
1921–22....	1,500,000	1,500,000	1,000,000	200,000	4,200,000
1922–23....	1,750,000	1,750,000	1,000,000	200,000	4,700,000
1923–24....	2,000,000	2,000,000	1,000,000	200,000	5,200,000
1924–25....	2,500,000	2,500,000	1,000,000	200,000	6,200,000
1925–26*...	3,000,000	3,000,000	1,000,000	200,000	7,200,000
1932–33....	4,250,000	4,250,000	1,000,000	300,000	9,800,000

* Reached the maximum this year, but later increased.

Types of instruction. Three types of schools or instruction are aided under the Smith-Hughes Vocational Education Act:

1. *The all-day or continuation school,* usually two years in length, and intended to give a good type of preparatory course for the different trades, such as carpenter, machinist, mason, baker, plumber, electrician, printer, shoemaker, or weaver; in commerce for the work of bookkeeper, stenographer, typist, auditor, or accountant; in agriculture, for the various types of farm work such as orcharding, dairying, poultry-raising, truck gardening, stock-raising and bee culture; and in the home economics field for such work as cook, dietitian, housemaid, institution manager, and house decorator. The school day usually is eight hours long, with a half day on Saturday. This provides ten per cent more schooling in two years than

[1] As significant of the national interest which a decade and a half of discussion had awakened in the question, every State had signified its acceptance of the provisions of the Act within five months of its enactment by Congress.

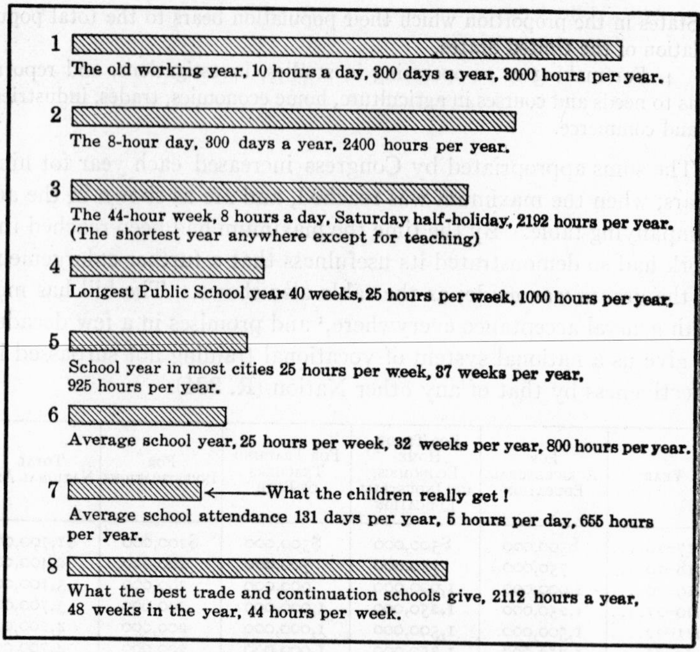

FIG. 154. A YEAR'S WORK IN INDUSTRY AND IN SCHOOL

the ordinary high school gives in four years, and a trade in addition. In these day continuation schools a sound preparation for the skilled occupations is given, as well as mechanical insight and industrial outlook. The instruction does not so much displace apprenticeship training as shorten it and make it more effective. There is every reason to believe that this type of all-day continuation school will ultimately become the general type for the continuation of the education of those headed for industry, the work being based on the completion of the work of the junior high school.

2. *The part-time classes*, with approximately the same aims as the continuation school, but intended for those who have already gone to work and can give but a few hours a week to vocational training.

3. *The evening-school class*, for the instruction of advanced workmen who need specialized instruction to increase their efficiency, and many helpers and assistants who need instruction in tool manipulation, methods of construction, and the fundamental principles underlying the work they are trying to do.

An analysis of the first sixteen years under the Smith-Hughes Law shows that there were, in 1932, approximately four hundred state directors or supervisors of vocational education employed by the forty-eight States, that the number of schools of all types operating under the law had increased to approximately 15,000, that 28,372 teachers were employed in the work, and that the total enrollment in these schools was 1,176,162. As an example of the value of the work, Figure 155 gives the results of a few weeks of training in a factory noted for its efficiency, and shows something as to the value of the work.[1]

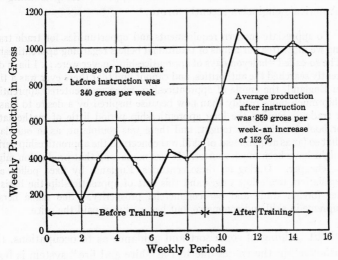

Average of Department before instruction was 340 gross per week

Average production after instruction was 859 gross per week - an increase of 152 %

FIG. 155. INCREASING PRODUCTION BY CORRECT TRAINING METHODS

The vocational high school is the most effective agency so far devised for the training of that 70 per cent of all our children who

[1] That vocational education pays large returns may be seen from the following statement, made in an address by Edward T. Franks, Vice-Chairman of the Federal Board for Vocational Education, in an address in 1929 before the Ohio Vocational Association.

He said:

"The 13,000 employed students of the Central Vocational School of Milwaukee, who attend school but eight hours per week, earn more money each year than the entire system of education costs the city for all kinds of public education. There were 63,600 part-time vocational students in New York City last year, and they earn annually, while attending school, more than $45,000,000. The vocationally trained cotton growers of the South produced 400 per cent more cotton per acre than the average of the cotton-growing States that year. A vocationally trained farmer in Ohio produced 1680 bushels of corn on his ten acres, while the average yield for the State was forty-eight bushels per acre."

cannot or will not continue in the regular courses of the high school,[1] and who have, at the rate of a million a year, been entering industries for which they have been but ill-fitted and in which they could have little hope of advancement or success (**R. 304**). It is also the most effective means for replacing and improving on the age-old and often much lauded apprenticeship training of workmen — a system now almost obsolete in most trades — and a system that always was exceedingly wasteful of time and effort and never was a very effective means of training. Of this old apprenticeship training one of America's engineers recently wrote:[2]

> To appreciate modern requirements and opportunities for trade training we must free our minds of traditional beliefs regarding apprenticeship. The so-called "halcyon days of apprenticeship" never were.... I have diligently searched the authorities, and cannot find that there ever was a time in England, the cradle of apprenticeship, when men entered apprenticeship much more readily than now because inspired by a desire to master a trade.... During the long apprenticeship period little of mathematics or book learning was taught, and there was complaint, as in our days, that so far as acquirement of skill was concerned the apprenticeship period might have been much shorter. It was made long that production might be cheaper. During all these centuries, England, by fixed policy and legislation, made low wages and this sort of apprenticeship the basis of her foreign trade and her commercial prosperity. She made herself supreme in skill and commerce, but her workmen paid the price.

Without training of some sort and guidance as to occupations, the "turnover" in the trades due to the "hire and fire" system is both large and costly to both industry [3] and the public, for to the latter the cost ultimately must be passed on.

[1] In discussing the need for some other type of training than that afforded by the regular academic high school, Thorndike writes:

"Our theories about schooling, recreation, and the higher life are all somewhat blinded by an unscientific expectation that somebody will grow wheat and bake bread and make shoes and build railroads and manage factories by some such necessary order of nature as makes the sun shine and the rain fall. This blindness is often accompanied by a certain condescension, or even scorn, toward productive labor, which is perhaps a relic of the long centuries of idealization of the leisure class. There is very real danger that schooling may unfit a community to produce by itself its own necessities, and lead it to depend on industrial mercenaries imported to do all the dirty work." (E. T. Thorndike, *Adult Learning*, p. 193.)

[2] H. E. Miles, in *Mechanical Engineering*, August, 1921.

[3] The American Engineering Council, in the *Report of the Commission on Waste in Industry* (1923), declared that the "hire and fire" system costs the metal trades in this country alone at least $100,000,000 a year. There is an estimated cost of from $50 to $250 for each employee "hired, trained, and separated." At $50 only, applied to 2,000,000 employees in the metal trades industry alone, the annual wastage is $100,000,000.

A century of evolution. We now find that the American high school, as a result of nearly a century of progress and evolution, has now evolved into a diversified American system of secondary education, in turn leading to entrance to higher schools or to life occupations and professions, somewhat as shown on the following chart.

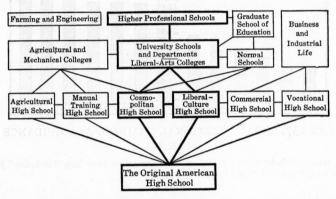

FIG. 156. THE RECENT EXPANSION OF THE HIGH SCHOOL
AND THE COLLEGE

Vocational guidance. Another outstanding development in educational work that has come as an outgrowth of the new interest in vocational education has been the organization of systems of vocational guidance and a follow-up service for young workers. Under earlier conditions such a thing as the vocational guidance of youth was unnecessary, but with the growing complexity of industrial society and the minute subdivision of the old trades, vocational guidance has recently assumed an entirely new importance. The idea underlying it is not primarily to find jobs for young people, but rather to provide parents and pupils with information as to the demands and opportunities in the different life careers, and the best means of preparing for and entering them. The real purpose is to sort out capacities and adaptabilities, to prolong preparation in school, and to steer young people away from vocations for which they have no natural aptitude and from essentially "blind-alley occupations."

The movement is quite recent, going back scarcely beyond 1907, when a bureau for advising young men in the choice of a vocation

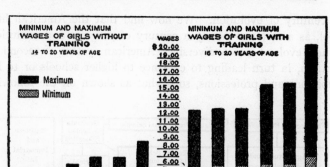

FIG. 157. WHAT VOCATIONAL TRAINING AND GUIDANCE
CAN DO

In training girls for better occupations and guiding them away from "blind-alley" jobs.
From a chart in Ellis's *Money Value of Education*, p. 26.

was opened in Boston. In 1909 this grew into a Vocational Bureau,
which soon became connected in its work with the public schools,
business houses, and manufacturing establishments. Lectures as
to careers were given to the upper classes in the elementary schools;
printed matter as to vocations was distributed; vocational counselors
were appointed in all the schools; and pupil record-cards were made
out. Boston soon became the center of the movement,[1] and from
there it has spread rapidly all over the United States. By 1910
thirty-five cities were at work on the idea. Today it is an educational conception accepted generally, and schools everywhere are
thinking and acting on the idea. Connecticut, in 1913, probably
was the first State to authorize definitely the addition of vocational-
guidance teachers to the schools. A decade later such teachers had
become common, with some States giving state aid for their salaries.

The study of life-careers for boys and girls has been introduced
into many schools, and intelligent planning for one's life-work has
been emphasized. Instead of leaving school and accepting the first
job that offers, regardless of adaptability or the future it may hold

[1] An interesting book that gives the early history of the movement, by the Director of the
Vocational Bureau of Boston, is Meyer Bloomfield's *The Vocational Guidance of Youth*.
124 pp. Boston, 1911.

or its influences on life and health, the attempt is made to save boys and girls from mistakes before it is too late to change. In giving such guidance the school not only is making its own education more effective, but also is protecting society from the dangers that arise when adults find themselves in work for which they have no aptitude and in which they cannot support a family.

More and more this service is becoming an integral part of the work of the day continuation and the part-time school, and a number of States and many cities now provide comprehensive plans for the vocational guidance of youth. The vocational-guidance and placement counselor, and the school-and-job co-ordinator, are thus new types of members of the educational staffs in our cities, and the vocational counselor is today found in connection with nearly all our larger cosmopolitan high schools.

III. UNIVERSITY EXPANSION AND EXTENSION

Expansion of the original college. In Chapter VIII we traced briefly the rise of the state university as the crown of the school system of the State, and the endowment by Congress, in 1862, of an entirely new type of higher instruction in the colleges of agriculture and mechanic arts. One of the earliest of these new institutions to become established, as well as at the time one of the most heavily endowed, was Cornell University, in New York, opened in 1868. This institution, and the State University of Michigan, together rendered a very valuable pioneer service, during the quarter-century following the opening of Cornell, in marking out new lines of collegiate activity and new relationships between the colleges and the high schools beneath. At Cornell University instruction in science, agriculture, and engineering was placed on an entirely new footing, and the instruction in the older subjects of the college curriculum was both broadened and deepened. Michigan was one of the first state universities to free itself from the hampering influences of state politics on the one hand and sectarian influences on the other; to open its doors to women on the same terms as men (1870); to begin the development of instruction in history (1857), education (1879), and government (1881), with a view to serving the State; and to examine and accredit the high schools (1871) and receive pupils from accredited schools into its freshman class without examination.

Before 1850 the colleges were small, had very limited library facilities,[1] and usually offered but one course, based on Greek, Latin, and mathematics, known as the classical course, and leading to the A.B. degree (R. 170). Brown offered a parallel course, without Greek and emphasizing more modern studies, in 1851, leading to the Ph.B. degree. Harvard organized the Lawrence Scientific School, in 1847, with instruction in science, and leading to the B.S. degree, and Yale made a similar organization in the Sheffield scientific School, the same year. Dartmouth and Rochester also established courses for the B.S. degree in 1852, Michigan in 1853, and Columbia a course for the Ph.B. degree in 1864. By 1880 our colleges were offering three or four parallel courses, much as the high schools did twenty years later. These led to different degrees — B.A., B.L., B.S., and Ph.B. Graduate instruction was also organized, and courses leading to the A.M., M.S., and Ph.D. degrees were in time provided. The first Ph.D. degree granted in the United States was by Yale, in 1861. Few others were granted by our universities before the opening of the first distinctively graduate university — Johns Hopkins, at Baltimore, in 1876.

Creation of new chairs and schools. With the creation of new chairs to represent new subjects of study, or subdivisions of old subjects, which became common after about 1875, the next tendency was to reorganize the colleges by departments, such as Greek, Latin, English, history, mathematics, physics, biology, etc. This became the common form of organization for the larger universities after about 1890, and still continues. With the very rapid increase in the quantity of knowledge, and the subdivision of old subjects into many new chairs, the more recent tendency has been to re-group the university into a series of colleges and schools. Today a large state university would include most or all of the following colleges, schools, or divisions, each subdivided into a number of departments or branches of knowledge, and often leading to separate degrees.

1. The college of liberal arts.
2. The college of engineering.
3. The college of agriculture.
4. The school of history and economics.
5. The school of pure science.
6. The school of education.
7. The school of household arts.
8. The school of fine arts.

[1] Thus the Williams College Catalogue of 1849–50 states that "the college library is open to the senior and junior classes the first Friday of the term and every Wednesday, and to the sophomore and freshman classes every Saturday."

9. The school of business administration.
10. The school of journalism.
11. The school of law.
12. The school of medicine.
13. The school of veterinary medicine.
14. The school of pharmacy.
15. The school of dentistry.
16. The school of forestry.
17. The school of mining.
18. The school of architecture.
19. The university-extension division.
20. The summer-session division.

Social significance of this great expansion. All this rapid development and subdivision and reorganization of the university into schools and colleges indicate the assumption of new service for the welfare of the State. That the State has appreciated the service has been shown by a university development previously unknown. Since about 1885, when the state universities began to turn their attention to serving and advancing the welfare of the State, university attendance and revenues have advanced by leaps and bounds. During the same period the stimulating competition of such privately endowed universities as Harvard, Yale, Columbia, Cornell, Johns Hopkins, Pennsylvania, Tulane, Chicago, and Stanford has also made itself felt. The growth in full-time resident student enrollment [1] may be seen from the figures, at different dates, for a dozen of our larger state universities and half a dozen of the more important privately endowed institutions, as given in the accompanying table.

University	1885	1895	1905	1915	1925	1930
*California.........	197	1781	3294	6,434	16,294	17,322
*Georgia...........	184	299	483	651	1,390	1,840
*Illinois..........	247	814	3597	5,439	11,212	12,709
Iowa.............	234	1133	1560	2,680	5,082	4,860
Michigan.........	524	2818	3832	5,833	9,422	9,431
*Minnesota........	54	2171	3633	4,484	10,170	12,490
*Nebraska.........	142	1397	2728	3,832	5,930	5,795
North Carolina....	230	229	666	1,088	2,288	2,749
*Ohio State........	64	805	1835	4,599	8,849	10,709
Texas............	151	630	1235	2,574	4,810	5,070
Washington.......	6	425	811	3,249	61,49	7,368
*Wisconsin.........	313	1520	3010	5,128	7,760	9,401
Chicago...........	—	1265	2373	3,803	5,484	5,679
Columbia.........	425	1943	4020	10,211	11,727	14,958
Cornell...........	461	1638	3230	5,598	5,397	5,725
Harvard..........	1586	3290	4136	5,226	7,608	8,218
Stanford..........	—	1100	1568	2,054	3,117	3,556
Yale.............	1086	2350	2992	3,300	4,722	5,259

* The state agricultural college in these States is combined with the state university.
Data for last two columns taken from Walter's statistics for autumn registration, as printed annually in *School and Society*.

[1] Summer session, extension, and part-time students are not included.

Development of the summer session. One of the most marked aspects of university development, during the past half century, has been the organization of summer sessions and the growth of summer-session enrollment. Probably the first summer school was the seaside laboratory conducted at Buzzards Bay, Massachusetts, in 1869, by Harvard and under the direction of Professor Louis Agassiz.[1] In 1873 Agassiz organized a summer school of marine biology for teachers on the island of Penikese, where he gathered together many of the foremost young instructors in science. In 1874, the Chautauqua Assembly was organized on Chautauqua Lake, in western New York, by Bishop J. H. Vincent, of the Methodist Episcopal Church. This organization provided numerous courses of popular summer lectures, outlined courses of study for personal use, and adopted textbooks and courses of reading for use throughout the year. It had a great vogue for a quarter of a century and more, and was widely imitated at many places in the United States. Probably the Chautauqua movement, more than the work of Agassiz, gave to the universities the idea of summer courses for teachers (**R. 306**).

Probably the first state university to organize a summer session was the University of North Carolina, where summer courses were offered, under private auspices, from 1877 to 1884, when the work was suspended, to be revived by the university in 1894. The University of Wisconsin began a summer session in 1887, at first under the auspices of the Wisconsin Teachers Association; Indiana University began summer instruction in 1889, and Cornell University in 1892. In 1891, the University of Chicago opened on a four-quarter basis, with the summer quarter organized as an integral part of the year's instruction. By 1910, the summer session, usually of six weeks' duration, had become common, and after the World War many universities reorganized their instruction on the four-quarter (Chicago) basis, while many other universities, colleges, and normal schools provided for summer sessions of from six to eight weeks, with the needs of teachers primarily in mind. By 1925, approximately one fourth of the teachers of the United States were in attendance at summer sessions. The rapid increase in summer-session attendance

[1] Louis Agassiz (1807–73), a professor of natural history at the College of Neuchâtel, Switzerland, was drawn to Harvard as professor of zoölogy and geology in the new Lawrence Scientific School at the time of its opening, in 1847, where he remained until his death in December, 1873.

may be seen from the figures for a few selected institutions, shown in the accompanying table.

UNIVERSITY	1913	1916	1919	1923	1926	1930
California..........	2363	3922	4322	10,258	9,875	7,294
Illinois............	713	1147	1314	2,064	2,254	3,088
Iowa..............	426	684	1290	2,253	3,085	3,493
Michigan..........	1408	1793	1961	3,054	3,666	4,329
Minnesota.........	531	649	1595	4,540	5,444	6,210
Nebraska..........	511	834	762	2,569	3,401	2,713
Ohio State.........	703	1181	1240	2,419	3,080	4,845
Texas.............	981	1477	1800	2,658	3,275	4,170
Washington........	—	1386	1527	2,109	3,249	3,686
Wisconsin..........	2120	3144	3213	4,710	5,165	5,088
Chicago...........	3771	5424	5012	6,375	6,474	4,957
Columbia..........	4539	8023	9539	12,675	13,858	14,016
Cornell............	1392	1628	2151	1,937	2,053	2,440
Harvard...........	797	1128	2692	2,292	2,844	2,486
Stanford...........	—	—	520	1,002	1,194	1,262

Statistics for 1926 and 1930 taken from Walter's registration figures, printed annually in *School and Society*. Figures for previous years taken from a table printed in the *Journal of the N.E.A.*
Many of the State Teachers Colleges, which have also provided for summer work, have experienced a quite similar increase in their summer session enrollments.

University extension.   By way of rendering a still greater service to the people of the State, our state universities and agricultural colleges have recently become engaged in what seems destined to become a very important new feature of their state service.   By the development of study centers, lecture courses, and scientific and technical instruction at many points within the State, by traveling exhibits, traveling libraries, correspondence study, and by short courses provided at public-school centers, our universities and agricultural colleges are today extending the advantages of higher education to the people of the State who have not been able to go to college.   Unlike the summer-session work, which is designed primarily for teachers, the extension service is carried on during the regular academic year and is designed for adults.   To the work already begun we have recently added the agricultural extension work provided for by the national government, through the Smith-Lever Act (page 598).

The University of Wisconsin has rendered notable service in this work (**R. 305**), and may be considered as a type of the best and an example for development elsewhere.   How it has extended its service to cover the whole State is shown by Fig. 158.   At the end

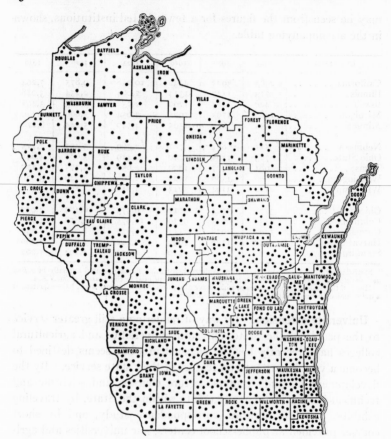

FIG. 158. UNIVERSITY EXTENSION WORK IN WISCONSIN

Each of the 1239 dots on this map represents a community in which use was made of one or more of the major services of the University of Wisconsin Extension Division from July 1, 1931, to June 30, 1932. Some service was rendered in every one of the State's 71 counties.

of a quarter century the University had an active extension enrollment of approximately 24,000 students, and during the preceding year 421 correspondence-study courses were offered in 845 subjects (**R. 306**). In addition, thousands of "package libraries" had been loaned to different communities in the State, and the university service had also included state and municipal advising and health instruction.

Such service can be made of the greatest value to the people of a State in elevating standards, developing public opinion, diffusing general and special knowledge, and building up a more intelligent democratic life. With democracies so dependent on learning and leadership as we now see them to be, and with the many intricate problems ahead of us in the new world civilization which will follow largely as a result of the World War, it is almost certain that our universities will be called upon to play a much more important part in the education of democracy in the future than they have in the past. The university-extension movement, as well as all the other educational expansions and extensions traced in this chapter, are significant of new social and industrial conditions and new national needs. As our social and political life becomes more intricate and more complex, and our world connections more extensive, education must broaden its work and enlarge its functions to prepare our people for the demands which lie ahead (**R. 306**).

Coincident with this rapid increase in students, faculty, schools, and courses has been the greatest number and amount of gifts of money to our universities ever given to aid higher education in any land, at any time. Since 1900 over two and a half billions of dollars have been given for educational and charitable and religious purposes, and a recent tabulation of all public gifts of $5000 or over, made in the United States since 1893, shows that 43% has been for schools and colleges, 37% for charitable purposes, 9% for religious purposes, 9% for museums and art galleries, and 2% for libraries. Such gifts are evidence of the public appreciation of the valuable services to the State and Nation rendered by our colleges and universities, both publicly and privately endowed. The States, too, have put millions into the equipment and maintenance of these higher institutions, believing in them as creators of advanced public opinion and as training schools for the future leaders of the State. In a recent article in the *Atlantic Monthly*, President Pritchett wrote:

> The rise of these great universities is the most epoch-making feature of our American civilization, and they are to become more and more the leaders, and the makers of our civilization. They are of the people. When a state university has gained solid ground, it means that the people of a whole state have turned their faces toward the light; it means that the whole system of state schools has been welded into an effective agent for civilization. Those who direct the purposes of these great enterprises of democracy cannot be too often reminded that the highest function of a university is to furnish standards for a democracy.

The prime business of a state university is to provide leadership and to furnish standards for the institutions of democracy, and in this capacity it has well been termed "the soul of the State." In times of agitation and change and the inauguration of new state undertakings, leadership and service are particularly the mission of the state university, and the faculty of a state university bears a relationship to the State not sustained by professors in endowed or denominational, institutions. In times of unrest and change, in particular, the state university must hold true to its course, and men trained in history and politics, in law and government, in pure and applied science, in medicine and engineering, and in ethics and education must throw the force of their influence in directions tending to secure the proper progress of the State and the Nation that the cost of progress — in a democracy always large — may be reduced to a minimum (**R. 307**).

QUESTIONS FOR DISCUSSION

1. Show the connection between the recent rapid development of the high school and the social and industrial changes since 1860, described in Chapter XIV.
2. What is the educational significance of the change of the high school from a book-study high school to a laboratory and shop high school?
3. What is the social meaning of the numerous parallel high school courses and schools (page 630)?
4. Contrast the American and European high schools in purpose.
5. Show the advantage, in a democracy, of a higher school to develop tastes and test capacities (page 631).
6. Why should ours be free, when the European school is a tuition school?
7. What does the rapid development of the junior high school indicate as to the reorganization in secondary education taking place?
8. What do you understand by "a determination of the objectives of the secondary school"?
9. Why should so much emphasis be placed today on a simplification of secondary-school programs, whereas two decades ago the emphasis was all on expansion?
10. What do you think of the importance of each of the Seven Cardinal Principles as objectives?
11. Were the six objectives of the Yale professors any better? Why?
12. Do you think the Eliot statement (page 635) a correct one? If so, how do you account for the present preponderant emphasis on the book subjects in the high school?
13. What do you think of the Flexner proposals (page 635)? Why? Compare them with Herbert Spencer's proposals (page 470).

14. What would be the result of the introduction of Bobbitt's plan into a large high school, on (a) present courses of study? (b) the teaching staff? (c) textbooks now used? and (d) on the pupils and their training?
15. Explain the breakdown of the old apprenticeship education.
16. Explain our long neglect of vocational training.
17. Explain our continued neglect of higher commercial training.
18. Explain our recent rapid acceptance of the agricultural high school, whereas the agricultural colleges for a long time faced much opposition.
19. Explain the continued emphasis by the high school of studies leading to the professions rather than the vocations, though so small a percentage of our people are needed in professional lines. How may vocational guidance help here?
20. Show the human and monetary value of vocational guidance.
21. Was it a strong point in the Smith-Hughes legislation that so many different trades and occupations were included, with options to communities as to what they shall offer? Why?
22. If the vocational school has so long a day (Fig. 154), why should not the ordinary high school put in longer hours?
23. Show the usefulness of the vocational high school in preparing for vocational work in the present time of rapid shifting of occupations.
24. Just what do you understand by: (a) vocational guidance? (b) blind-alley occupations? (c) school-and-job co-ordinator?
25. Explain the very rapid expansion of the university during the past half century, after its slow growth up to that time.
26. Explain the rapid development of summer-session work.
27. Explain why university extension is so desirable in a democracy.
28. Explain why American universities have received so much in benefactions, whereas the universities of England, France, Germany, Italy, and other lands have received little or nothing.
29. Would it be fair to say that the relative amounts of money given to education, charity, religion, museums, and libraries (page 657) are a fair estimate, in the minds of the American people, of the relative importance of each?
30. Show how a university may help to reduce the cost of progress in a democracy.

TOPICS FOR INVESTIGATION AND REPORT

1. The organization and work of a large technical high school for girls.
2. The organization and work of a large technical high school for boys.
3. The organization and work of a county or district high school of agriculture.
4. The organization and work of an evening vocational school.
5. The need for vocational education in the United States.
6. The Smith-Hughes Bill plans and work.
7. The organization and work of vocational guidance in some city school system.

8. The evening-school system of some large city.
9. The part-time day instruction in some city.
10. The university extension work done by your state university.
11. The library extension work organized by your state library.
12. The *Report* of the National Commission on Vocational Education.

SELECTED READINGS

In the accompanying volume of *Readings* the following selections, related to the subject matter of this chapter, are reproduced:

297. Committee: Why We Have Secondary Schools.
298. Inglis: Changing Ideals of Secondary Education.
299. Committee: Rapidly Changing Character of the Secondary School.
300. Russell: The Problem of the American Secondary School.
301. Bobbitt: Determining the Objectives of Education.
302. Dewey: Unity of the Public Educational System.
303. Commission: Vocational Education and National Prosperity.
304. Hoover: The Importance of Vocational Education.
305. Russell: Quantity, Quality, and Economy in Education.
306. Anonymous: The Extension Division of the University of Wisconsin.
307. Van Hise: The University and the State.

QUESTIONS ON THE READINGS

1. Do any of the objectives listed (**297**) appeal to you as being objectives that we do not need to care for? Why? Do you think that the secondary school of today cares for all the objectives listed?
2. Enumerate the reasons and forces which have caused the changes in ideals (**298**) listed by Inglis.
3. Contrast the task of the earlier high school with that of today (**299**).
4. Of the three points of view presented (**300**), which appeals to you as most accurate? Why?
5. If we were to accept Sir Michael Sadler's point of view (**300**), what changes in the administration of our secondary school would be necessitated?
6. Does Professor Monroe (**300**) point out a real danger in our secondary educational system? If so, how remedy it?
7. Does Bobbitt's reasoning (**301**) lead directly to the type of curriculum outlined in the text (pp. 637)?
8. Do you agree with Bobbitt's reasoning? Why?
9. Show how Dewey's article (**302**) naturally helped to stop the agitation for a separate vocational school system.
10. Assuming the argument of the Federal Commission (**303**) to be sound, what will be the result when all the nations train their workers vocationally?
11. Show how Mr. Hoover's address (**304**) presents a strong argument for vocational education as a sound investment for the Nation.

12. How may we reconcile quantity and quality (**305**) in education?
13. Would you say that such extension service (**306**) pays the State well: (*a*) materially? (*b*) socially?
14. Explain Van Hise's conception (**307**) that the university is "the soul of the State."

SELECTED REFERENCES

*Bloomfield, Meyer. *The Vocational Guidance of Youth.* 124 pp. Boston, 1911.

   A brief statement of the aims and purposes of the early movement. A more detailed statement may be found in the same author's *Youth, School, and Vocation.* (Houghton Mifflin Company. 1916.)

*Burton, M. L. R. "Functions of a State University"; in *School and Society*, vol. 12, pp. 355–69. (October 23, 1920.)

*Coffman, L. D. Inaugural Address as President of the University of Minnesota; in *School and Society*, vol. 13, pp. 703–11. (June 25, 1921.)

Eckelberry, R. H. *History of the Municipal University in the United States.* 213 pp. Bulletin 2, 1932, United States Bureau of Education.

Ellis, A. C. *The Money Value of an Education.* 52 pp. Bulletin 22, 1917, United States Bureau of Education.

Federal Board of Vocational Education. *Annual Reports*, 1917 to date, Washington.

Holt, W. S. *The Federal Board for Vocational Education; Its History, Organization, and Activities.* New York, 1922.

Koos, L. V., and Kefauver, G. N. *Guidance in Secondary Schools.* 640 pp. New York, 1922.

   A standard college textbook on the subject.

*Kingsley, C. D. "The High-School Period as a Testing-Time"; in *Proceedings of the National Education Association*, 1913, pp. 49–55.

   A good article on the high school as a testing-time, and the need for cosmopolitan high schools.

Lewis, Wm. D. *Democracy's High School.* 125 pp. Boston, 1914.

   An interesting statement of the new national problems the high school must face, as these affect both the boy and the girl.

Monroe, Paul. *Cyclopedia of Education.* 5 vols. The Macmillan Co., New York, 1911–13.

   The following articles are especially important:
   1. "Agricultural Education"; vol. I, pp. 58–68.
   2. "College, The American"; vol. II, pp. 57–79.
   3. "Evening Schools"; vol. II, pp. 521–27.
   4. "Household Arts in Education"; vol. III, pp. 318–31.
   5. "Industrial Education"; vol. III, pp. 425–43.
   6. "University Extension"; vol. V, pp. 684–89.
   7. "Vocational Education"; vol. V, pp. 740–42.

National Society for the Study of Education. *Agricultural Education in Secondary Schools. Eleventh Yearbook*, Part II, 1912. 101 pp.

662 PUBLIC EDUCATION IN THE UNITED STATES

National Society for the Study of Education. *Vocational Guidance and Vocational Education for the Industries.* *Twenty-Third Yearbook*, Part II, 1924. 435 pp.

> Section I on vocational guidance and placement; Section II on vocational education. Contains much descriptive matter of work then under way.

*Proctor, W. M. *Educational and Vocational Guidance.* 352 pp. Boston, 1925.

> The problem, and how to handle it. A very useful book.

Prosser, C. A., and Allen, C. R. *Vocational Education in a Democracy.* 580 pp. Boston, 1925.

> The nature, principles, and functions of vocational training, and its relation to general education.

Prosser, C. A., and Allen, C. R. *Have We kept the Faith? America at the Crossroads in Education.* 429 pp. New York, 1929.

> Thinks that we have not given vocational education proper support, and that our high school system is wrong in purpose and results.

Sears, J. B. *Philanthropy in the History of American Education.* 111 pp. Bulletin 26, 1922. United States Bureau of Education.

> Our standard study of the subject.

Shelby, T. H. *General University Extension.* Bulletin 5, 1926, United States Bureau of Education.

Van Hise, C. R. "Place of the University in a Democracy"; in *School and Society*, vol. 4, pp. 81–86. (July 15, 1916.)

> An excellent statement.

CHAPTER XX

THE EDUCATIONAL REVIVAL IN THE SOUTH

Conditions in the South faced. The reconstruction period in the South came to an official end with the withdrawal of federal troops and military rule by President Hayes, in 1877 (Chapter XII). For the next quarter-century the South was largely engaged in trying to find itself and determine its future. The reconstruction period had been more devastating than the war itself, it had lasted twice as long, and by its close most of the property which the war had left had been swept away. The Southern States were impoverished and burdened with debt. Governmental activities were demoralized. Agriculture was prostrate, and the plantations were in ruins. There were almost no industries. Taxable property, from which the means for the maintenance of civilization is derived, was small in amount and produced but little income. Everywhere, too, the problems of government and education were complicated by the presence of two races, destined to live side by side and to work out their respective destinies together, and with the utmost uncertainty as to their attitudes toward their common problems. The organization of the civil government and the restoration of some semblance of the former prosperity of the South naturally took precedence, while the creation of state systems of public instruction had to wait for new leaders, new impulses, and more prosperous times.

The labor unit in the South remained the Negro, as before the war, with now a new class of poor whites added (**R. 308a**). The Negro was now emancipated, ignorant, unambitious, largely spoiled by the mistakes of reconstruction, and less well trained for work than when he was a slave. The poor white, who had lost his property as a result of the fortunes of war and had been reduced to manual labor, found in the emancipated slave a competitor whom he could not rival [1] (**Rs. 238, 308b**). Post-war conditions called for a change from plantation to more intensive and smaller-scale agriculture, and the

---

[1] "Even the wealthy, when threatened with poverty, fled from the South... because everyone who knew the Negro looked with holy fear upon the day of his emancipation. With the well-fed chattel, the expensive slave, he could compete; but with the starving Negro of freedom he had not a ghost of a chance." (Paul B. Barringer. *Negro Education in the South.*)

development of the possible industries of the South was now most desirable, but the weight of an uneducated citizenship, white and black, coupled with the general poverty, for long retarded development. Well-intentioned Northern philanthropy often did not help in solving these problems, particularly as they related to the colored race (**R. 239**), as the ideals set up and the ambitions awakened during the reconstruction period too often belonged to a distant future rather than to an immediate present. A great need of the Southern States was education, but education of a type that would meet the conditions faced by them.

Officially, the Federal Government did nothing to help create systems of education for the region, aside from the small work of the Freedmen's Bureau, as all attempts (Chapter XII) to provide some form of national aid failed of enactment. In the South itself, the schools and colleges which survived the war or were established anew suffered seriously from social disorder, the mixed-school conception, lack of funds, fraud and mismanagement, and the political turmoil of the times, with the result that educational progress was impeded and the state systems of education were slow in developing. Between the close of the reconstruction period and the opening years of the twentieth century, education generally made but little progress in the States of the old South.

Actual conditions. The poverty-stricken condition of the South, as it relates to education, may be well illustrated by North Carolina. In 1886, statistics show that the total cost for the education of approximately 570,000 children in the rural and city schools of that State was but $771,719, and that this amount was divided among approximately 6600 different schools and 6700 teachers. The estimated valuation of the grounds, school buildings, and equipment for these schools was a little less than $700,000. The average length of the school term was but 60 days, and the average salary of the teachers a little under $80 for the school year. At least two thirds of the teachers were men. The total amount spent for the supervision of all the schools of the State, including nine separate small-city school systems, was a little less than $30,000 a year, of which approximately $19,000 was paid to the 96 county school superintendents of the State. Considerably more than one fourth of the white population ten years of age and over, and about 70 per cent of the colored population, was illiterate. There was no educational sentiment of importance in the State.[1] The University of North Carolina had been in existence for a century, but was only slenderly aided by the State and not open at all to women. There was no state normal school for white teachers, and only a meager system of short summer institutes that offered any kind of preparation for teaching. Yet this school system was all the people of North Carolina had been able to develop since 1870 to replace what before the war was one of the best school systems of the South.

By 1900, things were but little better, for in that year the amount provided by taxation for each child of school age in the South varied from 50 cents in Alabama and North Carolina to $1.46 in Florida and Texas, as against an average for the whole United States, the South included, of $2.84 per child. The annual amount raised by taxation for schools, per adult male, likewise varied from $2.65 for Alabama and North Carolina to $6.37 in Texas, as against an average for the United States as a whole of $10.93. The yearly school term varied from 70 days in North Carolina to 119 days in Louisiana and Virginia, as against 144 days for the United States as a whole. The average yearly salary for teachers varied from $84 in North Carolina to $192 in Virginia, as against an average of $310 for the whole United States. No Southern State had enacted a compulsory-attendance law before 1900; less than 60 per cent of the school population of the South was enrolled in school; and less than 40 per cent was in average daily attendance. Only one pupil in ten of those who enrolled reached the fifth grade, and only one in seventy reached the eighth grade. The percentage of illiteracy among the white population of the South was still three times the average for the United States as a whole. The almost total lack of school supervision, outside a few cities, left the teachers free to give instruction in whatever line they felt themselves best prepared, with the result that the teaching methods were poor and wasteful. There were few public high schools, and the elementary schools were but imperfectly graded and sometimes not graded at all. The average value of the rural schoolhouses, in 1900, was only about $100, and those of the Negroes

[1] "Some regarded the public schools as a public charity. Some opposed them on the ground that they were purely secular and did not teach morality. Still others opposed the whole idea of public education because the Negro shared in the division of the public funds. The leading churches were then and later actively opposed to state support of higher education, because they held that the state, by such support, entered into unfair competition with the sectarian colleges. In a word, the public schools were satisfactory to no class of people." (*Report of the United States Commissioner of Education*, 1907, vol. I, p. 330.)

even less. State and county supervision existed largely in name only. According to Knight,[1] the state superintendents "were generally politicians, lawyers, soldiers, or patriots, and the conditions of the office made them little more then clerks," while the county superintendencies "went to briefless young lawyers, broken-down preachers, or some other incompetent person as a reward for some political service." There were no professional standards, either in the laws or in public opinion, for either office.

The following statement, taken from the *Annual Report* of the State Superintendent of Education for South Carolina, for 1900, describes conditions as they existed somewhat generally throughout the South at that time.

> It is a misnomer to say that we have a system of public schools. In the actual working of the great majority of the schools in this State, there is no system, no orderly organization. Each county supports its own schools with practically no help from the State as a whole. Each district has as poor schools as its people will tolerate, and in some districts anything will be tolerated. Each teacher works along in her own way, whatever that may be, almost uninfluenced by the existence of any other school or school authority. Isolation reigns. This is not inspiring or stimulating.

New influences. While for a long time education in the South remained at a low ebb, and progress for a quarter of a century was discouragingly slow, a number of new influences were beginning to affect the problem and in time these exerted a cumulative force. The establishment of the Peabody Education Fund, in 1867, and the important service rendered by this Fund during the succeeding thirty-five years in stimulating the establishment of city school systems and in training teachers has been described in a previous chapter (XII, p. 439). The John F. Slater Fund, mentioned also in the same chapter (p. 441), established in 1882 for the benefit of the colored race, likewise for long rendered limited but important service in aiding in the training of teachers and the provision of industrial education for the Negro.

In 1868 there was founded, at Hampton Roads, Virginia, a new type of institution known as Hampton Normal and Agricultural Institute (**R. 309**). This institution has rendered a very important service to the colored race, and has been the parent of a number of

[1] Knight, Edgar W. *Public Education in the South.* p. 421.

similar schools founded elsewhere in the country.   The superintendent of public instruction of Virginia, Dr. Ruffner, declared it to be
"the most valuable of all schools opened on this continent for the
colored people."   Its founder, General Samuel Chapin Armstrong,
had headed a colored regiment during the war, and in 1866 had been
appointed superintendent of education for the colored people of
Virginia under the Freedmen's Bureau.   His training and exper-

FIG. 159.   THE FOUNDERS OF INDUSTRIAL TRAINING FOR
THE COLORED RACE

SAMUEL CHAPIN ARMSTRONG	BOOKER T. WASHINGTON
(1839–1893)	(1858–1915)
Founder of Hampton	Founder of Tuskegee

ience [1] had equipped him well to understand the needs of the Negro
race, and during the twenty-five years he directed Hampton, until
his death in 1893, he shaped the policy for the education of the
Negroes and the Indians (included in 1878) of America, while the
men and women he trained went out and became the leaders of their
people throughout the South and West.   The object of the institution was to train teachers and industrial leaders for the two races,
particular emphasis being placed on character building, the missionary spirit, agricultural instruction, vocational courses, and the
home-making arts.

[1] General Armstrong was born in the Hawaiian Islands, of missionary parents, and educated there and at Williams College.   For some years he was connected with the department
of public instruction of Hawaii, where he obtained that knowledge of the education of
backward peoples which proved of much use to him in his work for the Negroes of the
South.   Realizing the need of the colored people for industrial training, he founded Hampton
on the shores of Hampton Roads and began his great life-work.

Of the many educational institutions of similar type to which Hampton gave rise, probably the most notable is the Normal and Industrial Institute founded by a Hampton graduate, Booker T. Washington,[1] at Tuskegee, Alabama, in 1880, and opened for instruction July 4, 1881. This institution has followed and in some respects surpassed Hampton, and through its teacher-training work, industrial courses, hospital and nurse-training school, and extension division it has exerted a very important influence on Negro education not only in Alabama but throughout the South as well (**R. 309**).

New leadership. Here and there through the Southern States, in the late nineties, there were signs of the coming of a new period in the economic and educational life of the region. Economic recovery, though slow, had been increasingly in evidence, and by 1900 there were many indications that a change had at last set in.[2] A new thrifty middle class had arisen, determined to drop the old feuds and resolutely face the future.[3] The question of racial relationships had finally been settled by the firm establishment of white supremacy throughout the South. The Spanish-American War of 1898 had served, too, to unite North and South in a common undertaking, and as the soldiers of both sections lived and fought side by side in Cuba, a kindlier feeling on the part of both took the place of some of the old antagonisms and led to better mutual understandings.

The old theory that education at public expense was an invasion

[1] Washington was born a slave near Hale's Ford, Franklin County, Virginia, in 1858. His first education he obtained in a night school. When fourteen years old, he walked five hundred miles to Hampton and asked for admission. His entrance examination was to clean out a dirty room. So well did he do the job that he not only was admitted, but paid all his expenses there for three years by janitor work. After some teaching experience, he studied further at Wayland Seminary at Washington, D.C., then became an instructor at Hampton, and, in 1881, he became principal of the new Institute chartered by the Alabama legislature at Tuskegee, where he remained the rest of his life. His *Up from Slavery* tells the story of his life and work. He died in 1915.

[2] "Within twenty years, from 1880 to 1900, the South increased its wages paid to factory hands from $76,000,000 to $350,000,000; its production of pig iron from 397,000 tons to 2,500,000 tons; its output of coal from 6,000,000 tons to 50,000,000 tons; the number of spindles from 667,000 to 5,000,000; and the output of manufactured articles from $339,-791,898 to $1,173,422,565.

[3] "The young men of the present generation in the South are facing toward the future; and this, without destroying veneration for the past, has given new inspiration and a larger courage for the present. These young captains and young soldiers of industry refuse no reverence for the veterans of the civil war, on either side, but the men of this generation are determined to run it. The sons will preserve and magnify the fame of their fathers, but they will not foster or fight over again their feuds. They believe in factories quite as much as in pantheons, in energy more than in inquests, and in schoolhouses more than in graves." (Dr. McKelway, "The New Generation"; in *Report of the United States Commissioner of Education*, 1903, vol. I, p. 363.)

of parental obligation and that taxation for education was unjust and unwarranted, common throughout the South before the Civil War, had largely broken down. A new generation of leaders was beginning to be in evidence, and they, realizing the fundamental importance of education to the new South, attacked the faulty educational facilities of the time and the inadequate taxation for instruction as hampering influences on its development. The right of localities to tax for public schools was demanded,[1] and, when general legislation could not be obtained, special permissive legislation was secured instead. Typical of this period and this new attitude was the following statement, made in 1900, by the then State Superintendent of Education for Alabama, John W. Abercrombie.

> If our funds are not sufficiently large, what shall we do? Shall we fold our arms and wait until Alabama doubles in wealth?
>
> What we should do — what other States have done — what we must do, if we would properly qualify our people for citizenship, is to give to counties, townships, districts, and municipalities the power of taxation for educational purposes. If the people desire to levy a tax on their property to build a schoolhouse, or to supplement the state fund, for the purpose of educating their children, they should have the power to do it. The right of local self-government is a principle for which the southern people have always contended, yet, in the matter of providing for the education of our boys and girls, it is a right which the fundamental law of the State denies us.

The race issue, with its illiterate voting and mixed schools, which had checked the development of public education for a quarter of a century, was now eliminated as an issue in politics by the disfranchisement of the illiterates of both races and by constitutional amendments requiring literacy as an essential to citizenship and a qualification for suffrage. A premium was thus placed on the education of the masses, and the necessity for both general and local taxation for education was in consequence given a new emphasis. A demand now arose for the removal of constitutional limitations to local taxation for the maintenance of public schools.

Throughout the Southern States a new generation of leaders came to the front, and many of these took a strong stand for the development of the public school as a means of sectional regeneration.

[1] As a reaction to the waste and extravagance of the reconstruction governments, the Southern States had, rather generally, prohibited local taxation or so strictly limited it as to make educational support almost impossible.

Walter Hines Page (1855–1918), of North Carolina, must be rated as one of the ten or fifteen most influential men who provided leadership to America for the first two decades of the present century. Born and educated in North Carolina, he realized how nearly the lamp of civilization came to extinction in that section during the reconstruction period, and it became his consuming passion to rescue the South from the fate that had overtaken it. Another Southerner, born in North Carolina just as the Civil War was beginning, and who rendered distinguished educational service to the South during this period, was Edwin A. Alderman. He was professor of education at

FIG. 160
EDWIN A. ALDERMAN
(1861–1931)

the University of North Carolina from 1893 to 1896, and as such occupied one of the oldest chairs in the subject in the universities of the United States; president of this institution from 1896 to 1900; president of Tulane University at New Orleans from 1900 to 1904, and president of the University of Virginia from 1904 until his death in 1931. As one of the leaders in the Conferences for Education in the South, and as a platform speaker, he rendered distinguished service. Andrew Jackson Montague of Virginia, governor of that State from 1902 to 1906, and Charles Brantly Aycock, governor of North Caro-

lina from 1901 to 1905, exercised notable educational leadership during the first half-dozen years of the present century. Governor Aycock stumped the State on a progressive educational platform, and in his inaugural address, in January, 1901, he reviewed his campaign pledges and urged the legislature to make "ample provision for the education of the whole people" (**R. 310**). Legislative appropriations for public schools gradually began to increase, legislation as to taxation was changed to permit of larger local support, the administration of the schools was improved, and it was evident, shortly after 1900, that a new era in Southern education was about to dawn. The need of the time was for some organized agency that could carry on the work of educational propaganda, acquaint the people with actual conditions, and educate them to the new public-school idea. This fortunately was supplied by a new organization that came into existence almost by accident — the Conference for Education in the South.

The Conference for Education in the South. This Conference, which soon awakened wide interest and exerted an important influence on education in the South, owed its origin to the Reverend Edward Abbott, rector of Saint James's Parish, Cambridge, Massachusetts. In the summer of 1897 he made an extended journey through the eastern portion of the South, visiting schools and interviewing leaders. He had for many years been a member of the Lake Mohonk Indian Conference,[1] and was struck, in the South, with the isolation of the workers, the lack of co-ordination of effort, and the great need for acquaintance, co-operation, and stimulation.[2] Stopping for a time at Capon Springs, West Virginia, he interested the owner of the hotel there in inviting a selected list of thirty-four guests, twenty of whom were ministers of the gospel, to meet with him the following summer to consider the needs of Christian education in the South. Interest at first centered primarily in the church schools organized and maintained in the South for the colored people. A small group of interested people was brought together in the summer of 1898, important papers were read and discussions conducted, experts gave testimony and advice, and "a message and appeal" was adopted. Out of this beginning the important movement for the improvement of education in the South was evolved.

The second and third Conferences were held in 1899 and 1900 at Capon Springs, but with a larger registration of business men, and afterward at various places in the South. The event of the second Conference was an address by Dr. J. L. M. Curry, Agent of the Peabody Fund, which presented a survey of the needs of the South

[1] This Conference had assembled annually in the autumn, on the invitation of Mr. Albert K. Smiley, at his Lake Mohonk Mountain House, for a consideration of the needs of the Indians of New York State. The Reverend Edward Abbott, at Capon Springs, conceived the possibility of organizing a similar conference there to consider the needs of education in the South.

[2] "There were some dozen or more well-known Northern organizations engaged in maintaining schools in the South — some for white pupils and some for Negroes — and for many years they had been collecting and expending amounts aggregating annually some two million dollars or more. Yet these Northern organizations were each carrying on their operations with almost no regard to what the others were doing in the same field. Then in the South there were many large private schools and institutions, supported by religious denominations, which had no more to do with one another than the Northern schools. To think of bringing them into some sort of mutual helpfulness was no insignificant undertaking." (G. S. Dickerman, in *Report of the United States Commissioner of Education*, 1907, vol. I, p. 318.)

and an appeal for the improvement of every educational agency. This address changed the direction of the Conference, caused it to drop the word "Christian" from the title chosen the year before, to appoint a field agent [1] to study conditions and report, and to resolve to direct its energies toward universal education through state-established, -controlled, and -supported schools. At the third Conference Dr. Dickerman, who later became field agent for the organization, made an exhaustive report on conditions in the South. His conclusions were that

> the children of the rural communities of the South need schools which are adapted to the conditions which exist, and that to insure this the school must be developed on its own ground, and that this work must be done by the people of the South, especially in their public school systems:

and he recommended that they be aided in the effort they were making.

Bishop Dudley of Kentucky presided at the first Conference, Dr. J. L. M. Curry, agent of the Peabody and Slater Funds, at the second, and at the third Conference, Mr. Robert C. Ogden, of New York, was elected president, and he continued to serve in this capacity for a number of years.[2] To his energy, administrative skill, and generosity much of the success the movement was due. For many years a trainload of important people of the North went south to the Conference as his guests, and in this way Northern interest was awakened and deepened, and co-operation with Southern leaders made easier and more effective. By such means the Conferences were given a broad national spirit.

The fourth Conference, held at Winston-Salem in 1901, marked an important turning-point in the history of the movement because at that time it adopted a fundamental policy and organized an agency for effective work. At this Conference, Dr. Dickerman made another detailed report on educational conditions in the South, urged the necessity for improving the education of both races, reiterated his faith that the way lay through the building-up of the public school systems, said that the time had come for "some comprehensive undertaking to foster an educational spirit in the rural

---

[1] Rev. G. S. Dickerman, of New Haven, Connecticut, was chosen, to work in co-operation with Dr. Curry of the Peabody Fund. One important part of his work was to become acquainted with the Southern leaders and secure their attendance at the Conferences.

[2] From which the movement became known as the Ogden movement. Other titles used were the Southern Conference Movement, and the Southern Educational Movement.

portions of the South," and that the work must be directed by Southern people already in the field. The resolutions committee later brought in a resolution (**R. 311**), which was adopted, providing for the creation of a Southern Education Board for the better direction of the work the Conferences had marked out and the awakening of interest in public education throughout the South. This was done, and in a few years what at first had been a small movement, engineered largely by Northern leaders and with Negro education chiefly in mind, was changed into a national educational undertaking of which the South was deeply conscious and in which it was vitally interested (**R. 312**).

Co-operating closely with this movement, Mr. John D. Rockefeller, in 1903, obtained an incorporating Act from Congress creating the General Education Board,[1] the purpose of which was "to promote education within the United States of America, without distinction of race, sex, or creed." To this Board Mr. Rockefeller has, from time to time, given money and enlarged powers, and by 1930 he had turned over to it approximately one hundred and forty million dollars. The services of this Board to the South have been most significant, and a great variety of educational projects have been aided. From the first it kept in close touch with the work of the Southern Education Board, which came into being about the same time, often aiding it with funds. Probably the most important work of the latter Board in the South has been the financing of professors of secondary education in the state universities, and state agents for rural and secondary education in the state departments of education of most of the Southern States. The purpose of such grants was to stimulate the creation and development of a secondary school system for the South, something almost entirely lacking at the time the Conferences began to meet. Especially noteworthy, also, was a series of meetings of the school superintendents of the various States, financed by the General Education Board.

The southern revival. With the organization of the Southern Education Board for unification of effort [2] and educational propa-

---

[1] Co-operation between the two Boards was ensured by the appointment of seven men to membership in both. Representatives of both the Peabody and Slater Funds also were added to both Boards, thus ensuring close co-operation of all agencies engaged in the promotion of education in the South. The General Education Board stood for the national interest, and the other Boards for the fostering of local initiative.

[2] "It was a large effort, larger than anyone thought at the time. It was a proposal to unite

ganda in the South, a vigorous campaign of educational activity was begun, and for the next decade a great and wide-spread educational revival took place in the Southern States, paralleling in purpose and intensity that carried on two thirds of a century earlier in Massachusetts and Connecticut by Horace Mann and Henry Barnard. Local organizations were perfected in the different States, extensive and systematic field work was inaugurated and directed, and a bureau of investigation, information, and publicity was established [1] at Knoxville, under the direction of the University of Tennessee. Hundreds of able advocates of public education volunteered their services and were enlisted, the movement soon secured the hearty endorsement of the southern press and people,[2] and a series of educational campaigns was launched and carried through to successful completion. Of these, Dr. Dickerman,[3] who became field Agent for white schools for the Board, wrote, in 1907:

> For the campaign work in all its phases able advocates promptly came forward in the several States and enlisted in the work. Presidents and professors in the universities and colleges, lawyers, business men, and holders of office — the friends of progress and the moulders of popular opinion, were quick to see their opportunity and to improve it. The most practical school questions came up for discussion; local questions and those more general; better buildings and a higher grade of teaching for the particular community; improved legislation, wiser taxation, larger appropriations, and more efficient administration of the entire educa-

the educational forces, working more or less separately and often in isolation, in a dozen great States. Of some little consequence, too, were the Northern people who were endeavoring to do educational work in the South. To think of bringing them into some sort of mutual helpfulness was no insignificant undertaking." (Wycliff Rose, in *Report of the United States Commissioner of Education*, 1907, p. 318.)

[1] Dr. J. L. M. Curry, of the Peabody Fund, was made supervising director, with Dr. G. S. Dickerman and Booker T. Washington as field agents. Presidents Edward A. Alderman, of Tulane, Charles D. McIver, of the North Carolina Normal and Industrial College, and H. B. Frissel, of Hampton Institute, were made assistant directors. President Charles W. Dabney, of the University of Tennessee, was made chief of the bureau of investigation and publicity, with Professor P. P. Claxton of the same university, later United States Commissioner of Education, and Professor J. D. Eggleston, Jr., of Virginia, as publicity directors.

[2] "We hold out our hand to you, Mr. Chairman, and thank you for coming among us, but we say to you that we would be unworthy your coming did we for one moment hesitate to tell you that the education of all the children of the South is our work, and by God's help we mean to bear it. And we mean to carry it on until every child within the borders of the South, white and black, shall have a thorough education." (The Honorable Hoke Smith, in address of welcome, Fifth Conference, Athens, Georgia, 1902.)

[3] Dickerman, G. S. "The Conference for Education in the South, and the Southern Education Board"; in *Report of the United States Commissioner of Education*, 1907 vol. I, p. 307.

tional system of the State. People gathered in mass meeting at their court-houses, in churches, and in public halls, in the city and in the country alike, to hear men talk on education, to listen intently to discussions about the improvement of their children's schooling. Larger numbers came out to these gatherings than to any others. Political orators and spellbinders in a political campaign failed to secure the attendance or to arouse the enthusiasm of these college presidents, superintendents, and school teachers, who came with that message of a brighter hope and a higher service for the children.

Some of the outstanding educational campaigns [1] were those in North Carolina in 1902, Virginia in 1903, Georgia and Tennessee in 1904, South Carolina, Alabama, and Mississippi in 1905, and Arkansas and Florida in 1908. Some of these campaigns were continued for a number of years, until the whole State was awakened. As a result much new legislation was enacted, some state constitutions were changed, enlarged taxation for education was secured, and a new attitude toward public education came to prevail in the South. In less than a decade school revenues were doubled, and in a few States trebled, while a new interest in providing better school buildings, decreasing illiteracy, increasing local support, lengthening the school term, and securing better teachers were outcomes of the movement. A new interest in the development of high schools, the consolidation of small rural schools, the establishment of school libraries, and the creation of new teacher-training schools were likewise resultants. [2] Schools of education were developed in the state universities, the professional training of school administrators was begun, and the substitution of county-unit administrative organization in place of the old district system were also consequences of the educational revival. As a result most of the Southern States today have a much better form of educational

[1] In connection with these campaigns hundreds of "rallies" were held in the different States at which educational addresses were made and the needs of the schools were set forth. In Virginia, for example, 530 rallies were held in a single year, and in Tennessee over 300, with an average attendance of 1000. These rallies usually were followed by the organization of a School Improvement League to carry on the work locally.

[2] For example, between 1901 and 1906 the six States — Virginia, North Carolina, South Carolina, Georgia, Tennessee, and Louisiana — made an advance of 69 per cent in school expenditures, 78 per cent in the amount raised by local taxation, the value of their school property advanced 51 per cent, and the expenditure for teaching equipment 164 per cent. In high schools, Virginia reported 303 in 1907, where there had been but 19 three years before. Tennessee established 32 such schools during this period, and Louisiana increased the number from less than a dozen to 53. In the same period, in the seven States for which we have statistics, some 5000 school libraries were established, with an average of 100 books each.

organization and administration for their rural and village schools than is to be found in the majority of the Northern States.

A great regional disease. Closely connected with these educational campaigns designed to awaken interest on the part of the people of the South was one of the most important hygienic campaigns ever waged in any section of this country. As it was fruitful in educational results, it deserves mention in any statement as to the new educational movements of the region. For long the population of large portions of the South, particularly the sandhill and coast sections, had been sadly afflicted with what had been diagnosed as chronic anæmia, or continuous malaria, and no remedy for the trouble had been discovered. From Virginia to Texas the disease was prevalent. The outward symptoms were well known — swollen joints, emaciated body, protuberant stomach, greenish-yellow skin, sagging mouth, dull eyes, general lassitude, and inability to do much in either thinking or work. Children afflicted with the disease were stunted and had a prematurely-old expression.

In September, 1902, a well-trained employee of the United States Public Health and Marine Hospital Service, Dr. Charles Wardell Stiles, who had studied in the best medical schools of Europe,[1] suspecting the disease to be the same hookworm that was known in Europe and had recently been found by the Army Medical Corps to be widely prevalent in our newly annexed province of Porto Rico, set out with his microscope to study the so-called anæmia or malaria of the South. The proof being soon found, he returned to Washington with the announcement that the disease was hookworm,[2] and that it was widely prevalent throughout the South, where a

---

[1] Charles Wardell Stiles, son of a Methodist minister, was born at Spring Valley, New York, in 1867. After graduating from the Hartford, Connecticut, high school, he went to Europe for study, spending five years there at Paris, Berlin, Leipzig, the Trieste Zoölogical Station, and the Pasteur Institute. While in Paris a book on the hookworm disease was published and fell into his hands. Returning to the United States in 1891, he was appointed first consulting zoölogist in the Bureau of Animal Industry of the Department of Agriculture at Washington. Later he was transferred to the United States Public Health and Marine Hospital Service, and taught medical biology at the Army Medical School. The latter position opened to him the opportunity to make hookworm researches in the Southern States.

[2] The hookworm is a small worm, about as thick as a pin and half as long, with a number of hooks at the mouth end to enable it to hook onto the intestinal walls of the victim, suck his blood, discharge poisons into his system, and excrete eggs, which in turn hatch in any warm damp soil. There they may live for as long as six months, waiting for some barefooted passer-by, when they attach themselves to his feet, bore through into the blood stream, and finally land in the small intestine and affix themselves to the walls and begin a new cycle. The treatment is simple. A dose or two of thymol kills the worms, and epsom salts washes them from the system. The patient then has only to wear shoes and get well.

warm, moist climate and the habit of going barefoot had kept the pestilence alive and virulent. Brought in from Africa by former slaves, the disease had been passed on to the whites, who suffered more seriously from it, with the result that men of English, Scotch, and Irish stock, who elsewhere in America had built up our civilization and been leaders in church, and school, and State, in the South had become the so-called "poor white-trash" and were headed downward toward degeneracy and extinction. Stiles prepared a report on the disease, said that it could be stamped out at a cost of fifty cents per person and in a few days' time, and urged a national campaign for its elimination. This report was published as a bulletin of the Public Health Service, and Stiles expected that

> the country would be stirred, an aroused country would galvanize Congress, and Congress would provide the sinews for the kind of war contemplated — tons of thymol and epsom salts, and flying squads of sanitarians.

The publication, however, was almost unnoticed, and Congress, which had always been willing to appropriate money liberally for the elimination of cattle tick, boll weevil, hog cholera, or insect pests, was uninterested in wholesale human sickness in the South. The one tangible result of the publication was an invitation, a little later, to address the Pan-American Sanitary Conference on the subject, and the chief outcome of this was that a facetious newspaper reporter wrote up the address under the heading that "the professor" had discovered "the germ of laziness." The public-press joking and jeering which followed made impossible any organized action to relieve the sufferers, as almost no one took the idea seriously. For the next five years the matter rested, while "chronic anæmia" and "continuous malaria" took their ceaseless, deadly toll throughout the South, and children in the schools found themselves unable to study and often unable even to attend.[1]

The Country Life Commission incident. In 1908, in an effort to do something to improve the conditions surrounding life on the farms of the Nation, President Roosevelt appointed what became

---

[1] In one school, as an example, a local physician working with the Commission, found thirty-eight of the forty pupils infected, while forty-five of their brothers and sisters were too sick of the disease even to come to school. A year later the teacher of the school said:

"Children who before the treatment were listless and dull are now active and alert; children who could not study a year ago are not only studying now but are finding a joy in learning. There is a new spirit in the school. Most of the forty-five who were sick at home are now well and coming to school."

known as The Country Life Commission,[1] and Dr. Stiles was assigned as an attaché to travel with the Commission.   One morning,
while riding through the South, Stiles, Walter Hines Page, and Henry
Wallace, editor of *Wallace's Farmer*, were sitting in the smoking
compartment of a sleeping-car when the train stopped at a station.
Standing on the station platform was a miserable figure of a man,
presenting all the symptoms of a long-standing case of the hookworm
disease.   The following conversation ensued:

> *Wallace:* What on earth is that?
> *Page* (sadly): That is a so-called "poor white."
> *Wallace:* If he represents Southern farm labor, the South is in poor luck.
> *Stiles:* That man's condition is due to hookworm infection; he can be
> cured at a cost of about fifty cents for drugs, and in a few weeks' time
> can be turned into a useful man.
> *Page* (astonished): Is that really a hookworm case?   Can he really be
> cured?   You can make a healthy man out of that wreck?   Good God!
> Stiles, are you in earnest?

As the train went on, Stiles explained his studies, outlined the course
of the disease and what could be done to cure it, and told of his inability to interest either Congress or the South.   To Page, a Southern man, with his passion for bettering his native region, the story
was of enormous potential importance.   For generations he had
seen many of his country people disdained, written off as worthless
degenerates, and headed toward extinction, and now Stiles told him
that they were merely sick with an easily curable disease.   Free
them from the parasite that consumed their energies and a revital-
ized generation of Southern white men would result.   Page saw at
once how much of the South's past this theory explained, and how
much for the South's future it promised, and he lost no time in
getting in touch with those in the North who could and would act.

A great sanitary and educational campaign.   When the Country
Life Commission returned from its Western swing, the Secretary of
the newly organized General Education Board, Dr. W. Wallace
Buttrick, was waiting for Dr. Stiles.   When he found him, he said,
"Walter Page says you know something I must know immediately,"
and to Buttrick he told the story again.   Soon he was summoned to
New York City to tell it once more to Dr. Simon Flexner, director

---

[1] United States Country-Life Commission: *Report of the Roosevelt Commission on Country
Life.* 65 pp. Washington, 1909. The Chairman of the Commission was Liberty Hyde
Bailey, then Dean of the College of Agriculture, at Cornell University.

of the laboratories of the Rockefeller Institute for Medical Research, and then again to Mr. Rockefeller's chief personal and legal advisers in his philanthropies.   Stiles returned to Washington, assured that "the Rockefeller office will support this work," and in November, 1908, the newspapers announced that Mr. John D. Rockefeller had given one million dollars to combat the hookworm disease in the South.[1]

This announcement started a second installment of newspaper gibing and awakened some resentment in the South, but the Rockefeller Sanitary Commission for the Eradication of Hookworm Disease soon got under way.   By means of lectures, demonstrations, talks to local groups, newspaper publicity, and tactfully enlisting the co-operation of local physicians, the work made progress, though slowly at first.   During the first year 102,000 persons were examined, and 42 per cent were found infected and were then treated.   By 1914, half a million school children and nearly as many adults had been examined, with about the same percentage of treatments. When the World War draft combed the South for young men, from one eighth to one third of the draftees were still afflicted with the disease; but by 1927, after about 7,000,000 children and adults had been treated, the Annual Report of the International Health Board, into which the Commission had been merged, was able to say:

> At the present time it is fair to say that hookworm disease has almost disappeared from the United States, and is rapidly coming under control in many parts of the world.

This entire undertaking was one of the most effective educational campaigns ever waged anywhere.   From the first it was seen clearly that the sanitary campaign had to be largely a campaign of education.   The Southern people could not be held up and forced to swallow thymol and epsom salts; they had to be educated to want to do so.   Southern sensitiveness also had to be reckoned with, misunderstandings had to be cleared up, some sharp newspaper criticism had to be allayed by careful explanations, and co-operation had to

[1] With the newspaper gibing in mind, and fearing to offend the South, Mr. Rockefeller stated his gift as graciously as possible, saying that he would consider it "a privilege to act in any movement which offers assurance of relieving human suffering," and that it would be an especial pleasure "to feel that the principal activities of your Board will be among the people of our Southern States," whom he had come to know and to respect greatly and to whom he would like "to express in some measure my appreciation for their many kindnesses and hospitalities."

be secured. All this required both patience and time. The result, however, was well worth the cost in money, time, and effort, as a new race of people has since been in the making throughout the affected areas of the South. Heartrending caricatures of children, unable to study and with no desire to learn, have been changed into chubby, rosy-cheeked youngsters who go to school with interest and pleasure. Pitiful, sickly, poverty-stricken men and women, living as it seemed for generations under a curse, many of them illiterate and believed to be of a low grade of mentality, have been changed into useful and energetic citizens possessed of a desire to learn and know. In the words of the late President Eliot, of Harvard, it was "the most effective campaign against a widespread disease which medical science and philanthropy have ever combined to conduct," and the results of the campaign have been great in the impetus given throughout the South to the provision of better educational facilities for the children and the teaching of sanitary science and health habits in the schools.

Recent progress. The three decades since the beginning of this educational revival in the South have witnessed many changes and advances, so that today the city school systems compare favorably with those in other parts of the United States. New school plants have been erected, additional financial support has been secured, better training facilities for teachers have been provided by the States, good professional supervision has been instituted, good secondary schools are now maintained, and the children of both races have been provided with about the best educational advantages the cities can afford. In the rural schools, however — and the South is still essentially rural in the distribution of its population — the progress has been much less marked, despite determined efforts in a number of States and some noteworthy outside aid.

There are many reasons that will account for this situation. The Southern States are still poor, and they have an unusually large proportion of children of school age; [1] many rural schools must be maintained, and these often of two kinds; agriculture is still the predominating industry, and is still too much one-crop farming; the rural population per square mile is relatively low, and farm-tenantry

[1] In the Southern States the number of children of school age exceeds the number of adult males who must support the schools, ranging from about 1300 to 1500 school children per 1000 adult males, as against an average of about 800 children per 1000 males in the North and about 600 in the West.

is high; and the general level of well-being of the average rural home is still below that of most other parts of the Nation. These conditions, to be sure, are in large part a result of the plantation type of agriculture of the war and the reconstruction period. In the past thirty years the South has made a determined effort to improve the situation, realizing that the future well-being of that section is largely dependent on better educational advantages for the masses of the people, black as well as white. As Knight well points out, "measured by its own past record the South has made tremendous educational progress since 1900, but measured by national standards in education and by present educational needs, the South is still far behind the rest of the country." The school term is still a month and a half shorter than the average of the forty-eight States as a whole; the salaries and training of the teachers are materially lower than the average; in library facilities and secondary educational advantages the Southern States are at the bottom of the list; and the per capita expenditures for education are still quite low (**R. 313**). The South, however, has caught the spirit of the new education movement, and the different States may be expected, from now on, to advance their state systems of public instruction as rapidly as their material resources will permit. Of the progress so far made, Jones, in his summary of public school facilities in the South, says:

> The establishment on solid foundations throughout the South of a system of free public schools, governed by chosen teachers and maintained by the State, tells of a revolution in popular opinion with which it is not easy to find a parallel. The old antipathy to free schools, with the prevalent unpopularity of the teacher's occupation, has gone. Incomplete as are the outworkings of the system, inferior as are a great many of the schools, imperfectly qualified as are not a few of the teachers now employed, there is a vast significance in the beginning made — in the standards of achievement that have been set up.

Outside forces that have aided. Within the past two decades certain new organized efforts, originating outside the South, have materially aided the people of these States in handling their problem. Two of these have been national in scope, and the others that will be mentioned have been sectional and designed primarily to aid the region in dealing with the heavy burden of the education of the Negro.

The two national forces mentioned were the enactment by Congress, in 1914, of the Smith-Lever Co-operative Agricultural Extension Act (page 598), and in 1917 the Smith-Hughes Vocational Education Act (page 643).   Both bills were sponsored in the Senate by Senator Hoke Smith, of Georgia, and both Acts have been of special value to the agricultural South.   Under the Smith-Lever Act a large amount of valuable agricultural extension work has been carried on by county agricultural agents, home-demonstration workers, boys' and girls' club workers, and Negro extension workers in advising the farmers of the South, both white and black, as to crop production, soil protection, disease control, sanitation, child care, household management, and similar matters, with special work organized for the Negro farmers.   Under the Smith-Hughes Act, work of a somewhat similar nature has been done for the rural population through the medium of schools and classes in agricultural subjects, and, in addition, through part-time day and evening continuation education in vocational and industrial subjects for the youth of the cities.

The organized efforts which have been sectional and intended primarily for the benefit of the Negro, which will be mentioned here, are: The Anna T. Jeanes Fund of $1,000,000, established in 1908; the Phelps-Stokes Fund of $1,000,000, established in 1911; and the Julius Rosenwald Fund, established in 1915, and in 1920 raised to $20,000,000.   These have supplemented the work of the Slater Fund (page 441), established in 1882.

The income from the Slater Fund has been used mainly for the partial support of a large number of normal and industrial schools for the Negro race, and, at last report, 156 county training schools to prepare teachers for the Negro rural schools were being partially maintained.   The Jeanes Fund [1] income has been used chiefly to provide specially trained teachers to promote and supervise, under the direction of the county superintendents, rural and industrial education for the Negroes; to do extension work among their schools, and introduce the simple home industries into their work;

[1] Given by Miss Anna T. Jeanes, of Philadelphia to a board of trustees composed of five Northern men, five Southern men, and five men of the Negro race, for the purpose of aiding rural schools for Negroes.   The more important services of the Fund have been the work of the traveling supervisors, who supervise Negro-schools, and stimulate simple home industries, sanitation, the improvement of schoolhouses and grounds, and the formation of improvement clubs.   The counties and the colored people are asked to contribute a portion of the salaries of these supervisors.

and to provide county agents to travel about and create a sentiment for improved homes and schools and better sanitary conditions. The Phelps-Stokes Fund [1] has been used so far largely to make a careful survey of the needs of Negro education in the South; to establish fellowships for the study of the sociology of the Negro at certain leading Southern universities; to create a traveling foundation at Peabody College for the study of the needs of the Negro race; and to assist the work of the Southern University Race Commission.

The Julius Rosenwald Fund [2] has been the most important of the four, partly because of its larger resources, and partly by reason of the purpose to which its income has been put and the method by which it has been administered. Working in co-operation with the educational departments of fourteen Southern States, the income has been used to aid schools for the Negro race, to erect adequate school buildings, to promote school consolidation, to extend the school term, and to establish school libraries. A condition of the grants for buildings has been that the Negroes themselves must raise an amount at least equal to the grant made, either in money or donated labor, and that the buildings be of standard construction with reference to site, lighting, ventilation, and sanitation.   On June 10, 1930, the five thousandth Rosenwald rural school was completed,[3] and during the seventeen-year period up to the close of 1930, this Fund had aided in building 5075 rural schools for Negroes in 830 counties in fourteen Southern States, at a cost to the Fund of approximately four million dollars. To this same purpose the Negroes themselves gave $4,478,653, whites gave over a million, and the fourteen States supplied the remaining $15,800,000, making a total of $25,342,272, of which this Fund contributed 16⅔ per cent. The

[1] Established in 1909 by a bequest of $1,000,000 in the will of Miss Caroline Phelps Stokes, of New York, and incorporated as a Fund in 1911. The purpose, as stated in the will, included the education of Negroes, both in Africa and the United States."

[2] In 1914, Mr. Julius Rosenwald of Chicago, announced, through Tuskegee Institute, that he would give money to assist in the erection of rural school buildings for Negroes. Beginning in a small way the work ultimately grew to large proportions. At the time of his death, in 1930, Mr. Rosenwald was president of the Sears-Roebuck Company.

[3] The first school in this program was built in 1913 near Tuskegee, in Alabama. It was a single-room frame building, erected at the modest cost of $942.50. The five thousandth school was built near another great industrial institute for Negroes — Hampton. It is a consolidated school with accommodations for 300 pupils, who will receive instruction from six teachers in farming and trades as well as rudimentary academic subjects. The school is substantially built of brick at a cost of $20,000, to which the Fund contributed, on its regular schedule of aid, $2600.

schools erected in this seventeen-year period had a teacher capacity of over 13,000, and a pupil capacity of 612,495. All these schools have become public property when completed, and have added much to the educational facilities of the South. The Fund has also established a professorship of Negro life and schools at the George Peabody College for Teachers at Nashville, and granted a number of fellowships for advanced study to teachers and other Negroes of unusual promise.

The education of the Negro. The education of the Negro is one of the difficult problems which faces the South. With their large migration to the Northern cities at the time of and following the World War, the problem has now in part become one for the North as well. After nearly three quarters of a century, the difficulties of the question are still present and the complete answer has not been found, though the progress toward its solution has been remarkable (**R. 314**). No racial group in the United States offers so many problems of economic and social adjustment as does that of our ten million Negroes. In the South they constitute almost one third of the population; in Mississippi and South Carolina they number one half; and in the "black-belt counties" their proportion ranges from fifty to ninety per cent. In the seventy years since their emancipation took place, the illiteracy of the race has decreased from ninety-five to twenty per cent; approximately a million colored men, in 1930, were farmers of varying degrees of independence; and three quarters of a million own their own homes and one quarter million their farms. In the same period the death-rate among the Negroes has decreased one half, though it is still more than one and one half times that of the whites. Except in a few cities, the Negro teacher has completely supplanted the white as the teacher of the race [1] and as a people they are assuming an increasing responsibility for the education and progress of their members (**R. 314**).

However difficult the problem may be for a people with less than

[1] "This change has not been an unmixed blessing, and the schools have not always prospered as a result. While white teachers were in their management they themselves often became deeply interested in the children and ambitious for the prosperity of the school. Having considerable influence in the community, they were able to secure more favorable attention than would be given to Negro teachers. With the change, the schools under Negro teachers had no effective advocates, and so were constant losers. The amazing contrast between the public schools for white children and those for Negroes in nearly all parts of the South tells the story of this misfortune." (G. S. Dickerman, in *History of Negro Education*, Bulletin 38, 1916, United States Bureau of Education, p. 262.)

the average material prosperity to maintain two school systems, the economic future of the South depends upon the adequate training of the black as well as the white workmen of that section.   It is evident. now that the leaders there realize the economic importance of the Negro, as is evidenced by their efforts to improve the education of the people of the colored race.   The progress in the provision of educational facilities for them since 1900 has been greater than at any previous period, and today the race possesses some excellent schools.   Every Southern State has appointed a State Agent for Negro schools, and county supervision is maintained by a remarkable corps of Negro women.[1]   Normal and industrial institutes for the training of teachers and craftsmen are found throughout the South, many of which are state-aided or supported; publicly supported industrial and trade schools of secondary grade for Negroes are becoming more frequent; and the interest of college men throughout the region in the racial problem promises much in results for the future.   The earlier lack of interest in the question and a willingness to leave it to Northern missionaries and philanthropic effort is today being displaced by the realization that no one, except the Negro himself, is so deeply concerned in the success of the work or has so much at stake in it as the people of the South themselves.

QUESTIONS FOR DISCUSSION

1. Why did "well-intentioned Northern philanthropy" not help the South with its race problem in the decade or two immediately following the close of the war?
2. From the statement of "actual conditions" on page 664, estimate the daily expenditure for education per pupil, the daily pay of the teacher, the yearly pay of the county superintendents, and the average value of the schoolhouses.
3. Why was the rise of a new middle class a necessity for development in the South?
4. Show that education is in a sense a surplus luxury, and that sound taxation for education had to come after other essentials of government had been looked after.
5. Show that the statement of Dr. Dickerman (page 672) was thoroughly sound.

[1] This supervision, county by county, is maintained by a body of Negro women, known as Jeanes teachers, because the Jeanes Fund selected these women, helped in their training, and often paid the initial cost of their employment.   The Jeanes supervisor is guide and counselor in everything that has to do with Negro welfare and race relationships in her county.

6. Show how fortunate it was that the Northern leaders of the early Conferences gradually turned the movement over to Southern men to carry on.

7. Show the parallel between the Southern education movement and the revival carried on much earlier at the North by Mann and Barnard, as to means of propaganda and effectiveness.

8. Was the reception of Stiles's report by Congress and the public anything exceptional? Why?

9. Show the important educational implications of the work of the Rockefeller Sanitary Commission in the South.

10. Show the vast educational importance of the Smith-Lever work for the rural South.

11. Would you say that the progress made in the education of the Negro, in the years since his emancipation, has been rapid, or not? Why?

SELECTED READINGS

In the accompanying volume of *Readings* the following selections, related to the subject matter of this chapter, are reproduced:

308. Winston: Conditions the South Faced.
309. Jones: Industrial Train'ng for the Negro Race.
310. Aycock: On Legislative Duty.
311. Resolution: Creation of the Southern Education Board.
312. Dickerman: Sweep and Power of the Conference Movement.
313. Knight: Educational Problems of the Southern States.
314. Embree: Progress in Negro Education and Welfare.

QUESTIONS ON THE READINGS

1. What was the magnitude of this condition (**308a**) the South faced? Was the remedy prescribed a proper one at the time? Why?

2. Could the pitiable situation of the poor white (**308b**) have been avoided?

3. Why, if such institutions as Hampton and Tuskegee (**309**) are valued so highly, have we had so few of them and so many "cultural colleges" founded for the race?

4. Would you say that it was "good politics" for a governor to take such stands as did Governor Aycock (**310**)?

5. Characterize the tone and the purpose of the movement as it found expression in the Resolution (**311**) given.

6. Account for the sweep and the power of the movement (**312**).

7. What are the remedies for the conditions Knight portrays (**313**)?

8. Show that the picture presented by Embree (**314**) is a very hopeful one.

TOPICS FOR INVESTIGATION AND REPORT

1. The founding and work of Hampton Institute.
2. Booker T. Washington, and his work.

3. Educational services of Edwin A. Alderman.
4. Work of the Conferences for Education in the South.
5. Work of the Commission for the Eradication of Hookworm Disease.
6. National funds to aid education in the South.
7. Negro education; its problems and progress.

SELECTED REFERENCES

Coon, Charles L.   "Charles Duncan McIver and his Educational Services, 1886–1906"; in *Report of the United States Commissioner of Education,* 1907, vol. I, pp. 329–39.

   Describes the important work he did for North Carolina and the South.

*Dickerman, G. S.   "The Conference for Education in the South, and the Southern Education Board"; in *Report of the United States Commissioner of Education,* 1907, vol. I, pp. 291–328.

   Continues the article by Rose to cover the 1904–07 period.

Jones, Thomas J.   *Negro Education.*   2 vols., Bulletins 38 and 39, 1916, of United States Bureau of Education.   Vol. I, 422 pp., is a general summary report; vol. II, is a report by States.

   A survey of private and higher schools for the colored people in the United States, made by the Phelps-Stokes Fund.   Vol. I gives a good picture of the problem and results attained.

*Knight, Edgar W.   *Public Education in the South.*   482 pp.   Boston, 1922.

   The last two chapters deal with the period from 1900 on.

*Lingley, Charles R.   *Since the Civil War.*   New York, Rev. Ed., 1926.

   Chapters 3, 4, and 19 deal with the economic, political, and intellectual foundation and background, and conditions existing at the close of the last century.

Murphy, Edgar.   *The Problem of the Present South.*   New York, 1905.

   Chapter 8, on educational problems of the new South, good supplemental reading for this chapter.

*Rose, Wycliff.   "The Educational Movement in the South"; in *Report of the United States Commissioner of Education,* 1903, vol. I, pp. 357–90.

   A history of the rise of the Conference for Education in the South, and the work of the first six Conferences, 1898–1903.

*Sullivan, Mark.   *Our Times,* vol. III.   New York, 1930.

   Chapter IX, "An Emancipation," describes in some detail the work of Dr. Stiles and the General Education Board in the eradication of hookworm in the South.

Annual Reports of Jeanes Fund, Rosenwald Fund, and Slater Fund.
Proceedings of Conferences for Education in the South.
State Histories of Education in Southern States — See References at close of Chapter XII.

CHAPTER XXI

PROFESSIONAL ORGANIZATION

I. THE SCIENTIFIC STUDY OF THE PROBLEM

Our progress toward scientific organization. Up to the days of Carter and Mann and Pierce in Massachusetts, and Barnard in Connecticut and Rhode Island, our school development had been almost entirely along the lines of securing legislation, first to permit, and later to require, the establishment of schools; of organizing an administrative machinery to look after the schools thus established; and of creating a public belief in education for democratic ends and a sentiment that would support further progress. The development was highly empirical, each community and State following the lines of least resistance, without much regard to underlying principles of action. Carter and Mann tried to give a better organization to the schools of Massachusetts, as did Barnard to the two States to the south, while Mann sought by his *Reports* and addresses, and Barnard by his *Journals*, to introduce the improved teaching methods which American travelers abroad had described, and which both had observed in European schools. The schoolmasters of the time largely resented change, however, and few who taught felt the need of any training, so it was not until the movement looking toward a more scientific basis for our school practice had infused into it the psychology of Pestalozzi, the new ideas of Guyot and Krüsi, the administrative organization of Harris, and particularly the professional enthusiasm of Sheldon and Parker, that we really set to work in earnest to psychologize instruction, train would-be teachers for teaching, and put schoolroom practice on something approaching a scientific basis. The period from 1860 to about 1885 to 1890 was with us the great period of "faculty" psychology, subject methodology, and administrative organization and curriculum building. This period also was marked by the firm establishment of the public normal school, and the beginnings of the professional study of education in a few of the universities.

While more new ideas have come to us from abroad since the

decades of the eighties and the nineties, we have been particularly busy in working out many new conceptions of the educative process at home. As a result we today possess a truer psychology than Sheldon and his followers knew. The child-study movement of the eighties and the nineties (page 401) opened up entirely new conceptions as to the nature of child development. A new profession of teaching has been created within the past half century, and the study of the administration of public education has been organized into a new professional subject by our colleges and universities. Above all, our educational thinking has been colored through and through by the new social and industrial forces which have become so prominent during the past fifty years, and as a result we of today think in terms of a new educational philosophy, and direct the work of our schools along new lines and toward new ends.

The new scientific study of the problem. Within the past quarter of a century a number of new educational conceptions have come to the front which have already deeply modified our educational thinking and practices, and which promise to do more than any previous impulses to reorganize our educational work after a rational plan and to give scientific direction to our educational procedure. Within this period of time entirely new means of attacking educational problems have been developed through the application of statistical procedures, the use of standardized tests, and the devising of scales for the measurement of the intelligence of school children. While these new instruments are still imperfectly developed in so far as precision is concerned, so important have these movements become in terms of future educational work that they bid fair to change many of our teaching procedures and the whole character of the supervision of instruction in our schools. The scientific purpose of the new movements has been to enable us to determine educational results quantitatively, and to make it possible for us to evolve, by the careful measurement of schools and children, a series of standards of measurement (measuring sticks for school work) and units of accomplishment (time and effort evaluations of instruction) which can be applied to schools anywhere to determine, scientifically, the economy or wastefulness and the efficiency or inefficiency of the work being done. On the basis of such information the effectiveness of all kinds of instruction can be measured, and schools in different places can be accurately compared. The leader in this new movement has been Professor Edward L. Thorndike, of Teachers College, Columbia University, who has given thirty-five years of highly productive effort to the problem, and the work has centered chiefly in the universities which, since the beginning of the present century, have given serious attention to the scientific study of education. It has been in the universities that the best thinking on the problems surrounding the reorganization, administration, and the scientific study of education, and the most new and creative work has been and is being done.[1]

The university study of education. In no country in the world have the universities, within the past three decades, given the attention to the study of Education — a term that in English-speaking lands has replaced the earlier and more limited "Pedagogy" — that has been given in the United States, and, as a consequence, students from all over the world today come to American universities to train themselves, for service in their home lands, in the theory and practice and administration of public education.

Probably the first attempt to provide lectures on Pedagogy in any American college was made by what is now New York University, when a course of lectures on teaching by Thomas H. Gallaudet (1787–1851) was announced to be offered during the academic year 1832–33, but there is no evidence that the lectures ever were given.[2] The first actual experiment seems to have been made at Brown University, where the city superintendent of schools of Providence, Rhode Island, Samuel S. Green (1810–83), acted as Professor of Didactics from 1850 to 1855. In 1860 a course of lectures on the "Philosophy of Education, School Economy, and the Teaching Art" was given to the seniors of the University of Michigan. In 1873 a Professorship of Philosophy and Education[3] was established at the University of Iowa,[4] as a development out of a normal depart-

---

[1] In education, as in other lines of work, the old statement that the distinctive function of a university is not action, but thought, has been exemplified.

[2] Of this early attempt, T. F. Jones, in his volume entitled *New York University, 1832–1932*, p. 141, says: "Perhaps because of his ill health, perhaps because of lack of demand, Mr. Gallaudet seems never to have given instruction; no evidence has been found of his having done so."

[3] The exact title was Professor of Mental and Moral Science and Didactics.

[4] In 1923 important exercises were held commemorating the fiftieth anniversary of the founding of the first permanent chair in Education in the United States. The one professorship had in the meantime grown into a large and important College of Education. See *Fifty Years of Progress; Proceedings of the Celebration of the Fiftieth Anniversary of the College of Education.* Extension Bulletin No. 133, University of Iowa, October, 1925. 68 pp.

EDWARD LEE THORNDIKE
Professor of Education at Teachers College, Columbia,
since 1899

CHARLES HUBBARD JUDD
Director of the School of Education at the University of
Chicago, since 1909

TWO LEADERS IN THE PSYCHOLOGICAL STUDY OF EDUCATIONAL PROBLEMS

ment which dated back to the opening of the University [1] in 1855 (**R. 315**). This was the first permanent chair in the subject created in America (**R. 315**). In 1878 Iowa expanded the work into a College of Normal Instruction, leading to the degree of Bachelor of Pedagogics; in 1890 this was expanded into a Department of Pedagogy, and in 1907 into a School of Education.

In 1879 a Department of the Science and Art of Teaching was created at the University of Michigan, which became the second permanent university chair in the new subject in America. In 1881 a Department of Pedagogy was created at the University of Wisconsin, and in 1884 similar departments at the University of North Carolina, the University of Missouri, and at Johns Hopkins. In 1885 a chair in Education was established at Ottawa University, Kansas; in 1886 a Department of Education was established at Indiana University; in 1887 Teachers College, now a part of Columbia University, New York, was organized; and in 1891 both Chicago University and Stanford University opened, both on October first, with chairs in Education as part of their original faculty organization. From this time on the organization of chairs or departments of education was very rapid, increasing from 11 in 1891 to 83 by 1893, 174 by 1894, 220 by 1898, 244 by 1899, and 247 by 1902. Today, not counting teachers colleges, probably some 500 colleges and universities in the United States are offering courses in educational history, theory and procedure, and in school administration, and many of these institutions maintain large and important professional Schools of Education for the more scientific study of the subject and for the training of leaders for the service of the Nation's schools. In addition, somewhere near 300 public and private normal schools and teachers colleges also are offering training for teaching in public and private schools.

Development of new lines of professional work. Up to 1900, at least, the work offered in Education in the colleges and universities of the United States was quite elementary in character, and largely devoted to courses in the history and philosophy of education and to teaching methods and school management, but by about 1905 the beginnings of a change were evident, chiefly in that a number of

[1] The original Foundation Act of the University, of February 25, 1847, had specifically provided that there should be established a professorship for the training of teachers for the public schools. This was done with the opening of the University, in 1855.

promising young men had begun to turn to the subject as a field for scholarly specialization. Within a decade thereafter entirely new lines of study had been opened up, and the basis for new courses of instruction, new measuring techniques, and new procedures in investigation had been laid. Largely as a result of the foregoing, and wholly within the past three decades, one of the most significant movements in all our educational history has taken form and today modifies all our educational procedure.

Without attempting to be more than approximately exact as to dates, and without trying to name all the different workers who have contributed to the new movement, the development may be said to have been about as follows:

Between 1900 and 1905 an entirely new type of general history of education was developed, and by a decade later the students of Paul Monroe had worked out theses which laid a basis for a comprehensive history of American education,[1] which appeared in 1919. In 1904 Edward L. Thorndike made the beginnings of a new method of attack by applying statistical procedures to social and educational problems,[2] which was followed later by Rugg's textbook on *Statistical Methods*,[3] the first of a numerous progeny. In 1905 Strayer and Elliott published their pioneer studies as to costs in city school systems; in 1906 Cubberley published his studies of state school finances, and of teacher certification; and in 1910 Swift issued his monumental study of the history of permanent common school funds.[4] These early studies marked the beginnings of a long train of related investigations dealing with finance, cost accounting, budgets, business management, and teachers' status which have laid

[1] Important publications in this field were:
Cubberley, E. P. *Syllabus of Lectures on the History of Education*, 1902, 1904.
Dexter, E. G. *History of Education in the United States*, 1904.
Monroe, Paul. *History of Education*, 1905.
Graves, F. P. *History of Education*, 3 vols., 1909-13.
Parker, C. *History of Modern Elementary Education*, 1912.
Graves, F. P. *Student's History of Education*, 1915.
Cubberley, E. P. *Public Education in the United States*, 1919.
Cubberley, E. P. *History of Education*, 1920.
Cubberley, E. P. *Readings in the History of Education*, 1920.
[2] *Mental and Social Measurements*, 1904, 1907.
[3] Rugg, Harold. *Statistical Methods Applied to Education*, 1917.
[4] G. D. Strayer. *City School Expenses*, 103 pp.; Elliott, E. C., *Some Fiscal Aspects of Public Education in American Cities*, 101 pp., 1905; Cubberley, E. P., *School Funds and their Apportionment*, 255 pp., 1906; Cubberley, E. P., *The Certification of Teachers*, 88 pp., *Fifth Yearbook of the National Society for the Scientific Study of Education*, Part II, 1906; Swift, F. H., *History of Permanent Common School Funds in the United States*, 493 pp., 1910.

the basis for standard textbooks and for the scientific study of the problems of city and state school administration.

In 1909 the foundations of a new philosophy of education were laid by the publication of John Dewey's *How We Think*, followed in 1916 by his *Democracy and Education*. In 1924 Chapman and Counts published their *Principles of Education*, and this, with Dewey's books, provided us with an entirely new educational philosophy, based on the new biology, psychology, and sociology.

Beginning in 1909 with the work of Gulick and Ayres,[1] Dresslar and Rapeer [2] in 1913, and Terman [3] in 1914, the foundations were soon laid for a new schoolbuilding and educational and mental hygiene, which added other new subjects of instruction to our educational work. Today educational hygiene is a field by itself, and one of fundamental importance for educational work.

A new ability to diagnose. Back as early as 1897 Dr. J. M. Rice had startled the country by a series of articles in which he claimed that the results of teaching spelling could be measured by means of a spelling test.[4] His proposal was greeted with ridicule by many, but the idea of a series of standard tests gradually made headway. In 1908 C. W. Stone, a student under Thorndike, published the first standardized achievement test, dealing with the ability to reason in arithmetic.[5] This represented a most important new development in the scientific study of educational practice. In 1910 Thorndike published his *Handwriting Scale*, by 1910 Courtis [6] had his *Arithmetical Scales* well along toward completion, and in 1912 Hillegas published his *Composition Scale* and Ayres his first *Spelling Scale*.

So forcibly did this new idea as to the measurement of accomplishment and ability appeal to the younger schoolmen that these pioneer workers were soon followed by a large number of men and women

[1] Gulick, L. H., and Ayres, L. P. *Medical Inspection of Schools*. 276 pp. New York, 1909.

[2] Dresslar, F. B. *School Hygiene*. 369 pp. New York, 1913. Rapeer, L. W. *School Health Administration*. 360 pp. New York, 1913.

[3] Terman, L. M. *Hygiene of the School Child*. 417 pp. Boston, 1914; 505 pp., 1929. Terman, L. M., and Hoag, E. B. *Health Work in the Schools*. 321 pp. Boston, 1914.

[4] Rice, J. M. "The Futility of the Spelling Grind"; in *The Forum*, vol. 23, pp. 163–72, 409–19. (April and June, 1897.)

[5] Stone, C. W. *Arithmetical Abilities and Some Factors Determining Them*. 101 pp., 1908.

[6] S. A. Courtis, of the Detroit schools, has done a prodigious amount of work in developing and perfecting his various scales for testing arithmetical operations. He was one of the earliest workers in the field.

who were busy for the next ten years in developing, testing, and standardizing all kinds of accomplishment scales.[1] For each scale was worked out a "standard score," which means the amount of work with the tests which should be done by average pupils, of any age or grade. When Hines published his *Guide to Educational Measurements*, in 1923, he estimated that there were then over 300 standardized scales available for use.

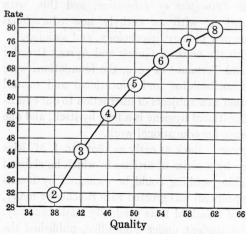

FIG. 161. GRADE NORMS FOR HANDWRITING

Based on Ayres' *Handwriting Scale*, Gettysburg Edition. From this graph any pupil can readily determine his normal score.

With these standard tests and scores we can now measure an unknown class and say, rather definitely, that, for example, the class not only spells poorly but is 12 per cent below standard; that the class is 8 per cent ahead of its place in speed of writing, but 15 per cent below on quality; that the children are from 6 to 16 per cent above grade in the four simple arithmetical processes, but 21 per cent below in ability to reason on simple arithmetical problems; that they can read orally 16 per cent better than the average class, but are sadly deficient in thought-getting ability from silent reading; and that, in composition, they are 10 per cent below standard and can write much better than they can think. Still more, we can determine

[1] At the meeting of the Department of Superintendence of the N.E.A. at Philadelphia, in 1913, quite a little of the discussion hinged around whether measurement and tests could be successfully applied to teaching and administration. In a general way, the younger men approved of the idea, and the older men doubted. The discussion was largely precipitated by two thought-provoking papers on measurement in school administration read by Professor Paul H. Hanus and Superintendent Frank E. Spaulding, two on measuring the efficiency of teachers by Superintendents William M. Davidson and Ben Blewett, three on school supervision by Superintendents Milton C. Potter, J. J. Keyes, and Frederick M. Hunter, and one on economy of time through testing, by Leonard P. Ayres.

just where the difficulty lies, not only with schools or classes, but for individual pupils in classes as well, as the Ayres Writing Scale (Fig. 161) graph reveals.

The next step from the perfection of standard scales, which could be used for diagnostic purposes, was a careful diagnostic study of learning procedures in the common school subjects, as arithmetic, reading, and handwriting, with a view to determining just how learning actually took place and, on the basis of such knowledge, the outlining of more scientific teaching procedures. The leader in this phase of the work has been Charles H. Judd, Director of the School of Education at the University of Chicago since 1909, aided by certain members of his staff. The careful psychological studies made there of silent *vs.* oral reading, number combinations, and muscular movements in handwriting have been especially significant.

Application to the school survey. In 1910 the school survey began,[1] a new movement destined to produce a large amount of important data as to school supervision and administration and to reveal the importance of the standardized scales as measuring instruments. The first school surveys were those made at Boise, Idaho, 1910 (31 pp.); Montclair, New Jersey, 1911 (28 pp.); Baltimore, Maryland, 1911 (112 pp.); New York City, 1911 (10 vols.); East Orange, New Jersey, 1912 (64 pp.); Portland, Oregon, 1913 (317 pp.); Butte, Montana, 1914 (163 pp.); Salt Lake City, 1915 (324 pp.); Cleveland, Ohio, 1916 (25 small volumes); and Grand Rapids, Michigan, 1917 (387 pp.). In the New York City (arithmetic only), Butte, and Salt Lake City surveys, standardized tests were used to measure pupil attainment for the first times.

Within recent years these tests have been used in school surveys in a large number of American cities, and those responsible for the conduct of the schools have been told, as a result of the tests, where their schools stood in the matter of instruction. Butte (1914), Salt Lake City (1915), Cleveland (1916), and Grand Rapids (1917) form good examples of the early use of these tests to diagnose con-

[1] There had, of course, been a few so-called surveys made here and there earlier. Two early ones frequently cited are the ones made by Francis Wayland at Providence, Rhode Island, in 1828, and the survey of educational conditions in Rhode Island made by Henry Barnard, in 1844. Other so-called surveys that might be cited were made in a few cities at an early date. Notwithstanding these, the first modern school surveys, as we now know them, were made as stated in 1910 and 1911.

ditions. In Butte, for example, the schools were found ahead of where they should have been in all formal drill subjects, and below where they should have been in all subjects involving reasoning or expression. In Salt Lake City, the schools were found to rank high and above standard in all subjects in which tests were given — spelling, composition, writing, reading, and arithmetic — but that the range of pupil abilities in classes and schools was too large, and that too much time was being given to these subjects at the expense of other studies. The Cleveland measurements showed much wrong emphasis in instruction, far too wide variations between schools and classes, and need of an entirely new type of school supervision to secure better results for the money expended. The schools of Grand Rapids, as a whole, were found near to where they should be, the attention needed being to individual schools, rather than to the school system as a whole. Quite similar results have been shown by many subsequent school surveys.

As the school survey movement developed it soon changed in character from an occasional survey made by outside experts, to a continuous survey of production made from within by the superintendent of schools and his staff. This change led to the creation of city bureaus of educational research to conduct testing programs, gather data, and interpret the results. Between 1911 and 1918 a number of such bureaus were established,[1] in the larger cities of our country. Soon their work was expanded from that of general survey and testing to include a wide series of studies relating to pupil placement, retardation, testing programs, salary schedules, curriculum reorganizations, statistics, finance, accounting, attendance, budget preparation, and other types of research studies, while many such bureaus have divisions that deal with misfit and subnormal children and do the work of a psychological clinic.

Since the World War, with the large amount of new school building construction undertaken, the school building survey has been developed and perfected, and school building scales and score cards have been worked out and standardized.[2] In 1925 a standard text-

[1] The first was at Rochester, New York, in 1911, chiefly for finance and accounting. In 1912 Baltimore created a bureau primarily for educational research, and in 1914 Louisville established one primarily for work as a psychological clinic. These three types of bureaus for research still exist, though the first and second types now are usually combined. The number of such bureaus rose from 1 in 1911 to 17 by 1915, 53 by 1920, and 108 by 1926.

[2] The most generally used scales are those devised by Professors Strayer and Englehardt, of Teachers College, Columbia, which rate school buildings on a scale of 1000 points. Three

book on the School Survey [1] appeared, which laid down the fundamental principles which have been developed and have since controlled for all types of school survey work.

Standard tests as a basis for course of study eliminations. The studies made with the use of the tests, too, have shown that in some school subjects we have been teaching far too much in quantity, giving too much school time to instruction in them, or over-emphasizing certain phases of the teaching of a subject to the neglect of other important phases. The children of Butte, for example, were learning to spell over 10,000 words, while all careful studies made of vocabularies show that 1000 words will cover the most commonly used and most commonly misspelled words, and that about 3500 words are about all that need be taught. In Salt Lake City children were being given 25 per cent more school time for writing than was necessary, and were being drilled to a degree of perfection in penmanship which was wasteful of time and energy. In Cleveland too much time was being given to oral reading, without results to warrant the expenditure. In Grand Rapids the composition tests showed the pupils to be over-drilled in the mechanics of composition, but poor in ability to think. On the basis of such studies, combined with studies as to the social usefulness of the various parts of the different school subjects, and studies as to the pedagogy of instruction, we have already been able to do something in the revision of our elementary school curriculum that has lightened the load and materially improved the instruction of what remains.

By creating such measuring sticks for school work, both supervisors and teachers are given a far more definite aim than ever before for the work they are to do. Waste of energy through over- or under-emphasis of certain phases of the teaching process may be prevented. Principals and teachers can tell, from a glance at the results of standard tests, charted on a standard score card, whether or not any room or group of pupils is up to standard; what are the weak points; whether a room or a school is making progress; and in what rooms the load and the teacher are not properly adjusted. Teachers, in particular, can know definitely what results are expected of them, and at all times whether or not they are

different score cards have been developed for City Schools, Rural Schools, and for High Schools.

[1] Sears, J. B. *The School Survey*, 440 pp. Boston, 1925. A textbook on the use of school surveying in the administration of public schools.

accomplishing them. Even pupils can, in some subjects, score their own records on standard score cards, calculate their growth in accuracy and speed, and compare their writing with the standardized writing of a writing scale hung in the room.

The underlying purpose. The important underlying purpose in the creation of all such standards for measuring school work and for comparing the accomplishments of pupils, classes, schools, or school systems, is to give to supervisors and teachers means by which they may, quite definitely, measure the effectiveness of the work they do, and learn from the charted results where to shift the emphasis and how to improve the manufacturing process. Teaching without a measuring stick of standardized length, and without definite standards (standard scores, or norms) for the work of the different grades, is much like the old time luck-and-chance farming, and there is no reason to think that the introduction of well-tested standards for accomplishment in school work will not do for education what has been done for agriculture as a result of the application of scientific knowledge and methods. This recent development of tests and measures for instruction is a movement looking toward scientific accuracy in teaching, and is comparable in importance to the introduction of the idea, in the sixties, of an orderly psychological development in children to which a methodology of instruction should be applied.

For the superintendent, standardized tests have meant nothing less than the ultimate changing of school administration from guess work to scientific accuracy. The mere personal opinion of school board members and the lay public, and even the old method of a comparison of school systems, have been in large part eliminated, and in their place has been substituted demonstrable proof as to the validity of a method or a procedure or the effectiveness of the administration or the supervision of a school system (**R. 316**). The development of standardized tests has meant a vast improvement in our ability to evaluate educational procedures, and as great an advance toward scientific organization as did the introduction of the conception of an orderly psychological development in the sixties.

The measurement of intelligence. Within the past quarter-century there has also been worked out and perfected another new and very important means of testing whereby it is now possible to measure and classify children on the basis of their intellectual capacities. In 1905 a French psychologist, Alfred Binet (1857–1911), as the result of fifteen years of work, published a scale for measuring the intelligence of school children. Later revisions were published in 1908 and 1911, and American revisions by Goddard in 1911, Kuhlmann in 1912, and Terman and Childs in 1913. Terman's Stanford Revision, now the standard American edition, appeared in 1916. This form of test, commonly known as the Binet, the Binet-Simon, or the Stanford Binet, is an individual test, and the intelligence of the pupil examined is expressed as an intelligence quotient (I.Q.).

Our entry into the World War, in 1917, gave new impetus to the testing problem, and resulted in the development of the Army Intelligence Scales,[1] by means of which a whole company could be

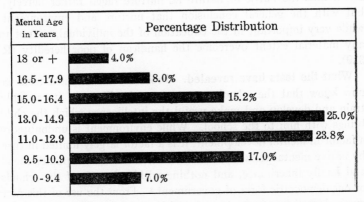

Mental Age in Years	Percentage Distribution
18 or +	4.0%
16.5 - 17.9	8.0%
15.0 - 16.4	15.2%
13.0 - 14.9	25.0%
11.0 - 12.9	23.8%
9.5 - 10.9	17.0%
0 - 9.4	7.0%

FIG. 162. ARMY INTELLIGENCE TEST RESULTS

Percentage distribution, by Mental Age, of the results of the examination of 1,700,000 army recruits on the Army Intelligence Tests, in 1917. Age eighteen is regarded as adult.

tested at one time. Over 1,700,000 army recruits were given the Army Alpha alone, and were sorted for army work accordingly. Intelligence testing was advanced a decade as a result of this procedure. Following the War the National Intelligence Test was

[1] These were in two forms — the Army Alpha, for those able to read English, and the Army Beta, for those unable to read English. The distribution of scores obtained for the 1,700,000 recruits tested by the Army Alpha were, mental age 18 (A) being called adult:

Letter Score	E and D–	D	C–	C	C+	B	A
Mental Age	0–9.4	9.5–10.9	11–12.9	13–14.9	15–16.4	16.5–17.9	18
Percentage	7.0%	17.0%	23.8%	25.0%	15.2%	8.0%	4.0%

developed, and this has had extensive use in our schools.[1] There are at present over thirty well-known group intelligence tests on the market, designed for use not only in the schools but also in the industries and the courts, with the Stanford Binet still the standard for use with individual children (**R. 317**).

The use of intelligence tests provoked an enormous controversy. The conception of the biological inequality of human beings, though clearly recognized as to size and strength and endurance and ability to perform, seemed particularly difficult for some educators to accept when applied to mental capacity (**R. 318**). The democratic ideal in education seemed at stake. Instead of being born free and equal, as our political maxims had taught us, we now found that we were born free but unequal, and unequal we were forever to remain. For a time the battle of nature *vs.* nurture raged rather fiercely,[2] but with the general conclusion that nurture and environment, while very important in the education of the individual, cannot to any material extent overcome the handicap of poor heredity (**R. 319**).

What the tests have revealed. From the use of these tests we now know that the school cannot create intelligence; it can only train and develop and make useful the intelligence which the child brings with him to the school. While environment is undoubtedly a factor in mental development, it is a factor largely limited in turn by native mental capacity, and this is a matter of the pupil's racial and family inheritance, and nothing within the gift of the schools or our democratic form of government.[3] From the use of this new measuring stick, too, we have found that there can be no arbitrary classification of children into such groups as dull, average, and bright. Instead, children shade off from one classification into another, all the way from idiocy at one end of the scale to superior genius at the other. As might be expected, most children fall into the relatively

[1] The first year the test was available 575,000 copies were sold, and the third year 800,000 copies were sold.

[2] This discussion culminated in the publication of the *Twenty-Seventh Yearbook* of the National Society for the Study of Education (1928), both Parts I and II being devoted to a series of papers and investigations relating to Nature *vs.* Nurture, and their influence on intelligence and achievement.

[3] A good example of attempted governmental interference to preserve democratic equality was the following regulation, adopted by the Senate of one of our 1933 legislatures: "No intelligence test, aptitude test, or other test designed to determine the mental classifications and fitness of an individual shall ever be used as a basis for grading, classifying, or segregating any children in elementary or high schools."

normal class, the curve shading off somewhat evenly in either direction, as Figure 163 shows.

By means of a series of carefully selected and standardized mental tests we are now able to measure and give each child an intelligence rating (intelligence quotient; I.Q.). From this rating (I.Q.) we know, within a reasonable degree of accuracy, the possibilities of the child in school work. Terman's studies showed that the distribution of the intelligence of children, between 5 and 14 years of age, is approximately as shown in Figure 163, the extremes in intelli-

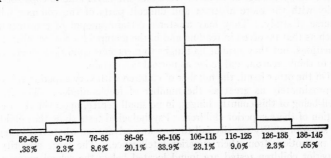

| 56-65 | 66-75 | 76-85 | 86-95 | 96-105 | 106-115 | 116-125 | 126-135 | 136-145 |
| .33% | 2.3% | 8.6% | 20.1% | 33.9% | 23.1% | 9.0% | 2.3% | .55% |

FIG. 163. THE DISTRIBUTION OF INTELLIGENCE AMONG CHILDREN

Based on the measurement of 905 unselected school children, five to fourteen years of age. From Terman's *The Measurement of Intelligence*, p. 66.

gence in the children he measured ranging from 56 to 145. On the basis of his work he suggested the following classification of children as to I.Q. and mental capacity.

I.Q.	*Classification*
Above 140.............	Near genius or genius.
120–140...............	Very superior intelligence.
110–120...............	Superior intelligence.
90–110.................	Normal, or average intelligence.
80–90..................	Dullness.
70–80..................	Border-line deficiency, sometimes classifiable as dullness, often as feeble-mindedness.
Below 70..............	Definite feeble-mindedness.

Educational significance of intelligence measurements. The educational significance of this new means of measuring intelligence is very large. Questions relating to proper classification in school, grading, promotion, choice of studies, schoolroom procedure, vocational guidance, and the proper handling of subnormal children on the one hand and gifted children on the other all acquire new meaning when viewed in the light of intelligence measurement. To quote Terman:

Wherever intelligence tests have been made in any considerable number in the schools it has been shown that not far from 2 per cent of the children enrolled have a grade of intelligence which, however long they live, will never develop beyond the level which is normal to the average child of 11 or 12 years. They may be able to drag along to the 4th, 5th, or 6th grades, but even by the age of 16 or 18 years they are never able to cope successfully with the more abstract and difficult parts of the common-school course of study. They may master a certain amount of rote learning, such as that involved in reading and in the manipulation of number combinations, but they cannot be taught to meet new conditions effectively, or to think, reason, and judge as normal persons do.

On the other hand, the number of children with very superior ability is approximately as great as the number of feeble-minded. The future well-being of this country hinges, in no small degree, upon the right education of these superior children. Psychological tests show that children of superior ability usually fail to reap any advantage whatever, in terms of promotion, from their superior intelligence. The large majority of superior children tested are found located below the school grade warranted by their intelligence level.

When these new tests of intelligence have been applied to the children who experience difficulty in getting along in the regular school a flood of light has been thrown on the problem. Low mentality, retardation in school, truancy, immorality, and criminal tendencies all seem to be tied up closely together. It may now be confidently asserted, on the basis of tests so far made, that approximately 2 per cent of the children in our schools are of such low mentality that they probably never will attain to a grade of intelligence above that normal for a twelve-year-old child; that among the children in our reform (industrial) schools 20 to 25 per cent are feeble-minded, and another 20 to 25 per cent of low-grade mentality; that approximately 25 to 30 per cent of our criminals and 30 to 40 per cent of our prostitutes are feeble-minded. Of the low-grade-in-intelligence members of these classes, very few have ever progressed beyond the sixth grade in school. Lacking in the ability to foresee and weigh consequences, and unable to exercise self-restraint, every low-grade or feeble-minded girl is a potential prostitute and every boy of the type a potential criminal.

Viewed in the light of this new knowledge, the importance of mental measurements to grade and classify intelligence, of the standard tests to determine lines of progress, and of the special types of schools for delinquents and defectives mentioned in Chapter XV — differentiated course of study, over-age classes, non-English-speaking classes, supplemental coaching classes, industrial classes, home schools, disciplinary classes, parental schools, state industrial schools — all acquire a new educational significance in the light of our recent discoveries as to the measurement and grading of intelligence. The recent development of standard scales and a scale for the grading of intelligence mark distinct forward steps in the improvement of our educational procedure. Just now they are both new, and the public and some educators seem afraid of them, but as they are learned by teachers and principals and their use made common, schoolroom methods will become more intelligent, children will be classified and taught better, and the needs of the slow on the one hand and the gifted on the other will be better cared for by our schools. Both standardized tests and intelligence tests represent important new steps forward in the process of making education a more scientific procedure.

A further and more recent development has been tests intended to measure special types of mental ability, such as will, temperament, emotions, moral attitude, administrative capacity, personality, mechanical aptitude, and other somewhat similar mental qualities. It is probable that the future development of mental tests will be markedly in this direction. The ultimate conclusion of the process likely will be the development of a comprehensive test, or series of tests, which will permit the all-around examination of an individual.

Education as a teaching subject has thus passed, it will be seen, through much the same stages as many other teaching subjects — agriculture, engineering, the sciences, economics, psychology — in that it made its crude beginnings first by claiming its field, then by working out and organizing its teaching materials, developing its techniques, and expanding its work in new directions. Today the subject offers challenges to thinking that each year are attracting to it some of the most promising young men and women who are entering the public service. While the business world has, during the past fifty years, drawn the best brains of the Nation into its field, there is good reason to think that the prizes in the business world will be less attractive in the future to those of large administrative capacity. The next generation of young people may well discover that the fields of government and of public education offer excellent opportunities to men of exceptional ability for adventure and usefulness.

II. ORGANIZATION OF THE TEACHING PROFESSION

Early educational organizations. As was described in Chapter VI, the early propaganda organizations for education were composed chiefly of public-spirited citizens drawn together for the purpose of awakening sentiment favorable to the creation and maintenance of systems of public instruction by the general taxation of property. A few of these early propaganda organizations, notably the American Lyceum (page 168) and the Western Literary Institute and College of Professional Teachers (page 169), had made a point of including teachers and educational leaders, as well as lay citizens, in their membership. During the decades between about 1820 and 1850 these propaganda organizations rendered notable service in the formation of public sentiment favorable to tax-supported schools.

Beginning about the same time, we find the first of the more strictly professional organizations of teachers themselves meeting for the consideration of more strictly professional problems. In New York and New England we find records of a few meetings of town and county conventions of teachers by or before 1830 (**R. 320**), and shortly thereafter of state conventions where the addresses were intended primarily for teachers and principals (**R. 321**). These, however, were informal organizations; the first formally organized state teachers' association not being formed until 1845.

Transitional associations. What is regarded as the first of the national associations of teachers, though it has always remained predominantly a New England organization,[1] was the American Institute of Instruction, organized in the State House in Boston,[2] in August, 1830 (**R. 322**). From the first this organization enrolled

[1] The first seven years of its existence all meetings were held in Boston, and of the total number of meetings held from 1830 to 1906, one third of the meetings were held in Massachusetts, one fourth in New Hampshire, and but one tenth were held outside of New England. Of the last, Montreal, Halifax, and Saratoga and Troy, New York, have represented the meetings held elsewhere.

[2] "On the 15th of March, 1830, a meeting of teachers and other friends of education was held at Columbian Hall, in Boston. It continued until the 19th. During these meetings a constitution was formed and plans for later meetings were made. A second meeting was held in August of the same year, at which officers were elected and plans were fully laid out. The name given to this organization was *The American Institute of Instruction*." *Am. Inst. Instr. Proc.*, Vol. I, pp. 3–7.

among its membership the leading scholars and educational statesmen of the time, and for many years the grammar-school men and
the public-school men took no part in its proceedings.[1]   The American Institute, like the Western Literary Institute, represented for a
time a transitional type of organization, its early mission having
been "to foster the public school sentiment and develop it into a
scheme which more nearly approximated a 'system' than was to
be found elsewhere in the United States" (**R. 322**).   For a decade
and a half the American Institute was a general New England
organization, but in 1845 it became a Rhode Island association.
For the next forty years the organization was left largely to the
care of Rhode Island schoolmen.   For a time it experienced financial
difficulties, but since about 1885 it has again been made more and
more a New England organization in scope and character and has
grown in importance and influence.   Its meetings have attracted
the leading public and private school and college men of New England
and its programs have always been of high grade.

Between 1831, when it ceased to be a Cincinnati and Ohio organization and became a more or less national institution, the Western
Literary Institute and College of Professional Teachers (page 169)
rendered much the same type of service in the West and South that
the American Institute of Instruction rendered for a time in New
England, and it is accordingly ranked as the second oldest educational
association in the United States.   While largely represented by the
four States of Ohio, Indiana, Illinois, and Kentucky, the association had branches and scattered membership in many other States
of the Union (see Fig. 51, page 170).   The first eleven meetings
(1831–41) and the last one (1845) were held in Cincinnati, and the
others in Louisville, Kentucky.   Three sessions were held each day,
for a five-day period, and the leading speakers [2] of the region and
the leading topics of the time were listed on its programs.[3]

[1] The public-school men of New England later formed state associations of their own
(Massachusetts, 1845; Connecticut, 1848) and limited membership to those actually engaged in teaching, thus excluding such men as Horace Mann, Thomas Gallaudet, Edward
Everett, Josiah Quincy, Edmund Dwight, and others prominent in the school revival and
the American Institute.

[2] Among the early speakers and officers of the Institute may be found such names as Lyman Beecher, Samuel Lewis, Calvin E. Stowe, William H. McGuffey, Joseph Ray, Samuel
Galloway, Henry Barnard, Albert Picket, Elias Loomis, Emma Willard, and Miss Catherine
E. Beecher — names that are of large historic significance in the development of public
education in the then West.

[3] Of this Institute, Henry Barnard has written: "It was not only one of the earliest educational associations of our country, but also proved itself to be one of the best, one of the most

It was but natural that the leaders in both these early associations should have been leaders in public thought, rather than public school teachers.   One hundred years ago there were few public schools, no city or county or state superintendents, very few high schools (page 259), no normal schools, and no professional literature except Hall's *Lectures on Schoolkeeping* (page 376) and the *American Annals of Education* (page 343).   The state university was still in its infancy, travel was by stagecoach, and no one was paid for making an educational address or for attending an educational meeting.   Yet these early associations provided a forum for the formulation of great plans for the development of public education and the advancement of the welfare of mankind.

National Association of the Friends of Education.   Ten years after the last meeting (1839) of the American Lyceum Association, and four years after the last meeting (1845) of the Western Literary Institute, a new effort was made for the organization of a national educational association through a convention of teachers, school superintendents, and friends of education generally.   This convention met at Philadelphia, on October 17, 1849, and continued in session for three days under the presidency of Horace Mann, with Henry Barnard chairman of the business committee of the convention.   The call for a "National Convention of the Friends of Common Schools and of Universal Education" was signed by 37 representative schoolmen, 12 of whom were state superintendents of public instruction, and several were presidents of colleges.

This convention formed a transition from the earlier type of organization, composed largely of college men and publicists interested in education, to the more modern type of educational organization composed primarily of teachers and supervisory officers of the schools.   Fifteen States were represented at this meeting.   Many of those present held responsible state and administrative positions; many also were practical teachers in the schools.   The discussions of the convention were confined closely to topics relating to the organization and administration of systems of public instruction

active, energetic, and laborious, and one of the most practical and widely influential. Started by practical teachers, it early enlisted in its cause the aid and co-operation of the most prominent professors and teachers in the colleges and high schools of the West, and through them exerted a beneficial influence upon teachers and schools generally, and, somewhat more indirectly, upon public opinion, legislative action, and public school systems."

adapted to the different sections of the United States.[1] In closing the last session of the convention, Horace Mann in his address said:

When, in the course of yesterday's proceedings, a resolution was introduced proposing to make this a national convention, I confess that, as I sat here in my chair, I felt myself trembling with emotion at the idea of the responsibility you were about to assume. Shall this body establish itself as a national convention? Shall we hold ourselves out to this great country as a source of information and a center of influence on one of the most important subjects that can be submitted to the human faculties? Shall we hold ourselves up here in full sunlight, and virtually say to the whole country, come here and fill your urns from our fountains of wisdom? Those views came over me with such force as almost to make me forget where I was, and the duties I had to discharge; for experience has led me to know something of the difficulties of the work. Yet it was the pleasure of the convention to adopt the resolution; and through the signatures of your officers you will severally subscribe to that conclusion. Now, by these acts, you have signed and sealed a bond. You have obligated yourselves to perform great duties, and you cannot deny or elude this obligation without a forfeiture of honor and character. If we fulfill the duties we have assumed this meeting will prove one of the most important meetings ever held in this country. If we fail in our respective spheres of action to fulfill these duties, this meeting will be the shame and ridicule of us all. By itself it is a small movement, but we can make it the first of a series that shall move the whole country. However insignificant in itself, it is great in its possibilities.

At the second Philadelphia meeting, in 1850, it was resolved to adopt a constitution and take the name of the American Association for the Advancement of Education. Subsequent meetings were held at Cleveland (1851), Newark (1852), Pittsburg (1853), Washington (1854), New York City (1855, 1857), Detroit (1856), and Albany (1858), after which this association ceased to exist. The formation of the National Teachers' Association, in 1857, composed primarily of actual teachers, absorbed the organization.

State Teachers' Associations. The first state teachers' association, in the modern sense of the term, was the Rhode Island Institute of Instruction,[2] which was organized in 1844, and held its first meet-

[1] The nine main topics considered by the convention were: administrative subdivisions of the State, school attendance, school architecture, grades of schools, course of instruction, teachers and their problems, support, public interest, and supplemental means (libraries, lyceums, lectures).

[2] Among those prominent in this early organization were John Kingsbury, the first president; Henry Barnard, state commissioner of education at the time; Nathan Bishop, for many years superintendent of schools in Providence; Samuel S. Green, Bishop's successor; Francis Wayland, president of Brown University; and Dana P. Colburn, principal of the Rhode Island Normal School.

ing at Providence on January 28, 1845. This organization and the Massachusetts Teachers' Association, formed the same year, may be regarded as a division of the American Institute of Instruction into two separate state groups, largely for the greater convenience in attendance of their respective memberships. These new organizations were soon followed by others of much the same type, each being largely an association of those actually engaged in teaching, and some, as in Massachusetts (1845), limited to teachers only. Within the next dozen years a number of state teachers' associations were formed, all being somewhat similar in purpose and clientele. The first associations to be organized were:

Order	State Teachers' Association of	Date of organization	First meeting held at
1	Rhode Island	Jan. 28, 1845	Providence
2	New York	July 30, 1845	Syracuse
3	Massachusetts	Nov. 25, 1845	Boston
4	Ohio	Dec. 31, 1847	——
5	Connecticut	Apr. 15, 1848	——
6	Vermont	Oct. 16, 1850	Montpelier
7	Michigan	Oct. 12, 1852	Ypsilanti
8	Pennsylvania	Dec. 28, 1852	Harrisburg
9	Wisconsin	July 12–14, 1853	Madison
10	Illinois	Dec. 27, 1853	Bloomington
11	New Jersey	Dec. 28, 1853	——
12	Iowa	May 10, 1854	Iowa City
13	New Hampshire	Nov. 27–28, 1854	Nashua
14	Indiana	Dec. 25, 1854	——
15	Missouri	May 22, 1856	St. Louis
16	North Carolina	Oct., 1856	——
17	Alabama	—— 1856	——

On page 343 we gave a list of the earliest educational journals, and here should be added a few of the early state educational journals. *The Rhode Island Schoolmaster* (1845–74), *The Massachusetts Teacher* (1848–74), and *The New York Teacher* (1852–65) are among those especially valuable historically. Of those which were more or less the organs of the state teachers' associations should be mentioned *The Ohio Educational Monthly* and *The Pennsylvania School Journal*, each claiming to be older than the other and both may be considered as beginning in January, 1852; *The Illinois Teacher*, published from 1854 to 1872; *The Indiana School Journal*, begun in 1856; and *The Wisconsin School Journal*, begun in 1871.

The National Teachers' Association. By 1857 the movement for the organization of associations of teachers themselves had proceeded far enough that a call was issued (**R. 323**) to "all practical teachers in the North, the South, the East, the West" to meet in Philadelphia in August to organize as a National Teachers' Association. The call was signed by the presidents of ten state teachers' associations.[1] The new association was to be primarily an organization of public school teachers, as distinct from college professors, administrators, and publicists, which all preceding national educational organizations had included. Its purpose was well stated in the opening remarks of the presiding officer (**R. 324**) of the gathering. Forty-three original charter members are listed as having signed the constitution at Philadelphia, August 26, 1857. The object in forming the association, as stated in the constitution, was "to elevate the character and advance the interests of the profession of teaching, and to promote the cause of popular education in the United States." The doubts as to the success of the undertaking, which the small number attending the first meeting awakened, were soon dispelled as the subsequent meetings, held at Cincinnati in 1858, Washington in 1859, Buffalo in 1860, Chicago, 1863, Ogdensburg, 1864, Harrisburg, 1865, Indianapolis, 1866, Nashville, 1868, Trenton, 1869, and Cleveland in 1870 were well attended. Due to the state of the Nation no meetings were held in 1861 and 1862, or in 1867 due to difficulties in obtaining a suitable meeting place. At first membership in the Association was confined to men teachers, but at the Indianapolis meeting in 1866 women were made eligible by substituting the word "person" for "gentleman" in defining eligibility.

National Education Association. In 1858, at a meeting held at Norwich, Connecticut, an organization was formed known as The American Normal School Association, and beginning with the Indianapolis meeting of 1866 this Association held its meetings regularly with those of the National Teachers' Association. In 1865, at a meeting held at Harrisburg, Pennsylvania, the National Association of School Superintendents was organized, and the first regular meeting of this group was held at Washington, in February, 1866, and a second meeting in August of the same year, at Indianapolis,

---

[1] The call was first proposed by the president of the New York Teachers' Association, prepared by the president of the Massachusetts Teachers' Association, and signed by the presidents of the State Teachers' Associations of New York, Massachusetts, Vermont, New Hampshire, Pennsylvania, Indiana, Wisconsin, Illinois, and Iowa. It was thus primarily a call for national organization on the part of the teachers themselves.

in connection with the National Teachers' Association. The plan of two meetings a year, one in February and one in connection with the summer meeting of the national association, was continued thereafter.

In 1869, the National Teachers' Association appointed a committee on revision of the constitution, and at the Cleveland meeting of 1870 this committee reported in favor of reorganization into a new body to be known as the National Educational Association, with four departments, viz.:

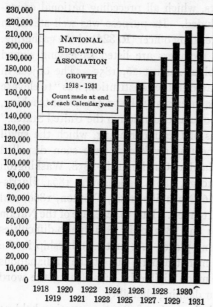

NATIONAL EDUCATION ASSOCIATION

GROWTH 1918 - 1931

Count made at end of each Calendar year

1918 1920 1922 1924 1926 1928 1930
1919 1921 1923 1925 1927 1929 1931

FIG. 164. GROWTH OF THE N.E.A. SINCE THE WORLD WAR

Permanent members enrolled, by years

1. School Superintendence
2. Normal Schools
3. Elementary Schools
4. Higher Education

The three independent national associations were thus affiliated into one national association under a new name, organized as departments, and provision was made for expansion in the future. The new Association, though formally organized in 1870, thus really dates back to the organization of The National Teachers' Association in 1857, and the present Department of Superintendence to the formation of The National Association of School Superintendents in 1865. Regular meetings of the Association have been held annually since 1870, with the exception of the years 1878, 1893, and 1906.

In 1895 the constitution was amended to provide for continuous or permanent membership in the Association to replace a temporary or yearly membership. At first the permanent membership roll grew slowly, but since the World War, due largely to an increased sense of national unity, the membership has experienced a remark-

able increase, as Figure 164 well shows.   In 1898 the position of
Permanent Secretary was created, and an office and office force
provided for.   In 1906 the Association secured national incorporation, by Act of Congress, and changed its name to that of National
Education Association.   In that year a *Fiftieth Anniversary Volume*
was issued in lieu of the meeting scheduled for that year for San
Francisco, which was abandoned because of the devastation wrought
there by earthquake and fire.   In 1916 permanent headquarters
were established at Washington, and an important new feature added
in the form of a Research Division.[1]   In 1921 the Department of
Superintendence also established the position of Permanent Secretary, with headquarters with the N.E.A. in Washington, and in
1923 the Department began the publication of an important series
of *Yearbooks*.   The seventy-five years of existence of this Association (1857–1932) is a record of increasingly important service [2] and
accomplishments (**R. 325**).

New problems of the teaching profession.   Coincident with the
recent remarkable growth of the National Education Association
has been an equally rapid expansion of the different State Associations.   These also have been reorganized, have greatly expanded
their membership, have employed permanent secretaries, many have
established research divisions, and all have become important factors
in state educational legislation.   So far, their greatest energies have
been used in the securing of larger school support, life-tenure legislation, and teacher-pension legislation, but there is good reason to
think that, as the members of these state associations become increasingly educationally conscious, they will address themselves
more and more to an intelligent legislative solution of the many
new and pressing problems of public education.   These new problems
are administrative, instructional, and personal, and relate to better
administrative organization — state, county, and city; to more

[1] Under the direction first of Dr. John K. Norton, and later of Dr. William G. Carr, the
Research Division has become a very important feature of the work of the National Education Association.

[2] For seventy-five years men and women of vision and courage have poured their best into
the work of the National Education Association.   Through it they have sought to improve
education and to lift the quality of American life and enterprise.   The schools today are
better because of this professional devotion and zeal.   The schools of tomorrow will be better
still.   In this corporate age they can be made better only through the co-operative effort of
all the teachers working shoulder to shoulder on their problems.   At no time have the schools
needed the Association more than now.   At no time has the individual teacher needed the
Association so much as now.   This need will increase during the years ahead.

adequate and more intelligent school supervision; the determination of teaching efficiency; curriculum reorganization; the physical welfare of both teachers and pupils; community service; adult education; educational extension; and the many subordinate problems arising from these larger issues.

That the public is gradually becoming more and more interested in the work of the public schools is yearly growing evident. The growth of national, state, and local Parent-Teacher Associations is a case in point. Organized in 1897 at Washington, as the National Congress of Mothers, and now known as the National Congress of Parents and Teachers, this Association today embraces a million and a half members, and its annual conventions are large and important gatherings of those deeply interested in the progress of public education. The local branches of this Association often render very important local educational service. Women's Clubs, Rotary Clubs, and Chambers of Commerce are illustrations of other local groups that today are interested in educational progress. These organizations represent something of the earlier attitude, when the so-called educational associations and conventions included in their membership representative citizens and leaders of thought outside of the school world, and when they moulded public opinion in a way that the present-day teachers' associations, intent on their personal problems, have so far largely failed to do. These more representative citizen organizations have it within their power to curb the manifest tendency of teachers' organizations to think primarily of their own interests, and to call them back to the consideration of the broader aspects of pupil welfare and national needs.

QUESTIONS FOR DISCUSSION

1. In what ways may the measuring procedures "change our teaching procedures and the whole character of the supervision of instruction in our schools"?
2. Can you see any reason for the very rapid development of university departments of education after about 1885 to 1890?
3. Show how the new standard measures: (a) mean ability to diagnose, (b) give a basis for course of study eliminations, and (c) mean more definite work in instruction.
4. What advantages would standardized records have over per cents in transferring pupil records from school to school?

5. How could a series of student-records be made useful in the work of vocational guidance?

6. Show how the introduction of standard measures means as great an advance in instruction as did the introduction of the conception of an orderly psychological development in the sixties.

7. Show how the school survey movement was a natural outcome of the new tendency to measure, developed after about 1905.

8. What new light do intelligence measurements throw on the question of differentiated courses of study and schools, as set forth in Chapter XV? What on the truancy problem? What on the problem of the education of "peculiar children"?

9. If not far from two per cent of our children are of very low-grade intelligence, have we as yet done much in providing special class instruction?

10. What do you think of the common statement that "the most neglected children in the public schools today are the very bright children"? Why?

11. Explain the mentality of a legislature that passes such a regulation as that given in footnote 31 on page 700. What forces are behind such actions?

12. Trace the transition in educational associations from the early propaganda organizations of laymen to the present "union type" of educational organizations.

13. How many and what departments form the N.E.A today?

14. How do you explain the very rapid increase in permanent membership in the N.E.A. since the World War as contrasted with the very small membership before that event?

15. How and why might the Parent-Teacher organization be more expressive of the public attitude toward educational questions than teachers' organizations?

SELECTED READINGS

In the accompanying volume of *Readings*, the following selections, related to the subject matter of this chapter, are reproduced:

315. Ensign: The First Permanent Chair in Education.
316. Cubberley: The Contribution of Standardized Tests.
317. Freeman: Brief History of the Mental Test Movement.
318. Terman: The Nature *vs.* Nurture Controversy.
319. Heilman: Heredity and Environmental Factors.
320. Annals: Early County Conventions.
321. Annals: Program of an Educational Convention of 1838.
322. Winship: The American Institute of Instruction.
323. Hagar: Call for a Convention to Organize a National Association.
324. Russell: Purpose of the National Teachers' Association.
325. Morgan: Seventy-Five Years of the N.E.A.

QUESTIONS ON THE READINGS

1. What influences would you think were prominent in inserting the teacher-training provision in the Enabling Act for the University of Iowa (**315**) as early as 1847?
2. State, in your own words, the contribution of tests to school administration (**316**).
3. Show that the historical development here described (**317**) was the same as for most other scientific advances, and illustrate by another development, if you can.
4. How do you explain the opposition to mental tests here described (**318**)?
5. State the different types of schools required were nature, or nurture, the great determining factor (**319**).
6. Characterize the early county institutes described in **320**.
7. Characterize the Detroit state convention described in **321**.
8. Estimate the importance and influence of the early meetings of The American Institute of Instruction (**322**).
9. Characterize the spirit and purpose of this "Call" (**323**).
10. What does this Address (**324**) reveal as to the purpose and spirit of the new profession?
11. Indicate three or four lines of desirable activity for the N.E.A. (**325**) for he next quarter century.

TOPICS FOR INVESTIGATION AND REPORT

1. The early chairs of education in the universities, and the character of the early instruction.
2. The early Standard Tests movement.
3. The early school surveys, and the lines of study they established.
4. The pioneer work of Binet.
5. The history and use of the Army Scales.
6. The nature *vs.* nurture controversy.
7. The American Institute of Instruction.
8. The American Lyceum and its institute program.
9. The American Association for the Advancement of Education.
10. The early State Teachers' Associations and their work.
11. The early State Educational Journals.
12. Early development of the N.E.A.
13. The National Congress of Parents and Teachers.

SELECTED REFERENCES

*Almack, John C., Editor. *Modern School Administration.* 382 pp. Boston, 1933.

Contains a series of articles dealing with the progress of educational administration during the preceding thirty-five years. Good historical sketches of school survey movement, curriculum work, administrative changes, etc.

Ayers, L. P.   "Economy of Time Through Testing the Course of Study"; in *Proceedings of the National Education Association*, 1913, pp. 241–46.

   A brief but suggestive article dealing with the possibility of applying standards and measurements, so as to secure a more economical use of the time of pupils.   Written when the testing movement was in its beginnings.

*Ayers, L. P., and Thorndike, E. L.   "Measuring Educational Products and Processes" (2 papers); in *School Review*, vol. 20, pp. 289–309 (1912), discussion, pp. 310–19.

   Two Harvard Teachers' Association papers, read early in the discussion, and dealing with the need for measurement in education.

*Bobbitt, Franklin.   *The Supervision of City Schools; Twelfth Yearbook* of the National Society for the Study of Education, Part I.   96 pp.   1913.

   An excellent discussion of the problem of efficiency measurements and standards.

Chapman, H. B.   *Organized Research in Education.*   221 pp.   Bureau of Educational Research, Monograph No. 7, Ohio State University, Columbus, 1927.

   An historical study of the early development, work, problems, and techniques of the different types of educational research bureaus.

Courtis, S. A.   "Educational Diagnosis"; in *Educational Administration and Supervision*, vol. I, pp. 89–116 (February, 1915).

   A very interesting article on the use of arithmetical tests and scorings, showing how the teacher may become an educational physician to her pupils.

*Judd, Chas. H.   *Measuring the Work of the Public Schools.*   290 pp.   Cleveland Education Survey, 1916.

   An excellent volume, showing standard measures applied as a means of educational diagnosis to both elementary and high schools in a large city-school system.

*Kandel, I. L.   *Twenty-Five Years of American Education.*   469 pp.   New York, 1924.

   A series of sixteen essays outlining development in the divisions of the subject of education during the period 1897–1922.

Monroe, W. S., DeVoss, J. C., and Kelly, F. J.   *Educational Tests and Measurements.*   521 pp.   Houghton Mifflin Co., Boston, 1924.

   A standard guide to the use of the standard tests, and an explanation of the meaning of the results obtained.

*Monroe, W. S.   *Ten Years of Educational Research, 1918–1927.*   367 pp.   Bulletin 42, Bureau of Educational Research, University of Illinois, 1928.

   Our standard history of the research movement.

*National Society for the Study of Education.   *Yearbooks.*
   12th Yearbook, Part I, 1913.   *The Supervision of City Schools.*   96 pp.
   15th Yearbook, Part I, 1916.   *Standards and Tests for the Measurement of the Efficiency of Schools and School Systems.*   160 pp.
   17th Yearbook, Part II, 1918.   *The Measurement of Educational Products.*   190 pp.
   27th Yearbook, Part I, 1928.   *Nature and Nurture; Their Influence on Intelligence.*   460 pp.

27th Yearbook, Part II, 1928. *Nature and Nurture; Their Influence on Achievement.* 350 pp.

National Educational Association. *Fiftieth Anniversary Volume,* 1906.

Pages 453 to 540 consist of a series of historical papers, dealing with the early Teachers' Associations and the history of the N.E.A.

*Russell, Jas. E. "The Scientific Movement in Education"; in *Proceedings National Education Association,* 1926, pp. 719–28.

Changes in thirty years, and the contribution of the scientific movement.

Terman, L. M. *The Measurement of Intelligence.* 362 pp. Houghton Mifflin Co., Boston, 1916.

Part I gives a simple explanation of the measurements, and points out their educational significance. Part II describes the measurements and explains how to give them.

*Terman, L. M. *The Intelligence of School Children.* Houghton Mifflin Co., Boston, 1919.

A very readable and valuable account of the results and significance of mental measurements. Written for the grade teacher.

Tiegs, E. W. *Tests and Measurements for Teachers.* 470 pp. Boston, 1931.

An excellent treatment of testing and measuring, with a consideration of the educational significance of the new movement.

Washburne, C. W. "Organizing Public Schools for Research"; in *Journal of Educational Research,* vol. 10, pp. 364–68 (December, 1924).

A good description of the organization and direction of research in a small school system.

Barnard, Henry. *American Journal of Education.*

See Index for articles on American Institute, National Teachers' Association, local teachers' associations, etc.

CHAPTER XXII

ADMINISTRATIVE REORGANIZATION OF AMERICAN EDUCATION

Wars usher in new problems. The Spanish-American War marked a turning point in the history of the United States. Before that event we had moved along quietly as a self-contained debtor nation, busily engaged in opening up and developing our country and in producing an exportable surplus to send abroad to apply on the debts we owed to Europe. While we were still following old established ways, the quarter-century preceding this War had nevertheless been a period of marked criticism of the public school. As a result the curriculum had been gradually expanded, and the school was being called upon to direct its energies toward newer and larger purposes. The Spanish-American War of 1898 and the Russo-Japanese War of 1904–05 served alike to concentrate attention more strongly on the importance of public education, as it was seen that it was "the man behind the gun" who won in each case. These wars served to reveal to the American people a new place in world affairs which they might be expected to occupy, and for which new types of training would be needed by our people.

The decades immediately following these wars were a period of great industrial development and national prosperity for us. Business and governmental undertakings of a scale previously unattempted were begun; the specialization of labor and the introduction of labor-saving machinery took place to an extent before unknown; new inventions destroyed old trades, and threw thousands of workmen out of employment; the immigration of peoples racially farther removed from our original stock reached a maximum; villages became more urban, and city life far more complex; the frontier practically disappeared; state governments assumed new services and functions; the national feeling was deepened and intensified; and our National Government was called upon to do many things for the benefit of our people which it had become clearly evident that our States could not do.

In 1914 came the outbreak of the World War, and early in 1917 we entered the conflict. The result of this titanic struggle was to usher in a new and changed world in which we have not yet found our bearings. Today we find ourselves in a world of confusion and conflict, burdened by debts, and oppressed by a narrow nationalism and intense national hatreds; our educational system subjected to increased strain and criticism; the need for a broad, general, and diversified training, adapted to the needs of the future rather than the present, everywhere evident; and the demand acute for fundamental educational administrative and taxation reorganizations that will enable us to produce a system of schools based on business principles and better adapted to serve the new educational needs of our national life. This call for a reorganization of our educational and fiscal administrative machinery, and for a redirection of both rural and city education, our leaders have for long been declaring and some good beginnings have been made, and there is today good reason for believing that our people are at last becoming conscious of this need. The necessity for financial economies alone, in the immediate future, may be sufficient to secure for us the reorganizations we have for long talked about and striven for in vain. What these reorganizations are, and the progress we have so far made toward securing them, we shall attempt to state in the pages which follow.

I. REORGANIZATION AND REDIRECTION OF RURAL AND VILLAGE EDUCATION

All progress sketched city progress. The reader probably has been impressed, before this, by the fact that practically all the educational progress so far sketched as happening within the past three-quarters of a century has been city progress. Unfortunately for rural and village education, this statement is only too true. The firm establishment of the Massachusetts district system in the States, described in Chapter IX, and the fastening on the schools, as a result of the early democratic movement, of a political instead of an educational basis for the selection of county and state school superintendents, as described in Chapter VII, have together combined to deprive the rural and village schools of our country of any real educational leadership, and to keep rural and village education from making the progress needed to meet the changed conditions of rural and village life. The cities, by the early elimination of their school districts (page 316) and their elective superintendents, have been able to draw to the management of their school systems the keenest thinkers and the most capable administrators engaged in educational work. In any line of work involving good organization and adaptation to rapidly changing conditions, nothing counts for so much as good leadership at the top. Of this our city school systems have for long had a monopoly.

The rural and village schools of most of our States, cut off by constitutional provisions or by state laws from securing such directive oversight from outside the county, and within the county only on a political basis, and split up into thousands of little unrelated school districts, unable adequately to finance themselves and inspired by no unity of purpose and animated by no modern conception of educational work, have gone along without much change since the days of the fifties and the sixties (**R. 326**). Too often the little rural school stands today as a forlorn and shrunken landmark of what used to be an important rural social and educational institution. The text-books have been revised and made uniform, to be sure, but

FIG. 165
ONE OF THE LANDMARKS

the new books adopted have been books written primarily with city and not rural needs in view. A uniform course of study has been introduced, usually of the formal and drill type, but until recently with but little adaptation to rural needs. Normal-trained teachers, trained primarily for city grade work, have been employed, but they have taught in terms of city needs, and have deserted the rural school for a city position at the earliest opportunity. Some formal agriculture has recently been introduced into the course of study, but with little provision for its supervision or adequate facilities for the work, and the city-trained teacher has usually not known what to do with it. The natural result is that our rural and village schools have remained bookish, their work unrelated to farm life or national needs, and their influence away from the farm. In consequence, country people have largely lost interest in them, and many have rented their farms and moved to town, in large part to obtain better educational advantages for their children.

The new rural-life problem. In the mean time, since the days when the district system flourished in all its glory, and when eighty per cent of our people lived on the farm or in the little village and under rather simple living conditions, a vast and far-reaching revolution has taken place in the character of rural and village life. Inventions, labor-saving machinery, steam, electricity, the automobile, improved roads and means for transportation, the radio, moving pictures, rural mail delivery, the increase of conveniences and comforts, the rise of the cheap illustrated magazine, the circulation of the city daily paper, new world interests, new agricultural knowledge, new and more distant markets, commercial large-scale farming, the rapid rise of farm tenantry, the influx of the foreign-born into rural districts, the decay of the rural church, the dying out of the old rural social life, the decline of the old farm and village industries, the coming of a new type of tenant farmer, the cityward migration of the best and the poorest of the rural population, the decline in interest in local government as larger national and world interests have come in, the intellectual revolution which has followed the industrial revolution, and the vastly increased mobility of the population due to good roads and the automobile — all these have combined to change the whole face of the rural-life educational problem.

To one who has given little or no thought to the subject it is hard to appreciate the great change in rural and village life which has taken place within the past half-century. It has been of far-reaching importance, and has touched every phase of rural life and education. Almost nothing is now as it used to be; almost nothing is done as it was a half-century ago; in almost no respect are the educational needs what they used to be. Nowhere has the social and industrial revolution wrought greater alterations than in the village or on the farm, and nowhere in our national life have the institutions of society made so little change to meet the new conditions. The result has been the rapid development of a rural-life problem of large magnitude and of great social, economic, and educational consequences, the solution of which lies largely in the provision of a new type of rural and village school, the complete reorganization and redirection of rural education, and the provision of an entirely new type of rural administrative and supervisory organization.

Effect of these changes on the rural school. Under the stress of these new life conditions the old supervision by the district school trustees has completely broken down, while the expanding scope of all education today has left the little independent district too small a unit to make any adequate provision for modern rural or village educational needs. Only in remote districts or in isolated country places does the district system longer render any important service. The boy or girl on the farm or in the little village does not today receive a fair deal, and can never hope to receive as good an education as the city boy or girl receives so long as the outgrown district system continues to attempt the impossible, and so long as local political availability rather than educational training and competence rules in the selection of those who are to supervise and direct our rural and village schools. If there is any clear and unmistakable lesson to be drawn from the administrative experience of our city school systems, it is that the prime essentials for good school organization and administration are the abolition of school-district control, the unification of all schools under one board and one superintendent for administration and supervision, much larger units for school finance, and the entire elimination of politics and local residence requirements in the selection of superintendents of schools. If rural people could only understand how much better schools they could have, often for the same money, if for the district system they substituted the county or some other even larger unit for administration, the district system would soon be placed where many other outgrown institutions of society now are (**R. 326**).

That the district system is wasteful of effort and funds, results in great educational waste, is unprogressive to a high degree, leads to an unwise multiplication of little schools, does not provide adequately for the needs of country and village boys and girls, and that any marked general educational progress is impossible under it, no longer admits of successful contradiction. Here and there one occasionally hears of a redirected rural or village school which is rendering a real service, but these are few in number, in the district-system States, and the progress made is too slow and too local to be of much value.

The school-consolidation movement. Having started the mischief in the early days of its history, Massachusetts was the first State to try to remedy the matter. As early as 1869 this State enacted legislation permitting the consolidation of school districts, and in 1882 finally abolished the district system by law and restored the old town system from which the district system had evolved (see drawing on page 70). After this abolition of the district system, the consolidation of schools in Massachusetts became more rapid,[1] and by about 1890 the idea spread to other States. Ohio, in 1892, was the first State west of the Alleghenies to permit the union of two or more districts to form a consolidated school. Indiana began consolidation in 1901, and, largely due to its earlier abolition (1851) of the district system, the idea soon made remarkable progress there. Between 1897 and 1905, some twenty States authorized the consolidation of schools and the expenditure of school money for the transportation of pupils, while certain other States, operating under some form of the county-unit system, slowly began the work of school consolidation.

Looking over the different States today, after from twenty to thirty years under permissive consolidation laws, we find a few States in which rather remarkable results have been achieved,[2] but a larger number in which but little — relative to the problem — has as yet been accomplished,[3] though in many cases a vast amount of energy and effort have been expended to accomplish these meagre results.[4] An examination shows, too, that the chief results have been accomplished in the county-unit States, the town-system States of New England where the district system was abolished earlier, or in a few township-system States where the district system did not have a foothold, while the smallest accomplishments have been in the district-system States (R. 327).

[1] By 1888 the consolidation movement had attracted so much attention that the State began to collect statistics as to the amount of money spent for the transportation of pupils to consolidated schools, which then was $26,000 a year. The progress of the movement in Massachusetts since 1888 may be judged from the fact that such expenditures now are about $600,000 a year. As a result, thousands of little one-room schools have been done away with, and a new type of education provided for the rural and village children of the State.

[2] Colorado, Indiana, Kentucky, Louisiana, Mississippi, North Carolina, North Dakota, Ohio, and Texas are examples of States where good results have been achieved.

[3] California, Illinois, Kansas, Nebraska, Missouri, Oregon, and Wisconsin are examples of States in which relatively little has been accomplished.

[4] Kansas is a good illustration here. After twenty-eight years of effort but 174 consolidated schools had been formed in the State, while 7228 one-room schools remained. In 40 of the 105 counties no consolidation had been effected. Yet good men had worked at the problem there, and worked hard, and the burdens of district taxation are heavy.

Essential features of the consolidation idea. The essential features of the plan are an agreement, usually by vote at an election called for the purpose, to abandon three, four, five, or more little district schools; to erect instead a good modern school building, such as is shown in Fig. 166, at some central place; to haul the children by automobile from their homes each day to this central school in the morning, and back home in the late afternoon; and at this central

FIG. 166. A CONSOLIDATED COMMUNITY-CENTER SCHOOL

Compare this with the schoolhouse shown on page 719 as a place for country boys and girls to go to school. This school has six classrooms, two laboratories, manual-arts and home-economics rooms, an assembly hall, and a branch county-library room.

school to provide graded instruction, a partial or complete high school, agriculture, manual and domestic work, and many of the advantages now enjoyed by city children. Such a school can also be made a rural community-center school by adding an assembly hall, branch library room, and playgrounds. The picture (Figure 166) shows such a school, containing six class-rooms, an assembly hall and library on the main floor, and a manual-training room, domestic-science room, and agricultural laboratory, science room, toilet rooms, and indoor playrooms in the basement.

It is only by making the school a center for the community life that the rural and village school can hope to exert the influence which it should. The development of a new and better rural and small-town life is largely a matter of education and guidance, and of the institutions capable of providing this leadership the school easily stands first, if it can but rise to meet the opportunities which confront it. It is this new conception as to the function and possibilities of rural education which has been behind the consolidation of schools and the reorganization of rural education during the past century.

As yet the movement has not experienced the success which its educational importance deserves.

County-unit consolidation. The trouble with all such voluntary consolidation of school districts lies in the fact that consolidation proceedings are very hard to get started, district jealousies and district inertia usually prevent the union district being made large enough at the start, and but few voluntary unions can be secured. The left-hand figure in the drawing in Figure 167 shows the usual result under a voluntary, district-vote plan. The one consolidated district may have cost ten years of popular education, and then probably is too small.

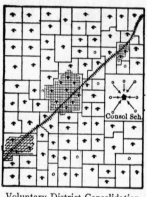 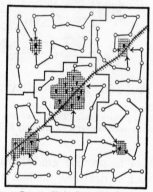

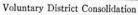

Voluntary District Consolidation   County-Unit Consolidation

FIG. 167. RURAL EDUCATIONAL REORGANIZATION

Eighty-eight school districts consolidated into five, providing schools of from 200 to 350 pupils each, instead of from five or six to fifteen or eighteen, as at present.

After nearly fifty years of trial and effort, we now see not only that voluntary consolidation is inadequate and too slow, but that the new rural educational demands require not only more rapid but also more extensive reorganization than voluntary effort can secure. Only by the use of a unit at least as large as the county can the right kind of consolidation and the right type of school be provided, and this must be superimposed on the districts by general state law. Such a planned county-unit consolidation is shown in the right-hand figure of the drawing above. The same result might be achieved, in six to ten years' time, by a county board of education proceeding gradually, step by step, in the abandonment of small, unnecessary, and inefficient rural schools. It could not be achieved in a century to come by dependence on voluntary district action.

In the right-hand half of Figure 167 the county has been dealt with as a whole, and a county-unit school system has been substituted for the district systems of the other figure. The central city school system may have been left under the control of its separate city board of education, though compelled to annex, for school purposes, a number of adjacent school districts, or it may have assumed the

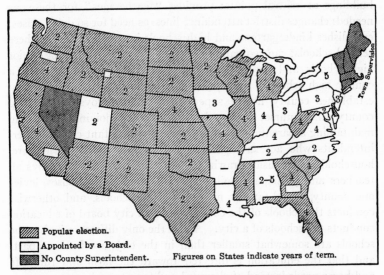

FIG. 168. PROGRESS MADE IN ELIMINATING THE POPU-
LARLY ELECTED COUNTY SUPERINTENDENT OF SCHOOLS

direction of all the schools in the county.[1] Otherwise the county has been consolidated by state law into one county school district; all the old small districts and their boards of unnecessary district school trustees have been abolished; and for the management of the new county school district the people of the county have elected a county board of education of five citizens, much as they elect a county board of five supervisors to oversee county expenses, build roads and bridges, and supervise the poor relief and county hospital

[1] Whether the central city should be absorbed into the county-unit school system, as in Georgia and Utah, or remain a school system separate from the county school system, is in part a matter of the size of the city and in part a matter of local conditions. There is much good argument for one unified system of schools for the whole county.

and poor farm. This county board of education is exactly analogous to a city board of education, and has substantially the same powers. It selects and appoints a county superintendent of schools, instead of asking the people to elect him, being free to go anywhere in the United States for him, or her, and to pay what they feel they can afford to get the man or woman they want for the office. With the aid of the county superintendent the county board then consolidates the small scattered schools; erects larger and more modern buildings at central points; provides "teacherages" for these, as needed; changes district attendance lines, as need for so doing arises; establishes kindergartens and high schools in connection with these central schools; can reorganize the school work by providing junior high schools and departmental organization; may provide for a county high school of agriculture and manual and household arts; establishes county health supervision, and employs a traveling county school nurse; unites with the city or adjoining counties in maintaining a parental school; and provides assistant county superintendents who act as supervisors of primary work, agriculture, household arts, music, drawing, etc. The board also employs all teachers and principals, builds and repairs all schoolhouses, levies one county school-tax for maintaining all schools, and otherwise conducts the schools of the county just as a city board of education conducts the schools of a city. About the only difference is that the schools are somewhat smaller than in the city, are farther apart, and that the education is directed toward the farm and rural-life and home needs instead of cityward and for city ends.

What such a reorganization would mean. Such county-unit consolidation is by no means theoretical, but is found well-developed in Louisiana, Maryland, Ohio, and Utah, in a more or less well-developed form in a number of Southern States, and in partial development in a number of other States. The school system which the United States organized for Porto Rico was organized on this plan, and the school system of Hawaii also is of the county-unit type. It has so many advantages, is so well adapted to meet the new rural-life problems, and under it rural education can so easily be redirected and enriched along the lines needed by rural and village boys and girls, that it or some modification of it now promises to be the coming form of educational organization for all territory lying outside the separately organized cities.

With about four or five such consolidated schools to an average Middle-West county, instead of eighty to a hundred and twenty little insignificant schools (see Fig. 167), or something like four to five hundred such consolidated schools to an average State instead of eight to twelve thousand little districts with their struggling little schools, the whole nature of rural life and education could be reshaped and redirected in a decade, and life on the farm and in the village would be given a new meaning. Such a change would also dispense with the need for the services of from 2500 to 3500 of the cheapest and most poorly educated rural teachers of the State, as well as some 24,000 to 36,000 district-school trustees — both of which would be educational gains of no small importance. In place of this army of school trustees, five citizens for each county, or about five hundred for a State, would manage much better than now all educational affairs of the rural and village schools. The Baltimore County, Maryland, county-unit school system, which has often been described, forms an interesting example of what can be accomplished by such an educational reorganization and redirection.

After a few years under such a county-unit reorganization each county would come to have a small number of modern-type consolidated schools, rendering effective rural service, and, if properly located, serving as centers for the community life. High-school education, directed toward rural- and village-life needs, would become common for all, instead of as at present only for city and town children; adequate professional supervision would direct the work; and the curriculum could be tied up closely with the rich life experiences of rural boys and girls. What now seems so wonderful and so exceptional, when carried through here and there by some especially intelligent and persuasive county superintendent, would then become the rule. The chief right of which the people of the rural districts would be deprived by such a reorganization would be the right to continue to mismanage and misdirect the education of their children by means of a system of school organization and administration the usefulness of which has long since passed by.

II. STATE EDUCATIONAL REORGANIZATION

The chief state school officer. Closely related to the county educational reorganization, which we have just sketched, is that of state educational reorganization. The need for reorganization here is fast coming to the front as another of our important administrative problems. As was stated in Chapter VII, when we finally decided to establish the office of state school superintendent,[1] we almost everywhere turned to popular election as the means for filling the office. As was explained on page 218, this at the time seemed the natural and the proper method, as the office then was conceived of as being much like that of a State Auditor or State Land Agent. The early duties were almost wholly financial, statistical, clerical, and exhortatory; the office required no special professional knowledge; and any citizen possessing energy, a strong personality, and a belief in general education at public expense could fill it. Many of the most successful early state school officers were ministers or lawyers.

Since these earlier days the whole character of our popular education has changed, and education at public expense has been transformed into a great state, one might almost say, a great national interest. From a mere teaching institution the school has been raised to the foremost place as a constructive agent in our democratic life. Public education today represents our greatest national undertaking, and, aside from the army, our most highly organized public effort. Since the first establishment of state school systems permission has everywhere been changed to obligation; functions formerly entrusted to the little districts have been taken over by the county, or the State; new and far larger demands have been made on communities; new aims and purposes in instruction have been set up; and entirely new problems in organization, administration, instruction, sanitation, and child welfare have been pushed to the front. The different State School Codes have become bulky, and school legislation has come to demand a professional knowledge and an expertness of judgment which formerly was not required. The exhorter and the institute worker have come to be needed less and less, and the student of education and the trained administrator more and more. As a result, a well-thought-out state educational policy now is a necessity if intelligent progress is to be made.

Election and appointment of experts. Only in the cities, though, has our administrative organization kept pace with our educational

[1] Between about 1830 and 1850 every Northern and some Southern States created either an *ex-officio* or a real state school officer to look after the rising state interest in education. Most of the new States to the westward created the office as soon as or shortly after they were organized as Territories, and the Southern States which had not done so previously soon after the close of the Civil War.

development along other lines. The school, in its development, has outrun the thinking of those who direct it in district, county, and State. Though the expert and professional character of the office of State Superintendent of Public Instruction is now quite generally recognized, the office itself, in most of our States, is still in a backward state of development and realizes but a small fraction of its possible efficiency. In two thirds of our American States, as shown in Figure 169, we still trust to political nomination, and to the popu-

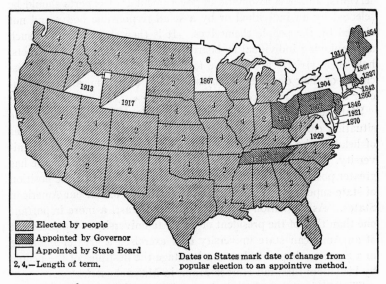

FIG. 169. METHODS USED FOR SECURING THE CHIEF
STATE SCHOOL OFFICER, AND TERM

lar election of residents of the State willing to enter political candidacy for a poorly-paid and a short-term office, to secure the head of our state school systems, though not employing the method to select the state geologist, state mine examiner, state horticultural commissioner, state bank superintendent, state architect, state highway engineer, state entomologist, state forester, secretary of the state board of health, secretary of the state board of charities and correction, the president of the state university, or experts for railway or public service commissions.

There is no reason, though, except the historical one, why we should elect the head of the state school system and not elect the other experts mentioned, or why we should appoint them and not appoint the head of the state school system. The argument so often advanced that by so doing we would be taking the schools away from the people represents either sheer ignorance or political clap-trap, or both, as a comparison with the other experts mentioned or with city school supervision at once reveals. What the people want is good government and efficient service from their public servants, and it is axiomatic in government that experts should be selected by an individual or by a small responsible body, and not elected by the people themselves. It is then the business of such an employing individual or board to oversee the experts it selects, hold them strictly accountable for results, protect them in the discharge of their duties from unjust attacks, and dismiss them whenever they cease to be competent.

State school officer and president of university compared. The situation can perhaps best be seen if we compare the two offices of head of the state school system and president of the state university. Probably no position in the whole state public service has greater possibilities for constructive statesmanship than the position of state superintendent of public instruction in one of our American States. As a position it is, potentially at least, a more important one than that of the president of the state university. No president of an American state university ever exercised a greater influence in a State or shaped to better advantage the destinies of the people by his labors than did Horace Mann in Massachusetts.

The chief reason why one is appointed and the other elected is that the college and the university have their roots buried back in the Middle Ages, and appointment of the rector, chancellor, or president has always been the rule, whereas the office of state superintendent of schools is a creation of the Andrew Jackson period in our governmental philosophy.[1] When our American States founded their state universities they organized them after the pattern of the ages; when they created the new office of head of their newly evolving democratic school systems they followed the then new democratic

[1] The chief state educational office arose as an evolution out of some clerical type of elected state office, in the days when the Jeffersonian theory, as to government, had reached its culmination in the spoils theory of the Andrew Jackson period, while these newer state offices, involving expert service, were a later development after scientific service had come to have a proper value placed on it.

idea of the people electing practically every public official. The governing body for the university (board of trustees, or regents) has often been elected by the people, but the president and professors have always been recognized as expert state servants, and appointed without reference to residence, politics, race, sex, or religion. Under such a plan our universities have made wonderful progress. Imagine the result, though, if you can, had the people nominated and elected, along political lines and always from among the citizens of the State, the president of the state university as they do the head of the state school system, and the heads of departments in the university as they do the heads of the county school systems in the State. It is hard to conceive what Republican Chemistry, Democratic Latin, Prohibitionist English, Union-Labor History, Progressive Anatomy, or Farmer-Labor Economics would be like.

That the office of head of the state school system has not measured up with that of the presidency of the state university is a matter of common knowledge, and it has not done so largely because the office has for so long been afflicted with the blight of partisan politics; been one of the lowest-salaried positions within the gift of the State; and because political expediency, rather than any educational standard, has been the measuring stick used in selecting candidates for the position. The people seldom have an opportunity to vote for a really good man for the office, as the best men usually cannot be induced to become candidates. Of a few States where the office is elective this at times has not been true, but not of many, and usually not for long in any State. In some of our States the traditions of the office have settled down to merely that of a retiring job for some old and reasonably successful practitioner from the ranks, and in consequence it has commanded but little respect or authority.

Lack of a consecutive state educational policy. As a result, few of our States today reveal, in their educational and legislative history, any evidence of having followed for any length of time a well-thought-out educational policy. Often the state oversight has been of a distinctively *laissez-faire* type, the officer acting largely as a clerk, statistical agent, tax distributor, and institute lecturer. School legislation has represented expediency, has been of the patch-work variety, and a conception of the State as an active and energetic agent for the improvement of educational conditions and the advancement of the public welfare has been entirely lacking.

When we turn to the State of Massachusetts we get an example of the opposite of these tendencies and results. Thanks perhaps to her strong aristocratic leanings, when the State Board of Education was created, in 1837, the State provided for the appointment by it of a Secretary to act as head of the school system, and not for the popular election of a chief state school officer. The result was the appointment of Horace Mann as the first Secretary, he holding the position, despite abuses and bitter attacks, until his election to succeed John Quincy Adams as a Member of Congress from Massachusetts, twelve years later. Had he been compelled to submit himself to the people every two or four years for re-election, there were times when he could not have been re-elected, and had the office been an elective instead of an appointive one, it is more than probable that Mann would have remained a lawyer and never been known as a school administrator.

Largely as a result of the Massachusetts conception of the importance of the chief state educational office, the leadership of that State in educational progress has been one of the marked features of our educational history. Since the establishment of the office of Secretary, in 1837, but nine persons have held the office up to the present time, and all have been educational leaders and statesmen of a high order. The present incumbent (1933; now called Commissioner of Education) was called to the position in 1916 from the head of the school system of Maine; his predecessor from a professorship of school administration at Teachers College, Columbia; and his predecessor from the position of assistant superintendent of the schools of Boston. One who has read the preceding chapters of this book cannot help but be impressed with the number of important educational advances which had their origin in Massachusetts, and the State has also been a leader in much other educational legislation which had not been mentioned. Though small in size and possessing no great natural resources, and for the past seventy-five years being slowly buried under a constantly increasing avalanche of foreign-born peoples who have corrupted her politics, diluted her citizenship, and often destroyed the charm of her villages, the State has persisted in a constructive educational policy which has been in large part her salvation. Had the selection of leaders for her schools been left to politics, it is hardly probable that the results would have been the same. What Massachusetts has for so long enjoyed in the matter of educational leadership other States ought now to begin to possess.

Democracy's need for leadership. No type of government has such need for trained leadership at the top as has a democracy, and no branch of the public service in a democracy is fraught with greater opportunities for constructive statesmanship than is public education. By it the next generation is moulded and the hopes and aspirations and ideals of the next generation are formed. To rise above office routine to the higher levels of constructive statesmanship is not easy, and calls for a high type of educational leader. Yet this higher level of leadership is what a state department of education should primarily represent. The improvement of society and the advancement of the public welfare through education is perhaps the greatest business of the State. A state board of education to determine policies and select leaders, and a chief state school officer (state superintendent, commissioner of education, or whatever title he may be given) to carry policies into execution and think in constructive terms for the school, should be the center up to which and down from which ideas for the improvement of public education should come (R. 328).

In both county and state the demand today is for intelligent professional leadership, that our people may receive greater return for the money they put into their schools, and that the children in them may receive a better-directed education than they are now receiving. The important steps in the process of securing these results consist in following the lines for reorganization which have been set forth — namely, the reorganization of school work to secure larger opportunities and greater effectiveness; the reorganization and redirection of rural and village as well as city educational procedure; the abolition of the outgrown district system for a larger administrative unit; the elimination of politics and popular election in the selection of experts; and the concentration of larger authority in the hands of those whose business it is to guard the rights and advance the educational welfare of our children. The need in our States is for governors with educational vision who will lead their legislatures in the imposition of a "New Deal" on the schools. The needed reforms, if they are to be attained in half a century to come, must be imposed from above.

III. TAXATION REFORM A NECESSITY

Need for tax reform. For at least three decades leaders in school administration have been pointing out the need for tax reform in our States as a necessary supplement to educational reform. Some progress has been made by a few States in the reform of their plans for general taxation, but the great majority still cling, wholly or in part, to the taxation methods of a century ago. In taxation for education, which is clearly a general state benefit and as such should be in some good measure equalized, we have made even less progress. As the survival of the old Massachusetts district school system still hampers the administration of education, so dependence on the district unit of taxation for the great bulk of support for education stands in the way of proper school maintenance. We are still in the ox-cart and stagecoach days, in most of our States, in the matter of school support.

A hundred years ago, when our plans for school support were first developed, wealth was far more evenly distributed than it is today. Agriculture was the chief industry of the time, the hidden wealth of the country had not been opened up and developed, means of communication were few and difficult, and the common industries of the time were carried on in the small villages or on the farms. Large industries had not been developed or centralized. Labor-saving devices had not removed the industries from the home to the central factory. Railroads were yet in their infancy. Telegraph, telephone, and electric power lines were unknown. Cities, with their aggregation of people and wealth, were few and small. The wealth of the time, also, was almost entirely visible and tangible wealth. Real-estate mortgages, which were recorded, formed almost the single form for the investment of money. What one man possessed did not differ greatly from that of his neighbors, and his land, barns, horses, cattle, wagons, crops, and household goods were all visible and easily taxed. The taxation of farms and home property, and of personal chattels and mortgages, naturally formed the fundamental basis of revenue for all kinds of governmental support. This simple state of affairs continued until well toward the latter part of the nineteenth century.

Rise of educational inequalities. Since those simple and somewhat primitive days the whole character of wealth, living, industry, government, and education have changed, and population and wealth are no longer approximately evenly distributed. As it is today, the development of the natural and climatic resources of the Nation, the concentration of manufacturing and wealth, and the evolution of many new forms of intangible property which are hard to find and tax, have developed taxing inequalities that are marked, and have made difficult for some communities and easy for others the support of such necessities as education, health, and government. Still more, the vast social and industrial changes of a century have brought about new political and economic and social needs that have made of education a greater state and national interest than ever before in our history. In consequence, the State has been forced to assume a control over education undreamed of in the earlier period of educational development. The scope of public education everywhere has broadened, and its per capita cost everywhere has increased.

As a result, the burden for the support of education, with chief dependence on district taxation and the old property tax as the chief reliance, is greater today than many communities can bear. With the maximum tax allowed by law they cannot meet the minimum requirements of the State, low as these minimum demands often are. District taxation and the old property tax have largely broken down as a means for school support, and the taxes now levied on farm and home property often are almost confiscatory in character. Yet the education provided for farm and village children is usually far from good enough. The remedy lies not in a cheaper type of schooling, but in much larger taxing units and in different forms of taxation. This calls for a much larger proportion of state school support, and the substitution of county for district taxation as a supplement to state support. The cost for anything so manifestly for the common good should be much better equalized than it is at present.

Cutting the schools to save on taxation. The great economic depression which has recently hung over the United States has brought this need for a better basis for taxation for education clearly to the front. The old taxation basis has failed to produce enough money to maintain the schools, and in consequence many schools have had to close or the teachers have taught without pay. Worse still, in the effort to reduce all expenditures the schools have been singled out for heavy reductions at the very time their burdens have been materially increased. As one speaker recently well put it, "A sword hangs over education throughout the United States" (**R. 329**). Much unintelligent "economy" has been proposed, and some of it practiced.[1] Appropriations for textbooks and school supplies have been greatly curtailed, repairs to schoolbuildings have been stopped, special classes have been abandoned, staffs for specialized services have been reduced or dismissed, research staffs have been discontinued, and specialized fields of instruction have been eliminated (**R. 329**). Yet at the same time the schools, and particularly the high schools, are crowded as never before, and the teaching load has been enormously increased. The school health service has been materially reduced and in cases entirely eliminated at a time when it is most needed.[2] Guidance service has been cut from the high school offering at a time when guidance is of greatest value. Special classes for misfits have been discontinued when misfits are in the schools in greatest numbers, and the regular classes are overcrowded. Supervision has been curtailed at a time when professional supervision is most in demand. Library appropriations have been reduced when the library is called upon for its maximum service. Instruction in music, drawing, home economics, manual arts, and gardening have been reduced or stopped, as "fads and frills," at a time when education for leisure-time activities is of vital importance. Kindergartens, junior high schools, visiting teachers, and school nurses, which we have worked long to secure and believe to be valuable additions to our educational systems, are swept away in a night by city councils voting for "economy."

It clearly is the right of the people through constitutional amendment, or acting through their representatives in the legislature, to fix the rates of taxation for schools which they are willing should be levied, but so long as the schools remain within the tax limits so set they should be allowed to determine their own budget and their own expenditures. This claim is made because of the fundamental

[1] "The sudden breakdown of our economic structure threatens all that has been accomplished through a decade of brilliant achievement. There are those who suggest even that the progress of more than a half-century be wiped out; that our schools go back to the Three-R curriculum which accompanied horse and buggy days. The present emergency is even more serious than the War." (*Journal of the N.E.A.*, March, 1933, p. 74.)

[2] "While health is proclaimed, theoretically, as of first importance, the elimination of services which aim at the protection of children from infection and malnutrition indicates that we do not practice what we preach. From reports recently received by the U.S. Office of Education it is evident that there is more need for safeguarding the health of the child today than ever before." (United States Office of Education, Circular no. 79, 1933, p. 15.)

importance of public education as a creative social service, and because tax-levying authorities tend too often to neglect this major claim. In cases of emergency, as the present situation has well shown, school authorities are willing to reduce expenditures according to their proper share, but without some independence in fiscal matters they will be forced to undesirable sacrifices.

It is too early as yet to write the history of public education in the depression, but enough can now be discerned to reveal the unintelligent procedures being practiced and to point out the need for tax reform for the support of education. We also can record as a notable service in the cause of human welfare the heavy sacrifices the teachers are making that the future citizenship of this Nation may not be deprived of any more of their educational rights than can be prevented.

That the leaders in public education in this country today face one of the most determined battles to preserve the schools from being sacrificed, that economies in other public services need not be made and that extravagances elsewhere may be untouched, there can be little question (**R. 331**). We are on the battle line, whether we wish it or like it, and the situation calls for both defensive and offensive tactics. We must defend the rights which we have won after long and hard fighting, and the opportunity now presents itself to take the offensive and to bring home to the American people the tremendous importance, for the future national life, that the educational services to our children be not in any serious manner curtailed.[1] France, Germany, England, Belgium, and Italy, despite their crushing financial burdens and their comparative poverty, have maintained their schools at a high level; there is no economic or public reason why America should not do the same. Reasonable cuts in maintenance charges will be assumed, but attempts to sweep aside the established guarantees and the educational progress of decades must be fought to a finish.

The fundamental reform demanded. What we need to do is to substitute the State for the school district as the prime source for

---

[1] "Our society is passing through a period of unprecedented economic distress. Economies can and must be made, but the services of education must be expanded and increased in efficiency to meet the needs of the crisis. We must fight not only to keep the schools open, but also to provide in them opportunities suited to the needs and capacities of all boys and girls. We must rededicate ourselves to the ideal of equality of opportunity. (George D Strayer, in *School and Society*, July 1, 1923, p. 7.)

school support.¹   The unit of support, too, needs to be shifted from a fixed rate of tax to a fixed amount per pupil to be educated, and this amount should be guaranteed and not be subject to city-council or state-legislative favor.   Only under such a fixed per-pupil guarantee can the schools pursue a somewhat even rate of progress.

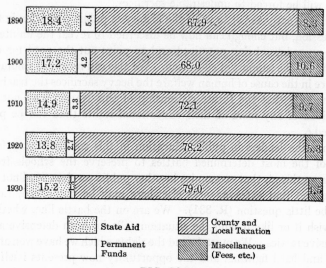

FIG. 170

SOURCES OF REVENUE FOR SCHOOL SUPPORT, 1890–1930

From Office of Education data

In most of our States today the percentage of state support for education is pitiably inadequate, and it has been slowly decreasing for half a century.   With the continued growth of taxing inequalities and the continued increase in cost for schools there is urgent demand that the State should assume a much greater percentage of the annual maintenance burden.   In most States such a shift of responsibility for maintenance is impossible without such a fundamental reform in methods of taxation as will permit of larger and surer revenues from all without unduly burdening the farmer and the

¹ In the Australian States all maintenance comes from the States.   In California, which has always been generous in state aid and has recently taken an advanced position in the matter of state support, the State will in the future provide $60 for every pupil in average daily attendance in the elementary schools the preceding year, and $90 for every pupil in high schools.   The remainder needed to conduct the schools will come from district taxation; under a county unit it would come from county taxation.

home owner. The increased pressure for adequate school support which the recent economic depression has brought to the front is almost certain to be an important contributing factor in the development of tax-reform movements in our States. In all probability, too, it will give added impetus, once recovery has been brought about, to the recent demand for some form of national aid to the States in the maintenance of what is, after all, a great national undertaking for the advancement of our people in general knowledge, political intelligence, health, morality, social adaptability, industrial efficiency, and economic competence.

IV. THE NATIONAL GOVERNMENT AND EDUCATION

Beginnings of a national interest. The somewhat accidental evolution of a series of grants of land from the national domain to the States for the establishment and aid of their school systems, described in Chapter IV, tended to make the Federal Government an interested and benevolent spectator in the growth of the state school systems, even though education as a function of government had been left to the States by Amendment X to the Federal Constitution (page 86). The educational revival of the forties had revealed to the leaders the limitation of means and the inadequacy of the administrative organization of the States for the upbuilding of systems of public education suited to the needs of a rapidly developing democracy, and the Civil War greatly increased the importance of the educational issue, both at the North and at the South. Out of these new influences a movement for the creation of a national office to study the educational problems of the Nation arose.

The National Teachers' Association, between 1858 and 1865, had given some attention to the problem, and in 1866, at the first meeting of the new National Association of State and City School Superintendents, afterwards the Department of Superintendence of the National Education Association, Mr. E. E. White, then State Commissioner of Education for Ohio, read a paper on a "National Bureau of Education." In response to a resolution then adopted, Hon. James A. Garfield, then a Member of Congress from Ohio, introduced and sponsored a bill in Congress to create such a Bureau "to collect statistics and facts concerning the condition and progress of education in the several States and Territories, and to diffuse information respecting the organization and management of schools

and school systems and methods of teaching." Through his persistent zeal and skillful leadership, Congress, by a narrow margin,
passed an Act, approved March 2, 1867, establishing a Department
of Education (but without cabinet rank) for the purpose of collecting facts, statistics, and information as to schools and school systems[1]
which would aid the people of the different States "in the establishment and maintenance of efficient school systems and otherwise
promote the cause of education generally throughout the country."
The President was to appoint a Commissioner of Education to head
the Department, who was to report annually to Congress.[2]   The
following year the opposition succeeded in reducing the Department
to an "Office," reducing the salary of the Commissioner, and eliminating the Chief Clerk, leaving him only two clerical assistants.[3]
Throughout all its subsequent history Congress has held the "Office
of Education" to a relatively minor position, with very limited
functions and very meagre support.   While the Federal Government has undertaken many important scientific and educational
services, Congress has from the first carefully contrived that almost
nothing originated under the direction of the Office (or Bureau)
of Education.   Even in its statistical and informational service
the different Commissioners have been badly cramped by utterly
inadequate appropriations.

The Education bills.   Faced by the many new problems and needs
in public education following the World War, a committee appointed
by the National Education Association, in 1919, proposed that public
education be in part nationalized by the transformation of the
Bureau (now Office) of Education into a Federal Department, with
a Secretary in the President's Cabinet; that adequate funds to
conduct educational investigations be provided; and that a sub-

[1] At the time of the establishment of this so-called "Department," statistics were available in Washington regarding education in but seventeen of the States.   Nothing was known
as to education in the other nineteen.   What had become of the vast land-grants for schools
was almost unknown.

[2] During the nearly sixty years of the existence of the Bureau, or Office, there have been
but nine Commissioners of Education.   The first appointee was Henry Barnard (1867–70),
followed by John Eaton (1870–86), Nathaniel H. R. Dawson (1886–89), William T. Harris
(1889–1906), Elmer E. Brown (1906–11), Philander P. Claxton (1911–21), John James
Tigert (1921–29), William John Cooper (1929–33), and George F. Zook (1933–   ).

[3] The new office was ordered to ascertain the condition and progress of education throughout the country, and was to be headed by a commissioner, with a chief clerk and two assistants, and was given $12,000 a year for maintenance.   The next year (1868) the chief clerk
was dropped, the salary of the commissioner was reduced from $4000 to $3000, and the
Bureau quartered in two rented rooms — a condition that continued for many years to come.

vention of $100,000,000 a year be granted by the National Government to the States to assist them in maintaining better their state school systems, but in particular to aid the States in the elimination of illiteracy, the Americanization of immigrants, the promotion of health education and physical education, the training of teachers, and the better equalization of educational opportunities (**R. 331**).

In 1919 a Bill to carry out these recommendations was introduced in both Senate and House, which became known as the Smith-Towner Bill, from the names of its sponsors. Failing of enactment, substantially the same bill was reintroduced in the next Congress, in 1921, and became known as the Sterling-Towner Bill. When this bill also failed, a substantially similar bill, widely endorsed as well as opposed by individuals and organizations throughout the Nation, was again introduced in the next Congress, in 1923, and became known as the Sterling-Reed Education Bill. No action being taken, a substantially similar bill was again introduced, in 1925, except that the proposed subvention to the States was now omitted, and the bill became known merely as The Education Bill.[1]

In 1923, a joint Congressional Committee on the Reorganization of Government Departments recommended the creation of a Department of Education and Welfare, and that same year President Coolidge so recommended in his Annual Message to Congress, but again no action was taken. Finally, in 1929, Secretary of the Interior Wilbur, with the approval of President Hoover, appointed a National Advisory Committee on Federal Relations to Education, of 51 members representing widely diverse interests, the purpose of which was to study the whole problem and to outline such policies and procedures as would constitute, in the words of Secretary Wilbur, "the proper chart by which to steer our educational course." This Committee reported to the President, in October, 1931, recommending that the direct control of education continue to be left to the States, but that the Federal Government should assist the States in carrying out the educational function by a greatly enlarged informational and research service, by grants of money determined by needs, and by all desirable forms of "intellectual co-operation." To meet these purposes best the Committee recommended the con-

[1] The Education Bill provided that, as a condition to sharing in the grants, the State must provide for a school term of not less than six months each year, compulsory school attendance between seven and fourteen for at least an equal period, and a law requiring the English language to be the basic language in all schools, public and private.

solidation of all educational functions of the Federal Government under a Department of Education with a Secretary in the President's Cabinet (**R. 332**), the Secretary to aid the President in the consideration of educational problems, plan and organize the national research and information service, and to "contribute constructively to development of the leadership which American education needs for its co-ordination and intelligent advance." Assistant Secretaries were to direct the technical work of the Department, supervise the research and publications, and maintain co-operative professional relations with the States and with educational institutions. No action has so far (1933) been taken on these recommendations by Congress, and at this stage the question of national aid and oversight rests.

The question of federal aid. The proposal to aid Education in the States by a grant of federal funds awakened deep opposition, as well as enthusiastic support. It was argued that the proposal was undemocratic, that the money of one State ought not to be taken to aid education in another State, that it was paternalism that would prove dangerous, and that the schools of religious organizations would suffer. Congress, always easily frightened by organized minorities, and the educational forces being but poorly organized in support of the Education Bills, never allowed the matter to get to a vote in either house. There have always been votes for Congressmen who spent national funds for the elimination of hog and chicken cholera, cattle tick and bovine tuberculosis, or in increasing yields from any animal or crop, and Congressmen also think that there still are votes for "saving the people's money" by *not* spending it for education and child welfare. In view of the many new nation-wide undertakings of far-reaching consequence inaugurated by the "New-Deal" administration since 1933, the objections of paternalism and undemocratic action seem puerile today. Nor can the supposed interest of any church be allowed to stand in the way of the adequate education of children in our public schools. Since the movement for a National Department of Education may be said to be steadily gaining ground, it probably will be successful before very long. There is plenty of relatively inexpensive work that such a department could do that would be very valuable to the schools of the Nation, and of a type that cannot be so well done by a subordinate Bureau or Office, and cannot be done at all by the States working alone.

It is also probable that, after the present period of post-war economy is over, some federal aid for the promotion of education in the States will be granted by Congress. Very probably the Department will come first, and the aid-grants will follow as a later development.

The problem before us. The question is largely one of what obligations the Federal Government has to the States in the matter of the maintenance of state systems of education, and how important education is as a national undertaking. If there are no federal obligations to the States in the matter, and if education is a benefit which is local and particular and specific and easily traceable, rather than indefinite and general and social and widely diffused, then the discussion of a Federal Department of Education and of federal subsidies to the States may be classified as "pork-barrel politics" and deserves but little consideration from thoughtful people. If, on the contrary, a general and social service is rendered, the particular benefits of which transcend state lines and are difficult to trace, and also if there are certain definite obligations that the Nation can be shown to have toward the States, then the question of federal aid is quite another matter. The writer takes distinctly this latter view (**R. 333**).

For a long time we have spent money liberally for the development of agriculture in the States, for animal-disease eradication, the control of pests, the improvement of rivers and harbors, the building of army camps and post offices and irrigation dams, and these expenditures have not been deemed especially paternalistic or undemocratic. In general, they have given good returns. For a decade and a half we have also been engaged in the creation of a great system of state and national highways, to which the Federal Government has made annual appropriations of from $85,000,000, to $125,000,000 — amounts as large on the average as were proposed for education in the Education Bill. For the year 1933-34 the amount is to be $400,000,000. Not only have the States been aided in proportion to their mileage of so-called "post-roads," but sparseness of population has been taken into consideration in making the grants. To these appropriations there has been almost no objection, yet highways, useful as they are, represent no such national interest as does public education, and they could be postponed for a time with far less loss to us as a Nation than will accrue from the serious curtailment of the education of the generation now in the schools.

When we consider the great inequalities between the States in their ability to support an adequate system of public schools, due to differences in wealth, sparseness of population, and presence or lack of natural resources, and how some of our States would need to expend a prohibitive proportion of their income for education to enable them to maintain schools of only average cost, while other States can maintain excellent schools on quite low expenditures, the need for a better equalization of the burdens for the maintenance of what is for the common good of all becomes evident. Only through some form of federal aid, with a view to the equalization of educational opportunity up to a certain determined minimum of length of school term, attendance, teacher-quality, and expenditure, can the disparity in ability to maintain schools be remedied within any reasonable period of time (**R. 332**).

Distinct national obligations. There are two other phases of the problem which present a much more definite national obligation to the States. These relate to the education of the Negro and the immigrant.

Up to the time of the Civil War, slavery was a national institution under congressional regulation, and the Negro was regarded almost wholly as a chattel without personal rights. The Emancipation Proclamation was an act of war in an effort to preserve the Union, and the amendments to the Federal Constitution which admitted the Negro to citizenship and made him a voter were not concurred in by the States in which the Negro then lived. Their approval was part of a coercive policy against the States that had been in rebellion. Devastated and impoverished as a result of the fortunes of war, these States were neither able nor willing to handle the problem thus thrust upon them by the National Government. These acts made the Negro a political as well as an economic factor in our national life, and the new freedom of movement has since made him an important health and public-welfare factor as well. In addition, two fifths of the illiteracy problem in the United States today is that of negro illiteracy. Considering him as a voter and a citizen, literacy and citizenship training have become important, and his peculiar mental makeup and character have made his vocational and industrial education almost a necessity. The South, so far, has not been able to handle the problem, and the present condition is a burden on the whole Nation in that it retards the economic development of the South. Until some federal aid is provided negro education in the South seems destined to remain a heavy burden, and of no great value to the Negro receiving it.

Another special obligation of the Federal Government to the States lies in the matter of the education of the immigrant and his children. By the Federal Constitution, the control of immigration was placed wholly with the Federal Government. There it has remained, and all attempts by States to regulate the admission of foreign-born within their borders has been resisted by the federal authority.[1] Between 1820 and 1914, the Federal Government admitted 32,102,671 foreign-born into our country, and dumped them on the States to educate, and control, and assimilate into our national life. Of the 11,726,506 who came to this country during the four years preceding the World War, 26.5 per cent were unable to read and write any language, and not over 12 per cent could speak English. An almost child-like faith in the public school as the "melting pot" has been expressed by Congress, even though the great bulk of the immigrants never come in contact with the day school and have to be reached, if reached at all, through evening, and adult, and citizenship, and vocational classes — classes that our cities are now eliminating as an economy measure. It seems only right that the Federal Government should assume some fair share of the burden now carried by the States in trying to educate and assimilate these foreign born and to instill into them that faith in American ideals which we regard as a birthright. Often, too, this labor has had to be carried on in the face of opposition from an alien home and clan and church.

A national conception needed. Vast changes in the habits, and thinking, and needs of our people have taken place within the present century. What the railroad, the telegraph, the newspaper, and the school began in the preceding century, the radio, the movies, the automobile, and the paved highway are completing in this one. State lines and state attitudes tend more and more to be absorbed into the national life, and the increasing responsibility of the Federal

[1] A good illustrative case was the attempt of California to regulate Japanese immigration and schooling, which was resisted as an interference with the treaty-making power of Congress.

Government is generally recognized. The parochial attitude tends to give way to the national attitude, and in all phases of our governmental service we are moving toward larger units for administration and control in the interests of effectiveness. The district system and the political system in education have done their work, and ought to give way to larger units of administration and well organized state control. We have a national school system in spirit, and, while leaving administrative control to the different States, public education ought to be nationalized in the thinking of our people. Probably this is one of the great tasks of the next quarter of a century.

In the development of our state school systems in the future the Federal Government has a large part to play. The large work it has done in promoting the general welfare and increasing the wealth of the Nation through agriculture, disease eradication, and health and public-welfare work point the way toward other opportunities for federal activity along lines equally important, especially with regard to child welfare, health, and education. If the vast sums the Nation now wastes on war work, expenses of past wars, and preparation for future wars might be diverted to productive enterprises, almost everything of a welfare nature could be achieved in behalf of our people.

QUESTIONS FOR DISCUSSION

1. Why should war be the cause of educational progress and reform?
2. How had "the man behind the gun" won the wars?
3. Why has educational reorganization become so important a problem today, whereas fifty years ago we were fairly well satisfied with the schools we had evolved and the plan of administering them?
4. What do you understand by the rural-life problem?
5. Show why the rural school has been left behind in the educational progress of the past fifty to sixty years.
6. How have invention and machinery affected the rural school?
7. When farmers are so willing to modernize their farm processes and equipment, why do they object so to the modernization of the school their children attend?
8. What are the fundamental needs of rural education today from the standpoint of: (a) administrative organization? (b) teaching? (c) curriculum?
9. What would the community-center rural school offer that cannot be provided by the little district school?

10. Enumerate the advantages of such a reorganization of rural education as is shown in Figure 167.
11. Point out the analogy between county-unit educational organization and good city school organization.
12. Why has school administration been so much slower in developing centralizing tendencies than other forms of the State's business?
13. State why the popular election of experts is always less likely to produce good public servants than is selection and appointment.
14. In the creation of the new state commissioners and agents for education, why did we not provide for their selection by popular election instead of by appointment?
15. How do you account for Massachusetts having shown evidence of a more carefully thought-out educational policy, and over a longer period of time, than other American States?
16. How do you explain the results shown on the map given as Figure 168, page 725?
17. Why must we almost of necessity wait for reform to be imposed from above? Why do not our State Teachers Associations supply the needed leadership?
18. Show how the county unit in school administration would pool the costs for education, equalize tax rates, and change the whole character of district taxation.
19. Show how the same would be done, on a still broader and more equitable scale, if the great burden for the support of schools were borne by the State.
20. Show why States depending on farm and home taxation have trouble today in maintaining their schools.
21. Why, when there is need for economy in school expenses, do communities economize at the expense of the recent and often more valuable additions to education?
22. What are the advantages of a per-pupil unit in taxation over a fixed tax rate in mills, or cents?
23. Distinguish between local and general benefits from taxation, and show the position of education in the matter of support.
24. Give some illustrations of the unequal distribution of natural resources, climate, and economic wealth that effect the maintenance of educational systems, as between the States.
25. Do you accept the reasoning as to national responsibility, in part at least, for the education of the Negro and the foreign born? Why?

SELECTED READINGS

In the accompanying volume of *Readings*, the following selections, related to the subject-matter of this chapter, are reproduced:

326. Deffenbaugh and Covert: School Districts in the United States.
327. Abel: Characteristics of the Consolidation Movement.
328. Commission: State Educational Reorganization.

329. Frank: The Sword over Education.
330. Cubberley: Education on the Battle Line.
331. Strayer: The Education Bill.
332. Natl. Committee: A Secretary for Education.
333. Cubberley: Equalization of Educational Opportunity.

QUESTIONS ON THE READINGS

1. What do the figures given in **326** reveal as to the wastefulness of the district unit?
2. What have been the essential characteristics (**327**) of the consolidation movement in the United States?
3. When the advantages of proper state educational reorganization seem so evident, why do these common objections (**328**) persist so powerfully as to block action? What is behind the objections?
4. In times of financial stringency, social and cultural and educational agencies are usually the first to suffer (**329**). Explain why this is so.
5. State the advantages, to the school, of a fixed per-pupil appropriation and of independence for the schools in budget making within the limits of funds granted (**330**).
6. Analyze the argument of Strayer for the Education Bill (**331**), and state the extent to which you agree, or disagree, with reasons.
7. Enumerate the advantages that would accrue to public education from having a Secretary for Education (**332**).
8. Add further points to the argument for a larger equalization of educational opportunity (**333**) as between the States.

SELECTED REFERENCES

Abel, J. F. *Consolidation of Schools and Transportation of Pupils.* 135 pp. Bulletin 41, 1933, U.S. Bureau of Education.

A comprehensive and useful document.

Bagley, W. C. "Do Good Schools Pay"; in *Journal of the N.E.A.*, vol. 12, pp. 211–16. (June, 1923.)

A study of education in the States, in the rank of their intelligence ratings, school efficiency ratings, and productive efficiency.

Cary, C. P. "The Making of a State Department of Public Instruction"; in *School and Society*, vol. 11, pp. 336–43.

Outlines standards, work, and costs.

Cubberley, E. P. *Rural Life and Education*, 2d ed. Boston, 1922.

Part I sketches the historical development of the rural-life problem.

Cubberley, E. P. *State School Administration.* Boston, 1927.

Chapters IX–XI deal with county organization, the rural-life problem, and state organization, and chapter XVIII with the question of national aid for education in the States.

Fitzpatrick, Edward A. "A Comprehensive State Educational Program"; in *School and Society*, vol. 15, pp. 186–91.

Need for an educational planning department in every State.

Harris, T. H. "Organizing a State School System for Effective Service", in *Elementary School Journal*, vol. 24, pp. 54–59.

A good general article on state educational organization.

Harris, T. H. "The County Unit"; in *Elementary School Journal*, vol. 23, pp. 768–74.

A description of the Louisiana county-unit plan, and a brief statement of its advantages.

Kieth, J. A. H., and Bagley, W. C. *The Nation and the Schools*. 364 pp. New York, 1920.

A detailed consideration of the precedents for national action, and the reasons for the different items in the proposed Education Bill.

Norton, J. K. *The Ability of the States to Support Education*. 88 pp. Washington, 1926.

An important study, relating to the ability of the States to meet their educational obligations.

Staffelbach, E. H. "Some Facts Concerning the Need of Federal Aid in Support of Education"; in *School and Society*, vol. 21, pp. 147–52.

Costs, burden, and relation to social income.

Strayer, George D. "National Leadership and National Support for Education"; in *School and Society*, vol. 11, pp. 674–81.

Advocates enactment of Smith-Towner bill, and points out the need for national leadership in education.

Fitzpatrick, Edward A. "A Comprehensive State Educational Program," in *School and Society*, vol. 13, pp. 189–91.

Need for an educational planning department in every State.

Hanus, P. H. "Organizing a State Department or Team for Educative Service."

A good picture of the work which administrative leadership involves.

CHAPTER XXIII

FUNDAMENTAL PRINCIPLES AND PROBLEMS

The national system evolved. In the chapters preceding this one we have traced, in some detail, the evolution of our American public schools from the days of their infancy to the present, and have shown the connection between our more pressing present-day problems and our evolution during the past. Starting with a few little church school systems, founded as an outgrowth of Reformation fervor and convictions, we have, in the course of nearly three centuries of educational evolution, gradually transformed the school from an instrument of the church to a civil institution, and have built up what are in effect forty-eight different state school systems. While these vary somewhat in their form of organization and the scope of the system provided, they nevertheless have so much in common, are actuated by so many of the same national purposes, and follow so closely the same guiding principles, that we may easily say that we have evolved what is in spirit, if not in legal form, a national system of public education. This we have felt, due to the thoroughly native character of the evolution which has taken place, has been reasonably well suited to the needs of a great democratic society such as our own.

In the course of this long evolution, despite much conflict and quite irregular development in different parts of our country, we have at last come to a somewhat general acceptance of certain fundamental principles of action. These may now be said to have become fixed, not only in our traditions but in our laws and court decisions as well, and to represent the foundations upon which our public educational systems rest. In this final chapter it may be well to review briefly some of the more important of these guiding principles before taking up the problems which lie just ahead.

The essential nature of education. To the enthusiasts of the Protestant Reformation we owe the idea that the education of all is essential to the well-being of the State; that it is the duty of each parent to educate his child; and that the State may enforce this duty by appropriate legislation. First conceived of wholly for the welfare of the religious State, and so enforced in the Massachusetts Laws of 1642 and 1647, in the church-period legislation of the Central Colonies, and somewhat in the apprenticeship legislation of all the Colonies, but particularly in the Southern Colonies, the idea of the right of the State to enforce education to advance the welfare of the State in time became a fixed idea in the New England Colonies, Rhode Island excepted, and from there was gradually spread, by the migration of New England people, all over the northeastern quarter of the United States. Becoming firmly established there by the middle of the nineteenth century, the idea spread, in the course of time, over the entire Union, and is now an accepted principle of action in all our American States.

In establishing schools of its own to enforce the obligation of education, the State has done so, not so much because it can educate better than can parents, though in most cases this is true, but because by itself taking charge of the conduct of schools the State can enforce better the obligation it imposes that each child shall be educated. Neither does the State establish schools because by state co-operative effort they can be established and conducted more economically than by private agencies, but rather that by so doing it may better exercise the State's inherent right to enforce a type of education looking specifically to the preservation and improvement of the State. With the passage of time, the growth of our Nation, and the extension of the suffrage to more and more diverse elements in our population, we have come to see clearly that an uneducated citizenship is a public peril, and to insist more strongly than before on the exercise of this fundamental right of the State. A natural corollary of this right to require education for the protection and improvement of the State is the right of the State to provide inspection to see that the obligation the State imposes is being fulfilled, and supervision to lead to the improvement of what is being done.

The right to tax to maintain. The provision of schools to enforce the obligation imposed by the State, though, requires money, and the better the schools provided the more they are likely to cost. Even state supervision of education, were the provision of schools left entirely to private or religious initiative, also would cost something. This cost must be defrayed from public funds, and these must come from individual, group, or general taxation.

Just how schools should be supported must be determined by a consideration as to their nature.   If they are only or largely of personal or local benefit, such as telephone service, street-lighting, sidewalks, or streets, then they should be supported by individual or local taxation.   Being conceived, though, as essential to the welfare of the State as a whole, then their support should be by the general taxation of all, and not from taxes or fees paid by the parents of the children educated.   The establishment of this principle, that the wealth of the State must educate the children of the State, required time and effort, for it virtually meant the confiscation of a portion of the fruits of the labor of all men, and in proportion as they by hard labor and thrift had been able to accumulate a surplus, and the use of the part so confiscated to educate the children of the State, regardless of whether or not the particular parents of the children educated had any surplus wealth to be so confiscated.

This is an essential state service to which all owners of property must be subject, and no man can expect to escape his share for support by sending his children to a private or parochial school. This of course he is free to do, as we have so far in our history not seen any reason for limiting this right of choice, but the exercise of such freedom and choice cannot be expected to relieve him of his proper share for the support of so essential a state service as public education.   Equally might he claim exemption from taxation for the maintenance of police because he is a law-abiding citizen, from the support of the fire department because he has built his house of concrete, from taxation to purchase and maintain parks because he has attractive grounds about his home and does not visit the parks maintained by the public, or from the support of the health department because he employs a family physician.

How far the State may go.   How far the State may go in levying taxation to provide general educational advantages is another matter which we have decided shall be left to the State to determine. Our government is a government by majority rule, and we have gradually established it as a principle of public policy that what the majority, acting through its accredited representatives, once decide to be for the public welfare can be ordered and provided.   When this involves new lines of action not only new laws, but at times amendments to the constitution of the State are necessary, but, once a clear majority has decided that something in the interest of the public welfare should or should not be done, it is not difficult to alter whatever laws or constitutional provisions stand in the way. When this has been done the courts have uniformly decided that the will of the majority, so registered, shall prevail. The early school taxation laws, the laws for the extension of the high school, the provision of state normal schools, the first compulsory attendance laws, free textbooks laws, laws for medical inspection and health supervision — these and others have been tested in and upheld by the courts.

So it may be safely asserted to have become an established principle of our American educational policy that the State may provide, or order provided, if it deems that the welfare of the State will be better preserved or advanced, whatever form of educational effort, type of school, aspect of inspection or instruction, or extension of education may to it seem wise to add. The needs of our democracy are alone the test, and these needs are to be determined by majority action and in the majority interest, and not imposed by the rule or to meet the needs of a class.

There is every reason to feel that this fundamental principle of action has not as yet in any way reached the limits of its application, but rather that the future is almost certain to see a great extension of educational advantages into new directions to meet the needs of classes of our people not now adequately provided for. In the fields of night schools, vacation schools, play-grounds and directed play, community-center activities, adult education, public music, civic-welfare education, health supervision, child welfare, school and university extension, and vocational guidance, to mention a few of the more certain directions of future state educational activity, we are almost sure to see marked extensions of the right of the State, in the interests of the welfare of the State, exercised to provide or order to provide.

Schools to afford equal opportunity. Another principle which we have firmly established in our educational policy is that the schools provided shall afford not only equal opportunity for all in any one class or division of the school, but also that full opportunity for promising youths to rise shall be offered by the State, and that this opportunity, as well, shall be equally free and open to all. In other words we decided early, and as a part of the great democratic movement in the early part of the nineteenth century, that we would institute a thoroughly democratic school system, and not in any way copy the aristocratic and monarchical two-class school systems of European States.   Accordingly we early provided in our state constitutions and in our laws for free public schools, equally open to all.   As soon as possible we abolished the rate-bill and the fuel tax, extended the free-school term, and provided free school supplies.   We replaced the tuition academy with the free public high school, and superimposed it onto the common school we had developed to form an educational ladder which ambitious youths might climb.   On top of the high school we superimposed the state college and university, similarly tuition free.   We freed the schools from the pauper taint, and opened the same or equivalent opportunities to girls as well as boys.   To make the school as common in its advantages as possible we also early eliminated all trace of sectarian control.

As a result we have today, in each of our American States, a school system free, non-sectarian, and equally open to all children of the State, and which any child may attend, at the expense of the State, as long as he can profitably partake of the educational advantages provided.   To reach an increasing number of the State's children, and to retain them longer in school, the State is continually broadening its educational system by adding new schools and new types of education, so that more may find in the schools educational advantages suited to their life needs.   In this way we widen the educational pyramid by increasing the opportunities for more and more to rise, and thus secure a more intelligent and a more enlightened democracy.   Under an autocratic or a planned form of government this would not be desirable, but in a democracy it is a prime necessity.

State may compel attendance.   The State, having adjudged the provision of education to be a public necessity, to preserve and advance the welfare of the State, the natural corollary of such a position is the right of the State to compel children to attend and to partake of the educational advantages which have been provided. The State may also compel their parents, by severe penalties if need be, to see that their children come to school for the period adjudged by the State as the minimum term and minimum number of years to be accepted.   We came to this position slowly and hesitantly, but today we may be said to have arrived at the point where we hold it the right of the State to compel each child to attend school every day the schools are in session and he is able to attend, and for a period extending up to at least fourteen years of age, with every probability that in the near future it will be extended up to sixteen. Having conceived a common school education, at least, to be the birthright of every American boy and girl, the State has finally stepped in to see that the children of the State are not prevented from obtaining their birthright. Nor can the State admit the needs of the parents for the labor of their children as an excuse for non-attendance, though the rejection of such a plea involves obligations on the part of the State to provide, in the form of poor-relief, the earnings of which the State by the exercise of compulsion deprives the parent.

The State may set standards. Any conception of the State as an educational agent, interested in seeing that schools are provided to preserve itself and to advance its welfare, naturally involves the right of the State to fix the minimum standards below which it will not allow any community or private or parochial school to fall. While either too much liberty or too much state oversight may result in weakness in the local school systems maintained, some state oversight and control must be exercised if strength is to be developed. In all such matters as types of schools and classes which must be maintained; the language in which the instruction is given; length of term to be provided; the care of children which must be exercised; the hygienic conditions; and the minimum rate of tax for schools which must be raised locally, it is essentially the business of the State to fix the minimum types, lengths, and amounts which will be permitted, and through the exercise of state inspection and state penalties to enforce these minimum demands. This we have clearly settled both as a right and a duty in our laws and our court decisions. It is also the right, as well as the duty of the State, to raise these minima from time to time, as changing conditions and new educational needs may seem to require or as the increasing wealth of the State will permit, and without waiting until all communities are able to make such advances. To do this will often involve reciprocal obligations on the part of the State, but these the State must expect and be prepared to meet.

Carrying the idea still further, we have also come to accept as an established principle that it should be the business of the State to formulate and carry out a constructive educational policy for the advancement of the welfare of the State by means of public education. Instead of being a passive tax-gatherer, distributor of funds, and lawgiver, the State, if it is to meet the educational problems of a modern world, must become an active, energetic agent, working for the moral, social, hygienic, industrial, and intellectual advancement of its people. The formulation of minimum standards from time to time, the protection of these standards from being lowered by any private or sectarian agency, and the stimulation of communities within the State to additional educational activity — these have now come to be accepted both as fundamental rights and duties of the State.

Public education not exclusive. Unlike some Continental European countries we have never been driven to the necessity of making public education exclusive. Instead, we have felt that the competition of private and parochial schools, if better than the public schools, is good for the public schools. Especially in the line of higher education have we profited by allowing the freest competition between the privately endowed colleges and the state universities. As a result such privately endowed institutions as Harvard, Yale, Columbia, Princeton, Johns Hopkins, Duke, Tulane, Chicago, and Stanford have fallen in whole-heartedly with our state and national purposes and have become really national universities.

On the other hand, our States have not as yet exercised their accepted rights of supervision, and often have allowed a competition from private and religious schools which was not warranted by any ideas of state welfare. In a few of our American States this situation has recently been taken in hand, and standards have been established which are clearly within the right of the State to establish. These involve the requirement of instruction in the English language, the provision of schools at least as good as the public schools of the same community, and full co-operation with the public school authorities in such matters as compulsory school attendance, health supervision, and statistical reports. These are legitimate demands of the State; they have been upheld by our courts; and they should everywhere be enforced by our American Commonwealths.

The present conviction of our people. Slowly but certainly public education has been established as a great state, one might almost say, a great national, interest of the American people. They have conceived the education of all as essential to the well-being of the State, and have established state systems of public education to enforce the idea. The principle that the wealth of the State must educate the children of the State has been firmly established The schools have been made free and equally open to all; education has been changed from a charity to a birthright; and a thoroughly democratic educational ladder has everywhere been provided. The corollary to free education, in the form of compulsion to attend, is now beginning to be systematically enforced. The school term has been lengthened, the instruction greatly enriched, new types of classes and schools provided, and new extensions of educational opportunity begun.

As a result of our long evolution we have finally developed a thoroughly native series of American state school systems, bound together by one common purpose, guided by the same set of established principles, and working for the same national ends. In consequence it may now be regarded as a settled conviction of our American people that the provision of a liberal system of free nonsectarian public schools, in which equal opportunity is provided for all, even though many different types of schools may be needed, is not only an inescapable obligation of our States to their future citizens, but also that nothing which the State does for its people contributes so much to the moral uplift, to a higher civic virtue, and to increased economic returns to the State as does a generous system of free public schools. The present position of the United States, industrially and commercially and socially, is in no small degree due to the extensive systems of public education which have been provided.

Our characteristic native development. We have evolved these fundamental principles of action, as has been said, only after long public discussion and conflict. Time was required to set forth the arguments and convince a majority of our people as to the desirability of accepting them, and still more time to permit the necessary extension from an acceptance in principle to an acceptance in reality. Still more, after their acceptance in a few States or a section of the Union, more time was required to permit the spread and general acceptance of the ideas by our people as a whole. As a result we have made progress but slowly and irregularly, and often a generation has been required to familiarize ourselves with and accept some new idea which has been a demonstrated success in other States or other lands.

Our educational development, as a result, has been slow and thoroughly native, and ideas reaching us from abroad have been carefully examined, questioned, tried, worked over, and adapted to our conditions before they have met with any general acceptance among our people. Consequently our American school systems are thoroughly "of the people, for the people, and by the people." This is both their strength and their weakness. They are thoroughly democratic in spirit and thoroughly representative of the best in our American development, but they also represent largely average opinion as to what ought to be accomplished and how things ought to be done. There are many improvements which ought to be carried out without delay, and which if made would add greatly to the effectiveness of our schools and consequently to our national strength, but which we shall probably have to wait for until a new generation arises, and achieve then only after a long process of popular agitation and discussion in which those in favor of the changes have out-argued those opposed.

National initiative without responsibility. The same "show me" spirit which has characterized our slow educational development has also characterized our instruction. We have thrown both teachers and pupils largely on their own resources, with the result that either the instruction has been very poor or both teachers and pupils have made marked development in initiative and in ability to care for themselves. The most prominent characteristic of many of our schools has been the former, but the latter has characterized so many schools, and so thoroughly characterizes our private and public life, that as a Nation we have gained a world-wide reputation for initiative and imagination and the ability to carry through successfully large undertakings. Living under a form of government which has given us large freedom both to commit mistakes or to make successes, not afflicted by a bureaucratic government which has imposed a uniformity destructive of initiative, with plenty of elbow-room for the man possessing ideas and energy, always willing to learn, thoroughly democratic in spirit, possessed of large common sense, able to see means and ends and how to relate the two, and willing to follow the leadership of any one of ideas and force or to lead ourselves, we have developed independence of action as a national characteristic. In no other country have the results of national attitudes, national training, and national restraint or freedom shown to better advantage in the general intelligence, poise, good judgement, moral strength, individual initiative, and productive capacity of a people than with us.

These characteristics have carried us along very well up to recent times, and all that is valuable in them we ought to retain. Certainly the splendid initiative of our youth, never shown to better advantage than during the participation of this Nation in the recent World War, is something which we cannot afford to lose. We have, however, lacked somewhat in state and national effectiveness because we exercise our initiative in such an individual manner. It has been largely a case of each fellow for himself, and only in cases of national emergency or danger have we co-operated well. The virtue which we now need to develop to supplement this splendid national trait is a stronger sense of intelligent responsibility for the common welfare, national as well as local, as expressed in some form of self-imposed democratic discipline. Our most prominent characteristic has been a democratic independence and the ability to take care of ourselves. The most prominent characteristic of the German boy, on the other hand, has been a blind obedience to the authority of the State. In between the two the English boy has preserved his initiative and at the same time learned to respect authority and to shoulder responsibility, and the results of this training were well brought out in the recent World War. The American boy showed splendid initiative and daring, but was restive under discipline; the German boy lacked individual initiative when forced to take care of himself, but did well what he was told to do; the English boy exhibited, in a high degree, both initiative and an intelligent sensitiveness to leadership which contributed much to the success of the common cause.

Probably one of our greatest future educational problems is that of striving to increase our governmental effectiveness on the one hand and individual responsibility for good government on the other, while at the same time retaining our democratic life and that training which develops initiative, force, and foresight. Just where the division between personal initiative and national discipline is to be drawn is a question that must be determined somewhat by the demands made by the welfare of the State. If good citizenship is the fundamental problem, then a large place must be found for individual initiative, and much must be left to self-imposed control. If, on the other hand, the safety of the State is the important consideration, then imposed discipline must take precedence over individual initiative and liberty of action. Though we now face no great danger from the outside which seems to imperil the safety of the State, still, since the welfare of any State must depend both on civil order and security, education in a democracy must of necessity combine both liberty of action and self-imposed discipline.

Why our educational problem is difficult. Contrasted with a highly organized Nation, such as Germany was before the World War, we seem feeble in our ability to organize and push forward a constructive national program for development and progress. The State was highly organized; the people homogeneous; the officials well educated, and selected by careful service tests; national policies were painstakingly thought out and promulgated; the schools were effectively organized into uniformly good institutions for the advancement of the national interests; the teachers were carefully trained in state institutions, and made into parts of a national army expected to follow the flag loyally; the Church was nationalized, and in part supported by the Government; religion was taught in all schools, and the weight of religion and the backing of the priesthood were used to support the State; and a great national army was maintained and used as an educative force for nationalizing all elements and training the people in obedience and respect for law and order.

With us, on the other hand, we have only our schools. Our government is what the people want it to be — good, bad, or indifferent. While in a monarchy the ruling government may be much better than the people could provide for themselves, in a democracy this can never be. The thinking men and students of fundamental questions in any form of government are relatively few. In a monarchy these are usually selected to rule; in a democracy they constitute a minority seldom selected for office, and often possessing but little power to mould majority opinion. Even in our universities professors work with a view to improving the future rather than the present. The classroom is often a generation ahead of public opinion. Everywhere our public officials are of the people, and representative of majority ideas. Though our States and the National Government have recently assumed many new functions, looking toward more centralized control and better public administration, each increase in state control has been objected to vigorously by those who fear that the coming of bureaucratic efficiency may reduce us to mediocrity and rob us of some of our splendid initiative. A national religion is inconceivable with us, and a great national army we do not need or want. We are thrown back, then, upon our systems of public education, the public press, and our political life as the great moulding and unifying forces in our most heterogeneous national life, and of these three the school easily stands first as the force which ultimately shapes the other two. Upon the public school teacher, then, and upon those who direct the policies of our schools, in reality rests the burden of the future of our free democratic institutions and the welfare of our national life. The children of today are the voters and rulers of tomorrow, and to prepare them well or ill for the responsibilities of citizenship and government rests almost entirely with the schools of our Nation. What progress we as a people make in national character from generation to generation is largely determined by how well the public school has seen national needs and been guided by that largeness of vision without which but little progress in national welfare is ever made.

The problems our schools face. In the schools our people, adult as well as the young, must be trained for literacy, and the English language must be made our common national speech. There, too, the youth of our land, girls now as well as boys, must be trained for responsible citizenship in our democracy, and so filled with the spirit and ideals of our national life that they will be willing to dedicate their lives to the preservation and advancement of our national welfare. In our high schools and colleges the more promising of our youth must be trained for leadership and service in the State, given a vision of our world place and its relationships, and prepared for constructive service along the lines of the highest and best of national traditions in statesmanship, business, science, and government. In our common schools and in special schools those who labor must be trained for vocational efficiency, and given a sense of their responsibility for promoting the national welfare. The school, too, must take upon itself new duties in teaching health, promoting healthful sports, training in manly and womanly ways, inculcating thrift, teaching the principles underlying the conservation of our human and material national resources, and in preparing the rising generation for a more intelligent use of their leisure time. This last involves training for appreciation and intelligent enjoyment by developing better the musical, artistic, and literary tastes of our people, and by training for avocational ends. That we are to have far greater leisure time in the future seems certain; the problem will be to use this increased leisure intelligently and to a good purpose.

Along with all these important aspects of the educational process must come the development generally among our people of a higher moral tone, that as a Nation we may rise and be equal to the advanced moral conceptions which we in recent years have set up internally and in our international dealings. National morality, though, is always an outgrowth of the personality, morality, and teaching of a people, and this in turn rests on proper knowledge, humane ideals, the proper training of the instincts, the development of a will to do right, good physical vigor, and, to a certain degree, upon economic competence. Mere moral or religious instruction will not answer, because it usually does not get beneath the surface of the problem. No Nation has shown more completely the futility of mere religious instruction to produce morality than has Germany, where religious instruction was universally required. The problem is how to influence and direct the deeper sources of the life of a people, so that the national characteristics it is desired to display to the world will be brought out because the schools have instilled into every child the conceptions and attitudes it is desired to see shine forth. Where America will stand in the affairs of the world, and the place it will occupy in history a century hence, will be determined largely by the ability we display in shouldering the new tasks, and in subordinating every personal ambition and every sordid motive to the great ideas of international right and justice, sterling national worth, and service to mankind. In the words of Lincoln we must "have faith that right makes might, and in that faith to the end dare to do our duty as we understand it." How we understand our duty, and how large the duty appears, ultimately goes back to the schools and the homes of this Nation.

Education a constructive national tool. Education today has become the great constructive tool of civilization. A hundred years ago it was of little importance in the life of a Nation; today it is the prime essential to good government and national progress. As people are freed from autocratic rule the need for general education becomes painfully evident. In the hands of an uneducated people democracy is a dangerous instrument. Too often, the revolver instead of the ballot box is used to settle public issues, and instead of an orderly government under law we find injustice and anarchy. When we freed Cuba, Porto Rico, and the Philippines from Spanish rule we at once instituted a general system of public education as a safeguard to the liberty we had established in these Islands, and to education we added sanitation and courts of justice as important auxiliary agencies. The good results of our work in these Islands will for long be a monument to our political foresight and our intelligent conceptions of government. In all lands where there is today an intelligent popular government, general education is regarded as an instrument of the first importance in moulding and shaping the destinies of the people.

In our own land, despite all our admirable progress, we still have a large task before us, and the task increases with the passing of years. We have here the makings of a great Nation, but the task before us is to make it. The raw materials — Saxon and Celt, Teuton and Slav, Latin and Hun — all are here. Our problem is to assimilate and amalgamate them all into a unified Nation, actuated by common impulses, inspired by common ideals, conscious of a moral unity and purpose which will be our strength, and so filled with reverence for our type of national life that our youth will feel that our form of government is worth dying for to defend. Never did opportunity knock more loudly at the doors of a Nation than it has at ours since 1914, and never was a Nation in better position to open its doors in response to the knocking. The place we shall occupy in history will be determined largely by how well we meet the emergencies of the present situation; how satisfactorily we solve the many new problems of the new world life after the World War; how well we respond to the calls of humanity for service; and to what extent we utilize the opportunity now presented to reorganize and unify our national life within. Many forces must co-operate in the work, but unless our schools become clearly conscious of the national needs and the national purposes, and utilize the opportunities now presented for new and larger national service, we shall, in part at least, fail to reach the world position we might otherwise have occupied.

Importance of the educational service. Education in a democratic government such as ours is the greatest of all undertakings for the promotion of the national welfare, and the teacher in our schools renders an inconspicuous but a highly important national service. In teaching to the young the principles which lie at the basis of our democratic life; in awakening in them the conception of liberty guided by law, and the difference between freedom and license; in training them for self-control; in developing in them the ability to shoulder responsibility; in awakening them to the greatness of that democratic nobility in which all can share; in instilling into them the importance of fidelity to duty, truth, honor, and virtue; and in unifying diverse elements and fusing them into the national mould; the schools are rendering a national service seldom appreciated and not likely to be overestimated. It was to create such constructive institutions for our democratic life that we took the school over from the Church, severed all connections between it and its parent, made it free and equally open to all, and dignified its instruction as a birthright of every American boy and girl.

QUESTIONS FOR DISCUSSION

1. Does the obligation to educate impose any greater exercise of state authority than the obligation to protect the public health?
2. What would be the result were we to relieve from school taxation those who send their children to private or parochial schools?
3. While schools have, at first, been established by majority action, is it not true that much further development has been made by a small but thinking minority? Illustrate.
4. Show that art and musical education would be a legitimate extension of public educational effort.
5. Does the provision of equal opportunity for all necessitate equal or equivalent schools or school rights? Illustrate.
6. Show why the essentially democratic American school system would not be suited to an autocratic type of government.
7. Show that compulsory school attendance is the natural corollary of taxation for schools.
8. What is meant by the State increasing standards which may involve reciprocal obligations on the part of the State?
9. Show that the demands of the State on private and parochial schools, mentioned on page 756, are legitimate demands.
10. Illustrate the difference between an acceptance in principle and an acceptance in reality.
11. Are the characteristics which we have developed in our young people those of a new or an old country? Why so?

12. Illustrate what is meant by intelligent responsibility for the common welfare.

13. What kind of discipline is represented by the Army? By the Boy Scouts? Are schools of both types? Illustrate.

14. Show that the weight of a priesthood and the force of religious instruction in the schools would be strong supports for an autocratic state.

15. We do much less in the training of teachers than do homogeneous monarchical nations having an army and a priesthood. Is this right? How do you explain this condition?

16. Have we done much so far in giving our students world vision? Why? Do we need to do so?

17. What are likely to be the effects at home of the standards of national honor we have developed abroad? Illustrate.

18. Show how our educational tasks increase with the years.

19. Show how the World War is likely to be of great advantage to us in the matter of assimilating and integrating our foreign-born.

SELECTED READINGS

In the accompanying volume of *Readings*, the following selections, related to the subject-matter of this chapter, are reproduced:

334. Pritchett: Our Educational Development.
335. Coffman: Education as a Social Development.
336. Coffman: Education and the American Governmental Philosophy.
337. Russell: Education for the Industrial Era.
338. Russell: Education for Liberty.

QUESTIONS ON THE READINGS

1. Restate in your own words, and in shorter space, the history of the evolution of the American school system as traced by Pritchett in **334**.

2. Similarly, restate the argument of Coffman (**336**).

3. Do you think that Coffman has stated well (**335**) the social development idea? Why?

4. Similarly, contrast the two types of educational systems as described by Russell (**337**).

5. Assuming that the technocratic type (**337**) is to prevail, what changes in the living standards of our people would necessarily result?

6. What dangers to our national life does Russell (**338**) sense?

INDEX

Abbott, Jacob, *The Teacher*, 325

Abbott, Rev. Edward, begins Conference for Education in South, 671–72

Abercrombie, John W., on education in Alabama, 669

Academies: character of training in, 113; curriculum, 249, 378; early interest in, 112–13; female, 251–52; Franklin's, 246; first established, 246–47; in South before the War, 425; number of, 247; organization and control, 248; Phillips Exeter, and Andover, 246; religious attitude of, 249–51; train teachers, 376–78; transition institution, 245–47, 255

Adams, John, at Harvard, 68f, 75f; on need for education, 90

Adjustments and differentiations, in elementary education, 519–28

Admission to college, subjects recognized and dates, 315

Adult education, forms of, 587–99; adult illiterates, 590–92, 594–97; agricultural extension work, 598–99; citizenship classes, 592–94; evening schools, 587–90; library service, 597; Moonlight Schools, 595

Agassiz, Louis, lectures to teachers, 385, 654

Agricultural and mechanical colleges: early demand for, 279; extension work of, 598–99; colleges established, 278–80; value of the land grants, 280

Agricultural Extension Act, 598–99

Agricultural high school evolved, 630

Alabama: early school legislation in, 130; educational development of before Civil War, 417–18; condition by 1900, 667; state university founded, 116

Alderman, Edwin A., services to the South, 670, 674f

Amalgamation and assimilation, 488–89

Amendment X, Federal Constitution, 86, 739

America, effect of discovery of, 10

American educational ladder, 273, 281

American Institute of Instruction organized, 170–71, 704–05

American Journal of Education, Barnard's, 228–29, 344

American Lyceum, 168–69, 704–05

American people, who constitute, 480–89

American school of the 3 Rs, origin of, 29; development of, 288–89

Andover Theological Seminary, an early manual-labor school, 364

Annals, the American, of Education, 343

Antioch College established, 275

Apperception, as Herbart developed it, 451

Apprenticeship training: in the Colonies, 34–36; in Virginia, 23; Indenture of, 34; apprenticing an orphan, 35; breakdown of, 638

Arithmetic, in colonial times, 47–49

Arithmetics, colonial, 47–49; Dilworth's, 47; Greenwood's, 47; Hodder's, 48; manuscript, 49

Arithmetics, later national: Colburn's, 294–95; 395–96; Grube plan, 396–97; Pestalozzi's work on, 394–95; Pike's, 294; Ray's, 295

Arkansas, educational development in before the Civil War, 419

Armstrong, Samuel C., work of, 667

Army draft revelations, 615–17; as to literacy, 591; as to mental age of recruits, 699

Assimilation and amalgamation, 488–89

Attendance, school — See Compulsory Attendance

Attitudes toward education: Colonial, 12–26; early constitutions, 94–97; early toward colleges, 114–16; early legislation, 97–105; the academies, 112–13; present-day conceptions, 756–57, 762–64

Awakening of interest in education, early, 163–66; in South — See South

Ayres' Handwriting Scale, 694

Bache, Alexander Dallas, Report on Education in Europe, 360

Baltimore, early Public School Society in, 126; the McKim school, 128

Baltimore County, county unit in, 727

Barnard, Henry: edits *American Journal of Education*, 228–29, 344; edits *Connecticut School Journal*, 227, 343; edits *Rhode Island School Journal*, 344; first U. S. Commissioner of Education, 229; on work of Cyrus Pierce, 381; opposes rate bill in Connecticut, 203;

organizes first Teachers' Institutes, 324; president University of Wisconsin, 229; scholar of the awakening, 228–29; work in Connecticut and Rhode Island, 226–28

Batavia plan, the, 522

Battledoor, the, 43

Battles for state-supported schools, list of the seven, 176–77

Beecher, Catherine Elizabeth, founds Hartford Female Seminary, 252

Bell, Andrew, and monitorial instruction, 128–29

Bible, use of in schools, 43, 46, 61; controversy over use of in Massachusetts, 234–35

Bingham, Caleb, his textbooks, 292; his *Young Lady's Accidence*, 295–96

Blair bill for national aid, 442–43

Blind, education of, 580–82; early beginnings of, 580; books for, 581; schools for, 582

Blow, Susan, establishes first kindergarten in St Louis, 457

Blue-backed Speller, Webster's — See Webster, Noah

Bobbitt, Franklin, proposals for reorganization of high school, 636–38

Boelte, Marie, opens kindergarten training school in New York, 457

Boston: beginnings of school grading in, 304–06; infant schools in, 138; kindergartens begun, 457; school examination of 1845, 331–32; school system in 1823, 306

Boston, Infant School Societies in, 138

Boston Latin School, 31, 306

Boston schoolmasters, Mann's controversy with, 225, 362–63

Braille Alphabet, for the blind, 581

Breckinridge, Robert J.: ancestry, 229–30; work in Kentucky, 187–88

Brooks, Rev. Charles: influenced by Dr. Julius, 361; work for normal schools in Massachusetts, 378–79

Buchanon, Pres., veto of first Land Grant College Act, 279–80

Buffalo, early school history in, 317; first city superintendent schools, 317

Buildings, school — See School Houses

Bülow-Wendhausen, Baroness, work in establishment of kindergartens, 456–57

Byfield, South, academy established, 246

Calvinism in New England, 13, 14, 25, 41

Cambridge promotion plan, 524

Capon Springs Conferences, 471–73

Carter, James G.: agitates for school reform in Massachusetts, 221–22; for schools to train teachers, 373; establishes one, 373; *Letters*, 221

Case School of Applied Science founded, 278

Catechism, the, 43–44

Catholepistemiad, the, 342

Catholics, demand division of school funds, 236–38

Central schools, 568

Cessions of land by Colonies, 83–84

Changes since 1898, 507–08

Chapman and Counts proposals, 634–35

Charity school conception, in New Jersey, 196–97; in Virginia, 23, 198; in Pennsylvania, 21, 191–96; in other Colonies, 24

Cheever, Ezekiel: as a teacher, 52; his *Accidence*, 49–51

Chemistry, beginning of instruction in, 276

Chicago, early school history in, 318–19; first high school in, 261; first graded course of study in, 319; first city superintendent in, 319

Chicago, University of, inaugurates the four-quarter system, 654

Child, the center in education, 516; teacher in such a school, 517–19

Child Health and Welfare, White House Conference on, 576, 610–11, 620–21

Child labor and the school, 571–72; national regulation of, 572–73

Child labor laws, first, 429

Child-study movement, 401–02

Child welfare work, 575–78, 604–22; research stations for, 578, 618

Children's Charter, the, 620

Christian Witness controversy — See Mann; Sectarianism

Christianity, its contribution, 2

Church, loss of influence over young, 499–501

Cincinnati, Hughes and Woodward bequests, 128

Cities, growth of in U.S., 142–43; number of, by decades, 143

City: begins schools before State, 180–81; early city superintendents, 217; early made schools free, 191, 200; effect on of rise in manufacturing, 148; growth of since 1860, 493–94; new problems of, 149; rise of, 143; research bureaus in, 696f; urban and rural in 1930, 493

City courses of study — See Courses of Study

City School Societies: in Baltimore, 126, 128; in New York City, 124–26

Civil school, rise of in New England, 73–75

Civil War, checks development at the North, 428–31; general effect on education, 427–31; post-war reconstruction period, 431–44

Classes, differentiated, 522, 526–28; to speed up work of school, 527–28

Claxton, P. P., 674f, 740f

Cleveland, early school history in, 319

Clinton, DeWitt: on Lancastrian schools, 134; president Public School Society, 124–26; recommendations to legislature on schools, 155, 175; supports the academies, 277, 376; supports high schools, 261

Coeducational colleges, beginning of, 275

Colburn, Warren: his *Arithmetic*, 294–95, 384, 395–96; use of in South, 423

College admission requirements, subjects and dates, 315

College education for women, 274–75; early Female Seminaries, 251–52

Colleges, colonial, 31–33, 264–65; character of, 114–16; curriculum, 32, 51; damaged in Revolutionary War, 82; lists of, and dates, 114f, 264–65; beginnings of reform of, 65–67

Colleges, national period: all small and poor, 266, 269, 278; admission subjects, 315; begin coeducation, 275; Dartmouth case, 272; established by 1860, 268; established by decades, 1780–1900, 270; expansion illustrated by Cornell, 651, and Michigan, 274; in the South, 425; new national attitude toward, 270–71; technical instruction added, 277

Colonial instruction, religious purpose of, 41–42; waning of in 18th century, 59–61

Colonial teachers — See Teachers

Columbia University, 115; chemistry added, 276; medicine added, 276 — Also see Kings College

Columbian Primer, illustrated alphabet of, 232, 292

Commission, the Country Life, 598, 677–78

Commission on Vocational Education, National, 641–43 — Also see Vocational Education

Commission on National Aid to Education, 741–42

Commissioner of Education, U.S.: establishment of office, 739–40; list of Commissioners, 740f

Committees of N.E.A.: on College Entrance Requirements, 543–44; Department of Superintendence, 545–47; Economy of Time, 544–45; Fifteen, 543; National, for Curriculum Study, 542–47; Ten, 542–43

Common School Journal, Massachusetts, 225, 343–44

Community center schools, 594–97, 724

Compulsory-maintenance attitude in the New England Colonies, 14–20; spread of, 25

Concentration, in studies, 540

Conference for Education in the South, 671–73

Connecticut: Constitution of 1818, 95, 238; early state legislation, 98; endowment funds, 177; fight against rate bill in, 202–04; law of 1650, 19; sale of Western Reserve, 179, 202; work of Barnard in, 226–28

Connecticut Common School Journal, 227, 343

Consolidated community-center school, 595–97, 723

Consolidation movement, 721–27 —Also see Rural Schools

Constitution, Federal: no mention of Education, 84; why this, 85–86; on religious question, 87–88

Constitutions, state, on education, 94–97; amendments to prohibit sectarian aid, 239

Content subjects, in elementary school, 518

Continuation school, 573–74; 646

Conventions, for propaganda, 171–73

Cook County Normal School, 547

Cooking, introduction into schools, 466

Cornell University, development of, 651; early manual instruction in, 462

Costs per pupil, by decades, 430

Cotton mill, first in U.S., 144; rapid development of spinning, 144

Country Life Commission, 598, 677–78

County school superintendent, how secured, and term. 725

County-unit educational reorganization, 724–27

Courses of study: differentiated classes and schools, 526–28; differentiated courses, 524–26; early legislation fixing subjects, 300; flexible grading and promotion plans, 521–28; handling the misfits, 520–21; parallel courses, 523–

24; school grading in Boston, 304-06; in New York City, 303-04; in Providence, in 1800, 301, in 1820-1848, 302-06

Cousin, Victor: Report on Prussian schools, 356-58; influence of in Massachusetts, 358; in Michigan, 216

Crary, Isaac E.: ancestry, 229-30; influenced by Cousin's Report, 357-58; work of in Michigan, 216

Crippled children, schools for, 583-84

Curriculum, elementary: completed, 471; Denver study of, 546; eliminating useless subject matter, 540-41; evolution of the, 473; new curricular problems, chart, Fig. 136, 548-49; overcrowded, the, 539-41; place of Parker and Harris in, 473-74; recent study of, 546-47; reforming by Committees, 542-46; study of in experimental schools, 545-46; result of the Industrial Revolution on, 505-06

Curriculum, secondary: Bobbitt's proposals for reform of, 636-38; College Entrance Committee report on, 543-44; Committee of Ten on, 542-43; Cardinal principles of, 633-35; Chapman and Counts on, 636; Department of Superintendence studies, 545; Eliot and Flexner proposals, 635-36

Curry, J. L. M., 439-40, 671-72, 674f

Dalton laboratory plan, 528-29
Dame school, the, 27-28
Dartmouth College case, 272
Davenport, *History of U.S.*, 298, 399
Days of schooling, by decades, 429
Deaf, education of, 577-80; sign language, 589; oral method, 579; work of Gallaudet for, 578
De Garmo, Charles, *Essentials of Method*, 454
Delaware: early constitutional provisions, 95; early school legislation in, 101; educational development before the Civil War, 409-10; lotteries to aid academies, 177
Dentistry, instruction in begins, 276
Degrees, early college, 652
Department of Superintendence, N.E.A., organization of, 709-10; curriculum studies, 545
Desks, early school, 330; in Quincy School, 312
Detroit, early school history in, 317-18
Development concept in education, 514
Dewey, John, his work, 506-07; his philosophy of education, 693; ques-

tions elementary school organization, 551-53
Dewey Laboratory School, Chicago, 547
Dickerman, Rev. G. S., work of in the South, 672-73, 674f
Differentiated classes and schools, 526-28
Differentiated courses of study, 524-26
Dilworth, Thomas: his *Arithmetic*, 47; his *Guide*, 46-47, 63, 296
Disciplinary classes, 568
Disciplinary conception of education, 514
Discipline, colonial, in colleges, 57f, 58f; in schools, 57
Discipline, in early American schools, 328
Disputation, in the colonial colleges, 33, 68
District system: abandonment of, 323; consolidation to eliminate, 721-27; curbing of in New England, 219-21; defects of, 321-23; exaggerated ideas as to importance of, 220; great day of, 315-23; how organized a county, 213, 320; in the early cities, 316-20; in New York, 214; merits of, 321-23; rural district management, 320-21
Dock, Christopher, his *Schuleordnung*, 325f
Draft, army, revelations of, 615-17
Drawing, begun by Massachusetts, 468-69; in early city schools, 428, 466; in English schools, 467-68
Drill subjects, listed, 518
Dummer Academy established, 246
Dunster, Pres. Henry, 32
Dutch, in Central Colonies, 12, 27
Dwight, Edmund, helps Mann establish first state normal schools, 379
Dwight, Henry E., *Travels in North Germany*, 356
Dwight, Nathaniel, his *Geography*, 297, 390

Education, alignment of interests in battle for, 163-66; arguments for and against, 165-66; new motive for after War for Independence, 88-91; opinions of leaders as to need for, 89-90
Education as a subject of study: development of new lines, 691-95; first chairs of, 691; new challenges in, 703-04; scientific study of begins, 690-91; university study of begins, 690-91
Education, a constructive national tool, 762-64; conviction as to, 756-57;

essential nature of, 750–51; equal opportunity to be provided, 751–52; how far the State may go, 752–54; our thoroughly native development, 313–15, 757–58; public education not exclusive, 756; State may set standards, 755–56; why our problem is difficult, 760–62

Education Bills, the, for Federal Aid, 740–42; the question involved, 742–47

Educational conceptions, changing: developmental, 514; disciplinary, 513; knowledge, 513; newer, 515–16

Educational consciousness, before 1820, 110–11

Educational journalism begins, 343–44; list of early journals, 343–44; early state teachers' association journals, 708

Edwards, Ninian W., in Illinois, 229–30

Elementary school: complete, 471; arrangement questioned, 550–54; early American school of the 3 Rs, 29, 298–99; early legislation fixing studies, 300; elementary school subjects become fixed, 298–300; as evolved by 1890, 549–50; evolution of by periods, 300–14, 473; origin of in Protestant Revolts, 9; President Eliot questions arrangement, 523; three types of subject matter, 518

Eliminations of subject matter, 540–41

Eliot, Charles W., addresses, 523, 550–51; chairman Committee of Ten, 542–43; proposals as to secondary education, 635

Elizabeth Academy, in Mississippi, chartered, 251

Elmira College established, 275

Endowment funds for schools, early state, 177–79

English Grammar Schools, colonial, 63–64; private and evening, 64; subjects taught, 63

English immigration to the United States, 480–81, 484

English influences, early, transplanting of to the new world, 26, 340, 342

Erie canal, effect of, 145

European background, our, 1

European travelers, early, 354–62

Evening English Grammar Schools in colonial times, 64

Evening schools in cities, 428, 587; adult education, 588–92; citizenship classes, 592–93; change in purpose of evening schools, 588; under Vocational Education Act, 582, 646

Expression subjects, the, 518

Extension of the school, 563–99; adult education, 587–96; agricultural extension work, 598–99; chart showing, 589; compulsory attendance effects, 563–76; education of handicapped children, 577–87; library extension service, 597–98; university extension, 655–58

Faculty-psychology period, 400–01, 688

Farm tenantry in 1930, 495

Federal aid for education: beginnings of interest in, 739–40; creation of office U.S. Commissioner of Education, 739–40; Commissioners, 740f; new national concept needed, 745–46; national obligations, 744–45; the Education Bills, 740–42; the question of national aid, 742–45; the National Advisory Committee on, 741; recommendations of, 741–42

Feeble-minded, education of, 583–84; early classes for, 584; cities providing, 584

Fellenberg, Emanuel, his manual-labor school, 351, 363; early manual-labor schools in the U.S., 363–65; colleges evolved out of, 364; governors recommended, 365

Female academies created, 251–52

Ferguson, Katy, school for the poor, 122

Flexner, Abraham, proposals as to the secondary school, 635–36

Florida, educational development before the Civil War, 420

Foreign born in the U.S., 485; in schools, 504; literacy of, 590–93

Foreign influences on American education, 354–65; general results of, 365–66

Foundation elements in our civilization, three important, 1

Foundations, educational, to aid the South — See Negro Education

Franklin's Academy, 246; one purpose to train teachers, 372

Freedmen's Aid Societies, 437–39

French influences on American education, early, 341–42

Froebel, Friedrich, 455–59; develops the kindergarten, 456; the idea of, 458–61; spread of, 456–58; proposals as to hand work, 461–62

Fuel tax, the, 189f

Fundamental principles established, 750–57

Gallaudet, T. H.: announces course of lectures on pedagogy, 690; early advocate of teacher training, 373; tries to educate feeble-minded, 583; work for deaf and dumb, 578

Galloway, Samuel, 229–30

Gardening, school, 613–14; early work in, 613; value of, 614

Garfield, James A., work in establishing office of U.S. Commissioner of Education, 739–40

Gary school plan, the, 530–32

Genesee College established, 275, 364

German immigration to the U.S., 483

German Sects in Pennsylvania, 20, 25

Geography, early American texts, 297–98; instruction in revolutionized, 393–94; Parker's proposals for, 540

Georgia, first constitutional mention, 95; early school legislation in, 102; educational development in before the Civil War, 413–14; university of created, 115, 413, 426

Girard College founded, 360

Goodrich, Samuel, his histories, 298

Governors demand schools, 154–56, 174–76

Graded school evolved, 300; did not copy the *Volksschule*, 366; divided into class grades, 311–14; and recitation groups, 309–11; early school grading in Boston, 304–06, New York City, 303–04, Providence, 306–07, and 28 other cities, 309; high school fitted on, 314–15

Grading and promotional plans, 521–23; differentiated courses, 524–27; differentiated schools and classes, 526–28

Grammars, early American, 295–97

Grammar School, English, 63–64

Grammar School, Latin — See Latin

Grant, President, proposal to amend U.S. Constitution, 240

Greece, its contribution, 2

Green, Samuel S., early professor of Didactics at Brown, 690

Greensboro College for Women established, 275

Greenwood, Isaac, his *Arithmetic*, 47

Griscom, John, *A Year in Europe*, 354; comment on by Jefferson, 354f; describes Edinburgh high school, 355

Grube method in Arithmetic, 396–97; its vogue, 397

Guyot, Arnold, agent Massachusetts State Board of Education for geography, 385, 393–94

Gymnastics — See Physical Education

Hall, G. Stanley, work in child psychology, 402

Hall, Samuel Read: course of study, 375; *Lectures on Schoolkeeping*, 325, 376; opens first teacher-training school, 375; tablet to, 375f

Hampton Institute founded, and work of, 464, 666–67

Hancock, John, on education, 90; enters Harvard, 68f

Handicapped children, education of, 577–87; early beginnings of, 577; blind, 580–82; crippled, 582–83; deaf, 577–80; feeble-minded, 583–84; significance of the work, 584–86

Hand work — See Manual Training

Harper, Wm. R., questions our school organization, 551–53

Harris, Wm. T.: contributions to educational theory, 473–74; organizes elementary science course, 392, 469; opens first public kindergarten, 458; work as superintendent at St. Louis, 472; U.S. Commissioner of Education, 740f

Hartford Female Seminary established, 252

Harvard College: first admission requirements, 30; founding of, 15, 31; listing of students, 75; Plymouth Colony aids, 19; prominent colonial students, 68f; growth to 1800, 266; protection in constitution, 95; size in 1815 and 1832, 114; separates divinity, 276; law, 276; medicine, 276; scientific school, 278

Harvard, John, will of, 15f

Hawley, Gideon, work of in New York, 215

Haywood, Atticus G., agent of the Slater Fund, 441

Health supervision, begins, 607; health of teacher, 622; how Federal Government might aid, 619; mental hygiene, 621; pre-school health and development work, 617–18; rapid expansion of work, 608–10; reduction of death rate in a century, 619; size of the problem, 610–11

Heister, Governor, on Lancastrian Schools, 155

Herbart, J. E.: education and work, 449, 450–53; taught with Pestalozzi, 350

Herbartian ideas in Germany, 453–54; in the U.S., 454–55; the leaders, 454; type studies, 541

Herbartian Society and its publications, 454

High school, battle to establish, 245–64; Boston report on, 254; first in New York City, 256; first in U.S., 253–56; first in Chicago, 261; evolution of subjects of instruction in, 315; junior high school evolved, 631–32; list of before 1850, 259; Kalamazoo decision, 263; Massachusetts law of 1827, 257; new courses and schools, 254–57, 629–31; new conceptions as to, 632–33; origin of name, 253, 355; number by 1860, 262; rapid development of, 255; recent expansion of, 627–31, 649; struggle to maintain when established, 259–61

High school curriculum — See Curriculum, secondary

Histories, early U.S., 298

History teaching, beginnings of, 399; early American texts, 298, 399; Herbart's development of, 451–52

Hoar bill, for national aid, 442–43

Hodder's *Arithmetic*, 47–48

Holbrook, Alfred, work of at Lebanon, Ohio, 383f

Holbrook, Josiah, and the American Lyceum, 168

Home and Colonial Infant Society, 353, 386, 387

Home life changed by Industrial Revolution, 496–501

Hookworm in the South, campaign against, 676–80

Hoover Advisory Committee on Federal Relations to Education, 741; its recommendations, 741–42

Horace Mann School, in experimental curriculum study, 548

Horn, Ernest, his experimental school at Iowa, 548

Hornbook, the, 42–43

Hughes, Thomas, and the Cincinnati high school, 128

Illinois, early school legislation in, 99; first constitutional mention, 94; settlement of, 108–09

Illinois College founded, 106

Illiteracy: after Civil War in South, 442; attempts to remedy, 442–44; adult illiterates in the U.S., 590–92; citizenship classes for, 592–93; Moonlight schools, 595; New York literacy law, 593–94; of army recruits, 591; who constitute, in the U.S., 594–95

Immigrant, national responsibility for, 745

Immigration: assimilation and amalgamation into racial stock, 188–89; our original stock, 480–81; the tide, 481–86; today a cosmopolitan mixture, 486–87

Indiana: battle for school taxation in, 183–87; constitutional provision as to education, 96, 109; early school legislation in, 99; influence of French refugees at Vincennes, 342; settlement of, 108; state university founded, 116

Indiana University created, 267; becomes coeducational, 275

Industrial plants in the U.S., in 1833, 147

Industrial Revolution, the, 489–96; effect of on home and child life, 497–501; on the school, 501–06; John Dewey as interpreter of changes, 506–07

Industrial schools, state, 568–69; who in these, 568–69

Infant School Societies: in Boston, 138; in Eastern cities, 138; in England, 353; in New York City, 139–40; in Philadelphia, 141; in Providence, 139; origin of, 137

Institute of Instruction, American, 170–71, 704–05

Instruction, early American — See Teachers

Iowa, state university of: coeducational in 1856, 275; first permanent chair in Education, 691; work of Child Welfare Research Station in, 618

Irish immigration to U.S., 482–83

Italian immigration to U.S., 485

Jackson, Andrew, significance of election of, 152

Jay, John, on need for education, 90

Jeanes Fund, the, 682

Jefferson, Thomas: aided Public School Society of Washington, 126; his proposed plan for Virginia, 102, 341; on need for education, 89; propagandist for French ideas, 341

Jena, center for Herbartians, 453–54

Johnson, Marietta L., and her experimental school, 347–48

Jones, Margaret E. M., spends year at Oswego, 387

Journalism, educational, begins, 343–44; early state teachers' association journals, 798

Judd, Charles H., work at Chicago, 548, 695

Julius, Dr., description of Prussian normal schools, 361

Junior college evolved, 556–58; number of public colleges, 1930, 556

Junior high school evolved, 554–56, 631–32; pupils in, 631

Kalamazoo case, and decision, 263

Kentucky: Early legislation in, 103; educational development in before Civil War, 414; struggle in to prevent misappropriation of school fund, 187–88; superintendent of common schools, 216

Kidd, John, grant for schools at Cincinnati, 128

Kindergarten: contribution of, 460–61; first in U.S., 457; as developed by Froebel, 455–56; essential idea of, 458–59; spread of, 456–58

King Philip's War, 58, 62

Kings College: becomes Columbia, 115; opening announcement, 61, 65; prayer at opening, 265f; purposes in founding, 265

Know Nothing party, on religion in the schools, 239

Knowledge conception of education, 513

Kriege, Matilde, kindergarten training school at Boston, 457

Krüsi, Hermann, Jr., agent Massachusetts State Board for drawing and arithmetic, 385, 387f; work with Sheldon at Oswego, 387

Ladder, the American educational, 273

Lancaster, Joseph, in England, 129; in the U.S., 131

Lancastrian monitorial system, the, 128–37; early schools in U.S., 129, 132; essential features of, 131–33; later decline of, 137; Manuals of, 133; Model School to train teachers, 373; value of, 134–36; wide adoption of, 129

Land grants, Federal, to the States, 178, 193; for universities, 116; to Ohio, 92, 116; value of, 93

Land grants in Texas, 420

Land grant colleges — See Agricultural and Mechanical Colleges

Lands, cessions by Colonies, 83–84; early state grants of, 177

Lange, Alexander, and school reorganization, 553

Language instruction as modified by Pestalozzi's work, 391

Language study, early texts for, 296–97

Larson, Gustav, introduces sloyd work at Boston, 465

Latin Grammar School, of New England, 16, 29–30; at Boston, 31; decline of, 243, 248, 252; early foundations, 16f; difficulty in maintaining, 61, 69; locations of, 30; for boys only, 251

Law, instruction in begins, 276; early law schools, 276

Laws, early state, 97–105

Lee, Genl. Robt. E., on South's problem, 432

Leonard and Gertrude, 346

Lewis, Sam; work in Ohio, 229–30

Library extension work, 598–99

Lincoln, Abraham: approves land-grant college act, 280; changes in living since his day, 491–93; to people of Sangamon County on education, 1832, 156–57

Literature, added by Herbart as a study, 451–52

Living changes, due to Industrial Revolution, 492–96

Log colleges, in Pennsylvania, 22

Lotteries, for schools, 177, 178

Louisiana: early state legislation in, 102; educational development in before the Civil War, 416–17

Ludwick, Christopher, grant to Philadelphia charity school, 127

Luther, Seth, on education, 157

Lyceum, American — See American Lyceum

Lyon, Mary, establishes Mt. Holyoke, 250, 275

McIver, Charles D., 674f

McGuffey, William H., his Readers, 293–94; use of in the South, 423

McKim, John, gives a free school to Baltimore, 128

McMurry, Charles, Frank, and Lida, 454

Madison, Pres. James, on need for education, 90

Madison, James, changes as president at William and Mary, 66

Maine, early legislation in, 98

Mann, Horace: Annual Reports, 224–26, 361–62; controversy with the Boston schoolmasters, 325, 362–63; great work in Massachusetts, 221–26; his campaigns, 224f.; Mann vs Smith controversy, 234–35; Massachusetts Common School Journal, 225, 343–44; on taxation for education, 182; president National Association Friends of Education, 706–07; sectarian fight, 233–35; Seventh Report on drawing, 428; grading, 311, 361–62; on oral instruction deaf, 579; on Pestalozzian methods, 385; work in establishing normal schools, 378-82

Manual labor schools, early foundations, 363-64

Manual training: first manual-training high schools, 463-67; idea developed, 461-62; reaches the U.S., 462-63; in elementary schools, 465-66; the educational discussion as to value of, 466-67

Manufacturing: beginnings of in U.S., 144-48; cotton spinning established, 144; distribution of plants, 1833, 147; effect of on city development, 144; effect of on living, 492-96; industrial transformation by 1850, 145; new social problems resulting, 145; great extension of after 1860, 490-92

Manuscript Arithmetics, colonial, 48-49

Maryland: early educational legislation, 101, 181; educational development before the Civil War, 410; first constitutional mention, 94; lotteries for schools, 178

Marwedel, Emma, early kindergarten teacher in California, 457

Mary Sharp College established, 275

Mason, Lowell, introduces music in Boston schools, 355

Massachusetts: amends constitution to prohibit sectarian aid, 238; begins instruction in drawing, 468; creating supervision in, 221-24; consolidation of schools started, 721-22; early service in establishing high schools, 259-61; early state school legislation, 98; eliminates sectarianism, 233; establishes Normal Art School, 468; establishes first school for idiotic and feebleminded, 583; first constitutional provisions, 95; legislation as to studies, 300

Massachusetts laws: laws of 1634 and 1638, 14; law of 1642, 17; law of 1647, 18; importance of these, 18-20; laws of 1654-1693, 19-20; law of 1789, 288-89; laws of 1827 and 1835, 257

Massachusetts Institute of Technology founded, 278

Mayo, Charles and Elizabeth: introduce Pestalozzian procedures into England, 352-54; organize Home and Colonial Infant Society, 353, 386, 387; their object lessons, 353, 392

Medical Inspection — See Health Supervision

Medicine, first schools of, 276

Meeting House, in New England, importance of, 64, 69, 74

Men teachers, decreasing percentage of, by decades, 401

Mental hygiene, 622; health of teacher, 622

Meriam, J. L., and his experimental school, 547

Methods of instruction, of colonial teacher, 53; early American teacher, 327-28; effectiveness of, 331-33

Miami University created, 115, 267

Michigan: attempt to divide school fund in, 238; concentrates 16th section fund, 358; early settlement of, 109; early school legislation in, 109; lotteries for the university, 178; superintendent of public instruction created, 215-16, 358

Michigan, university of: begins technical instruction, 278; becomes coeducational, 275; development by 1852, 274; early foundation, 342; the Catholepistemiad, 342

Middle Ages, the, 3

Migratory laborers, schools for children of, 595

Mills, Caleb, Addresses, 185-87; his ancestry, 229-30

Milwaukee Trade School established, 640

Mirania, College of, 65

Mississippi, early legislation in, 103; educational development before the Civil War, 417

Missouri, educational development before the Civil War, 418-19

Montessori, Dr. Maria, her method, 459-60

Morrill, Justin S., and land-grant colleges, 278-79

Morse, Jedediah — his Geographies, 297

Mt. Holyoke Seminary established, 252, 275

Murray, Lindley — his English Grammar, 296-97

Music, in city schools, earliest introductions, 355, 428

National aid — See Federal Aid

National Association of Friends of Education formed, 706-07

National Association of School Superintendents formed, 709; becomes the Department of Superintendence, N.E.A., 710; Yearbooks, 711

National Congress of Parents and Teachers, 712

National education, beginnings of, 91

National Educational Association formed,

709-10; its growth and work, 710-11; Research Division established, 711

National Normal School at Lebanon, Ohio, 400

National Teachers Association founded, 708-09; investigates Oswego movement, 387-88; becomes the N.E.A., 709-10

National University: Washington's interest in establishing, 266-67; his will, 267

Native American party of 1841, on Church and State, 239

Neef, Joseph, his two books on Method, 354; where taught, 354, 385

Negro education: education of, 431-32; labor unit of South, 663-64; national responsibility for, 744-45; results of emancipation of, 431-32

Negro education, Funds to aid: Freedmen Aid Society, 437-39; Jeanes Fund, 682; Peabody Fund, 439-41; Phelps-Stokes Fund, 682; Rosenwald Fund, 682-83; Slater Fund, 441-42

Newark Academy established, 247

New England: educational beginnings, 14; First Fruits, 15; Primer, 44-46, 63, 69; towns, how settled, 60, 64, 69; town disintegration, 68-70; westward expansion of, 100, 105-08

New Hampshire: constitution of 1792, 95, 238; early legislation, 98; law of 1680, 98

New Harmony, Indiana, Neef at, 354

New Haven, early town plan, 71; first meeting house in, 69

New Jersey: beginning of school fund, 189f.; early school legislation in, 101; elimination of pauper school in, 196-97

Newlon, Jesse, and work in curriculum study, 546, 548

New Orleans, college of, 341

New York City: evening schools organized in, 587; conditions in 1833, 149; Infant School Society in, 139-40; Lancastrian Schools in, 129-32; Primary Schools organized, 140; Public School Society in, 124-26; religious controversy over division of school funds, 236-38; school for crippled children, 582; school grading in, 303-04; school subjects in 1819 and 1822, 303-04

New York State: academy curriculum, 249; creates first State Superintendent of Schools, 214-15; early legislation in, 98; fight against rate bill in, 200-02; first constitutional mention of educa-

tion, 94; Lancastrian system in cities of, 132; rate bill in, 200-02

New York Trade School established, 640

New York, University of State of, 341

Normal Schools; first state, 378-83; find their place, 399-401; noted private normal schools, 400; small early attendance, 380

North Carolina: early constitutional provisions, 95; early legislation in, 103; educational development before the Civil War, 411-12; educational status in 1886 and 1900, 664-65; Lancastrian schools in, 129; university early provided for, 95, 115; university begins summer instruction, 654; work of Calvin Wylie for, 411-12

Northern philanthropy in South: Freedmen's Aid Societies, 437-38; General Education Board, 673; Jeannes Fund, 682; Peabody Fund, 439-41; Phelps-Stokes Fund, 682; Slater Fund, 441-42; Rosenwald Fund, 682-83; Sanitary Commission, 678-80

North West Territory: early development in, 105-08; educational attitudes assumed by States, 108-09

Oberlin College established, 275, 364

Object lessons developed by Mayos, 353; lead to study of elementary science, 392

Ogden, Robert C., services to the South, 672

Ohio: early constitutional provisions, 96; early legislation, 99; growth of school taxation illustrated, 183; land grants to for schools, 92, 230; land grants to for religion, 92f., 230; land grants to for colleges, 115, 267

Ohio Company, land purchase of, 267

Ohio University created, 115, 267

Old Field Schools, 424-25

Olmstead, Denison, early advocates teacher training, 372

Oneida School of Science and Industry founded, 364

Open-air classes established, 582-83

Oral and objective teaching, 388

Oral method with the deaf, 579

Oswego movement, the, 385-89; normal school established, 388; spread of its graduates, 389

Owens, Robert, and origin of Infant Schools, 137-38

Page, David, Theory and Practice of Teaching of, 325

Page, Walter Hines, services to the South, 670, 678

Parental schools, 568

Parent Teacher Associations, 712; National Congress of Parents and Teachers, 711

Parker, Col. Francis W.: his contribution to educational theory and practice, 474–75; his theory of concentration, 540; his *How to Teach Geography*, 394, 474; work on curriculum, 547

Parochial school in the Colonies, 20–22, 25

Part-time schooling laws, 573–76, 646

Pauper school: attendance at in Colonies, 22–25; battle to eliminate, 189–98; in New Jersey, 196–97; in Pennsylvania, 191–96; in Virginia, 198

Peabody College for Teachers established, 441

Peabody Education Fund established, 439; work of, 440–41

Peabody, Elizabeth, introduced kindergarten at Boston, 457

Peale, Rembrandt, introduces drawing at Philadelphia, 428

Pedagogical Seminary established, 402

Peirce, Cyrus, work at Lexington, 381

Pennsylvania: battle in to eliminate charity school conception, 191–96; early constitutional provisions, 96; early dependence on charity schools, 21; early school legislation, 101; Lancastrian schools in the cities of, 132; mixed religious basis for schools, 20; propaganda societies in, 168; the law of 1834, 192–96; type of parochial school attitude, 20–22

Pennsylvania, University of: early curriculum, 65–67; in 1815, 114

Permanent state school funds, beginnings of in the States, 177–79

Permissive taxation, proceeds general, 180–82

Pestalozzi: contribution of, 347–49; consequence of his ideas, 249–50; educational experiences of, 346–47; ideas described by American travelers, 354–60, 384; inspiration of, 344–46; Mann's *Seventh Report* on, 361–63; scene of his labors, 347; spread of his ideas, 350–54; where he left the educational problem, 449; work and influence of, 344–54

Pestalozzian methods: effect of on school instruction, 388–96; introduction to the U.S., 384–88

Petty or dame school, 27

Phelps-Stokes Fund, 682–83

Philadelphia: early charity schools in, 127; Lancastrian Schools in, 129; Infant Schools in, 141

Philanthropic influences, early, 120–28; in aid of South, 439–42, 673, 682–83

Philbrick, John, develops graded school at Boston, 311

Phillips Exeter, and Andover, established, 246; aim of, 250–51

Ph.D. degree, first American, 652

Physical education begins, 461, 606–07; German *Turnen* introduced, 461

Physical defects in school children, 608–10; army draft revelations, 615–17

Physicians, training of by end of colonial period, 276

Pickett, Albert, 169, 343

Pierce, John D.: ancestry, 229–30; edits a School Journal, 343; influenced by Cousin's Report, 357–58; work in Michigan, 216, 357–58

Play activities, in kindergarten, 458–59; in schools, 611–12

Platoon school, the, 531–33; platoon organization, 532, 533

Playgrounds, some early, 612

Plymouth Colony laws, 19

Porter, Noah, on taxation for schools, 204

Primary schools, in Boston, 138–39; in New York City, 140–41; organization of in New York, 141. — Also see Infant Schools

Princeton College founded, 31, 31 f.; in 1815, 114; Old Nassau, 32

Professional education, rise of in the U.S., 275–76

Progressive school, the, 532–33

Project idea, the, 542

Promotional plans: Dalton, 528–29; differentiated, 524–28; flexible, 521; Gary, 530–31; platoon, 530–32; Winnetka, 529–30

Propaganda, early educational. 167–68; educational conventions for, 171–73; propaganda societies, 167–71

Protestant Revolts, 6; results of, 7

Providence: began schools, 180; began school grading, 306–07; early courses of study, 301–03; early School Societies in, 127; Infant Schools begun, 139; what and how a teacher taught in 1820, 302

Prussia adopts Pestalozzian ideas, 351–52

Prussian schools, early reports on — See Cousin, Bache, Mann, Stowe

Psalter, the, use of, 43, 46

Psychology becomes the master science, 400–01; as Pestalozzi knew it, 348, 450; as Herbart left it, 451–53; the faculty concept, 348, 451

Public School Societies, early in cities, 123–28; in Baltimore, 126, 128; in New York City, 124–26; in Philadelphia, 127; in Washington, 126

Public School Society of New York City, 124–26; gives up its work, 126, 237

Purdue University, 278

Puritans in New England, 14

Quakers, educational work of in New Jersey and Pennsylvania, 21, 26

Quincy School at Boston, 311–12, 604; plan of, 312

Raikes, Robert, and his plan for Sunday Schools, 121

Railroads, early development of, 145

Rate bill: cities abolish early, 200; early use of, 198; fight against in New York State, 200–02; final abolition of, 205; use in Connecticut, 202–04; use in New York City, 199

Ray, Joseph, his *Arithmetics*, 295

Readers, early American, 290–94; McGuffey's, 293–94; Webster's, 291–92

Reconstruction period: cost of, 436–37; Presidential plan, 433–34; Congressional plan, 434–35; resulting legislation, 435–36

Referendum: use of in Indiana, 185–87; in Pennsylvania, 193–94; in New York, 200–02

Reformatory and charitable education, Griscom first describes European, 355 — Also see Industrial Schools

Rein, Wm., work at Jena, 454

Religious attitude of the Academies, 250–51

Religious basis for education, 12

Religious faiths of early colonists, 13

Religious purposes in early instruction, 41–42; waning of, 59–61

Religious question, how the Constitution solved, 86–88 — Also see Sectarianism

Rensselaer Polytechnic Institute established, 276–78; its large early work, 277

Reorganization of the school: questioning of the arrangement, 550–52; reorganization completed, 559; significance of the movement, 558–60; the 8–4 plan as evolved, 549–51; the later 6–3–3 plan, 554–56; the junior high school in the plan, 554–56

Research bureaus, city, rise of, 696f.

Revival in the South, about 1900, 673–74 — Also see South

Revival of Learning, the, in Europe, 4

Revolutionary War — See War for Independence

Reward of Merit, A, 327

Rhode Island, early legislation in, 103; work of Barnard in, 226–28 — Also see Providence

Rhode Island Common School Journal, edited by Barnard, 344

Rhode Island Institute of Instruction, 705, 707

Rice, Dr. J. M., early measurement of Spelling, 693

Ritter, Carl, his work on teaching of geography, 393–94

Rockefeller, John D., establishes General Education Board, 673; aids Sanitary Commission for Eradication of Hookworm, 679

Rockford Seminary established, 275

Rome, its contribution, 2

Rosenwald Fund, its work, 682–84

Rousseau, and his *Émile*, 344–45

Runkle, John D., introduced manual work at Massachusetts Institute of Technology, 462–63; the course there, 463f.

Rural and village education: county-unit consolidation, 724–27; reorganization and redirection of, 718–27; the rural-life problem, 720; the rural-school problem, 719–21; the school consolidation movement, 721–24

Rural vs. urban population in 1930, 493; changes in rural living, 494–96; rural tenantry, 495

Russell, Wm.: early advocate of teacher training, 373; editor of *American Journal of Education*, 343

Russell, Wm. F., summary of current educational problems, Fig. 136, page 549

Safety Education, 614–15

Saint Louis: opens first high school in Missouri, 419; opens first kindergarten in the U.S., 458; work there of Wm. T. Harris as superintendent, 472

Sampler, a, 299

Santa Barbara promotional plan, 525

Scales, pedagogical — See Tests

School gardening, 613–14; early work, 613; value of, 614

School grading — See Graded School

School houses: an early Providence contract for, 328–29; early American,

328–30; early school desks, 330; modern elementary school building, 605; new types of, 604–06; use as a community center, 595–97

Schoolmaster, colonial, regulations as to in the Anglican Colonies, 24f.

School of the 3 Rs, origin of, 29; development of, 288–89

School Societies, 123–28; for propaganda, 167–71 — Also see Public School Societies, and Infant School Societies

School supplies, first free, 205–06

School support, sources of, by decades, 738

School survey movement, 545, 695; early surveys to use standard tests, 695; results of, 696

School taxation, recent cuts in, 735–37 — Also see Taxation

School textbooks — See Textbooks

Schools, alignment of interests in battle for, 164–66; local nature of all early schools, 212–13

Schools transplanted, to the American Colonies, 26

Science instruction, elementary: grows out of object lessons, 392, 469; Harris' course, 392, 469; Spencer's challenge as to, 470–71

Scrivener, the, 49

Sears, Barnas, his work, 439–40

Secondary school, origin of in Europe, 5 — Also see High School

Secretary for Education, in President's Cabinet, 740–42

Sectarianism: attempts to divide the school funds, 235–39; becomes a public issue, 238–39; battle to eliminate, 230–40; constitutions amended to prohibit, 239; fight in Massachusetts, 235–39; in Michigan, 239; in New York City, 236–37; proposal of President Grant, 240; of Governor Seward, 237, 238

Secularization of American education — See Sectarianism

Seguin, Edward, work for the idiotic, 583

Sense perception — See Pestalozzi

Seward, Governor, proposal for sectarian schools, 237, 238

Sewing, early instruction in, 299, 466

Sheldon, Henry, his work at Oswego, 385–89

Sheppard-Towner Maternity Act, 576

Simpson, Stephen, on schools, 157–58

Sixteenth Section grants, 92–94

Slater Fund established, 441–42

Slater, Samuel: factory schools, 122; first cotton mill in America, 144

Smith-Hughes Vocational Education Act, 643–46, 682 — Also see Vocational Education

Smith-Lever Co-operative Agricultural Extension Act, 598–99, 682

Smith, Benjamin F., Report on Prussian schools, 361

Smith, Walter, organizes art instruction in Massachusetts, 468

Smith, William, Provost at the University of Pennsylvania, 65–66

Snyder, Governor Simon, asks the legislature for schools, 154

Societies, Public School — See Public School Societies

Society for the Promotion of the Gospel in Foreign Parts, in the Anglican Colonies, 24

Soldan, Louis, exploits Grube method, 396

South Byfield Academy established, 246

South Carolina: early legislation in, 102; educational development before the Civil War, 413; by 1900, 665–66; university established, 115

South, the: awakening there before the Civil War, 408–22; after close of War, 431–32, 680–84; conditions by 1900, 665; Conference for Education in, 671–76; educational revolution after 1898, 663–85; hookworm control campaign, 676–80; national attempts to aid, 442–43; new influences in, 666–71; negro problem after War, 431–32; negro education since, 684–85; recent progress, 680–84; slow progress before 1900, 663–66; the reconstruction period, 431–37

Southern Education Board, 673–76

Southern schools — See South

Spanish-American War, changes since, 507–08

Speakers, early texts, 292

Spellers, Noah Webster's, 290–92

Spelling school, the, 322

Spencer, Herbert, his Essays, 470–71; effect of publication of, 471

Speyer Experimental School, 547

Springfield tests, the, of 1846, 332–33

State aid fixed the system, 188–89

State attitudes, early, by States, 94–103; summarized, 97, 104

State constitutions, early, on education, 94–97; amendments to prevent sectarian aid, 239

State control, beginnings of, 213–19

State educational reorganization, 727–33

State industrial schools, and inmates, 568–69

State special schools maintained, 585

State Superintendent of Public Instruction: early work and duties, 217–19, 727–28; elective basis begun, 217–19; election *vs.* appointment, 728–31; first officers, 213–16; by 1861, 216–17; lack of educational policy, 731–33; need for leadership, 733

State Teachers' Associations, early, 707–09; early Association *Journals*, 708

State university: battle to establish, 264–73; early establishments, 115, 267, 272, 426; become coeducational, 275; early attempts to transform colonial colleges into, 114

Sterling-Reed Education Bill, 741

Sterling-Towner Education Bill, 741

Stevens, Thaddeus, on value of schools, 155; fight for the Pennsylvania free school law, 195–96

Stiles, Charles W., his work for hookworm control, 676–79

Stowe, Calvin E.: ancestry, 229–30; his trip to Europe, 359; his *Report*, 169, 359–60

Subjects in elementary school instruction, three groups of, 518

Suffrage, extension of, 150–54; dates for, 151; educational significance of, 153–54; new demands on schools resulting from, 154–58

Summer and winter terms, 289, 325

Summer sessions in universities: early ones, 654; growth of, by decades, 655

Sunday School movement, 121–23; earliest schools, 123; first in New York and Philadelphia, 122; importance of in South, 122

Superintendent — See Supervision, and State, County, and City

Supervision, battle to establish, 212–21; creating in Massachusetts, 221; early city superintendents, 216–17; first state superintendents, 214–16

Survey movement, the, 545

Swett, John: ancestry, 229–30; work in California, 229

Taxation for education: beginning of, 179–87; growth of illustrated by Connecticut, 204, Indiana, 183–86, and Ohio, 183; reform of plans for now a necessity, 737–39; right to tax for established, 751–52; rise in taxing

inequalities, 734–35; state aid fixed the system, 188–89

Taylor, Orville, edits *Common School Assistant*, 343

Teacher, health of, 622

Teacher, in old type school, 513–16; in newer type, 517–19

Teacher training in U.S.: academies first provide, 376–78; beginnings of, 371–75; by 1860, 324; first city normal schools, 383; first state normal schools, 378–83; first teacher training school, 375–76; noted private schools, 400

Teachers' Associations: American Association for Advancement of Education, 707–08; American Institute of Instruction, 704–05; early propaganda, 375–76; noted private schools, 400

Teachers' Associations: American Association for Advancement of Education, 707–08; American Institute of Instruction, 704–05; early propaganda organizations, 171, 704; early transitional Associations, 704–06; first State Teachers' Associations, 708, and Journals, 708; National Association of Friends of Education, 706–07; National Educational Association, 709–11; National Teachers' Association, 708–09

Teachers, colonial, 51–55; an advertisement for, 62; a teacher to let, 54; cargo of, received, 55; character of their instruction, 56–58; discipline, 57; indentured servants as, 54, 55; licensing of, 53f., 55; many duties of, 52f., 55; Latin School teachers, 52, 58

Teachers' contracts, colonial, 48

Teachers, early American, and their equipment and method, 323–28; boarding-around arrangements, 325; effectiveness of work of, 331–33; in South before the Civil War, 424–25; methods, 327; morals, 326; purposes in instruction, 330–31; turning out of, 328

Teachers' institutes, beginnings of, 324

Teachers' profession, new problems of, 711–12

Technical education: beginnings of in America, 276; early engineers, 277; land-grant colleges established, 278–80; Rensselaer School founded, 276; the state universities begin technical instruction, 278; West Point established, 276

Tennessee: early legislation in, 103; educational development before Civil War,

415-16; state university beginnings, 115

Term of school, lengthening of, by decades, 429

Terms, summer and winter, 289, 325

Tests, Boston of 1845, 331-32

Tests, intelligence, beginnings of, 698-99; controversy over, 700; I.Q.s, 701; significance of, 701-03; the Army scales, 699; what they have revealed, 700-01

Tests, Springfield of 1846, 332-33

Tests, standard, beginnings of, 693-95; underlying purposes of, 698; use in course of study elimination, 697-98; use in school surveys, 695-97

Texas, educational development of before Civil War, 420-22; land grants for schools, 420

Textbooks, in early Colonies, 42; in South before Civil War, 423; new textbooks before 1850, 289-99; these change instruction, 289; the first free, 205

Thorndike, Edward I., work in developing measurements, 690, 692

Three Rs, the American school of: origin of, 27; development of, 288-89

Threshing before the maching age, 146

Town, in New England: break-up of, 70-75; how settled, 60, 64, 69

Transplanting of European civilization to America, 26, 58

Troy Seminary established, 252

Tubercular children, open-air classes for, 582-83

Tuskegee Institute, 464, 668

Type attitudes toward education of the Colonies, by 1750, 25-26; origin of, 12-14; the compulsory-maintenance, 14-20; the parochial-school, 20-22; the pauper non-state, 22-25

United States, in 1783, 83; a cosmopolitan mixture today, 486-88

Universities, private, work of in our national life, 270-71, 757

Universities, state, prime business of, 658 — Also see State University, and University Expansion

University expansion, 651-55; attendance, by decades, 653; early degrees, 652; expansion of original college, 653; new chairs and schools, 652-53; the original college, 651-52; summer session attendance, by decades, 655

University extension, 655-58; work of the University of Wisconsin, 655-57

University, national — See National University

Usher, the, and class, 310

Vacation schools, early, 612; value of, 613

Valparaiso Normal School, 400

Vassar College established, 275

Vermont: early constitutional provisions, 96; early legislation in, 98

Village and rural education — See Rural

Virginia: apprenticeship training in, 23; early settlers of, 22, 25; early legislation in, 23; early state legislation, 102; educational development before the Civil War, 410-11; pauper school in, 198; state university established, 115, 272; type of non-state attitude Colony, 22-24

Vocational education, 638-49; beginnings of with us, 639-41; National Committee on, 641-43; its findings, 642-43; Smith-Hughes bill for, 643-45; types of instruction provided, 645-46; results of the work, 647-48

Vocational guidance, 649-51

War for Independence: effect of on colleges, 82; on education, 88-91, 120, 288, 408; new motive for education, 88-91

Washburne, Carleton, 529, 546

Washington, Booker T., 667-68

Washington, City of, early schools in, 126; lotteries for, 178; Public School Society in, 126

Washington, George, on education, 89; interest in a national university, 266-67; will, 267

Washington University, establishes first manual training high school, 463-64

Webster, Daniel, on education, 156

Webster, Noah: his blue-backed *Speller*, 63, 290-92; his *Grammatical Institute*, 296; his *History*, 298, 399; his *Third Part*, 291-92; use of *Speller* in the South, 423

Western Academic Institute and Board of Education: formation of, 169; work of, 169-70, 359, 704-05

Western Literary Institute and College of Professional Teachers, 156; work of, 169-71

Western Reserve, sale of by Connecticut, 179, 202

Western Reserve College founded, 364

White, Andrew D., on early shop instruction at Cornell, 463

White House Conference on Child Health and Welfare, 576, 610–11, 620–21

Wilbur, Secretary R. L., appoints National Advisory Committee on Federal Relations to Education, 741

Wiley, Calvin H.: ancestry, 229–30; work in North Carolina, 411–12

Willard, Emma, establishes Troy Seminary, 250, 275

William and Mary College: founded, 23, 31; early pre-eminence, 67; curriculum reform at, 67, 68; divinity abolished at, 87f., 114

Wilson, H. B., and curriculum reform, 544

Winnetka plan, the, 529–30

Winter and summer terms, 289, 325

Wirt, Will, and Gary plan, 530

Wisconsin, early legislation in, 110

Wisconsin, University of: university extension, 655–57; schools of, 654–55

Wolcott, Governor, on Lancastrian schools, 135

Woodbridge, Wm. C.: edits Annals of American Education, 343, 374; his Geography, 297; his Letters on European schools, 355–56; plans a teacher-training school, 374

Woodward, Calvin M., 463–64

Woodward high school, Cincinnati, 128

Worcester Polytechnic Institute founded, 278, 364

Workingmen demand schools, 157–58; support public school movement, 173–74

World War, an accelerating force, 549

Writing: colonial teaching of, 49; Spencerian forms, 398; under Pestalozzi's influence, 397–99

Yale College: founded, 16; early curriculum, 33; early government of, 30f.; first admission requirements, 30f.; instruction begun in chemistry, 276, in divinity, 276, in law, 276; protection of in state constitution, 95; purpose in founding, 265; Sheffield Scientific School established, 278

Ziller, Tuiskon, develops Herbart ideas, 453–54

7/99 8